MINIS...

&

MISSION

MATTERS

(Various Contributors)

Edited:
RICHARD JACKSON

Published in 2015 by FeedARead.com Publishing

First Edition

All profits from the sale of this book and any donations made will be channelled to the Cliff College (CCITC) A/C and used to continue this pioneering "Partnership in Training" programme.

A CIP catalogue record for this title is available from the British Library.

Further information about the CCITC Programme is available from:

The CCITC Coordinator: Revd Richard Jackson MA BD
Tel: +44 (0) 1617182548
2 Almond Drive, Sale, Cheshire, M33 5QZ
Email: rev.rj@ntlworld.com

or

The CCITC Director, Revd Dr Stephen Skuce BD MPhil
Tel: +44 (0) 1246584215
Cliff College, Calver, Hope Valley, Derbyshire S32 3XG
Email: S.Skuce@cliffcollege.ac.uk

Web site: www.cliffcollege.ac.uk

"MINISTRY & MISSION MATTERS"

CLIFF COLLEGE
INTERNATIONAL TRAINING CENTRE (CCITC)

RESPONDING TO A GOD-GIVEN VISION

LECTURES DELIVERED DURING
PIONEERING PARTNERSHIPS OF TRAINING
FOR
MINISTRY AND MISSION
(2001-14)

SHARED WITH THE

CHRISTIAN COUNCIL OF SIERRA LEONE (CCSL)
(2002-4)

METHODIST CHURCH SIERRA LEONE (MCSL)
(2005-6; 2009; 2012-14)

METHODIST CHURCH CUBA (MCC)
(2005)

METHODIST CHURCH NIGERIA (MCN)
(2006-8; 2008-10; 2010-12; 2012-14)

METHODIST CHURCH UGANDA (MCU)
(2014)

3

TABLE OF CONTENTS

CLIFF COLLEGE INTERNATIONAL TRAINING CENTRE (CCITC-INTRODUCTION)..... 10

MODULE 1: OLD TESTAMENT MISSION 13
(Revd Dr Michael Thompson MA BD).. 13
LECTURE 1: JONAH AND HIS MISSION 13
LECTURE 2: THE SERVANT AND HIS MISSION 13
LECTURE 3: BLESSED IS THE ONE WHO FEARS THE LORD (PSALM 112) 15
LECTURE 4: WHAT ABOUT THE FUTURE? 16
LECTURE 5: THE PROPHETIC VISION 17
LECTURE 6: THE APOCALYPTIC HOPE 18
LECTURE 7: MISSION AND MORALITY 19
LECTURE 8: THE QUESTION OF SUFFERING 21
LECTURE 9: CONDITIONS AND CONVERSIONS 22

MODULE 2: NEW TESTAMENT MISSION...25
(The late Capt. Nicola Garnham MA BSc)... 25
LECTURE 1: INTRODUCTION-WHAT IS MISSION? 25
LECTURE 2: THE PEOPLE OF GOD AND MISSION 27
LECTURE 3: JESUS AND HIS MISSION 29
LECTURE 4: THE KINGDOM OF GOD AND MISSION 30
LECTURE 5: THE DISCIPLES AND MISSION 31
LECTURE 6: THE HOLY SPIRIT AND MISSION 33
LECTURE 7: THE EARLY CHURCH AND MISSION 34
LECTURE 8: PETER AND MISSION 35
LECTURE 9: PAUL AND MISSION 36
LECTURE 10: US AND MISSION 38

MODULE 2a: NEW TESTAMENT MISSION-PRACTICAL 40
(Revd Dr Malcolm McCall MA RN) 40
(& Mrs Janet McCall BA Dip.Ed.) 40
LECTURE 1: INTRODUCTION: GOD'S ULTIMATE PURPOSE 40
LECTURE 2: THE WOMAN AT THE WELL IN JOHN'S GOSPEL 43
LECTURE 3: MISSION AND EVANGELISM IN LUKE/ACTS 46
LECTURE 4: EVANGELISM AMONG THOSE SERIOUSLY INTERESTED 48
LECTURE 5: EFFECTIVE CHURCH PLANTING AT ANTIOCH 50
LECTURE 6: EFFECTIVE NURTURING OF A NEW CHURCH PLANT 52
LECTURE 7: PREACHING AND CHURCH PLANTING IN LYSTRA 53
LECTURE 8: PREACHING AND MAKING CONNECTION IN ATHENS 55
LECTURE 9: MISSION ENCOMPASSES ALL CREATION 57
LECTURE 10: JESUS THE CENTRE 60

4

MODULE 3: MISSION/EVANGELISM-PRACTICAL 63

(Revd Dr Martyn Atkins BA) 63
LECTURE 1: HISTORY OF MISSIONARY MOVEMENTS
.... 63
LECTURE 2: RETHINKING MISSION
.... 67
LECTURE 3: PURPOSE IN MISSION-WORKING FOR CHANGE
.... 70
LECTURE 4: CONVERSION AS EVENT AND PROCESS
.... 72
LECTURE 5: CATECHESIS AS TEACHING AND NURTURE
.... 76
LECTURE 6: MISSION & CULTURE-BRIDGING THE GAP
.... 79
LECTURE 7: MISSION IN AN URBAN CONTEXT
.... 82
LECTURE 8: EVANGELISM & SOCIAL ACTION
.... 86
LECTURE 9: THE BODY OF CHRIST OR EVERY MEMBER MATTERS
.... 89
LECTURE 10: SOME CONTEMPORARY TOOLS FOR MISSION
.... 92

MODULE 3a: EVANGELISM PICTURED-PRACTICAL 96

(Major Alan Burns MA BSc).. 96
LECTURE 1: MISSION AND THE KINGDOM OF GOD
.... 96
LECTURE 2: 5 "P" EVANGELISM
.... 102
LECTURE 3: MISSION IN THE BIBLE
.... 109
LECTURE 4: PRACTICAL EVANGELISM
.... 117
LECTURE 5: EVANGELISM AND CHURCH GROWTH
.... 124

MODULE 3b: EVANGELISM TODAY-PRACTICAL 131

(Revd Phil Clarke BA MA) 131
LECTURE 1: SINGING THE LORD'S SONG
.... 131
LECTURE 2: PERSONAL EVANGELISM
.... 134
LECTURE 3: MODELS OF EVANGELISM IN THE GOSPELS
.... 139
LECTURE 4: MODELS OF EVANGELISM IN THE ACTS OF THE APOSTLES
.... 141
LECTURE 5: PAUL'S METHODS OF MISSION AND OURS
.... 144
LECTURE 6: MOBILIZING THE LOCAL CHURCH FOR MISSION
.... 147
LECTURE 7: CONNECTING WITH CULTURE
.... 149
LECTURE 8: CONTEMPORARY MODELS OF MISSION CHURCH
.... 152
LECTURE 9: EVANGELISTIC PREACHING
.... 154
LECTURE 10: STYLES & CONTEXTS FOR EVANGELISM
.... 157

MODULE 3c: YOUTH MINISTRY-PRACTICAL..161

(Revd Dr Steve Emery-Wright MDiv BA) 161
LECTURE 1: THE IMPORTANCE OF MINISTRY TO TEENAGERS AND EMERGING ADULTS
.... 161
LECTURE 2: UNDERSTANDING PHYSICAL DEVELOPMENT AND ITS IMPLICATIONS
.... 165
LECTURE 3: SPIRITUAL GROWTH
.... 169
LECTURE 4: A THEOLOGY OF YOUTH, A THEOLOGY WITH YOUNG PEOPLE, ROLE OF MINISTER
.... 174
LECTURE 5: THE THEOLOGY OF CONTEXTUALISATION/INCARNATION OF MISSION WITH YOUTH
.... 178
LECTURE 6: UNDERSTANDING YOUTH CULTURALLY AND PRACTICING CULTURAL EXEGESIS
.... 180
LECTURE 7: HOW YOUNG PEOPLE UNDERSTAND WORSHIP
.... 182
LECTURE 8: EMPOWERING YOUNG PEOPLE AND THE CHURCH FOR MISSION
.... 184
LECTURE 9: WHAT ARE YOU SEEKING TO ACCOMPLISH. SPIRITUAL FORMATION IN YOUTH?
.... 190

LECTURE 10: TAKING YOUR MINISTRY DEEPER: TOOLS FOR REFLECTION 194

MODULE 4: CHURCH GROWTH AFRICA-HISTORY 197
(Revd Dr Kehinde Olabimtan BTh MED) 197
LECTURE 1: EARLY CHRISTIANITY OF EGYPT AND NORTH AFRICA 197
LECTURE 2: NUBIA AND ETHIOPIA 203
LECTURE 3: CHRISTIAN MISSIONS IN MEDIAEVAL AFRICA 208
LECTURE 4: MODERN MISSIONARY MOVEMENTS IN AFRICA 214
LECTURE 5: PIONEERING IN WEST AFRICA 220
LECTURE 6: PIONEERING IN WEST AFRICA 2—SOME RELIGIOUS ENCOUNTERS 225
LECTURE 7: PIONEERING IN SOUTHERN AFRICA 231
LECTURE 8: PIONEERING IN EASTERN AFRICA 237
LECTURE 9: THE ROMAN CATHOLIC MISSIONS IN THE MODERN ERA 243
LECTURE 10: INDEPENDENCY, INDIGENIZATION AND OTHER DEVELOPMENTS 250

MODULE 4a: CHURCH GROWTH AFRICAN-TODAY 257
(Revd Dr Usman Habib MA) 257
LECTURE 1: HISTORIOGRAPHY OF THE NEW GENERATION CHURCHES 257
LECTURE 2: MISSIOLOGICAL/EVANGELICAL ADVENTURE OF NGC 260
LECTURE 3: ADDRESSING THE FEAR OF SPIRITISM THROUGH FAITH 264
LECTURE 4: MARKETING THE GOSPEL - STRATEGIES 267
LECTURE 5: NGC USER OR SEEKER SENSITIVE SERVICES 270
LECTURE 6: MENTORING: AS LEADERSHIP DEVELOPMENT PRINCIPLE 273
LECTURE 7: ULTRA-MODERN WORSHIP CENTRES 277
LECTURE 8: THE WORD OF GOD AS THE POWER BEHIND NGC'S GROWTH. 280

MODULE 4b: CHURCH GROWTH-EXPRESSIONS 283
(Revd Dr Deji Okegbile MA) 283
LECTURE 1: INTRODUCTION 283
LECTURE 2: DEFINITION FOR FRESH EXPRESSIONS OF CHURCH. 285
LECTURE 3: WHY FRESH EXPRESSIONS OF CHURCH? 287
LECTURE 4: METHODISM—A MODEL OF FRESH EXPRESSIONS OF CHURCH 289
LECTURE 5: SEARCH FOR FRESH EXPRESSIONS OF METHODISM IN NIGERIA 291
LECTURE 6: FRESH EXPRESSIONS OF METHODIST LITURGY 294
LECTURE 7: FRESH EXPRESSIONS OF METHODIST SACRAMENTAL CHARACTER 296
LECTURE 8: FRESH EXPRESSIONS OF CHURCH LEADERSHIP 298

MODULE 5: HOLINESS, SPIRITUALITIES & MISSION 301
(Revd Dr Jennifer Smith BA MPhil) 301
LECTURE 1: INTRODUCTION AND OVERVIEW 305
LECTURE 2: EARLY METHODISM AND THE WORLD OF THE WESLEYS'. 311
LECTURE 3: WESLEY ON 'WORKS OF PIETY' 318
LECTURE 4: WESLEY AND THE 'MEANS OF GRACE': WORKS OF MERCY 323
LECTURE 5: DISCUSSION: (NO ASSOCIATED HANDOUT FOR STUDENTS) 326
LECTURE 6/7: HOLINESS AND THE MISSION OF THE CHURCH I & II 326

6

LECTURE 8: REVISION AND REFLECTION ON LOCAL ISSUES (INTERACTIVE) 331

MODULE 5a: HOLINESS, WESLEYAN SPIRITUALITY 332
(Revd Kenneth Todd BA MA BD).. 332
1: FIRST, THE POLITICAL KINGDOMS OF TODAY NEED AN OPTION FOR THE POOR. 332
2: SECONDLY, THE WORLD TODAY NEEDS SALVATION. 335
3: THIRDLY, CHRISTIANS TODAY NEED THE ASSURANCE OF SINS FORGIVEN. 337
4: FOURTHLY, THE CHURCH TODAY NEEDS THE DYNAMIC OF HOLINESS OF HEART AND LIFE. 338

MODULE 6: WORSHIP & PREACHING-TRADITIONAL 341
(Revd Prof Achim Härtner M.A.) 341
LECTURE 1: THEOLOGY OF WORSHIP AND PREACHING–INTRODUCTION 341
LECTURE 2: THEOLOGY OF WORSHIP AND PREACHING–WHAT ARE WE DOING AS WE PREACH? 347
LECTURE 3: THE SERMON – GOD'S DOMAIN OR HUMAN ARTWORK? 357
LECTURE 4: PREACHING FOR HEARERS 366
LECTURE 5: TYPES OF HEARING AND PREACHING 372
LECTURE 6: STRUCTURES OF SERMONS – INVITATIONS TO LISTEN 384
LECTURE 7: THE PREACHER AS ARCHITECT- BUILDING PLANS FOR SERMONS 395
LECTURE 8: TEN STEPS FROM THE BIBLICAL TEXT TO THE SERMON 405
LECTURE 9: DELIVERING A SERMON 413
LECTURE 10: THE USE OF SYMBOLS IN WORSHIP AND PREACHING 424

MODULE 6a: WORSHIP & PREACHING-PRACTICAL...438
(Mr Peter Worrell LP)... 438
LECTURE 1: WHAT IS WORSHIP? 438
LECTURE 2: PATTERNS OF WORSHIP 442
LECTURE 3: THE CONTENT OF WORSHIP 446
LECTURE 4: OPEN TO THE WORD 451
LECTURE 5: OPEN TO THE SPIRIT 457
LECTURE 6: MUSIC AND WORSHIP 459
LECTURE 7: BIBLE MATTERS 463
LECTURE 8: WORSHIP AND MISSION 468
LECTURE 9: WORDS AND BEYOND WORDS 472
LECTURE 10: WHERE NOW? 478

MODULE 7: ENCOUNTERING OTHER RELIGIONS 485
(Revd Dr Stephen Skuce BD MEd M Phil: Director CCITC) 485
LECTURE 1: WHAT IS THE JEWISH FAITH? 485
LECTURE 2 WHAT IS THE MUSLIM FAITH? 489
LECTURE 3: WHAT IS THE HINDU FAITH? 508
LECTURE 4 WHAT IS THE BUDDHIST FAITH? 521
LECTURE 5: WHAT IS THE BAHÁ'I FAITH? 536
LECTURE 6: WHAT IS THE SIKH FAITH? 539
LECTURE 7: WHAT IS THE CHINESE FAITH? 546
LECTURE 8: "A FIRM AND GENEROUS FAITH" 547

LECTURE 9: TOWARDS AN AUTHENTIC WESLEYAN INTER-FAITH UNDERSTANDING 559

MODULE 8: MINISTRY LEADERSHIP-HISTORIC 565
(Revd Prof David Dunn-Wilson MA M.Phil BD Ph.D FRSA).................................... 565
LECTURE 1: "THE KEYS OF THE KINGDOM 1" 565
1: THE ROMAN LEADERSHIP STRAND 566
2: THE JESUS LEADERSHIP STRAND 567
3: THE APOSTOLIC LEADERSHIP STRAND 568
4: THE EPISCOPAL LEADERSHIP STRAND 570
5: THE CHRISTENDOM LEADERSHIP STRAND 573
6: THE NIGERIAN CONNECTION: 574
LECTURE 2: "THE KEYS OF THE KINGDOM 2" 576
1: THE NON-CONFORMIST STRAND 576
2. THE RENAISSANCE LEADERSHIP STRAND 578
3: THE PROTESTANT LEADERSHIP STRAND 579
4: THE SECULAR LEADERSHIP STRAND 582
5: THE INDIGENOUS LEADERSHIP STRAND 584
6: THE NIGERIAN LEADERSHIP STRAND? 585

MODULE 8a: MINISTRY LEADERSHIP-PRACTICAL 587
(Revd Richard Jackson MA BD International Coordinator CCITC) 587
LECTURE 1: BIBLICAL LEADERSHIP: OLD TESTAMENT 587
LECTURE 2: BIBLICAL LEADERSHIP: NEW TESTAMENT-GOSPELS/ACTS 589
LECTURE 3: BIBLICAL LEADERSHIP: NEW TESTAMENT-EPISTLES 592
LECTURE 4: CALLED TO BE MINISTERS 594
LECTURE 5: CALLED TO BE LEADERS 597
LECTURE 6: CALLED TO BE VISIONARIES 600
LECTURE 7: CALLED TO BE THEOLOGIANS 602
LECTURE 8: CALLED TO BE PASTORS 605
LECTURE 9: CALLED TO BE (AD)--MINISTRATORS 608
LECTURE 10: CALLED TO BE—WHAT? 611

MODULE 8b: MINISTRY LEADERSHIP-PENTECOSTAL 615
(Dr Ben Pugh) 615
LECTURE 1: PENTECOSTALS BELIEVE THAT LEADERSHIP IS CHARISMATICALLY ORDAINED 615
LECTURE 2: PENTECOSTALS BELIEVE IN PLURALITY IN LEADERSHIP 618
LECTURE 3: PENTECOSTALISM HAS A STRONG BELIEF IN 'SPIRITUAL AUTHORITY.' 622

MODULE 8c: MINISTRY LEADERSHIP-PASTORAL 627
(Revd Dr Heather Morris MA) 627
LECTURE 1: THE NATURE OF PASTORAL CARE: THE PASTOR AS SHEPHERD 627
LECTURE 2: THE NATURE OF PASTORAL CARE (2) 631
LECTURE 3: PASTORAL CARE AND EVANGELISM 638
LECTURES 4 AND 5: PASTORAL CARE AND THE DEVELOPMENT OF REFLECTIVE PRACTICE 644
LECTURE 6: PASTORAL CARE IN THE CONTEXT OF GRIEF AND LOSS 652

LECTURE 7: PASTORAL CARE AND PHYSICAL ILLNESS 664

LECTURE 8: CHARACTER AND LISTENING 669

MODULE 9: SOCIAL RESPONSIBILITY & MISSION 677

(Revd Albert Beah MA) 677

LECTURE 1: CONCEPT OF MISSION FOR COMMUNITY DEVELOPMENT 677

LECTURE 2: CONCEPT OF MINISTRY FOR COMMUNITY DEVELOPMENT 685

LECTURE 3: CONCEPT OF COMMUNITY 695

LECTURE 4: CONCEPT OF DEVELOPMENT 699

LECTURE 5: CONCEPT OF COMMUNITY DEVELOPMENT 705

LECTURES 6 & 7: STRATEGIC AND PARTICIPATORY PLANNING FOR COMMUNITY DEVELOPMENT 712

LECTURES 8 & 9: PROGRAMMING FOR SUSTAINABLE DEVELOPMENT 720

LECTURE 10: CHALLENGES FOR COMMUNITY DEVELOPMENT IN MISSION 724

MODULE 9a: COMMUNITY MINISTRY & MISSION 728

(Revd Cameron Kirkwood MA CNAA) 728

LECTURE 1: A COMMUNITY CHURCH IS INCARNATIONAL 728

LECTURE 2: A COMMUNITY CHURCH HAS VALUES 730

LECTURE 3: THE IMPORTANCE OF WHERE WE ARE 732

LECTURE 4: A COMMUNITY CHURCH IS INVITATIONAL 734

LECTURE 5: A COMMUNITY CHURCH IS RELATIONAL 736

LECTURE 6: A COMMUNITY CHURCH IS A MINISTERING COMMUNITY 738

MODULE 10: APPLIED EVANGELISM PROJECT 743

(Supervision by MCN Lecturers & Diocesan Staff) 743

ONE FINAL WORD! 743

APPENDIX 1: CORE TEAM-INVITED TRAINERS 745

(2002-14) 745

CORE TEAM (ORGANISING, LEADING TEAMS & LECTURING ON A VARIETY OF SUBJECTS AT DIFFERENT TIMES IN

SEVERAL COUNTRIES) 745

INVITED SUPPORT TRAINERS/LECTURERS (2002-14): MANY CONTRIBUTING TO MORE THAN ONE CCITC

PROGRAMME. 746

APPENDIX 2: ASSOCIATED BOOKS 748

CLIFF COLLEGE INTERNATIONAL TRAINING CENTRE (CCITC-INTRODUCTION)

THE PREFACE

This book **'MINISTRY AND MISSION MATTERS'** is being published as a companion volume to **'GOING AND GROWING' published by 'Feed a Read' in November 2014.** 'Going and Growing' shared the history of the Cliff College International Training Centre from its inception in 2001 through to 2014. This companion volume provides a sample of the kind of teaching that has been delivered during the in-country 'Residentials' which are at the heart of this successful partnership in training programme.

The Core Training Team of CCITC is supplemented for the residential training by invited lecturers who are experts in their field. A brief introduction to the lecturers and indications of their qualifications at the time they first lectured on the programme is associated with their details, listed in Appendix 1. Further information about their actual involvement during different phases of the programme can be found in the companion book 'Going and Growing' mentioned earlier. Most of those invited to share in the programme have previous experience overseas and of working in diverse cultural settings. Lecturers offer their time and particular expertise free. The cost of travel, visas and out of pocket expenses for a visiting team of 6-8 people utilised for the 2-3 weeks residentials, twice a year are met from our budget, which is largely funded by the Methodist Church in Britain, MMS(Ireland) and through the generosity of associated sponsors/personal donations.

The visiting lecturers, who are partnered overseas with local college lecturers, engage in a mutually profitable exchange of insights, lecture notes and other materials that enrich their continuing ministry both in the colleges and in the UK. The visiting team is well supported by the Rectors (Principals) and the College Tutors at our residential centres, who meet with the students for tutorials during the year, mark their assignments and assist in the final assessment.

What is shared in this book is just some of the teaching/training that has been given under most of the International Diploma In Applied Ministry And Mission (IDIAMM) Modules. With a variety of lecturers from England, Ireland, Germany, Sierra Leone, Nigeria and the USA offering their gifts freely, readers should note that these notes are presented without the embellishments, anecdotes and these days power-point visuals that most lecturers use to enliven their presentations. As this editor has learned, the idiosyncratic nature of lecturers reveals something of their personality in their presentation. Whilst trying to correct any 'glaring errors', I have been reluctant to tamper with 'style', except where it verged on the profligate in the use of paper and an increased number of pages. Readers will note also that we have left, as with the originals, the references that reveal something of the context and culture which was being addressed when these lectures were being delivered. The years spanned (2002-15) have led to some helpful cross-fertilisation of teaching between modules.

Whilst most modules are addressed through a full series of lectures, students are expected to utilise a variety of resources, materials and books (up to £700 worth provided free to every trainee on the programme) to complete their assignments and projects. Obviously, this is not a book to be read cover-to-cover, but anyone interested in the ministry and mission of the church, both here and overseas, will find much in these presentations to stimulate your own thinking. You will be enriched, as so many of our trainees have been, by the various themes and perspectives shared by lecturers from diverse cultural backgrounds seeking to help others 'apply' what they have discovered about 'Ministry & Mission Matters'.

Limitations within this publication mean that some more interactive teaching on vital subjects are not included here though they are no less important to the overall further training programme provided for church leaders largely in West Africa. The residential blocks include: lectures on Communicating in English; Study Skills; a series of interactive lectures exploring how adults learn; and responding to community concerns relating to HIV/Aids, social responsibility, raising funds for projects and alternative styles of leadership. Practical training in communicating to others what has been learned is a key aspect of the training programme.

Our thanks go out to all who have in any way contributed to the success of this pioneering programme. In this publication, no serious attempt (other than by the lecturers themselves) has been made to acknowledge all sources used of material gleaned from other publications. Our apologies to anyone who feels that their copyright has been infringed or their point of view not given an adequate airing. Please be happy with us that what is shared in these pages is now contributing to the evangelistic outreach of large numbers of students cum practitioners of ministry and mission in Africa and through them elsewhere. Requests for similar programmes are received from churches and colleges in many parts of the world. We cannot respond to most of these because we lack the resources, but we trust that by focusing upon strategic centres like Nigeria in West Africa, the ripple effect of knowledge and enthusiasm for the 'Good News' will begin to make its own impact on the whole region.

We can testify personally, and now in a documented way, that what began as a spontaneous response to the 'Troubles' of the 1990's that devastated Sierra Leone has grown into an effective partnership in training programme, much appreciated by the churches with which we have been privileged to be involved.

As indicated earlier the International Coordinator or Director of CCITC will happily respond by email to anyone seeking further information. Cliff College will be pleased to receive any donations that will help to promote and extend this programme. With untapped short-term training resources and funding provided through bi-lateral programmes as well as nationally through the World Church Relations office and the CCITC, 'The world is my parish' might again become our Methodist watchword in the UK. Supportive friends/sponsors continue to help us respond to the training needs of our partner churches in the 21st Century. There is no copyright on the concept of **'Doing Training There, Together with Them'**, Our hope is that our pioneering work will help the church(es) multiply, 'partnership in training' initiatives because: **'MINISTRY & MISSION MATTERS'**.

Richard Jackson (Revd)
International Coordinator,
Cliff College International Training Centre (CCITC)

MODULE 1: OLD TESTAMENT MISSION

(Revd Dr Michael Thompson MA BD)

RELIGION & MISSION THEOLOGY IN THE OLD TESTAMENT

LECTURE 1: JONAH AND HIS MISSION

JONAH IS A PERSON CALLED TO ENGAGE IN MISSION, A SPECIFIC MISSION.

NOTE:
(a) This is a story, and

(b) Jonah is portrayed as a disobedient prophet.
The call (1:1-2); the response (1.3); the storm (1:4); the faith of the sailors and the plight of Jonah (1:16-17).
The prayer of Jonah from the belly of the fish (chapter 2).
The renewed call, Jonah's response & the response in Nineveh (3:1-9).
Jonah's distress (4:1-8).
The Lord's response – the real message of the book–(4:9-11).

(c) What does this book have to say to us today?
(i) Are we hearing God's call to us?
(ii) The message about God's love for all.
(iii) What about Luke 15:29-32?
(iv) The strength we need for the task (Jonah 2: esp. vv. 1-2 & 10).

LECTURE 2: THE SERVANT AND HIS MISSION

ISAIAH: 40-55, THEIR BACKGROUND AND SETTING:

Leaving Babylon to go back to Jerusalem. Thus Isa. 40:3-5. So much of these chapters is thrilling good news, yet within them is some very sombre news: the four passages about a 'servant' (Isa. 42:1-4; 49:1-6; 50:4-9; 52:13-53:12).

1. Isa. 42:1-4 is about servant being given a mission to a wider world (compare Jonah).
2. Isa. 49:1-6 also has an international theme. What is the meaning of 'justice' here?

3. Isa. 50:4-9 In this third passage the servant faces opposition and receives blows and insults (v.6), but is confident about the Lord's help (vv.7, 9).

The fourth passage is much longer and more complex, but can be broken into parts:

4a. Isa. 52:13-15 is an opening speech by God and offers a summary of what follows – servant's success and exaltation, but had much to endure. How other people were startled at his appearance, at first despising him, but by the end coming to see there was much more than that in his sufferings.

4b. Isa. 53:1-3 is about the servant's sufferings, and this told by an unknown group, who come to see that through what the servant did they have received healing (53.4-6). Here, 53.6b sounds like the ritual of the scapegoat in Day of Atonement ritual in Lev.16.

4c. Isa. 53:7-9 tells about servant's sufferings, but that 'he was stricken for the transgressions of my people' (v.8). In fact, that his death was 'an offering for sin' (53.10-11) – a word used elsewhere in the OT (e.g. Lev. 5.1-26; 7.1-10; Ezek. 40.39) of a sacrifice offered so that certain sins might be forgiven, but nowhere else does the OT speak of a human person being offered; normally it is goat or sheep, turtle dove or pigeon.

4d. Isa. 53:12 sums it all up: servant receives great honour having borne the sins of many; looks as if he will have new life, but no details are given.

What does all this mean for us? It is great insight that comes out of the weakness and dispossession of the life of exile in Babylon. So Jesus warned his disciples about the fact that following him would involve them, as well as him, in taking up the 'cross'. I suggest that these four servant passages in Isa. 40-55 are not just about Jesus, but are also about us, about how the work of God will be done in future times.

Who is the servant? I suggest not one person, but here are four pictures of how the life of discipleship will have to be lived out. It will need great dedication, but there will be a great reward.

PS. 112 IS ABOUT THE BLESSINGS THAT COME:

To those who put their trust in the Lord. That is, it is about the deliverance of God. Note about this psalm:

1. It is an acrostic psalm–each line begins with the next letter of Hebrew alphabet.
2. There is relationship between Ps 111 and 112; same words and phrases are used, though sometimes with different meanings.
Perhaps Ps. 111 is about the praise of devout people, while 112 is about the outworking of faith in God in a person's life.
3. Not easy to date these psalms, though many think they are post-exilic.

Ps. 112 begins with 'Hallelujah' (as do also Ps 111: 113:–also see end of Ps 104), but this is outside the acrostic structure. Perhaps it is to show that it is psalm of praise.
v1. 'Blessed' (*'ashre*)–compare Sermon on the Mount (Matt. 5.1-12) is the 'one' (literally 'the man'–Hebrew *'ish* [man] as distinct from *'ishah* [woman]). This person is 'blessed' because they 'fear' the Lord, that is, 'reverence, worship' him. This person delights in the commandments of the Lord. Which 'commandments' are these?
v2. Speaks of consequences of this 'fear' of the Lord, and this thought is continued in v. 3: it is prosperity and success. Such a viewpoint is also to be found in OT in Deut., Kings, Chronicles, whereas a rather different view is set forth in Job, Ecclesiastes and certain psalms (37, 49, and 73). The OT cannot come to any 'solution' to problems of sufferings of devout and apparently innocent people, but is able to speak about the preciousness of the relationship that a believer has with God (see e.g. Ps. 73:21-28).
v4. The devout one reflects various qualities of God as they are revealed in his/her life:

'Gracious', meaning 'show favour', that is favour God shows to us;
'Merciful', that is, 'show compassion', 'comfort' as in Isa. 40:1;
'Righteous' which perhaps has two basic meanings,
'Good', i.e. 'good person', and in the sense that.....
God's righteousness is his will to deliver his people.

v5-6. Are about the good and long-lasting renown and influence of such devout people. However, (**vv. 7-8**) such people may suffer misfortunes in their lives.

v9. Is about the generosity to others on the part of truly devout people, a verse taken up by St Paul in 2 Cor. 9:9. 'Horn' is symbol of strength, while Hebrew *kabod* can mean either 'glory' or 'honour'.

v10. The final verse is about the frustrations experienced by the ungodly. Note in vv. 8 and 10 the play on the word 'see': in 8b the righteous 'see' the fate of the wicked, while in 10 the wicked 'see' the vindication of the righteous.

LECTURE 4: WHAT ABOUT THE FUTURE?

What does the Old Testament have to say about the future? In this session, we consider some of the more general things that the Old Testament writers present about hope for the future, but in later sessions we shall consider two particular, more specific, topics, what I have called *The Prophetic Vision* and *The Apocalyptic Hope*.

(a) Deliverance in the Old Testament
We should recall what has already been said on the subject of the Old Testament and deliverance in the session on Ps. 112, and also what it was that people such as Moses, Jonah, and 'the Servant' of Isa. 40-55 were called to proclaim, offer, or bring into effect.

(b) The Day of the Lord
Note the following: Amos 5:18-20; Isa. 2:9ff; Zeph. 1:14-16.
See also: The day of vengeance of the Lord (Isa. 61:2). And: 'the great and terrible day of the Lord' (Mal. 3:2; 4:1 and 5).

(c) The theme of Providence in:
The Joseph Story (Gen. 37-50 – see esp. 45.4-8 and 11);
The book of Ruth; and the completed book of Isaiah

(d) Some Visions of the Future in the Book of Isaiah
    Isa. 2:2-4   Isa. 9:2-7   Isa. 11:1-9

(e) Death The Pit (Ps. 16:10; 28:1 etc.)
    Sheol (Gen. 42:38; Num. 16:30, 33 etc.). This seems to involve separation from God (see Isa. 38:18; Ps. 6:5), and the setting of Sheol is portrayed as being under the earth, that is at the farthest possible distance from God. Further, death is apparently a total breach with the world of the living, and represents a terrible and constant threat to human life.

16

(f) Hope of Life after Death
The 'translations' of Enoch (Gen. 5:24) and Elijah (2 Kings
2:1-15); Restoration of Israel in Hos. 6:1-3; 'Resurrection' of Israel in
Ezek. 37:1-14; the future life of the Servant in Isa. 53:10-12; Defeat of
death in Isa. 25:8 and 26:19; 'Many shall be raised...' (Dan. 12:2-3)
(g) 'Nothing can separate us from the living God...'
See Ps 16:9-11; 49:15; 73:23-28

LECTURE 5: THE PROPHETIC VISION

THREE ISSUES ABOUT LIFE IN THE WORLD–SOCIAL JUSTICE, MERCY, FELLOWSHIP
WITH GOD PROCLAIMED BY FOUR HEBREW PROPHETS: AMOS, HOSEA, ISAIAH,
MICAH.

(a) Social Justice:
Amos We could have gone here to Is 1:15-17; 5:7-8 or Micah 3:1-3,
but instead we go to Amos. In the prophecy of Amos note: Situation of
general prosperity at the time: 1:1, 3:15, 4:1, 6:1, 4-7. The man called
to be the Lord's prophet: 7:10-15. His teaching about social justice:
2:6-8; 5:14-15, 21-24 (esp. 'justice', *mishpat*, in 5:15, 24).
(b) Mercy:
Hosea's concern about Israel's faithlessness to God. See Hos. 1-3.
Which came first: experience of faithlessness in marriage, or insight
into people's faithlessness to God? Hosea proclaimed God's mercy,
loving kindness (*cheseth*) to his people (see 2:9). God requires this
from them to himself (6:6 not the non-lasting sort of 6:4), also between
themselves (4:1, 10:12, 12:6). See in particular 11:1-9 on this theme.
(c) Fellowship with God:
Book of **Isaiah** opens with picture of people who are not in the desired
fellowship with God (1:2-4). What instead is required? See 2:5, 6:1-13
(Note here: holy God, human sinfulness, called to service, the
message); 7:1-9 (Note: political crisis; call to faith, trust).
(d) Micah 6:8 sums up these three prophetic issues:
> He has told you, O mortal ('adam) what is good; and what does
> the Lord require of you but to do justice (mishpat), and to love
> kindness (cheseth), and to walk humbly (or 'modestly', even
> 'carefully') with your God.

Note here: The call to social justice (as seen in Amos); the desire that there should
be kindness; and the call to live the life of humble fellowship with God. Note also:
that it is 'your God'; that all this is a call to live a life of personal fellowship with the
one who is my/your/his/her/their Lord.

Only one 'apocalyptic' book in OT (though parts of other books in 'proto-apocalyptic' language), and that is Daniel, a book in two languages, and two parts. Only second part in apocalyptic language.

Chs 1-6: series of stories about Daniel and his three friends, in which one way or another they triumph over their captors.
Chs 7-12 are very different, and consist of four visions about the course of history from the Babylonian exile and up to the Greek kingdom. Apocalyptic is about 'revelation', esp. of heavenly mysteries and eschatological events. Did it develop from prophecy, or wisdom, or from parts of both? In the Bible, we have Daniel and Revelation from this tradition, but in inter-testamental era, there were many others around. Also, have proto-apocalyptic in Isa. 24-27, 34; Ezek. 38-39; Zech. 9-14; Joel 3.

Note the symbolism (to protect authors and those addressed); also the issue of 'surplus of meaning'.
Note also emphasis on dualism, division of world into good and evil; there are few shades of grey in this literature! Further, this is literature that comes out of desperate times, when good can only come through the direct action of God, it being beyond human ability to change things. That is, book of Daniel comes out of the clash of Jewish religion with the unbending Hellenistic kingdom.
Note: Two canonical forms of book of Daniel, also the two languages.

The Plan of the book of Daniel is as follows: Part 1

Ch.1: Three Jewish young men demonstrate that their way of life is superior to the captors' way.
Ch.2: Nebuchadnezzar's dream, and Daniel's interpretation of it.
Ch.3: Nebuchadnezzar's statue to be worshipped the burning, fiery furnace.
Ch.4: Another dream of the same king.
Ch.5: Belshazzar's banquet, the writing on the wall, Daniel the interpreter.
Ch.6: Daniel in the lions' den, but is protected.

Then in Part 2, four apocalyptic visions. Now Daniel is the dreamer, and an angel interprets:

Ch.7: Growing terror of Greek empire; God's judgement in hands of 'someone like a son of God'.

Ch.8: Ram and Goat representing Persian and Greek empires respectively.

Ch.9: Daniel's prayer of intercession and interpretation of prophecy in Jer. 25:11-14, 29:10.

Ch.10: Vision of a heavenly messenger.

Ch.11: Historical summary from Persian Empire to the Greek ruler Antiochus Epiphanes.

Ch.12: Resurrection and final retribution.

The message here is that the world is in a violent situation, beyond any prophet's preaching to remedy, and that all must be left in God's hands. Therefore the only thing God's people can do is to remain faithful to God, patiently leaving things in his care and purposes. Yet, and especially in the less violent situations portrayed in the first part of the book, the faithful people of God are shown to be 'right', even at times 'triumphant', demonstrating remarkable 'wisdom' and 'understanding'. The readers of the book of Daniel in every age are surely intended to understand these things, and in such times to live in the ongoing faithful practice of their faith.

LECTURE 7: MISSION AND MORALITY

WHAT CONTRIBUTION DOES THE OT MAKE TO CHRISTIAN ETHICS?

We do need to acknowledge the problems:
E.g. Ps. 137:8-9; Exod. 21:23-24; Lev. 24:19-20; Deut.19:21; Josh. chs 6, 11, etc. Compare Matt.5:44; Luke 6:35. However, we can pursue various approaches to the OT in our search for ethical guidance, as follows:

Imitation of God:
E.g., see Deut. 10:17-19, which stresses as God has loved his people, so should they love other people. Thus, Deut. gives emphasis to caring within the Israelite community–see Deut. 24:12-13, 14-15, 17, 19-21. And all this because ... Deut. 24:22. Words 'imitate, imitation' may not be used here, but the principle is present.

The Ten Commandments:

See Exod. 20 and Deut. 5:6-21, and also collections of laws in Exod. 34:14-28. In the Ten Commandments note how the emphasis is on what God has done first, and that he then calls for wholehearted acceptance of his lordship. That is, grace comes before law! First part of the Commandments is about relationship between people and God, and second about people and people.

Note Sabbath

In Exod. 20:8-11 and Deut. 5:14-15, and the different reasons given in these texts for its observance. The weekly day of rest came to have wide effect in lives of Jews and Christians. Ex 20:12 Deut. 21:18-21 and 27:16 stress family life, while Ex 20:13=Deut. 21:21 concerns the sanctity of life–perhaps the principle here is that life belongs to God. Then also are the prohibitions against adultery (Ex 20:14=Deut. 22:22); theft and stealing (Ex 20.15=Deut. 5.19 and see also Josh. 7:24; Ex 21:16; 1 Ki 21); bearing false witness (Exod. 20:16), for when this happens the judicial system cannot function properly. The final Commandment (Ex 20:17) lifts them onto a different level–one is not to 'desire' what belongs to another person. **Note how all this** comes out of the people of Israel 'knowing' God, and from the fact that he has dealt with them in such caring and loving ways. To obey these Commandments is to live as God acts and lives.

The Contribution of the Hebrew Prophets:

In particular about 'justice' (*mishpat*) and 'righteousness' (*tsedaqah*). See Isa. 5:7; 1:16-17. See also the warning in Amos 5:21-24. Further, Micah 6:8. Again, see the incident of Naboth's vineyard (1 Ki 21), and also what was happening in a later age (Micah 2:1-2; 6:11-12; Isa. 3:14; 5:8; Amos 2:6-7a; 8.4-6). Note about care for those who are suffering or dispossessed: (Amos 4:1-3; 6:4-6; Isa. 3:16-17; 5:11-13; Micah 3). Also about corruption in the legal system: (Isa. 5:22-23; 1:21-26; Amos 5:7, 12; Micah 7:3; Ez. 22:12). See also the condemnation of worship that comes out of unrighteousness situations: (Hos. 6:6; Am 5:21, 24; Isa. 1:13b; 1:12-17; Jer. 6:20).

Finally, no doubt there was sin and failure in the life of ancient Israel, and there is still the problem of such things as Samuel hewing Agag in pieces (1 Sam. 15:33), but equally there is surely in the OT much to guide us in our ethical search today. Nor have we been any more successful in leading moral lives than the people of ancient Israel?

Suffering is the common experience of us all, and of all peoples in the world. There is a special problem for those who believe themselves to be held in the care of a God of love, care and strength. Does the Old Testament give us any help with this? Here are four Old Testament responses to questions about suffering:

(1) Are we suffering because we have sinned?

This is the point of view of the books of Kings–which have been called a corporate confession of sin that resulted in the exiles of 722 and 587 BC. See 2 Ki 17, especially verses 7-18, and 2 Ki 24:1-7. It is also there in the books of Chronicles–see the two sides of this in 1 Chron. 10:13-14 (when you sin–see also 1 Chron. 10:13-14), and 2 Chron. 20:20 (when you believe in God). It is also there in many of the Old Testament prophets–see, for example, Isa. 3:13-4.1.

(2) Has another god caused the suffering?

While parts of the OT accept that there are other gods it says that they must not be worshipped or obeyed (see Ex 20:3-6; Deut. 5:5-7). But in Isa. 40-55 we have developed monotheism (belief in existence of only one god), and this prophet says that the Lord God of Israel is the creator of all things (Isa. 40:21-23, 28), that there is only one true God, Yahweh the God of Israel (40:12-31; 43:8-13; 46:5-13). The prophet says that idols are useless objects (40:18-20; 41:21-24; 44:9-20; 46:5-7). See also Isa. 45:5-7.

Note that in the OT, Satan: (Usually 'The Satan') is a servant of God who does certain works for God in the world (see Job 1-2; Zech. 3:-2), being in a 'heavenly council'. However, in intertestamental times, and in the NT, he has become a being who stands in opposition to God and who seeks to frustrate God's purposes. He becomes known by various other names, e.g. Beelzebul, Belial, 'the devil', 'the evil one', 'the ruler of demons'. Note his fate according to Matt. 25:41.

(3) Is God teaching us through suffering?

Amos 4:6-11 seems to be suggesting that God put suffering on the people of Amos's day in order to teach them to come back to him. However, this teaching seems to have failed, because Israel did not understand what God was trying to say to them through a series of disasters. Part of the contribution of Elihu to the great debate about suffering in the book of Job is that suffering may educate us in the ways that God wishes us to live. The speeches of Elihu are in Job 32-37, and within these see 36:1-25–in particular 36:8-12, 15-16.

(4) Shall we ever understand these things or will they remain a mystery?

Jeremiah suffered greatly as he served as a prophet of God, and he cried out to God. See Jer. 11:18-23; 15:15-21; 17:12-18; 18:18-23; 20:10-13. These are the so-called 'Confessions of Jeremiah', and they are like individual lament psalms (e.g. Ps 3-7; 9/10; 13; 17; 22 etc.) Jeremiah was assured that though the sufferings would go on, even so the Lord would be with him. See Jer:15.20-21; 20:11.

The book of Job is a great debate about the sufferings that apparently righteous people experience, and although various views are presented (Eliphaz, Bildad, Elihu, the Poem about Wisdom [ch.28], perhaps even in the Prologue [1:1-2.13; 42:7-17]). Job is not satisfied, and from the beginning to the end of the book he cries out to God (see e.g. Job 3 and 29-31). When eventually God appears and speaks to Job, he gives no answer to Job's problems and complaints. He does make Job aware of how much Job does not understand about the world and the creation. Yet God has spoken to Job! And that seems to have given satisfaction to Job–see 40:3-5; 42:1-6. So perhaps at the end of all the great debate, the book of Job says to us that in such innocent sufferings there is great mystery.

LECTURE 9: CONDITIONS AND CONVERSIONS

QUESTION: WHEN CONVERTS COME TO OUR CHURCHES, WHAT CONDITIONS WILL WE LAY UPON THEM?

E.g., Must they give up all connections with Traditional Religion? What about wives? Is there any help for us in the OT on this subject? Consider the historical situation for Jewish people after the exile and when they had returned to Jerusalem, and where they were joined by others (converts, proselytes). Jewish people had spent around 50 years in Babylon and elsewhere. Clearly some had served in foreign courts and had had to become eunuchs. Others had married foreign wives. In the OT, we can see three main attitudes towards such people as they came together in Jerusalem.

(1) The books of Ezra and Nehemiah take a strict line on this subject. We see this in Ezra's prayer of confession in Ezra 9 (see v.14) and in the making of a covenant that Jewish men will send away foreign wives and children (Ch. 10). The matter is spoken about also in Neh. 13:23-27–and note here the issue of mixed marriage in the priesthood (13:28-29). So in this approach, 'Thus I [Nehemiah] cleansed them from everything foreign ...' (Neh. 13:30).

(2) Chapters 56-66 of the book of Isaiah take a different approach in these matters. Here the temple is to be a house of prayer for *all* peoples, and foreigners who join themselves to the Lord (converts, proselytes) will be joyful in the temple, and moreover their burnt-offerings and their sacrifices will be acceptable on the altar, even 'to minister to him' (Isa. 56:6-7). It is understood that at this time as well as there being the gathering of the outcasts of the people of Israel (presumably from their exiles) the Lord will 'gather others to them' (56:8). Notice also here the welcome to the eunuch (56:3-5) and compare Deut. 23:1. What is happening here? Is an earlier law being set aside? See also Ezek. 44:7-9.

(3) The books of Chronicles, it is generally agreed, come from this same period of OT history, and perhaps present something of a compromise between the above two approaches. While the Chronicler's main concern is with Judah and Jerusalem, and thus leaves out history and kings of the northern kingdom (nothing here about Elijah and Elisha!) he does speak of events when some steps towards reunification are taken. Thus, see the very different treatment in 2 Chron. 28 from what is given in 2 Kings 16. See especially the 'sermon' of the prophet Oded in 2 Chron. 28:9-13, and the response to it in vv.14-15. See for other such incidents: 2 Chron 30:10; 34:6-7, 33; 35:17-18.

Perhaps in the post-exilic community the Chronicler wanted his people to adopt a moderate position, one that was neither 'separatist' (Ezra-Nehemiah) nor 'assimilationist' (Isa. 56-66).

Thus: When the converts come to our churches what conditions will we lay down? Shall we be 'separatist' or 'assimilationist' or 'compromisers'? Is the OT any help? Or may we agree to differ?

MODULE 2: NEW TESTAMENT MISSION

(The late Capt. Nicola Garnham MA BSc)

LECTURE 1: INTRODUCTION-WHAT IS MISSION?

The New Testament is a missionary document containing preaching, model mission history, and letters written primarily by missionaries while on mission.

FIRST, WE NEED TO DEFINE WHAT WE MEAN BY MISSION.

Traditionally the term mission has sometimes been confused with the term 'missions', the focus is on the activity of the church or ecclesiastical group. In his book *'Transforming Mission'* David Bosch, for example, lists a number of different meanings for the word mission used within the context of the church. These include: the sending out of missionaries; the activities undertaken by missionaries; the geographical area where missionaries are sent; the agencies which despatched the missionaries; the non-Christian world or mission field; a local congregation dependent on the support of a more established church; and a series of special church services or campaigns.

It is perhaps a consequence of this wide divergence in usage that the term mission has become somewhat misunderstood. But the key to beginning to grasp an understanding of 'mission' is the derivation of the Latin word–*missio*-to send. From this is derived the term *Missio Dei*-The Mission of God. It is essential to realize that God is the prime missionary; mission is not just another job for the Church to fit into its programme.

Mission [is] understood as being derived from the very nature of God. It [is] thus put in the context of the doctrine of the Trinity, not of ecclesiology or soteriology. The classical doctrine of the missio Dei as God the Father sending the Son, and God the Father and the Son sending the Spirit [is] expanded to include yet another "movement": Father, Son, and Holy Spirit sending the church into the world.[1]

---

1 (David Bosch, Transforming Mission: paradigm Shifts in Theology of Mission. Maryknoll, N.Y.:Orbis, 1991, 390.)

1. God is the main and most important protagonist of all missionary activity–mission is initiated developed and completed by God.
2. Mission is a communal activity–it begins with the participation of the three persons of the Trinity. It is initiated, developed and completed in community.
3. People of God are both the subject and object of God's mission.

God's mission started with creation, which laid the foundation and continues through the Old Testament. People were to be God's people.
The mission continues with the Mission of the Son. He died for us all, in order that we can be alive. God himself was on his way to heal us from sin.
God's mission is fulfilled in the sending of the Holy Spirit, pouring out God's love, in our hearts and inspiring us for our mission to bring life and love to other people. God's mission will meet his final goal when God dwells among his people as their God and they will be his people. The Mission of the triune God is nothing other than God's love in action. Because God is love, God is in mission seeking for us in order to show us his love.

Defining mission The 'five marks of mission' originally set out by the Lambeth conference of 1988 which is now used fairly widely ecumenically:
1. Proclaiming the good news of the Kingdom
2. Teaching, baptising and nurturing new believers
3. Responding to human need by loving service
4. Transforming unjust structures of society
5. Striving to safeguard the integrity of creation and sustaining and renewing life on earth.

Christian mission has been defined as:

....quite simply, the participation of Christians in the liberating mission of Jesus...it is the good news of God's love, incarnated in the witness of a community for the sake of the world.[1]

To participate in mission is to participate in the movement of God's love toward people, since God is a fountain of sending love.[2]

---

1 (Hering, 1980:78 quoted in Bosch, Transforming Mission, 1991, p. 519)

2 (Bosch, Transforming Mission, 1991, p. 390)

"Mission" describes...everything the church is sent into the world to do[1]

Mission embodies the total impact of the church on the world: it's involvement with the social, political and moral life of the community and nation where it is placed.[2]

Mission is about creating a community that cares for the world in the way God does.[3]

Mission is the participation of the people of God in God's action in the world.[4]

Questions for discussion:
1. How do the flowing aspects of God's nature shape God's mission: love, justice, holiness, mercy?
2. People may participate in mission for a variety of reasons, good and bad. List some good motives and some bad motives.
3. What opportunities for mission have the church you belong to found recently?
4. Discuss the statement 'Evangelism is mission but mission is more than evangelism'

Through the sending of His Son into the world, God demonstrated and revealed the motivation of His missio–his love for the whole world. ***God loved the people of this world so much that he gave his only Son, so that everyone who has faith in him will have eternal life and never really die.*** *John 3:16 (Contemporary English Version)*

LECTURE 2: THE PEOPLE OF GOD AND MISSION

MISSION IN THE OLD TESTAMENT

We cannot divorce the New Testament from the Old Testament, the Old Testament is fundamental to our understanding of mission in the New Testament. Jesus uses the Old Testament scriptures to announce and explain his mission. If there is a 'missionary' in the Old Testament, it is God himself. The word 'selah' which is translated 'send' occurs over 800 times in the Old Testament and over 200 times takes God as the subject. Selah implies:

---

1 John Stott, The Contemporary Christian, 1992 p.341

2 (Michael Green, Evangelism through the Local Church, 1990)

3 Alex McManus, Leadership. Summer 2003, p.41

4 Carlos F. Cardoza-Orlandi, Mission: An Essential Guide

- There is a purpose.
- The sending party has authority.
- There is a reluctance to disobey.

In the Old Testament, we see God sending his people, his servants, the prophets and also his promise to send a saviour.

Two important themes to note in our exploration of mission in the Old Testament are **creation** and **covenant.** The **creation** stories underline God's care concern and creative purposes for the world. Ken Gnanakan notes that 'Mission is God himself entering into our world and seeking to restore us and our environment to the glory that God intended.'[1] God showed that his mission is anchored in his **covenant,** for in the promises God made with Abraham, Isaac and David he had said that he would bless the whole world through them. Interestingly, Matthew's gospel begins with the genealogy of Jesus showing that he was a direct descendant of Abraham's.

Abraham-Gen 12: 1-5

God called Abraham, to leave his home and to go where God sent him. But this call does not only impact on Abraham and his family. Although God called a particular people, He did not restrict his purposes to this group but clearly declared that all the people on earth would be blessed through Abraham and his descendants. Abraham has no direct mission to the nations; he is not sent to call them to God. But he has a kind of 'indirect' mission; being faithful to God, leaving his country and his relatives, being a stranger in his world but nevertheless blessed by God.

Jonah-Jonah 1-4

This short book contains a wealth of insights into both our human condition and the mission of God. As well as telling us about a reluctant missionary, the book reveals a great deal about the graciousness of God in his dealings with Jonah and with the people of Nineveh. Here we see that God is more of a missionary than we are and that often he works in ways and among people that are unexpected. Jonah is frightened and he also misunderstands and misrepresents God, however God gives him a second chance.

---

1 Kingdom Concerns,1993, p.59

Questions for discussion:
1. Has God's desire for all nations to know him ever been rescinded?
2. What lessons can you/your church learn from Jonah's experience?

LECTURE 3: JESUS AND HIS MISSION

The Word became flesh and made his dwelling among us. We have seen his glory, the glory of the One and Only, who came from the Father, full of grace and truth. John 1:14 (NIV)

'The real starting point of the primitive Christian mission lies in the conduct of Jesus Himself.'[1]

THE MISSION MANIFESTO OF JESUS: READ-LUKE 4:16-30.

In His sermon at Nazareth Jesus proclaimed to the assembled congregation His understanding of Himself and His work. It is, if you like, the mission statement of Jesus. It acts as an introduction to the public ministry of Jesus and for this reason is very significant.

The following points should be noted:
• Luke tells us that Jesus returned to Galilee after He had been filled, empowered and anointed by the Holy Spirit. In this way, the writer underlines that the Holy Spirit was fundamental to Jesus carrying out his mission.
• The centrality of the poor in Jesus' mission. There can be no doubt that Jesus had a particular concern for the economically oppressed and His teaching emphasized that the coming of the Kingdom of God was particularly good news for the impoverished. This category could be extended to include all those who are marginalised or disadvantaged in society.
• The words 'the year of the Lord's favour' refer to the year of Jubilee, the year of release. According to Leviticus 25:10 every fiftieth year there was to be a balancing of the economic system, all property was to be returned to its original owner. It allowed for a periodic redistribution of land and wealth, the cancellation of debt and the freeing of slaves.
• Another unexpected factor in Jesus' announcement was that his words were ones of forgiveness and healing, not of vengeance and

---

1 Martin Hengel quoted in David Bosch Transforming Mission, 1991, p. 31

wrath. In fact, the harsh words of Isaiah 61:2b have been omitted from the quotation. The Messiah has come, not to bring destruction and retribution but to announce a year of favour for both Jews and their opponents. It is this foretaste of the Gentile mission, the suggestion that outsiders could be admitted to God's kingdom, which provoked the outburst of fury from the people in the synagogue.

Questions for discussion:
1. What part of Jesus' announcement is most significant for your church's ministry?
2. What sort of people might be excluded or marginalized from worship today? How could you break some of those boundaries?
3. Discuss how, in His ministry, Jesus went on to put into practice these principles.

LECTURE 4: THE KINGDOM OF GOD AND MISSION

The main theme of Jesus' teaching as recorded in the Gospels of Matthew, Mark and Luke is the coming of the Kingdom of God (Greek *Basileia*-the rule of God or God's way of doing things*)*. Matthew usually uses the term "Kingdom of Heaven", while Luke and Mark use "Kingdom of God". An explanation for this is that Matthew's Gospel was addressed to a Jewish audience who would avoid the direct use of the name of God. Mark and Luke addressed their gospels to a more general audience who would be unfamiliar with the term "Kingdom of Heaven".

Much of Jesus' teaching on the Kingdom of God is given in the form of parables. As Jesus proclaimed, taught and lived out the reality of the Kingdom he became involved in every area of human life, spiritual, social, economic. The rule of God is central to His understanding of His own mission. He challenged His hearers to break out of their narrow, nationalistic ideas about what the rule of God meant and He challenges us to appreciate fully what it means to bring the future reality of the Kingdom of God into the present. **Two features of Jesus' preaching about the Kingdom should be noted:**
- God's reign is both future and already present; it is both gift and promise.
- God's reign arrives where Jesus overcomes the power of evil, nevertheless the counter forces remain a reality.

"The calling of the church in every culture is to be mission. That is, the work of the church is not to be an agent or servant of the culture. The churches' business is not to maintain freedom or to promote wealth or to help a political party or to serve as the moral guide to culture. The church's mission is to be the presence of the kingdom. . . . The church's mission is to show the world what it looks like when a community of people live under the reign of God"[1]

"Kingdom people seek first the Kingdom of God and its justice; church people often put church work above concerns of justice, mercy and truth. Church people think about how to get people into the church; Kingdom people think about how to get the church into the world. Church people worry that the world might change the church; Kingdom people work to see the church change the world." [2]

"This is Jesus' missionary ministry: the long expected reign of God is being inaugurated...among the lowly and the despised"[3]

Questions for Discussion:
1. Define the Kingdom of God in your own words.
2. Why is the Kingdom of God a good model for mission?
3. Could your church be described as a sign of God's Kingdom?

LECTURE 5: THE DISCIPLES AND MISSION

Then Jesus came to them and said,
"All authority in heaven and on earth has been given to me. Therefore, go and make disciples of all nations, baptizing them in the name of the Father and of the Son and of the Holy Spirit, and teaching them to obey everything I have commanded you. And surely I am with you always, to the very end of the age." Matthew 28:18-20 NIV

EARLY IN HIS MINISTRY, JESUS SELECTED THE TWELVE TO BE HIS DISCIPLES

The word disciple from the Greek *mathetes* means a student or apprentice, one who learns by observing and doing, not just by reading and listening. (Matt 4:18-22) Later on, when they had spent some time with him, Jesus sent out the disciples with his authority (Matthew 10:1-42) They later came back and reported to Jesus all that they had done (Luke:10).

---

1 Robert Webber, The Younger Evangelicals, 2002, 133

2 (Howard Snyder, Liberating the Church, 1983:11)

3 Schotoroff & Stegemann quoted in Bosch, Transforming Mission, 1991, p. 33

After His death and resurrection Jesus commissions His disciples for mission (Matthew 28:16-20), sometimes known as the great commission.

- The foundation of the mission is the authority of Jesus
- Go–the emphasis is on movement or being sent. This word could also be translated as 'as you go'.
- Make disciples, not just converts, members, attendees or interested parties.
- Baptizing them, including them in the community.
- Teaching them, instructing them on life in the Kingdom.
- All nations or people groups, a universal mission.

The theme of discipleship is central to Matthew's gospel and to his understanding of mission and the church. The final verses of the gospel must be read in the light of all that has gone before; it is in essence a handbook for disciples. For Matthew teaching is not an academic exercise, it is a matter of the will rather than the intellect. The apostles are to teach the new disciples to submit to the rule of God as revealed in the life and ministry of Jesus. The 'Sermon on the Mount' (Matthew: 5-7) expresses the essence of the teaching of Jesus on discipleship.

"Jesus was short on sermons, long on conversations; short on answers, long on questions; short on abstractions and propositions; long on stories and parables; short on telling you what to think, long on challenging you to think for yourself; short on condemning the irreligious, long on confronting the religious." [1]

Questions for discussion:
1. If the people who come as newcomers to your church become like the people who are already there will that change the world?

2. To what extent do we as Christians fail to live according to the teaching of the Sermon on the Mount. How does that affect our mission?

---

1 Brian McLaren, More Ready Than You Realize p.15

THE NEW TESTAMENT WRITERS GIVE A VITAL ROLE TO THE HOLY SPIRIT

The Holy spirit is vital to the life of the community and their empowering and equipping for mission. Since the time of William Carey, when there has been great emphasis among evangelicals on the Great Commission, there may sometimes have been a tendency to overlook the role of the Holy Spirit in mission. There is a danger that thoughts about mission can focus on what we are to do rather than who we are to become, in the power of the Spirit.

Luke's purpose in writing his two part work, the gospel account and the book of Acts, was to show how the first Christians began to work out in their own context how to continue the mission of Jesus. He is careful to make the link between the ministry of Jesus and the story of the early Christian community and to note that it is the Spirit who will sustain and direct the work. **Read: Luke 24: 44-49 and Acts 1: 3-8**

In the gospel of John, we see again that the Holy Spirit is crucial for mission. In the 'farewell discourses' of John 14-16 John uses the Greek word '*paraclete*' which has a range of meanings including comforter, encourager and mediator. The Holy Spirit will be with the community to teach and guide them in the way that Jesus has done. At the end of the gospel, Jesus commissions His disciples, "As the Father has sent me, I am sending you", and then immediately they are filled with the Spirit. **Read: John 14:15-31, 16:5-16 and John 20:21-22**

"The same Spirit in whose power Jesus went into Galilee also thrusts the disciples into mission. The Spirit is not only the initiator and guide of mission, but also the one who empowers the mission."[1]

"Why did God send us His Holy Spirit?...There can be no doubt from a candid examination of the New Testament account that the prime purpose of the coming of the Spirit of God upon the disciples was to equip them for mission. The comforter comes not in order to allow us to be comfortable, but to make us missionaries."[2]

---

1 David Bosch Transforming Mission, 1991 p.113

2 Michael Green, Evangelism in the Early Church

"The presence of the Spirit so enriches the post-Easter community that its state is better than that of Jesus' own disciples...The paraclete does not simply replace the presence of the risen Christ in the community but intensifies it." [1]

Question for Discussion:
1. What do the words of Jesus 'As the Father has sent me, so I am sending you', mean for your mission and ministry.
2. What principles of mission can we learn from the incarnation?

LECTURE 7: THE EARLY CHURCH AND MISSION

In the book of Acts, the first history of the mission of the Church, we have Luke's compilation of oral accounts of how a localized Jewish movement began to spread throughout the then known world. As the apostles grappled with their understanding of who Jesus was they also came to understand more about His mission.

The Holy Spirit empowered the Apostles' and Early Church to:
Speak for God
- In their own languages Acts 2:14,37
- In other languages Acts 2:6-11
- In debate Acts 6:10
- Boldly Acts 4:29,31

Serve Others
- Through administration of aid Acts 6:1-6
- In famine relief Acts 11:27-30
- By signs and wonders Acts 3:1-8
- By living a missionary lifestyle Acts 2:42-47

Be Faithful
- Pray effectively Acts 12: 5-17
- Endure threats and abuse Acts 4:21-25
- Face martyrdom Acts 7:54-58

Gain Specific Guidance
- To start a new work Acts13:1-5
- To speak to individuals Acts 8: 26-31
- To break boundaries Acts 15: 24-29

---

1 Senior and Stuhmueller The Biblical Foundations for Mission, 1983, p.287

"The New Testament writers were not scholars who had the leisure to research the evidence before they put pen to paper. Rather, they wrote in the context of an 'emergency situation', of a church which, because of its missionary encounter with the world, was forced to theologize" [1]

"It is in encounters with the Holy Spirit that the early church works out its purpose. Theology is forged in the white heat of experience, where the apostles are moved or challenged or dumbfounded by the Spirit of the living God. If they become missionary apostles it is only because God does not give them much choice." [2]

Questions for discussion:
1. What can we do in our churches to ensure that we are open to the Holy Spirit?
2. When have you seen God working in new and unexpected ways?

LECTURE 8: PETER AND MISSION

PETER'S DISCIPLESHIP AND JOURNEY OF FAITH

Peter's journey of faith and his growing understanding of what it meant to be a follower of Jesus was a long and complex one:
1. When Jesus first called Simon Peter to follow Him, Peter had little idea of what he was getting into. Mark 1:16
2. He was an early witness to healing ministry of Jesus. Mk 1:29-31
3. He joined a group of companions travelling with Jesus. Mk 1:36-39
4. Peter was one of the three who formed an inner circle around Jesus. Mk 5: 37
5. He often acts as spokesman for the group. Mark 8:27-29
6. Peter is often portrayed as being impulsive. Mark14:29
7. Peter denied ever being with Jesus. Mark 14:6-72
8. He was the first apostle to preach about the resurrection. Acts1:14
9. He healed a lame man in the name of Jesus. Acts 3:1-10
10. Peter is the first apostle to be associated with the Gentile mission. Acts 10

---

1 David Bosch, Transforming Mission, 1991, p.16

2 Michael Riddell Threshold of the Future, 1998, p.17

THE SIGNIFICANCE OF ACTS 10

This story is of pivotal significance for the mission of the early church. The fact that Luke devotes a whole chapter to recording the details demonstrates the weight that he gave it. Some points to note from the chapter are:

➢ God is working here in unexpected ways, outside the orthodox religious community.

➢ Why was the journey necessary? Mission is a two way street. Cornelius had something to learn from Peter and Peter had something to learn from Cornelius.

➢ Peter's journey to Caesarea takes him right out of his comfort zone; it is difficult for us to grasp the gulf that existed between Jews and gentiles. Peter had a huge barrier to cross. Mission is always in the direction of others and away from ourselves.

➢ When Cornelius tries to worship him Peter corrects him but does not reject him.

➢ Peter gives an apparent pagan, time to tell the story of what he knows of God and of his activity in his life.

➢ Peter is amazed as he sees God doing something unprecedented, yet he recognizes that God is present and at work.

"We must be prepared to let God do genuinely new things within the history of mission... The people of God have many times been called upon to go beyond their boundaries. This is not a comfortable experience"[1]

Questions for Discussion:

1. Describe you own journey of discipleship and the way in which your understanding of mission has grown and developed.

2. What situations that you are faced with mean that you may need to 'think outside the box' in order to see God working in new ways.

LECTURE 9: PAUL AND MISSION

STARTING POINT FOR PAUL'S THEOLOGY AND HIS MISSION WAS HIS CONVERSION.

"The Apostle of the Damascus Road Experience" This is recorded in Acts 9:1-19 and is also referred to by Paul in his letters, for example Gal 1:1-17, 1 Cor 15: 8-11, 1 Cor 9:1-2, Phil 3: 3-11.

---

1 Mike Riddell, Threshold of the Future, 1998 p.27

Paul never identifies himself as a teacher, a thinker, a philosopher; he is always simply and plainly a messenger, an apostle, one sent with a message to deliver. Paul pursued a clearly thought out **mission strategy.** He especially concentrated on great cities, particularly the major seaports. He preached in the capital, Rome, and in Athens, the world's cultural centre. Philippi was the "chief city" of Macedonia (Acts 16:12), as was Corinth in Achaia and Ephesus in Asia Minor. Antioch, Troas and Thessalonica were all great seaport cities. His aim was not just to win individual converts; it was to plant influential regional churches. Establishing solid churches in such cities would provide centres for carrying the gospel throughout the world. Another characteristic of his practice is the way Paul works alongside colleagues such as Barnabas, Timothy, Priscilla and Aquila and Titus.

Michael Green in *Evangelism in the Early Church* (1970, p.286), identifies three main **missionary motives** common to the 1st century evangelists, all of which are identifiable in Paul. They are a sense of **gratitude** (Gal 2:20, Rom 5:5), a sense of **responsibility** (1 Cor 9:16, 19-23) and a sense of **concern** (Eph 2: 12-13, Rom 3: 23).

The content of Paul's **preaching and his mission theology** is reflected in his letters to the fledgling churches. It was the ministry of Paul to preach the Gospel to the Gentiles. His particular call as an apostle was to lay the foundations for new churches and to proclaim the Gospel at places where Christ had not already been preached. Thus Paul's theology was a theology of mission: a theology which explains to newly founded churches their foundations in Jesus Christ and how to build on it; and a theology which defends the mission among the Gentiles (1 Thess; 1,2 Cor) against those who question it or oppose it (Romans; Galatians; Philippians). Central to his theology is his conviction that it is through Jesus Christ that we are saved.

[We need] "to... extrapolate from Paul, to allow him to 'fertilize' our imagination and, in dependence on the guidance of the Holy Spirit, to prolong, in a creative way, the logic of Paul's theology and mission amid historical circumstances that are in many respects very different from his."[1]

---

1 David Bosch, Transforming Mission, 1991, p. 170

Questions for Discussion:
1. Compare, contrast, and then discuss Paul's approach to evangelism in different contexts.
2. What models are being employed and how does Paul try to connect with the culture of the people he is trying to reach? Acts 13: 14-48 (In Pisidian Antioch), Acts 14: 8-20 (In Lystra), Acts 16: 1-40 (In Philippi), Acts 17: 16-34 (In Athens), Acts 19: 1-20 (In Ephesus)

LECTURE 10: US AND MISSION

In his book "The Contemporary Christian" (1992) John Stott says, *'Our mission is to be modelled on Christ's. Just as his love for us is like the Father's love for him, so his sending us into the world is like his Father's sending him into the world* (p.342*).*

As we have explored mission in the New Testament over the last few days we have seen that we are collaborating with the Mission of God in the world and that our mission is rooted in the mission of Jesus. Mission means that we are sent in the power and with the enabling of the Holy Spirit.

The New Testament provides us with a foundation for mission, however we cannot simply lift principles and models from a 1st century context and expect them to work in our communities. Just as the Christians of the New Testament based their mission on the mission of Jesus and were willing to be guided by the Holy Spirit so we must be wiling for God to work in and through us to send us out into mission in new and unexpected ways.

Mission models for our world?
What models for mission are helpful to us in the 21st century in Nigeria or in London?
Mission as disciple making
Mission as caring for creation
Mission as seeking justice
Mission as signs and wonders
Mission as social activism
Mission as …

Late one Sunday night in Whitechapel, when I was about twelve or thirteen years of age, I was walking home with the founder when he led me for the first time in my life into a drinking saloon. I have never forgotten the effect that the scene produced upon me. The place was crowded with men, many of them bearing on their faces the marks of brutishness and vice, and with women also, dishevelled and drunken, in some cases with tiny children in their arms. There in that brilliantly lighted place, noxious with the fumes of drink and tobacco, and reeking with filth, my father, holding me by the hand, met my inquiring gaze and said, 'these are our people; these are the people I want you to live for and bring to Christ.'

Bramwell Booth

At times, participating in mission can seem daunting, but let's be reminded of the words of Jesus:

Anyone who has faith in me will do what I have been doing. He will do even greater things than these, because I am going to the Father. And I will do whatever you ask in my name, so that the Son may bring glory to the Father (John 14:12)

MODULE 2a: NEW TESTAMENT MISSION-PRACTICAL

(Revd Dr Malcolm McCall MA RN)

(& Mrs Janet McCall BA Dip.Ed.)

LECTURE 1: INTRODUCTION: GOD'S ULTIMATE PURPOSE

AIM:

To grasp the amazing scope of God's "first and last" mission purpose in Scripture in such a way that it becomes the heart of our mission and ministry

INTRODUCTION:

What does "Mission" mean? Mission is the activity of God. He is a sending God–messengers, prophets, leaders and His own Son (Luke 20:9–19). A missionary is God's fellow-worker (1 Cor. 3:9). But note use of the word "missional" because of unhelpful connotations of the word "missionary"–especially for some in the "majority world", the Global South. So, the **mission belongs to God**, and mission is also the response of the Christian community (Isa 6: 1–8: see also John 20:21–23, though this will be considered more closely in Lecture 5)

For relationship with "Mission" in OT (see Luke 24:44) Note: The purpose of mission is to reveal God, who is always present (Ex 3:1-14; Matt 1:23; Jn 1:14; Ps 139:7-12. To consider:

"God's mission comes first, then the Church" (Dakin, T).,

"What is the heart of a global perspective on the Church?" in Mission-shaped Questions, (ed. Croft, S., CPH, London, 2008), p43).

How to distinguish between "mission" and "evangelism"? Note that Methodist Church Nigeria is "repositioning for evangelism". Note also the difference between the words "evangelistic" and "evangelical".

THE HEART OF THE MATTER:

Rev. 5:9 and 7:9-10; also 21:- "a new heaven and a new earth". Here the mission described in Gen 12:1-3 finds its ultimate fulfilment. The Vision is for the reconciliation of all creation in Jesus. In Him alone, the whole potential of all Creation can be realised.

Jesus Himself makes the connection between what was revealed to Abraham and its fulfilment in Himself: "Your father Abraham rejoiced at the thought of seeing My day; he saw it and was glad" (Jn 8. 56) Paul develops and explains the nature of this connection, especially in Romans and Galatians: In Romans 4, Paul explains that Abraham is "father of us all"–that is, the father of "those who are of the faith of Abraham". (verse 16, cf. NLT translation: "Abraham is the father of all who believe.") In Gal 3:6-18 comes to the wonderful conclusion (writing to his fellow-Jews): *"He (God) redeemed us in order that the blessing given to Abraham might come to the Gentiles through Christ Jesus, so that by faith we might receive the promise of the Spirit" (NIV)* The end of chapter 3 gives an insight into the nature of the church and into Kingdom values, which has radical implications for us all: "you are all one in Christ Jesus" (28). But don't miss the huge scope of God's purposes for those who have put their faith in Jesus (26): *"Now that you belong to Christ you are the true children of Abraham. You are his heirs, and now all the promises God gave to him belong to you" (verse 29, NLT).* In this way, Paul "anchors" his mission to the Gentiles in the beginnings of God's covenant with His OT chosen people through Abraham.

No wonder, then, that Jesus says, *"Go and make disciples of all nations" (Matt.28:19)* and *"Go into all the world and preach the Good News to all creation" (Mark 16:15).* That has been God's declared purpose since Genesis 12:3!

The Scriptures may be understood as the narrative of how God has been, is, and will work out that purpose centrally through the Person and work of His beloved Son Jesus. What a privilege, what a challenge, what a battle!

A MORE DETAILED LOOK AT REVELATION 5.9 AND 7.9-10

Revelation chapters 4–7 sees the whole universe "from the vantage point of God's throne at its centre. The meaning of the history of the world is symbolized in a scroll in God's right hand which none is found worthy to open, except Christ, pictured as the Lamb who was slain" (Wright, op. cit., p249). The cross of Christ is the key to the unfolding purpose of history, to the unfolding mission of God, because (&.9-10):

41

1. It is redemptive. Cf. Rev.1:5b: "All praise to Him who loves us and has freed us from our sins by shedding His blood for us" (NLT). Forgiveness, cleansing, healing, freedom!!

2. It is universal. Cf. Rev. 5:9

3. It is victorious. The Lamb wins! Cf. Rev. 12:11: The redeemed overcame the enemy by the blood of the Lamb. He and His redeemed people will reign on the earth (ibid. p250)

APPLICATION FOR CHURCH LEADERS:

The "connecting link", and between Gen 12:3 and Revn 7 is that Abraham is *"the father of all who believe,"* and we who believe have been redeemed *"in order that the blessing given to Abraham might come to the Gentiles"* (i.e. people "from every nation, tribe, people and language")

Nothing on earth can compare with "all the families of the earth" (Gen. 12:3, NKJV) being blessed through our sharing the Good News of Jesus with them. May we be spoilt for any other purpose than this– to see God's Kingdom advancing throughout the planet, to see God's Kingdom come.

Now then, the challenge to Church leaders is,

Do we in fact have and seek the "faith of Abraham" to go ahead of our people, leading them in these things? Are we ready to leave everything, and go, at God's command (Genesis 12:1, 4)?–perhaps to Northern Nigeria? Will we obey God, even if it means giving up everything and everyone else? Perhaps for us, it is not a geographical moving, but rather a willingness to stand on our own if need be, even within the church, when others misunderstand us or actually oppose us? What about the local churches in which God has called us to minister? Do they realise that the first call on their time is to mission? Do they recognise Methodism as a "Mission Movement"? Are they eager to "reposition for evangelism? What are we doing to help them?

CONCLUSION

"It is the risen Jesus who alone is worthy to open the scroll, signifying the meaning of all history. And His worthiness and authority to do so rests on the cross, which is redemptive, universal and victorious (Rev. 5:9-10). Christ crucified and risen is the key to all history, for He is the One who accomplished the mission of God for all creation. If, then, it is in Christ crucified and risen that we find the focal point of the whole Bible's grand narrative, and therein also the focal point of the whole mission of God, our response is surely clear. Before we set about the essential task of working out what it means in practice that Jesus said to His disciples, *"As the Father has sent Me, I am sending you" (Jn.20.21),* in terms of our personal participation in God's mission in our context and generation, we first of all need to kneel with Thomas before Christ and confess, *"My Lord and my God"* (Jn.20:28)" (Wright, ibid, p535).

IMPORTANT NOTE:

You are required to produce an **Assignment** of around 1,500 words on this Module, to be presented to your National Tutor (i.e. your Group Tutor who is on the Staff at Umuahia/Sagamu). The title for the assignment will be given at the end of this set of lectures.

Also, at the end of these lectures, there will be an **Examination** on this module, to be taken during the Residential. Please don't hesitate to ask questions about these requirements, as they are an essential part of gaining the necessary credits for your Diploma from this module.

LECTURE 2: THE WOMAN AT THE WELL IN JOHN'S GOSPEL

AIM: How to do one-to-one "fishing for folk"–reaching a whole community at the same time!

Introduction: Water shortages in Nigeria–situation in Zonkwa.

Ex 17:1-7: People quarrelled with Moses–*"Give us water to drink".* People grumbled against Moses–*"Why did you bring us up out of Egypt . . . to die?"* Meribah=quarrelling; Massah=testing.

"Strike the rock and water will come out for the people to drink."

People tested not Moses, but the LORD: *"Is the LORD among us or not?"*

Cf. 1 Cor.10:4: *"they drank the same spiritual drink; for they drank from the spiritual rock that accompanied them, and that rock was Christ".*

John 7:37-39: Jesus' explicit *"Come to Me and drink"*–and the explanation that Living Water = Holy Spirit (but not yet given because Jesus not yet glorified) but to be given at Pentecost (see Acts 2:38-39)

Repent–be baptised by water (!)

Received gift of the Holy Spirit - be baptised by the Holy Spirit.

John 4:1-42: "The Woman at the Well:

Had 5 husbands/no husband/ partner. Must feel social outcast to choose unsociable and hottest time of day to draw water. Must have been dehydrated even fetching water! Town must have been distance away because disciples took time to return from buying food. Woman must have been trying to find fulfilment in life: 5 husbands/no husband/partner – digging her own cistern which could not hold water – trying to find an alternative stream. In C.S.Lewis, Silver Chair, the Lion representing Jesus says to a girl trying to find an alternative water-supply, *"There is no other stream"* (c.f. Jer.2:13: **the** Spring of Living Water) Jesus doesn't say in NT, "I AM the living water" as He does say, *"I AM the living bread"* **but** in OT Jer.2:13 states, *"My people have . . . forsaken Me, the Spring of Living Water"*- and they have dug "broken cisterns" that cannot hold water (cisterns=water tanks and channels).

Picture woman going to well–sees someone there, thinks, "Bother! I try to come when no-one is around and now . . . it's a man . . . and a Jew at that! Well, a man won't be talking to me–I'm only a woman. And even better, he's a Jew, so he would never lower himself to speak to me, a Samaritan. Divine appointment: Woman and Jesus at well alone together. Had common need of all human beings: water. If anything, Jesus seems more vulnerable than the woman. *"You have nothing to draw with and the well is deep"*, as she points out. We see Jesus later, even more vulnerable on the Cross, thirsty again! *"I thirst"* (John 19.28). He was there for our sake, suffering thirst for us, sharing our humanity. Yet out of His side flowed blood and water when the soldier stabbed His body with a spear. He promised: *"Whoever drinks the water I give will never thirst. Indeed, the water I give will become in him a spring of water welling up to eternal life"* (John 4:13-14).

Jesus, the Son of God, suffered thirst and asked a Samaritan woman for a drink. Then He suffered on the Cross for our sins–thirsty–taking our place so that we might have living water through Him.

Verse 16 seems like a fishing technique to "catch" the woman. (c.f. Jesus' promise: "I will make you fishers of men") *"Go call your husband." "I have no husband." "You are right"* – no husband. From this "word of knowledge," the woman recognizes Jesus as a prophet.

Then, *"I know Christ is coming." "I who speak to you am He"*, as Jesus reveals Himself to her.

Verse 29 further fishing technique–this time through the woman: *"Come see a man who told me everything I ever did. Could this be the Christ?"* Woman's words draw them: testimony always needs to draw people - beyond the one who testifies about Jesus - to Jesus. c.f. I Peter 3:15: *"Always be ready to give a reason for the hope that is in you"*.

Cf. Jesus asked His disciples, *"Who do you say I AM?"* Simon Peter answered, "You are the Messiah, the Son of the Living God" (Lk 9:20)

Verse 42: *"We no longer believe just because of what you said; now we have heard for ourselves and we know: this man really is the Saviour of the world."* (Believe with a second-hand faith to believing with a first-hand faith: knowing: He is Saviour of the world (c.f. Matt. 16.17)

CONCLUSION:

No accidental meeting–Jesus had to go through Samaria (verse 4: why? Because of the woman and her village, to bring them to salvation). Human side of the Son of God: tired (6); thirsty (7) but offering woman living water (10); probably hungry (8) but with food the disciples didn't know (32, 34)

Jesus broke down barriers between: Man/woman; Jews/Samaritans; Christ/woman of disrepute; Worship of Jews/worship of Samaritans; Place to worship/"spirit and truth" worship; "Messiah coming"/"I AM HE"

Jesus' technique: "Go call your husband and come back"

Honest answer: "I have no husband"; Truth-revealer: "You are right"

Conclusion: *"You are a prophet . . . . I know Messiah is coming. He will explain everything to us."*

Woman's technique: *"Come and see a man who told me everything I ever did"* Drawing townsfolk to Jesus; Stating His supernatural knowledge *"Could this be the Messiah?"* Doesn't conclude for them but suggests these go together. Her testimony excited them enough to go to Jesus and invite Him to stay.

We need to break down barriers and invite, *"Come and see"*.

FURTHER BIBLICAL STUDY:

Isaiah 44:3; John 7:37-39; Revelation 7:17; 21:17; 22:1; 22:1

To discuss: Where are the "flash-points" in this narrative?

AIM:

To underline the indispensable role of the Holy Spirit in the work of mission and evangelism.

INTRODUCTION:

Who is the "main character" in Luke/Acts apart from Jesus?

THE PERSON AND WORK OF THE HOLY SPIRIT IN THE GOSPEL OF LUKE:

Note how the accounts of the activity if the Holy Spirit in the Gospel of Luke prepare the reader for the dynamic role played by the Holy Spirit in the mission and evangelism described in Acts:

The Holy Spirit will come upon Mary so that she will give birth to Jesus. (Luke 1:35)
The Holy Spirit causes Zechariah to speak prophetically about his son John, and the salvation that is to come. (1:67-79)
The Holy Spirit directed Simeon to the temple Courts. (2:27)
Jesus will baptize you with the **Holy Spirit** and with fire (2:16). Note texts on the 2 entrances to Cliff College in the old days!
The Holy Spirit authenticated the person of Jesus. (3:21 -22)
Jesus, full of the Holy Spirit, was led by the Spirit in the desert. (4:1). c.f. Gal. 1:15-18.
The Holy Spirit anoints Jesus for His public ministry. (4:18-19)
Jesus promises the Father will give the Holy Spirit to those who ask. (11:13)

Jesus promises "power from on high" (24:49) in the context of understanding the Scriptures (44-46) and of preaching (47) and witnessing (48). All this can hardly be separated from Acts 1:8.

> *"It was the risen Jesus . . . who opened the eyes of the disciples to understand the Scriptures, by reading them in the double light of his own identity as the Messiah and of their ongoing mission to all nations in the power of the Spirit" (Wright, ibid. ps.534-535).*

See how **these themes are continued and developed in the Acts missional narrative. Acts of the Apostles might be described as "Acts of the Holy Spirit".**

1. The first Christians are all **baptized in the Holy Spirit**
E.g. Acts 2:1-4; 4:31; 8. 15-17; 10:44-47 (and 11:15-17); 19:1-8.
2. He gives assurance to what they are doing and what they preach
E.g. Acts 11:15-17; 15:28 Rom.8:16=Own personal experience 1976!
Favourite text of John Wesley-note his father's deathbed comment,
  "The inner witness, Son, that is what matters- the inner witness."
3. He points to Jesus: E.g. Acts 4:8, 12
"He will glorify Me" (John 16:14). If words and deeds do not point to
Jesus, they are not of the Holy Spirit: if they do, it is a good indication
that it is the work of the Holy Spirit. Acts 2:38, and 4:10-12 and 17:31
as examples. *"The more mission happens, the greater Jesus is seen to
be."* (Dakin in Mission-shaped Questions, p.46)
4. He provides for real fellowship ("koinonia") among believers
E.g. Acts 2:42-47; 2 Cor.13.14: CEV-*"may the Holy Spirit join all
your hearts together"*
5. He guides "He will guide you into all truth" (John 16:13). Note
Acts 13:1-4, especially in relation to mission. Also, the Holy Spirit
shows what is "good", breaking through cultural, racial and spiritual
boundaries and limitations
6. He gives power to be effective witnesses But you will receive
power when the Holy Spirit comes on you; and you will be My
witnesses in Jerusalem, and in all Judea and Samaria, and to the ends
of the earth" (Acts 1:7 – 8) NB: This same theme of Jesus is recorded
at the end of all 4 Gospels–twice as a command (Mark 16:15; Matt.
28:19) and twice as a statement or promise (John 20:21; Luke 24:49).
"Whom have you brought with you?" People need not feel daunted by
the whole matter of witnessing–what is at the centre of our beings is
bound to come out in our words and life-style (Matt.12.34-37).
7. He causes healings and miraculous signs and wonders *"Stretch
out your hand to heal and perform miraculous signs and wonders
through the Name of your holy Servant Jesus."* After they prayed, the
place where they were meeting was shaken. And they were all filled
with the Holy Spirit (Acts 4:30 -31).
8. He sends out on Mission Acts 8.–Philip; Acts 10:19–"the Spirit
said to Him"–so in this way Peter was led on to share the Good News
with Gentiles–a revolutionary step for a Jew. Acts 10:44, 47–it was the
receiving of the Holy Spirit by Gentiles in Cornelius' house that
persuaded Peter they should be baptised. Acts 13:1–5 –Antioch; Acts
16:6–10.

Many of the places Paul and the others wanted to visit were "closed" to them by "the Spirit of Jesus". And then He opened the way to go to Europe! Any Christian mission and evangelism must be Holy Spirit initiated!

In all these instances, the Holy Spirit causes them to cross cultural, racial, geographical and religious boundaries and limitations. The Council of Jerusalem is led by the Holy Spirit to recognise all this as "good" (Acts 15:28). Note: even earlier, in Acts 11:1-18, the Jerusalem Church had recognised the leading of the Holy Spirit in all this (15-18).

APPLICATION TO CHRISTIAN LEADERS:

Sign over Cliff College entrance: *"Did you receive the Holy Spirit when you believed?" (Acts 19:2)*
First followers filled more than once – see Acts 4:31b;
1 John 2:27–"abiding anointing"; Ephesians 3:16, 20–always more!
Eph. 5:18–"Be filled with the Spirit"–present, continuous, imperative!!

LECTURE 4: EVANGELISM AMONG THOSE SERIOUSLY INTERESTED

AIM:

To learn how to reach a whole nation with the Good News!

INTRODUCTION:

Leaving the 99 sheep to find number 100! See Luke 15:1-7

Context of Acts 8:

Believers fled the persecution in Jerusalem, preaching the Good News about Jesus. (cf. seeds being scattered) One was Philip, who brought the Good News to Samaria–*"So there was great joy in that city"*. May not be the Apostle Philip! A magician saw that Philip's message was more powerful than his magic and he also believed–*"he was amazed by the great miracles and signs Philip performed"* (See Mark16:20).
Philip impacting many, many people in the city of Samaria–it would be terrible to stop now! **But** an angel of the Lord told him (cf. "the Spirit of the Lord", later in verses 29 and 39).

"Go south-Down desert road (between Jerusalem and Gaza)."

Philip obeyed, free will still there, but obeyed, though he must have wondered who/how many he could preach to on a desert road! Ethiopian eunuch in chariot came up, sitting reading Isaiah 53. The eunuch could not really worship because he did not have the Spirit of God or the Truth (John 4:24) Holy Spirit's detailed instruction: *"Go over and walk along beside carriage"*. Philip ran–had to get to the carriage before he could walk! Sometimes we have to do something "strong" in initial obedience to God–Philip ran!

Heard man reading aloud: *"Do you understand?"* We must be sensitive to what is happening around us. We must be listening to God. Communication with Him is so important! Cue! How do we know what to say? If Philip had asked for a lift, maybe the eunuch would have said, "No". *"How can I?"* sounds full of frustration. Then he begged Philip to get up and sit with him.

Examine passage: Isa.53
He was led like a Lamb silently going to be killed. He was humbled and had no justice. Killed, so no descendants. Eunuch asked who it was about. The eunuch has been asking many relevant questions. Philip was enabled to understand the "heart-beat" of the eunuch. Perfect lead-in to preaching the Gospel!

Philip began where the Eunuch was (see Paul in Athens later-Acts 17:22), using Isa.53, and then leading on to other passages, to preach the Good News about Jesus. We need to be led in the way the Holy Spirit shows us. Came to water. Asked to be baptised. Water in desert is amazing–but just when the Eunuch was ready to be baptised! Spirit of the LORD (c.f. Angel of the Lord and the Holy Spirit) caught Philip away to Azotus (c.f. when Jesus ascending back to heaven, Luke24.50-53). Eunuch never saw him again, but went on his way rejoicing.

One man met one man–and a whole country was able to hear the Gospel through one key person, a high-ranking African under Queen Candace. Possibly the ancient Christian church in Ethiopia goes back to the conversion of this key official? Philip left the crowds because God told him to.

Philip never went himself to Ethiopia–rather like 'Gospel Smuggling'!!

Can we provide examples in our own ministry of the detailed leading and instruction of the Holy Spirit? Are there any ways in which we might more clearly and regularly know the detailed leading of the Holy Spirit in our daily ministry? What does it mean in our own local situation to "begin where the person is"–as Philip did with the Ethiopian eunuch?

LECTURE 5: EFFECTIVE CHURCH PLANTING AT ANTIOCH

(ACTS 11, 13 and 14)

AIM:

To identify New Testament principles of church-planting so that they may be applied our own situation.

1.   The Planting of a Missional church (Acts 11:18-22)

What were the "ingredients" in the planting of the Antioch Church which enabled it to be so vibrant, robust and dynamically growing?

a) Persecution! verse 19. *"The blood of the martyrs is the seed of the church."* Through history, and in the present day, where does the church grow most amazingly? Where there is persecution!
b) Reaching out over cultural and ethnic boundaries: verse 20. "God gives special grace and attractiveness to those who live and minister as aliens in a foreign land for the sake of the Gospel."
c) "The hand of the LORD was with them": verse 21. "If Your Presence will not go, do not carry us up from here" (Exodus 33:15)
d) Help from a more established and mature "mother church:" verse 22. Note how the Methodist Circuit system (and the whole Methodist Church organisation) is designed to work, with weaker, smaller, younger churches being helped by larger, more mature churches

2.   The Development of a Missional church (Acts 11:23-30)

Within a year or two (it would seem) the Church in Antioch had developed enormously in maturity, in strength, in numbers, and in service. What were the causes of this encouraging growth?

a) "The grace of God": verse 23. Cf. verse 21 above. No grace, no permanent spiritual growth and fruit. "We can all put on a good performance, but only God can provide a permanent harvest."

b) Encouragement from a "good man, full of the Holy Spirit and of faith:" verse 24. Barnabas=son of encouragement. What most Christians and struggling churches most need is encouragement!

c) Teamwork–each "playing to his strengths," doing what he was gifted by the Holy Spirit to do–Barnabas, encouraging; Paul, teaching.

d) Spending time on priorities: teaching, presumably daily, for a whole year: verse 25. How easily any Methodist minister seems to get side-tracked by trivialities!

e) Listening to the prophets, and responding in active service by sending financial help to their fellow believers: verses 27–30. They did not just say it–they did it! "It is not that we love anyone less–just that we love our sisters and brothers more!"

4.   The outreach of a missional church (Acts 13:1-4; 14:21-28)

Within a short time, perhaps less than a year (for Paul was still with them), the new young church at Antioch was engaged in church-planting itself in Cyprus and Asia Minor (present-day Turkey)! At least 5 churches were soon planted. So the new church-plant quickly became a church-planter! What factors enabled this to happen?

a) Worship, fasting and prayer: 13. 1-2

b) Obedience to the prompting of the Holy Spirit: verse 3

c) Laying on of hands and sending them off: verse 3. We are all "goers" or "senders". It's just that the "senders" stay and pray!

d) The Church in Antioch sent their best men!

e) The "goers" re-connected with the "senders". Very important to let those who stayed behind to pray share into all that God does through the "goers".
Cf. the crucial principle in 1 Samuel 30:24:

the share of the one who goes down into battle shall be the same as the share of the one who stays by the baggage; they shall share alike.

(NB: Don't neglect the significance of Acts 14:26-28.)

AIM:

To discover from Paul's first mission journey (and especially Acts. 14:21-28) principles of "growing" a new church-plant.

SOME BASIC PRINCIPLES:
1. "Then they returned"
"Like new-born babies, crave pure spiritual milk" (I Peter 2:2). "You need milk" (Hebrews 5:12 – examine context). The need for pastoring c.f. John 21:15–"Feed my lambs"–and I Peter 5:1-4 **Return to them!**
2. "strengthening the disciples" (22)
See Ephesians 3:14-2. Note Psalm 59:9: "You are my Strength."
Seek the LORD Himself to strengthen them!
3. "encouraging them to remain true to the faith" (22)
See Acts 11:22-30. We can assume that the way Barnabas did it in Antioch (23) was the way Paul and Silas did it elsewhere:
a) "a good man, full of the Holy Spirit and faith"–personal spiritual integrity
b) ""went . . . to look for Saul" – team ministry, and identifying the right people to help build up the new church
c) "for a whole year Barnabas and Saul met with the church and taught great numbers of people"–no substitute for meeting together for teaching!   **Encourage them!**
4. "we must go through many hardships to enter the Kingdom of God" (22)
See Matt 10 – especially verse 22; Luke 9: 57-62 Mark 9: 34-38
Gal 2:19 (NB–cannot go on to v 20 unless we start at v 19!)
Prepare them for difficulties, adversities, hardship, suffering and spiritual battle!   **Prepare them!**
5. "appointed elders" (23)
The whole question of leadership and authority Matt. 18:15-20; 28: 18
Provide proper spiritual authority – thank God for MCN!
6. "committed them to the LORD" (23)
See Jude 24-25. Important that we recognise it is not our good nurturing or pastoral ability that causes new Christians and new church-plants to grow. 2 Cor 12:9-10 apply quite as much to this area of our life and ministry as any other–though that should not become an excuse for laziness on our part!
Recognise it is only the LORD who can do it!

Planting a new church is not the end of the matter, but only the beginning! Seeing people won for Christ is bringing them (by God's grace) to the starting line of the race, not to the finishing tape!

LECTURE 7: PREACHING AND CHURCH PLANTING IN LYSTRA

AIM:

To discover the apostolic method and message in speaking to a completely non-Jewish crowd–just the sort of people we will be addressing in our own evangelism-in order to identify key elements which need to be part of our own evangelistic ministry

1. "ACCOMPANYING SIGNS"
See Mark 16:20 signs, wonders and miracles are the natural accompaniment to the preaching of the Gospel. Cf. Acts 3

2. THE CHARACTER OF THE MESSENGERS
They were horrified to think of the pagan priests offering sacrifices to them!

This incident reveals the danger of identifying what is done in the name of Jesus as having been performed by people, and then treating them like gods. The church today needs to be aware of this danger, for personality cults can end up treating those with a remarkable ministry as if they are on the same level as Jesus. (Paul Mumo Kisau-of Nairobi, Kenya–in The African Bible Commentary, p.1325).
See Acts 3 again, verses 12-13

3. CONNECTING WITH THE CROWD (Verses 15 – 17):

We bring you Good News, that you should turn from these worthless things to the living God".
The living God, who made the heaven and earth and the sea and all that is in them.
In past generations He allowed the nations to follow their own ways, yet He has not left Himself without a witness in doing good – giving you rains from heaven and fruitful seasons, and filling you with food and your hearts with joy. (NRSV).

Other translations of verse 17a:

Yet He has not left Himself without testimony. He has shown kindness by giving you . . . . (NIV).
but even then He did not leave you without evidence of Himself in the good things He does for you. (JB). c.f. Rom 1:19-20

4. THE CORE OF THE GOSPEL

Clearly, Luke does not here provide a full account of Paul's preaching of the Gospel on this occasion. He only summarizes Paul's introductory shouted plea to the crowd, emphasizing the terrible misunderstanding the crowd was falling into. We are assured that Paul and Barnabas focused totally in this region on "proclaiming the Good News" (14:7), and we are aware that in verses 15–17 the basic Good News is by no means fully proclaimed. The full proclamation of the Gospel was Paul's whole concern wherever he went (1 Corinthians 1. 17; Romans 1:15 - 16).

From other places in Acts and Paul's letters, then, what was the core of Paul's Gospel message?

1. The cross (1 Cor. 1:17)

2. The resurrection and imminent return of Jesus (1 Thessalonians 1:9-10: note how similar the language of v 9 is to Acts 14: 15)

3. Repent! (Acts 13:24)

4. Believe in Jesus, be forgiven and be free! (Acts 13:38-39)

5. Live together in the church in a new Kingdom lifestyle – which will involve you in persecution! (Acts 14:21-23)

5. CONFLICT!

See verses 19–20; c.f. 2 Tim 3:12; 1 Pet 4:12–19; 5:9; Lk 9:23– noting that cross is a one-way ticket to death by way of hideous torture!

6. CONTINUING CARE FOR NEW CONVERTS

New church-plants need lots of nurture! See verses 21 – 23 again

AIM:

To explore "making connections" when preaching the Gospel to a Gentile crowd with no biblical background.

INTRODUCTION:

Esther reading 3:11–4:3. Shake hands–why? Connections! Esther touched the golden sceptre between her and death. Our golden sceptre =Jesus.

Acts 8: 26-40. Philip made connection with Ethiopian eunuch where the man was at – in the desert, but also in Isa.53.

1. Religious: People's attempts to make connection with God through "religion:" Trying to earn salvation or trying to appease Him.

Hausa word for God–"Allah"–used in Bible-translation. Good, because there is only one God, one true God – we know Him through Jesus: *"No one comes to the Father except through Me"* (John 14:6b). The unknown God can be known through Him. This was Paul's technique in Athens: the unknown god you already worship – He is the One I have come to tell you about. Even as Christians, we can be "religious" without realising it. Dennis' story of minister under another's leadership: religiosity in a) Prayer b) Bible study c) Worship

2. Reach out: Lk 8:43–48: We can reach out not just physically, and be reached out to. It can be by calling/inviting like Jesus with Zacchaeus (Lk 18:1-10)

3. Repent: 2 Cor. 7:10–one way godly–not like Judas Iscariot. Jesus must become greater, I must become less . . and less . . and less (John 3. 30). "1" before "000s" (c.f. Job 33:22-24). Repent and be baptised for forgiveness (Acts 2:38)

4. Resurrection: God will judge with justice by a man sent from God (John 3:16). God's proof to all by raising Him from the dead (Acts 2:22-24). Accredited by the Resurrection: Jesus Christ as Son of God.

Three occasions recorded in Acts when Paul preached particularly to Gentiles who were pagan worshippers of the "gods" of Greek culture, but had experienced little contact with Judaism:

1.   **Lystra** (Acts 14: 8-20). Lame healed–Barnabas called "Zeus" and Paul "Hermes". They insisted that they were only human themselves, and that people needed to turn from "these worthless things" to the living God: their Creator and Benefactor.

2.   **Athens** (Acts 17:16-34). The discussion at the Areopagus may have been a public enquiry because the introduction of a new god was not a religious problem to the people, but the civil authorities needed to "check out" the "track record" of the new deity and see if the sponsor could afford to set up a temple, provide sacrifices and pay priests, etc. BUT Paul shows God doesn't need their accreditation – He is in judgement on them! He didn't need service or housing: He provides for all the human race.

3.   **Ephesus** (Acts 19:9-10). Paul gave 2 years of systematic lectures. Healings (19:9-10). To truly converted believers (19:17-20). Resulting in sales of idols decreasing in Ephesus. 19:23-27: man-made gods = no gods.

Paul's message was a challenge to:
1.   Lystra, because a monotheistic message
2.   Athens, because of intellectual and civic pride
3.   Ephesus, because of economic interest

In **Lystra** and **Athens** Paul emphasises God as the One living Creator of heaven and earth (Acts 13:15 and 17:24) and the Providence of God (13:17 and 17:25). In Lystra this is evidence of God's kindness, giving joy even to pagans. In Athens he gives proof that God longs for people to seek Him, though He is not far from us.

Paul uses pagan poetry to illustrate this (17:27-28). In both Lystra and Athens, Paul says God has been patient with them over this pagan ignorance in the past (13:16 and 17:30), but now there needs to be a turning away from worship of worthless things (13:15) because they are inadequate for the Divine Being (17:29).

NB: Pagans in Thessalonica also turned from idols to serve the true and living God (1Thess.1:9.) In Athens Paul speaks of judgement, and links this with the Resurrection (Acts 17:31).

NB: Paul is not calculatingly offensive against Artemis/Diana (Acts 19:37). Interesting how Paul's attitude changes depending on whether he speaks to believers or unbelievers. To Roman Christians (Chap. 1) he lays out a theological argument with the Christians, highlighting the wrath of God, whereas in Acts he is an evangelist preaching to pagans and highlighting God's kindness. To both, he emphasises Judgement.

To the Roman Christians, idolatry is rebellion and brings wickedness and perverted thinking: "lie". In Athens, idolatry is seen as from ignorance and worthless and "absurd". He did nothing to blaspheme Artemis/Diana their goddess. Also, interestingly, Paul uses no OT quotations when addressing Gentiles.

CONCLUSION:

Paul starts where the Athenians are, using their religiosity, poetry and curiosity. He actually takes what opposes the worship of the Christian God and converts it into an advantage (e.g. The "unknown god" altar). He dares to discuss intellectually, because Athenians spend their time doing that, but he is careful not to blaspheme or "knock" their deity. He begins by speaking to their cultural understanding.

Bibliography:
Special reference to: Wright, Christopher, The Mission of God (IVP, Nottingham, England, 2006; ISBN 978-1-84474-152-6)

LECTURE 9: MISSION ENCOMPASSES ALL CREATION

AIM:

To look at the NT "big picture" within which we are repositioning for evangelism, and thereby be more maturely effective in our mission.

1. Review Paul's preaching in Athens and Lystra:

What was the "big picture" within which Paul set his preaching to non-Jewish listeners?

This is seen in the preaching recorded in Acts, especially on the two occasions when we have a record of the sermons to completely Gentile listeners who had no previous knowledge of the OT revelation. (Cornelius, in Chapter 10 was already a "God-fearer", "respected by all the Jewish people".)

In **Lystra** (Acts 14. 8-20) and in **Athens** (17: 16-34), Paul starts with the God of all creation. He "emphasizes God as the one living Creator of heaven and earth (13:15; 17, 24). In both he stresses the providence of God in giving humans all the necessities of life, even life and breath itself (13:17; 17:25). In Lystra he offers this as evidence of the kindness of God bringing joy even to pagans; in Athens he offers it as proof that God longs for people to seek him, though he is in fact not far from any of us (supporting this from pagan poetry–17:27-28). In both places, he notes that God has been patient and tolerant of pagan ignorance in the past (13:16; 17.30). But in both he also calls for a decisive turning away from the worship of "worthless things" (13:15), which are hopelessly inadequate for the divine being (17:29)" (Wright, ibid, p.181).

Note: How might a study of Paul's preaching in Lystra and Athens affect our own evangelism? Paul's evangelism was uncompromisingly effective but it was not calculatingly offensive.

2. The "big picture" in Paul's letters:

See the missiological significance of **Ephesians 1:9-10**: God's purpose in Christ involves the whole of time and "all things in heaven and on earth" (10);

1 Corinthians 15:20-28: the Mission involves "all dominion, authority and power" (24), including death (26) - "everything" has been put under Jesus (27); **Romans 8:16-25:** "the creation itself" (21); **Colossians 1:15-20**: "all things were created" by Jesus (16) and for Him (16b). Through Jesus, God's purpose is "to reconcile to Himself all things, whether things on earth or things in heaven" (20). Each of these passages deserves a set of lectures devoted solely to them!

3. Romans as a "missional tract"

One way in which the cosmic sweep of the Mission affects Paul's thinking when he writes to the Christians at Rome is that he himself is constantly thinking "globally". See especially 1:8-17: Paul's vision extends "all over the world" (8), "both to Greeks and non-Greeks" (14); 15:8-32: Paul is planning to go to Spain (24). "I hope to visit you while passing through and to have you assist me on my journey there, after I have enjoyed your company for a while" (24).

Crucially, too, note 16:25-26:

"so that all nations might believe and obey Him".

In this setting, the whole doctrine of **election** takes on a different focus. "Election is of course . . . election unto salvation. But it is **first of all election into mission**" (Wright p.264). We are saved to serve, to seek the lost – "chosen instruments" to pass on the message of salvation to others. "God's calling and election of Abraham was . . . that he and his people should be the instruments through whom God would gather that multinational multitude that no man or woman can number" (ibid.) The election argument in Romans 9-11 ends with this:

"The gifts and the call of God are irrevocable" (11. 29). What call? Surely the missional call of Isaiah 6. 1-8, implied also in Genesis 12. 1-3–the call to share in the missional purpose of the LORD God Himself.

Romans 11:32 would bear this out: **"so that He may have mercy on them all."**

If this is the case, a church which is not a missionary church is hardly a church at all. And a Methodist presbyter who is not on a mission needs either to repent or resign! For God's call to us is essentially a call to share in His mission purposes:

"woe to me if I do not preach the Gospel!" (1Corinthians 9:16) – in order "to win as many as possible" (19)

Is that where I am at in my ministry?

4. Application for our own ministry, mission and evangelism:

a)   "Methodism **is** mission." In light of this lecture, how do you now understand this statement? What are we going to do about it? What are the challenges and difficulties?

b)   "Evangelism precedes the Church." Is this statement true?

c)   How will this vision of "the big picture" practically affect your life and work as a Methodist minister? What changes will be required in your churches and in your own life?

AIM:

To reinforce, from John's Gospel, the central Truth about evangelism –that Jesus Himself is the only reason, the only Empowerer, the only Way to bear "fruit" that will last.

INTRODUCTION:

"Apart from Me you can do nothing" (John 15:5). Do we really believe that? Do our lives and ministries as evangelists demonstrate (live out) that truth? Do we walk the talk? Of course, **the whole of the NT** points the same way: E.g. Mark 1:1: *"The beginning of the gospel about Jesus Christ, the Son of God"* and

Jesus Himself is the **only** Saviour–so there is no evangelism apart from him–there is no salvation apart from Him (Acts 4:11-12). We have nothing to preach if we don't centre on Jesus. and

Jesus Himself is the **only** Foundation of everything (Col. 1:17). We must not slip away from Him as the Foundation, the Cornerstone. We must not seek anything within the church or for other believers which is not founded entirely on Jesus:

(1 Cor. 3:11–"no one can lay any foundation other than the one already laid, which is Jesus Christ"). Yet in a particularly amazing way, **John continually focuses us on the Person of Jesus.**

Jesus, be the Centre, Be my source, be my light, Jesus.
Be the fire in my heart, Be the wind in these sails,
Be the reason that I live, Jesus.
Jesus, be the Centre, Be my hope, be my song, Jesus.
Jesus, be my vision, Be my path, be my guide, Jesus.

An early recognition of the Truth in John's Gospel:
"He must become greater; I must become less" (John 3:30).
Read the context in verses 27 – 36: Life is only to be found through believing in Jesus (36)

1.   Jesus the Centre in John Chapters 5–12

Look for a phrase or sentence in each of these chapters which demonstrates this truth. A summary of this truth may be found in Jesus' words in John 14:6: "No one comes to the Father except through Me."

2.   The crucial request

"Sir, we would like to see Jesus" (12:24). In some pulpits, that request is placed on a piece of paper on the lectern, to remind the preachers constantly of their task.

3.   The revealing picture of the Vine, the branches, and the fruit: John 15:1-17

Consider the implications for us in our lives, our evangelism, our ministries, of these words of Jesus:

Verse 5: "Abide:": "Go on growing in Me" (Phillips); "Remain united to Me" (GNB); "Live in Me" (LB); "Make your home in Me, as I make mine in you" (JB) "Stay joined to Me" (CEV)

Verse 10: "obey My commands"

Verse 12: "love each other as I have loved you"

Verse 16: "ask in My Name"

Note especially Jesus' summary in verse 16: *"I chose you and appointed you to go and bear fruit – fruit that will last".* Even our coming to this time and place in our lives, to this Course, is a result of **His** choice. The only lasting fruit (souls won for Christ and made like Him) is entirely dependent on **Him.**

4.   Jesus sends us out to do what He has done

Jn 20:21–23 He focused on doing God's will completely (Jn 6:38) and on speaking God's word only (John 12:49). So we are to do the same if we are truly His. Jesus sends us out to do what He has done! Bishop Leslie Newbigin (quoted by Revd Dr Martyn Atkins) used to say that the most important word in Jn 20 19-23 is **"as".**

Note: Jn 13:1-17 is a crucial element in the "as": missional activity involves actions as well as words, service as well as proclamation!

CONCLUSION:

Fruitful evangelism–with fruit that lasts–depends entirely (from the perspective of our responsibility) on us living a Gal 2:20 life-Crucified–dead and buried–no longer us–Jesus only.

All for Jesus – all for Jesus, This our song shall ever be:
For we have no hope, nor Saviour, If we have no hope in Thee
All for Jesus – Thou hast loved us; All for Jesus – Thou hast died;
All for Jesus – Thou art with us; All for Jesus crucified.

MODULE 3: MISSION/EVANGELISM-PRACTICAL

(Revd Dr Martyn Atkins BA)

THE PRACTICE OF MISSION/EVANGELISM-THEN AND NOW

LECTURE 1: HISTORY OF MISSIONARY MOVEMENTS

Some Definitions of Evangelism:

WJ Abraham *'Evangelism is best construed as that set of actions which are governed by the intention to initiate people into the Kingdom of God.'[1]*

Evangelism   *1. The preaching or promulgation of the gospel.*
                 2. Evangelicalism.
Evangelist   *1. Any of the writers of the four gospels.*
                 2. A preacher of the gospel.
                 3. A lay person doing missionary work ...
Evangelize   *1. Preach the gospel to.*
                 2. Convert (a person) to Christianity

D T Niles, *(missionary in India) 'One beggar telling another beggar where to find food'.*

Harvie Conn *'Evangelism is giving God's message of life in such a way that it is understandable in every culture and in every situation, as one becomes involved in the ministry of listening and serving as well as speaking'.*

David Bosch *'...that dimension and activity of the church's mission which, by word and deed and in the light of particular conditions and a particular context, offers every person and community, everywhere, a valid opportunity to be directly challenged to a radical reorientation of their lives, a reorientation which involves such things as deliverance from slavery to the world and its powers; embracing Christ as Saviour and Lord; becoming a living member of his*

---

1 Abraham WJ The Art of Evangelism (Sheffield: Cliff College Publishing, 1993) p33

community, the church; being enlisted into his service of reconciliation, peace, and justice on earth; and being committed to God's purpose of placing all things under the rule of Christ. [1]

The Lausanne Covenant, 1974 '... *to evangelise is to spread the good news that Jesus Christ died for our sins and was raised from the dead according to the Scriptures, and that as the reigning Lord he now offers the forgiveness of sins and the liberating gift of the spirit to all who repent and believe.*'

HOW DID IT ALL BEGIN?

Great Commission–John 20:21 'As the Father has sent me, I also send you'. Matthew 28:20 'All authority has been given ....Go therefore ...'
Acts 2-beginning of the Christian church and the missionary movements that followed. History of Christian Mission - Early church (to 325AD)
Jewish church–people influenced by the apostles after Pentecost.
The church in Jerusalem-Temple worship-animal sacrifices - male children circumcised-Old rituals followed-old law books read
Very soon, this church expanded to include Gentiles–Acts 10

NICAEA (FROM 325 – 600AD)

Preaching to the Greeks. By AD300, possibly half the urban population in some Roman provinces were Christian.[2] By 325AD, Christian Jews were in the minority.
Council of Nicaea convened by King Constantine, Nicene Creed (Note: little to do with behaviour of Christians as in the Sermon on the Mount, but all about doctrinal statements and belief.)
Or by setting out what we believe, do we put barriers in place for those who believe differently?
Christian centres around the eastern Mediterranean. Key language of the church was Greek. The 'bold confession ... that Jesus was Lord ended in a compromise where the emperor was to rule 'in time' and Christ in 'eternity'[3] Non-Christian faiths were regarded as inferior to Christianity. Christianity spread outside the Roman Empire.

---

1 Bosch Transforming Mission (Maryknoll: Orbis Books, 1991) p.420

2 Bosch p.192

3 Bosch p.302

YES! *Freedom from persecution*
order/rules /uniformity/creeds
political influence
finance and other resources
comfortable place to be–no argument!
easy/non-demanding
credibility (imputed)
hierarchy
accountability

NO! *no room for diversity*
no freedom/flexibility
no individuality/individualism/cultural diversity
no personal awareness
church taken for granted
false security
lukewarmness/nominality/complacency/apathy
restrictive
link between Christianity & Western culture/politics
non-missionary (evangelical) activity

MIDDLE AGES (600–1500AD)-MEDIEVAL ROMAN CATHOLIC MISSIONARY ERA:

Literary culture based on Latin, the language of the sacred books and the liturgy
Power remained in the hands of the clergy–the ordinary people could not read
Christianity was synonymous with the class system–accompanied social change
Ecclesiasticization of salvation; marriage of state and church

PROTESTANT REFORMATION/ ENLIGHTENMENT (1500AD ONWARDS.) MODERNITY I

The Age of Reason–Descartes, *'I think, therefore I am'*
Scientific method–observe, analyse, understand - control of natural world–people no longer victims of nature–superstition banished–authority of Church/tradition questioned.

---

1 Bowen R ...So I Send You (London: SPCK, 1996) p 153

Individualism–freedom to think, behave as we wish–tolerance of private options outside the area of public truth, including religious belief. Concept of purpose eliminated from scientific study.

Missionary activity: 'One way traffic' for Christian expansion.
Political: individual enthusiasm/lack of control by central government
Economical :surplus of cash
Religious: Christian self-confidence, missionary expansion, Mission compounds.

Karl Barth–the church does not exist for itself, 'It exists as it is sent and active in its mission'.[1]
Gustav Warneck–European colonial expansion could open the door for missions, but … should be independent of colonialism .. advocated indigenous 'people's churches'.
Bruno Gutman–theology of creation - missionaries must respect existing social systems – gospel of Christ must fit into the basic social framework, not destroy it.
Anti-colonialism–new awareness and respect for indigenous peoples

THREE NEW MOVEMENTS. 2

a. Pentecostal Movement–Latin America
b. Theological Education by Extension–Guatemala
c. Liberation Theology–Base communities–Brazil

Africa [3] The Indigenous Movement–many churches either left the main-line churches or were expelled from them
Movements of Renewal-reflected priorities of local culture, community and relationships. Challenged other aspects of local culture e.g. OK to admit failure Translated gospel into concrete action
Leaders of Revival not clergy but laity. Clear pattern to worship, everyone contributed, relevant and full of praise Administration seemed chaotic compared with missionary standards. Most importantly, 'walk in the light' with one another.

---

1 Barth K Church Dogmatics (vol.IV, pp. 724ff) quoted in Bowen p.12
2 Bowen p.170 ff
3 Bowen p.131 ff.

'MISSION'

Various definitions: mainly these describe authority and structure:

Evangelism = *propagation of faith*
Event = *evangelistic project or activity*
Agency = *sending organisation*
Foreign field = *conversion of heathen*
Style of church = *charismatic, liturgical, liberal*

The church in mission mode.
Sign-pointer, symbol, example, model.
Sacrament-mediation,
Representation, anticipation.

GOD'S MISSION – MISSIO DEI

O.T.

1. Distinctiveness of Israel among the nations.
2. God gives promises linked to covenant.
3. God chooses Israel who is in the centre of His purposes.
4. God's compassion embraces all nations in judgement and mercy.

N.T. Four key missiological features of the ministry of Jesus (D Bosch[1]):

1. The reign of God, now and not yet, the Kingdom
2. Continuity with the Torah
3. Discipleship training
4. Easter hope as the missionary message.

EARLY CHRISTIAN MISSION
Proclaimed a last chance for Israel.
There was no intention to establish a new religion.
Jewish opposition and the geographical spread of Christianity into the Gentile world increasingly distanced Christianity from its Jewish roots.

---

1 Bosch D Transforming Mission (Maryknoll: Orbis Books ,1991) pp31-41

NEW TESTAMENT MISSION

Matthew-mission as disciple making. Written for Jewish Christians in context of Jewish insurrection against Romans. Jesus is for the Jewish people, yet his implications are for the whole world. Proclaims to 'outsiders'; teaches Jews; importance of deeds alongside words. God's reign-justice and righteousness leading to personal and communal holiness. Making disciples-'teaching' 'baptising' modelled on Jesus' example. Promise of support through Jesus' continued presence with them. **Key words: 'send', 'go', and 'proclaim', 'heal', 'exorcise', 'make peace', 'witness', 'teach' and 'make disciples'.**

Luke: Writes for a Gentile church and therefore has different emphases to Matthew.
Jesus' ministry unfolds in three stages: Galilee 4:14-9:50; Journey from Galilee to Jerusalem, 9:51-19:40; Events in Jerusalem, 19:41 to the end of the Gospel.
Gentile mission is introduced in Luke: 4:16-30, encounters with Samaritans, Luke 9:51-56; 10:25-37; 17:11-19 Jerusalem is a key symbol of opposition. The Gospel is for the poor especially, but also the rich, all need to repent.
Paul: Loyalty to the first apostles but sharp awareness of his call to the Gentiles
Paul's motivation: 2 Cor: 5 "He has committed to us the message of reconciliation." (v19)

Take account of: (v10)	The **judgement** of Christ
Be motivated by: (v14)	The **love** of Christ
Experience: (v17)	The **power** of Christ
Extend: (vv18-19)	The **ministry** of Christ
Focus on: (vv20-21)	The **death** of Christ

PAUL'S THEOLOGY:

1. **Paul's missionary calling**: Gal 1:11-17 - revelation to Paul from Jesus himself; commission from God - goal was the conversion of the Gentiles; context was the history of Israel (3:8)
2. **Paul's stewardship of the Gospel**: Eph 3:1-13 dependent on grace; focused on an open secret; kingdom extended to the Gentiles

3. **The success of Paul's mission**: Rom 15:14-33 God's grace v15; Gentiles believe v16; totally dependent on Spirit's power, 18-19; Fulfilling Christ's mission v19; new mission fields, vv20, 21

4. **The logic of Paul's Gospel**: Rom 1:1-17 Paul set apart v1; mission to the Gentiles v5; serving wholeheartedly v9; eager to proclaim v15; unashamed of the message v16

5. **The Gospel in God's plan**: Rom 1:1-17 God's promise vv1-2; content a brief creed vv3-4; purpose v5; gospel of Christ is a saving power. vv16, 17

6. **Paul's ambition**: Phil 1 & 2 service; sacrifice; standing firm; for me to live is Christ and to die is gain v21

7. **Paul's commission**: Eph 6:10-20; Phil 1:5, 27; 2:16 Commitment to the Gospel, partnership; contending, holding fast

PAUL'S MISSIONARY METHODS:

1. Adapted strategy to locality   (1 Cor 9:16-23)
2. Went to all strata of society   (Rom 1:14, 15)
3. Championed the cause of the Gentiles   (Gal 3:28)
4. Concentrated on strategic cities   (Rom 1:10)
5. Used the local church as a base   (1 Thess 1:7.8)
6. Proclaimed a full Gospel   (Acts 20:26, 27)
7. Had complete confidence in the message (Rom 1:15)
8. Nurtured believers towards maturity   (Col 1:28)
9. Consolidated earlier work   (Rom 15:20, Acts 15:30, 36)
10. Set an example to be followed   (1 Cor 11:1)
11. Trained young leaders   (1 Tim 4:8)
12. Maintained a pioneering spirit   (2 Cor 10:15-17)

MISSION IN CONTEXT (DAVID BOSCH)1

Affirms that God has turned toward the world and includes elements of liberation and 'God's preferential option for the poor'.

Involves the construction of a variety of 'local theologies';-from accommodation to indigenisation; total and on-going integration; is aware of the danger of relativism and the danger of contextualisation.

---

1 pp426 - 432

Reads the signs of the times-realises every member has responsibility for mission.

Does not use the crucial nature and role of the context as the sole and basic authority for theological reflection.

It moves away from conquest of other faiths to dialogue

Remembers the importance of symbol, piety, worship, love, awe, and mystery, moving to a developed theology of mission integral to the life of the church.

Succeeds in holding together in creative tension theoria, praxis and poiesis (faith, hope and love).

Missiology saves the church from parochialism and informs missionary practice.
It puts soteriology (doctrine of salvation), Christology, ecclesiology, eschatology, creation and ethics in the context of the contemporary world.
Mission is action in hope marked by six salvific events: incarnation, cross, resurrection, ascension, pentecost, parousia.

LECTURE 3: PURPOSE IN MISSION-WORKING FOR CHANGE

'The centre of all we do in the church is neither evangelism nor social action but the coming of the rule of God into our midst.'[1]
'Change is an anxiety-arousing and difficult business for everyone, including those of us who are actively pushing for it'[2].
At the same time, '... humans are more complex than we often assume. We both fear and seek change.'[3]

MOTIVATION FOR CHANGE

People motivated by in-born needs:

---

1 Abraham WJ., The Art of Evangelism (Sheffield: Cliff College Publishing, 1993) p.34

2 Lerner H., The Dance of Anger (London: Thorsons 1989) p.3

3 Senge PM., The Fifth Discipline (London: Random House 1990) p. 155

Abraham Maslow's 'Hierarchy of Needs'[1]

1. Biological and Physiological needs   **2. Safety needs**
3. Belongingness and Love needs   **4. Esteem needs**
5. Self-Actualization needs

Agents of change: psychological and sociological factors 'Capacity for Life'
Task of Christian evangelism: to declare truth about God as revealed in person of Jesus Christ
Motivation that underlies the task: God-given desire[2] The Church of England's Commission on Evangelism, (adopted 1918, reaffirmed 1945)
Motive for evangelism
The challenge for the church
Postmodern pressures not to conform or commit[3]
Reject the metanarratives of faith as being of no consequence.

Methods of evangelism by the church-By its existence; Proclamation; Church Growth'; 'Initiation into the Kingdom of God'[4]
Some successful ecumenical initiatives (at least in UK)
Limitations
Stereotypical evangelism
Permission evangelism

New initiatives

The main inhibitor of growth is fear[5]
Christians have two unique stories to tell.

Bibliography

Abraham WJ., *The Art of Evangelism* (Sheffield: Cliff College Publishing, 1993)
Armstrong RS., 'Evangelism' in Richardson A & Bowden J*A., New Dictionary of Christian Theology* (London: SCM Press Ltd. 1983)
Bosch DJ., *Transforming Mission* (Maryknoll, New York: Orbis Books, 1999)

---

1 Chapman A.,' Maslow's Hierarchy of Needs' (http://www.businessballs.com/maslow.htm,) 2.6.2004

2 Simpson ML., Permission Evangelism (Colorado Springs: Cook Communications Ministries 2003) p.24

3 Simpson, p.35. See also p.86

4 ibid. p.31

5 Main J., Moment of Christ (London: Darton, Longman & Todd Ltd. 1984) p.28

Chapman A., Maslow's Hierarchy of Needs

Glasser A., 'An International Perspective' in Hill M. ed. *Entering the Kingdom* (Bromley, Kent; MARC Europe, 1986)

Finney J., *Finding Faith Today* (Swindon: British and Foreign Bible Society, 1992)

Frost R., *Essence* (Eastbourne: Kingsway Publications Ltd. 2002)

Frost R., *New Age Spirituality* (Eastbourne: Kingsway Publications Ltd. 2001)

Green M., *Evangelism through the Local Church* (Sevenoaks: Hodder and Stoughton, 1990)

Green R., *Only Connect* (London: Darton, Longman and Todd Ltd. 1987)

Guinness O., *Time for Truth* (Leicester: Inter-Varsity Press, 2000)

Gumbel N., *Questions of Life* (Eastbourne: Kingsway Publications Ltd. 1993)

Hill M., (ed.) *Entering the Kingdom* (Bromley, Kent; MARC Europe 1986)

Lerner H., *The Dance of Anger* (London: Thorsons 1989)

Main J., *Moment of Christ* (London: Darton, Longman & Todd Ltd. 1984)

McGrath AE., *Bridge-building* (Leicester: Inter-Varsity Press, 1992)

Nazir-Ali M., *From Everywhere to Everywhere* (London: William Collins & Co. Ltd., 1990)

Newbigin L., *The Open Secret* (London: SPCK 1978)

Scott-Peck M., *The Road Less Travelled* (London: Arrow Books, 1990)

Senge PM., *The Fifth Discipline* (London: Random House, 1990)

Simpson ML., *Permission Evangelism* (Colorado Springs: Cook Communications Ministries, 2003)

Snyder HA., *Models of the Kingdom* (Nashville: Abingdon Press, 1991)

Trustees for Methodist Church Purposes, *The Methodist Worship Book* (Peterborough: Methodist Publishing House, 1999)

Wheatley MJ., *Leadership and the New Science* (San Francisco: Berrett-Koehler Publishers, Inc. 1999)

LECTURE 4: CONVERSION AS EVENT AND PROCESS

'DAMASCUS ROAD EXPERIENCE'

Conversion=major change in life–sometimes called a Damascus Road Experience. Complete reversal in thinking; in way of being; or in way of living; or in all three areas of life. What happened to Paul? What changed a born and bred Jew (Phil 3:5, 6) into a 'bondservant of Jesus Christ? (Phil 1:1) Was Paul 'converted' or called?[1] Conversion suggests a changing of religions–Paul did not change his religion. Paul is not described as tormented and full of guilt because of sin.

Bosch: Paul underwent a radical change in values, self-definition and commitments therefore 'conversion' or 'transformation' are appropriate. For Paul his transformation was ongoing: 'Not that I have already attained or am already perfected: but I press on ...' (Phil 3:12)

---

1 Bosch D Transforming Mission (Maryknoll: Orbis Books, 1991) p.125

1. A BIBLICAL MODEL:[1] Acts 2:38

Repentance and faith: What we do=recognition of who we are in relation to God, a turning point, a new way of being, public declaration
Water Baptism: What the Church does=public acknowledgement and acceptance into the fellowship of the church
Spirit Baptism: What God does=spiritual affirmation, sealed with the Spirit
Something missing: Incorporation=belonging, so other elements can be added e.g. Awakening, which is what regeneration is about
Renunciation = what is left behind
Incorporation = 'and they devoted themselves to …'

2. AN 'ECCLESIOLOGICAL' MODEL: 'church' comes first

Personal commitment, corporate belonging, and openness to the Spirit.

3. CONVERSION AND INITIATION MODEL: W Abraham *The Art of Evangelism*, 'although evangelism is about proclamation, its intention should be to bring people into the reign of God on earth'.[2]

METHOD IN EVANGELISM

Moral Dimension=involves receiving the Christian moral tradition summed up in the great commandment to love God and our neighbour.
Experiential dimension=involves experience of conversion/new birth - sins are forgiven and we enter a covenant relationship with God.
Theological dimension=Christian intellectual heritage - ecumenical creeds of the early church.
Horizontal dimension=entering the church of Christ in baptism/confirmation, joining ourselves to the saints and martyrs of the ages.
Operational dimension=committing to work as agents of the kingdom, equipped by the Holy Spirit to do the works of the kingdom.
Disciplinary dimension=classical disciplines - prayer, fasting, means of grace.

---

1 Pawson D The Normal Christian Birth

2 Abraham W The Art of Evangelism (Sheffield: Cliff College Publishing, 1993) p.61ff

4. ASPECTS OF INITIATION INTO THE CHURCH

Conversion
- repentance
- forgiveness of sin
- born again into the kingdom and become children of God.
- no single pattern – times of crisis/ times of process
- ongoing growth and development

Baptism into new community that lives in and for the kingdom of God
- church and kingdom inextricably linked
- public witness
- personal commitment to the rule of God

Morality
- love of God with heart, soul, mind, strength
- love of neighbour as of self

Creed
- intellectual heritage
- scripture and creed belong together
- manifesto of Christian community

Spiritual gifts
- dynamic and varied
- power to fulfil one's individual role as an agent of God's kingdom

Spiritual disciplines
- means of grace
- sustenance
- responsible obedience

5) AGENTS IN INITIATION

- God, Father, Son and Holy Spirit
- the evangelist
- the church
- the person or persons evangelised

6) ELEMENTS IN THE PROCESS

- ➤ Conversion (radical confrontation with God, a turning)
- ➤ Community (shaping focus)
- ➤ Baptism (separation from conversion–a marked feature)
- ➤ Morality (life of love, rule of life)
- ➤ creed (worldview, believing certain things, maybe altering a previous worldview)
- ➤ Spiritual gifts (whole body)
- ➤ Spiritual disciplines (basic to growth)

7) LITURGICAL INITIATION

- ➤ The divorce of sacramental baptism from experiential faith
- ➤ John Wesley and Methodism. being born again, again!
- ➤ Communion. All age worship.
- ➤ A sacramental-less or ritual-less initiation is unbiblical and a contradiction in terms.

8) LEARNING

a.   **Five elements of Christian Initiation:**

1. Church;
2. Welcome;
3. Prayer;
4. The Way;
5. The Goal;

b.   **Co-ordinates of Effective Initiation**

Dynamic before structure;
Discovery rather than delivery;
Transformation above information;
Kingdom not just church;
Community not just individuals;
Confrontation not just comfort;

1. Catechesis–Jumping hurdles? Opening windows? Opening doors?

2. What is catechesis?
Greek verb Catecheo, 'to echo', to teach orally'.
Narrow sense-the oral teaching of a **catechist** by which those under instruction=**catechumens**=are **catechised.**
The whole programme of training/learning is referred to as a **Catechumenate.**
The **catechesis** of a particular church is formalised in a **catechism.**
Broad sense-catechesis that extends beyond rote learning. Clearly linked to initiation but seen in wider terms such as nurture, education, Christian growth and maturity.

3. Some examples of catechesis
a) **The very earliest catechesis** is the whole, or a large part of the New Testament.
Kerygma-the initial gospel proclamation designed to introduce a person to Christ and to appeal for conversion.
Form criticism–examines traditions about Jesus as they developed during the period of oral Transmission (c 30-65AD)
Redaction criticism–examines the role of the Evangelist as author, theologian and editor of written sources used for the composition of the gospels.

b) The Patristic Model-Insights from **St Cyril of Jerusalem**

Stage 1: The pre-catechumenate period of preparation emphasising instruction, testing and ritual struggle including exorcisms and blessings.

Stage 2: Entry into catechumenate- preparatory period for baptism-included:
➢ the presentation of the candidates to the baptised congregation
➢ formal interrogatory examination and admission to the congregation
➢ further rites of purification and illumination
➢ public profession of faith
➢ 'conversion' was explicitly expected and implicitly assumed.

Stage 3: Complex baptismal rite that was full of symbolism
➢ included themes associated with confirmation-anointing of the Holy Spirit and admission to communion.
➢ attendance at the whole of worship with the whole community

Stage 4: 'Post-baptismal catechesis' or (technically) 'mystagogical teachings'.
➢ 'deeper' things of faith–often called 'the mysteries'.
➢ sometimes the Eucharist was not received until this stage.
➢ 'home-coming' celebration rites
➢ sometimes rites of renewed faith for the whole congregation.

c. Sunday schools and catechisms: 17th century England, infant baptism the norm. Formal catechetical process and many of its rituals disappeared. Still have parents/godparents.

Later-regulated, written catechism (some denominations)-people baptised in infancy required to learn before confirmation. This poses several questions:

➢ Can you be born a Methodist, or Anglican, or Baptist?
➢ What must have happened for the infant to be nurtured in the Christian faith?
➢ Does Christian nurture begin before or after conversion?

4. Learning from the (idealised) early Church/Patristic model:

➢ they took it seriously
➢ Baptism was the central act, even though it was not the end of the process.
➢ **Integrated teaching, multi-media method, whole person teaching environment e.g.**
✓ an emphasis on faith building via bible teaching
✓ use of liturgy and ritual. Ceremony was important.
✓ ritual exorcism was a key element
✓ there were periodic presentations
✓ often each catechist had a sponsor/mentor
✓ there was a clear element of what we now call group dynamics

5. Identifying aims of (idealised) Early Church/Patristic models

➢   knowing God through personal encounter
➢   creating a Christian world view
➢   creating a Christian identity. A new name was often given at baptism – here is a new person in Christ.
➢   crating a Christian lifestyle/value system. A counter-culture.
➢   provide Christian resources.
➢   sustaining faith, often in a difficult environment.
➢   place within a Christian community, in terms of contribution and reception.

6. Contemporary models of catechesis as models of initiation

➢   Rite of Christian Initiation of Adults (RCIA
➢   The Adult Catechumenate Produced by Catechumenate Network, adapted from RCIA.
➢   Some evangelical/charismatic examples
➢   *Good News Down your Street. Saints Alive.*
➢   *Alpha.* Developed by team at Holy Trinity, Brompton, London.
➢   *Emmaus: the way of Faith.* Bible Society, Church House Press and the National Society.
➢   *Disciple.*

7. Observations

Different models and ecclesiological emphases are probably right.

All models now work on a process basis and all evangelical/charismatic models now work on a crisis through the process basis.

Most models aim at the church 'fringe'. So a prior realisation, aim, and strategy is that the church needs to be growing a constant fringe.

Relevance and Mystery is the great balancing act.

How do we steer between the deadness of 'rote' learning and over-subjectivism?

The models share *principles* much more than they share *content*. *What* is taught, and *catechised for what?* remain big questions.

Still some way to go, especially in charismatic/evangelical models, to use rituals and symbols to powerful effect.

8. Some questions?

1. Is this whole business central to the life of the church or peripheral?
2. Is it taught by lay people or the theologically trained? Is the congregation involved?
3. Are there public rites at various stages?
4. Is it sociologically appropriate?
5. What pattern of Christian conversion is implied or assumed?
6. What are the charismatic expectations?
7. What educational method does it use? Does it allow for exploration?
8. Is it appropriate for people of different ages, especially the young?
9. Does it integrate congregational worship? How are sacraments used within it?
10. How is the world regarded?
11. What happens when it is over?

LECTURE 6: MISSION & CULTURE-BRIDGING THE GAP

1 Historical background:

•   **First Christian missionaries** were Jews. Peter & Cornelius Acts 10. Paul worked with masters and slaves to Christianise their attitudes even though slavery was seen as part of the order that was passing away.

•   **Conversion of Constantine** 312AD

•   **19th Century**–Four new ideas

1. **Commission** Need for all Christians to hear and heed the Great Commission.
2. **Colonialism** The East India Company appointed Chaplains to serve in the areas where they traded
3. **Compassion** Ending of slave trade through commerce and Christianity
4. **Civilization** When Stanley met Livingstone and King Mutesa of Buganda he wrote to *The Daily Telegraph* (1875) 'this enlightened and progressive ruler' relied upon Christianity to bring light and hope to his country and called for a 'pious and practical missionary'.

2. Seeing things differently

➢   **Communication often fails,** because people hear and see things differently
➢   **Dynamic Equivalence,** translating *meaning* of words; transmitting new ideas

3. The Nature of Culture

➢ 'the integrated system of learned patterns of behaviour, ideas and products characteristic of a society.'
➢ involves beliefs, values, customs, institutions that bind society together with a sense of identity, value, security and continuity.
➢ a bridge linking different generations .
➢ a wall separating people from those who want to invade or change their culture.
➢ people cannot escape their culture–it is within them.
➢ people can defend themselves against another culture or can deliberately enter another culture (e.g. Jesus).

4. When different cultures meet

➢ **Conflict**   Simon Kimbangu called to preachand heal. Missionaries rejected his African ministry='not Christian' some still do
➢ **Co-existence**
➢ **Competition**
➢ **Cross-fertilisation** Each culture gives to the other=celebrate the differences.

Questions
When should a country be called backward? When it is heavily in debt (Brazil)? When most of its people are illiterate? When private gain at the expense of others is rewarded (Britain)?

5. Cross-cultural Communication: two dangers

➢ Life and teaching similar to prevailing culture-Church no longer the bearer of God's judgment and promise. Becomes guardian of the culture and fails to challenge it.

➢ Language and lifestyle different from local culture-church becomes a ghetto-no contact. Therefore unable to challenge traditional ways of life; or attacks local culture so strongly that it fails to communicate or cuts converts off from own culture.

80

Four ways to communicate:
a) Isolation: remain in separate worlds – you just don't understand
b) Extraction: you come into my world e.g. converts to mission compounds–evangelised islands rather than bridges of witness
c) Identification: I enter your world–mostly I learn new things
d) Reciprocation: Mutual exchange where we learn from one another

6. An Indigenous Church:
Roland Allan complained (1912) that mission Churches in most parts of the world were:
a)   *not indigenous*=i.e. not rooted in their local culture
b)   *dependent*=on parent Churches for money, ideas and leaders
c)   *all alike*=fail to reflect God-given riches and differences.
   European style buildings, liturgies, music, behaviour, rituals, rely on foreign leadership.

A truly indigenous Church:
a) All activity in patterns of the local society,
b) The Church often begins independently, without work of missionaries.
c) The Church is not founded, but *planted* in soil of the local culture.
d) New converts taught simply and clearly-translate teaching into living and doing.
e) Takes responsibility in ways which make sense in terms of own local culture.
f) Uses its own financial resources; discovers its own spiritual gifts, discovers new revelations, new aspects of the Gospel, and new forms of Christian living, in direct dependence on the Holy Spirit.
g) The 'parent' Church often does not recognise the indigenous Church.

7. Form and Function
The Function (or Meaning) of any practice is its purpose. e.g. ritual to recognize ending of life, 'Letting in the New Year'.
➢   **Forms** vary from culture to culture
➢   **Christians are called to discern** which Forms of traditional culture in their society can be used in the service of the Gospel and which are incompatible–usually best to leave this to those who understand them best.

8. Jesus and Culture

➢ Jesus constantly identified with the culture of his day: priests, peasants, rabbis, Gentiles and challenged it by doing the unexpected; forgiving paralysed man, raising widow's son, eating with Zacchaeus.
➢ Jesus did not deny the existence of demons–he defeated them
➢ Jesus continues to challenge the fear of demons and offers liberation.
➢ Jesus also challenges the European world view which denies spiritual and supernatural realities
➢ Jesus also culturally challenged–Matt 15:21ff–Canaanite woman
➢ A pre-packaged Jesus is restricted to one agenda and cannot surprise us.

9. Inculturation

➢ If we are to communicate the gospel, it is important that we understand other cultures/world views. Different things make sense according to what you believe.
➢ The process of re-thinking is called 'Inculturation'.
➢ The aim of inculturation is to make Christianity feel truly at
➢ home in the cultures of each people

Four principles:

1) **The message must be relevant to the cultural context**
2) **The message must be stated simply**
3) **The message must be interesting**
4) **The message must be attractive**

LECTURE 7: MISSION IN AN URBAN CONTEXT

What is distinctive about city centre church and ministry?

1. CONTEXT:

a. Dominant features: commercial, retail, civic, leisure, judicial and educational.
b. There may or may not be residential accommodation.
c. Transient population: extremes of power/powerlessness, wealth and poverty.

2. IDENTITY:

a. Often collaborative style/with or without a gathered congregationand own premises .

b. Partnership with other churches, groups and agencies who share Kingdom values.

3. ROLE TO:

a. Demonstrate the love of Christ for all who live, work and spend time in the city.

b. Provide opportunities for varieties of worship for transient people.

c. Offer pastoral care and nurture for Christians and non-Christians.

d. Fulfil a representative and prophetic role.

e. Support Christians in the work place.

4. TENSIONS AND CHALLENGES:

a. Constant change/new and varied models of ministry/need to reflect, adapt, reshape.

b. Many injurious changes in society.

c. The responsibility of being a flagship church.

d. The explosion of the leisure industry-new patterns of Sunday life.

e. The redevelopment of city centres-continual change of population.

f. The demands of a seven-day, 24 hour city.

g. The effective deployment of resources and personnel.

FINDING A THEOLOGICAL BASE. LEECH1-SEVEN ELEMENTS: 2

1. **Each small Christian community=locus for theological activity.**
2. **Activity need not only be intellectual.**
3. **Theological work must involve a cross-section of people.**
4. **Theological work is ongoing activity.**
5. **Theology is messy.**
6. **Prayer is central.**
7. **Theology involves belief. Apologetics seeks to open up the door of faith.'**[1]

---

[1] Leech K 'Doing Theology in an Urban Context' in Eastman M & Latham S (eds) *Urban Church* (London: SPCK, 2004) p.7

[2] Stott J *Issues facing Christians Today* (London: Marshall Pickering1990) p.26

Biblical themes:
Jesus: Great Commission (Mt 28:16-20) manifesto in Lk 4:16-20.[2]
Incarnation: primary (Phil 2:5-11) belonging, being, caring, feeling.
Servant: being there, 'born as one of us, Mary's Son'.
Shalom: salvation, justice, peace-Nu 6:24-6; Eph 1:14-18; Col 1:20
Kingdom: 'Where there is no vision the people perish' Prov 28:19 AV
The value of the individual: People become anonymous.
Face of the poor: Poverty challenged and opposed throughout the Scriptures. (Mt 11: 28)
Justice, jubilee, liberation: God is just and wills justice for the whole of his creation.
Principalities and powers: Paul (Eph. 6:10-18). Jesus (Luke 4:1-13).
City: Jesus enters, weeps for and judges the city/gives vision of new
          Jerusalem. All of life is in the city.
          The glory is that Jesus is already there, waiting.

BIBLICAL MODELS FOR URBAN MISSION

Jesus:
- Incarnation–arriving, 'digging in'.
- Healing-'being used ' by people in need
- Parables–looking around for messages already there
- Acted Parables–attempts at action
- Disciple groups–working with small communities
- Crucifixion–consequence of Jesus-style action
- Resurrection–new life, transformation
- Parousia–glimpses of a 'New City'

Paul: Bosch[3]-Paul's own understanding of his mission Rom 15:15-21
- Paul thinks regionally, not ethnically
- Chooses cities that have a representative character
- Lays foundations for a Christian community–from these strategic centres the gospel will be carried into the surrounding countryside and towns
- His vision is world-wide and ecumenical

---

[1] Green M *Evangelism Through the Local Church* (Sevenoaks: Hodder & Stoughton, 1990) p.113ff
[2] Leech p9ff
[3] Bosch DJ *Transforming Mission* (Maryknoll: Orbis Books 1991) p128ff

- He founds local churches
- Nurtures these through occasional pastoral visits/letters, and sending fellow-workers to them
- Intercedes on behalf of his congregations, and counsels them about a variety of very practical and down-to-earth matters
- Waits for them to grow in spiritual maturity; stewardship; and to become beacons of light in their environment
- He refuses to duplicate effort
- He encourages colleagueship-with intimate circle, independent co-workers and with representatives from local churches

Bowen:[1] -many valid models of urban mission-just a few to start us thinking:
- give power away
- utilise local radio and TV, telephones or newspapers
- plant new congregations
- educate
- provide intensive youth worship

Gospel Values
- make it clear that everyone is a child of God
- lay a table where all are welcome, where strangers find a home
- recognize that everyone has an offering to bring
- find faith where no one else looks for it
- notice people whom others ignore or diminish
- celebrate the 'greatness of the small'
- give space for everyone to fail, to learn, to grow
- make mercy and generosity servants of renewal
- never force an entry into other people's lives
- warn against making rules more important than relationships
- love finds joy in being spent; being broken or vulnerable also reveals God's presence
- expect change to be possible for everyone
- patiently wait to find each person's 'touching place'
- promise that, wherever Christ is, his promises are fulfilled

---

[1] Bowen R ...So I Send You (London:SPCK 1996) p190ff

Twentieth century-separation of evangelism and social action.
Evangelicals have stressed personal spiritual growth and conversion.
Liberals emphasised issues of justice and freedom-liberation theology.
Cognitive dissonance is to believe one thing but to do something else.

New Testament model
No separation of social and evangelical
No division between body and spirit, social need and spiritual need

This has resulted in:
- stronger social dimension since the 1970s,
- increasing liberal interest in evangelism.
- a major increase in thinking and teaching about trade justice.

Michael Green (*Evangelism Through the Local Church*)
*If evangelism in the church is going to have any significant meaning,
other than adding a few more members to the Christian community,
those who are concerned about spreading the good news of Jesus
Christ
must ask what the good news is all about.*

- 'Who do we worship?'
- 'Who do we serve?'
- What does this mean in terms of our attitude and lifestyle?
- How should we mix religion and politics so that faith is relevant to the real world?
- What is the political and religious significance of issues that confront us today?

A Christian Aid survey:

'The Gospel, the Poor and the Churches', 1994, saw **Poverty as**:
- homelessness,
- hunger
- unmet needs,
- lack of power and control over one's life.
- the fault of the developing world

But what about global responsibility? Christian action for a fairer world-**Belief in:**
1. The wholeness of people-body, mind and spirit
2. The wholeness of the Gospel-a broad view of salvation-Luke 4:18, 19
   Gospel is about restoring people to what God intended them to be in the beginning.

The Bible combines charity and revolution in its approach to injustice
- **Matt 25:31-46** Sheep and goats.
- **James 5:1-6** Social injustice is condemned
- **John 10:10** Working for personal & social transformation
- **Col 3:15** Peace of Christ as arbiter in decision-making
- **Eph 4:13** Maturity measured against stature of Christ. Holds together doctrine of creation (Gen 1:26-30) and Fall (Rom 2:2).

The Kingdom in New Testament terms must include:

a. Corporate/individual, social/spiritual aspects-Lk 4:16ff; Is 61; Is 9:6-7
b. Radical Kingdom values
c. Battling against the darkness
d. Challenging the evils of the status quo
e. The issues of rich and poor
f. The marginalised (women, the poor, the disabled).
g. The religious and political establishment-Matt 9:35

Conversion transforms-**Repentance** has social aspects.
Grace is free, discipleship is costly.

Motives for Social Action-Three types of social concern:
1. Relief   2. Development   3. Structural change.

Key theological doctrines relate to social concern:
- **God**-continually involved in his creation and hurting for it.
- **Sin**-spoils God's creation (Eph 5:11 - 'deeds of darkness').
- **Incarnation**–Christ among us in order to save us.

1. The Lausanne Covenant 1972
2. Influence of American evangelicals.
3. The Charismatic Movement.

In Biblical terms, *'neither evangelism nor social action make full sense divorced from the fact of the Christian community as the visible, earthly expression of the Kingdom of God'.*[1]

Developing a Theology of Evangelism and Social Action:

1. The way we see the world.
➢ Our background and influences
➢ Our value system
➢ Seeing the world from the other point of view.
➢ Danger of judgmentalism on one hand and collusion on the other
2. Thinking straight.
➢ Abandoning dualism
➢ Exploring the two opposite heresies of legalism and licence.
3. Wholistic world view.
➢ Commitment to education, living out 'kingdom centred Christianity'

John Stott: "Our Biblical convictions about creation and stewardship should put Christians in the forefront of environmentally concerned people".

WHAT ARE OUR GROUNDS FOR A BIBLICAL ECOLOGY?

(1) God created all creation good (Gen 1:31)
(2) God commanded us to be wise stewards of the planet. (Gen 2:15)
(3) God created all of creation to worship him (Psalm 148:7-12)
(4) Jesus came to redeem the whole cosmos (Jn 3:16; Rom 8:19-21)
(5) Environmental problems always affect the poor most.
What is democracy if your air is too polluted to breathe?
What is economic development, if your lands too poisoned to farm?
What is international law, if rich countries dump toxic waste on poorer nations?
Environmental justice is fundamental to the Gospel.

Suffering and a God of love
(Do many evangelicals have a simplistic view of suffering?)

---

1 Snyder The Community of the King (Downers Grove: Inter-Varsity press 1977) p.13

Liberation Theology

Reign of God comes in power in Jesus. God is the liberator: Releasing his people from captivity in Egypt (Exodus); demanding justice (Is. 1:11-17, 58:1-11; Amos 5:21-26; Mic 6:6-8; in the mission of Jesus (Lk 4:16-21) Christianity therefore unavoidably political:

God's message is truth, justice, peace and liberation

Question: What experience do you have of putting social action and gospel together?

LECTURE 9: THE BODY OF CHRIST OR EVERY MEMBER MATTERS

WHAT IS THE BODY OF CHRIST?

Community of disciples that carries on Christ's ministry.
Christian Community in action.
Challenge–to raise up new leaders and renew Body of Christ in action.

Those who make up the Body of Christ=The Church is the whole people of God:

- Laity and clergy
- Individuals and groups
- Families
- People of all kinds united in Christ

Characteristics of the Body of Christ:

- **Alive**-reflects triumph and joy of Easter, not gloom of Good Friday
- **Covenantal**-its heart is a covenant between God and his people
- **Gifted**–each member gifted for the common life and ministry (Rom 12:3-8)
- **Renewing**–constant need of renewal, reform, challenge. Each generation must respond anew to the Gospel.
- **Missional**
a. Breathes in holiness and study, so can breathe out faith in action;
b. Gathers for worship and nurture, scatters for witness and service

Body of Christ in Action:
Kerygma (proclamation)–tell the story of God's love in Jesus
Koinonia (community)–live together in God's grace; a family where persons are received, renewed, reformed in the likeness of Christ
Diakonia (service)-share God's grace in love/service, reaching out to people where they are

Your participation

- Focus on a need
- identify your gifts and resources
- seek support of others
- work as a team

Putting it into Practice
a. Translating Christian life-style in community into 'naming the name'.
b. Avoiding quick fix solutions.
c. Releasing people from a constant round of meetings
d. Enabling them to 'give a reason for the hope which is within them'
e. Possibly creating specific situations and events where this can happen.

Ultimately, no one will share the most important things in their lives unless:
     (i) They are convinced of the truth of them;
     (ii) They are excited about them.

ENCOURAGING PEOPLE IN PERSONAL WITNESS

Don't assume that people in church have a strong enough faith to share it; be sure that those you encourage to witness to their faith actually have a faith; consider whether you need to start a stage back in discipling. Once established: faith sharing becomes meaningful; faith is strengthened by sharing.

God does give them courage, words and understanding as they share. They find that people are more open to the message than they had anticipated: they find that prayer makes a difference; they discover that many people are on a spiritual journey. Grappling with apologetic issues stretches and often strengthens faith.

Tell your own story of coming to faith. Christians are normal people.
An unimpressive gradual conversion story connects with many people's experience
What Christ means to me today more significant than experience from years ago
Witness is seen essentially in personal experiential terms
Personal testimony can lead on to less subjective methods
Telling your story may be costly as it involves vulnerability
It involves openness to new people and ideas

POSSIBLE DANGERS:

Danger of many testimonies is that they appear to be in a time-warp:

- Because they have little reference to contemporary issues and ...
- May not appear relevant to an unbeliever in the 2000s.
- Your actual experience may be wonderful and true for the person who describes it, but must not be forced upon anyone else.
- What is true for 'Person A', need not be for 'Person B'.

Go beyond telling your story:-More than relating personal experience.

Paul's approach to the sceptical, intellectual, plural Athenians (Acts 17) is directly instructive:

1. He takes a close look at Athenian society
2. He is informed about their philosophy and literary culture.
3. He is able to use these as bridge points for the Gospel.
4. He states key aspects of the Gospel (but not every key aspect)
5. He enables a variety of responses.

Classic passages on an approach to personal witness:

John 4   Jesus and the woman at the well;
Acts 8:26-40 Philip and the Ethiopian;
John 3   Jesus and Nicodemus;
Luke 18   Rich young ruler;

Role models

Christians need Christian leaders who model faith sharing:
- by talking naturally about Jesus, in formal religious situations/in ordinary conversation.
- not so much a special activity a living relationship with Christ
- that shows itself in a concern for justice and poverty, compassion for the needy and lost.
- keep in touch with 'not yet Christians', spend time, share meals, be concerned long term .....

So Be Yourself:
Confrontational=Peter, Acts 2:14-40
Intellectual= Paul Acts 17
Testimony=of blind man healed in John 9
Over a meal=Matthew, Luke 7:36-50
Invitational=the Samaritan woman in John 4

a. Have a clear plan in mind for describing the key elements of faith.

b. Engage in Christian apologetics-suffering, evil, science, morality.

c. Avoid any kind of pre-packed message-instead listen to 'where people are coming from'

d. Think in terms of long term discipleship, not just instant conversion.

LECTURE 10: SOME CONTEMPORARY TOOLS FOR MISSION1

ALPHA:

Looking for answers: an opportunity to explore the Christian faith. Fun, evening/day–series of talks addressing key issues relating to Christian faith. For everyone–especially those wanting to investigate Christianity. Adaptable to any contexts: workplace; social venue; private home; Armed forces; all denominations; prisons;

---

1 Editors Note: Most of the courses described in this lecture have been updated or superseded in the intervening years since these lectures were first delivered in post-conflict Sierra Leone. They are included here for interest and to maintain historical integrity.

Student Alpha; Youth Alpha.

Started 1993; Bible-based; focuses on person of Jesus and his relevance to life today. Based on 15 'talks'; includes preferably a weekend away or at least a whole day to cover the 4 sessions on the Holy Spirit. Talks available on video but also in book form so can be presented 'live' and adapted for local use. There is a personal handbook for each participant.

Relies on the effectiveness of personal invitation, sharing of food, safety of small groups. People valued for themselves/experience of life. Questions encouraged, nothing too trivial, insights welcomed. None of us know what another's life is really like[1]. Follow-up course of 9 sessions includes a study guide.

EMMAUS: THE WAY OF FAITH

A course designed to welcome people into Christian faith/life of the church. Rooted in an understanding of evangelism, nurture and discipleship modelled on the example of Jesus in the story of the Emmaus Road, it aims to involve the whole church in these areas. It works by encouraging a journey of faith that is life-changing, enduring and has an impact on the community, as well as the individual.

Three stages–Contact, Nurture and Growth.

Contact, encouraging the vision of the local church for evangelism, giving practical advice on how to develop contact with those outside the church. **15-week:**
Nurture course covering basics of Christian life;
Growth through four books that help Christians to deepen their understanding of Christian living and discipleship.

What are the obstacles to overcome if you are running an Emmaus Nurture course?

1. Lack of boldness
2. Rushing things. Nurture courses need to have firm foundations, and the following matters have to be seen to:

---

a) Ensure the leadership of the church know the course and are enthusiastic about it

b) Who might be invited on the course? Initial four week course for church leaders

c) What would be the best venue for the sort of people who are to be invited?

d) Who is going to lead the course and do they need any training?

e) How can the whole congregation be involved in this?

3. Courses change as they are repeated. Persevere. Churches often stop nurture groups after one or two sessions because numbers are fewer. BUT research shows that it is only after the third or fourth course that outsiders are touched

4. Leaders need the right gifts. Teacher–who can teach adults; Evangelist–lead to Christ; Administrator–get them there in the first place; Pastor–who can care for them.

5. What happens next? There has to be follow up-best to keep a group together

What is special about Emmaus? It tries to answer three questions:
  1. How do we get a group of people together?
  2. What is the best way of helping people to make the Christian truth their own?
  3. What happens after the course?

WALK TO EMMAUS

Spiritual renewal program to strengthen local church through development of Christian disciples and leaders. Modelled on Christ's servanthood-encourages disciples to act in ways appropriate to being "a servant of all".

The Upper Room, a ministry unit of the General Board of Discipleship of The United Methodist Church, sponsors the Walk to Emmaus and offers it through local Emmaus groups around the world. Although connected through The Upper Room to The United Methodist Church, The Walk to Emmaus is ecumenical. *Excerpted with permission from What Is Emmaus? by Stephen D. Bryant. Copyright © 1995 by The Upper Room.*

ESSENCE

A new tool for Christian mission Frost R, *Essence* (Eastbourne: Kingsway Communications, 2002)

- based on Christian spirituality
- for those with an interest in spirituality/New Age philosophy
- six week course or residential weekend
- experiential introduction to Christian faith in culturally relevant way
- small groups – confidentiality, intimacy
- practical, 'hands on' experience
- preferably not on church premises–informal, comfortable setting
- Advertise alongside New Age material in coffee shops, health centres, libraries, etc.
- Participants pay for sessions – covers cost of materials, room hire, etc.

FOUNDATIONS 21

- **Discover your own discipleship pathway** and direction for Christian ministry.

- **Access a rich blend** of personal and group material to suit your lifestyle and learning style.

- **Receive help in your spiritual journey** from others both locally and via the Internet.

- **Benefit from a whole range of multi-media resources** including over 6 hours of video, more than 3,500 web pages and thousands of web links.

- **Enjoy daily** updates, inspiration and challenge to enable you to grow in your faith and become a more effective disciple of Jesus Christ.

MODULE 3a: EVANGELISM PICTURED- PRACTICAL

(Major Alan Burns MA BSc)

LECTURE 1: MISSION AND THE KINGDOM OF GOD

DEFINITIONS (FROM A SALVATION ARMY PERSPECTIVE)

Evangelism

To evangelize is so to present Christ in the power of the Holy Spirit that people will put their trust in God through him, to accept him as their Saviour and serve him as their King in the fellowship of his church. Archbishops committee into the evangelical work of the Church 1916

Tell the story of fisherman Pete!

Mission

The gospel has come to you on its way to someone else! The word mission has behind it the idea of movement because primarily it is about God sending and our being sent–this aligns with the mission of Jesus. "As the Father sent me, so I send you," Jesus said to his disciples. The idea of a Mission station is an odd one–as things stand still in stations! The church is missionary by nature–it is at its best when moving! The difficulty about using words like evangelism and mission is that we use them inter-changeably but are never sure why. Evangelism as we have noted is about the activity of making people into disciples of Jesus Christ. Mission is about the church being sent out into the world and includes everything that the church does as it moves out.

The theological foundation of mission is important here. The Roman Catholics use the term 'Mission Dei'–the mission of God–to describe how the Father, Son and Holy Spirit relate to one another. It is a relationship of movement and the word relationship is the one that should be in the front of our minds as we think of mission. The Father sends the Son and the Spirit. What Mission Dei does in fact, is to describe what God is like. The church is like God in this sense–it is a movement because it is sent by the Father. The church does not have to invent its mission. It is God's mission! It exists by mission-it is the kingdom of God! So as the church is sent out into the world–it reflects the nature and life of God himself. I think this is the closest we get to understanding mission.

Missionary Attitude versus Missionary Activity

There is a key distinction between a missionary attitude and a missionary activity. The missionary attitude of the believer is important in the context of the church. The church may engage in missionary activities but still not really have a missionary attitude! The church may conduct a campaign, or a recruiting initiative, but that alone does not make the church missionary. A church I led held open air services in a busy London street, and was proud that it had done so for over 125 years. We marched out of the hall with a large band and we made a noise on Oxford Street in London. This was undoubtedly a missionary activity and one which the church placed high value upon– you would be hard pressed to persuade the folk to give it up and why would you want to?

But the big question is this: does the church have a missionary attitude? Did the individuals see this as mission? I couldn't help but observe the habit of this for many of them. Very few would lay down their instrument in order to speak to someone–maybe they found their brass instrument useful to hide behind–I don't know. My point is that if we really want to be a missionary church, then the key factor is the missionary attitude of the members. If those people in my church were witnesses to Jesus in their daily lives, would we need to march the streets?

Our concern is for those to whom we are being sent! In that way a church becomes missionary in attitude and as such really is a continuum of the life of Christ, it finishes the mission that Jesus came to do. This is how I best understand what the Body of Christ is. Mission is an attitude of mind–this attitude is at the heart of what it means to be church and is reflected in the very heart of God himself. This is who God is and what God does is based on "God so loved the world …."

Sent–to their ground!

Who's ground? The whole idea behind being sent is to consider whose ground mission takes place. If I belong to a church where the theology is 'come to church' then I am inviting the unchurched to my space and my territory. When I was converted I used to take Salvation Army (SA) literature to public houses and the challenge of witness on their ground was exciting and it allowed the people I met and spoke to set the agenda in a setting that they controlled and were comfortable in. Christians actually spend a lot of time on the ground of the unchurched but our problem may be that we don't see ourselves as sent by God.

I was listening to a testimony of a teacher whose church was making her the Sunday school leader. Her teaching and relational skills with children seemingly made her an obvious choice for this role. The church invited her to the front for prayer and for the ceremony of making her the leader in front of the congregation. She was not impressed. "Why have they never invited me to the front for prayer before. I have been teaching in front of classes of 30 kids for 15 years, not Sunday school or church kids and the church never once thought to pray for my teaching for them. What's more important; our kids in church or the kids in school every day where I go to live out my faith in non-church territory? Did she have a point? What does your church do to resource people who are sent out to the world every week into many places where they are witnesses?

The Kingdom of God

The most spoken about theme in the gospels is the Kingdom of God. It is probably therefore the most important issue. It seems to me that it is vital we make this the most important theme of our preaching and our mission. What did Jesus mean by it? The Old Testament taught the kingdom as something that would occur in the future. For example;

Dan 2:44 At the time of those rulers the God of heaven will establish a kingdom that will never end. It will never be conquered, but will completely destroy all those empires and then last forever.
And ....
Dan 4:34 "When the seven years had passed," said the king, "I looked up at the sky, and my sanity returned. I praised the Supreme God and gave honor and glory to the one who lives forever. He will rule forever, and his kingdom will last for all time."

One day God would put the world right by saving his helpless people! In the teaching of Jesus, the rule of God was the central theme. One of the interesting observations in all the gospels is that there seems to be an issue over where to start when telling the story of Jesus. Each author seems to opt for starting the story in a different place, for very good reasons I am sure! Mark begins with the baptism of John; Matthew with Abraham; Luke begins with Adam; and John has to go even further back to the beginning of 'the Word'. What is apparent is that the Kingdom is about the reign of God, the absolute sovereignty of God over everything, creation and the cosmos, the beginning and the end. In answer to the question "Who is Jesus", they all had to make a decision–Jesus is the source and goal of the cosmos. This is the story of the reign and rule of God, Alpha and Omega!

Mark in the first chapter of his gospel records:

Mk 1:14 *"After John had been put in prison; Jesus went to Galilee and preached the Good News from God."*
Mk 1:15 *"The right time has come," he said, "and the Kingdom of God is near! Turn away from your sins and believe the Good News!"*
Matthew affirms the same:
Mt 12:28 *"No, it is not Beelzebul, but God's Spirit, who gives me the power to drive out demons, which proves that the Kingdom of God has already come upon you. "*
*And **Luke**:*
Lk 4:18 *"The Spirit of the Lord is upon me, because he has chosen me to bring good news to the poor. He has sent me to proclaim liberty to the captives and recovery of sight to the blind, to set free the oppressed*
Lk 4:19 *and announce that the time has come when the Lord will save his people."*
Lk 4:20 *Jesus rolled up the scroll, gave it back to the attendant, and sat down. All the people in the synagogue had their eyes fixed on him,*
Lk 4:21 *as he said to them, "This passage of scripture has come true today, as you heard it being read."*

The Kingdom had arrived. It was here in Jesus himself. He demonstrated its arrival through signs and wonderful works. The power of the kingdom could be clearly seen in what Jesus did and who Jesus was. There was no distinction between the different types of kingdom activity. He preached, healed, discerned, and surprised his audience The Holy Spirit enabled Him to help and minister to people:

John 3:34 The one whom God has sent speaks God's words, because God gives him the fullness of his Spirit. Jesus not only showed them God's power, but he shared human weakness. People could reject, persecute and even kill Him. And here is the mystery: it is by the way of suffering, rejection and death, the way of the cross, that the reign of God is brought to earth.

Jesus bears witness to the reign of God not by overpowering the forces of evil, but by taking their full weight upon himself. Yet it is in that seeming defeat that victory is won.[1]

So, parables and stories explain it. It has to be revealed by the action of God in human life. Many do not see it although it is right in front of them. The supreme parable of course is the cross, a mystery to many. God's rule is not yet because Jesus has not returned! His second coming will be the time for final judgment.

His teaching on the Rule of God was especially important for the poor, the weak, the oppressed: he taught that justice was an essential part of the Kingdom and Rule of God, certainly a lot more important than religious observance and ritual which often kept people out of the system! Justice is an essential part of the Kingdom of God:

Mk 12:32 The teacher of the Law said to Jesus, "Well done, Teacher! It is true, as you say, that only the Lord is God and that there is no other god but he.

Mk 12:33 And you must love God with all your heart and with all your mind and with all your strength; and you must love your neighbor as you love yourself. It is more important to obey these two commandments than to offer on the altar animals and other sacrifices to God."

Mk 12:34 Jesus noticed how wise his answer was, and so he told him, "You are not far from the Kingdom of God." After this nobody dared to ask Jesus any more questions.

---

1 Newbigin, Lesslie The Open Secret, (SPCK London 1995) p, 35

Roger Bowen[1] **points out 12 ways** in which we can reflect the rule of God in our lives and in our churches:

1. Having Jesus at the centre of our lives and preaching.

2. Announcing good news for all people *now*.

3. Being open to all the gifts and powers of the Holy Spirit.

4. Admitting our sin and weakness and our need for help.

5. Looking forward to the growth of God's reign on earth.

6. Praying that God will work and rule among us.

7. Showing love to all, especially the poor and outsiders.

8. Welcoming *all sorts* of people into God's family.

9. Being ready to suffer and keep on loving.

10. Working for justice in our own community and nation and in all the world.

11. Repenting of sin and living holy lives.

12. Expecting God to change things in surprising ways.

The Life of the Kingdom!!

Important for evangelism? It has to be rooted in the concept of the Kingdom/reign/rule of God.

All creation is invited to share in the blessing of salvation provided by Jesus Christ. And to share in what is coming (eschatological) the final consummation of God's justice and love. We eagerly anticipate His glory!

---

1 Roger Bowen, So I send you London:SPCK 1996

5 "P" EVANGELISM

✎PRESENCE
- ☼ NEEDS MEETING - HOW MANY ARE HELPED? - social concern and social action (Matthew 5-8)

✎PROCLAMATION
- ☼ HOW MANY HEAR THE GOSPEL - gospel events, gospel witness, gospel affirmatives, gospel promises, gospel demands

✎PERSUASION
- ☼ HOW MANY DISCIPLES ARE MADE - personal relationships, call to commitment, elementary instruction, early incorporation - initiation rite

✎PARTICIPATION
- ☼ HOW MANY ARE INVOLVED IN MINISTRY - discover, develop and deploy your giftedness in ministry within the body

✎PERFECTION
- ☼ HOW MANY ARE REACHING MATURITY - personal holiness, personal spiritual growth - spiritual disciplines

PRESENCE: HOW MANY ARE HELPED? It is simply the church being there. It may be the presence of the church building or a notice board, or a Salvationist in uniform, or not.

Can you give some examples of presence evangelism in your church?

PROCLAMATION: HOW MANY HEAR? Telling the story-gospel events, gospel witnesses, gospel affirmatives, gospel promises, and gospel demands. In this course, we shall be looking at ways to do this personally, telling others about Jesus.

PERSUASION: HOW MANY ARE CONVERTED? They know the facts; now they need to commit.

PARTICIPATION: HOW MANY GET ACTIVE? Date with Destiny is an attempt to help people to get involved in ministry.

PERFECTION: HOW MANY ARE REACHING MATURITY IN CHRIST?

Holiness = becoming like Christ in character, personal spiritual growth and development.

EVANGELISM INVOLVES ALL OF THIS:- The Engel Scale

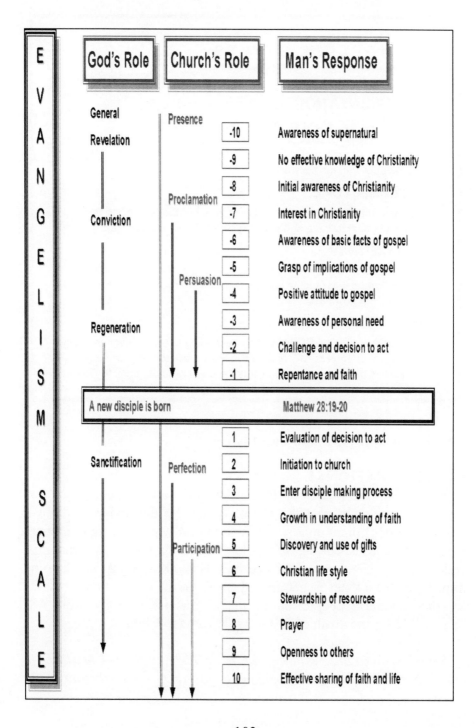

E V A N G E L I S M S C A L E	God's Role	Church's Role		Man's Response
	General Revelation	Presence	-10	Awareness of supernatural
			-9	No effective knowledge of Christianity
		Proclamation	-8	Initial awareness of Christianity
	Conviction		-7	Interest in Christianity
			-6	Awareness of basic facts of gospel
			-5	Grasp of implications of gospel
		Persuasion	-4	Positive attitude to gospel
	Regeneration		-3	Awareness of personal need
			-2	Challenge and decision to act
			-1	Repentance and faith
	A new disciple is born			Matthew 28:19-20
			1	Evaluation of decision to act
	Sanctification	Perfection	2	Initiation to church
			3	Enter disciple making process
			4	Growth in understanding of faith
		Participation	5	Discovery and use of gifts
			6	Christian life style
			7	Stewardship of resources
			8	Prayer
			9	Openness to others
			10	Effective sharing of faith and life

EVANGELISM STYLES

EVANGELISM STYLES

⊛ CONFRONTATIONAL

⊛ Peter Acts 2 - stood up in the power of the spirit and preached on the day of Pentecost. He confronted people with the truth of their actions. This was in keeping with his personality

⊛ INTELLECTUAL

⊛ Paul Acts 17 - went to the philosophers in Athens. He had the intellectual training and capacity to meet them on their own ground

⊛ TESTIMONIAL

⊛ Blind Man - John 9. When they brought him to court he did not confront neither did he reason. He said *"Here is what I know - I was blind but now I see"*.

⊛ RELATIONAL

⊛ Matthew - Luke 5:29 - How can I best relate to my colleagues at work, school or university? Matthew threw a party for them which actually earned him the right to their trust, and to introduce them to God.

Finding the approach that best fits you!

CONFRONTATIONAL

Ready, aim, fire, sums up Peter. Full force and instantly! Can you imagine trying to correct the son of God-Peter did and you might if you have a confrontational style! Walking on water, diving overboard when he saw Jesus, cutting off a soldier's ear, all in the confrontational style of Peter. If he was convinced he was right there was no stopping him. It needed a Peter to get up and speak on the day of Pentecost. He let thousands of people know in no uncertain terms who was responsible for the death of Jesus. 3,000 came to Christ.

Some people are waiting for a confrontational Christian to challenge them. They need someone to ask them where they are with Christ in a direct and bold way.

INTELLECTUAL

Logical, reasoned, prepared presentation of the gospel, maybe the reason why Paul excelled in writing such good letters. The intellectuals at mars Hill (Acts 17) would not have liked Peter's confrontational approach. They needed logic, a laying out of the evidence and not a list of platitudes.

This means not only declaring the gospel, but defining the gospel and defending it. It is an increasingly important part of evangelism in this secular age. Note too how Paul changed his own style, adjusted to the situation that he found himself in– and picked on the statue to the unknown God!

Acts 17 – Paul in Athens

- *Starts with their agenda*
- *Uses their authorities*
- *Identifies with them and finds common ground*
- *Demonstrates incredible self-sacrifice and risk*
- *Affirms, then challenges*
- *Invites further dialogue, leaves the way open*
- *Includes Jesus as understood and leads them beyond their understanding*
- *He looked, listened, learned and lived among the people*

TESTIMONIAL

One man had something happen in his life that was worth talking about! This man refused to go down the intellectual route: he would not have a theological debate; *"one thing I know, once I was blind but now I see!" (John 9:25).* He steered away from confrontation and spoke definitely from his own experience.

Most people need to hear testimony. What has happened to you? How is God working in your life? They may not respond to challenge or argument, but a personal account of your faith could influence them powerfully. Paul adopted this in Acts 26:

Acts 24 -26 - Paul with the Romans

- *Answers their questions and starts with their agenda*

- *Uses their authorities*

- *Identifies with them and finds common ground*

- *Affirms, then challenges*

- *Tells his faith story, bears witness honestly*

- *Includes Jesus as understood and leads them beyond their Understanding*

- *He looked, listened, learned and lived among the people*

- *Uses their languages*

It does not need to be dramatic!

You may have been brought up in church and never had a Damascus road experience. But God has become real to you and you may be in a position to talk about the difference between religion and Christianity. Your living relationship with Christ is your testimony.

RELATIONAL

Friendship evangelism. In my opinion the most effective for today. Some people will never be reached except through the long haul of an interpersonal relationship. Having cups of tea with them and chatting about everything under the sun. The relationship slowly deepens, and different levels of intimacy begin to unfold.

You patiently listen-their trust develops. Sharing meals and having people round at home. Matthew threw a party for people that he worked with over the years, Luke 5:29). The danger is that we build friendship with hidden motives-what of our integrity?

EVANGELISM STYLES ... continued

✦ INVITATIONAL

✦ Woman at the well - John 4: Even having requested discretion from this woman, Jesus was faced with the whole town coming to hear him after she was let loose!

✦ SERVICE

✦ Dorcas Acts 9 - She made articles of clothing. This maybe less verbal and involved the skill of the hands - but God uses that too!

INVITATIONAL APPROACH

Many non-Christians are open to this approach-come to church. 25% of people would come to church if a friend invited them. Obviously, you just have to be selective in what you invite them to.

SERVICE APPROACH

Acts 9:36. People who naturally notice needs that others have, other people may not even see them, but delight in meeting those needs. Dorcas was 'always doing good and helping the poor', and was well known for it.

Mother Theresa is one of the greatest evangelists of the 20th Century. You may not be able to stand up and preach, and argue the case, but can you make a good meal, or fix a car, or.....

Bill Hybels =The formula!

```
THE EVANGELISM
FORMULA


HP + CP + CC = MI
```

Bill Hybels presents a formula for evangelism-a way of reaching God's lost people! HP + CP + CC = MI
Maximum Impact is the end result-to have the greatest possible spiritual impact on those who are around us. This is God's purpose for the church=MI! We are to be his witnesses, empowered by His Spirit to reach people for Christ. We are to arrange our lives in order that we may have the maximum spiritual impact on those around us. Fishers of men - it's our responsibility to put that challenge into action.

THE INGREDIENTS ARE SALT AND LIGHT.
SALT-makes people thirsty and spices things up. It preserves. Stimulates thirst. Adds excitement to taste. Holds back decay. You are the salt of the earth. But salt needs two conditions in which to work-POTENCY AND PROXIMITY.
HP = High Potency
CP = Close Proximity
We must be a strong concentration of Christ's life and influence which gives our lives power to demonstrate his presence. We need to be close enough to people we are hoping to reach for the power to have its effect. Salt without savour is worthless.

LIGHT-the main thing he emphasises is that under a bushel it has no effect. CC = Clear Communication. We have to learn how to declare the basic principles of the gospel effectively. I'm afraid that many Christians have opted for simply living out their faith in an open and consistent manner, the people around them will see it, want it, and will somehow work out for themselves how to get it! Every part of this formula needs to be fulfilled if we are to be effective evangelists.

THE SENDER

FROZEN LANGUAGE CLERICAL
- Religouswords, jargon, long words "Ions""
- Language of the pulpit Theology

FORMAL LANGUAGE
- Those amazing forms tax returns, insurance documents watch the small print!!

INFORMAL LANGUAGE
- Polite - but still friendly

CASUAL LANGUAGE
- Relax with friends talk about football etc. neighbours politics

INTIMATE LANGUAGE
- The language of family the language of love

LECTURE 3: MISSION IN THE BIBLE

Mission in the Old Testament

In His book "Transforming Mission" David Bosch comments that 'the difference between the Old Testament and the New Testament is mission'[1]. There have been those who suggest that mission is absent from the Old Testament. However, he goes on to point out that the Old Testament is vital to our understanding of mission. His key point is that Israel has been created by God as a nation, having been rescued, redeemed by God who led the nation out of Egypt. Therefore, Israel and its history represent the arena and context for the activity of God. The basis of his relationship with Israel was his covenant made at Mount Sinai. Through a number of key individuals, the activity of God can be seen in the nation's history. The God of Abraham, Jacob, Isaac, Moses, are evidences of his work in Israel's historical past, but reveal Israel as his choice nation through whom to work his purposes. The mission of God can be seen clearly, as we look at the Old Testament.

---

1 Bosch David, Transforming Mission, (Orbis Books, New York, 1991) p, 17

109

Although it may be harder to detect than in the New Testament, it is there. It may be true to say that His mission seemed to exclude other nations and to be focussed on Israel in particular. That may be why it is difficult to define.

For example, **Abraham's call** to leave Ur in Genesis 12 was coloured with the idea that in choosing Israel from the nations they were not different from the 70 or so other nations (Genesis 10) that existed at the time. All of the nations had refused to listen to God and respond to him. The choice of Israel was not made to exclude the others. In fact, we know that the opposite is true. It was to be through Israel that the nations of the world were to be blessed and find God's favour. It was by grace that Israel was chosen! They were not simply to receive God's blessing and favour, but they were to carry it to others! And yet God's choice became more and more narrow! **Isaac**, and not Ishmael was chosen, **Jacob** and not Esau, **Judah** and not Israel and so on. It's the exclusivism that seems at odds with the New Testament, and which makes it difficult for us to see the mission of God. But as prophets like Amos remind the people then and us now also, as well as being privileged, Israel carried responsibility. The Old Testament's great events point us in the direction of God's mission. What are they? The 'Exodus' reminds us of the struggle of a nation for freedom. Preachers in Africa have often drawn inspiration from such stories as they symbolise their struggles to be free.

The Book of Jonah contains another interesting missionary insight. Is it the book about a reluctant prophet or a gracious God? Jonah travels in the opposite direction in response to God's call! Jonah slept while the pagan sailors prayed! They heard and repented while Jonah moaned and complained! Jonah is like the sleeping church, awakened to reality preaches his message. The people repented and Jonah did not! Ninevah responded to his preaching while he complained that God was too generous and merciful! Remember his sulk Jonah was very unhappy about this and became angry.

Jon 4:2 So he prayed, "LORD, didn't I say before I left home that this is just what you would do? That's why I did my best to run away to Spain! I knew that you are a loving and merciful God, always patient, always kind, and always ready to change your mind and not punish.

Jon 4:3 Now then, LORD, let me die. I am better off dead than alive."

Jon 4:4 The LORD answered, "What right do you have to be angry?"

The interesting question here was why Jonah was angry? Could it be that the truth was that he desired the grace and mercy of God exclusively for the Jews – and was offended because Ninevah repented and was shown mercy? This revealed the exclusivist in Jonah and could it be that it may be present in Christians today? Is the good news of Jesus available for every tribe and nation?

Here are Roger Bowen's conclusions to the story of Jonah:
1. God is more missionary than we are.
2. We are often afraid of mission and do not want to evangelise
3. We often misunderstand and misrepresent our God.
4. True love for God can often be found outside the church.
5. It is often hard for us to see what is happening when God works in new ways.
6. Mission does not make us successful, it makes us amazed and humble.

Surely, the great lesson from the Old Testament is that we are not saved in order to feel good and get heaven. We have a responsibility to see ourselves as sent and to behave like the God we follow. Self-emptying, self-surrendering, committed to reaching others, caring for the poor and marginalised. The primary character of the Christian is to be like Christ. What is the fruit of a Christian?

THE GOSPELS
The basic idea in reflecting on the gospel is that we always should use the life and character of Jesus as our model for mission. The key theme here in the gospel is the Kingdom of God, the reign or rule of God. It is an incredible story in that respect, that a king arrives, heralds a kingdom with a group of 12 simple fisherman and one or two others. This baffled the religious leaders of his day. But in everything he did from his care for the poor and marginalised, to his death as a criminal, he encouraged his followers to share his ministry of weakness knowing that God was with and in them by His Spirit–building a kingdom!

111

MARK

Mark's gospel is often been credited as being a direct straightforward account of the story of Jesus. When I trained as an SA officer they gave me an assignment that was most helpful, to write my own commentary on the gospel of Mark But we have to remember that the gospel was written to give Christians guidance for their life, and not simply a chronology of the life of Christ or even background information. Christians were facing upheaval and the collapse of the familiar structures of Judaism. Challenges about lifestyle and witness were prevalent. It was time of rapid change and upheaval to which Mark wanted to speak into. In order to help the reader to have pegs around which to base the story, the book is written around 3 confessions: Remember that this book is a mission document to guide people who are sent out into the world as witnesses!

1.   God's Confession of Jesus:
Mk 1:11 And a voice came from heaven, "You are my own dear Son. I am pleased with you."
2.   Peter's confession of Jesus:
Mk 8:29 "What about you?" he asked them. "Who do you say I am?" Peter answered, "You are the Messiah."
3.   The centurion's confession of Jesus:
Mk 15:39 The army officer who was standing there in front of the cross saw how Jesus had died. "This man was really the Son of God!" he said.

Bowen identifies 5 key aspects of Jesus life and ministry around which Mark builds his account:

1.   Jesus used the ordinary language of the world in His teaching
2.   He was open to outsiders
3.   He delivered people from oppression of all kinds=physical, religious, social and political
4.   He commissioned the twelve to continue his work
5.   He suffered and died in weakness at the hands of His enemies.

A key concept is that although his followers were to share his power, Mark made a lot of their weakness and inability to see the true significance of his mission or their own. Ultimately, they both betrayed and forsook him! Weakness will always be a feature of

Christian mission, it may even be the key! The church will not grow because it is strong, but because it is weak. The relationship between strength and weakness is a key feature of Mark's account. It should be a key theme of the life of the church. Fear of failure and lack of strength are conditions that release the power and strength of God. Do not pray to be strong, but to be weak! God works through human weakness. Power evangelism and weakness evangelism are closely linked!

LUKE

Luke is writing to a non-Jewish reader (Theophilus) and his orderly narrative has him in mind. The key verse is 4:21 which he lays alongside Isaiah 61:1-2: He taught in the synagogues and was praised by everyone: Lk 4:16-21

> **Luke 4:16** *Then Jesus went to Nazareth, where he had been brought up, and on the Sabbath he went as usual to the synagogue. He stood up to read the Scriptures v17 And was handed the book of the prophet Isaiah. He unrolled the scroll and found the place where it is written, v18 "The Spirit of the Lord is upon me, because he has chosen me to bring good news to the poor. He has sent me to proclaim liberty to the captives and recovery of sight to the blind, to set free the oppressed v19 and announce that the time has come when the Lord will save his people." v20 Jesus rolled up the scroll, gave it back to the attendant, and sat down. All the people in the synagogue had their eyes fixed on him, v21 as he said to them, "This passage of scripture has come true today, as you heard it being read."*
> **Isa 61:1** *The Sovereign LORD has filled me with his Spirit. He has chosen me and sent me to bring good news to the poor, to heal the broken-hearted, to announce release to captives and freedom to those in prison. v2 He has sent me to proclaim that the time has come When the LORD will save his people and defeat their enemies. He has sent me to comfort all who mourn, v3 To give to those who mourn in Zion Joy and gladness instead of grief, a song of praise instead of sorrow. They will be like trees that the LORD himself has planted. They will all do what is right, and God will be praised for what he has done.*

It is worth noting that it is the Spirit of God who is at work, reference to the Spirit who will be sent to his followers in due course.

One of the great concepts here is the **Centrifugal and Centripetal** nature of mission. Let me explain:

CENTRIFUGAL MISSION:

is where message is sent outside to non-believers.

CENTRIPETAL MISSION:

brings outsiders into the church. See page 41 of Bowen's book. Go out and proclaim. Attract in, and then send out.

Key themes of Luke: Jesus came in the power of the Spirit, the new age was to be the age of the Spirit of God. All the activity of the Spirit is focussed on Jesus himself. Jesus had a special concern for the poor, not only finance and money, but those who were deemed outsiders of society, particularly religious society. The lepers, women, children, tax collectors, and the Samaritans are featured in Luke.

Their immorality or status prevented them entering the temple. Jesus welcomed them at his table. In Luke's gospel, Jesus eats good food with bad people! In Luke's gospel, Jesus declares that God's heart is with the lost before the found. Luke 15: 3 lost stories!

JOHN'S GOSPEL – The prologue – 'Be There' (incarnate mission)

THE BOOK OF ACTS

This book charts the growth of the early church, the crucial decades in world history! AD 33 to AD 64.

In that time, Christianity reached every corner of the globe and became the largest religion in the world.

Once the Spirit came upon them, they spread from Jerusalem, Judea, Samaria and to the uttermost parts of the earth.

Now there is an evangelism strategy!

An Acts 1 Focus (1)

PHASE ONE: JERUSALEM MINISTRY:

- Lost sheep (all churches)
- Networks of friends, etc.

PHASE TWO: JUDEA MINISTRY:

- Unchurched atheists in community

An Acts 1 Focus (2)

PHASE THREE: SAMARIA MINISTRY

- Different "people groups" in
  community (cross cultural)

PHASE FOUR: UTTERMOST PARTS MINISTRY

- New plants beyond present "drawing area"
  (corps having baby corps, who have baby
  corps, who have baby ....)

They worked outwards from a warm centre. Modern churches often operate not from an outreach perspective, but from an 'in drag' one! We trawl our registers and look for those who used to come to church, who were baptised or married in church, and try to interest them afresh. They learned this from Jesus who invested his time with the twelve and the three within the twelve. He moved out from there. The church did the same. Acts 1 charted the beginning of evangelism in the early church–not Acts 2. they obeyed God, stayed in Jerusalem (vs 12), they prayed (14), they were united (14) and they were open to the Spirit. Get the centre of the fire hot and people will be warmed on its outskirts and be drawn in. A church on fire is an irresistible church!

They believed in every member ministry. What really happened was not done only through the preaching of Paul and Peter, but by Christians wondering about chatting to their friends and neighbours, informal missionaries they have been called. These days evangelism is expensive, minister oriented, dependent on the skills of an evangelist, which many churches don't seem to have so they opt for a visiting specialist to conduct a campaign! The early church equipped every member to be a witness, they didn't preach, they simply knew how to say "Jesus Christ is alive and I know Him"! It's a conversation stopper if ever I heard one!

They worked most effectively on the god-fearing fringe of the synagogue. All churches have a fringe. (Explain PAL). What about the winter migrants who turn up at Christmas & Easter! Think of it! One festival proclaims that the Lord has come among us and the other proclaims that even death cannot keep him down! He is the God who is here and He is the God who is alive!

They had joyful worship! There's a shock, joy in worship. I know Christians who are allergic to joy! I can go to church where the music is good, the preaching good, but we expect the whole thing to be over in an hour, and joy would not be the main characteristic of what happened in that time! I don't want to go on about this, but when did we start sitting in rows staring into the back of each other's heads?

They concentrated on giving oversight to those who they led to faith. I love this. No hit and run tactic! After care was a valued principle of the early church. Programmes of instruction, quite elaborate from what we read were the order of the day, "They devoted themselves to the apostles teaching, and to the fellowship, the breaking of bread and to prayer"! (2:42) Members knew that they were loved and cared for, they were trained, they understood their faith and so they grew. The new converts in Acts were not simply believers, they were brethren, they belonged!

LECTURE 4: PRACTICAL EVANGELISM

GROWTH CONCEPTS

- The power of analogy in solving problems:
  Getting my church folks involved in evangelism is like getting a tortoise to run!
- How do you get a tortoise to run?
- What does that suggest you might do?

Suggestions, please!

GROWTH CONCEPTS

What's the fruit of an oak tree?
Another OAK TREE!

"By their fruits you shall know them!"

See John 15:
So-what is the fruit of a Christian? Another Christian! What is the fruit of a church? Another church!!

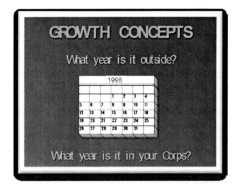

The evidence from inside the church sometimes belies the year it is outside-it feels we are going back a number of generations! Always go to church and ask what year is it? The music will be a clue–the dress will be another–the language another!

The way we package what we offer has an effect on the way people respond!!

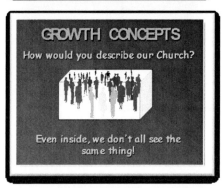

Exercise: Stand people up and ask them to describe the room-all from different perspectives!

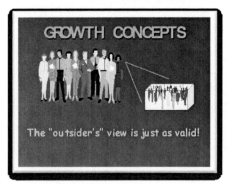

We need to listen to what those outside our Church & Corps are "telling" us about what we do and offer. Bear in mind that it is not always in words that they tell us, their actions can speak volumes too!!

REGENT HALL CORPS - our plans for balanced growth

NURTURE *Deepening Christians*	EVANGELISM *More Christians*	WORSHIP *Worshipping Christians*	SERVICE *Servant Christians*

Holiness meeting
 	
Discipleship
  - Date with Destiny
  - 2:7 Series
  - Planned Giving
  - other 'discipleship'
    courses
 	
House group
development
 	
Raising the prayer
profile
 	
Home League
	'Salvation' meeting
	  development
	
	Open air meeting
	  development
	
	Alpha course
	
	Welcome team
	  development and
	  follow up
	
	Book/ cafe ministry
		Participation in
		  worship
		
		Place of music in
		  worship
		
		Our Sunday
		  ministry
		
		Develop a 'seeker
		  friendly' meeting
		
		Youth/student
		  worship
			Care in our Community
			  - soup run
			  - advice centre for
			    homeless
			
			Care in our family
			
			  - House group
			    development
			  - Pastoral care
			    system

At my last church (above) even the image to shoppers on Europe's busiest street had something to say about who we are and what we offer. I took two photos and asked what people saw.

The results led to a change in the frontage which was more attractive and modern for a church in that location. It actually looked as inviting as the shops around it!

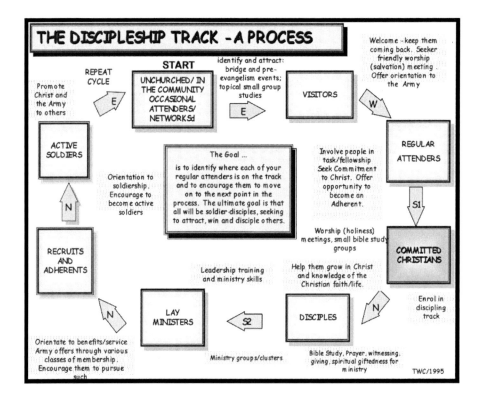

THE DISCIPLESHIP TRACK - A PROCESS

Welcome - keep them coming back. Seeker friendly worship (salvation) meeting. Offer orientation to the Army

REPEAT CYCLE

Promote Christ and the Army to others

E

START
UNCHURCHED/ IN THE COMMUNITY OCCASIONAL ATTENDERS/ NETWORKSd

identify and attract: bridge and pre-evangelism events; topical small group studies

E

VISITORS

W

ACTIVE SOLDIERS

Orientation to soldiership. Encourage to become active soldiers

The Goal ...
is to identify where each of your regular attenders is on the track and to encourage them to move on to the next point in the process. The ultimate goal is that all will be soldier-disciples, seeking to attract, win and disciple others.

Involve people in task/fellowship Seek Commitment to Christ. Offer opportunity to become an Adherent.

REGULAR ATTENDERS

S1

N

RECRUITS AND ADHERENTS

Leadership training and ministry skills

Worship (holiness) meetings, small bible study groups

Help them grow in Christ and knowledge of the Christian faith/life.

COMMITTED CHRISTIANS

N

LAY MINISTERS

S2

DISCIPLES

Enrol in discipling track

Orientate to benefits/service Army offers through various classes of membership. Encourage them to pursue such

Ministry groups/clusters

Bible Study, Prayer, witnessing, giving, spiritual giftedness for ministry

TWC/1995

THIS TRACK EMBRACES ALL OF THE ABOVE IN A LOGICAL SEQUENCE.

Helpful because it shows the "big picture" into which we must fit the key roles/purposes which we have outlined. Several steps:

1. Re-organise for mission with the MISSION CLUSTER MODEL

2. Be sure that all present programme activity advances the roles (NEWSS) in a way that balances each. Where are the gaps? We may need to add or delete programmes to help us to achieve this.

3. Use this track to formally identify where people are on the continuum and to move them along to the step. Recognise the need for balanced personal growth.

4. Place people (staff and lay) by their spiritual giftedness, natural talents, personality and compassions (all God given for ministry). Ensure each role is adequately resourced with the right people.

5. Categorise budgets by roles and ensure that each roles receives the necessary allocations.

6. Evaluate the effectiveness of each role and the balance of them all at least annually.

EVANGELISM APPROACHES

✍DIRECT APPROACH

- Do you ever think about spiritual matters?
- "Who, in your opinion, was Jesus Christ?"
- Do you ever wonder what happens to us when we die?
- What do you think a Christian is?
- What is your spiritual background? Were you taught particular spiritual perspectives as you grew up?

✍CONVERSATIONAL BRIDGES

- Business - Relocation - moving house - Hobbies and spare - time - Nature - Music - Sport - Shared struggles - Holidays

✍INVITATIONAL APPROACH

- make sure the event is excellent and sensitive to seekers - put some information in their hands that they have a visual reminder - offer them a lift or accompany them!

BUILDING RELATIONSHIPS

✍Starting Spiritual Conversations

- The Direct method
  - Do you ever think about spiritual things?
  - Where do you think you are on your spiritual journey?
  - If you ever want to know the difference between religion and Christianity just let me know!
- The Indirect Method
  - Using the already happening conversation to share your faith
- The Invitational Method
  - Invite to an event
  - Offer to transport them
  - Do something before or after the event

BUILDING RELATIONSHIPS
WITH THOSE WHO DO NOT BELONG

BUILDING RELATIONSHIPS

✐ **Starting Spiritual Conversations**
  ⊕ **Transition the conversation when talking about:**
  - Weather or nature
  - Hobbies
  - An upcoming holiday like Christmas, Easter etc
  - The latest TV show
  - Finals of sports tournaments
  - A personal difficulty that someone is going through

All of the above focus upon the other persons areas of concern!!

KNOW YOUR OWN STORY (TESTIMONY)
AND BE READY TO SHARE IT

WHAT IS YOUR STORY?

✐ **Your Story is Important!!**
  ⊕ Your friends are interested!!
  ⊕ They can relate to a story

✐ **Organise your story around 3 handles (Acts 26)**

⊕ BC	=	Before Christ
⊕ C	=	Conversion
⊕ AD	=	After Christ

✐ You need an overall theme

✐ You need a concluding question

KNOW GOD'S STORY (BIBLE+)
AND BE PREPARED TO SHARE IT

WHAT IS HIS STORY?

GOD
- God is loving – 1 John 4:16
- God is holy – 1 Peter 5:15
- God is just – 2 Thessalonians 1:6

Us!
- We were created sinful
- We deserve death – physical and spiritual
- We are helpless - morally bankrupt - sinners!

Christ
- Christ is God and became a human person
- Christ died as our substitute
- Christ offers forgiveness as a gift

You
- You must respond
- You must invite Christ to be your forgiver – the leader of your life
- You can be transformed by the Holy Spirit

BE SENSITIVE AS TO WHERE PEOPLE
HAVE REACHED ON THEIR OWN JOURNEY

CROSSING THE LINE

Assess their readiness
- Have you come to the point where … or are you needing to think it through more?
- Where would you say you are in the process?
- Are there any reasons why you would not want to ask God into your life?

Pray
- You should guide the prayer
- Ask for God's forgiveness
- Ask for God's leadership
- Thank God for accepting the prayer

Celebrate their commitment
- Keep in mind that all people do not react in the same way!
- What matters is the step of faith – not the emotional feeling evoked
- Share Luke 15:10 – the angels rejoice!!

Follow up
- Other Christians
- Personal Prayer
- Bible Reading
- Discipleship Programme

I would like to examine today the relationship between evangelism and Church Growth. This is important to mission and evangelism because while these subjects deal with the question 'what is to be done' - Church Growth could be said to deal with the question who is to do it? We should be interested in the church and its growth. Jesus after declaring the kingdom of God is here, then called the disciples to follow him and be in community with him.

"The calling of men and women to be converted, to follow Jesus, and to be part of his community is and must always be at the centre of mission".[1]

The father of the Church Growth movement is Dr Donald McGavran. The simple question he posed was: 'Why do churches in some parts of the world grow, and others do not?' McGavran was an American, who spent most of his ministry as a missionary in India. His view was that people should not be taken out of their culture to hear the gospel, but should hear the good news within it. In this way, new Christians become *Bridges of God* (title of his book) rather than islands of faith (mission stations). Basically, the church multiplied within culture, in groups of people who came to faith and led others to faith. He defined this concept as church growth and founded the Institute of Church Growth. Listen to his definition of Church Growth:

Church Growth is that science which investigates the nature, function and health of Christian Churches as it relates specifically to the effective implementation of God's commission to make disciples of all nations. Church Growth strives to combine the eternal principles of God's Word with the best insights of contemporary social and behavioural sciences.

He observed in India, and I think the same holds true for Africa which was also a missionary target, that missionary methods differed and affected the success or lack of in churches. Specifically, the method based on the mission station approach. McGavran argued that this approach detaches converts from their indigenous culture and community and links them to a foreign mission station.

---

1 Newbigin, Lesslie The Open Secret, (SPCK London 1995) p,121

They are required not only to conform to the gospel lifestyle imperatives, but to ethical and cultural standards of the said station. The effect is twofold. One the convert is transplanted into an alien culture and is not in a position to influence and win relatives and neighbours to the faith. Secondly, the mission's energies are exhausted in their efforts to bring the converts and their children into conformity with the standards being imposed by the station. Both of the above combine to halt growth. Schools and hospitals are features of these stations, but in the provision of these, the church stops growing. McGavran traces this failure to a misreading and misunderstanding of the Great Commission. The primary business being to baptise and to teach. The mission station approach halted growth because it devoted its energy and resource to something other than discipling.

Some Reflections on Culture

"Any attempt at communicating the gospel involves the culture of the evangelist and their life experience-their understanding of what the gospel actually is."

"A missionary cannot present a pure, unadulterated gospel, but only a gospel embodied in, and shown in the culture of the missionary."

"The Christian Faith cannot exist in a form separate from the culture of its adherents."

"Contextualisation consists of the challenge to one cultural group to make sense of their understanding of the gospel with another cultural group."

"To communicate 'in the language of those to whom it is addressed...clothed in symbols which are meaningful to them. Those to whom it is addressed must be able to say, "Yes, I see. This is true for me, for my situation.'" Lesslie Newbigin, The Gospel in a Pluralist Society

"i.e. framing the gospel message in language and communication forms meaningful to the local culture-focussing the message on crucial and relevant issues in the lives of those to whom it is addressed."

"This is a never ending task due to the fluid, changeable nature of culture."

"Faith must be rethought, reformulated and lived anew in each human culture, in depth and right to the culture's roots."

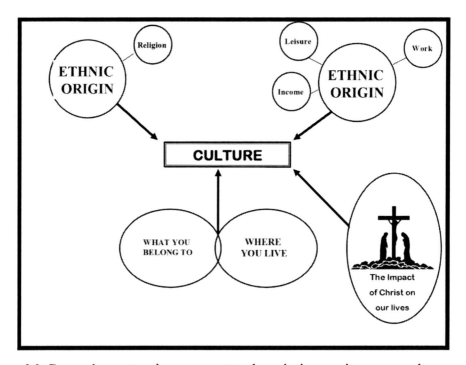

McGavran's contrasting concept to the mission station approach was the 'people's movement'. This strategy has resulted in the non-stop growth of churches because missions direct their energy and resource to discipling. By contrast, the strategy of a 'people's movement actively seeks and fosters the corporate decisions of whole social groups to accept the gospel. This avoids the breaking of natural relationships. Basically this means that people within a culture 'gossip the gospel' within their family and friendship networks. People become Christians without social dislocation so that the resulting churches have leaders and loyalties intact. Churches are more stable, are self-supporting and to bear up better under persecution.

The homogenous principle
One of the controversial areas linked to the discussion of culture is that of the homogenous principle – birds of a feather! The concept at its root is one that states that people should not have to leave their own culture – to cross any unnecessary boundaries or barriers in order to become a Christian. Therefore, local churches should come from one tribe or from one homogenous group. In this way, new Christians are attracted to the church and will not have to dislocate themselves from their own culture or change their behaviour to a huge extent.

There are points in its favour:
- People can speak their own native language or dialect
- Christians can value their own culture without being dominated by the host cultural group
- Converts from other faiths within that culture, will find it difficult enough becoming Christians without adding another set of barriers for them to cross.

And there are problems:
- Jesus brought together people who were totally different. Simon the freedom fighter and Matthew a tax collector!
- The church has always been a fellowship of Jew and Gentile, rich and poor, slave and free, male and female. This is part of the gospel. The good news is that Jew and Gentile get to share together in the one body of Christ. People need to see a multi-cultural church. How does that equate to churches of separate groups. This may hinder evangelism?

Receptivity
Another evangelism concept developed within Church Growth is that churches should concentrate on areas of the population that are deemed to be 'receptive' to the gospel.

Barriers to Growth and Church Pathology
The pragmatic approach of Church Growth theorists is revealed in a determination to get to the facts and to state them candidly. We surely need to know why a church is growing and why a church is declining. Face the brutal facts before it is too late! Church Pathology–a definition of pathology: *"The scientific study of the nature of disease and its causes, processes, development, and consequences."*

Church Growth seeks to define what kind of growth is good or bad. Not all growth is good, leaves instead of fruit for example!

The definition of good growth is as follows:
- **Conceptual** growing *up* into maturity as Christians
- **Organic** growing *together* in relationships
- **Incarnational** growing *out* into society and meeting need acts of kindness and mercy
- **Numerical** growing *more* in numbers, new people becoming Christians and joining the church through evangelism.

The concept is that by achieving balance in each of these the church grows.

127

THERE ARE FOUR KINDS OF NUMERIC GROWTH:

1) *BIOLOGICAL GROWTH*

2) *TRANSFER GROWTH*

3) *RESTORATION GROWTH*

4) *CONVERSION GROWTH*

A church can table its growth on a graph: classical in church growth pathology! The emphasis in Church Growth terms should be in restoration and conversion growth.

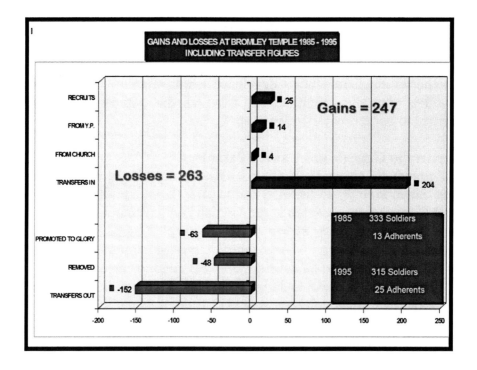

Balance=Church Health=Dependent on a healthy body with properly functioning systems.

N Nurture
E Evangelism
W Worship
S Service   BODY
S Service   COMMUNITY

**I always use
the NEWSS
acrostic
as an
alternative
mnemonic.**

THE PURPOSE DRIVEN CHURCH

Churches grow *warmer* through FELLOWSHIP

Churches grow *deeper* through DISCIPLESHIP

Churches grow *stronger* through WORSHIP

Churches grow *broader* through MINISTRY

Churches grow *larger* through EVANGELISM

THE PURPOSE DRIVEN CHURCH

Evaluation of Church Growth and Evangelism

Positive:

- Value of Listening and understanding before speaking.
- Thought out the principles of mission and state them clearly.
- Evangelism should lead to the numeric growth of the church and this has been explicitly stated in Church Growth.
- Church Growth basis its teaching on evangelism on the fact that approximately 80% of church members joined a church because of contacts with other Christians within the church. Friendship is a key to Church Growth evangelism.

Negative:

- Relied too much on human management skills and not enough on theology and history which shows that God's work is not predictable, management cannot explain everything that God does!
- Does not answer questions. What is growth or what is church?
- It has over-emphasised growth in numbers and not placed emphasis on other areas of growth.
- The danger that leaders become superstars.
- Too much emphasis on external results–our programmes could be biased to produce them alone!
- A magic wand approach to theology and evangelism–if we are desperate, we'll try anything! For example, is friendship evangelism manipulative? Surely, a hidden motive in developing friendship is suspect?
- Too much on emphasis on church membership and not enough on what it really means to come under the rule of God–disciple and teach.

MODULE 3b: EVANGELISM TODAY-PRACTICAL

(Revd Phil Clarke BA MA)

LECTURE 1: SINGING THE LORD'S SONG

THE TERM 'EVANGELISM' IS WIDELY MISINTERPRETED.

It is not: Pressurising people to believe
Conducted only by 'experts' addressing large crowds
Impossible in a plural society

Evangelism means literally to 'gospelise'–to tell the message about Christ with the intention that people commit themselves to him. This is a task for the individual Christian and for the church as a whole. 'The evangel is Jesus–not religion, or a feel good factor or a particular expression of theology. God is the evangelist' - Michael Marshall.

Here are some classic definitions of evangelism:

To evangelise is so to present Jesus Christ in the power of the Holy Spirit that men shall come to put their trust in God through him, to accept him as their saviour and serve him as their king in the fellowship of his church.   *William Temple.*
Evangelism is those actions that are governed by the intention to initiate people into the Kingdom of God. William Abraham.
Evangelism is 'One beggar telling another beggar where to find bread'.   *Daniel Niles.*

Bible Society's Church Growth material described evangelism as being about:
• **Presence** – being there, connected to the people we seek to share Christ's love with.
• **Proclamation** – declaring the Good News on the basis of 'being there' with people.
• **Persuasion** – enabling people to make their own decision to follow Christ.

Many Christians find this difficult, for various reasons–e.g.: poor role models, embarrassment, lack of faith, concern to keep friendships, worry about being asked difficult questions (many of which no one has answers for) ...Many have negative images about what evangelism is, thinking of it as being hard sell/pressurising people to believe, for experts only, programme centred ...

MISSION IS EVERY WAY IN WHICH THE KINGDOM OF GOD IS DEMONSTRATED IN GOD'S WORLD. EVANGELISM IS EVERY WAY IN WHICH THE KINGDOM OF GOD IS DECLARED IN GOD'S WORLD.

'The nature of God and the mission of God is revealed through incarnation'-Eddie Fox and George Morris. It is not that the church of God has a mission but that the God of mission has a church—without mission we are not church.

We often assume that the world at large is resistant to the Gospel, yet there is a search for security, wholeness, affirmation, relationship, acceptance ...The Gospel addresses these things: We have a mission and a message. We are called to be 'fishers of people' (Mark 1:17) There must be a catch!

Jesus sent out his inexperienced disciples almost immediately– they learned on the job: (Luke 9 & 10). Observe Jesus' model of apprenticeship training in evangelistic ministry—watch and hear me, come with me and share in this ministry, now you go and do the same, then come back and share the results with me.

Three misconceptions about mission and evangelism:

- That this is optional–no, it's a command!
- That this is something we do for God–no, God does it through us!
- That a church has to be perfectly ready to engage in mission.
  No, you never will be fully prepared!

To evangelise is an activity we can describe as:

- momentous–incredible privilege
- multi faceted– takes many forms–word, deed, sign
- shared–in partnership with others
- contested–opposed by the powers of evil
- divine–God's mission, Holy Spirit inspired

'The mission of Jesus and the mission of the Spirit are nothing other than movements of life; movements of healing; of liberation; of righteousness and justice' - *Jurgen Moltmann.*

'To clarify the nature of mission is to answer the question, what is the church for...? It is a community in response to the Missio Dei, bearing witness to God's activity in the world by its communication of the Good News of Jesus Christ in word and deed'-*Andrew Kirk.*

To be effective in this task we must be connected but distinctive–salt and light (Matthew 5:13–16). Connected with those whom we seek to reach with the Gospel, but not so immersed in the culture that we are indistinguishable from it in life-style, character and values. One of the problems in witnessing for Christ is that the church has 'lost the plot'–majored on the minors, become an institution more than a movement disconnected with the society it is called to reach. We need to re-state the Gospel of God's grace in Christ, received through personal faith and surrender of our life to Jesus Christ.

The Psalmist asks 'How can we sing the Lord's song in a strange land?' (Psalm 137:4). We must recognise firstly that the land is 'strange' (changed/changing) and, secondly, know what the 'song' (message) is. Western Missioners must continually re-learn the obvious: Jesus was not white, middle class or Methodist. Commend him to others avoiding these pitfalls!

"SECULAR PEOPLE"

George Hunter's profile of 'secular' people in the USA indicates that they are: essentially ignorant of basic Christianity, are seeking life before death, are conscious of doubt more than guilt, have multiple alienations, are untrusting because they are insecure, experience causes in history as being 'out of control' and cannot find 'the door'. He believes that those who can reach such people: will have an understanding of modern culture; live by the faith they commend; have a passion for a missionary church; make a deliberate decision to reach beyond the Christian culture; will not write people off; identify with the people they are called to reach; encourage the church to witness in word and deed; be gripped by a core of convictions and engage in Christian apologetics.

What are our motives for sharing faith in Christ: Sometimes this is to do with guilt or compulsion or the need to recruit for church. The Apostle Paul sets out a better motivation in 2 Cor 5:10–21:

➢ v. 10 Anticipating the judgement of Christ
➢ v. 14 Convicted by the unmerited love of Christ
➢ v. 17 Experience the transforming power of Christ
➢ v. 18–20 Continuing the ministry of Christ
➢ v. 21 Focusing on the death and resurrection of Christ

All this is driven by the Holy Spirit whose essential role in the life of the individual and the church is to:
- **Restore: to its original condition**
- **Refresh: with a new supply**
- **Renew: arrange for a continuing validity of 'refreshing'.**

LECTURE 2: PERSONAL EVANGELISM

Most people become Christian through the witness of a friend or family member (85%, John Finney). We should have a strong emphasis therefore on equipping every Christian to share their faith first of all with those who are close to them. This is daunting to some but it should be as natural as breathing (Rowan Williams) – if you have good news you naturally want to share it – indeed, you cannot keep it to yourself.

THE NEW TESTAMENT DESCRIBES THE WORK OF THE EVANGELIST IN VARIOUS EVOCATIVE TERMS
:

- The fisherman–Luke 5:10
- The shepherd–Matthew 9:36
- The farmer–Matthew 13:3
- The ambassador–2 Corinthians 5:20

What do these descriptions suggest to you?

When we understand the journey of faith for most people as being a gradual process influenced by many people and experiences, rather than a sudden crisis is encouraging and enabling of Christian witness. We would not generally expect people to grasp sufficiently the Gospel message and decide to follow Christ the very first time they hear about him.

Think about your own faith journey. Identify the steps that led you to become a Christian and how you have grown in faith since then. The Engel scale explores the journey to Christ and afterwards, from a person having no interest in faith through enquiry to conviction and commitment.

In Luke 19:1–10 Zacchaeus becomes a follower of Jesus.
What might have been his steps to faith? Possibly these....
- Complacency–'I can't be bothered to think about this'
- Curiosity–'Maybe I should enquire about this'
- Conviction–'I believe this to be true'
- Commitment–'I will take action now'
- Change–'I will put things right with God's help'

Receiving Christ as Saviour is likened in the New Testament to:
- Soil receiving seed–Mark 4:3 – 8
- Child receiving gift–Romans 5:15
- Host receiving guest–Revelation 3:20
- Bride receiving bridegroom–Revelation 19:7
- Believer receiving bread and wine–1 Cor 10:27 - 29

EMMAUS ROAD v DAMASCUS ROAD
For many people the way to faith in Christ is more of an Emmaus Road (Luke 24) than a Damascus Road (Acts 9) experience, a gradual awakening rather than a sudden crisis. Even some 'Damascus Road' experiences may not be as sudden as sometimes they appear–(Acts 9:22, 26). Identify the steps that led Saul/Paul to follow Christ–belief in God, familiarity with the scriptures, contact with credible Christians, observing martyrdom for the sake of Christ...

Paul however may never have developed as a Christian without Ananias–Acts 9 & 10 (and later Barnabas–Acts 11, 13, 15). Perhaps your role could be like that of Ananias–interpreting 'God moments' and courageously witnessing to unlikely converts. Increasingly in the West, we find that people are turned off by organised religion but are often open to spirituality.

In personal witness, testimony is a good tool. Your story may not seem dramatic but it may well connect with your hearers– especially if it is backed up by a changed life. Practice telling your own story–you

135

may want to write this out to map out your journey with God and clarify your thinking about it. What are the steps that led you to Christ, the people and circumstances that influenced you? What difference does Jesus make to you today and how does he affect your life in practical ways? Use ordinary non-religious language to express this. Share your story first with someone who may be sympathetic to you – not everyone will be! Your story is about Christ in you today not about your life in the past. Know what to say and how and when to say it.

Be prepared for many disappointments in personal witness and don't blame yourself for these–Your role is to share the message of God's love, people make their own choice. Many hear the message and reject it. Some appear to receive the message but when difficulties come along they give up–The Parable of the Sower illustrates this graphically: (Matt 13:1–9 & 18–23).

Jesus passionately offered the love of God but he did not force people to believe, neither did he chase after them when they hesitated in order to offer more acceptable terms! (Luke 18:18–30). Paul's letters indicate that some believers fell away from their first commitment during hard times or through material distractions.

OUR STORY AND THE BIBLICAL STORY

Sharing our own story of coming to faith is not a substitute however for explaining the Gospel message as set out in scripture. We must avoid making the story simply our story–it is bigger than all of us. Whilst telling our story does fit the spirit of our age with its interest in spiritual experiences, it will also engender the idea that we all have our own stories which are all equally valid. That is why we need to state the uniqueness of Christ as revealed in the Bible and his centrality to the message we proclaim. Jesus promised the Holy Spirit would guide our witness for him–giving us the words we need, protecting us from harm, opening opportunities and hearts to receive him.

Hospitality is a good context for Christian witness. Many of Jesus conversations in the Gospels took place at the meal table. He consistently ate and partied with the disreputable, but with all levels of society in order to share the love of the Father with them. (Luke 7:36-50) Simon; Luke 19:1-10 Zacchaeus). In the UK over the past twenty years Alpha has been the most effective evangelistic tool=Video Gospel presentation and conversation over a meal.

Think out how you would express the key aspects of the Christian message–a suitable tract or Gospel leaflet may help you. Think how, having described what God has done in Christ, you would enable someone to turn to Christ as Saviour. You will need to be a good listener, giving people opportunity to express their journey, views, doubts, concerns and needs, as they feel able. Be flexible in approach according to the needs and understandings of your hearer. However, some structure for sharing the Gospel and key points enabling someone to turn to Christ may be helpful:

One simple pattern is:

A – Admit you are a sinner
B – Believe that Christ died for you and rose again to give you life
C – Consider that it will be tough to be a Christian
D – Decide to follow Christ

It is very important to listen carefully to the person you are speaking with. This is part of love and respect. Be aware that there are frequently asked questions/barriers to faith. Be ready to respond to these acknowledging that you do not have all the answers and that the nature of faith is to believe on the basis of compelling evidence but without complete proof in any scientific sense.

A degree of trust is required–we use trust all the time in life so that act of trust is not alien to us. Often the battle for the will and the challenge of handing over control is the big issue. For Christ to be our Lord we must submit to him and that is what many people, including church-going people are reluctant to do.

It is the work of the Holy Spirit to bring people to conviction and new life but he uses our prayers and witness in this work. Though we are all fallen and sinful people, God is already at work in our lives enabling us to surrender to him ahead of our choosing to follow Christ.

This is the great Wesleyan principle of prevenient grace–grace that goes before us.

Consider some of the key barriers to belief and be ready to 'give a reason for the hope that is within you' (1 Peter 3:15) Apologetics.

The most likely stumbling blocks to belief are:

➤ **undeserved or random suffering,**
➤ **other religions,**
➤ **relativism / pluralism,**
➤ **scientific advance,**
➤ **the weakness of the church/bad past experiences of church/Christians....**

These matters cannot be lightly dismissed and we have a responsibility to seek some understanding of these issues. Simplistic answers to complex questions are unhelpful. Be unashamed to say that you do not have all the answers to hard questions asked by enquirers who have very genuine and difficult questions. Also, be aware that some people may keep asking questions as a way of avoiding the challenge of commitment.

Prayer before your conversation and a prayerful attitude in general are important since evangelistic conversation is not about winning an argument or convincing someone of the truth of the Christian message but a change of heart – a spiritual event brought about by your witness and God's transforming power.

Personal witness is part of daily life but may be initiated by certain circumstances or events–bereavement, tragedy, joyful events, new directions/opportunities, mission events, worship, preaching....

What might be the essential personal ingredients for faith sharing?

• **Sure**: confident in what and whom you believe
• **Simple**: able to express faith in Christ in clearly so that someone else can understand
• **Sympathetic**: seeking to understand where the other person is coming from
• **Systematic**: knowing how to express the key elements of faith in Christ and how to receive Christ as Saviour.
• **Surrendered**: soaked in faithful and persistent prayer.

The New Testament is intended to be a missionary document. (Luke 1:1–4, John 20:31). The biggest clue to Christian witness and personal evangelism is not simply in the lives of the first disciples and early Christians but in the nature of God himself revealed in his coming in Christ. Incarnation is at the heart of the mission task–the God who becomes one of us in order to draw us back to God. Atonement is the heart of our message–Christ died and rose again to bring us life.

JESUS COMES AS.....?

So we must ask: how did Jesus come? What were the characteristics of his coming? Small, vulnerable, in poverty, in humility, alongside the ordinary people. Philippians 2: 6–11 describes the humility of Jesus who leaves the glory of the Father's presence on a rescue mission. Whilst there are many vivid examples of faith sharing in the Gospels the ultimate model is that of the missioning God who 'becomes one of us' in order to save us.

Charles Wesley expresses it thus:

'God comes down, he bows the sky, and shows himself our friend:
God the invisible appears: God the blest, the great I Am,
Sojourns in this vale of tears, and Jesus is his name.....
Emptied of his majesty, of his dazzling glories shorn,
Being's source begins to be, and God himself is born!'

Hymns & Psalms 101

God sends his own Son in love at great cost but freely to a broken world (John 3:16). In the past, he loved and sent, in the present we are invited to believe in him so that in the future we may have eternal life. This life begins as we trust Christ today. The message is an invitation to: life=John 14:6; a party=Matthew 22:1–10; belief=John 20:26–29.

John 1:1–18 describes the coming of Christ, the Word, in terms of life, light and truth. Divinity is revealed to humankind. God becomes a human being in order to rescue his fallen creatures. (Rom 5–8: 2 Cor 5:14–21, Eph 1, 2 ff) describe this salvation plan focussed in the cross and resurrection of Jesus. Jesus expresses the style of mission his followers are to exemplify: 'As the Father sent me, so I send you'

(John 20:21). We ask therefore, 'how did Jesus come?' and find in our response the beginning of true evangelism. John 17 also expresses the ideas of sending and being sent in Jesus' prayer before his passion.

THE JESUS WAY OF INVITING OTHERS

In inviting people to follow Christ, there are some wonderful examples in the Gospels:

Mark 1–The calling of the first disciples–from their work and familiar settings to follow him. There is a sense of urgency and excitement.

Luke 7–The Roman officer expresses faith that Jesus can heal his servant and Jesus says he has never found this kind of absolute trust among the Israelites.

John 3–Jesus and Nicodemus. The religious leader is challenged to start again with God (be re-born) if he is to receive eternal life.

John 4–Jesus and the woman at the well. He knows all about her but still cares deeply for her and, having listened to her questions, offers her life. She goes away amazed to tell others.

Matthew 17–Peter, James and John see Jesus transfigured and hear the voice from heaven attesting to the real identity of Jesus. Truth is revealed directly to them on the mountain.

Luke 24–Jesus, the stranger, reveals his identity to the two disciples after his resurrection as they journey to Emmaus and he breaks the bread in their home.

John 20–Thomas' doubts are answered as he meets and recognises the risen Christ.

John 21–Peter expresses his love for Jesus and Jesus accepts Peter, despite all his failings.

These characters and many more provide us with illustration and inspiration. Relatively little is offered in the Gospels in terms of a manual of evangelistic methods. The disciples are told to 'go into all the world and make all nations my disciples' (Matt 28:19 – 20). They are to teach and baptise in the knowledge that Christ will always be with them. After he has ascended to heaven, the Spirit will be sent to facilitate the mission task.

Luke 9:1–6 & 10:1-20 show Jesus instructing and sending out the 12 and the 72 – a foretaste of what would be achieved later in the mission of the church in the Acts of the Apostles.

The book of Acts is the best missionary handbook you could ever have, combining the practice of evangelism and reflection on practice (praxis) in a variety of contexts and through several key apostles inspired through the Holy Spirit. As Luke's second volume, the Acts of the Apostles describes the continuing ministry of Jesus through his followers. It displays his interest in healing, miraculous signs, colourful characters, mission alongside the poor and the Gospel for all–specifically the Gentiles ('the outsiders'), as first expressed in the ministry of Jesus in Luke's Gospel.

THE ACTS OF THE HOLY SPIRIT

It is clear that the empowerment and overwhelming/baptism of the Holy Spirit is key to the whole venture. First, the disciples wait (Acts 1:8). Then they receive (Acts 2:1–4) and begin to declare the message of repentance for sins and salvation in Jesus name to the world (v14–42). Believers are baptised as a sign of faith in Christ. Thus, the Great Commission of (Matt 28:19–20) begins to be fulfilled.

THE HOLY SPIRIT INSPIRES

A lively growing community of believers is established. Their life-style is an expression of their message (Acts 2:43–47). Identify some of the features of this vibrant early Christian community:

- **Expectation**–of Christ's return, of God's activity through the proclamation of the Gospel
- **Experience**–clear and often dramatic evidence of the Holy Spirit's work
- **Explanation**–responding through preaching and testimony to the questions raised by the Holy Spirit's work
- **Explosion**–rapid growth of the numbers of believers
- **Expansion**–geographical and cross cultural growth fulfilling the Great Commission
- **Expression**–the message validated by the changed lives and values of the believers

The first Christian community is characterised by:

- **Koinonia**–fellowship, a strong practical and spiritual commitment to other believers

- **Marturia**–suffering through witnessing to Christ
- **Diakonia**–humble service, alongside those who were most needy, servant ministry
- **Metanoia**–transformed lives through the power of the Holy Spirit

The first half of the Book of Acts illustrates many features of a vibrant church:

Chapter 3–signs, wonders, challenge to believe
Chapter 4–Opposition, apologetics, prayer, unity, caring
Chapter 5–Discipline, judgement, supernatural healing,
Chapter 6–Shared leadership, light and darkness
Chapter 7–Biblical preaching, ultimate sacrifice......

Healing accompanies the declaration of the Lordship of Christ (Acts 3:1–10). This elicits both excitement and consternation and provides an opportunity for Peter and others to declare by whose power and in whose name these miraculous things are done.

So these first 'followers of the way' begin to talk about Christ as a way of explaining what people see before them.

They are deeply committed to prayer (Acts 4:23–31); bold to ask for courage to go on they experience a release of spiritual power. Talking to God about people precedes talking to people about God. At several points in Luke's account, we are told that the word spread– (Acts 6:7, 12:24 & 19:20).

PERSECUTION AND PERSONALITIES

Opposition is severe but repression, initially by the Jews, and even martyrdom, as today, spreads the message further–Acts 6 & 7. The Gospel seems to spread beyond Jerusalem as much from the effects of persecution as by intentional evangelistic strategy. The Jewish Christians are slow to appreciate the implications of the Great Commission concerning the Gospel for all–persecutions without and dissention within continue but there are many evidences that the non-Jewish world is ready to receive the Gospel–Acts 10, 11 & 15. (Also, that the Jewish church of the first century exhibits some of the same problems as the institutional church of Christendom in the 21st).

Acts 8 involves the apostle and evangelist Philip and demonstrates an exciting expansion of the Gospel into Samaria and a remarkable example of personal witness to an Ethiopian official. Note the many supernatural instances aligned to human obedience and openness to opportunity.

Acts 9 opens a new episode of missionary advance with the conversion of Saul/Paul. Luke clearly believes this to be a key event since he records it three times (also in chapters 22 & 26 as Paul makes his defence before the authorities). Ananias is in the role of evangelistic counsellor and takes a big risk in offering the hand of fellowship to Saul, believing that his conversion is genuine. Without this risk-taking obedience, Saul might never have matured into the great missionary apostle he became.

Barnabas is a key figure in the missionary expansion of the church:

➢ In generosity towards the church's mission (Acts 4:36–37)
➢ as a friend in need following Saul's conversion (Acts 9:27)
➢ seeking out Saul to share with him (Acts 11:24–26)
➢ partnering Saul's mission sent from congregation (Acts 13:1–3)
➢ parting from him, following disagreement (Acts 15:36–41).

Acts 13:1–3 sees the church at Antioch identify and send its best people for the work of evangelism in other places. (Not simply exporting its problem cases!) The extensive travels of Paul in the Gentile world begin here and continue to the end of the Book of Acts.

Acts 16 describes the entry of the Gospel into Europe at Philippi. It incorporates the establishment of a new congregation, liberation from demonic and unjust relationships, signs and wonders, confession of faith and baptism, demand for justice and public accountability.

Acts 17 describes the engagement of the Gospel with the philosophical elite of Athens where engages with the local culture, confronts points of confusion and speaks of resurrection. This appears to have been one of the less fruitful occasions.

The story, quite rightly, is incomplete by the end of Acts–the mission continues. Paul has eventually reached Rome declaring the Gospel for all (Acts 28:28).

The Apostle Paul's missionary adventures and methods are described in the Acts of the Apostles by Luke and in the Letters of Paul himself.

"MISSIONARY METHODS: ST PAUL'S OR OURS." C.F. ROLAND ALLEN

Here are some of the principles that emerge:
1. Adapted strategy to locality (1 Corinthians 9:16–23)
2. Went to all strata of society (Romans 1:14–16)
3. Championed the cause of the Gentiles (Gal. 2:11–21, 3:28)
4. Concentrated on strategic cities (Romans 1:10)
5. Used the local church as a base (1 Thess 1:7-8)
6. Proclaimed a full Gospel (Acts 20:26-27, 1 Cor 2:1–5)
7. Had complete confidence in message (Rom 1:15, 1 Cor 1:24)
8. Nurtured believers towards maturity (Col 1:28, 2:6-7)
9. Consolidated earlier work (Romans 15:20, Acts 15:30 & 36)
10. Set an example to be followed (1 Cor 11:1-2 Tim 3:10–14)
11. Trained young leaders (1 Tim 4:8, 2 Tim 4:1–5)
12. Maintained a pioneering spirit (Acts 28:28, 2 Cor 10:15–17)

POST-CHRISTIAN PRINCIPLES

In discussing missionary contexts and methods, we can learn much from Paul and his partners as they proclaimed Christ and planted congregations of Christian believers around the Roman empire of their day. It may be that, in the largely 'post Christian' (post Christendom) society of the West today, we need to engage again with these principles and to evangelise on the assumption that people do not know the Gospel (or have not heard in a way that they can relate to). Paul spoke out the message about Christ in a plural, philosophically and spiritually inquisitive but uncommitted sometimes cynical context.

The salt and light principles of Matthew 5:13–16 apply again here: We are to be connected with our society but distinctive from it in order to be effective witnesses to Christ. Sometimes we have been connected where we need to be distinctive and distinctive where we need to be connected. The task is enormous. Every generation and society needs to hear the Gospel in a language or form that is understandable and appropriate. The Holy Spirit will help us to get this right but it will involve risk–the expression of faith in action.

These principles can be implemented personally and in the local church. The purpose of the church is to worship God and to bring others to faith in Christ as Lord and Saviour. Sometimes this simple goal is ignored or forgotten and the church looks more like a yachting club existing for the entertainment of its members rather than a life boat station out there to rescue the perishing. Ask the question: 'What on earth are we here for?'

Ten years ago, British Methodism described its four-fold purposes as: worship; service; learning and caring; evangelism.

MISSION STATEMENTS AND METHODS

The local church needs to express its purpose in a mission statement that is Biblical, understandable, transferable and short embracing the ideal that the church is the only organisation that exists for the benefit of its non-members (William Temple) e.g.:

- Elm Ridge Methodist Church, Darlington: 'Compelled by Christ's love to be God's church in today's world' (2 Cor 5:14)
- Darlington Methodist Circuit: 'By all means to save some' (1 Cor 9:22)
- Eastbourne Methodist Church, Darlington: 'Open at the edges– committed at the core'
- Thrum Hall Methodist Church, Rochdale: 'This church exists to be the people of God: worshipping him, sharing the Good News, serving others'.
- From Willow Creek Community Church, South Barrington, Chicago: 'All people matter to God so they must matter to us'.

The mission statement must be simple and clear to be memorable, defining what our church exists for and what it does. Growing churches find their focus outside themselves as 'engaging faith communities' (Robert Warren). We are called to be the joyful bold disciples of a Jesus led counter culture, called into being by the Father and empowered by the Spirit – our purpose must reflect this. Go on to expand your church's mission statement in terms of how this objective and purpose can be achieved. This is strategy and it can only be tackled once the overall purpose is clear. Once we have clarity, there we can begin working out our purpose in practice.

145

To achieve an effective and relevant strategy we need an up to date understanding of:

- **Our community**: areas of change, growth, need and opportunity in the catchment defined by geography or networks.
- **Our church**: our calling, identified strengths and weaknesses
- **Our Gospel**: what we believe about God and people, how we express this
- **Our values**: what is most important to us about God and people, acceptable means to achieve our goals.

It is necessary to return to these foundational principles regularly in order to check out what we are doing against our stated aims and beliefs.

OUR STRATEGIC GOALS SHOULD BE:

- **Specific**
- **Measureable**
- **Ambitious**
- **Realistic**
- **Time bound**

Another way of coming at this would be to use the Parable of the Sower and other Parables of the Kingdom (Matthew 13):

- **Break up the ground**
- **Sow the seed**
- **Reap the harvest**

How will we accomplish these three tasks? How will the 'Innovators' pass on their vision, confidence and enthusiasm to the 'Implementers', remembering that is Jesus who will build his Church? (Matt 16:18)

Strategic directions might look something like this:
- **Developing eventful, inclusive and participative worship**
- **Growing as an open, welcoming, learning community**
- **Engaging the wider community**
- **Making more faithful disciples**

146

Ultimately, however, what most churches need is not a new strategy or a new idea but new life through the Holy Spirit.

One psychiatrist asked a church leader, 'If I gave my patient a prescription for love, could they bring it to your church?'

LECTURE 6: MOBILIZING THE LOCAL CHURCH FOR MISSION

'The church exists by mission as a fire exists by burning' Emil Brunner 'I am not afraid that the people called Methodists should ever cease to exist .... but I am afraid lest they should only exist as a dead sect, having the form of religion without the power and this undoubtedly will be the case unless they hold fast both the doctrine, spirit and discipline with which they first set out'. John Wesley

DESIGNED FOR DECLINE OR GEARED FOR GROWTH

History and experience tells us that some of Wesley's concerns have proved to be well founded. The historic denominations in the West have been in decline for a century. We see the symptoms of decline in many situations:

1. Low expectations and negative attitudes–a wish to die with dignity
2. Nominalism–linked to church but uncommitted to Christ
3. Remnant mentality–hanging on, entrenched views, unwillingness to change
4. Disconnected to the community it is called to reach, cultural blindness
5. Institutional, bureaucratic, inflexible responses
6. Leadership tensions

(Adapted from Ray Pointer, Church Growth, and primary research)

Rather than dwelling on problems however, we will do best to see the characteristics of growing and healthy churches:

1. Anointed and enabling leadership, prophets more than managers
2. Recognised and released gifts in all God's people
3. Passionate spirituality, faithful prayer, eventful worship, Holy Spirit renewal
4. Functional structures, people not programme orientated, open to change
5. Holistic small groups, cells, Alpha courses, disciple training
6. Appropriate evangelism especially through friendship
7. Loving relationships, compassionate service

Adapted from C Swartz (Natural Church Development); own research

147

Most churches work on a 'come' model of witness–come to us, meet us on our ground, engage with our programme, do things our way–and you will be welcome. This model assumes that people know what the church stands for, accept those values and merely require invitation. This has been the Christendom model and is now ineffective in a society where less than 10% of the population have any meaningful contact with church. We might visualise the situation as akin to being cut off in a meander loop which becomes an isolated pond instead of being in the flow. There is need to reconnect with the flow for the pond or it will soon dry up.

WE NEED TO 'MIND THE GAP': *(Note-Recorded announcement on London Underground helping to avoid accidents.)*
- **Credibility gaps**–the church and some Christians have a poor reputation with some.
- **Cultural gaps**–there is a huge difference between the life of the church and the world at large in values and practice.
- **Communication gaps**–the style and language by which Christians communicate does not often resonate with un-churched people.

A different approach to local church evangelism is needed, one that takes into account the widening gap between pew and pavement (c.f. Wall Street and Main Street) and engages with a plural, secular, spiritually inquisitive but doctrinally ill-informed society. There are many ways in which the first century model takes this into account and can be adapted for today: A changeless message for a changing world.

GROWING CHURCHES

Even in overtly secular societies, some churches are growing and effective in evangelism today. We need to learn from models that work without simply replicating their methods in a different context. Many, though by no means all, of these examples are found in the new churches. They are generally:

1. Light on structure, cell based, positive and direct on leadership,
2. Biblically conservative, charismatic,
3. Independent, post denominational,
4. Contemporary in worship style,
5. Not majoring on pastoral care,
6. Gathered rather than neighbourhood congregations,

7. Intentional concerning personal witness,
8. Operating seeker sensitive activities,
9. Dependent on prayer,
10. Anticipating high levels of commitment expressed through
11. sacrificial giving,
12. Engaging many in ministry but fewer in decision making,
13. Connected to younger and un-churched people....

Some steps towards becoming an effective mission focussed congregation could lead us back to our roots as:
- **One–diverse in expression but united in Christ–inward in community**
- **Holy–dedicated to living entirely for Christ–upward in worship**
- **Catholic–universal, inclusive–rooted in history**
- **Apostolic–true to founding dream/beliefs–outward in mission**

This is expressed practically and authentically as sharing, encouraging, supporting, forgiving, truth telling, respecting, trusting and committing – adapted from Rick Warren. We need to move away from a model where 80% of the people are passive and 20% do everything (and give most of the money), towards the ministry of all God's people.

LECTURE 7: CONNECTING WITH CULTURE

Over the last twenty years in Europe and America, we have been emerging painfully from a secular modernist world of 'enlightenment' into what has been termed postmodernism with new challenges and opportunities for Gospel witness.

POSTMODERNISM

Postmodernism: notoriously difficult to define but exhibits interest in:
1. **Spirituality without commitment**
2. **Environment without a Creator**
3. **Words without agreed meaning**
4. **Individuality without belonging**
5. **Present without future**
6. **Choice without responsibility**
7. **Tolerance of all approaches to faith and life**
(Adapted from Peter Brierley).

149

Faith is not excluded entirely from this mind-set but tends to be unfocussed. In Christian witness and observation of the media, we will quickly encounter the 'spirit of the age' to be:

- Ignorant of the story of the Bible and of basic Christian belief, pervasive pluralism.
- Seek life before death, individualistic, at times hedonistic, seeking present fulfilment
- Conscious of doubt more than guilt, influenced by science more than theology
- Influenced by negative images of the church as an institution
- Are alienated by fundamentalism and judgementalism, authority and formality
- Untrusting and sceptical because insecure, apathetic, in constant flux
- Upholding individual freedom of choice as the ultimate virtue

Much of this may sound depressing and negative but there are still opportunities for Christian witness. A major difficulty is that we are often in Britain trying to present a message to people who think they know what the message is (though they don't in fact) and have already rejected it on the basis of unsympathetic media coverage and bad personal experiences of church. People may still acknowledge a spiritual need but there is a huge gap between the church and the search. We are all influenced by the culture around us – it is part of who we are. Recognising this and working with it is part of an incarnational approach to evangelism. Too often Christians are in a ghetto of their own making, shouting their message from a distance and wondering why no one listens.

EFFECTIVE CHRISTIAN WITNESSES ARE THOSE WHO:

Understand modern culture–connected and often positive about society
Live by the faith they commend–integrity, an attractive holiness
Have a passion for a missionary church and express faith naturally but intentionally outside church
Care deeply about the people they are called to reach–mirroring Christ's love for the world.
Witness in word and deed–show positive outcomes to believing.
Are gripped by a core of convictions–what beliefs/values motivate us?
Engage in Christian apologetics–use the scientists, engage with the big questions

(Adapted from George Hunter)

Contextualisation of the Gospel message and method is not compromise it is starting where people are. Look for good examples of this, possibly from other cultures and contexts. You do not need to replicate these but you can learn much from them. A whole church which is open at the edges and committed at the core embraces this concept. Vincent Donovan states:

'An inward turned Christianity is a dangerous counterfeit, an alluring masquerade. It is no Christianity at all.... A Christian community is basically in existence for others. A church that turns in on itself will die'.

Our major and essential task is to re-connect with the younger generation, working people including the growing range of ethnic minorities. For this to happen the church must change its mode and mindset from that of a 'come and join us' institution to that of a radical living on the edge community with a clear sense of purpose.

Six characteristics of a missionary church (or of a missionary):
1. Being before doing–less activist, more reflective, enjoy God not just God's work
2. Human before Christian–approachable, vulnerable, relational
3. Belonging before believing–growing into faith within a family of believers
4. Listening before speaking–hear the questions first
5. Travelling before arriving–pilgrimage is a missionary paradigm
6. Spirituality before creed–seek an experience of God then interpret it
(adapted from Robert Warren, Sheffield, UK)

The task of mission and evangelism is holistic–it always has been: (Luke 4:16–18): Jesus in the Synagogue reading (Isaiah 61:1–3):
'The Spirit of the Lord is upon me because he has appointed me to bring good news to the poor, to proclaim liberty to the captives and recovery of sight to the blind, to set free the oppressed and announce that the time has come when God will save his people'.

Rick Warren (Saddleback Church, California)
Identifies Christ's five purposes for the church he leads:

151

1. **Magnify–Celebrate God's presence in worship**
2. **Mission–Communicate God's word in evangelism**
3. **Membership–Incorporate God's family in fellowship**
4. **Maturity–Educate God's people through discipleship**
5. **Ministry–Demonstrate God's love through service**

LECTURE 8: CONTEMPORARY MODELS OF MISSION CHURCH

Churches grow when disciples are made. This is the work of the Holy Spirit released through prayer and planning.

STRATEGIES FOR EVANGELISM

We need to develop a strategy for evangelism in the local church and to keep this under review in an on-going process of developing ways of being church in a changing context:

- Establish the facts–about the Gospel and the community we serve
- Identify the task–overall strategy
- Set goals–identify specific objectives
- Equip members–provide opportunities for training and experience
- Review progress adjust strategy in light of changed circumstances

Often a SWOT analysis is employed as a simple tool for evaluating the mission context and effectiveness of a congregation:
STRENGTH WEAKNESSES, OPPORTUNITIES, THREATS.

Our image of church will define our approach to mission: army, body, castle, community, family, life boat, school, team, club, orchestra....
George Carey identifies the characteristics of a growing church as:
- **Prepared to face disturbing news**
- **Concerned with God's mission not its own existence**
- **Geared to the deepening of faith**
- **Harnessing the ministry of all its members**
- **Aiming for quality in worship**
Clarity of purpose is very important. For instance, a railway does not exist fundamentally to run trains but to transport people and goods. Similarly, church does not exist fundamentally to run programmes but to declare and live the Gospel in such a way that people become disciples of Jesus Christ.

We must ask:
 1. Why are we here? – Purpose
 2. What is our aim? – Goal
 3. How is this accomplished? – Method

Churches growing through evangelism are often looking out for what God is doing and seeking to join him in it. They have many characteristics in common:

1. A passion for God,
2. People orientated values and vision,
3. Awareness of the prevailing culture,
4. Agreed evangelistic strategy,
5. Financial commitment to outreach,
6. Regular teaching to equip the congregation for mission,
7. Involvement in and accessibility to the local community,
8. Discipleship programme, + seeker friendly worship and events,
9. Identifying and releasing gifts for mission,
10.   Inter-church co-operation,
11.   Dissatisfaction with transfer growth,
12.   Engender a stakeholder rather than a consumer mentality,
13.   Willing to risk failure,
14.   Imagine new possibilities–dreaming the Kingdom dream....

We can see this put into action clearly in some new forms of church which find their origins in the earliest Christian communities where new wine required new wine skins (Luke 5:38).

Cell Church comprises of: small primary units of Christian belonging which express New Testament models of discipleship, church planting and evangelism designed for the multiplication of congregational units as communities of the Kingdom based on every member ministry. These cells provide an informal atmosphere where the Gospel is expressed in varied accessible ways without pressure.

CLASS MEETINGS AND CELL CHURCHES

The overriding concept is that the cell is there to multiply – either a cell grows and multiplies or it decays and dies. There is a cell group leader but the emphasis is on every part of the cell being involved. This is a more dynamic model than most house groups and has some social implications similar to the South American base communities.

153

The format and intention of a Cell Group meeting owes much to the Wesleyan Class Meeting:

Welcome–ice breaker, introduction, explanation
Worship–Prayer and praise
Word–Understanding and applying the Bible
Witness–Testimony to what God is doing in our lives and resulting actions

Instead of assumption: church=building + minister + Sunday service
Cell church offers: church=community, faith, action. (Robert Warren)

Authentic marks of the mission church are to be: self-propagating, self-governing and self-financing (Henry Venn et al).

The leadership of such churches, whether cells or church plants reaching beyond a culture familiar with conventional church, is less about laity and clergy, presbyters and deacons but rather about (Ephesians 4:11–12):

*apostles, *prophets,   *evangelists, *pastors and teachers

The cell church model will mean a re-think of the nature of church where the small unit rather than the whole congregation is the primary unit of church and the commitment of the members is first to the small group and secondly to the larger unit. This allows great flexibility in the styles of worship and community that can be created, reaching many different people and needs. Many new spiritual movements have begun in this way through history and today.

LECTURE 9: EVANGELISTIC PREACHING

It is sometimes assumed that one preaches to the converted but in most churches, there are those who are uncommitted or enquiring into faith. Therefore explaining the Gospel and calling people to commitment through preaching both inside and outside the church is both appropriate and relevant. Paul states in Romans 1:16–17 that he is 'unashamed of the Gospel for it is the power of God for salvation to those who believe'.

Later in Romans 10:13–15 he says 'For whoever calls on the name of the Lord will be saved. How shall they call on him in whom they have not believed? .... And how shall they hear without a preacher ....'

William Abraham declares:

In announcing the Good News, we need to abandon the image of proclamation that is so prevalent in Protestant tradition. That image, represented by the solid, tripartite sermon, usually read from a manuscript, is a culturally relative phenomenon. What matters is that the Good News of the Kingdom be transmitted with flair and in culturally fitting forms. That announcement, furthermore, is to be heralded less in the church and more in the market place and in the world at large. Moreover, as the Gospel is made known formally and informally it will spill over into other acts of speech. It will lead into basic instruction, into offering relevant explanations, into dialogue and conversation, and into offering a reason for the hope that is within one. It is artificial to limit this to formal acts alone or to some hygienic act of preaching fashioned according to some standard mode, although there is an obvious place for the well planned, formal heralding of the Good News in appropriate places.

The message of the Gospel requires a response offering a balance between what God has done in his sovereign will, the Calvinist emphasis, and his desire for us to trust and follow his Son, the Arminian emphasis. The preacher can, following a declaration of what God has done, enable this response. This includes the unpopular concept in today's world of conviction of sin leading to repentance as well as emphasising the love of God for sinners shown in the cross of Christ.

William Sangster referred to preachers as 'vulgarizers'–making sublime truth accessible to ordinary people. John Stott states 'the preacher is a herald ... charged with the solemn yet exciting responsibility of proclaiming the Good News of God, the apostolic kerygma.'

A clear sense of calling is essential to the preaching ministry. This comes in a huge variety of ways but it should always be checked out through prayer, reading Scripture and advice from mature believers. Jesus must be central to the proclamation, especially his death and resurrection as the atoning sacrifice for sin.

We learn much from Jesus' methods:

- he taught mainly through story-parable (Luke 15)
- he used everyday situations to declare the message with clarity and vitality (Matthew 13)
- he caused alarm by saying the unexpected or controversial (Lk 13)
- his words were accompanied by actions including compassion and miracles (Luke 13)
- he appealed to all levels of society (John 3 & 4)
- he encountered severe opposition (Matthew 23)
- he gave more detailed/difficult teaching to the inner circle of followers (John 17)
- he encouraged others to declare the same message (Luke 9-10)

The preaching of the Apostles emphasised the death and resurrection of Jesus and challenged people to believe–many thousands did and joined the fellowship: (Acts 2 & 4). This was a continuation of the prophetic proclamation of men like Isaiah, Jeremiah and Ezekiel whose oracles are recorded at length in the Old Testament.

Harvey Cox argues 'The effectiveness of preachers such as Billy Graham and Festo Kivengere .... has been their ability to interpret the Gospel vividly into the experience of their hearers. This is not about the communication of ideas but the use of vocabulary which illuminates and interprets aspects of people's world. An inner dialogue takes place between God and people through the preacher.' Therefore, evangelistic preaching, birthed in prayer and study, must include:

Information–about the Gospel of Jesus Christ, clarity, reasoned faith
Ownership–personal sincerity, conversational style, common ground
Conviction–conveyed passionately, dramatic tension, honesty
Response–expected and enabled for various needs

Maintain good eye contact–do not read from a script but use some well thought through notes as a guide. Be faithful to scripture but key into your hearers' experience by using appropriate illustration. Be passionate and be yourself. Vary pace and volume. Avoid unnecessary repetition. Use story remembering that Jesus taught in parables.

Be ready to explain the reason and need for response early in your address, returning to this in your final challenge. Give time to allow this to happen at the end and have suitable people and literature prepared beforehand and available to help in the conversation and prayer situations that result. Local and culturally appropriate follow up of new believers or those who have received a new experience of the Holy Spirit is vital.

LECTURE 10: STYLES & CONTEXTS FOR EVANGELISM

There is no single approach to evangelism and the mission of God that is appropriate in every situation. Here are several styles and contexts, you will think of many others. Traditionally we have thought of context and network in terms of geography, so our most obvious and natural context would be those who physically live near us. This may not be the case now as community is defined in a huge variety of ways–workplace, leisure grouping, electronic/internet groupings....

THE FRIENDSHIP ROAD(S) TO FAITH

More people come to faith by friendship than programme. However, one can complement the other and the local neighbourhood is still a significant factor in mission strategy. Beware of quick fix solutions – great trees grow from small seeds – but it takes time!

Vision and creativity are spiritual gifts. It is good to dream the Kingdom dream: 'Wouldn't it be great if God ....' (Complete the sentence). Vision is caught not taught, but it does need to be clearly explained and it is not simply the latest bright idea. Vision looks to the horizon and seeks to take others there.

Keep returning to the vision and tease out the values that underpin it. When the values are agreed the vision will be clearer and will be owned–a mission shaped church forms.

THE ALPHA COURSE:

One of the most effective evangelistic tools over the past 20 years has been the Alpha Course, pioneered by Nicky Gumbel at Holy Trinity, Brompton and spread internationally. Alpha incorporates key elements in evangelism: invitation on the basis of friendship, hospitality, informality, opportunity for relaxed enquiry, experiencing the Holy Spirit, good quality presentation leading to the challenge of commitment. Other small group activities for enquirers are also effective–short courses, Cell Groups, informal sharing and ministry.

Short term missions led by visiting teams are helpful supplements to a local congregation's evangelistic efforts even when team members are inexperienced and in training. An extra boost of personnel with particular skills and enthusiasm can attract others, train the team themselves, boost confidence and ignite new life in the congregation. This can be extended by planting a team in a communal house for a limited time in a neighbourhood to create a missional community witnessing to others, building trust and friendship to reach people who would never normally come to a church building.

PREACHING AND WORSHIP:

The proclamation of the Good News with Sunday worship or at special events has traditionally been one of the main contexts for evangelism. We cannot assume that all those present in a church setting are Christian but if such presentation of the Gospel is restricted to this, we will miss 90% of the population. Seeker services usually of a relaxed contemporary style will provide opportunities for people to come and hear the message but this does assume that people come onto our territory and to some extent do things our way – assumptions which need to be challenged. Good quality presentation in preaching, drama, music, projection.... is important. Although this is a visual age, many people still listen to and are moved by powerful oratory. Therefore, the crusade / revivalist style of evangelism still has a role alongside other methods depending on the context.

PUBLICISED EVENTS

Local and national media give opportunity for witness where there is a compelling story or event. The whole electronic revolution opens up possibilities for good or ill.

Healing services or remembrance events for people recently bereaved may attract none church people. They need not happen always in church.
Outdoor witness on the high street or in the park has always been part of the church's witness. The emphasis needs to be on fun, sound

bite rather than sermon, praise songs more than seven verse hymns....
It's a reminder that the cross of Christ was a public event, the early
proclamation was in the public arena not hidden away from view and
to reach un-churched people we must be alongside them and on their
turf not ours. Take care to avoid the 'cringe factor' – be gracious not
judgemental and abrasive, make the event fun to watch or be part of –
not just traditional church outdoors!

Children, youth and family targeted activities have a great variety
of forms from holiday clubs to sports, food and party events. These
may be some of the least threatening styles of outreach but effective
non-the-less.

Rural–Urban: Geographical and social context provides opportunities
and some limitations to evangelistic witness. We need to adopt varied
styles for town centre, suburb, village.... It is good to discover what
works in a particular situation. You will need to take some risks. All
growing congregations have a list of failures – things tried in good
faith but which flopped. Be ready to recognise when something isn't
working and change the approach.

Other possibilities:
Outreach connected to social action expresses the practical outcomes
of faith in Christ. It grabs attention and expresses Christ's love in
tangible ways. Most importantly, it is modelled on the ministry of
Jesus to the whole person. Recent expressions of holistic mission
include:

Healing on the Streets–prayer ministry meeting the needs of people
down the high street or in accessible centres/coffee bars.

Labyrinth–keying into the spiritual journey idea but exploring the
claims of Christ interactively rather than just a maze of ancient paths
with 'touchy feely' experiences along the way.

Biblefresh–interpreting the Bible in practice to mark the 400th
anniversary of the translation of the Authorised Version and linking
with Bible Society initiatives.

Regional outreach events, youth events/camps, music festivals,
environmental events....

Outdoor hospitality–open invitation to a Kingdom party.
Prayer backs up these events and is an integral part of the evangelistic strategy. This can be expressed in a great variety of ways from prayer triplets to prayer concerts, walks, vigils,

New people will change your church. This presents a huge challenge to those who have been comfortable with the same pattern for a long time. Often they have simply assumed that this is the right way to do things, even when there is little fruit.

The leader's main role is to hear what God is saying to the church and to move the church towards God's purposes in God's ways. This is a vulnerable place to be. It will take courage, ability to communicate a vision and to bring people on board with it, then to implement it without waiting for the laggards.

Jesus did not wait indefinitely for people to decide and change. He worked with a dedicated group of learners, sometimes slow learners and they began a movement that changed the world. You are part of this movement. There is no limit to what God can do.

We conclude with a quotation from early in this lecture series:

**"MISSION IS EVERY WAY IN WHICH THE KINGDOM OF GOD IS DEMONSTRATED IN GOD'S WORLD.
EVANGELISM IS EVERY WAY IN WHICH THE KINGDOM OF GOD IS DECLARED IN GOD'S WORLD."**

This broad definition should give us plenty of scope for imaginative ways of demonstrating and declaring the love of God in God's world.

MODULE 3c: YOUTH MINISTRY-PRACTICAL

(Revd Dr Steve Emery-Wright MDiv BA)

COURSE DESCRIPTION: YOUTH MINISTRY AND MISSION

This course explores the unique nature of young people and youth ministry placing it within the context of ministry in general. The course provides grounding in: the theology of youth ministry, studies in the formative needs of adolescents, contextual missiology, the role of the minister, volunteer development, mentoring and family support, resource development and selection, and coordinating a multidimensional youth development ministry within the context of all age ministries.

LECTURE 1: THE IMPORTANCE OF MINISTRY TO TEENAGERS AND EMERGING ADULTS

My personal desire is to learn from you. You have experienced youth ministry and you have engaged in youth ministry. You know your home communities and situations, I do not. You will teach me and all of us. You are not only a student in this course but also a teacher. For this reason you will be expected to engage in conversations and debates in this class.

Youth = 13-20 year olds (the focus of this course).
Emerging adult = 20-30 year olds.
This tends not to be the African categories but the academic literature uses these age groupings.

THE GOAL OF THE LESSON IS TO ESTABLISH WHY CHRISTIAN WORK AMONGST CHILDREN AND YOUNG PEOPLE IS IMPERATIVE FOR EVANGELISM AND MISSION.

A possible objection to specialised youth ministries

Why should we be breaking ministries down into specialties? Dividing families up, some might even argue breaking down the families. Is it not better to do youth mission and ministry holistically – reaching out to families and caring for youth and children within the context of family? Does specific children's and young people's mission work exacerbate the division's in our society rather than the reconciliation of the Gospel.

161

I think there is some real truth to the criticism that children and youth mission is potentially divisive. But having said this I believe there are compelling reasons for making these age groups a priority for mission and ministry. In the prioritising children and youth, the church actually discovers interconnectedness.

SIX BROAD REASONS AS TO WHY CHRISTIAN WORK AMONGST CHILDREN AND YOUNG PEOPLE IS IMPERATIVE FOR EVANGELISM AND MISSION.

1. Biblical Reasons: Provide me with a few bible verses that would indicate the importance of this emphasis.

Deut 6: 4-9. Keep these words that I am commanding you today in your heart. Recite them to your children and talk about them when you are at home and when you are away, when you lie down and when you rise. Bind them as a sign on your hand, fix them as an emblem on your forehead, and write them on the doorposts of your house and on your gates.

Matthew 19: 13-14. Little children were being brought to him in order that he might lay his hands on them and pray. The disciples spoke sternly to those who brought them; but Jesus said, 'Let the little children come to me, and do not stop them; for it is to such as these that the kingdom of heaven belongs.'
Educational Ideals in the Ancient World by William Barclay 1959

In Ministerial preparation, trainees spend time in Biblical studies, historical and systematic theology, homiletics and pastoral care, even evangelism and mission but little if any of this focuses on children and youth. They get overlooked. I would argue that Evangelism's primary focus needs to be in youth and children's work.

2. The age of decisions: Teenagers and young adults are at the stage when they are asking ultimate questions (senior citizens are the second largest group). **How many of you became Christians before the age of 25?** Various studies have put the figure at around 85% –below 14 the most fruitful age–with new people making faith commitments falling off between the age of 14-18 but still higher than adults (Brierley 2002: 171) Children and youth are seeking and willing to change. "To ask why is human; theology directs us to the source of all meaning. Children ask the basic questions, adolescents ask the difficult and ultimate questions, and adults get tired of asking questions." (Borgman, 2004:12)

3. Age of Identity development: The teenage years are a time of identity development within the context of a community and family but also in contrast to parents. "Who am I separate from my parents?" This often requires differentiation, a necessary space to question the "faith" of the parents before it is owned and embraced or altered (Westerhoff 2002-Will Our Children Have Faith?). There are no second generation Christians. In that sense, all of youth ministry is a mission activity.

The act of identity formation creates a need to be with other teenagers separate from their parents (but not necessarily other adults). Worship and church attendance is an anti-cultural activity for teenagers in some cultures (Mayo etc. 2006: 16ff). To attend a church without young people reinforces the attitude that to worship they must reject their "youth identity" but if there are a significant number of young people present then faith is affirmed as an acceptable activity for young people in spite of the cultural trend.

In some countries, the average age for leaving church is 10–for others it is when they move away from family. Something is going wrong. To a large extent church fails to provide them with an opportunity to interact with God or the people around, they are marginalised. (Nye 2002:84ff). It is clear that many young people have become alienated from church before they hit their teen years but this does not mean they are spiritually disinterested.

4. The unique neurological place of Tweenagers and early teenagers: Brains have two great growth spurts–2 years old and 11–at the onset of puberty.
Neurological reasons: Neurological research has demonstrated that the growth of the brain during early adolescence does not occur evenly. The consequences of this are heightened emotions with experiences interpreted through emotions–this includes religious experiences. [R E. Dahl http://www.wccf.org/pdf/dahl.pdf 2008]

One missiological implication of this is what researchers call the "use it or lose it" principle. That is, whatever aspects of the brain are used during puberty become hard-wired for life. Music/sport/ foreign language is best learned before 12/TV. The brain in a real sense expands to make room for God. This age is the most open to God because of this.

5. Cultural: They are caught between the traditions of their church and the rapid change of their culture. The church needs to engage in cross cultural mission to young people. Many mainline churches express themselves in a culture that is foreign to young people. There is a disconnect between the symbols and language of their culture and the culture of the church. This is caused by at least two cultural factors. First, the rapid change in culture–that can be seen in young people's distrust of institutions, the need to engage and create, and discovering meaning individually. There is also the cultural divide between high culture and common culture. Often within the church culture, there is an embracing of "high culture" over and against "common culture" in which most young people exist.

Vincent Donovan wrote the excellent book Christianity Rediscovered–the story of how he sought to evangelise the Masai through a conversational process of contextualising the gospel cross culturally. In so doing, he too rediscovered the Gospel. Upon returning to the US, he noted that youth culture had become a strange foreign tribe to the church. He suggests the same cross cultural missiological process needs to be used. He writes,

"In working with young people, do not try to call them back to where they were, and do not try to call them to where you are as beautiful as that place might seem to you. You must have the courage to go with them to a place that neither you nor they have ever been before." (1982: vii)

6. Ecclesiologically: The church desperately needs the young people.
A. An anthropologist from University of Michigan has studied religions around the world... young people's numinous experiences ensure that the rituals engaged with retain their depth and meaning–they don't become "mere ritual" unable to transform lives (Rappaport 1999: 377ff). David's ability to think the impossible...A young Samuel's ability to hear and respond to a call...Mary's audacious 'yes' and willingness to sacrifice all.

B. The church needs young people because many of the innovations and advances within the church take place first within the young groups. Young people lead the church from Modernity to Post-modernity – they empower the church to engage with culture.
C. Passion of youth ignites our passion. They ask the awkward and critical questions that adults have become too comfortable or polite to ask.
D. Ordained ministry often ignores youth.

These compelling Biblical, developmental, social, physiological, cultural, ecclesiological reasons challenge the church, and challenge you and me to prioritise our mission to children and youth. What is your take on all of this? What are your thoughts and questions?

LECTURE 2: UNDERSTANDING PHYSICAL DEVELOPMENT AND ITS IMPLICATIONS

Goals:
1.   To examine physical development as it relates to youth work and mission
2.   To examine neurological development as it relates to youth work and mission
3.   To explore identity and social development as important work for teenagers

Defining Youth: Emerging adults

The United Nations, for statistical purposes, defines 'youth', as those persons between the ages of 15 and 24 years. All United Nations statistics on youth are based on this definition. By that definition, therefore, children are those persons under the age of 14. Article 1 of the United Nations Convention on the Rights of the Child defines 'children' as persons up to the age of 18. This was intentional, as it was hoped that the Convention would provide protection and rights to as large an age-group as possible, and because, there was no similar United Nations Convention on the Rights of Youth.

Many countries also draw a line on youth at the age at which a person is given equal treatment under the law–often referred to as the "age of majority'. This age is often 18 in many countries, and once a person passes this age, they are considered to be an adult. However, the operational definition and nuances of the term 'youth' often vary from country to country, depending on the specific socio-cultural,

165

institutional, economic and political factors. Within the category of "youth", it is also important to distinguish between teenagers (13-19) and young adults (20-24), since the sociological, psychological and health problems they face may differ.

Africa–the Nigerian Church often draws the line at 30 or at marriage–Why? UK 13-18, USA 12-18, Developmentally... It is Adolescence (The term used when we speak of teenage development) is a time of great transition. We can speak of youth culture and the concept of youth as a modern construct–developed in the past 100 years or so but adolescence is not a construct it is something that has always happened.

LUKE 2:52 "SO JESUS GREW BOTH IN HEIGHT AND IN WISDOM, AND HE WAS LOVED BY GOD AND BY ALL WHO KNEW HIM".

1. What's Happening Physically (in particular in terms of sexuality?
    [They] are passionate, irascible, and apt to be carried away by their impulses. They are slaves to their passions...If the young commit a fault, it is always on the side of excess and exaggeration for they carry everything too far, whether it be their love or hatred or anything else. They regard themselves as omniscient and are positive in their assertions.–Aristotle
What is happening to make this so? The onset of puberty is the often cited physical beginning point of adolescence.
Girls (?Women 14.5 year old) was the average age for first menstruation a century ago–it is 11.5 today (10-14) for white US women slightly earlier, for African American women and slightly higher for Asian. Breast development 2 + years before and pubic hair 1+ years before. Adolescence is getting earlier–Our church programs often do not reflect this

Boys have not drastically reduced in age 1-2 years later than girls–Testicular growth about 11-12 range (beginning earlier and later) – pubic hair 12+. 13-14 First ejaculation for most boys. This wide range has psychological implications for both late developers and early developers. The difficulty with the terms 'youth' and 'adolescence'–the ending markers have become unclear and are Western–but no disagreement that these changes occur.

166

1. What is happening neurologically?

Two brain growth spurts–birth and at the onset of puberty. (Terrible 2's and early adolescence–any similarities?) The pre-frontal cortex (CEO of brain involved in the decision making, controlling moods, and evaluating situations) grows.

Implications:

i) "Use it or lose it" principle. That is, whatever aspects of the brain are used during puberty become hard-wired for life. Music/sport/ foreign language is best learned before 12/TV. Sexual ethics and habits–Masturbation habits, sexual patterns etc.

ii) The function of the brain that **develops strategies and organizes** information is also underdeveloped among adolescents. High risk activities because they don't recognise the danger and feel invulnerable/sexual risk taking but balanced with lack of social skills for some. Because it is developing, it is also sensitive to substance abuse.

iii) Reading emotions. Early teens they use a gut-level part of the brain (temporal lobes) to interpret emotions. Misread photographs of fear and interpreted as anger etc.

iv) Sleep–9-10 hours per night. OK for less over short periods but over long periods has an adverse effect on brain development. Information retention: less sleep=less information retention. Direct correlation between academic success and amount of sleep students.

Cognitive development and abstract reasoning. The way they see the world changes.

2. What is happening in terms of Identity Development–it is the time of life for decisions.

i) Differentiation–leaving parents–separating yet want to be close– reasons for conflicts. Sometimes contributing factor for sexual activity.

ii) Individuation–African context... implications for worship, church, youth work, dress, etc.

iii) Identity development–key work of adolescence. Ability to think abstractly–what others think about me and what I think about what they think. Trying on identities and experimenting with identities. Role of the parents in these factors.

3. What is happening socially?
i) Douvan and Adelson (1966:186-197) in their research on female friendship in adolescence noted, the three distinct stages of early 11-13, middle 14-16, and late:
In the early stage, friendship centres on activities rather than interaction.
In the middle stage, the emphasis is on security, that a friend should be loyal.
In the late stage of 17 plus there is a more relaxed shared experience because they are feeling more secure in their own self-identity. Coleman (1980:94-96) in his research found that friendship is no less important for males at this age but females express more anxiety about their relationships, particularly in middle adolescence. Fuhrman (1986:103) observes that females may express more anxiety concerning friendships because their orientation at that age is towards trust, sensitivity and intimacy as opposed to 14–16 year old males who have an activity orientation in their friendships. Conformity to the peer group in terms of dress style is important in adolescence (Elkind 1994:205). It is another way to distinguish themselves from the parents as well as provide the sense of security that comes in belonging. This conformity is at its height in early adolescence and begins to diminish from 14-15 onwards (Elkind 1994:238-251). Specifically in terms of dating
ii) Sexuality is important to spiritual growth and development.
Major source of strong emotions most positive but also a source of stress. Important in identity development, relational skills. Risks– genital sexual activity, infections, pregnancy, sexual victimization, romantic breakups are one of the strongest predictors of depression and suicide attempts. Move from boyfriend in name and status to boyfriend as romantic other.

Decrease in prayer, worship, and church attendance. Friendship and the peer group of adolescence can also be viewed developmentally. Friends and peers are considered to play an important role in the development during this stage. Frith (1984:22) emphasises this from a cultural understanding when he writes, "references to youth culture are usually references to people of the same age doing things in groups." Berndt's (1979:606-616) research demonstrated that adolescent's susceptibility to peer pressure increases while reliance upon parental opinion decreases.

Meaning, making and a three legged stool. Family, Friends and Self-concept are three key aspects for shaping faith in terms of meaning in life, purpose, guidance, and hope. Is this true in Africa? The vulnerability of three legs indicates the need for a strong fourth leg.

There is a long and rich tradition in viewing young people within the framework of the developmental stage model which continues to exert great influence within the educational system and other institutions including the church (Wyn/White 1997:51; Gerali 1998:36). Stage theories understand young people in terms of inherent biological and psychosocial processes and provide a starting point for the analysis of young people (Gesell 1956:4). The work Erickson (1968) in psychological and identity development Piaget (1958) in intellectual development, Kohlberg (1981), in moral development, Fowler (1981) for spiritual development and many others have identified stages to assist in understanding the development, attitudes, and actions of a person at any given stage. The adolescent (the term the developmental theorists use for young people) stage or stages of development is generally associated with the teenage years before moving to the responsibilities of young adulthood (Clark 2001:42)

1. Moral Development

Lawrence Kohlberg (1969) and moral development. He proposed that children form ways of thinking through their experiences which include understandings of moral concepts such as justice, rights, equality and human welfare. Kohlberg followed the development of moral judgment beyond the ages studied by Piaget, and determined that the process of attaining moral maturity took longer and was more gradual than Piaget had proposed. On the basis of his research, Kohlberg identified six stages of moral reasoning grouped into three major levels. Each level represented a fundamental shift in the social-moral perspective of the individual.

Stage 1: the preconventional level, a person's moral judgments focuses on avoiding the breaking of rules that are backed by punishment, obedience for its own sake and avoiding the physical consequences of an action to persons and property. As in Piaget's framework, the reasoning of Stage 1 is characterized by ego-centrism and the inability to consider the perspectives of others.

169

Stage 2: there is the early emergence of moral reciprocity. The Stage 2 orientation focuses on the instrumental, pragmatic value of an action. Reciprocity is of the form, "you scratch my back and I'll scratch yours". The Golden Rule becomes, "If someone hits you, you hit them back." At Stage 2, one follows the rules only when it is to someone's immediate interests. What is right is what's fair in the sense of an equal exchange, a deal, an agreement. They tend to be self-identified with these rules, and uphold them consistently; viewing morality as acting in accordance with what society defines as right.

Stage 3: awareness of shared feelings, agreements, and expectations which take primacy over individual interests. Persons at Stage 3 define what is right in terms of what is expected by people close to one's self, and in terms of the stereotypic roles that define being good - e.g., a good brother, mother, teacher. Being good means keeping mutual relationships, such as trust, loyalty, respect, and gratitude. The perspective is that of the local community or family. There is not as yet a consideration of the generalized social system. My family, My tribe, My gang who is important

Stage 4: marks the shift from defining what is right in terms of local norms and role expectations to defining right in terms of the laws and norms established by the larger social system. This is the "member of society" perspective in which one is moral by fulfilling the actual duties defining one's social responsibilities. One must obey the law except in extreme cases in which the law comes into conflict with other prescribed social duties.

Stage 5: These individuals reason based on the principles which underlie rules and norms, but reject a uniform application of a rule or norm. Moral growth comes when previous ways of determining actions no longer fit. Moral dilemmas bring growth. Example of the test question…

In Europe, a woman was near death from a special kind of cancer. There was one drug that the doctors thought might save her. It was a form of radium that a druggist in the same town had recently discovered. The drug was expensive to make, but the druggist was charging ten times what the drug cost him to make. He paid $400 for the radium and charged $4,000 for a small dose of the drug. The sick woman's husband, Heinz, went to everyone he knew to borrow the money and tried every legal means, but he could only get together about $2,000, which is half of what it cost. He told the druggist that his wife was dying, and asked him to sell it cheaper or let him pay later. But the druggist said, "No, I discovered the drug and I'm going to make money from it." So, having tried every legal means, Heinz gets desperate and considers breaking into the man's store to steal the drug for his wife.

This is important for religious education is most clearly understood in terms of our Methodist Holiness of Heart tradition. The motivation for our actions denotes spiritual maturity. Without the One who provides the principles this theory falls apart.

2. Faith Development Theories.

James Fowler–stages of faith… Not really faith but how the brain will understand faith.

Infancy and Undifferentiated Faith
Stage 1. Intuitive-Projective Faith
Stage 2. Mythic-Literal Faith (teenagers)
Stage 3. Synthetic-Conventional Faith
Stage 4. Individuative-Reflective Faith
Stage 5. Conjunctive Faith
Stage 6. Universalizing Faith

Stage One: Intuitive-Projective faith. It usually occurs between the ages of three and seven. Imagination runs wild in this stage, uninhibited by logic. It is the first step in self-awareness and when one absorbs one's culture's strong taboos. The advantages of this stage are the birth of imagination and the growing ability to grasp and unify one's perception of reality. Also dangerous in that the child's imagination can be dominated by unrestrained images of terror and destruction and the exploitation of the fertile imagination by enforced taboos and indoctrination.

Stage Two: Mythic-Literal faith. The runaway imagination of stage one is here harnessed, and linear thinking becomes normative. Found mostly in school children (although one can maintain this state for life), stage two persons have a strong belief in the justice and reciprocity of the universe, and their cosmic powers are almost always anthropomorphic. A person in this stage is both "carried and 'trapped' in" their own narrative. Stage two can be dangerous because the relentless belief in reciprocity forces the individual into a strict, over-controlling perfectionism; their religious system will without doubt be either legalistic or else they will be overwhelmed with feelings that they cannot be forgiven.

Stage Three: Synthetic-Conventional faith. The majority of the population finds its permanent home in this stage. It is a stage characterized by conformity, where one finds one's identity by aligning oneself with a certain perspective, and lives directly through this perception with little opportunity to reflect on it critically. One has an ideology at this point, but may not be aware that one has it. Those who differ in opinion are seen as "the Other," as different "kinds" of people. Authority derives from the top down, and is invested with power by majority opinion. Dangers in this stage include the internalization of symbolic systems (power, "goodness" "badness") to such a degree that objective evaluation is impossible. Furthermore, while one can at this stage enter into an intimate relationship with the divine, one's life situations may drive one into despair. Such situations may include contradictions between authorities, the revelation of authoritarian hypocrisy, and lived experiences that contradict one's convictions.

Stage Four: Individuative-Reflective faith. This is primarily a stage of angst and struggle, in which one must face difficult questions regarding identity and belief. Those that pass into stage four usually do so in their mid-thirties to early forties. At this time, the personality gradually detaches from the defining group from which it formerly drew its identity. The person is aware of him or herself as an individual and must--perhaps for the first time--take personal responsibility for his/her beliefs and feelings. This is a stage of de-mythologizing, where what was once unquestioned is now subjected to critical scrutiny. This stage is not a comfortable place to be and, although it can last for a long time, those who stay in it do so in danger of becoming bitter, suspicious characters who trust nothing and no one.

Stage Five: Conjunctive faith moves one from stage four's rationalism to the acknowledgement of paradox and transcendence. In this stage, a person grasps the reality behind the symbols of his or her inherited systems, and is also drawn to and acknowledging of the symbols of other's systems. This stage makes room for mystery and the unconscious, and is fascinated by it while at the same time apprehensive of its power. It sees the power behind the metaphors while simultaneously acknowledging their relativity. It is an overwhelming, ecstatic stage in which one is radically opened to possibility and wonder.

Stage Six: Unclear:

Some Problems with Fowler's theory:
1.   Not so much as stages of faith as 'The Psychology of Human Development and the Quest for Meaning': Stages of an aspect of faith. Not faith in a Biblical or theological sense.
2.   Jesus' understanding of faith is directed toward the future. It brings about the future. It has to do with an event, transcending and transforming any given state of equilibrated development.
3.   Faith comes forth in the encounter with other people. Preeminently in the person of Jesus, but also with others who invoke faith. Others witnessing to faith
4.   Faith is concrete rather than general and abstract.
5.   Faith Saves
6.   Other arguments about specific areas/stages are also made.
John H. Westerhoff III Westerhoff compares four styles of faith to rings of a tree trunk. The analogy is simple: it is a maturing tree that starts with one ring of faith and as it matures, develops up to four. Faith is an action which includes thinking, feeling, and willing and it is transmitted, sustained, and expanded through our interactions with other people of faith in a community of faith".
Stated simply, the styles, moving from the core outward are (1) experienced, (2) affiliative, (3) searching, and (4) owned faith.

1. Experienced faith is the basis of one's spiritual journey. "A person first learns Christ not as a theological affirmation but as an affective experience". This can be called tactile faith-one enhanced by sensory experience (e.g., clasping hand in prayer, kneeling or standing in church.)

2. Affiliative faith focuses on the sense of belonging within the community. Faith begins individually and then moves outward communally. The logical extension of experienced faith is belonging to or identifying with a specific community or religious tradition. Rites of passage, like baptism or The Lord's Table, facilitate this belonging.

3. Searching faith, often evident in late adolescence and young adulthood. Searching faith encompasses three characteristics: doubt, experimentation and commitment. *"In order to move from an understanding of faith that belongs to the community to an understanding of faith that is our own, we need to doubt and question that faith".*

4. Owned faith, the largest tree trunk ring, "conversion"-whether gradual or sudden, which involves one's searching faith becoming one's owned faith. Owned faith is maturing faith, one that allows the individual the fullest expression of God's power and love.

It is helpful to know these theories to understand:
a) that one size does not fit all;
b) to develop programmes that are appropriate to age;
c) to know that doubt and struggles are a part of maturing faith;
d) to create dilemmas can be good;
e) to move away from seeing faith simply as understanding.

Ultimately, spiritual growth is growing in our love for God and love for neighbour. The more we can understand about ourselves and others the more we can foster this growth.

LECTURE 4: A THEOLOGY OF YOUTH, A THEOLOGY WITH YOUNG PEOPLE, ROLE OF MINISTER

What is your theology of Young People? Groups of 2 x 5 minutes.
How does God view young people? What if they are baptised or unbaptised?
What is their role in church? Their gifting?
What is the responsibility of the church towards them?
What is their responsibility to the church?
Our theology of young people will tell us much about our own theology.

How is God at work among the young people in Nigeria?

Children and young people are not simply adults in waiting but fully human now (though many churches don't treat them as if they are). The implications of this are that...

Created in God's image!

In human form God in Jesus was a teenager who ministered to others.

Reflect something of the very nature of God as teenagers

They share with all humans a fallen nature and a need to experience God's healing restorative love. (This is the one area not ignored by historical theology. They debate whether a child is accountable for sin while ignoring the child present in the church.)

Children and young people respond to God's salvation in ways that are appropriate for their age. (Just because a worship style, Bible Study style, way of being church is appropriate for adults does not necessarily mean it's appropriate for young people any more than a European style of worship is appropriate for West Africa.)

Children and young people are equal partners with adults in the life of the Church.

Young people are often marginalized within the leadership of the church. Failure to consult young people is a similar problem to the marginalization that took place in Acts 7. We need to find the same kind of creative responses.

Learning is for the whole church–adults, children and young people

Young people do need mentoring but they also mentor

They are not the church of the future they are the church of today

The church needs young people to revitalize their faith and worship and to keep the church contextualized to changing culture.

Mission and ministry is for and with children and young people, as well as adults

Name young people who did amazing things in the Bible. They were gifted and empowered by the Spirit. Our church must not quench this.

Yet young people because of their developmental, social and cultural place in society need special attention from the church.

The call to evangelism comes at whatever age.

We are called to be witnesses to young people as well as to empower young people to be witnesses with their culture.

The concept of the 'Priesthood of all believers' includes children and young people

The Holy Spirit works through children and young people as well as adults

The ignoring of children by Theologians outside of the issue of baptism and original sin has been a recurrent theme throughout history. Jerome Berryman, *Children and the Theologian: Clearing the Way for Grace* (New York: Morehouse Publishing, 2009) argues that this is due to the fact that most had little or nothing to do with children.

Others theorize that it is just that they are a hidden group, considered to be adults in waiting, and therefore can be ignored. This has changed in the past 50 years.

Helpful theologies of young people have been written by Karl Rainer, Kenda Dean and Steve Emery-Wright.

Kenda Creasy Dean (*Practising Passion* Cambridge: Eerdmans, 2004) presents an excellent theology of young people that both empowers **young people** and **the church**.

Divine Passion is revealed as God's	Addresses adolescent desire for:	Meets Developmental need for:	Authenticated by:
Fidelity	Steadfastness	Acceptance	"being there"
Transcendence	Ecstasy	Feeling part of greatness	"being moved"
Communion	Intimacy	Camaraderie	"being known"

Divine passion as God's:	Visible in the Church as:	Historic trajectory	Forms of practice in YM	Leadership
Fidelity "being there"	A sacred solidarity	Didache	Compassion Youth events	Coaches
Transcendence "being moved"	Holy momentum (pilgrimage/retreat)	Leitorgia	Play Praise and lament	Trail guides
Communion "Being known"	The sacrament of one another	Koinonia	Chastity prayer	Mentors Icons

What is the theology expressed in your church towards young people?

IN THE UK THE ESSENTIAL FEATURES OF YOUTH MINISTRY SINCE 1990 ARE:

1.   Youth ministry is Relational / Incarnational
2.   Youth ministry recognizes the priority of worship
3.   Youth ministry relies on the transforming power of God
4.   Youth ministry recognizes that mission is holistic
5.   Youth ministry is a long term process
6.   Youth ministry recognizes the importance of discipleship
7.   Youth ministry seeks to empower young people in/for ministry

The theology that currently supports most of youth ministry worldwide at this time in history is an incarnational theology.

INCARNATIONAL MINISTRY MEANS:

1.   Like Christ, we are sent out to incarnate the good news into our local cultures.
2.   It means that we seek to be in ministry next to people, relationally like Jesus Christ.
3.   It means that we are willing to risk vulnerability.
4.   It means that it will also challenge the culture.

1. Tell me the Story of the Methodist Church in Africa...

The African church planted by the Europeans did not use incarnational theology. As David Bosch (1992:297) wrote, "the gospel always comes to people in cultural robes."

Richard Niebuhr *Christianity and Culture,* shares five ways Christians understand culture. The incarnation theology would be in the middle of these 5 saying that culture is both Good and Evil. We can only understand and express ourselves from within a culture. It is a gift from God. But, though the good news is incarnate in the culture, it also always challenges that culture.

To be incarnate in a culture means to value the way people live and empower them to help you understand the Gospel within that culture. Vincent Donovan *Christianity Rediscovered.* He explored the Gospel with the Masai and in the process rediscovered it. As I quoted in a previous lecture...

In working with young people in America, do not try to call them back to where they were, and do not try to call them to where you are, as beautiful as that place might seem to you. You must have the courage to go with them to a place that neither you nor they have ever been before. (p. vii)

2. It means that we seek to be in ministry next to people– relationally like Christ. Both Kosuke Koyama *Water Buffalo Theology* and Richard Dunn *Shaping the Spiritual Life of Students,* speak of 3 mile and 2 mile per hour ministry–ministry at the speed of the people.

For Ministry with your Christian young people this means not simply to come with your agenda – the church's agenda but to enter their world with their needs and their agenda without relinquishing your own. This is exemplified in Jesus Ministry with the Woman and the Well and various healings. For evangelism this means not only going into the culture with young people with your witness and with eyes wide open to what God is already doing there. It means being with young people not just so they will become Christians but because Christ loves them.

3. Incarnational theology therefore means that we are willing to risk vulnerability. We no longer have all the answers because we realise we understand with our own cultural robes. Teenagers have different robes and their understanding and experience may well be different. We need to learn from them. To be with people in their culture means a willingness to stand by them in their pain… It can mean a cross.

4. To be Incarnational also means that we challenge the culture. The Gospel is incarnated into culture but it also challenges all cultures. It is both contextualised and decontextualised. What does this mean for teenagers in the global youth culture? In Nigeria?

Possible problems with incarnational youth ministry…

Andrew Root's (*Revisiting Relational Youth Ministry*) critiques the use of incarnational theology. Instrumental incarnation is not Christ-like. By this he means to be with others for hidden motives other than to love like Christ is wrong. That kind of friendship evangelism is not Christ-like. To become friends or to love like that is not friendship or love, only manipulation.

Steve Griffiths (*A Christlike Ministry*) Says incarnational theology is too limited. He creates a broader based Christological underpinning that includes.

- Incarnational
- Crucified
- Resurrected
- Ascended
- Eschatological
- Jesus: Kingdomship and Discipleship

A good start but does not develop fully enough because he leaves out Pentecost! What about Community???

You can see that there is room for you to write a book that underpins an understanding of youth ministry and therefore all ministry.

LECTURE 6: UNDERSTANDING YOUTH CULTURALLY AND PRACTICING CULTURAL EXEGESIS

Finger at the ceiling trick... Different perspective

Hwa Yung (*Mangoes and Bananas*) argues that what is necessary for the mission/ministry in a culture is that it must be contextual to that culture. Meeting and even arising out of the cultural distinctiveness of the people, their needs, while being faithful to the Christian tradition.

GLOBAL YOUTH CULTURE

Rapidity of change	Consumerism
Growing individualism	Entertainment
Identity through consumption	Target marketing
Digital communication	McDonaldization
Global companies	Globalization
Glocalization	Global tolerance or reaction toward tolerance.
Other aspects	

Postmodernity is primarily a phenomenon of Western culture. One cannot speak of the postmodern without first speaking of modernity and modernism, for it is from within Western culture that the modern view of the world has arisen. The postmodern is, therefore, a movement which has arisen in reaction to the modernism of Western civilization. At the same time, "it is a part of the broader and deeper changes going on in the world today." This is because of the widespread influence of Western culture throughout the world and the fact that the process of modernization continues to bring capitalism, urbanization, technology, telecommunications, and Western popular culture to virtually every corner of the globe. Although primarily a Western cultural movement, the postmodern is having an effect upon the intellectual life of many cultures, including those of Asia. (Daniel Adams) Mandatory education; mass media; global market; images; time; materialism; secularisation??; loosening of family ties; lengthening of transition time to adulthood; technology; global targeting of youth, the lack of markers and rituals for adulthood

Engaging in cultural exegesis is the start of being able to contextualise the Gospel. Missionaries have learned the lessons from Anthropologists. One lesson they have taught us is that while working with people from a different subculture we must also study the culture and make ourselves aware of differences and similarities.

Take for example the culture of the British Methodist Church and the young people in Great Britain. Cultural exegesis is essential. Knowing the young people you work with and not assuming your culture/values etc. are the same as theirs. Anthropologists have provided us with the tools to begin this study in a very limited way based on **Survey; Interview; Observe:**

Using these simple tools you can find out how much their attitudes differ from "When I was young!" Their activities in leisure time. Music and movie tastes. What are your spiritual habits? What is your perfect worship? Engaging with the young people to know them. Contextualisation. You will also discover how your young people are different; the young people your church is not reaching, how you relate and compare with other churches.

Cultural Exegesis Tools:

As A Participant Observer Observe; Habits; Dress; Language; Values and beliefs (harder to spot); Symbols (music, movies, other things they may consume); Experiences. This requires an evaluation first of ourselves using this list (basic to salvation actually) in order to understand where we are standing. It requires to a certain degree setting aside our own values so we can observe not judgementally.

In groups of four, develop a list of the distinctive culture of 13-19 year olds in Nigeria. How does this differ from church culture?

Now you will need to test the list by interviewing young people you work with and asking their opinions of youth culture outside of church. Once you understand the differences you can begin to understand how they might worship and engage in church differently. This information will allow the church to work together with young people to create worship, fellowship, mission engagement, discipleship methods that are appropriate for them.

LECTURE 7: HOW YOUNG PEOPLE UNDERSTAND WORSHIP

What is worship?

- Worship is an invitation of God to respond to God's word in the world and in our lives – in the power of the Spirit.
- Allowing our spirit to be set alight by the Spirit of God.
- Showing God's worth. How many have had 'worship wars'?
- The Gospel in motion–Lex orandi lex crendeni-assuring orthodoxy–[this is worship in truth]

Why is it so important?

- It shapes our beliefs
- It shapes our actions
- Because God is who God is…
- It is the foundation for missions
- Other reasons

Why is it so important for teenagers?

- For all of the above reasons plus…
- They are at the age of identity development and this will shape their whole future.
- Without meaningful worship, young people may well drop out of, or change church the church they attend.
- In a world that says it is not cool for young people to worship, being with other young people in worship both affirms their faith and declares that young people are supremely concerned with faith.

1. In the word.

2. In the sacrament (the drama that expresses the truth beyond the word).

3. In the culture (contextualized) of the worshipper. The worshipper must engage and for this to happen it must be grounded in their culture.

4. In the possibility of transformed living (decontextualised).

Worship has been contextualized through the ages. The history of liturgical development is really a history of contextualisation. Revival and church growth in West Africa could only happen after worship became African. Each of these deserves a lecture of its own, but let's put these things in the context of the young people…The church tries to provide worship for young people. It may be able to do this if it is sufficiently connected to the culture the young people inhabit. Often however it misses the mark.

I would argue from our understanding of worship that the church should not create worship for young people but empower young people to worship. WHAT IS THE DIFFERENCE?

Creating worship with young people means:
- An assurance that God has gifted them as the body of Christ
- It means that they know more about their culture than you do
- It means that they can lead the church to ground worship in their culture
- It means that they need our permission, our help, our teaching of tradition while allowing them the freedom to play with it.

Early Church… Serious Play and Discovery

ACTS-NOT A FIXED WAY OF WORSHIP–huge variety. Temple to pray, on the beach, in the home. Singing, praying, teaching, preaching, charismatic and high

Like what went before and also strove to be different

Contextual–different in Jerusalem, Samaria, Corinthians, in the images of Revelation.

Prayer, Word, Holy Communion, Song

Out of my 15 years of research with young people…

In Europe, the church failed to do this. The music, the expression of worship, the creation of worship, even the purposes of worship were grounded in 'enlightenment'. A world foreign to young people. One of the major reasons that young people stopped attending church in the 1970's – 2000 was because they could not relate to worship. They wanted to worship, but just were not empowered to.

In Asia, it was very different.

The Singaporean church was planted by the Europeans but… In the 1980's the young people began to reshape the church. In the hierarchical society where young people defer to the elders, how this happened did not make sense to me. But several things made it possible.

1.   The church's openness to the Spirit
2.   The pragmatic nature of the church
3.   The leadership's willingness to risk with the young people.
4.   Now their youth programmes are focused around empowering the young people to participate in, and in some cases even shape worship.

This process begins with working with young people in discovering how they understand and express worship.

HOW DO NIGERIAN YOUNG PEOPLE UNDERSTAND WORSHIP? HOW IS IT DIFFERENT FROM THE WORSHIP OF THEIR ELDERS?

HOW CAN YOU DISCOVER THIS INFORMATION MORE ACCURATELY?

LECTURE 8: EMPOWERING YOUNG PEOPLE AND THE CHURCH FOR MISSION

Aim lower, think smaller, give up and go have a cup of coffee.
Now keep these in mind for a few minutes as we listen again to the words of Deuteronomy 6: 4ff in maybe the best known passage in the Old Testament–the passage every practicing Jew would repeat every day at the beginning of their prayers,

Hear o Israel the Lord your God, the Lord is one, Love the Lord your God with all your heart, with all your soul and with all your strength. The commands I give you today are to be on your heart– Impress them on your children. Impress them on your children. Talk about them when you sit at home and when you walk along the road, when you lie down and when you get up.

The Jewish faith placed the emphasis on children and young people. The synagogue and Jewish culture as a whole is known historically and continues to be known today for the emphasis it places upon children. They taught formally and informally–as they sat at home and as they walked along the way. The early church picked up on this priority.

1. AIM LOWER

So in seeking to fulfil the call to go and make disciples they aimed low. In the everyday moments and in the formal teachings they aimed low. So many churches when they think church growth think adults. Instead think Children and Youth... That is where the commitments are made. In fact, that is where the family are most often changed.

There are developmental reasons for aiming low. It's the time of life when people develop their identity, including their spiritual identity. Young people are the most open to making decisions for Christ. Children ask the little questions; teenagers ask the really big questions; we grown-ups are too tired and busy to ask. Young people are seeking for directions and answers in life even if they do not acknowledge that they are really spiritual questions. People usually make a Christian commitment before the age of 25...

Straits Times did a survey and discovered in Singapore...65% of young people commit (of all religions). In the Christian faith it is safe to say somewhere between 60-80%. Let's take the survey here–how many of you committed yourself to Christ before the age of 25?

FISH WHERE AND WHEN THE FISH ARE BITING.

It's also the time of life when our brain develops. There are two great growth spurts in the human brain. At 2 years old and 12 years old. It shrinks after that, pruning is what it's called. This is a sharpening of what is being learned, an opening of the neuro pathways. The habits and concepts that will last a lifetime are learned and reinforced.

The teenage brain doesn't develop evenly though. The part that feels and expresses emotion develops first and then the ability to control it and judge it comes later. This means that young people when

185

compared to adults experience and judge the world more through their feelings. Their passion for life and love is most fundamentally a search for someone who will be there, who they can rely upon through life. Their passion is for something outside of themselves bigger than themselves. Their passion is a search for something that makes life worth living.

In 2009, there was a shooting spree at a school in Finland. The young gunmen referred in their video to the April 26, 1999 massacre in COLUMBINE. Two lads in long black coats went into the school with guns and home-made bombs, targeting Christians. They went into the library. One of the gunmen recognised Cassie Berwell as a Christian. He asked her are you a Christian? She looked at him frightened because she knew the repercussions of her answer. "Yes" she said: she was dead before she hit the ground. The event in that library became famous within a day of the shooting. And Cassie wasn't the only one. Valeen and her yes; John Tomlin drawing people into his hiding place until there was no room for him; And Rachel Scotts, who was shot but her calmness and serenity moved all who saw her. There was also the teacher who was safe but kept going back in to rescue students until he too was shot. By the end of the morning, 18 people were dead and many others wounded.

I tell you this story because of what happened next. Within two days, the emails were flying around the world. I received one in the UK and not from my brother who lives in Columbine. WHY? What was it about this incident that captured people's attention…It was the passion of people expressing faith that was not only worth living for but worth dying for… This passion led literally thousands of others to faith. This passion that discovers a love for God and there is nothing they won't do, won't sacrifice, to follow their Christ. This is the first love of the church in Ephesus and the love that our church must not lose.

Right now, the message they receive and hear in our global society, is to get a good education, so you can achieve the lifestyle that will make you comfortable. Over half the young people in the region indicated that goal. It's not enough, but when asked what's important they say family and friends. We as a church have a bigger message that addresses their passion. If we are talking about a missional church we are talking about a church where reaching out to young people is a priority. The great mission field of a local secondary school, Junior Church or Polytechnic or University.

AIM LOWER

2. THINK SMALLER

I mean as a church, think of younger people in all that we do. Church budgets focus on a variety of things, including the young people's department. But that's part of the problem. It's seen as a department: we hire a youth worker and let them organise a few volunteers and that's the youth programme taken care of.

What is common to all churches with a history of thriving youth ministries…? The same thing that is common to all growing churches (by the way, they tend to go hand in hand; a church with a vital youth program usually is a growing church). What is the common element? We didn't find a particular programme, particular youth activities, a particular structure, particular training, youth worker, or particular kinds of congregations. Throw out all your ideas that there is a magic bullet in the form of curriculum, demographics, facility, or location, location, location. *A culture of youth ministry that permeates everything.*

It was what is described in **Deuteronomy 6 where the young people were intimately involved in all ministries and all ages were involved in caring for them.**

The Jewish and early Christian church also sought to resource the whole family, not just the parents but the grandparents as well in nurturing the developing faith of the young person. The family remains overwhelmingly the most influential element in most young people's faith. PARENTS, GRANDPARENTS, SINGLES

A church will not really grow until it aims lower and thinks small, that is until the whole church understands that youth ministry is not a side issue but central to all that they do and central to the work and ministry of the church. I'm not saying neglect any other age NO! I'm saying that rather to include all ages, but especially young people

187

because they are out of sight and are often out of the mind of the church. We tend to think that what we do here is the real church, the real ministry. This attitude cuts a whole segment, the most fruitful segment in terms of evangelism out of the church.

examplarym.com Churches in the US that are growing have large numbers of young people and children. The church has a focus of the presence of God and their mission to young people. The most influential person in the youth and children's programme was the Pastor. The pastor creates the culture and sets this vision!!!

THINK SMALLER
3. GIVE UP

How does a church have this culture of youth ministry? Give up thinking you have to do everything for the young people, instead think of what we can do with young people. What they have to offer. I hate it when people tell me the youth are the church of the future; they have failed to see that they are the church of today. They need your love, wisdom and direction and we as a church need their passion, their new commitments to revitalise constantly our life. To keep us near our first love. Young people have gifts and talents and passion to offer. Look at the Gospel reading. It's a wonderful passage with so much in it, but one aspect was that Jesus was engaged in learning and teaching. He was interacting with the adults and they were learning from him. He was a young adolescent – this can be seen by the irritating comment he made to his mother after they had travelled three days back to find him – "Well mum you knew where I would be…" If I had said that to my mother, she would have been furious. Jesus was a teenager yet he had gifts to offer the synagogue and they listened.

We often cut off young people's gifts from the rest of the church. The excitement of their new commitments. We must learn to hear their stories affirm and even be inspired by them. We can even learn from the way they relate the Bible to their own contexts. I was talking about Mary with a group of teenage girls and they said, "Wow, a baby meant she was willing to give up her teenage friendships for God". I never looked at it that way. Think of the teenagers in the Bible and what they had to offer. David, Jeremiah, Mark, (possibly some of the apostles) Timothy, the lad with two fish and 5 loaves, and Mary. What would have happened if they had not been allowed to exercise their gifts to the whole church? Give up our idea that it's one-way-traffic with youth and embrace God's gift of young people for the whole church.

GIVE UP

4. GO HAVE A CUP OF COFFEE.

How does a church have this culture of youth ministry? Adults have a cup of coffee with the youth and they get to know the young people. It's your responsibility. Don't leave it all to the youth workers. If you want to be a church that reaches the school, you need to be a church that sees young people and respond to them. Most young people want encouraging supportive relationships with adults! A study was done where full time Christian leaders were asked to name significant relationships that shaped their faith. On average, they named 6 adults. Do the maths: youth don't have enough youth workers to achieve this. So discover ways to have a cup of coffee with young people in church. Not all just one. Work with your adult youth leaders and figure out ways and places where you can mix. You don't have to know their culture, the latest pop song, you only need to care.

Let me tell you about Jessie Maria–87 years old when I first arrived at the church. We created a youth led service and Jessie attended, she turned off her hearing aid first though. She learned the young people's names. She spoke to them. The youth group put a newsletter out and each month featured a young person. One of the questions they were asked was, who do you admire the most? Jessie was the most popular answer. She died when she was 95. Her funeral was packed with young people.

"Hear O Methodist Church the Lord your God, the Lord is one, Love the Lord your God with all your heart, with all your soul and with all your strength. Impress them on your children. Impress them on your children. Talk about them when you sit at home and when you walk along the road, when you lie down and when you get up."

GO HAVE A CUP OF COFFEE.

How do you fulfil the great commission?
**AIM LOWER;   THINK SMALLER;   GIVE UP;
AND GO HAVE A CUP OF COFFEE.**

Outline & Review

1.   Why is this, an important question? Age decisions are made, dropping out of church, marginalisation of young people: 80% of children have a sense of God's presence; 60% of teenagers; and 30% of adults in the UK.

a. Biblical Reasons: Provide me with a few bible verses that would indicate the importance of this emphasis.

> ***Deut 6:4-9.*** *Keep these words that I am commanding you today in your heart. Recite them to your children and talk about them when you are at home and when you are away, when you lie down and when you rise. Bind them as a sign on your hand, fix them as an emblem on your forehead, and write them on the doorposts of your house and on your gates.*

> ***Matthew 19:13-14*** *Little children were being brought to him in order that he might lay his hands on them and pray. The disciples spoke sternly to those who brought them; but Jesus said, 'Let the little children come to me, and do not stop them; for it is to such as these that the kingdom of heaven belongs.'*
> Other verses and examples...

b. Developmental Reasons: The age of decisions.

The act of identity formation creates a need to be with other teenagers separate from their parents (but not necessarily other adults). Worship and church attendance is an anti-cultural activity for teenagers (Mayo etc. 2006: 16ff). To attend a church without young people reinforces the attitude that to worship they must reject their "youth identity" but if there are a significant number of young people present then faith is affirmed as an activity that is acceptable for young people in spite of the cultural trend.

Children on the other hand enjoy the presence of their parents but the average age for leaving church is in their 10th year (Brierley 2002: 111).

The unique neurological place of Tweenagers and early teenagers: One missiological implication of this is what researchers call the "use it or lose it" principle. That is, whatever aspects of the brain are used during puberty become hard-wired for life. Music/ sport/foreign language, prayer is best learned before 13.

Another implication is that the function of the brain that develops strategies and organizes information is also underdeveloped among adolescents. High risk activities because they don't recognise the danger and feel invulnerable. Because it is developing, it is also sensitive to substance abuse. There is a reason that the mortality and morbidity rate rises 300% in adolescence. This information has great implications for the need to do advocacy in creating healthy activities for young people and restorative work as opposed to punitive for negative behaviours.

This brain development also assists in explaining why early adolescents, boys in particular, have difficult sitting still. Sitting still for a 20 minute sermon let alone a 40 minute sermon is a real feat!

c. Cultural Reasons: Because they are caught between a culture that is changing faster than the church, so in terms of missions the church needs to engage in cross cultural mission to young people.

d. Ecclesiological Reasons: Church desperately needs young people.

A. An anthropologist from University of Michigan has studied religions around the world... young people's numinous experiences ensure that the rituals engaged with retain their depth and meaning – they don't become "mere ritual" unable to transform lives (Rappaport 1999: 377ff). David's ability to think the impossible... A young Samuel's ability to hear and respond to a call... Mary's audacious 'yes' and willingness to sacrifice all.

B. The church needs young people because many of the innovations and advances within the church take place first within the young groups. Young people lead the church from Modernity to Post-modernity–they empower the church to engage with culture.

C. Passion of youth ignites our passion. They ask the awkward and critical questions that adults have become too comfortable or polite to ask.

2. A brief overview of Youth Discipleship.
Westerhoff–Stretching the boundaries
Robert Kegan says that growth happens when our faith understanding no longer fits the dilemmas our cultural or personal world throw at us… Teenagers are moving from self-gratification orientation towards interpersonal mutuality…The trouble is consumerism keeps people stuck at self-gratification.

3. What Youth spirituality might look like for:
a. An Early Teen
Group orientation   Camps   Action prayer
Service   Belonging   Adventure
What traditional spiritual disciplines might look like
Catechesis–moving from childhood faith intentionally   Family
b. A   Middle/late teen
Group disciplines   'Powerful'   Numinous experiences
Interior development and exterior action   Worship
Empowerment Family   Stretching faith especially in late teens

4. What are you wanting to achieve? Remember it is two<-->way.

COME UP WITH A LIST AND ASK WHAT IS MISSING

SEEK SPIRITUAL GROWTH, BOTH ALONE AND WITH OTHERS

1. Are heard referring to having prayer, devotions, and meditation times.
2. Ask sincere and searching questions about the nature of a life of faith in God.
3. Prefer and attend gatherings where they can learn more about the Christian faith.
4. Accept opportunities for learning how to speak naturally and intelligently about their faith.
5. Are involved in Bible study and/or prayer groups.
6. Join Christian groups to build friendships and learn how to be a friend.

BELIEVE GOD IS PRESENT IN THE WORLD

7. Speak openly about seeking or experiencing God's guidance.
8. Are heard asking each other about what God has recently done in their lives or the lives of others.
9. In times of trouble, reassure others that God is active to make things work out all right in the long run.
10. Occasionally speak of having been keenly aware of the presence of God.

11. Speak publicly about their relationship with Jesus Christ.
12. When providing a rationale for their actions will cite specifics of their faith.
13. In conversation with family/friends brings up topics of faith or Christian living.
14. Pray for people especially needing God's help.

ARE ACTIVE WITH GOD'S PEOPLE

15. Regularly attend worship services.
16. Have willingly participated in two or more of the following: taught Sunday School, Bible class, or Vacation Bible School: served with a group to improve conditions at school or neighbourhood: made a presentation before a faith group or in worship: helped in raising money for a Christian project or mission trip: served on a congregational or denominational committee or task force
17. Regularly contribute money to a congregation or faith project.

POSSESS A POSITIVE, HOPEFUL SPIRIT

18. Enjoy being together, as evidenced by their laughing, singing, and conversation.
19. Show a gracious, loving attitude to people not easy to like (e.g., the difficult, rude, shunned, loser).
20. Have friends of widely diverse socioeconomic, ethnic, and religious background or persuasion.
21. Have been heard describing the Christian faith as a necessary force in society, helping people develop attitudes of understanding, sympathy, and cooperation.
22. Are known for their general optimism, trust, and positive expectation of other people, being convinced that one person can do much to make the world a better place.
23. Are eager, responsive, and cooperative rather than unresponsive, disinterested, and apathetic.

LIVE OUT A LIFE OF SERVICE

24. Give portions of time and money for helping people.
25. Attend conferences or workshops that present the challenge of service professions such as the ordained ministry.
26. Speak out publicly against specific social injustices.
27. Try to offer comfort or support to a friend or neighbour in the event of a death or tragedy either by talking or by action (personal presence, help with routine tasks, transportation, visit in hospital, etc.).
28. Defend a friend or acquaintance who is being talked about when he/she isn't there.
29. Organize and participate in study or action groups to address injustice or immorality.
30. Are involved in activities of service related to church, community, or world.
31. Are assuming responsibility for some aspect of their youth ministry.

LIVE A CHRISTIAN MORAL LIFE

32. Are heard referring to seeking help from Scripture in deciding what is right and wrong.
33. Actively seek to discourage friends from cheating at school.

34. Have a reputation for not participating in activities such as lying, stealing, substance abuse, etc. Have a reputation for honesty, integrity, hospitality, and acts of kindness.

LECTURE 10: TAKING YOUR MINISTRY DEEPER: TOOLS FOR REFLECTION

Practical theological reflection is a process of discerning the will of God in order to take ministry deeper.

Praxis   theory/theology   praxis loop

Distinguishes practical theology from other theologies in that it starts with practice. Reflective practice often involves a 4 step loop or better described as conversation.

1. **Describe Your Context**
2. **Interpret your ministry**
3. **Determine Your Norms**
4. **Implement Specific Action**

1. Describe Your Context

What's going on in your ministry?

What's happening when your young people gather together for church?

What practices take place on a regular basis?

What are the roles of the leaders and the young people?

2. Interpret your ministry

Why is what is happening, happening?

How does the "culture" of your church influence your ministry?

What are the aims of the practice in your ministry? (why are they practiced?)

Why are the roles of the leaders and young people what they are?

Who is not being heard and why not?

3. Determine Your Norms

(relate this reflection to the issue being developed in step two)

What should be happening in your local ministry?

What core Biblical principles form the basis of your ministry?

Does your ministry consider other theological perspectives or only your own?

What areas of scriptures do you struggle with?

How do others understand it differently from you and what is their theological position?

Who is not being heard and why not?

194

4. Implement Specific Action

How can you faithfully implement a new plan of action?
What concrete practice can you implement immediately?
What are the long term goals you are aiming for?
What obstacles are you likely to face and how will you address them?

*Adding the voices.

The voices of the community! Because of Jesus' emphasis on the marginalized, I would particularly include this voice. In order to do this you need to understand your own bias. This is hard to do and requires humility and listening to others. It is only when we do this that we are able to hear God's voice.

A Critical Conversation – (Stephen Pattison)

A 3 way conversation.

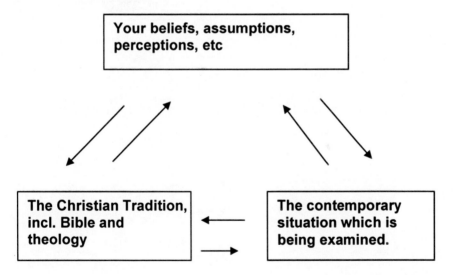

MODULE 4: CHURCH GROWTH AFRICA-HISTORY

(Revd Dr Kehinde Olabimtan BTh MED)

AFRICAN CHURCH GROWTH IN CHURCH HISTORY

LECTURE 1: EARLY CHRISTIANITY OF EGYPT AND NORTH AFRICA

EGYPT

The earliest association of Christianity with Africa is found in the refugee story of baby Jesus. His parents fled to Egypt from the threat of Herod the Great in order to secure his protection. However, the flourishing of the Gospel in that part of the African continent did not occur until about 100AD, and this occurred in three successive stages: Jewish (100AD), Hellenistic (200AD), and Coptic (300AD).

THE JEWISH PHASE

At the time of the birth of Jesus, Alexandria in the Nile Delta had become a large and perhaps the most significant centre of Jewish settlement in the Diaspora, with the Jews there numbering about a million. Two of the five sections to which the city was divided were dominated by Jews, their synagogue and their culture. As a coastal city, it was a flourishing commercial city, hence cosmopolitan. It was also an intellectual centre. The earliest known Jewish intellectual from Alexandria was Philo, "philosopher and Bible expositor, international and cosmopolitan Jewish scholar, deeply influenced by Hellenistic culture" and committed to establishing understanding between Hellenism and Judaism. There were other Jewish scholars of the most conservative strands in Alexandria who were using allegories to interpret the scriptures. Perhaps the most significant output of the intellectual life of Alexandria was the Septuagint, the Greek text of the Hebrew Bible.

The trajectories blazed by Christianity in Alexandria must, however, be understood in context. In the various successions of empires around the Mediterranean basin, Egypt had come under one power after another; but the conquest of Alexander the Great in 332 BC left the most enduring cultural and intellectual impacts on the land of the Pharaohs. The Greek language became the medium of communication, not only for the Greek settlers and traders in Alexandria but for the urban population in general. This was the process that produced Hellenistic Jews in Alexandria as in other cities of the empire of Alexander.

The first group of Christians trickled into Alexandria as missionaries, refugees and traders; but tradition, taken from Eusebius' *History,* attributes the founding of the See of Alexandria to St. Mark, the evangelist who was martyred in AD 68. However, the first historically known Alexandrian Christian was Jewish Apollos, "whose Hellenistic eloquence was a great challenge to Paul at Corinth". From all indications, he had been instructed "in the way of the Lord" in Alexandria (Acts 18:24, 1 Cor. 3:4-7). However, not much was known about Jewish Christianity in Egypt until recent centuries, the most revealing being unearthed in 1948 at *Nag Hammadi.* It indicated the tragedy that befell the community as it did elsewhere: wandering into the error of Gnosticism. Because many Jewish Christians fell into the error, they lost their influence on the Church and eventually withered away.

HELLENISTIC PHASE

With its Hellenistic intellectual heritage the ultimate legacy Alexandrian Christianity bequeathed the church came through its theological school. The city flourished to become the metropolis of the entire Mediterranean East with greater significance than Athens. And although the Romans conquered the city in AD 30, it retained its Greek ethos and extended its influence as far away as Rome. It is, therefore, understandable that theology in the proper sense of the word started from Alexandria, where fertile minds were at work advancing and refuting theological ideas. To assuage the thirst of young Egyptian Christians *Pantaenus* founded the catechetical school in 180AD and was succeeded by Clement, his disciple, in AD 200. The school attained its zenith under Origen in AD 220-54.

In continuing the school he inherited from Pantaenus, Clement impressed on his students to avoid the pitfalls inherent in the teachings of the philosophers, but he also challenged them to appropriate the best of their philosophies that were consistent with the Gospel—"whatever is good, whatever is beautiful." But it was Origen who would crown the effort of the Alexandrian school with his systematic exposition of Christian texts and daring application of Hellenistic insights to their interpretation for living.

He started with Scripture, establishing a secure text by comparing the various versions and interpreted it, always looking for a deeper (often allegorical) meaning of the text. Then he explained the biblical faith further by bringing it into the contexts of Greek philosophy and presenting it as a systematic unity. Finally, he pointed out the ways of perfection to the Christian soul. It is for this reason that he is venerated as the first biblical scholar, theologian, and master of asceticism, a man to whom all theologians…were deeply indebted.

Like Clement, his predecessor, he fostered in his students the same attitude towards Greek learning as indicated by his letter to one of them (Gregory):

I beg you to draw from the Greek philosophers such things as can be made curricular or preparatory studies to Christianity, for geometry and astronomy, such things as may be useful for expounding Holy Scripture. The philosophers say that geometry and music and grammar and rhetoric and astronomy are the handmaidens of philosophy. Let us say that philosophy itself is the handmaid of Christianity.

In recognizing all truths as God's truth, Origen opened our eyes to the importance of context in our understanding the activities of God in the world, a process veritably demonstrated in the incarnation of Jesus when "the word became flesh.

Alexandrian Christianity also contributed to the evangelization of Africa and evolved into a patriarchate; in this, the city was second only to Rome. Eusebius produced a long list of bishops who led the church in Alexandria after St. Mark, but the first one known in history was Demetrius (AD 189-231). Under his episcopate, the church flourished and he ordained bishops outside Alexandria whom he supervised. Thus, he established the patriarchate of Alexandria made up of over a hundred bishops and enjoyed the recognition of the Church in the East. The most famous of the Alexandrian bishop was Athanasius (AD 328-373), an astute defender of orthodoxy with regard to the person of Jesus in relation to the Father. He opposed Arianism to uphold the full divinity of the son. Origen's speculation was of less value to him and he would stick to the simple words of the scriptures and cultivate the fellowship of the simple Christian folks and religious men of his time, the monks.

The word "Copt" is used in modern times to describe non-Arabicized Egyptians; but it was first used for non-Hellenized Egyptians. While Alexandria remained cosmopolitan and cultivated the intellectual traditions from the North, its rear was largely populated by these unsophisticated masses of peasant farmers. They lived in the country-side and Upper Egypt where they survived on the Nile. Tradition holds that Demetrius was the first bishop to send missionaries among them. The success of the mission is attested to by the events that followed twelve years later. When Emperor Septimus Severus forbade conversion to Christianity in Egypt a large number of young Coptic Christian converts from Thebes, 500 miles south of Alexandria, were lined up for execution. In AD 250, during the persecution of Decius, Coptic liturgical books were burnt indicating that the liturgy of the church had evolved. By AD 300, the full Bible had been translated into the Sahidic dialect of Upper Egypt. In AD 330, Athanasius even preached in the Coptic language in Alexandria.

The traditional religion of the people of Upper Egypt prepared them for the message of Christianity. Traditionally very religious, their many divinities had been reduced into the triad of Osiris, the father; Isis, his sister and spouse; and Horus their son. Horus would lead the good souls after death to Osiris where they will share his divinity and immortality; Isis is the mother who already protects them in this world. In this way, the idea of resurrection and eternal life and the veneration of Mary the mother of God became a new version of their old faith.

The hallmark of Egyptian Christianity was martyrdom. Under Diocletian, their witness attained an unsurpassed height. Between AD 303 and 306 daily average of execution was between twenty and thirty, and this even became the reference point from which they reckon date, beginning with the *Era Martyrum*, which was the reign of Diocletian that began in AD 283.

For those who survived the bloody martyrdom, there was another form of discipline that would fit man for eternity. In this regard, Egyptian Christianity bequeathed the church the monastic discipline. This discipline was initiated by *Antony* who left the comfort of life and family to live in the desert alone in contemplation. Many young people followed in his trail but had not the discipline to keep focus and either despaired or lost themselves in some idle extravagances. It was *Pachomius* who then introduced the discipline of the monastic life in community, in a structured daily life of prayer and work. Monasticism made Egypt the land of saints as many people thronged there from all over the Christian world of the time to join with the contemplatives.

Following the Christological controversy of the fifth century, the Coptic Church cut itself off the churches at Constantinople and at Rome. Its position that overemphasized the divinity of Christ over and above his humanity, though triumphed at the Council of Ephesus (431), was defeated at the Council of Chalcedon (451). Its patriarch, Dioscorus, was deposed and another was appointed by the emperor. The church would not acknowledge the new patriarch but chose to face its own future alone. After the Arabic conquest of Egypt in AD 640, the church shrivelled as some converted to Islam. It was more economical to be a Moslem than to be a Christian.

NORTH AFRICA

The North Africa known to the world in the days of St. Augustine was restricted to the land around Carthage with Numidia as its hinterland and Mauritania as its distant limit, largely unknown. It roughly corresponds to the three countries known today as Tunisia, Algeria and Morocco (The Maghreb).

The main ethnic groups were the indigenous and poor Berbers and the Phoenicians who founded Carthage in 814 BC. The Phoenicians dominated the western half of the Mediterranean Sea as maritime traders and their Punic language served as the lingua franca of the region. The Romans destroyed Carthage in 146 BC and colonized the country as ex-service men settled in the land. The origin of the Church in this province is shrouded in obscurity, but its Latin character and juridical dependence on Rome betrays a Roman origin.

The earliest knowledge of the Church in Roman North Africa was in connection with the martyrdom of its Christians, the most popular being *Felicitas and Perpetua.* The former was an African slave girl who brought her mistress Perpetua to the faith. This underscored the church as a movement among the lower class but with gradual accretion of the middle class.

The **theological school at Carthage achieved for the western half of the Mediterranean what Alexandria achieved in the eastern half.** Its leaders were Tertullian and Cyprian. The former started formulating theology in Latin about 180 BC when educated Christians in Rome thought it could only be done in Greek. Tertullian avoided philosophical speculations but focused on ascetical and moral questions. His austere lifestyle was not acceptable to many; in the end, he pitched his tent with a Montanist sect from Asia Minor. A generation after, his theology was reworked by Cyprian the bishop of Carthage.

The church in North Africa reached its zenith under the exploits of St. Augustine, the Bishop of Hippo. His mother was Monica, a Berber woman married to a Roman. His was the culmination of all the theological achievements of western Christianity. The depth of his own religious personality is reflected in his autobiographical 'Confessions'. In the field of theology, he is above all hailed as Doctor Gratiae, the Teacher of Grace. He showed the overall importance of the grace of God in the work of salvation against the human asceticism of the monk Pelagius and the moralism of Tertullian….Against African separatism he constantly confessed his adherence to the universal church, while never ceasing to be a true son of Mother Africa. The glories of the Church in North Africa had a long shadow cast on it during the Donatist controversy. At its roots were religious, economic, social and political factors each of which had contrast in the situation of the peasant Christians of the hinterland (Numidia) and the educated middle class of Carthage. The one hundred years of schism was followed by the invasion of the vandals who, having converted to Arian Christianity, forced Arianism on the Catholic Church until Emperor Justinian conquered and dislodged them. **It was the Islamic occupation of Carthage in 697 AD that spelled the death knell of Christianity in North Africa. Why?**

1. **The indigenous Berbers were barely touched by the Gospel. The church looked towards Rome.**
2. **The church did not indigenize. The liturgy was in Latin. No literature in Punic or Berber language.**
3. **There was no virile leadership.**
4. **The church had spent itself in a century-long internal controversy that had weakened it.**

For Further Reading[1]

NUBIA

The Christian kingdom of Nubia in the heartland of Africa, North East, thrived after the Arab conquest of North Africa. It was known in the Bible as Kush but the Septuagint rendered it "Ethiopia", the land of "Sunburnt faces." At the time of Christ, the kingdom was ruled by queens who were called *kandake*. The eunuch baptized by Philip was an official of the court at Meroë. By the 4th century, Nubian monks had visited Egypt and Coptic Christians fled to Nubia during the Arian controversy. From all indications monks, soldiers and merchants may have brought Christianity to their Nubian homeland.

The official conversion of the state took place under Justinian the Great who organized imperial missions in the 540's. His aim was to evangelize dangerous border tribes in order to transform them into friendly neighbours. In Egypt, the Nubians constituted this class of people. Julian, an Alexandrian Copt, had convinced Empress Theodora to have the Nubians converted to Christianity, but Justinian was not disposed positively towards a Coptic-Monophysite missionary. His wife, however, being Monophysite at heart went ahead to appoint Julian as the first missionary. Julian evangelized the northern kingdom of Nobatia. The emperor's orthodox missionaries worked in the central kingdom of Makuria. The southern kingdom of Alodia asked for missionaries from Nobatia but when the entire people were united under Makuria, they all acknowledged the Coptic Patriarch in Alexandria.

Almost all available evidences regarding the inner life of the Nubian Church is connected with church buildings. By 1200, Makuria had seven dioceses, many churches and monasteries. The less developed southern territories recorded about 400 churches, and those in Soba, its capital, were decorated with gold. Excavations in Nubia have unearthed mural paintings in the Byzantine tradition and books in Greek, Coptic and Old Nubian. A Nubian lectionary found may indicate a partial translation of the Bible. This and the evidence of

1 Baur, John. *2000 Years of Christianity in Africa*. Nairobi: Paulines Publications Africa, 1994, pp. 21-30.

Falk, Peter. *The Growth of the Church in Africa*. Jos: African Christian Textbooks, 1997, pp. 25-58.

Walls, A.F. "In Quest of the Father of Mission Studies." *International Bulletin of Mission Research* 23, (1999), 98-105.

black bishops, dating back to the 10th century, are proof of a remarkable degree of indigenization. The fortunes of Nubia began to suffer reversal with the takeover of power in Egypt by the Turkish Mamluks in 1172. These Turks were more hostile towards Christianity than their Arab predecessors. In the ensuing political intrigues and military alliances with their neighbours, the Nubians lost out and suffered reprisals in repeated raids. The loss of political sovereignty and the destruction of most church buildings were a heavy blow to the "royal" Nubian Church. It was further weakened by a process of Arab settlement that encouraged inter-marriages of Arabs and Christian Nubian women. By virtue of the matrilineal laws of Nubian society (remember the kandake!) much land fell into Muslim hands.

The church and its leadership appears to have suffered violently in the hand of their invaders from about 1250 and not much was heard about it after 1450.

ETHIOPIA

The roots of Ethiopian Christianity can be found in its legendary connection with the Hebrew nation. Oral tradition about the visit of Queen of Sheba to Solomon has been developed into an elaborate legend, making Ethiopian kingship and priesthood a continuation of Solomonic dynasty with the capital at Aksum assuming the name Siyon. However, Ethiopian tradition knows three steps in the advent of Christianity: Philip's eunuch brought the faith; Frumentius the priesthood; and the Nine Saints the monastic life. The appropriation of the eunuch is a wrong appropriation, due to Ethiopia's piety rather than historical fact, just as the very name Ethiopia. Both originally belonged to Nubia. But it true that the first Christians arrived in the Kingdom of Aksum at an early time. They were Hellenistic traders, and the king permitted them to have their own prayer house.

The well-established trade route from the Mediterranean through the Red Sea to Ethiopia and India is also background to the official conversion of Ethiopia. A Syrian philosopher took his two disciples *Frumentius* and *Aedesius* on a journey to India and was shipwrecked. Soldiers brought the two young men to the court at Aksum and as they were well educated, they were entrusted with important posts, especially the schooling of the two princes Ezana and Zazana. Having completed this major task, they were allowed to leave. Aedesius went home and reported the story to the philosopher *Rufinus* who wrote it down. But Frumentius, who was very zealous to uplift the young Christian community, went to Athanasius, Patriarch of Alexandria, and asked for a bishop to be sent to Aksum. Athanasius found it best to send Frumentius himself as bishop and sent him back. So it is really Frumentius who brought the priesthood to Ethiopia, and throughout the centuries, the country has always received its bishop from the Patriarch of Alexandria. There is no further information about Frumentius' return, but the Ethiopian Church venerates him highly as St. Abuna Salama—Our Father of Salvation.

King Ezana seems to have been relatively late in accepting the Christian faith. He waged many wars in one of which he destroyed the Nubian Kingdom of the Kandake in Meroe. He had his victories recorded on five stone slabs. The first four inscription call him "Son of God Ares" but the last one, which acknowledges his earthly father Ella Amida, attributes his achievements to "the power of the Lord of Heaven, who in heaven and on earth is mightier than everything that exists" and "who made me a Lord." This shows a change from the traditional divine kingship to the biblical sacred kingship by adoption; its Christian sense is verified by a cross appearing on his coins.

It took a long time for the whole country to be evangelized. The greatest share in this missionary work is to be attributed to the monks. They arrived in various groups shortly before and after the year AD 500. They came from Egypt but were not Egyptians. They included many ascetics who came from all over the world to Egypt, and after a period of monastic training went on to other countries. The most famous among the monks, however, were the *Nine Saints,* with whom tradition identifies the proper advent of monasticism. It seems they were leaders of communities which included priests and nuns. The most prominent of them was St. Michael Aregawi, whose monastery Church of Debra Damo still exists. With the advent of the monks there also began the educational and literary work of the Church. The translation of most books of the Bible, chiefly from Greek and Syriac, is attributed to the Nine Saints. The pious but uncritical mind of the Ethiopians added to the Bible a number of apocryphal books. In fact, the whole Ethiopian literature remained through the centuries almost exclusively hagiographical and ascetical, while all education began around "parish" churches and was completed in monasteries.

The period between the advent of Islam (AD 640) and the restoration of the Solomonic dynasty (1270) is called the Dark Age of Ethiopia. It marks the age of isolation from the outside world and of expansion into the interior of the African continent. Early relationship between Ethiopians and the Arabs was cordial as the Ethiopians sheltered early Moslems fleeing persecution in their home land in the Arabia. But when the Jihad took off and they seized North Africa, they gradually seized the control of the route along the Red Sea. Ethiopians, who at first exacted tax from the settlers on their coast eventually lost out, and it became dangerous to venture out to Alexandria. Thus shut out from the rest of the world, they had no bishop (Abun) consecrated and looked inward, expanding into the interior of Africa. It led to the eventual creation of Ethiopia as a geographical and as an ethnic term.

The expansion towards the interior brought with it the incorporation of some indigenous religious elements. Churches were built on former places of sacrifice, called adbar; fertility cults and sacrificial meals at harvest time were continued, and survived even till our times. The Solomonic dynasty of Aksum lost its primacy to the Agaw tribe in Lasta. Their dynasty was in effective control from 1137 until the restoration of the Solomonic one in 1270. The only surviving descendant of the last Aksumite king, *Yikuno Amlak* had been educated and protected by the monks. He reigned in Shoa but moved around until the new capital was built in Gondar. His grandson Amda Siyon took up the challenge of conquering the menacing kingdoms around, and under him the epos Kebra Nagast (The Glory of Kings) was written, which traced the dynasty back to Solomon.

The zenith of Ethiopian Christian culture came a century later, under Zara Yakob (1434-1468). He wanted his kingdom to be both truly Ethiopian and truly Christian. He thus imposed the faith on the pagans in the new province, favoured monasticism and literature, tuned up the morals of his citizens with a code that included monogamy—a law from which he felt exempted. With him began a religious nationalism that was to last until the time of Haile Selassie. It expressed itself in Amharic Christianity as it had grown through the centuries and was believed by its adherents to be the most genuine Church of Jesus Christ.

At the beginning of the golden age of Ethiopia, two great monastic personalities gave direction to the leaderless life of the monks and instilled new purpose and order in their movement. They were St. Takla Haymanot (c.1215-1313) and Ewostatewos (Eustatius, c. 1273-1352). Takla Haymanot built Debra Libanos, the country's leading monastery, in Shoa. Its abbot later on was given jurisdiction over all monks and enjoyed the highest religious authority beside the bishop; as an indigenous person, he often had even greater influence. Takla Haymanot is regarded as the greatest Ethiopian saint, the restorer of the Solomonic Kingdom and the monastic legislator.

Ewostatewos' central monastery became Debra Maryam in Tigre. He was a controversial figure on account of his observance of the Sabbath in addition to Sunday. Failing to get the approval of the Patriarch of Alexandria, he went to Armenia where he died after 14 year exile. His disciples were persecuted and excluded from priesthood. But Zara Yakob eventually rehabilitated them and their Sabbath observance as a specific Ethiopian movement in contrast to the Alexandrian Church.

CLASSICAL FEATURES OF ETHIOPIAN CHRISTIANITY

1. The church was faithful to its Alexandrian Coptic Patriarchate roots, cherishing its apostolicity, following orthodox theology, accepting its "metropolitan", the abun (i.e. father) as guarantee of continuity of priesthood.
2. It manifested indigenous elements wherein the Emperor—*Negus Nagaste,* king of kings—was the *de facto* head of the Church, the pillar of faith.
3. The liturgy was rich in Eucharistic prayers and is still being celebrated in *Ge'ez,* the ancient language of Aksum.
4. The liturgy is also mixed with traces of traditional religion, such as animal sacrifices at the dedication of a church, and some practices from the Old Testament, such as the law of ablutions and the observation of the Sabbath.

For Further Reading[1]

1 Baur, John. *2000 Years of Christianity in Africa.* Nairobi: Paulines Publications Africa, 1994, pp. 31-39.

Falk, Peter. *The Growth of the Church in Africa.* Jos: African Christian Textbooks, 1997, pp. 67-73.

After the disappearance of the Church in North Africa and Nubia, the weakening of the church in Egypt and the isolation of that of Ethiopia, European princes began to take interest in the evangelisation of the continent of Africa in the closing decades of the 15th century. Some factors were responsible for this interest.

From about AD 1000 the princes of Spain and Portugal began the war to reclaim their land from the Moslems who had swept through North Africa to invade the Iberian Peninsula. While this struggle was going on, in 1453, the European Christian world was shocked to hear that the Turks had invaded Constantinople and had converted the church building Hagia Sophia into a mosque. It was the tonic European Christendom needed to renew the effort at liberating the holy land. Thus in Portugal the young prince, Dom Henrique, decided to take the war into Moslem territories and began to seek for sea route through which Portugal could launch a rear attach against the Moslems.

On the other hand, Europeans were seeking for alternative routes to the East, by way of the sea, in order to avoid passing through the hostile Moslem territories in their quest for spice and silk in India and China respectively. These needs accelerated early in the 15th century the development of maritime activities led by the Iberian powers. And the driving force behind this development was Dom Henrique, later known as Henry the Navigator even though he never sailed himself. His historian later indicated that in his determination to free former Christian lands of the presence of the Arabian invaders, Henry had it in mind to effect his purpose by joining hand with Prester John, believed to be the king of a Christian kingdom in the heart of Africa. The success of the maritime activities Henry the Navigator sponsored and organized brought Europe into contact with Africa and the rest of the world. With the prospect of commerce, the vision of crusade against infidels soon transformed into the Portuguese maritime world empire, the *Conquista,* sponsored and led by the kings themselves.

Hildebrandt, Jonathan. *History of the Church in Africa*. Achimota: Africa Christian Press, 1990, pp. 21-37

Sundkler, Bengt and Christopher Steed. *A History of the Church in Africa*. Cambridge: CUP, 2000, pp. 30-41.

The maritime activities of Portugal, as well as that of Spain in the westward direction, received papal blessing to convert indigenous peoples to the faith of the Church. Pope Alexander VI issued the bull in May 1493, vesting in the Iberian princes the royal patronage, the *padroado,* in their overseas territories. This meant that they were responsible for sponsoring missions to the peoples they encounter in their maritime activities. In their own eastward sphere where they had undisputed monopoly, the Portuguese built forts along the African coast, from *El Mina* in the Gold Coast to Mombasa on the East coast of Africa. From these forts and the other Islands, they discovered off the coast of West Africa they settled and traded with indigenous peoples. They had encounters with African kings and chiefs and sought to plant churches among them.

Although the Portuguese succeeded in spreading themselves from northwest Africa (Madeira) to Goa in India, their significant religious activities were concentrated on few places: Ethiopia, Kongo, Angola, Matamba and Monomotapa kingdom of Zimbabwe. But the monopoly of the Portuguese was only temporary, for soon after the discovery of the sea route to the East other European powers—the Danes, Dutch, English and French—also became interested in the prospects of overseas trade. Their presence was also not without religious motives. It was, however, in Kongo that a long and chequered history of church, state and conversion played out.

KONGO

The Portuguese sailors reached the mouth of Zaire River in the 1470s and were ready to add the area to their overseas possession. But the beginning of religious work there can be dated to 1483 when the Portuguese priest Diogo Cao took four Kongolese to Portugal to learn the language and return to serve as interpreters among their people. From 1491, the evangelisation of the people began at Soyo, the coastal district of the kingdom of Kongo. The team was led by father Vicentes dos Anjos in the company of four other priests and the young Bakongo. The first baptism took place on Easter day 1491 when the *Mani Soyo* and one of his sons were baptized in the presence of some 25,000 people. In May 1491 Nzinga Nkuvu, the *Mani Kongo,* was baptized and immediately ordered that all idols were to be burned. The baptism of the king was soon followed by that of the queen and one of the princes, Mvemba Nzinga, baptised Afonso. The energetic thrust of

209

the foreigners provoked a vehement reaction from the custodians of traditions and in 1495, the recently baptised noblemen and the prince fled to the adjacent town of Sundi, while the old king returned to his harem and ancestors. In the exile at Sundi, two Portuguese priests trained the young prince in western education and in the Christian faith. When his father died in 1506, Mvemba Nzinga, strengthened by ten years of refugee experience, established himself as the new king of Kongo.

Mvemba instituted reforms in his domain. He established schools for boys and girls and sent his son Henry to Lisbon for further training where he learned Latin. Henry was later consecrated "suffragan" bishop "of Utica" in North Africa. As Mvemba brought Kongo closer to Portugal, more missionaries were sent to his domain. At the time of his death in 1543, half of the population had been baptised. But a sore point remained in the association of Kongo with the Portuguese. Their menace of slave-dealing was a burden on Kongo. Relations with the merchants in Luanda and slave dealers of Sao Tome made matters untenable. It led in 1665 to a war between the Portuguese and Kongo forces during which the proud city of Sao Salvador (formerly Mbanza Kongo) with its cathedral and its eight churches was virtually destroyed. The king, Antonio I Afonso, was beheaded, together with his chaplain and relative, the first black Capuchin Francisco de Sao Salvador Roboredo. Civil war and decay followed and soon there were three contenders to the throne.

The coming of Italian Capuchins temporarily redeemed the situation in Kongo. They entered the kingdom in 1645, and their effort proved to be the most extensive evangelisation effort in Black Africa before modern times. In the last twenty eight years of the century, the Capuchins recorded surprising results in terms of Baptism. Thirty seven preachers together reported a total of 341,000. This was made possible because of the inclusive approach to conversion. Usually the people followed the example of their ruler. At his baptism, a herald would announce what was expected of the crowd, and the masses assembled in the market places would queue up to the baptismal font. But there were exceptions. The day after the ruler's baptism at Ngobila, Father Caltanisetta asked him to have the herald announce that all were to be baptised, but the ruler refused, feeling that each one should be free to decide him or herself. The priest was surprised when he took matter into his own hand by wanting to start baptising indiscriminately and the people fled into the bush. In another situation, traditional worshippers spread rumours that those who consented to baptism would suffer sudden death. But rumours could also serve the purpose of the church as those who come forward to "eat salt" were promised bliss.

With respect to indigenization, preparation for baptism was done by Kongolese interpreters—married lay men, from noble families, and some trained in Portugal. The first Kongolese catechism was available in 1556 and it was the first book to be produced in the Bantu language. In the 18th century, the Kongo church slowly but inevitably faded away. This may not be rashly concluded as a result of lack of roots; the problem was more complex.

WARRI

Besides the Kongo and Angola, there was only one other territory with significant attempt at evangelization in mediaeval Africa: the little Itsekiri kingdom of Warri. In 1570, the Olu invited Augustinian missionaries from Sao Tomé and had his crown prince baptized Sebastião. During his own reign, Sebastião personally instructed his people. He sent his son Domingos to be educated in Portugal, from where he returned with a European wife instead of becoming a priest according to his father's wish. This Catholic tradition of the rulers continued with some interruptions until 1807, but it did not spread beyond the court.

At the end of Sebastião's long reign, the Bishop of Sao Tome remarked that *"true Christianity is almost wholly confined to the king and the prince; the rest call themselves Christians to please the king. They take their children to baptism with the greatest reluctance, believing that a baptised child will die immediately."* This account does not take into cognisance the fact that the kingdom was not supplied with priests, and this continued throughout the reign of Sebastião's successors. The eight friars sent by Propaganda Fide were misdirected to Benin from where they were expelled after reprimanding the king for human sacrifice. A long plea from Olu Antonio yielded two Capuchin fathers who exercised a fruitful ministry in Warri for six years (1657-63).

In 1770, the governor of Sao Tomé sent a canon, João Alvarez, who was himself an Itsekiri. He was soon joined by an Italian Capuchin, but the mission was compromised by the bad behaviour of Alvarez, and the scandalized people of Warri came to the conclusion that "the Almighty has never intended Negroes to be priest." The account of Christianity in Warri shows how heavily the evangelization depended on trade. Once the Portuguese merchants found the local trade unprofitable, no ship called at Warri, and it was difficult to find priests who would stay in such isolated places for a long time. By the middle of the 19th century, the mission had faded out. Report also confirms what the history of the Kongo had proved: the power of resistance to assimilation of the African traditional religion. Even more than in the Kongo the axiom, "Once the king converts, the whole people follow", was proved false.

SOUTHERN AFRICA

When Bartholomew Diaz and Vasco da Gagama negotiated the Cape of Good Hope on their way to and from the East the contact of Europeans with the indigenous people of South Africa began. The contact was casual in the first two centuries as the Cape only served the purpose of provisioning for European sailors—Portuguese, Dutch, French and British. From 1652, however, a sustained contact that would prove most traumatic for the indigenous people began. That year Jan van Riebeck arrived with his 126 Dutch compatriots as settlers at the Cape, where they built a fort.

At first, the Khoikhoi saw van Riebeck as a symbol of goodwill. The Dutch East India Company insisted that the indigenous people were free and should be paid wages for their services, and this was upheld by the settlers. A Khoikhoi girl, Eva, who served with Mrs van Riebeck gained proficiency in the Dutch language, was taught Christianity, and served as interpreter to her people. She adopted a new lifestyle and was baptised and married to a Danish doctor. In 1713, the Khoikhoi were decimated to near extinction by smallpox. Towards the end of the century, tensions between the Dutch and their Khoikhoi and slave servants took violent forms. In 1788, 200 servants led by millenarian vision burnt their Dutch clothes and killed their white animals, prophesying the end of the world and threatening to kill all whites.

212

The Dutch farmers introduced slave labour, first from Guinea and Angola and later from Mozambique, Madagascar, India and Indonesia. The slaves often longed for freedom but none of them would receive manumission papers without baptism. In the economic interest of the settlers, many masters did not discuss religion with their slaves and as much as it was possible kept them away from Christian instruction. The situation was jolted with the arrival in the Cape of a Moravian missionary George Schmidt who had joined the group in Holland. From 1737, he spent seven years in the country before he was repatriated as a "heretic" by the Dutch Reformed *predikants.* But the precarious foothold he secured would prove enduring. He acquired a small farm and called it Genadendal, a model mission station. There he taught his indigenous converts the Christian faith and agriculture and organized them into prayer cells. Far away from home and without the possibility of visits from home, he was ordained by letter, and he started baptising his converts. His success threatened the Dutch establishment church and he was sent home from the colony. But before leaving, he handed his Dutch New Testament to Magdalena, one of his converts.

CONCLUSION

The second attempt to plant Christianity ended, like the first, in failure. Some factors can be adduced for this.
1. Trade received primacy in the contact of Europeans with the indigenous people; where evangelisation conflicted with trade, the traders sooner or later often carried the day.
2. Slave trade in particular decimated the continent and created credibility problem for European missions.
3. Missionaries did not make serious effort to indigenize the faith apart from a few translation of the catechism. They did not see value in indigenous cultures for their enterprise; hence, when traditional religious instincts gave Christianity apparently exotic expression the product was considered heretic.
4. There was no concerted effort to develop indigenous clergy. Too much focus was on the aristocracy.
5. The missionaries were sometimes paternalistic and looked down on the people.

For Further Reading[1]

1 Baur, John. *2000 Years of Christianity in Africa.* Nairobi: Paulines Publications Africa, 1994, pp. 42-98.

With the exception of the ancient Churches in Egypt and Ethiopia and a few lost outposts along the coast, contemporary Christianity in Africa goes back to the 19th century. Its beginning is centred on the peoples of sub-Saharan Africa. The conversion took place in an astonishing short time and embraced an extremely large sector of population. As the starting point of the whole epoch, the Year 1792 could be mentioned. It saw the foundation of the first Protestant missionary society to work among indigenous peoples of the world, the Baptist Missionary Society. And so Protestantism is the most important new ingredient that helped foster modern Christianity in Africa.

For half a century (1792-1842) Protestant missionaries were practically alone in the field, and until the nineteenth century ended with World War I, Protestant evangelists were far more numerous than Catholic ones. The major reason for this is that in the previous century the Protestant churches in Europe had experienced a great revival movement, while the Catholic Church had suffered a serious decline from which she started recovering but quite slowly after the Napoleonic Wars (from 1815 onwards). The Protestant movement combined evangelicalism (living according to the Gospel) with evangelism (preaching the Gospel), and thus began their missionary activities. It sprang from among leading revival groups like the Pietists and Moravians in Germany, the Methodists and the Evangelical wing of the Anglican Church in England.

The greatest single impulse came from the English Baptist William Carey, and the leading missionary country was Britain. Other missionary societies that came into existence following the precedence set by Carey's Baptist Missionary Society (BMS) were:

1. *London Missionary Society (LMS):* founded in 1795; interdenominational but practically Congregational–the society to which David Livingstone belonged.

Falk, Peter. *The Growth of the Church in Africa*. Jos: African Christian Textbooks, 1997, pp. 73-86.

Sundkler, Bengt and Christopher Steed. *A History of the Church in Africa*. Cambridge: CUP, 2000, pp. 42-80.

2. *The Scottish missionary societies*: founded in 1796: the Edinburgh Society, the later *Church of Scotland Mission (CSM);* and the Glasgow society, the later *Free Church of Scotland Mission (FCSM)*–both founded the Presbyterian churches of Africa

3. *Church Missionary Society (CMS):* founded in 1799 by the evangelical wing of the Church of England–the most influential society in the British colonies.

4. *Wesleyan Methodist Missionary Society (WMMS):* was founded in 1813

5. *Universities Mission to Central Africa (UMCA):* was formed in 1858, following Livingstone's appeal. It became Anglo-Catholic in outlook.

6. German Evangelical *Basel Mission (BM):* formed in 1815 on the European continent and French Reformed Paris, formed 1824, excelled.

7. *American Board of Commissioners for Foreign Missions (ABCFM):* in the United States was formed in 1810. It was congregational in outlook.

The *American Baptist Foreign Mission Society (ABFMS):* was also formed in 1814.

The British and Foreign Bible Society: an interdenominational organisation founded in 1804 provided the greatest single support which Protestant missions received.

It is important to note that the whole Protestant missionary movement was originally of Evangelical inspiration, and present-day Protestant churches in Africa are still eighty percent evangelical.

The Catholic missionary revival followed the Protestant one.

The earlier missions had been entrusted to the kings of Spain and Portugal; in the new missionary awareness, it was going to be the task of the whole church. The work was supported by the faithful, directed by the Pope, and carried out by a host of missionary societies, old and new. The papal reorganization took place under Gregory XVI (1831-46) and was effected through the "Propaganda" (the Congregation for the Propagation of the Faith). The leading Catholic country, for missionary as well as spiritual activity was France.

It gave birth to:

The Holy Ghost Fathers (CSSp), renewed by Libermann in 1848;
The Fathers of Lyon (SMA), founded by Brésillac in 1856; and
The White Fathers (WF), of Cardinal Lavigerie founded in 1868.
Besides these, a host of Sister's congregations and a number of priestly communities were founded, many of them specially dedicated to mission work. Among these are the:
Oblates of Mary Immaculate (OMI) in Southern Africa and the
Montfort Fathers (SMM) in Malawi.

Among the old orders that resumed work in Africa were the:

Jesuits (SJ); Franciscans (OFM); Dominicans (OP); Benedictines (OSB); and the Vincentians (CM).

Perhaps the greatest innovation in the work of evangelisation was the cooperation of women. The Protestant missionaries took their wives with them. These women were usually eager to share their domestic skills with their African counterparts. They also enjoyed the assistance of young lady volunteers, who frequently worked with distinction, such as Mary Slessor in Calabar. Catholic missionaries sought the cooperation of the Sister's Congregations from the beginning. The most important one were started by the founders of the Father's Societies, such as the **White Sisters, the Comboni Sisters, the Mill Hill Sisters, the Missionary Benedictine Sisters, the Precious Blood Sisters, and the Consolata Sisters.**

INITIATING FACTORS

The greatest single factor that was at the origin of the African missions and promoted the work of evangelisation for many decades was *the anti-slavery movement.* It was initiated and encouraged by a group of evangelical Christians in England, called the Clapham Sect, and led by William Wilberforce. Due to their efforts, slavery was declared illegal in Britain in 1772, the slave trade banned in 1807, and slavery abolished in all British Dominions in 1833. Other European states followed the British move, but the enforcement of the law was largely left to the British navy.

The fight against the Arab slave-trade was started by Livingstone and on the European continent carried on chiefly by Lavigerie. Its double effect was to arouse Christian missionary interest in Europe and to remove one of the former obstacles to a fruitful missionary activity in Africa. To liberate slave children and to make up for the former slave-trade were leading motives for the support of the missions in Africa.

Thus, modern African missions can be said to have originated as a form of reparation for the historical injustice committed by the Christian nations against Africans.

A second factor that favoured modern evangelisation was *the extensive geographical exploration* **in the 19th century.** Around 1800 Africa still remained the only continent where the interior was still unknown to the outside world. So it naturally attracted the interest of the explorers who purposely or unwittingly opened new paths for the missionaries. In some cases, the missionaries themselves became explorers, as did Livingstone. Colonialism may be called a concomitant rather than an initiating factor, for the missionary enterprise was well on the way when colonial occupation of Africa began. However, it too generated missionary interest, especially in countries which acquired their first overseas possessions at that time, such as Germany and Belgium.

Yet the all-important factor was that the colonial empires with their infrastructures of communications, health-care, law and order transcending the tribal community though regrettably enforced by military power provided the framework in which most of the Christian churches were established.

There is the temptation to compare the situation with the ancient Roman Empire that offered to the apostles and early missionaries such tremendous opportunities that Origen dared to call it a plan of Divine Providence notwithstanding the persecutions of which he himself was a victim. That the later Christian Roman Empire also influenced Christianity in a negative sense, affecting its very substance, is another point of similarity with the colonial period in Africa inasmuch as it hindered the acceptance of the pure faith in a genuinely African garb.

In contrast to earlier centuries there was from the beginning unanimity about the missionary goal of *building up churches* and not just saving souls. Evangelical missionaries like Moravians and Plymouth Brethren were more concerned with creating a small elite group of convinced believers. Missionaries of the great historic churches, like the Lutherans and the Catholics, laboured at once to have whole regions evangelised. They passed from village to village, erecting a school or a place of prayer and entrusted it to catechists and evangelists. **Another well-known principle was** *"Africa must be converted by Africans."* The effect of the harsh tropical climate on missionaries made this necessary as many Europeans could not survive its strain. Happily, this principle was spontaneously put to effect by African lay evangelists who on their own initiative took the Gospel to their people far and wide. Examples abound in the return of Yoruba recaptives to their homeland from Sierra Leone, the Baganda evangelists who took the Gospel to many East African peoples, and the migrant workers of South Africa who took the message to their homesteads. This effort was complemented by the missionaries' policy of developing native clergy. In the 1850s, CMS Secretary Henry Venn developed for the Anglican mission the policy of preparing *self-supporting, self-governing, and self-extending* churches under a native ministry and an indigenous episcopate, though there were contemporary cultural limitations on what that might mean.

A third distinctive feature of modern missions was a more positive approach to *African culture* **as compared with former centuries.** As a rule, the missionaries were eager to learn the African languages; many also studied indigenous customs and history. Outstanding was at least the linguistic work, to which Protestant missionaries were especially devoted, as the translation and distribution of the Scriptures was for them the most important means of evangelisation. It may be asserted that for many peoples the printing of the Bible in their language was synonymous with Christianity having become indigenous. Strangely enough, there was no serious study of a most important area: the traditional religions.

THE WEST INDIAN CONNECTION

In 1772, the British High Court declared slavery illegal on British soil. In 1807, slave trade was banned. And finally, in 1833 it was abolished in all British dominions. By the time, the slaves were declared free in the West Indies, Western missions had started their exploits in West Africa, howbeit with a high rate of attrition. This was chiefly due to the tropical weather that proved inclement to their health. It became clear that Europeans were not likely to make much success of mission in Africa all alone. And so after the emancipation act of 1833 the Negro population of the West Indies became a potential source of recruitment for African missions. The first attempt was made by the Basel Mission in 1840. Its enterprise in Ghana had broken down after a 12 year trial, mainly on account of fever; it was hoped that Africans from the West Indies would be more resistance to the climate. Two years later a company of 24 emigrants from Jamaica, including six families of farmers, settled down at Akropong. The barrier of language and feeling of superiority prevented the West Indians from achieving much.

A second attempt was made by the Baptist Missionary Society of Jamaica. In 1841, two missionaries arrived at Fernando Po on an exploratory visit and started work among the liberated slaves at Port Clarence (now Malabo). Three years later, they returned from home with reinforcements of evangelists, teachers and settlers. They were forced to quit in 1846 when Spain reoccupied the island, having earlier leased it in 1827 to Britain to control the slave trade. They transferred their headquarters to Douala in the Cameroons. When the territory became German, they moved to Congo in 1879. Generally, the West Indians found it difficult to live on African soil. In the face of displacements, only a few families remained in the service of the mission, the last of them dying in Zaire in 1932. The main contribution of the mission itself was Bible translations in the local languages.

The most successful attempt was made by Scottish Presbyterians who, working in Jamaica, were urged by their Negro-Christians to bring the gospel to their people in Africa. After prayers and collection of funds, the missionaries in England honoured the invitation of some chiefs from Calabar to send missionaries to their country. Calabar was the homeland of most Negroes of Jamaica and attracted quite a number of volunteers. The first group arrived in 1846, composed exclusively of Scottish and Jamaican missionaries. Happily, the initial idea of recruiting farmers was discarded and teachers were recruited instead. They proved to be good in their calling, and as late as 1920, some of the best schools were run by them.

For Further Reading[1]

Modern Christian beginnings in West Africa can be dated to the last decades of the 18th century. In 1787, some 400 poor Negroes in London and Liverpool were settled in Sierra Leone in the hope that they would flourish in their own land. Without adequate plan made for their survival, they suffered from the climate and the hostility of the indigenous people as well as that of the slave-traders. They also lacked cohesion and moral ideals to survive their new environment having been twice uprooted. Only a small group among them survived. In 1792, a better conceived scheme saw the resettlement of 1100 freed slaves from Nova Scotia in Canada. These were disbanded soldiers who fought on the side of the British army in the American war of independence. They had all converted to Christianity and they arrived at their new settlement with their pastors, mainly Methodists and Baptists. The hope to be the catalyst to set the conversion of Africa in motion did not materialise. The indigenous people made life difficult for them; the Sierra Leone Company that was managing them introduced tax in the face of high cost of goods and services in the aftermath of the war between Britain and France. The revolt of the Nova Scotians in 1800 coincided with the arrival of 500 maroons, run-away slaves, from Jamaica; these joined hand with the troops on ground to quell the revolt. In 1808, the British government took active control of the settlement. **The banning of slave trade introduced another dimension to the settlement of Sierra Leone.** The suppression of the trade in the face of its revival in Western Africa saw the further settlement of more people in Sierra Leone. This provided the opportunity for a lasting missionary success. Thousands of liberated slaves were brought to Sierra Leone and settled in the towns established by the government; by 1825, there were about1800 of them resettled. These were the people among whom missionaries worked by establishing schools and churches, Church Missionary Society (CMS) being the principal mission organisation.

1 Baur, John. *2000 Years of Christianity in Africa.* Nairobi: Paulines Publications Africa, 1994, pp. 103-115.

Falk, Peter. *The Growth of the Church in Africa.* Jos: African Christian Textbooks, 1997, pp. 91-101.

Fryer, Peter. *Staying Power— The History of Black People in Britain.* London: Pluto Press, 1984, pp.113-132.

Sundkler, Bengt and Christopher Steed. *A History of the Church in Africa.* Cambridge: CUP, 2000, pp. 81-96.

Evangelism was their primary concern, general literacy the second; then followed social welfare to equip the people with skills. Regent town under William Johnson turned out to be the most successful mission effort. As the final stage in their educational system, CMS established the Fourah Bay College in 1827. In 1876, it was affiliated to Durham University as a degree awarding institution in West Africa.

YORUBA LAND

Among the most enterprising liberated slaves were the Yoruba. Some of them bought a seized and auctioned ship and started a regular trade along the coast and eventually found themselves in Badagry. They reconnected with their homeland and some of them decided to return home for good. Many of these returnees were of the Egba stock and, on their return, settled at Abeokuta among their kindred. Sodeke, the leader of the city, welcomed the Egba refugees and was particularly pleased with the educated home-comers from Sierra Leone. The Methodists among them wrote from Badagry to Sierra Leone asking for missionaries to be sent to them. The Methodist pioneer missionary in the Gold Coast *Thomas Birch Freeman* was sent on a reconnaissance visit in 1842 and went as far as Abeokuta. He left behind his companion William de Graft in Badagry to start work among the returnees based there, while he returned to the Gold Coast. The following year agents of the CMS paid a visit to Abeokuta and eventually began their Yoruba mission in 1846 under the leadership of *Rev. Henry Townsend.*

The starting of the work at Abeokuta was seen by missionaries as offering good prospects in the evangelisation of the interior of Africa, but events did not proceed without challenges. Abeokuta was susceptible to attack from their Dahomean neighbours, and one of such attacks was waged in 1851 with heavy casualty on the assailants through the help of missionaries. The city was also involved in the civil war going on among the Yoruba people at the time missions arrived. Internally at some points, and particularly in 1849, there was a widespread persecution of converts to Christianity. The precarious situation of the city, hence the mission, made the missionaries to look further afield for other prospects of mission. This led to the establishment of Ibadan mission by David Hinderer in 1851. From Ibadan, mission spread to Iseyin, Oyo, Ogbomoso, Ilesa, and Ondo. These stations were often manned at the beginning by scripture readers

221

recruited from Sierra Leone. The expansion of CMS Yoruba mission was accompanied by translation of the Bible into Yoruba, a resource that helped to create a unified identity for the people after decades of civil war. The American Baptists also worked in Yoruba land in this period and gained foothold.

LIBERIA

Black Americans had, before the Emancipation, interest in the evangelisation of Africa. As with Sierra Leone, Liberia was not a mission field but a place to resettle freed African slaves in the United States of America; it was thought that in Africa they might be happier. The first group arrived in 1820 and were directed by Freetown missionaries to Cape Mesurado, which became Monrovia, while the country was called Liberia. Among the first missionaries, the Baptist minister Lott Carey excelled but he soon died in 1828. Missionaries from America were attracted to Liberia because of the settlers, but they were hindered by high death rate. The settlers themselves were the greatest obstacles to the work of evangelisation. They kept aloof from the indigenous people and held on to their American way of life. They deprived the indigenous people any civil rights, grabbing their land. And they prohibited what the local people were living on: trade in slaves and liquor. Their attitude made the coastal people not to welcome missionaries lest they get into the interior and undo their grip over them. It was only in the last quarter of the century that visible progress was made when the great deployment of Afro-American missionary activity took place in the years 1877-1900. Baptists, A.M.E. (African Methodist Episcopal Church) and A.M.E. Zion took the lead. They were less successful than the Methodists and the Baptists societies who came with mixed white and black personnel. It is due to the joint effort of all of them that after 150 years of Liberia evangelisation, at least one-fifth of the local population have accepted the message of the Gospel.

GHANA (GOLD COAST)

Christianity first came to Ghana in the 18th century. Among the earliest known names in this regard are Thomas Thompson, a missionary of the Society for the Propagation of the Gospel (SPG) and Jacobus Capitein, a liberated slave trained in the Netherlands and later served as a chaplain of the Dutch Reformed Church at the Elmina Castle. While Thompson's effort was sustained and led to the emergence of the Methodist movement in the Gold Coast, Capitein's fizzled out. Thompson had gone to work in the West Indies and had experienced some challenges in working among the slave population of the plantations. He thought it might be better to go and work at the very source from where these people were shipped to the West Indies. He therefore came to the British castle at the Cape Coast as a teacher chaplain from 1752 to 1756. His method was to distribute widely among the people religious literature published by the Society for the Propagation of Christian Knowledge (SPCK). He also arranged for the training in England of four young men from Cape Coast. The only survivor was Philip Quarque, who was ordained Anglican minister and continued Thompson's work from 1766 to 1816. Quarque opened regular catechumenate classes and received more books from SPCK. One of his successors applied the same method. These baptised boys became evangelists to their people. In various places, they gathered young men and formed Bible bands with a Christian rule of living.

When in 1834 these bands requested missionaries from the SPCK, Methodist missionaries were sent to them with J. R. Dunwell leading the train with his arrival on the New Year day, 1835. The only one who survived more than a few months was *Thomas Birch Freeman,* son of an African freeman and an English lady. Working from 1838 to 1890, he was the proper founder of the Methodist Church in Ghana. The establishment of a fellowship in the much dreaded Ashanti kingdom was Methodists' most spectacular success, although establishment of a mission there did not take place until the British occupation of 1896. The Methodist movement produced the early nationalist among the Fanti people.

The other early evangelising society in the Gold Coast was the Basel Mission. They were invited by the Danish traders to their castle Christianborg near Accra in 1828. All save one of their nine early missionaries died so quickly that they sought to salvage their work by asking for the assistance of West Indians. In 1836, they moved to Akropong in the Akwapim Hills, which became their headquarters. The Basel missionaries, being mostly from the German Lutheran Church, followed Martin Luther's ideal of a "folk church", preserving the people's cultural identity. For this reason, they consistently used the vernacular in teaching and preaching. The Twi and Ga languages, sub-groups of Akan and Ga-Dangbe clusters respectively, were developed by them through a grammar, a dictionary, and the translation of the Bible, thus raising these languages to a literary level. During the First World War, the Basel Mission was expelled from the Gold Coast for being predominantly German and its work was taken over by the Presbyterian Scottish Mission of Calabar.

Along with the Basel Mission there worked in Ghana the North German Bremen Mission, which gave birth to the Ewe Evangelical Church. Attracted by Thomas Birch Freeman's reports, they arrived in 1847 and decided to evangelise the Ewe, the major ethnic group of Togoland, extending to the Volta River. Faithful to their Lutheran tradition they developed a Christianity based on the indigenous language, with Ewe schools and literature, and a church community that in its structure was closely modelled on the people's past. Thus, they awakened the national consciousness of the Ewe who had so far lived in isolated clans. The full evolution of a unified Ewe church was, however, hampered by international politics of the First World War. The 1919 Treaty of Versailles divided German Togoland into British and French mandates; the British mandate merged with the old Gold Coast after a referendum in 1956 and the French mandate became the Republic of Togo in 1960. Ewe Presbyterian Church later adopted as their new name Evangelical Presbyterian Church.

THE NIGER DELTA

The last major effort of Protestant missions to be launched in 19th century West Africa was the Niger mission. Its prelude was the ill-fated Niger Expedition of 1841. The expedition was embarked upon in the bid to replace the trade in slaves with legitimate trade in agriculture as propounded by *Thomas Fowell Buxton.* Led by J.F. Schön and Samuel Crowther, the expedition turned out a failure, especially because of the death of its white members whose constitutions were not agreeable with the climate. With the medical breakthrough of the discovery of quinine as a remedy for malaria, a new initiative was launched in 1854 which travelled up to 250 miles beyond the Niger-Benue confluence without a single fatality. In the face of the prospects, the new expedition opened up—establishment of agricultural settlements and opportunities of Christian mission among the indigenous people along the banks of the Niger—Crowther was commissioned to begin the work with Sierra Leone staff in 1857. In 1864, he was ordained Bishop of Western Equatorial Africa beyond the Queen's domain.

The mission led by Crowther worked among the Ijaw people of the Niger Delta, then known as Oil Rivers, employing the school as method of evangelisation. This was because the various trading houses involved in the Palm oil trade in the delta needed literate clerks who could do business with white men on behalf of their masters. The work of the mission was however dogged by intrigues and mutual jealousies among the ruling families who also controlled trade in the delta. The mission itself was frustrated by the growing racial feelings between the Sierra Leonean recruits of the mission and the British staff that managed the steamer that conveyed mission agents on the Niger. This was further complicated by the introduction into the mission young graduates who were now staffing the CMS from the late 1880s. And what is more, discipline broke down among the Sierra Leonean recruits of the Niger mission and this provided the alibi the young missionary recruits needed to dismiss and retire them. Debate continues whether the young recruits were racially motivated in dismantling the team put together by Bishop Crowther or whether they were responding to the moral crisis and mission method of the agents out of religious conviction. In spite of the difficulties that attended mission work in the delta, the churches founded there thrived, albeit with tension between protagonists of Christianity and defenders of indigenous religions.

For Further Reading[1]

LECTURE 6: PIONEERING IN WEST AFRICA 2—SOME RELIGIOUS ENCOUNTERS

The evangelization work of Protestant missions in Africa was an encounter with Africa's traditional institutions of religion, politics and family life. But nowhere in this encounter did the gap between the cultural world of European missionaries and their African prospects was as traumatic as their contrasting religious worldviews. Wherever mission deeply penetrated African society there was a reaction. In West Africa, three theatres of this encounter will be explored.

---

1 Baur, John. *2000 Years of Christianity in Africa*. Nairobi: Paulines Publications Africa, 1994, pp. 110-125, 127-129.

Clarke, Peter B. *West Africa and Christianity*. London: Edward Arnold, 1986, pp. 30-85.

Falk, Peter. *The Growth of the Church in Africa*. Jos: African Christian Textbooks, 1997, pp. 102-141.

Sundkler, Bengt and Christopher Steed. *A History of the Church in Africa*. Cambridge: CUP, 2000, pp. 179-248.

Nananom, a divinity connected with the Fante tradition of origin, had emerged as a national divinity of the people with its grove located at Mankessim. With its fame developed a cult of priests who held powerful sway over the people and were held in awe. Through these priests, Nananom emerged as an oracle "able to give guidance to men stumbling in the darkness of imperfect knowledge… [and was] expected to give audible advice when consulted." But the cult was more than a cult of divination. It included in its operational strategy a "spy system…set up by the priests', through which 'information of a most detailed kind was collected about all sorts of people". The result was such that "when men and women…came seeking confirmation of their suspicions, the oracle spoke of such intimate details that no doubts arose about the supernatural powers of Nananom." This was the situation when Thomas Birch Freeman arrived in the Gold Coast in 1835.

Events that led to the exposure of the fraud of the priests of Nananom began to unfold in the year 1849. That year an old Fante man, Kwesi, left his village, Asafa, to camp at Obidan because of malicious gossip that he was involved in witchcraft. Obidan was located midway between Asafa and Mankessim. About the same time, a member of the Methodist Church at Anomabu, Kwasi Ata, came to found a church in Asafa. In Ata's later contact with estranged Kwesi, they forged a friendship that resulted in the founding of a Christian fellowship at Obidan. Being in the vicinity of Mankessim, the development made the priest of Nananom uncomfortable. In view of the growth of the fellowship at Obidan and the unrestrained enthusiasm of its members in their tirades against the cult of Nananom, the stage was set for a clash. The potential for violence continued to build up when in successive events Kwasi Ata shot a deer around the Mankessim grove and one of the junior priests of Nananom, Edwumadzi, embraced the Gospel and joined the growing band of Christians in Obidan. This was too much for the votaries of Nananom, and they waited for an auspicious moment to nip in the bud the growing threat to their institution. The opportunity came when the renegade priest led two other Christians to cut wood from the grove earlier violated by Kwasi. They made a good use of the opportunity. The chief of Mankessim, Edu, "led a great company of excited men to Obidan, brutally flogged and imprisoned the Christians, burnt down their houses and destroyed their farms."

The arbitration of Brodie Cruickshank, then the Judicial Assessor of the British administration at Cape Coast, in the matter led to more revelations about the cult. Not satisfied with Cruikshank's verdict on their action, Edu, on behalf of the cult, appealed for a re-hearing of the case. Their plan to kill by poisoning three members of the Methodist Church at Anomabu who stood for the Christians at Obidan during the first hearing leaked out and was confirmed to be true during the second hearing. The intended contrivance of the deaths of the three advocates was to serve as evidence of the power of Nananom and its revenge for the violation of its territory by the Christians. In rapid succession, authenticated revelations came up from former priests of the cult on the deceptions, frauds, and immoral escapades of the priests of Nananom. All these stripped the cult of its awe and cast it in a bad light among the people over whom it had had full sway. In the harsh judgement that followed, public flogging and imprisonment, the myth surrounding the cult evaporated. The triumph of the Christian community knew no bounds and was captured in the words of the Wesleyan superintendent of Anomabu Circuit as he wrote that:

The confidence of the people here and in the neighbourhood has been much shaken. The national gods of the Fantes, Hanamu (sic), are now forsaken; no one consults them. No human power could have done this, only the preaching of Christ crucified. The people are at this time hesitating between two opinions; all our energies are therefore required to win them for Christ. In Asafa, paganism is tottering and there are hopes of its downfall on some future day, thus making way for the triumphant advance of the gospel chariot.

AKYEM ABUAKWA (GOLD COAST)

At their entry into Kyebi around 1850, Basel missionaries enjoyed the acceptance and the goodwill of the chiefs and people of Akyem. This was not unconnected with the appreciation of the growing improvement in the material culture of the people of Akuapem where the missionaries had hitherto stationed. There, Andreas Riis' building exploits had earned him the title *Osiadan*, the 'house builder.' The result was that in the first fifteen years of their mission work in Kyebi, Basel missionaries enjoyed a good relationship with the people of Akyem Abuakwa.

227

[The Okyehene, Atta Obuom] readily sold the mission land for the construction of a mission station at Kyebi and even listened to two sermons from Suss on the difference between 'right' and 'wrong'. Obuom counted the Basel missionaries among his political advisors and twice invited them to sit with his Council to debate on pressing political matters. On another occasion, he employed two missionaries as his emissaries. Okyehene Obuom took keen interest in the affairs of the Kyebi Primary School. In 1863, he enrolled his son at the school and did not object to his baptism during the third quarter of 1866. Occasionally the Okyehene showed signs of hostility towards the missionaries. Such behaviour occurred in moments of aberration and proved transient.

There is no doubt that such an environment of mutual goodwill was what the missionaries needed to plant the Gospel among the people. As long as the missionaries kept away from local politics and added value to the living standard of their hosts by training them in new vocations like carpentry, masonry, and improved farming techniques, the goodwill continued. But after the demise of Okyehene Obuom, events took a turn for the worse, unleashing a season of recriminations and social turmoil in Akyem Abuakwa. What went wrong?

Basel missionaries had in fifteen years poured human and material resources into the work in Akyem. Schools had been built, churches had been established, and several evangelistic overtures had been made to the people; but in their estimation, the results did not justify the resources expended. In the view of the missionaries, the school system did not appear to be making the desired impact of securing converts; the few converts were school pupils, pawns and household slaves who were allowed by their owners to attend church or be baptised.

This in itself certainly cast the church in a bad light as essentially a community for the disadvantaged and the servile. It is therefore not surprising that it could not make much impact, having drawn its followers from among the un-influential, many of whom were still strangers and captives.

But Basel missionaries would not, like their Wesleyan counterparts in the Fante country, fold their hands bemoaning their lot in Akyem; rather, they intensified their methods of conservation and vigorous expansion. To conserve the little gains they had made, the missionaries encouraged their converts to move from their homes among their people and settle in their mission stations, which they called *Salem*, but which the local people called *oburonikurom*, Whiteman's village. Occasionally, the missionaries defied the orders of the paramount chief and threatened his authority with that of the British governor on the coast. In desperation, the missionaries reached for all the slaves in Akyem society, including those serving in the palace and those dedicated to the gods. The missionaries bought over slaves and encouraged them to pay their ransom fees by rendering to them services in the Salem. Many slaves saw in this the opportunity to buy back their freedom and were assisted to pay-off their masters.

The implication of this was not lost on the people. The labourers to farm the fields were being lost. The missionaries were not interested in fragmenting Akyem Abuakwa society, although that was the immediate effect of their strategy at conserving their gains. But in being overly concerned about what they considered as a slow pace in the progress of their work, they drove themselves to desperation. They even reached for state functionaries among whom they succeeded in winning over Yaw Boakye, the chief state drummer.

The missionaries' frustration with their inability to generate bandwagon effect led to their undermining the traditional institutions of Akyem Abuakwa. With effort intentionally directed at the palace, conversion to Christianity meant loss of personnel necessary for state functions. While Okyehene Amoako Atta I, did not oppose the conversion of persons, slave or freeborn, he could not stand watching his state functionaries abandon their duties and, in his reckoning, undermine the wellbeing of the state. He protested vehemently:

Must I let my horn-blowers, my drummers, my pipers…my sword bearers and executioners, my hammock-carriers, etc., become Christians? If I do, then I can no longer carry out my (fetish) ceremonies, nor can I receive foreign embassies worthily. Whoever has an obligation to serve me…will never be allowed to become a Christian.

In the protracted crisis that ensued, the British colonial government annexed Akyem Abukwa, hitherto a protectorate, and incorporated it into the Gold Coast and proscribed domestic slavery and pawning. At a stage during the crisis, the Okyehene was banished to Lagos but reinstated five years later. His return led to the final showdown with the mission during which he died in the custody of the colonial government at Accra. The crisis created economic difficulties in Akyem Abuakwa, and members of the royal household who could not adjust to a new life-style in the absence of the king took to extortion and crime to maintain themselves.

IBADAN

Consequent to the internecine wars that ravaged Yoruba land in the nineteenth century, Ibadan emerged as the military base of Oyo warriors and, later, the settlement of displaced peoples of the country. Samuel Johnson wrote that the city, ever at war with its neighbours, was 'destined by God to play a most important part in the history of the Yorubas, to break the Fulani yoke and save the rest of the country from foreign domination…to be a protector as well as the scourge in the land.' The leaders of the fledgling city were at the height of their belligerence when the Rev. David Hinderer visited them on May 16, 1851, in an exploratory mission of planting the Gospel there.

The Basel-trained, German missionary of the Church Missionary Society had, shortly after the abortive Dahomian invasion of Abeokuta, received permission from Sokenu and other Egba chiefs to take the Gospel to Ibadan. Although Ibadan was not at peace with its neighbours at this time, Egba chiefs granted the request of the missionary. Well received by the Baale of Ibadan, the paramount chief, and other four influential chiefs of the city, David Hinderer explained to them his mission. The first rebuttal came from the Baale's Osi who, being a staunch Moslem, opposed the missionary's intention. He vehemently resisted the plan in the verbal attack, *"Awon obaiye je ni iwonyi"*. (These are the world spoilers), "There is no country they enter but misfortune will follow for that place".

A dissenting response, and no less forceful, was offered by the Otun: *"But white men are at Lagos, Badagry, and Abeokuta; why should we be the last to receive them, and whatever be the consequence to others let the same be to us also."*

The imminent impasse was avoided through the counsel of the Balogun who advised that *Ifa*, the national god of divination, be consulted, and on the basis of its counsel, the chiefs could decide the fortune, or otherwise, of the missionary and his message in Ibadan. The outcome of this consultation favoured the presence of Rev. Hinderer in the city, and he was soon accorded a warm reception and properly accommodated to carry out his work unhindered. The search for a final solution to the wars was initiated by the Alafin Adeyemi in his letter of October 15, 1881, to the British governor in Lagos, W. B. Griffiths; this was with the advice of the indigenous church agents at Ibadan. Although it proved to be a long and tortuous search, it marked the involvement of the fledgling Christian community of Yoruba land in the socio-political currents of the time. The role of Ibadan agents of CMS in the crisis was redemptive and contributed to rescuing Yoruba people from their precipitous state, to later usher in a festive mood of thanksgiving throughout the land in 1892. Can we then conclude that Ifa's divination was right when it endorsed Hinderer's mission to Ibadan in 1851?

For Further Reading[1]

LECTURE 7: PIONEERING IN SOUTHERN AFRICA

The history of the church in Southern Africa is one of the most intriguing stories of Christian mission on the continent. The intersection of commerce, race, politics and religion in the southern end of the continent was, indeed, the manifestation of human nature both in its worst and in its most beneficent elements. And this was not just between Europeans and the indigenous people of the land but also among Europeans themselves. At the roots of this were the settler culture and the forces of disintegration and migration that was at work in the region.

---

1 Addo-Fening, Robert. Akyem Abuakwa 1700-1943: From Ofori Panin to Sir Ofori Ata. Trondheim: Norwegian University of Science and Technology (NTNU), 1997.

Bartels, F L. The Roots of Ghana Methodism. London: Cambridge University Press, 1965.

Johnson, Samuel. The History of the Yorubas—From the Earliest Times to the Beginning of the British Protectorate. Lagos: CMS, 1921.

Reindorf, Carl Christian. The History of the Gold Coast and Asante. 2nd ed. Accra: Ghana Universities Press, 1966.

The Dutch settlers lost the control of the Cape to the British government in 1795. In the unfolding policies of the new power, greatly influenced by British missionaries, citizenship in the colony was liberalized and all races were declared equal. The Boers (Dutch settler farmers), who were disaffected by the policy, embarked between 1836 and 1840 on the "Great Trek" northward from the Cape in search of the Promised Land. Literally fighting their way through, the trek destabilized the Nguni communities of the Eastern Cape and others within the vicinity, further compounding the disturbed situation already created by the wars among the Zulu nation, the *Mfecane*. The wars, which had knock-on effects just short of Lake Victoria in East Africa, as displaced people groups under pressure were forced to move and create space for others who had been displaced, and so creating in succession new lords and new vassals. Much of the pioneer work of Christian missions in 19th century Southern Africa took place in this environment of instability and shifting power base. Protestant missions were at the vanguard of the movement to evangelise the people while the established Church of England and the Roman Catholics would join the work fifty years later.

THE MORAVIANS AMONG THE KHOI-COLOURED

Shortly before the realities of large scale wars and displacements began to unfold in the 19th century, half a century after the expulsion of George Schmidt from the colony by the Dutch settler-farmers (Boers) for baptising himself his Khoi converts, the Moravians returned in 1792 to Genadendal. The Dutch East India Company had relaxed its law which then permitted them to return to their work in South Africa. On arrival, they were surprised to find that the convert community left behind by Schmidt were still meeting but under the pear tree planted by the missionary. Now aged Magdalena (Lena) still read the Dutch New Testament she inherited from the missionary but with the assistance of a helper, she having lost her sight. Genadendal became the mission station from where the Moravians re-launched their work.

The Moravians were known for their schools, especially the infant school. At Genadendal, the infant school provided early form of teacher training. The institution relied on indigenous leadership. The Khoi "captains" of the place held great authority, with a baton as symbol of office. It is characteristic of the atmosphere of the place that one of the regulations read: "The missionaries derive their authority from the congregations." Most of the missionaries were Prussians who had served in other Moravian fields for upward of six years. They were hardworking, enterprising and patriarchal. They also had the additional virtue of being highly musical. The hymns and the congregational singing were a great help in attracting people to the chapel. However, in spite of the stated principle that missionaries derive their authority from the congregations Moravians were poor in indigenising their church in South Africa. Seventy years after the renewal of the mission the field superintendent, J.F. Kuhn, objected to the ordination of a Coloured leader Joseph Hardenburg. In disagreement with the Elders' Conference in Herrnhut, Germany, he insisted in 1862 that it would be premature to do so and so refused the leader ordination.

THE LONDON MISSIONARY SOCIETY

Another mission that worked in the Cape was the Congregationalist London Missionary Society (LMS). Its two pioneer missionaries were more experienced and of the middle age in contrast to the young missionaries of the period. John Philip was a Scot and more of an administrator than a missionary; he gave out information to western missions about opportunities for service in South Africa. Active in the Western Cape and seen by the Boers as a meddler, he facilitated in South Africa the enforcement of 1833 proscription of slavery in British dominions and thereby triggered the protest of the Dutch farmers in the "Great Trek".

Johannes Theodore van der Kemp was Dutch with a degree in medicine from Edinburgh. He came to the Eastern Cape about 1800 and sought to work among the Bantu-speaking people, the Xhosa, but the endemic state of warfare among them made things difficult. He spent about a year among them and was respected by the people as a healer and a competent rainmaker. Having been greatly influenced by the Moravians after his conversion he established the Bethelsdorp "institution", near Port Elizabeth after the Moravian Genadendal, as a place of refuge for the many displaced coloured peoples. He was accused by the government at Cape Town for not making efforts to clothe the Coloureds and not encouraging them in the habits of industry, thrift, cleanliness, and subservience to the White ruling class.

233

There was no evidence that van der Kemp was not interested in the material improvement of his congregation as he sought to give them education. Even in this, he was involved in bitter dispute with the governor concerning the teaching of literacy to the Coloureds. His lifestyle did not endear him to the government as he went about bare-footed like the people among whom he worked and, worse still, married a Malagasy woman.

Bethelsdorp's first decade was characterised by poor growth. It lay on a poor soil, and water was scarce. Its shelters were temporary huts as the people looked forward to moving to more promising site. Worse still, the able-bodied men of the community were often away to Boer farms as labour hands. Teaching in the faith was irregular with students often absent and missionaries often ill; catechumens underwent long period of instruction; baptism was often delayed due both to the scruples of the candidates and the hesitations of the missionaries. The coloured members of the congregation served as the deacons and deaconesses. The Khoi converts served as interpreters when new mission stations were established at Kat River, Griquatown, Theopolis and Kuruman.

The major role the LMS played in early 19th century South African mission was akin to the role of the CMS in West Africa, drawing from the goodwill of liberal evangelical circle in Britain to advance the interest of indigenous people. But the "independent" policy of the mission resulted in its early withdrawal from the Cape for work further north, beginning with Kat River mission. Perhaps the most widely acknowledged achievement of LMS was the result of the travels of David Livingstone.

The missionary doctor, born 1813 in Blantyre, Scotland, made his way deep into Africa by the force of his will. His initial ambition was to be a medical missionary to China, but Robert Mofatt of Kuruman succeeded in shifting his focus towards Africa, giving him his daughter Mary in marriage. Livingstone found the South African field over-populated with missionaries and was at once determined to look for new grounds further north into the interior of Africa. Within a few months of arrival in Africa he was on an exploration tour of Bechuanaland (Botswana) 400km north-east of Kuruman. There he encountered *Sechele,* chief of Kwena, a Tswana Bantu people. Breaking off from his colleagues in the south, he temporarily settled among them with his wife at Kolobeng, learning their language and adopting their lifestyle as he taught them the Christian message. Sechele whet his appetite for exploration when he told him about a great lake and a powerful chief to the north (*Sebetwane of the Makololo*).

Following the lead and concluding that the future of mission lay in that direction, he crossed the Kalahari Desert in the company of two hunters and discovered the lake Ngami. After this experience in 1849, he did not look back but became, till his death in 1873, more of an explorer in search of mission prospects on the continent than being a missionary himself. Livingstone's exploratory achievements were acknowledged by the Royal Geographical Society, but he was more appreciated by his Christian constituency only after his death which stimulated missionary efforts in Eastern Africa. He brought home to British audience the ravages of Arab slave trade in East Africa and put pressures on the government to set up colonies in Africa to spread Britain's beneficent civilization and heal "the open sore of a continent".

PRESBYTERIANS AND METHODISTS

The evangelisation of the numerous Bantu along the eastern coast was a most hazardous enterprise on account of their conflicts with the Boers. It was eventually the Scottish Presbyterians who were able to establish, from 1824, a permanent centre among the Xhosa north of the Great Fish River: *Lovedale.* Under the leadership of James Stewart in the 1860s, the place was to develop into the greatest educational centre of Southern Africa, a famous training school for teachers and pastors. In the same year, 1824, the Methodists opened their first mission called Wesleyville, which soon evolved into a chain of six stations along the coastline, a sign that they were to grow into the church with the largest African membership in the country; only in recent years were they overtaken by the Catholics.

THE BOERS AND THEIR SETTLER THEOLOGY

A leading spokesperson of the Boers said that the main reason for the Great Trek was not so much the freedom given to the slaves but "their being placed on an equal footing with Christians, contrary to the laws of God and the natural distinction of race and colour, so that it was intolerable for any decent Christian". And the only real objection Boers had to the preaching of the Gospel was that missionaries did not teach that whites were a superior race. The economic and power relations between the settlers and the indigenous peoples created and reinforced this mind-set among the Boers. Without white labour, manual work was largely done by coloured people and was regarded as "Kaffir work". And they found justification for their anthropology from the Bible, essentially from Genesis 9. According to them, like the popular Christian interpretation of the period, the Cushite (Greek: Ethiopians) were all Africans and they had inherited the curse of Ham; the evidence of this, according to the interpretation, is the strong African sexuality, of which polygamy seemed to be one of the most obvious signs. But while a Catholic missionary like Father Comboni would pray for the salvation of the "unfortunate children of Ham", the Calvinist Boers just classified them as a "cursed race", in contrast to their own community of the elect. From this perception, their attitude towards the indigenous peoples of Southern Africa flowed for nearly two hundred years till the last decade of the twentieth century.

FRONTIER SPIRITUALITY

Generally, all the missions enforced the observation of "The Sabbath". In the Moravian institutions, the singing of hymns in the Dutch language prevailed and the converts enjoyed them. But for the Khoi the first chapter of Genesis—on the creation, the Fall, the Flood, and the anticipation of the last judgement—attracted keen attention. Experiences of dreams and visions were greatly influenced by apocalyptic images, leading to crying, repentance and conversion. The psychological environment of powerlessness in the face of violence, displacements and uprooted-ness also informed spirituality as this prayer formulated by the Griqua indicates:

Lord, save thy people. Lord, we are lost unless Thou savest us.
Lord, this is no work for children. It is not enough to send thy Son.
Lord, Thou must come thyself.

Certain symbols, such as blood and wounds were particularly disturbing to the Moravian Khoi. A Moravian historian writes:

The efforts of the missionaries centred around the impression of the Cross of the Saviour on the heart of their flock.... A little boy, when asked to state his faith, took off his *kaross* (cloak of animal skins with the hair on) and pointing to his side, head, and feet, said: "Those the saviour has suffered for me". When the moon was red one evening another child was also instantly reminded of the Saviour's wound, and a man dreamt that he saw a stream of blood pouring forth from the moon. Significantly, the moon played an important part in the traditional religion of the Khoi. A possible continuation of the old ritual practices were Christian prayer meetings held in the open air at the time of the full moon.

For Further Reading[1]

LECTURE 8: PIONEERING IN EASTERN AFRICA

The roads that led to the evangelisation of the peoples on the eastern part of the African continent in the 19th century led from three directions—from the north, from the east coast and from the south. The first party, coming from the north through the Nile and among whom was Johann Ludwig Krapf, aimed at reaching the Galla people (the Oromo) of Ethiopia. The party fell short of its goal being frustrated by the Ethiopian prince, Sàhela Selàssè. Krapf devised another route from the east coast to reach the people and thereby flagged-off in 1844 Protestant missions from that direction with base in Zanzibar. The third road led from the south as a result of the continuing effect of David Livingstone's explorations on the Zambezi and the Shire Highlands (Malawi). Effectively we can explore the mission from the east coast and the one from the south.

MISSION FROM THE EAST COAST

The first missionary to knock at the door of the Sultan of Zanzibar was Dr Johann Krapf. He was given permission to stay at Mombasa and "to convert the unbelieving world". In the first two years, while waiting for a companion from his mission, the CMS, he translated the New Testament into Swahili. When John Rebmann joined him, the two moved to Rabai Mpya, among the "pagan" Giriama people, the largest of the nine groups of the original costal population derogatorily call Wanyika (Bush people). The missionaries' message of "fallen man" and 'merciful God" was a failure among them; they regarded sin only as a social evil and God's love as experienced in rain and palm wine. They were forced looked further and in the process sighted the snow-capped Kilimanjaro and the Chagga people who lived on its slope. The people were interested in contact with Europeans chiefly for the reason of trade. Krapf and his successors could not grant their request of a mission staffed by artisans and a doctor.

1 Baur, John. *2000 Years of Christianity in Africa*. Nairobi: Paulines Publications Africa, 1994, pp. 188-206.

Falk, Peter. *The Growth of the Church in Africa*. Jos: African Christian Textbooks, 1997, pp. 142-188.

Hildebrandt, Jonathan. *History of the Church in Africa*. Achimota: Africa Christian Press, 1990, pp. 172-180.

Sundkler, Bengt and Christopher Steed. *A History of the Church in Africa*. Cambridge: CUP, 2000, pp. 323-374.

A more promising mission among the Akamba turned into disaster when their chief, Kivoi, was murdered by robbers while exploring with Krapf if Tana River was navigable for access to interior people. The Akamba chiefs forgave the missionary, who had shot into the air to scare the robbers rather than kill them. Krapf was invalided to Europe in 1853 while Rebmann continued for another twenty years, concentrating with a colleague J. J. Ehrhardt on literary activities.

They considered it premature to attempt to begin mission in the interior. Their attempt to establish a firm base on the coast by running an agricultural estate also failed.

BUGANDA AND MISSION FROM THE SOUTH

In his search for a way for the gospel to Central Africa, David Livingstone realised that the route from the south was impossible because of the Kalahari Desert and the desperate activities of the Boers for survival. The other option was to locate an east-west highway from where missions could reach "central Africa" and the Arab slave trade suppressed. From 1852, he succeeded in crossing the continent from Luanda on the west coast to Quilimane on the east coast in two and a half years. He was assisted by Makololo porters and troops. His success in crossing the continent led his mission organisation, the London Missionary Society (LMS), to send two missions to the Zambezi and the emergence of the *Universities' Mission to Central Africa (UMCA)*. Livingstone still had a larger vision of what could be done in Africa and determined to return to Africa to open wide path for Commerce and Christianity. His idea was in line with that of Thomas Fowell Buxton who saw the promotion of legitimate commerce as the remedy against slave trade in Africa. His further exploration in this regard led to his loss of contact with the wider world during which Henry Morton Stanley went in the search for him. It was Stanley, having in his subsequent visit crossed Africa from the east coast to the west and discovered the court of Kabaka, who broadcast to western missions the generous prospect of evangelising Buganda.

When the missions arrived in Buganda, Kabaka Mutesa I (1857-84) became a man at cross-roads, faced with four religions which were in turn coupled with four political powers. He walked the road of traditional religion, strongly supported by his chief; he met successively Islam from Zanzibar, Protestantism from England and

Catholicism from France. He went along each road a few steps, and then returned to where he had come from. As a shrewd politician, he attempted a policy of balance of power.

The Moslems were the first foreigners to appear in Buganda. Coming in 1844, they were traders and messengers of their faith. While Mutesa's father had expelled them, the son experimented with the religion of book, encouraged his people to follow the faith and built mosques for them. The converts proved more committed to the faith and challenged him for refusing circumcision. After Stanley's visit they put more pressure on him fearing he was about to convert to Christianity. When the Egyptian ruler sent Gordon Pasha to find the source of the Nile, he feared the contact between Egypt and the Moslems in his domain might prove treacherous. To preserve himself, he purged his court by having seventy chiefs burned, while Moslems were killed countrywide and hundreds fled to the coast.

In response to Stanley's sanguine comment about the prospect of making converts in Buganda, the CMS sent a religious-technical mission, one priest and seven laymen, under the leadership of Alexander Mackay. The first two missionaries arrived in June 1877. Mutesa agreed to Bible lessons and in turn asked them to make gun powder. He saw in these British missionaries a welcome way to balance the Arab. On their side, the CMS were full of hope to establish the Anglican Church in the Bugandan Kingdom. They were, therefore, disappointed when within two years they had to face competition from the Roman Catholic White Fathers. The CMS could not persuade Mutesa to expel the Catholics; he even enjoyed the controversies between them although he regretted that the Catholics could not secure him the advantage of protection by France. Within a year, he received baptisms from the CMS and from the Catholics, reached out olive branch to the Moslems again, and performed human sacrifices to appease a local divinity. Soon he declared Islam as a state religion and confessed why it was difficult to follow the Christian faith, "Our wealth in women kills us". Until Mutesa's death everything remained quiet, as he played one faith against another.

But the missions were making progress among the masses while the king was busy toying with religions. The young Baganda movement towards Christianity was under way. The number of people from the court, especially the pages, who came to read and to hear the Good News, increased from day to day. The term "reader" became identical with "Christian" and "man of the new elite". They were not only convinced at heart but grew also very apostolic in mind. Among them were to emerge, three years later, martyrs of the African church.

Kabaka Mutesa I died in 1884 and was succeeded the following year by his eighteen year old son Kabaka Mwanga, an unstable character capable of unpredictable actions. What is more, he was not only addicted to homosexuality but also to the smoking of cannabis. At the beginning of his reign, he was under the influence of the Arabs and the traditionalist chiefs led by Kattikiro Mukasa (the *katikkiro* was the office of Kabaka's chief administrator). To consolidate their position they instilled in him the fear of British aggression as demonstrated by the recent occupation of the Tanzanian coast by Germans. He then became suspicious of Mackay. When the missionary refused to be accompanied by an official from his court while travelling south, Mwanga burned three of his young Christians.

He killed the first East African Bishop, James Hannington, and his fifty porters for approaching Buganda from a forbidden direction. But the news leaked through some of the court pages that the decision to kill the bishop was taken at Mwanga's court council. The man held responsible for the indiscretion was Majordomo Joseph Mukasa Baalikuddembe, aged twenty-five, the leading Christian at the court. Joseph had often shielded the pages from the evil desires of the king and even tried to convert him. He pleaded with him not to kill the bishop and reproached him after he did. In a fit of rage, Mwanga condemned him to be burned. In the following months, there were a number of incidents that caused tension to build up, such as the mysterious fire that destroyed the court at Mengo, and Princess Nalumansi's profanation of the national divinities.

But most infuriating for the king was the growing disobedience of the pages, resisting his private desires and prohibition against visiting the missions. This challenge to the Kabaka's traditional absolute authority was the main reason that provoked the persecution. He once told Fr. Lourdel, head of the Catholic mission, "I am master here, I am Kabaka, I do not want anybody to resist me".

The persecution was by no means systematic or general. The main victims were the pages on whom Mwanga's outbursts of anger fell after he discovered that even his most beloved playboy had become a catechumen. Some thirty of them were condemned to death, together with their leader Charles Lwanga. Other victims were sorted out by the katikkiro: mainly leading Christians— the royal bandmaster and chief of Kigowa, assistant chief of Ssingo county, the two Protestant leaders (the blacksmith and the gatekeeper). Others were just caught up in the storm of unleashed anti-Christian feelings; some chiefs killed even non-Christians to please the Kabaka. The day of the great holocaust was June 3, when thirty-one were burnt alive on the pyres of Namugongo, mainly pages. At the end of the persecution one hundred or more had died. The Catholic Church had twenty-two of them beatified in 1920 and canonized in 1964. Their courageous testimony brought forth a new wave of conversions, and soon Mwanga was told by the katikkiro that there were so many Christians that their extinction would be impossible. After the persecution, Mwanga remained as unpredictable as ever. He made two Christian leaders, Protestant and Catholic, commanders of new regiments. Under them two Christian parties developed, each mustering some one thousand men.

The Moslems had only eight hundred but received a lot of arms from the Arabs; they were the most dangerous party. Suddenly, Mwanga fell back for support on his discontented traditionalist chiefs and planned to get rid of all "foreigners". The plan leaked and the Christians joined forces with the Moslems to depose Mwanga and install his eldest brother, Kiwewa, in his stead. The latter made the Catholic regiment leader his katikkiro. The confederacy lasted for only forty-two days.

The Moslems unexpectedly fired on the assembled Christian chiefs, who fled to Ankole. The new king was deposed for refusing circumcision and replaced by his more compliant brother, Kalema. The rule of the Moslems lasted about two years during which all missions were plundered and missionaries expelled; they took refuge at the southern end of the lake. Mwanga joined the White fathers now ready to attend catechism class. An alliance between the Catholics and the Protestants eventually saw Mwanga reinstated after ten months of civil war in which the Moslems were defeated.

Matters did not end with the defeat of the Moslems. The Christians turned against one another: the Catholics, Bafranza, against their Protestant counterparts, Bangereza. The competition for political offices connected with large grants of land became often more important than the religious issue. An interesting issue was that the Kabaka, as an institution, remained a powerful symbol, but in the case of Mwanga, who had lost all moral authority, he was no more than a pawn in the political game. Perhaps most unfortunate in the unfolding scenario was the fact that the two parties were deprived of their influential leaders as a result of deaths.

The final showdown between the two Christian groups was caused by the sharing of offices after the war against the Moslems. The ecumenical arrangement in which state offices had been equally awarded to the Catholic and the Protestant office holder broke down as more catechumen joined Catholics. The war that ensued brought about the intervention of the British government, leading to the declaration of Buganda and its adjoining kingdoms first as a protectorate and later as a colony.

THE SPREAD OF THE GOSPEL

However much the Catholic-Protestant confrontation is to be deplored, it also had positive side-effect of precipitating conversion in Buganda, making it the first Christian country south of the Sahara. Almost overnight, the controversy shifted from traditional faith or Islam or Christianity to Protestant or Catholic. Yet in actual figures the two churches counted in 1890 only 2,000 members each, together not even one percent of the total population. Twenty years later, their share was well over 40% in Buganda and some 7% in the rest of Uganda.

During the twenty years between the erection of the Protectorate and World War I, when Britain extended its power into the neighbouring kingdoms and the whole area together with Buganda became modern Uganda, Christianity spread along the same lines, usually in competing race between Protestants and Catholics.

Protestants had the advantage of a majority of Baganda chiefs whose services were commonly used to establish the British

242

administration and who propagated their own church. The advantage of the Catholics lay in the number of their missionaries. But for both church traditions, the lay apostles played a most important role.

In the Anglican Church, a revival movement, initiated by the missionary George Pilkington, took place in 1893-4 and aroused a storm of evangelism, bringing Baganda evangelists as far as the Congo and the Sudan. They set out, in their hands the Bible that Pilkington had arranged to have translated for them by an African-European team. They founded churches in other ancient kingdoms of Toro, Bunyoro, and Ankole. Although the Anglicans were ahead of their Catholic counterparts in moving into new territories, the latter soon overtook them in some of the kingdoms.

For Further Reading[1]

LECTURE 9: THE ROMAN CATHOLIC MISSIONS IN THE MODERN ERA

It is widely acknowledged that Protestant agencies pioneered Christian mission in the modern world. Consequently, the role of the Roman Catholics in the extension of the Christian message to "the end of the world" in this period tends to be underestimated or completely ignored. Yet it should be acknowledged that although they were slow in taking off, their exertions were no less vigorous than those of their Protestant counterparts. And what is more, the pioneer of their efforts in modern Africa was a woman, *Mother Javouhey* (St. Anne Mary Javouhey) who founded the *Congregation of St. Joseph of Cluny*. In 1819, she sent her first sisters to take charge of the hospitals in St. Louis and Goree, the first colonies of France in Africa. Her attempt to set up a Christian village on the river Senegal failed, yet her journey to Bathurst and Freetown on the invitation of the British Governor, who wanted his hospital reorganized, convinced her that civilization must go together with Christianity in the conversion of Africa. When she sought Papal approval for her congregation, the Superior of Holy Ghost Fathers protested, fearing unpleasant competition in the French colonies. Mother Javouhey's lasting achievement is that she shook off the despair of her church and proclaimed a new age in mission after centuries of failed attempts and un-sustained efforts.

1 Baur, John. *2000 Years of Christianity in Africa*. Nairobi: Paulines Publications Africa, 1994, pp. 224-242.

Sundkler, Bengt and Christopher Steed. *A History of the Church in Africa*. Cambridge: CUP, 2000, pp. 562-592.

However, the man who eventually jump-started organized Catholic mission work in modern times was Fr. Francis Liebermann (1802-52).

Described as "an epileptic Jew, trying to help the most despised members of another despised race, the Negro slaves", he received conservative Jewish education, the values of which he abandoned for agnosticism at the first opportunity to leave his father's control. But he eventually found peace of soul in the Catholic Church. He read theology but shortly before the sub-diaconate, he was struck down by epilepsy. Though consequently barred from the priesthood he remained in the seminary, where he received encouragement from two of his colleagues to found a society for the evangelisation of the Negro slaves soon to be emancipated in the French colonies. His plan matured. His health improved. And he was ordained a priest, after which he opened a novitiate for his *Society of the Holy Heart of Mary.*

The society had as its basic ideal "to announce the holy Gospel and establish His kingdom among the poor and most neglected people in the Church of God". Concretely, it should be in the service of the whole Negro race and aim at both an African clergy and an African civilization. The African he was talking of were those in the French colonies of Reunion, Madagascar and Haiti. His spiritual doctrine of surrendering oneself to God's providence and guidance through the Spirit left him open to any future adaptation. The opportunities of his society for service in Africa were complicated by the Holy Ghost Fathers who saw themselves as the legitimate society to function in French territories. The problem was solved when his society merged with theirs and Liebermann became the leader of the resultant society. He died in 1852, broken by nervous disorder that came upon him again in the last months of his life.

Liebermann's chief principle in mission was the establishment of an indigenous church and not just the baptism of as many as possible. He insisted on carefully deliberated planning for the future. *"The ten souls you save by a hurried and ill-conceived step, by a measure which produces an immediate good result, may perhaps mean the loss of more than a hundred thousand."* The *conditio sine qua non* for an indigenous church was "to form a native clergy rooted in the country, a native hierarchy".

The first means to achieve this was to be *the missionary's personal holiness, preserved by community life.*

The second was *national detachment and missionary adaptation* (i.e. crossing cultures).

The third was to *bring to the African both religion and civilization.*

MISSIONS IN WEST AFRICA

Assisted by other smaller societies the three major missionary movements of the Catholic Church with significant impact on West Africa, beginning from the 19th century, were the Society of African Missions (SMA), the Holy Ghost Fathers and the White Fathers. The first two worked in the forest belt of West Africa having come into the region by way of the sea; the first eventually extended its work beyond the Niger and Benue rivers and successfully established the Catholic faith in what is today Northern Nigeria. The third made its entry into the Western Sudan from North Africa.

Early Roman Catholicism in Nigeria dated back to the activities of "Padre Antonio", a catechist who had been educated as a slave in a Brazilian monastery and had come back as a pastor to his former companions. He built a chapel for them, held services and catechism classes, baptised children, blessed the marriages, visited the sick and buried the dead. At the opening of the SMA mission in Lagos, their first permanent holding in Africa, Pa Antonio was succeeded by an ordained priest in 1868. But the Catholic Yoruba Church was hedged in from three sides: by the traditional religion, Islam and Protestantism. It could hardly grow into mighty tree. The pews of Lagos Cathedral, the building completed in 1881, were for many years filled more by migrant Igbos than Yorubas. In the late 1890s, Abeokuta and Ibadan had at least a Catholic presence. The Abeokuta mission became popular as a medical centre only, and the importance of Ibadan rested in the seminary erected in 1908, which in 1929 produced the first three Yoruba priests.

The phenomenal success of the Catholics in West Africa was, however, achieved among the Igbo people of South-eastern Nigeria. Their missionaries made their way into the interior through the Niger River from whose banks SMA Fathers and the Holy Ghost Fathers evangelised the people. The former, with base at Asaba worked on the west bank while the latter, with base at Onitsha evangelised the east bank. It was on the east bank that the "miracle of school" promoted the work of Catholic mission in West Africa under Bishop Shanahan. Their success was not unconnected with the situation of the CMS mission in Onitsha when they arrived. Bishop Crowther offered them their first land holding in Onitsha. The gesture was however unreciprocated as the Holy Ghost Fathers, in the spirit of the time, were set to conquer the whole country for the "true faith".

The Catholics became popular for their charitable work, especially the free distribution of medicines. Fr Lutz had medical training and used his skills to win many Anglican children to his school. Next followed the crisis of the CMS Niger mission in which the new missionaries dismissed the "native agents" and enforced a stricter discipline. As a result, not a few of their members, including catechists, joined the Catholics. These two developments did not make the mission's work to grow phenomenally. The ultimate catalyst was the colonial conquest of Igboland, especially beginning with the 1901 expedition against the Long-Juju of Arochukwu. The intransigence of the Aros in refusing any foreign visitor, black or white, was seen as the major obstacle to the opening up of the country for trade and missions. Therefore, the missionaries supported the military expedition, and missions moved in after the dismantling of Aro dominance of the country. The arrival of a new regime in which Christianity and education became the means to appropriating new opportunities put missions in position of advantage.

It is against this background that we must appreciate the "school miracle" of Bishop Joseph Shanahan. He used the school as the exclusive means of evangelisation and abandoned the policy of liberating slaves and used subsidies from Rome for the schools. He was convinced that through the school the whole country would be won to Christ as the school children become "tiny apostles" to their homes and families. He left his base at Onitsha to the charge of his priests and brothers and combed the interior of Igboland, making impressions with his humanity and spirituality. His generous view of the Nigeria endeared him to his converts. The result: the number of Catholics doubled almost every third year. In 1931, when Shanahan retired, it just reached the 100,000 mark.

246

The White Fathers concentrated their efforts in Mali (then called French Sudan) especially in the more hilly regions south-east of the Niger and adjacent Burkina Faso (then Upper Volta); they reached as far as the northern parts of Guinea and Ghana. In these regions, there were ethnic groups which had not yet or only partially become Moslems, though Islam constituted a powerful presence in the whole Sudan belt. Like the Holy Ghost Fathers, they began their work among liberated slave children in the hope that it would later attract the surrounding indigenous peoples. It rather cast their work in a bad light as something for the servile class. They also had to contend with the anti-clerical attitude of the government in Paris who ordered the mission to close its orphanages and dispensaries while schools would then be run by colonial authorities. Some of the colonial agents also made efforts to frustrate and nauseate them. All these add to the unfavourable attitude of indigenous peoples towards Europeans in general because of their forced occupation of their territory.

In spite of their difficulties, White Fathers recorded success among the Mossi people of Burkina Faso. Their kingdom covered the greater part of the country. The White Fathers established their base at Ouagadougou (Wagadugu) in 1901 where the mission concentrated on the evangelisation of adults. Slowly a few Christian villages grew up; they counted 7000 in 1931. This modest success was amplified by the establishment of nursing schools which strengthened the health services of the White Sisters and their discovery of vaccines against river blindness, a devastating disease among the people. These achievements commended the mission to the people and earned them a good standing before the colonial government. They were therefore allowed to start their schools again, resulting in a flock that at the end of the 1940s had grown to 50,000. The fruits of the adult conversion method became visible in the days of Independence. That the first president of the country was a Catholic may be incidental. That the country's archbishop became the first francophone African cardinal could be attributed to the zeal of the White Fathers.

It was among the Dagati people of Northern Ghana that the White Fathers achieved their greatest success. They had been encouraged by a British representative to the French colonial office in Wagadugu to occupy Northern Ghana. At Navrongo, the people were only interested in the priests' dispensary. Polygamy was a major, though not the only obstacle. The Fathers then moved to the opposite north-western corner of the country where they opened a dispensary among the Dagaa. In two years, the mission was counting 7000 catechumen. Then the "rain miracles" followed. The converts were blamed for the drought of 1932 because they refused to sacrifice to the spirits.

When the elders sent to Fr McCoy to pray to God for them, he gave then conditions under which he would do so: no sacrifices to the spirits, no prohibition of visits to the mission, and no forcible marrying of their daughters. When all agreed he led them in prayer to God to whom they had never dared to pray before and rain fell overnight. The news spread over the whole area and on the average twenty delegations visited the mission per day. A new mass movement of conversion set in and spread to the Dagaa living on the other side of the Volta River.

MISSIONS IN SOUTHERN AFRICA

Having earlier been refused residence in 1818, the Catholics returned to South Africa in 1820 when the colony was opened to them. Ten years later, they were given full civil rights to operate, and in 1837, Rome re-erected the Vicariate Apostolic of the Cape of Good Hope and entrusted it to the Dominicans. There were just enough priests to serve immigrant Catholics in an environment where the Boers were very hostile. The proper work of evangelisation was, however, initiated by the French *Oblates of Mary Immaculate (OMI),* who arrived in 1852. They started work among Catholic immigrants in the new Vicariate Apostolic of Natal, which extended from Durban to Namibia and from River Kei to the Limpopo. Their hesitant beginning of mission did not impress the proud Zulu nation. Their teachings were countered with sophistic questions and general unbelief. Frustrated they moved to Basutoland (modern Lesotho) where the Protestant Mission of Paris was already at work among Chief Moshoeshoe's people. Despite meeting the request in 1865 of Basotho for a sewing school for their womenfolk, they refused to send their daughters there for fear that they might be converted and then insist on monogamy. For similar reasons later attempts at an indigenous sisterhood and priesthood failed.

The beginning of successful missions in South Africa can be dated to the aftermath of the Zulu War of 1878-79 when the British defeated Cetewayo, a grandson of the famous Shaka the Zulu. Until then the Lutherans had laboured to no success; now in the aftermath of their defeat they were open to European civilization. This opened the opportunity for the founding of the *Marianhill* by Abbot Francis Pfanner, who arrived from Austria in 1882. With the thirty monks in his party, he founded the *Trappist Monastery*. Seeing a vast un-evangelised field, he gave priority to missionary ideal over the monastic. In ten years, his mission grew into 300 members, built several outstations in addition to the central one. He populated these estates with "pagan' as well as Zulu converts, thus creating Christian villages that were open to the indigenous people. These people he initiated into new agricultural methods. His evangelising method was his work philosophy, which applied to him and every member of his communities: "Nobody has to work more than I do."

Pfanner hated apartheid; the only discrimination acceptable to him was to be in favour of the poor. In his school, the sons of rich farmers could be admitted only if there was enough room. In promoting female education, he went for young farmers' daughters in Germany, because the task ahead demanded "valiant women," not "lady sisters". Taking into account the African love for colours, he clothed the ladies with a red skirt, black cape, and white blouse and veil. Europeans called them "Red sisters"; but the Zulu acclaimed them as *Amakosazana,* princesses. They became missionary vanguard to Zulu homes, teaching the women and girls agricultural and domestic arts, chiefly by their example. The institution prospered except that the attempt to admit Zulu girls failed. Pfanner's missionary ideal over the monastic vision of his society brought much tension but his method triumphed. At his death in 1909, there were 49 Catholic mission stations between the Cape and the Zambezi, and 28 of them had been built by monks of Marianhill. Among about 600 Protestant stations in the region, not many could match them. In 1936, the mission received its final form as *Congregation of the Missionaries of Marianhill (CMM).*

For Further Reading[1]

---

1 Baur, John. *2000 Years of Christianity in Africa*. Nairobi: Paulines Publications Africa, 1994, pp. 134-152, 192-196.

Just as Protestant missions took the lead in bringing Christianity to modern Africa, beginning from the 19th century, the sociological effects of Christianity on Africa began to manifest, first, in their churches. Before these effects began to manifest Africans, Christian converts and non-converts had encountered another group of Europeans: the colonists in search of material benefits in Africa for their governments in Europe. In some places, they followed missions; in others, they preceded missions.

At the outset, there was cooperation between the two groups, missionaries and colonists. This cooperation gradually gave way to mutual suspicion as they realized that their motives for being in Africa were not really compatible. The missionaries came to uplift the exploited; the colonists came to exploit. In the end, suspicion became mutual antagonism. The time and the speed at which this development took place varied from place to place, but they did almost everywhere. For example, in West Africa the CMS was getting ready to work alongside British colonial regime in Sierra Leone at the time Van der Kemp (of the LMS) was locked in antagonism with the British governor at Cape Town. Yet another LMS missionary, C. Helm, would later counsel Lobengula of Ndebele (Zimbabwe) to give mining concession to a shrewd empire builder like Cecil Rhodes in the hope that the Ndebeles would be the better for it.

ETHIOPIANISM

As the relationship between missionaries and colonists evolved from one stage to another, the same reality of evolving relationship played out between the missionaries and their converts as the churches they established took roots among the people. After the partitioning of Africa at the 1884-85 Berlin Conference European colonists and young missionaries in the field began to relate to Africans, no longer in the spirit of benevolent service with which they started among the people. In the new climate of colonization and unhealthy racial feelings towards Africans, the converts began to sense a different attitude from the missionaries. The ideal vision of an African church that is self-governing, self-sponsoring, and self-extending gave way to the entrenchment of colonial churches where African agents were to remain under the tutelage of European missionaries. This was accompanied by perceived denigration of everything African by some missionaries.

In West Africa and Southern Africa, the immediate response of the fledgling African clergy was self-affirmation. This was centred on the text of Psalm 68:31, *"Ethiopia shall soon stretch forth her hands to God"*. This text of the Bible nurtured, among African Christians, the hope of the conversion of Africa, of future glory for the Negro race, and of Christian theocracy embracing the entire continent. Thus, *Ethiopianism* as an African ideological movement was born, marking the first stage in African Christians' response to the new development in their churches and states.

In West Africa, as well as in South Africa, Ethiopianism led to the withdrawal of a few of the clergies from mission churches and the erection of new church structures where African values and idiosyncrasies were permissible; otherwise, it was not different from mission churches in form and liturgy. In West Africa *Ebenezer Baptist Church, Lagos*, and *Methodist Church, Eleja,* also on Lagos Island, represented the new development. In South Africa, Rev. Mangena Mokone's *Ethiopian Mission* (pulled out of the Methodist Church) and Rev. Samuel Brander's *Ethiopian Catholic Church* (pulled out of the Anglican Church) were products of this consciousness. In West Africa the movement did not evolve beyond this stage, whereas in South Africa, where racial feelings eventually degenerated into the policy of separate racial development (apartheid), Ethiopianisma flowered into resistance movement in church and state, strengthened by relationship with Africans in North America under Bishop Henry Turner of the Methodist Episcopal Church (AME Church). The churchmen's resistance led to the formation of South African Native National Congress, in 1912, which later became the African National Congress (ANC).

INDIGENIZATION— THE PROPHET MOVEMENT

Following the schismatic movement of the Ethiopian churches was the movement for indigenization. This movement had been incipient all along in the attempt to entrench Christianity in Africa; in various ways, the churches of Nubia, Ethiopia, and Kongo expressed it. Although it is implicitly self-affirmative, and so shares the tendency towards independency, it is different from Ethiopianism which is consciously political. The movement towards indigenization was more of an intuitive appropriation of Africa's innate religiosity for the faith of the Church.

251

It began in the second decade of the 20th century. As a rule, a prophet or prophetess, gifted with healing powers, gathered a group of followers which soon became so distinct from other church members that they had to form their own church. Some of the first founders were Isaiah Shembe in South Africa, Wade Harris in Ivory Coast, and Garrick Sokari Braide in the Niger Delta. The largest movement was found in South Africa, especially among the Zulu where prophets and followers call themselves *amaSiyoni,* Zionists.

Among the Yoruba a parallel movement started when in the great epidemic of 1918, people, experiencing the inefficacy of the medical help of the mission church, gathered in prayer groups and were called *Aladura* (people of prayer). There arose a large number of Aladura groups and some of them spread all over Anglophone West Africa, especially in Ghana where they became known as *Sumsum Asore* (spirit churches). Various other countries saw simultaneously but independently the rise of prophets, notably Simon Kimbangu in the Belgian Congo, Zakayo Kivuli in Western Kenya, and John Maranke in Zimbabwe. Like Aladura and Zionists, their churches little affected the mission churches; they mostly absorbed their marginal members barred from baptism and won a similar if not higher number of followers from among the traditionalists.

Nevertheless, Wade Harris' and Garrick Braide's movements had positive effects on mission churches. Harris' movement broke the hard ground of Ivory Coasts for the Roman Catholic mission in a country where colonial authorities were unsympathetic of religion and the people were indifferent to the religion of their foreign masters. Braide brought a wave of revival to the CMS Church in the Niger Delta which Rev. James Johnson's bishopric could not manage.

It should be said also that the prophet movement in Africa suffered much in the hand of colonial governments. As popular grassroots movements, the authorities were not comfortable with their influence, and they were seen as potential seedbeds of nationalist rebellion. Harris, Braide and Kimbangu, among others, suffered imprisonments; Harris and Braide survived jail but had the wind removed from their sails. Braide died a broken man. Kimbangu died in his 30th year in prison.

The years just before and immediately after independence also witnessed some fermentation in African Christian history. On one hand, the colonial governments relaxed their grip on "dangerous" movements. Suppressed groups, like the Kikuyu churches in Kenya and the Kimbanguists in the Belgian Congo, resurrected again and were permitted to form churches. Moreover independent churches won the sympathy of the new African politicians, and the traditional population not yet touched by mission schools found the independent churches to be the easiest gate to enter into the new age as well. Except for tiny Swaziland, an official establishment of Independent churches did not take place anywhere. On the other hand, their relationship with their governments cooled down in most countries. They had little to offer in nation-building and development projects, and with few exceptions, they were apolitical. And among the new independent churches that originated in this period very few were individually of any importance. As in the European Church Reformation, so independency in African Christianity ushered in multiple splits into more and more bodies. This became the distinctive mark of the age, especially between 1970 and 1995.

The leaders of Christian independency in Africa were aware of the uncontrolled fission going on in their movements and so they adopted measures towards unity. This has taken two different forms.

First, an attempt to join the mainstream churches' councils in which case it proved very difficult for them to receive recognition. By 1985, seven had been admitted to the *World Council of Churches (WCC),* 15 to *All Africa Conference of Churches (AACC)* and a small number in each country were allowed to join the national council of churches. The second endeavour was to unite among themselves. There were many attempts at doing this but almost all failed or the unions never functioned. In 1978 a successful continental council was founded, The *Organization of African Independent Churches (OAIC).* Its first major objective had been a better training for the churches' leaders. This was sponsored and organized by the World Council of Churches' *Theological Education by Extension (TEE).*

Still, the mid-1950s and the years of independence witnessed some soul-searching in the churches established by Western missions.

In the climate of Pan-Africanism, some among the indigenous leaders of these churches saw the need for the churches' structures and liturgy to conform to Africans' religious and cultural sensibilities. The roots of this advocacy can be found in the conference called by Prof. Kofi Busia at Accra, Ghana, in 1955 under the theme "Christianity and African Culture". The conference, through its convenor and Prof. Baeta defended the continuity between African religions and Christianity and called on the churches to use African culture as the only language to proclaim the Gospel in Africa. In the same year, Francophone Africans priests were already seriously working in this direction, publishing their findings in 1956: *The Bantu Life Unity* by Vincent Mulago, *The Philosophy of Rwandan People* by Alexis Kagame and *Black Priests Question Themselves.* The first two were doctoral dissertations in the step of Fr. Tempels' *Bantu Philosophy* while the third was a collection of essays by students in Europe: Mulago, Kagame, Hebga and Mveng. In this their first theological production the authors demanded a real Africanization of the church: *"Are we, African priests, going to defend our hidden complex of being 'poor relatives' in the Church of God for ever? Or we will be sowers of Christian enthusiasm, which will force each one of us to rethink this problem of African fundamental theology?"*

In Anglophone Africa, the works of Professors Bolaji Idowu and John Mbiti took up the challenge of Professors Busia and Baeta, publishing works that were affirmative of African culture and religiosity and seeking bridgeheads that could connect Africa's past with the gospel. In arguing the case for this movement, Bolaji Idowu wrote in his *Towards an Indigenous Church* that:

[W]e may...compare the Church to a powerful, living stream which flows into and through the nations, giving of itself to enrich the people and transforming the land, bringing from and depositing in each something of the chemical wealth of the soils which it encounters on its way, at the same time adapting itself to the shape and features of each locality, taking its colouring from the native soil, while in spite of all these structural adaptations and diversifications its esse and its differentia are not imperiled but maintained in consequence of the living, ever-replenishing, ever-revitalizing spring which is its source.

It should be stated that what these churchmen were arguing for in the historic churches of Western missions were the things charismatic prophets of independent churches have already been doing intuitively.

Although many mission churches in Africa have become liberal in incorporating certain indigenous forms into worship, especially with regard to spontaneity and music in worship, the real work that Idowu called for, that is creatively bridging inherited Western Church liturgies with African religious and intellectual resources, is yet to commence among Protestant Churches. Yet it should be mentioned that in Anglophone Africa a good beginning has been made by Bishop Sarpong of the Catholic Diocese of Kumasi in Ashanti Region of Ghana. On the other hand, Catholic priests in Francophone Africa have made much progress both in form and content. The Protestant churches are yet to make a serious beginning in this respect.

And the chances that the churches of Protestant missions in Africa will do so do not seem bright at present. The reason is because another form of Pentecostal-charismatic movement has emerged from early 1990s in urban Africa. In its external form, it is sold out to western value system of clothing, music, wealth and urbanism. Although it draws much of these from the United States of America it is transnational in spirit and vision and, at bottom, denigrates Africa's indigenous religions which are considered as having no value for advancing the cause of the Gospel in Africa. As a matter of fact, indigenous religions and cultural practices are seen as spiritual and social draw backs whose vestiges incapacitate their victims even when they have become Christians. They are therefore undesirable and are to be remedied by the process of spiritual deliverance through prayers.

SUMMARY

The history of the church in Africa is a long one whose roots are deep in antiquity. Critics, both in the Western world and on the continent of Africa, have often insinuated that Christianity is a white man's religion used to soften Africans before their final subjugation in the colonial era.

This assertion is highly prejudiced and does not take into account the dynamics that gave birth to missions and the altruistic motives that made men and women lay down their lives in droves for the spiritual and social regeneration of Africa. This is not to argue that all missionaries did well. It only means that each situation of missionary encounter with African society must be evaluated in its context; that is considered within the realities that shaped and informed the encounter. And when this is done, in spite of all the minuses that accompanied missions, it will be seen that, at bottom, Christian missions elevated Africa.

It also needs to be said that Africans were no passive recipients of the faith of the Church. Like other people who received it from "outsiders" at one time or another, they sought to make it their own through the process of indigenization, which to them should be normative. And although this often brought misunderstanding between them and missionaries in earlier centuries, the bursting of the wineskin in the 20th century indigenous Prophet movement in Africa and the intellectual affirmations that followed it in the years of political independence indicate that Africans are indeed capable of making the faith theirs.

The final point issues from the last one. Without disregarding the critical pioneering role of European missionaries, the ultimate credit for the evangelisation of the continent must go to African evangelists, both in the agency of the missions and outside it. Many of these were men and women returnees from abroad as liberated slaves or migrant labours who came into contact with Christianity away from home and brought the tidings of the gospel to their own people in the nooks and crannies of Africa. Silent heroes, we may never know some of them in this world.

MODULE 4a: CHURCH GROWTH AFRICAN-TODAY

(Revd Dr Usman Habib MA)

CONTEMPORARY: NEW GENERATION CHURCH (NGC)

The purpose of this course is to investigate the immediate causes of the New Generation Churches' growth and contrast it with the decline in the mainstream or missionary Churches and to find a positive way forward.

LECTURE 1: HISTORIOGRAPHY OF THE NEW GENERATION CHURCHES

It is no longer a story that Nigeria shares a significant part in the unprecedented growth of Pentecostal/Charismatic Churches in the world Christianity today. Pentecostalism/Charismatic Churches are best understood as multifarious movements concerned primarily with the experience of the working of the Spirit and the practice of Spiritual gifts. In this sense, the term would include at least three categories:

(1) 'Classical or denominational' Pentecostals originating in the North American Holiness movement with historical links to the Azuza Street Revival in Los Angelis (1906-8), although Kalu Ogbu does not seems to agree that the Nigerian Pentecostalism originated from the Azuza Street and is not an extension of the American electronic Church;'

(2) The Charismatic movement in the older Churches, still a force to be reckoned with; and

(3) The Independent and indigenous Churches, fellowships and ministries that now form the majority of Pentecostals worldwide. These are the Churches referred to as New Generation Churches in this course.

Richard Burgess, in his analysis noted that, *'Some authorities believe that the global centre of gravity as far as dramatic Church growth is concerned has shifted in the 1990s from South Korea to Nigeria, Africa's most populous nation.'* What is today known as Pentecostal/Charismatic Churches in Nigeria began as a result of the spiritual transformation, witnessed among the African Indigenous

257

Churches (AIC) founded by Africans during the colonial era-missionary Churches. The Christ Army Church, formed in 1910s-1920s, was the first on the list, followed by the Aladura Churches, a Yoruba word for 'prayerful'. These include:

'Eternal Sacred Order of the Cherubim and Seraphim Society (ESOCSS),' founded in 1925 and the
'Church of the Lord Aladura' (CLA), founded in 1930s

In the early 1920s, a group led by Garrick S. Braide formed a prayer fellowship to find the cause of an influenza disease of the local populace, as the missionary Churches could not help to solve most of the needs felt by the people, such as witchcraft, healing body sicknesses, sorcery and poverty. They broke away from the Anglican Church and affiliated to the Faith Tabernacle; an American based Church in Philadelphia and called themselves the Precious Stone (diamond) Society. The group's quest was to contextualize Christian teachings in African ways in order to solve an 'ailing' problem.

This could be considered as the beginning of the Pentecostal Christianity in Nigeria, as these revivalist movements championed an experiential manifestation of the Spirit in the life of believers. Joseph Babalola, a member of the Faith Tabernacle, also led a revival that converted thousands in 1930s. This led to the affiliation of Babalola with the Apostolic Church in Great Britain; this relationship was short lived as a result of disagreement over the use of modern medicine. Thus, he formed the **Independent Christ Apostolic Church (CAC)** in Nigeria, which was estimated to have over a million members by 1990. This chain of revival has continued to date. Foreign Pentecostal denominations such as:

The Assemblies of God (1939) and the **Foursquare Gospel Church (1954)** were also introduced during this period.

During the 1960s–1970s, originating in evangelical student revivals, a wave of expansion spawned new Churches. This was the period of the Nigerian civil war (1967-1970), when the Scripture Union and the University campus students generated a proliferation of new Pentecostal denominations, which together represent the dominant expression of Nigerian Christianity. The leader of this move was

Benson A. Idahosa. He established, the **Church of God Mission International (CGM INT) in 1968**. William F. Kumuyi, established the **Deeper life Bible Church (DLBC) in 1975** and **David O. Oyedepo, founded the Living Faith Ministries Worldwide, also known as Winners' Chapel' in 1982.** Prior to this period, the **Redeemed Christian Church of God, founded by Pa Josiah Akindayomi in 1952,** was already thriving in Pentecostal spirit and theology. There are host of others in this group, but for the purpose of this course, these few are named. The membership of these Churches is running into hundreds of thousands.

REVOLUTIONARY TRANSFORMATION OF THE NGC

David Bosch argued that, *'Since in virtually all disciplines, there is a growing awareness that we live in an era of change from one way of understanding reality to another there has to be shift in paradigms.'* However, in his argument, Bosch insists that paradigms do not completely change totally in theological sense as it does in scientific sense, because, an old paradigm that seems completely out of fashion can be resuscitated by the acts of the Holy Spirit. Yet, the needs for a new look into what will enhance and advance the kingdom of God is very imperative. William Kane asserts that, *'Change is inevitable; it is perpetual, here and real.'* The men mentioned above, noted with great zeal the need to embrace the fact that the condition of Christianity in Nigeria as at late sixties and early seventies requires a shift in paradigm of operation. They adopted various methods that resulted into what we see today as the Pentecostal/Charismatic boom. When we refuse change, we impede development and progress in every life's adventure. Changes in the NGC include:

EMBRACING THE REALITY IN CULTURAL DIVERSITY

The missionary Churches undermined the cultural differences between the Europeans and the Nigerians they sought to convert, thereby, promoting a complete cultural shift that affect their mission, which led to their resistance in most cases. The theory of *'homogenous unit principle'* of Donald A. McGavran was faulted in the Nigerian context. 'Homogenous Unit principle' allow communities to maintain their cultural identity even when professing faith in Christ without a change in class or cultural shift. Hence, the development of the African indigenous Churches, to promote Christian worship in the African context, results in the birth of Pentecostal/Charismatic

259

Churches. Philip Jenkins noted that, *'Dancing or swaying is considered inappropriate for solemn or religious settings in the European culture, while to the Africans physical movement was perfectly normal.'* Prohibiting dancing is viewed as deviance from African culture. Jesus was careful about this fact while introducing the gospel manifestoes (Matthew 5: 17-18). Paul was conversant with cultural identity while planting the gentile Churches. (Galatians 2:11-14). Harvey Cox suggests two vitally important and underlying factors that:

'for any religion to grow in today's world it must possess two capabilities.' First, *'it must be able to include and transform at least certain elements of pre-existing religions which still retain a strong grip on the cultural subconscious of its people,'* Secondly, *'it must also equip people to live in rapidly changing societies.'*

These two 'key ingredients' he observed in Pentecostalism. The next session will give us more insight into the use of these keys.

For further reading[1]

LECTURE 2: MISSIOLOGICAL/EVANGELICAL ADVENTURE OF NGC

INTRODUCTION:

In the first session, we considered the historiography of the NGC Churches to be acquainted with how they came into being; their revolutionary transformation; and the failure of the missionaries to embrace the cultural reality that gave rise to these Churches. In this session, we will consider the Missiological/evangelical changes, worship innovations and their emphasis on the Person and gifts of the Holy Spirit.

Scriptural focus: Matt 28:18-20; Mark 16:15-20; Luke 24:46-49; Acts 1: 6-8, 2:2-41, 3:1-11- 4:1-4, 23-37-5:1-16, 13:1-4, 16:25-34 etc.

---

1 K. Ogbu, African Pentecostalism: An Introduction, (New York: Oxford University Press, 2007).

R. Burgess, Nigeria's Christian Revolution: The Civil War Revival and its Pentecostal Progeny (1967-2006), (Colorado Springs, CA: OM Authentic Media, 2008).

D. P. Ukpong, 'The Presence and Impact of Pentecostalism in Nigeria,'

www.glopent.net/members.frdonalpresence_and_impact_of_pentecostalism_Nigeria.pdf.

D. J. Bosch, Transforming Mission: Paradigm Shifts in Theology of Mission, (Maryknoll, NY: Orbis Books, 2008).

In many parts of the world, Pentecostals are notorious for rather aggressive forms of evangelism and proselytism, and Nigeria is no exception. From its beginning, the Pentecostal movement was characterised by an emphasis on evangelistic outreach, and Pentecostal mission strategy placed evangelism as its highest priority. Evangelism to them meant to go out and reach the 'lost' for Christ in the power of the Holy Spirit (Matthew 28: 18-20 and Mark 16:15-20), songs like 'only Jesus can save' and 'there is no other way' were their scriptural slogans. Many of these men were lay Church members who were mostly untrained and inexperienced, their only qualification was baptism in the Spirit and a divine call, their motivation and task was to evangelise the world before the imminent coming of Christ. So to them evangelism was more important than education or civilisation. Although a few of them manage to complete their university degree. Grant McClung noted that, the Pentecostals eschatological belief in *'Premillenialism, dispensationalism and the belief in the imminence of Christ's return forged the evangelistic fervour of the movement in its infancy.'* Thus, mission has advanced, resulting in Church planting across the nation and beyond.

According to Burgess, Nigeria is becoming known as one of the foremost missionary sending nations of the world, exposing Christian communities in the global North to African Pentecostal spirituality. For example, two of the largest Churches in Europe today were planted by Nigerian missionaries:

Embassy of God in Ukraine, founded by Sunday Adelaja in 1993, has over 20,000 membership in its headquarters Church and over two hundred congregations across several nations.

Kingsway International Christian Centre (KICC) founded in London by Matthew Ashimolowo, started in the 1980s with eleven people, by 2002 had approximately 5,000 members at its headquarters Church, as well as several satellite Churches. Nigerian-based Pentecostal denominations are also establishing Churches across the nation and all over Africa.

And a couple more churches with widespread ministries:

The Redeemed Christian Church of God has over 3000 congregations in Nigeria.

Living Faith Ministries Worldwide is everywhere and has the largest single auditorium in the world with a seating capacity of 50,000 in Lagos in one service.

NGC CHANGED WORSHIP STYLE

The NGC no doubt have immensely transformed the worship style introduced by the missionary Churches of the European. Seemingly quiet, dull and mournful type of worship that was against African culture of beating of congas, drums and playing of flute to stir ecstatic display of worship and dancing. God loves varieties, hence, he made the Africans jubilating people, with a lot of acrobatic carnival-like worship. This is attractive to worshippers. It is a winning way to attract people to God; the NGC founders knew it and applied it. Idahosa introduced the contemporary gospel music in the 1970s, for his television programme, 'Redemption Hour.' The NGC also encouraged the use of modern instruments, with the exception of, the **Deeper life Bible Church** of William Kumuyi.

Religious music in Nigeria has witnessed a remarkable innovation since the outburst of Pentecostalism. Many people had discovered a new dimension of being a Christian through the so called gospel music. The fluidity of Pentecostal rhyme and rhythm has made it easy for people to sing and play the same tune in various languages and in diverse cultural ambiences. Pentecostal music is homogenising the cultural spectrum of the country. According to Columbus Udofia, **'Music is a central part of African culture and especially in African religious culture.'** No wonder the youth of various ethnic backgrounds and religious affiliations can now come together to sing and enjoy a common religious tune.

EMPHASIS ON THE HOLY SPIRIT AND GOD'S GIFTS (1 Corinthians 12: 3-14:40).

The emphasis of the NGC on the Holy Spirit and God's gifts has helped in no small way to boost the growth of Pentecostal/Charismatic Churches in Nigeria. The established Churches turned away from the power of the Holy Spirit and resorted to scholasticism, while referring to these gifts as signs of demonic powers, just as the Jewish Rabbis of Jesus days accused Him of possessing the power of Beelzebub, for operating in the power of the Spirit (Matthew 12:22-32). The Church

Growth theories are built on the manifestation of the Holy Spirit empowerment that enabled the evangelists, pastors and even the missionaries in the soul winning project. Wagner argued that *'...it is only the direct work of the Holy Spirit which can ultimately transfer a person from the power of Satan to the Power of God and cause a sinner to be born again.'* The Holy Spirit's role in conversion of the individual cannot be explained by human understanding. Paul affirmed that no one can confess Christ as Lord without the help of the Holy Spirit (1 Corinthians 12:3). Gary McIntosh posits that, *"The growth of the Church is always brought about by the action of the Holy Spirit."* The Holy Spirit is the life-giver; He helps the Church in fulfilling the promises of God in Church Growth without depending on human effort. He added that Churches which grow are those which earnestly seek the gracious power of God. Acts of the Apostles are full of the impact of the Holy Spirit involvement in the early Church Growth (Acts 2-4).

The Holy Spirit's involvement in Church growth is inestimable in value. The NGC preachers are conversant with this fact that without the presence of the Holy Spirit, who empowers and convicts the lost and the saved of their sinful nature, no one, by his or her human skills, can make any Church to grow (1 Corinthians12:3). The growth of the Church is by divine prerogative. Therefore, the Holy Spirit is the most active personality to effect this growth. McIntosh stresses further that there must be, *'Life giving Church trust in the sovereign work of the Holy Spirit for the growth of their Church.'* Human ingenuity cannot multiply the Church of God. The Word of God by which the Church's discipleship programmes are organized is inspired by the Holy Spirit, who uses them to convict the sinners and rebukes the backsliders (John 16:7-13; Acts 2:37, 9:31). The need of the Holy Spirit's empowerment in our today's ministries cannot be over emphasized. It was the Holy Spirit who turned the Upper Room prayer meeting of one hundred and twenty members into a mega Church of three thousand one hundred and twenty members in just one day (Acts 2:41). The next lesson will tell us about how NGCs' faith overcame the fear of spiritism and the effect of prosperity gospel.

For further reading[1]

1 C. P. Wagner, *Spiritual Power and Church Growth*, (London: Hodder and Stoughton, 1996).

G. L. McIntosh, *Biblical Church Growth: How you can Work with God to Build a Faithful Church*, (Grand Rapids, MI: Baker Books, 2003).

INTRODUCTION:

The last session centred on the effects of Missiological/Evangelical adventures of the NGC; how they changed the gospel worship of the European into African context; and their emphasis on the power and gifts of the Holy Spirit. In this lesson, we will explore the dynamics of the faith of the NGC preachers in overcoming the fear of spiritism that usually 'harass' or cause psychological trauma to worshippers. Occultism in Nigeria is not a new phenomenon to any of you, I suppose. We are basically looking at what we already know or have in one way or the other practised.

Scriptural focus: Acts 13:6-13, 44-45, 19:11-22, 23-41; Job 5:12-14; Isaiah 54:17 Etc.

ADDRESSING THE FEAR OF SPIRITISM THROUGH FAITH

The faith of the NGC preachers in tackling demoniacs and the power of spiritists, especially that of witchcrafts and wizardry has been tremendous in this regard and must be commended as well. The bold faith of Late Archbishop Benson A. Idahosa of blessed memories cannot be forgotten: the stories of how the dead were raised to life through the power faith in God; cancellation of world council of witches meeting in Benin City in the 1980's; and the encounter with the Ogboni cults are living testimonies with us in Nigeria.

Rev Joseph Babalola, founder of the (CAC)'s faith over forces of darkness is unmatchable. The present crop of leaders of the New Generation Church and their unprecedented faith demonstration in conquering opposing powers to establish the Churches is comparable to the legends of faith stories in Hebrews Chapter Eleven. Healing; deliverance; revelation of dreams and visions; and miracles; are all characteristics of the NGC. These promote attraction from the populace who are miracle seekers. Thus, NGC preachers magnify miracles as chances to reach seekers. Deliverance ministry exploits cannot be ignored in this lesson, as some have professed to be set free from demonic influences. Some of the NGC preachers claim to be called into the ministry of deliverance as well. I specifically believe that deliverance is inclusive of what we are called to preach, nothing is particular about it (Matthew 28:18; Mark 16:17 and Luke 4:18-20).

B. Idahosa, *Faith Power to Achieve Your life's goal*, (Benin City, Gifts-Print Associate,1997)

Since people live naturally in fear, this has offered an escape route from this dreaded scourge of spiritism.

PROSPERITY GOSPEL

Achunike observed that, *'We belong to a society that is flamboyant, a society that worship wealth or money or possession.'* To be poor under such condition is considered disgraceful and unimaginable. Poverty is a canker in Nigerian society that needed to be eradicated with all available energy. This is what the NGC prosperity preachers offer as bait to attract teaming worshippers, who are searching for means to overcome the canker of poverty. Where the 'carcass is, the eagles must gather there. (Matthew 24:28).' The NGC preachers of prosperity do not sound apologetic in their declaration of their prosperity message. They proclaim it with all the energy of divine backing. Kalu Ogbu asserts in his analysis that, *'Within a decade Benson Idahosa reshaped African Pentecostalism in five years. He brought the prosperity gospel, the Episcopal polity, televangelism, megachurch with mega projects and theological education that sponsored a large group of African students who spread the faith and deliverance theology throughout the continent.'* Philip Jenkins calls these Churches *'health and wealth'* Churches.

Donatus Ukpong quoting David Oyedepo *'I know that God deals with people on covenants terms. From that time the yoke of poverty was broken in my life and I knew I can never be poor!'* Kingdom prosperity is a matter of revelation, when you discover your part it becomes easy to attain. John the Baptist said, 'A man can receive ONLY what is given him from heaven (John 3:27).

Do not condemn what you know nothing about, even though many critics of prosperity gospel either condemn it out-right or ignorantly spoke against the NGC flamboyancy and display of wealth and extravagance. Some attribute this to be an American influence, as Musa Gaiya observed in the writings of Paul Gifford and Rijk A. Van. The gospel is a complete package for everyone whom God calls, therefore, we are licensed to enjoy its total package (3 Jn 2-5, James 1:25 and Ps 1:1-3, 35:27 and Job 36: 11).

There are certain basic principles the NGC churches believe about the scripture that facilitate their prosperity gospel. These are included in the following factors enumerated below:

1. Consistent tithing: of all income at least 10% according to scriptures (Mal 3:6-12, Matt 23:23, Heb 7:1-10, Gen 14:18-20 and 28:20-22; Deut 14:22).

2. Fellowship offering: giving of freewill offering is a command by God in the scripture. He says 'none shall appear before me empty handed' (Deut 16:16-17, Mal 1: 6-8, 2:18, 3:6-10; 2 Cor 8:1-6).

3. Bounty offering (Seed faith): Something freely provided or an act of generosity in anticipation of divine approval. (1 Cor 16: 1-3; 2 Cor 9:1-12).

4. Thanksgiving offerings: For every good God perform in our lives demand thanksgiving with testimony and offering. (Ps 96:6-9; Amos 4:5 Ps 50:14).

5. Vows and Pledges: These are solemn promises made to God in anticipation of divine help. Therefore are to be altered with caution according to Solomon (Ecc 5: 3-5; Ps 50:5; 1 Sam 1:10-12; Deut 23:21-23).

6. Prophets' offering: This is special offerings given to ministers by the flock by way of appreciation or encouragement for their work in the vineyard of the Lord. We cannot refuse these gifts. God will not come down to bless you. He will use men and women on earth. See these passages (Matt 10:40-42; Rom 16:1-3; 1 Cor 9:1-14, 16:15-18; Phil 4:10-19; 3 John 2-5).

7. First fruit offering: This is commanded by God to be given at the beginning of every year (Ex 23:14, 16-17; Prov 3:9-10; Ez 44:30-31; John 3:16; Rom 8:23).

8. Project offerings: Tithes and offerings in the Bible are not meant for building, they were meant to be eating by the priests and Levites. It was God's salary for their work in the temple, but because we now have organized systems, we can no longer practice that now. See (Deut 18, Ex 25, 1 Chron 29:1-10 and 2 Sam 24:24.

9. Offering for the less privileged: This includes the widows, orphans, destitute and the poor around us. (Gal 2:10-11; Matt 25:31-46; Prov 3:27-28).

10. Property offerings: This is the giving of personal belongings either to the Church, work of God or evening to a struggling minister

(Acts 2:42-47, 4:32-37, 5:1-11; Phil 4:10-19 and 3 John 2-5). Missionary offerings still attracts blessing as well, the practice of all these opens the door of blessings to the NGC churches.

For further reading[1]

LECTURE 4: MARKETING THE GOSPEL - STRATEGIES

INTRODUCTION:

In the last lesson, we tried look at how these NGC churches addressed: the fear of spiritism through the dynamics of faith; and the meaning and effects of the prosperity gospel; to the Nigerian worshippers. This lesson will consider strategy of marketing the gospel by the application of marketing strategies, the dynamics of the NGC unceasing prayers and feminist involvement in their ministry and their impacts in the NGC growth.
Scriptural focus: Matt 16:13-20 & 11:28-30; Acts 15:1-10, 28-31 etc.

MARKETING THE GOSPEL - STRATEGIES

The founding proponent of this theory is George Barna, believes that, *'The basic concept of marketing is not only transferable to the Church, but necessary if the Church is to make any headway in this century. Thus Church marketing is the performance of both business and ministry activities that impact the target audience with the intention of ministering to and fulfilling their spiritual, social emotional and physical needs.'* Douglas Webster noted that, *'Unless we package and promote the gospel in a way our target audience can appreciate, we will be left without an audience.'* Stressing further, he said, *'The major problem plaguing the Church is its failure to embrace a marketing orientation in what has become a market-driven environment.'*

People are looking for what satisfies their spiritual quest and what will quench their thirst for God by offering them all the needed economic, social emotional and physical happiness.

1 K. Ogbu, *African Pentecostalism: An Introduction,* (New York: Oxford University Press, 2008).

M. A. B. Gaiya, *The Pentecostal Revolution In Nigeria,* Occasional Paper Centre of African Studies, (University of Copenhagen, 2002).

P, Jenkins, *The Next Christendom: The Coming of Global Christianity,* (New York: Oxford University Press, 2007).

B, Idahosa, *The Undamageable Faith,* (Benin City, Nigeria: Gifts-Prints Associates,1995)

Marketing is all about the performance of business activities that direct the flow of goods and services from the producer to the consumers, to satisfy the needs and desires of the consumer and the goals and objectives of the producer. We have all the theological training and knowledge we need from the Bible Institutions and Seminaries, yet, when we assume Church Leadership duty, we are faced with business realities. Barna, noted that, *'The Church is in business of ministry: searching out people who need the gift of acceptance, forgiveness and eternal life that is available in knowing Jesus Christ. For the local Church to be a successful business, it must impact a growing share of its market area.'* The NGC churches have taken advantage of these marketing strategies to explore the world of soul-winning and it is paying off. The following factors below offers us some Church marketing strategies:

a. Make your service consumer oriented culturally.

b. Develop good public relation and build on a pleasing personality that is attractive.

c. Be a good communicator. Jesus was a communicator specialist (Matt 7:28-29; Lk 4:22, 32). He spoke with eloquence that could be credited to modern advertising and marketing agencies, yet full of spirituality.

d. Jesus identified his target audience, determined their needs and delivered His message directly to them (Lk 19:1-10).

e. Jesus understood his product thoroughly, developed an unparalleled distribution system within the grasp of every consumer, without the product losing its value (Lk 4:18-20).

FERVENT UNCEASING PRAYER

Prayer is one of the characteristic features of the New Generation Churches in Nigeria. Allan Anderson, a notable observer and commentator of global Pentecostal/Charismatic revival, observed that:

> *'Some of the largest gatherings of Christians in the world occur in the camp grounds of these Nigerian Churches, where literally hundreds of thousands of people attend all-night Friday meetings in places with names like Redemption Ground and Canaan Land. The older Churches are struggling to keep pace with the jet-setting entrepreneurs who head up these new organisations.'*

These gatherings reveal the state of spiritual hunger and thirst for divine presence (Matt 5:6; Jn 7: 37-39). Oswald Sanders, noted that, *'The spiritual leader should outpace the rest of the Church, above all in prayer. And yet the most advanced leader is conscious of the possibility of endless development in his prayer life.'* This is the key to divine breakthrough in ministry as demonstrated by Christ (Lk 4:1-20; Mk 1:35).

The NGC churches no doubt have awakened the Nigerian eagerness for spiritual life in secular world and a desire for an experiential communion with God in prayers. People are now giving serious attention to their prayer life. Donatus Ukpong noted that, *'Pentecostalism is noted for encouraging a spirituality that abhors confinement and standardization, while provoking an intimate experience of the Holy Spirit. Night vigil, Holy Ghost camp meeting and power must charge hands of different ministries to affirm this fact. Worshippers travel long distances just to attend these meetings. Several testimonies given at these occasion become means of evangelism to attract non-Christians to these gatherings.'*

FEMINIST INVOLVEMENT IN MINISTRIES

Women are no doubt a very powerful means of outreach ministry. The NGC gave a very good opportunity to the women in their ministries to showcase their feminist attractive influence. This has paid off to these New Generation Churches and their counterpart in the missionary Churches are struggling to gain such recognition in a hugely hierarchical setting that seldom gives place to the women, but prefers to have them like the Apostle Paul warned, remaining quiet in the Church (1 Cor 14:34; 1 Tim 2:11-12). The older generation have so stuck to these passages that they have become a stumbling block through their own ego. Jesus sent the message of resurrection through a woman; the first person to see Him after resurrection was a woman; at the upper room prayer meeting that ushered in the coming of the Holy Ghost included women; (Jn 20:11-18; Acts 1:13-15).

The age we live in is an age of communication and this is done by influence and persuasion. This is why the business world is employing women more than men to facilitate their job and attract the right customers. Politicians are seeing the importance of women in governance; therefore, they are creating room for them. I am not in

269

agreement with putting immature, arrogant and prideful women in position of authority and spirituality (1Tim 3:4-8). Soul winning is the ultimate task Jesus left for the Church and the women are good instruments for this kind of business. We must use them in this regard (Prov 11:30). Where they are placed in leadership, they are always more careful and cautious than men and they seem to dread failure, therefore, their effort pays off.

For further reading [1]

LECTURE 5: NGC USER OR SEEKER SENSITIVE SERVICES

INTRODUCTION:

The just concluded lesson focuses its attention on three aspects of the NGC growth strategies: marketing the gospel; unceasing fervent prayer and feminist involvement in ministry. In this lesson, we will be looking at what it means to organise a 'User or Seeker Sensitive Service' or Church and how we develop a strong youth enhancement Church programmes.

Scriptural Focus: Matt 16:18 & 25:14-30; 1 Cor 3:5-15; Lk 11:23 etc.

NGC USER OR SEEKER SENSITIVE SERVICES

These NGC Churches are very enterprising in nature in that they apply business approach in running their Church business. David Oyedepo asserts that,

> *One of the reasons why most ministries ordained of God fall short of expectation or collapse completely is due to their unbusiness-like approach to ministry. Many ministers still think that ministry is just going to Church on Sunday to preach well-prepared messages (Luke 2:49; Isaiah 48:17).*

As we observed in the lesson on marketing the gospel strategies, George Barna advanced that User or Seeker Friendly Churches provide people with an accessible way to worship God; a

1 A. Anderson, *An Introduction to Pentecostalism,* (Cambridge: Cambridge University Press, 2008).

D. D. Webster, *Selling Jesus: What's Wrong with Marketing the Church,* (Downers Grove, IL: Inter-Varsity Press, 1992)

G. Barna, *Marketing the Church: What They Never Taught You about Church Growth,* (Colorado Springs, CO: Nav Press, 1988).

K. Ogbu, *African Pentecostal: An Introduction,* (New York: Oxford University Press, 2008).

J. O. Sanders, *Spiritual Leadership: Principles of Excellence for Every Believe,* (Chicago, IL: Moody Publishers, 2007).

M. B. A. Idahosa, *The Female Minister,* (Benin City, Nigeria: Gift-Prints Associates, 2005).

comfortable place to bring their friends; and a sensitive, creative community they can belong to; one that is wise enough not to get in the way of the task at hand; which is reaching the world for Jesus Christ. Gone are the days when men and women were so heaven conscious and bound, that in the church they became an earthly nuisance. The Biblical slogan for sensitive commitment that Christ left us with is *'Occupy till I come'* (Luke 19:13, check NIV version). Barna noted that, *'It will be increasingly difficult to convince the unchurched that our faith is pertinent to the 21st century if the tools of our trade are from the last century.'* The present advancement in technology and ITC calls for a rethink in the way we run our Churches with 18th/19th century formula or ideas. Where business exists, profiting becomes the ultimate target.

Ministry is not about programmes. Ministry is about people. Jesus did not minister through programmes, the early Church did not appoint programme directors, neither did the Bible exhort us to create programmes. But these three sources encouraged a focus on people through meaningful relationships. User Friendly Churches consistently demonstrate the ability to identify individuals within the Church who are able to minister to people with a special need. Here are some suggested approaches, they are not exclusive, know your environment and adopt your strategies:

a. Sensitive to the need of the brethren (John 6:1-13; Mark 8:1-9).
b. Provide for the less privileged (Matt 17:24-27).
c. Create a secure environment of worship (Matt 14:13-14).
d. Church must emphasize relationships (Acts 2:42-47)
e. Share material possessions (Acts 4:32-37).
f. Provide an organised setting (good smart sensible ushers, well dressed choir, car park, care giving Sunday school teachers for children and a well-timed service).
g. Preach contextualised sermons or messages that address the issues of the moment or resolves the need of your seekers, and then they will come back again.
h. Make worship appealing and contemporary, such as agrees with your culture.
i. Make use of good Public Address Systems (Note: Increasing the volume of your microphone is not a sign of anointing, but such noise can deafen your audience).

The leaders of NGC Churches acknowledge the fact that for their ministry to be complete, it must identify and address the needs of the children and youth. Remaining relevant among kids is perhaps more exclusive than among adults. Barna noted that, *'Raised in a society with a cut-throat competition, today's youth have come to expect excellence from Church. They are quality driven, unwilling to accept mediocrity.'* Youth love competitive activities that help to challenge their curious and enthusiastic mind to explore their world. Jesus made room for them, while his Apostles tried to restrain them from coming close (Luke 18:15-16). Youth and children are a considerable part of what constitutes the Church today, if we neglect them, there is no Church for tomorrow (Deut 6:6-9). When they are not properly engaged they engage themselves in the entire internet scams, pornographies, robbery, drug addiction and all forms of sexual promiscuities (Proverbs 22:6).

According to Jonathan Park, *'Christian leaders who invest in themselves will find it easy to invest in others, because they know the value of such investment.'* Aim to be the kind of leader who gets the best from others and who does the best for them.' Investing in others as a leadership task demands a concerted effort on the part of the leader to carry it out. George Ambler noted that,

Leaders must ask a legacy question, what next? The ultimate test for a leader is not whether he or she makes smart decisions and takes decisive actions, but whether he or she teaches others to be leaders and builds an organization that can sustain its success when he or she is not around.'

The mission of God must be our mission; therefore must provoke a mission minded thoughts. Ambler added, *'My success is determined by the seeds I sow. Not the harvest I reap.'*

Roxburgh and Romanuk assert that,

The leaders need to cultivate the people of God for a missional future. This explains that God's future is among God's people, leaders investing in the Youth amounts to preparing for the future. This means investing in emerging leaders must be made an issue of priority.

272

Blanchard and Hodges affirmed that,

'One aspect of a job well done as a servant leader is how well we have prepared others to carry on after our season of leadership influence is completed. Our leadership legacy is not just limited to what we accomplished, but it includes what we leave behind in the hearts and minds of those with whom we had a chance to teach and work.'

Paul highlighted in scripture how a leader should invest in his youth, '...I hid nothing that was profitable to you' (Acts 20:20). Church leaders must emulate Paul's model of encouragement to Timothy in the following ways:

First, gave him a big assignment to challenge false doctrines (1 Tim 1:3);

Secondly, encouraged them to get skills they need (2 Tim 2:15);

Thirdly, to be disciplined (2 Tim 2:3-7);

Fourthly, to also be willing to involve and teach others (1Tim 3:1-13, 2 Tim 2:2);

Furthermore, embolden them when they are fearful (1 Tim 4:12). This should include in family life, prayer for them, financial dealings in Church (1 Tim 6:6-12), based on scriptural standards.

For further reading[1]

LECTURE 6: MENTORING: AS LEADERSHIP DEVELOPMENT PRINCIPLE

INTRODUCTION:

The last session dealt with how we can organise a User or Seeker Sensitive Church within our area of operation; and developing some youth enhancement programmes or training; to get the children and youth involved in the programme of God's mission in this 21st century. This session focuses on mentoring as a leadership development principle and Effective discipleship models to prepare tomorrow's Church.

Scriptural focus: Deut 31:1-7, 14, 23; 1 Sam 3-4; 1 Ki 19:15-21; Lk 6:12-16 Etc.

---

1 G, Barna, *The Frog in the Kettle: What Christians Need to Know About Life in the 21st Century,* (Ventura, CA: Regal Books, 1990).

G, Barna, *User Friendly Churches: What Christians Need to Know About the Churches People Love to Go to,* (Ventura, CA: Regal Books, 1991).

D. O. Oyedepo, *Exploits in Ministry,* (Lagos, Nigeria: Dominion Publishing House, 2006).

A. J. Roxburgh and F. Romanuk, *The Missional Leader: Equipping the Church to Reach a Changing World,* (San Francisco, CA: Jossey-Bass, 2008).

John Mallison posits that, *'Christian mentoring is a dynamic intentional relationship of trust in which one person enables another to maximize the grace of God in their life and service.'* These include relationships, intention, trust, maximising, mentoring and service. These are basic components upon which the concepts of mentoring are built. Anderson and Reese noted that, *'Spiritual mentoring is one of the most influential ways to help us grow into intimacy with God, accept our identity and discover our unique voices for kingdom responsibility.'* What is also unique in this definition is the word *'intimacy'*, which is another word for *'relationship'*. Thus mentoring is developed on the strength of relationship. This is the secret of NGC ministers, why people prefer to relate with them closely rather than uniformed ministers.

Mallison noted that the origin and meaning of the word mentoring comes from Greek mythology. In Homer's Odyssey, mentor was the wise and trusted companion and friend of Ulysses and the guardian of his house during his ten-year absence at the Trojan wars. He acted as teacher and adviser of Ulysses' son Telemachus, helping him to develop sound values, attitudes and behaviour so that he would mature to be an upright, wise and courageous adult.

Wickman and Sjodin advanced that, *'The word mentor means a wise and trusted teacher or counsellor.'* Mentoring therefore focuses on the development of an individual's total being, spiritually, mentally, intellectually and physically to enable him/her to mature into useful serviceable adult. According to Wickman and Sjodin, *'A mentor is someone who helps us learn the ways or principles of this life, someone who has our interest at heart.'* The duty of a mentor is to teach mentoree or protégé the principles of success in a chosen career by way of guiding him/her through the processes involved. Protégé or mentoree is the student of the mentor.' The mutual relationship of sharing between these two individuals is what aids the possibility of mentoring. This kind of relationship is vital to promote mutual trust.

Stanley and Clinton stressed that, *'Mentoring is a relational experience in which one person empowers another by sharing God-given resources. Barnabas exhibited this virtue as an influencer to Paul, as he saw potentials in Saul (later the Apostle Paul) when others kept their distance (Acts 9:26-29). Barnabas was never afraid of the past of Paul but saw God's gifting of leadership in him. He drew him close and encouraged him through those early days and patiently stayed with him, knowing that time and experience would soon temper and mature this gifted young leader (Acts 13-15). Mentoring requires closeness, encouragement, teaching and patience between the mentor and mentoree.* Wright affirmed that, *'Mentors offer a safe place to gain perspective.'* He helps others to gain understanding of their purposes in life.

Mentoring others is not something most people learn in school. It does not require a college degree to mentor; it is both a skill and willingness between the mentor and mentoree to agree with each other. Mentoring allows the incumbent leadership to train or disciple the emerging generation leadership to succeed it; by passing on legacies of the pioneer leader.

Gibbs noted that, *'The most significant test of leadership is not present performance but the legacy that the leaders leave behind them.'* Thus, commitment is required in this direction of mentoring to ensure a successful training programme of mentorees. This Kingdom mentoring mind-set can follow a variety of approaches:

Firstly, mentors care about those who follow them; their primary interest is not what they can gain from the relationship, but what they can give to it. Ultimately, they fulfil Paul's admonition to look out not only for their own interest, but also for the interest of others (Phil 2:4).
Secondly, Mentors convey wisdom and skills. Through modelling and coaching, and eventually by turning over responsibility to their followers. Kingdom-style mentors seek to make their disciples more capable than they have been (Matt 10:25).
Thirdly, mentors correct their followers when they are wrong and do not avoid confrontation (Acts 15:36-39). Later Paul changed his approach and asked Timothy to bring John Mark to him (2 Tim 4:11).
Finally, mentors connect their followers to significant people and training that will further their development and increase their opportunities. Brian Winslade encouraged that, *'Mentoring that builds discipleship and spiritual formation is part of that authentic Christianity'*. Let us continue to invest together in mentoring, especially in the lives of the young generation leaders.

This focuses on the need for effective discipleship, it is used here as a form of training. However, Discipleship is the kingdom way of recruiting labourers for the continuity of Christ's kingdom on earth before he returns. Bob Deffinbaugh noted that:

'The life of Jesus and his disciples gave us example of discipleship model. The relationship between Jesus and his disciples was more personal than pedagogical.'

It was quite different from what happened between the Judaizers, Rabbis and their followers, where there was no intimacy whatsoever between the parties. The Great Commission is a command for leaders to make disciples (Matt 28: 18-20).

Sanders admonished that, *'In order to carry out his full trust, the leader must devote time to train others to succeed and perhaps supersede him.'* Early noted that, *'Second generation leaders stand on their predecessors' shoulders...because of all they have been given (taught) through their predecessors.'* Discipleship development process is still the recommended way to get people established into Christian-fold, and thereby raise leaders for the next generation. Interestingly, despite the short duration of John the Baptist's ministry, he was able to train his disciples. Twenty years after the Church began, Paul met them at Ephesus, still maintaining John's legacy (Acts 19:1-7). NGC leaders considered this principle as a workable one and adopted it. Let us begin to embark upon training believers as disciples. Jesus' pattern in the New Testament will be very helpful, although in many of these, NGC church did not understand the dynamics fully.

For further reading[1]

---

1 J. Mallison, *Mentoring to Develop Disciples and Leaders*, (West Chutswood, Australia: Openbook Publishers, 1998).

K. R. Anderson and R. D. Reese, *Spiritual Mentoring: A Guide for Seeking and Giving Direction*, (Guildford, Surrey: Eagle IPS Ltd, 2000).

F. Wickman and T. Sjodin, *Mentoring: A Success Guide for Mentors and Protégés*, (New York: McGraw-Hill Companies, 1997).

W. C. Wright, *Mentoring: The promise of Relational Leadership*, (Milton Keynes: Paternoster Press, 2004).

J. C. Maxwell, *Mentoring 101*, (Nashville, TN: Thomas Nelson Inc, 2008).

P. Jenkins, *The Next Christendom: The Coming of Global Christianity*, (New York: Oxford University Press, 2007).

INTRODUCTION:

Mentoring and discipleship are two leadership activities that keep the Church steadfastly growing. When people discover they have a stake in your ministry, they commit their whole being and resources into the work. In this lesson, we will consider the effects of Ultra-modern infra-structural worship centres and the use of Mass Media/Information technology in the preaching of the gospel by the NGC churches.

Scriptural Focus: Matt 10:1, 9-11; Lk 19:30-32, 22:7-13, 35; Acts 17:15-29.

ULTRA-MODERN WORSHIP CENTRES

In this lesson, I must warn that every Church is a unique Church with its own settings. In all these formulas that are being analysed in this course, they should be impersonated with caution. We must rely on the leading of the Holy Spirit to tell us *'what is applicable in your area or context (Acts 13:1-4; Rom 8:14).'* There is the need to do a general review of what others have done to get to where they are. This is the whole concept behind this teaching about the Contemporary New Generation Churches. As George Barna noted:

'People are different, and they respond in different way to stimuli, therefore, learn from their experience but avoid replication of such models, if God is not leading you to do so. Learn to generate your own ideas and thoughts through your observation and learning.'

Kalu Ogbu noted that, Benson Idahosa was the first to embark upon the building of a mega-church project in Benin City with a capacity of about two thousand-seats, known as:

Miracle Center at Airport Road, by 1 Giwa Amu Street, Benin City, Nigeria in 1975-8. Later he moved to the

Faith Miracle Center (a.k.a Faith Arena with a capacity of 10,000 seats) in 1984-86.

This **'Faith Dome'** was an enigmatic work of architecture that attracted streams of worshippers who wanted to identify with a man of success, a voice that sought to liberate people from the crutches of poverty. Since then, we have seen many different palatial kinds of structure with theatrical decorations presented on the altar of the NGC Churches.

The turning of a forest into a modern City, a great feat by David Oyedepo is an amazing wonder in Canaan Land, Otta, Ogun state, Nigeria. Where Philip Jenkins noted and caledl these, *'health and wealth'* Churches. These Churches have proved very attractive to the middle classes as well as the poor. Perhaps the best example of the great show place is the **Faith Tabernacle, which reportedly seats (50,000) worshippers.** Other flourishing ministries are **Mountain of Fire** and miracle ministries, **Deeper life Bible Church** and The **Redeemed Christian Church of God, with their massive Redemption Camp meeting ground at Lagos/Ibadan Express Way.** Hundreds of thousands are daily attracted to these places of worship because of the comfort and beauty the environment provides. An under-developed environment does not attract a well-to-do or an aspiring person to worship. People want to be where they can be challenged or inspired to aim higher, this is what these environments provide.

THE USE OF ELECTRONIC MEDIA/INFORMATION TECHNOLOGY ENHANCES CHURCH GROWTH

The Nigeria of the 1960s and 1970s was quite different from the one of the twenty first century. Life is not static, technology has advanced, and the Church cannot afford to be behind. The NGC Churches must be commended for their effort in using the mass media/information technological provision to boost the delivery of the gospel in recent times. The initiator of Televangelism was the late Benson Idahosa of blessed memories, as observed by Ogbu, a Pentecostal commentator.

Musa Gaiya noted that, the NGC preachers adopted the mass media means as an importation of American influence, affirming Idahosa as the leading figure. Stressing that, *'One important attribute of these kinds of Churches is their creativity, particularly in the use of the media, radio, television, newspaper, posters, bill-boards, electronic mail and the internet.'* He analysed the method as, *'In Nigeria one can be prayed for through the television by placing one's hands on the television set.'*

The NGC he noted have affectively taken over the home video industry, some of the popular Christian video industries are Christian Dior Production, Liberty Films and The mount Zion Film Production.

278

Chris Oyakhilome of the Christ Embassy and Chris Okotie of the Household of God Churches cannot be ignored in the gospel communication through the use of media exposition. Donatus Ukpong noted that, The Pentecostals have encouraged the use of mass media for religious programmes and this is fast becoming normal for the mainline Churches in the country.

This medium of preaching the gospel has offered a lot of opportunities to the unchurched people and non-Christian adherents to listen to the gospel in their closet unnoticed. I have seen and heard of Muslims who said they love listen to preachers like Olubi Johnson, Chris Oyakhilome, late Benson Idahosa, Enoch Adeboye, William Kumuyi, just to name a few. These secret Jesus admirers and disciples claimed that the power of the gospel has helped to influence their thinking and faith in God. All of us cannot be televangelist and radio gospel broadcasters, but if God is leading you into it, then learn the art of mass media communications before venturing into it. More practically, do ensure that you settle the issue of the financial involvement before going in (Lk 14:28-31). This is a good counsel.

Letter writing through internet, telephone counselling, GSM text messages can help us to reach our audience and congregations in a much easier way now than ever. Let us explore these means to the advantage of the gospel. Church history taught us that God used Alexander the great to establish a language culture (Greek) in European world; and used the Romans to establish good road networks and means of postage; before Jesus was born to carry out his mission of human salvation. These means facilitated the spread of the message of salvation faster than anticipated. So in our world we can use the internet and mass media tools to facilitate the gospel and glorify our Lord before his imminent return.

For further reading[1]

---

1 G. Barna, *User Friendly Churches*, (Ventura, CA: Regal Books, 1991).

K. Ogbu, *African Pentecostalism: An Introduction*, (New York: Oxford University Press, 2008).

P. Jenkins, *The Next Christendom*, (Oxford, Oxford University Press, 2007).

M. A. B. Gaiya, '*The Pentecostal Revolution in Nigeria,* Occasional Paper (Centre African Studies, University of Copenhagen, 2002).

INTRODUCTION:

The previous lesson revealed to us how the NGC churches developed through the establishment of Ultra-modern infra-structural worship centres to attract the crowds they enjoy; and how they have taken advantage of the ITC technology to the full; as a dividend for the gospel. In this final session, we will look at the emphasis on the Bible as the divine tool for Christian excellence and how to avoid the use of unnecessary theological terminologies to prove our scholarship before our members who are averagely educated. Then, we will review the whole talk at the end.

Scriptural Focus: 1Tim 4:12; 2 Tim 2:15; Heb 4:12; Tit 1:10-14; Isa 55:8-11; Jn 1:1-5, 6:63, 15:1-8.

THE WORD OF GOD AS THE POWER BEHIND NGCS' GROWTH.

Donatus Ukpong asserts that, *'Pentecostalism has reawakened a general desire and love for the bible as the written Word of God, and as a perennial document of authentic Christian moral life.'* He stressed that, *'Many are nowadays taking the Bible seriously and it is no longer considered as a book meant for the clergy. There are many Bible study groups in the mainline Churches in Nigeria and some of them are operating vital ecclesial ministries.'* This view is a result of what the use of the Word of God by the NGC ministers has provoked in the missionary Churches, that would not lay strong emphasis on the Bible, rather preferring to use the writings/sayings of Church fathers to entertain their worshippers. It shows that the NGC laid strong emphasis on the Word and the result is what encourages the super-power Churches to follow suit. The Church Growth Movement traces their theories on God's revealed Word, that whatever is not based on the living Word is considered heretic. Snyder reminds us that, *'...the Bible is the supreme and final authority concerning the Church's life and growth.'* The Word of God in the Bible is fundamentally a book that contains the guiding principles about the Church's operation, what it should be, and its function to the world. As the Word grows in the hearers, so faith for the impossible grows alongside. The case of Paul in Asia was a good example of how the increase in the Word of God resulted in Church Growth and establishment:

'...all that dwelt in Asia heard the Word of the Lord Jesus, both Jews and Greeks...And many who believed confessed and turn from their evil deeds...So the Word of God grew exceedingly and prevailed'

(Acts 19:8-20). The theory of the healthy undiluted use of the Word of God enhances Church Growth. There is enough provision in God's Word on how to grow the church. In the first place, the Church is not man's forethought but God's. Therefore, the best place to refer to, on the issue of Church Growth, would necessarily be the Word of God.

The parable of the sower in Mark's Gospel Chapter Four is a good example how the Word of God can grow the church effectively. When planted on a good ground, 30%, 60% and 100% is the expected harvest (Mk 4:4-20). The Acts of the Apostles gave a number of ways the Word of God affected the work of the early church (Acts 4:4, 6:7, 12:24). Notably, in Ephesus, it was reported that, as the Word grew, the Church multiplied, because they believed in the Word spoken (Acts 19:10, 18, 20). In the Great Commission, the Lord of the Church commanded that the disciples be taught the entire commandment that He gave them (Matt 28:19). Thus the Word of God as a theory in NGC is a relevant prerequisite for Church growth today. God watches over the application of his Words to confirm them where necessary (Isaiah 55:11 and Jeremiah 1:12).

UNNECESSARY USE OF THEOLOGICAL TERMINOLOGIES

The NGC preachers are not the types that were trained in seminaries and monastic centres with degrees in Theology or Psychologies/philosophies of religion; Hermeneutics of the Bible; Cosmological exegesis and all the 'ologies of religion.' They were simply filled with the Holy Spirit and had some knowledge of the Bible and understanding of the eschatological implication of Jesus return, if the world is not evangelised for him. These simply stirred the fire of Pentecostal awakening and the result is the NGC Church boom everywhere. They did not possess what is known as religious vocabulary, but were drunk in the power of the Spirit like the Apostles; hence, the visibility of the Apostles' result is noticed all over.

Do not misunderstand my intentions here, I am aware of (2 Tim 2:15) and I do strongly believe in education of ministers, to enable them to preach sound doctrines and to understand perfect interpretation of the Bible. No Doctor or Lawyer practices without first passing through professional screening, Artisanship or Law school. But consider (Tit 1: 10-14, 2:8-15, 3:14).

281

Where the use of theological vocabulary cannot heal a sick person, why open your mouth? Why use the word 'missiology', in Sunday service where 60% are primary/secondary school leavers and 25% are illiterate, instead of simply saying 'mission'? Why say my message is about, 'Eschatology' in Bible study where the educated hardly close from their office to attend, when you could easily say 'End-time'? Why use 'Ecclesiology', when it is even more convenient to say quite simply 'Church'? Jesus never attended any school of his days, nor did some of his Apostles. The simplicity of his message was an epitome of fire that left the peoples' heart burning and their minds pondering, 'what words are these?' They said, *'He spoke like one who had authority.'* (Matt 7:29). He mesmerized the educated Rabbis of his day, He made the Lawyers a congregation of fools and turned the religious bigots into religious recalcitrants (Matt 21:23-27, 22:15-46, 23:2-30). Knowledge in theology is well encouraged, but let it not become an uncomfortable yoke to the simplicity of gospel.

When you get to an academic environment do as the occasion demands, become the Webster Dictionary there and remember to simplify when you are back at Church. A humble educated person who ministers pleases God more than arrogant educated confusionists. Jesus would rather use a fisherman than use the most educated, but untransformed theologian. Your training should not hinder the gospel (2 Cor 12:6-7).

GENERAL REVIEW OF THE COURSE

Questions and Answers, student comments and feed back.

For further reading[1]

1 H. Snyder, 'Renewal Review,' *Evaluating The Church Growth Movement 5 Views*, G. L. McIntosh, (Eds) (Grand Rapids, MI: Zondervan, 2004).

H. Cox, *Fire From Heaven*, (New York: Addison Wesley Publishing Company, 1995).

A. C. Thiselton, *New Horizons in Hermeneutics: The Theory and Practice of Transforming Biblical Reading*, (Grand Rapids, MI: Zondervan Publishing House, 1992).

P. Ballard and J. Pritchard, *Practical Theology in Action: Christian Thinking in the Service of Church and Society*, (London: SPKC, 2006).

MODULE 4b: CHURCH GROWTH-EXPRESSIONS

(Revd Dr Deji Okegbile MA)

FRESH EXPRESSIONS OF CHURCH FOR MISSION: A RENEWED INITIATIVE FOR CHANGING TIME.

In order to overcome the current decline in membership and spirituality in the Western church, the church is engaging in mission bearing in mind the massive shift in global/post-modern culture. The purpose of this course is to awaken the church in Africa to the global challenges facing mission and evangelism. The course is to help the church to think of effective approach on how to improve mission and evangelism. The 12 kinds of fresh expressions in the Western context can prompt deeper reflection in the African context.

FRESH EXPRESSIONS OF CHURCH: LANGUAGE AND PRACTICE OF MISSION.

LECTURE 1: INTRODUCTION

The world is changing, the Christian community in the United Kingdom which is of pivotal importance to Christian mission in the world are repositioned to lead the way among Western nations in engaging with the massive shift in global post-modern culture. With at least 60% of the United Kingdom population now beyond the reach of the churches, and the proportion growing each year, the rest of the world can benefit from the British approach. The publication of Mission-shaped Church report in 2004 engaged the imagination of the Church of England, and the Methodist Church. Together with other denominations throughout United Kingdom, they have adopted the language of forming 'Fresh Expressions' of church. This is described as a 'mixed economy', and a normal part of engaging in God's mission (Croft).

Fresh Expressions of Church as a missional practice is about finding and engaging in God's mission for a changing world and church. Christians are stepping out in faith and beginning fresh expressions of church: new or different forms of church for a changing culture. Fresh expressions are a form of church for the Western changing culture, established primarily for the benefit of people not yet church members.

283

1. Alternative worship communities: A loose network of groups trying to connect Church, and especially worship, with particular shifting segments of popular culture. It seeks to be responsive to post-modern culture with a multi-media approach.

2. Base Ecumenical Communities (BEC): Offers a gospel of liberation with origins in Latin America (Brazil–1950s). A church of the poor, for the poor.

3. Café church: It is relational. Pub church, café church, churches meeting in leisure centres are offering new ways to meet in community across United Kingdom. The weekly and monthly patterns of meetings and gatherings includes: reading and discussing the newspapers in a pub; meeting for a meal with Holy Communion in a café owned by the church; and playing sports in a local gym. The strapline is, 'Church for people who don't go to church.' Its members devised the pattern of gatherings by reflecting on how their personal interests could be used to bring new life to others.

4. Cell church:

5. Churches arising out of community initiatives:

6. Multiple and midweek congregations:

7. Network focused churches:

8. School-based and school linked: congregations and churches.

9. Seeker church: Environment where life issues and Christian insights can be considered. The Seeker approach was pioneered by Willow Creek Church in Chicago in an attempt to create an experience of worship and teaching in which 'seekers' will be comfortable.

10. Traditional church plants:

11. Traditional forms of church: Inspiring new interest.

12. Youth congregations: Focus on children; Focus on under 5's and their families.

12+. Other new developments:

HOW TO CREATE FRESH EXPRESSIONS OF CHURCH.

In the mission shaped introductory course on how to explore the 'why' of creating fresh expressions of church, a six weeks course looking at the ever-changing nature of the social communities is put in place. The course is also about why the church needs to rethink its approach to those communities in meaningful and relevant ways.

The six sessions of the course are designed to present those changes in an informative and interactive way suitable for clergy and lay alike.

1. Rediscovering mission and what that means for church: Explores the mission of God as the foundation for any expression of church.
2. Changing world, changing church: Explores how the rise of consumerism and networking has affected our culture and how the Church might respond.
3. Re-imagining Church community: Explores the need for fresh expressions of church to be community-focused.
4. Re-imagining the Church-worship: Explores how fresh expressions of church are re-imagining worship.
5. Re-imagining Church-leadership and discipleship: Explores the type of leadership needed in fresh expressions of church and how to facilitate discipleship.
6. Where do we go from here? A time for evaluation, by providing space for people to respond to the need for Fresh Expressions of Church.

LECTURE 2: DEFINITION FOR FRESH EXPRESSIONS OF CHURCH.

Mission-shaped Church deliberately does not define the term 'Fresh Expressions of church' but describes a range of twelve different types of activity. The overall picture is very fluid, but as at May 2006, a definition which is to be refined further is:

'A FRESH EXPRESSION IS A FORM OF CHURCH FOR OUR CHANGING CULTURE ESTABLISHED PRIMARILY FOR THE BENEFIT OF PEOPLE WHO ARE NOT YET MEMBERS OF ANY CHURCH.'

It will come into being through principles of listening, service, incarnational mission and making disciples. It will have the potential to become a mature expression of church shaped by the gospel and the enduring marks of the church and for its cultural context.

FRESH EXPRESSIONS OF CHURCH AS A MEANS OF RENEWING VISION ARE:

A. Missional: Serving people outside church. One of the key elements of fresh expressions of church is the focus on mission as the main motivation. What is fresh about mission? Haven't we been doing some mission and evangelism for a long time? Since New Testament times, Christians have been called to see the gospel embedded in different

285

cultures in appropriate ways. So that's not a new development. Some of the examples of Fresh Expressions as enumerated above in UK context are new and fresh for a particular culture and they may not have been tried before (although they may be familiar to Christians elsewhere). Some are genuinely innovative.

B. Incarnational: Listening to people and entering their culture. Incarnational mission in terms of the way things are established and a sense of journey, growth and development. Incarnational mission is essentially mission after Jesus' pattern and style. People beginning with Fresh Expressions of church are generally speaking, not going with their hands full of what they have to offer. Nor do they have in mind a particular set pattern of what a Fresh Expression will look like. This is much more like a shared journey. The journey begins and continues with listening to the context and the wider community. It continues with loving service, exactly the pattern Jesus commends and demonstrates. As people listen and serve so new communities are formed. In those new communities, people come to faith. Only at a later stage in the process/journey does worship begin.

C. Educational: Making discipleship a priority by calling people to faith in Jesus Christ, and equally being committed to the development of a consistent Christian lifestyle appropriate to, but not withdrawn from, the culture or cultures in which it operates. *'If we fail in the area of making disciples, we should not be surprised if we fail in the area of leadership development.'* Discipleship promotes missional leadership.

D. Ecclesial: Forming church and relationships. A community of faith is characterized by a friendly welcome and hospitality with an open ethos and style for new members. Church in all its forms goes through death and resurrection just as its Lord did. Fresh Expressions of church are currently the key means of incarnating ecclesial resurrection, and by implication, death.

Every Fresh Expression of church is different. Some are in rural areas and others in the inner city. Some are in new housing areas. Others are primarily for young people or children, (single or married). Some are based in schools or homes. Each is a new adventure for the gospel (Steven Croft, Claire Dalpra and George Lings).

E. Spirituality of fresh expressions of church. The spirituality of fresh expressions of church is the spirituality of risk. It is argued that one of the consistent threads of running through many fresh expressions is God's call to take risks, to step out beyond comfort zones.

When Jesus called Simon the fisherman, who had caught nothing all night long, Jesus says, *'Put out into deep water, and let down the nets for a catch.'* (Luke 5:4). Simon was offered a deeper invitation from a familiar shoreline and comfortable shallows. Simon became Peter, the rock upon which God built his Church.

Discussion: How and where might God be asking something similar of you or your church?

LECTURE 3: WHY FRESH EXPRESSIONS OF CHURCH?

A fresh expression is a new form of church for our changing culture through loving service, community formation, evangelism, discipleship making, and evolving worship. Fresh Expressions of church are a more welcoming and open community, offering ways for all ages to learn about faith through worship and preaching that have depth and relevance, and inviting people into life-changing discipleship and service. *'We live in turbulent time of change. Many, beyond the borders of church, are desperate for some sense of spiritual reality. Fresh expressions of church are the green shoots of the future.' (Stuckey).*

FRESH EXPRESSIONS OF CHURCH ARE ABOUT LIFE CHANGING THEOLOGY THAT RESPECTS THE AUTHORITY OF THE BIBLE:

1. Showing Gospel themes: Essentially evangelical, showing how the good news becomes most clearly audible and visible. Fresh Expressions incarnate naturally different aspect of Christian faith and values in a way that is not always evident in the life of inherited church.

2. Modelling the mission of God: Theology of the *missio-Dei*–the understanding of God as primarily and essentially a missionary God, Father, Son, and Holy Spirit. Fresh Expressions naturally embody doctrine rather than simply speak or assent to it.

3. Focusing on the kingdom: Agreed goal of *missio Dei* thinking, namely the coming of the kingdom, or reign of God. The chief end and

287

focus of sharing in God's mission is the coming of the kingdom. Missiology shapes ecclesiology. The church is for God and the world and only then, in any sense, for itself. This contrasts sharply with the impression given by many inherited churches, especially those in decline, or wrestling with the costs of keeping huge buildings running, or appealing for large sums to sustain historic ministries. Fresh Expressions of church are not just keeping the show long ago planted.

4. Nothing new under the sun: Churches in every age, place and time, whether 10, 100, 1,000 years ago, were once planted and 'Fresh.' Fundamentally, all church began as a Fresh Expression in that place, time and culture.

5. Constantly changing church: The New Testament bears testimony to Temple-church and synagogue church in different social and geographical settings, catering for quiet different groups of Christian believers. With the arrival of 'Christendom' came dedicated sacred spaces modelled on basilicas and 'cathedrals', seat of power. Communities of monks produced their own 'Fresh Expressions' partly in rejection of the opulence and perceived decadence of Christian Rome, hundreds of years before those magnificent medieval monasteries and abbeys, many now in ruins, were built. The reformers developed their own forms of church out of a revised ecclesiology, and whether Catholic or Protestant, 'Christian Europe' followed the essential territorial pattern of diocese and parish, with its dedicated buildings of a certain form.

Seventeenth and eighteenth century England developed associations, classes and societies as Fresh Expressions of church, through the Methodist movement. Fresh Expressions of church are not new, but are natural to Christian faith and history. They are about major renewal of the Christian Church involving discovery or re-discovery of many different models of church.

6. Witness and evangelism: Invaluable method of Christian witness and evangelism in our contemporary pluralist, multi-faith cultural context. Fresh Expressions of church can offer a different model of being Christian and being church in place of 'building+priest+stipend' stereotype of inherited church.

7. Serving the community: Offering 'flat servanthood,' and not as landlord, but partners with others in communicating a different expression of Christianity in a community.

8. Being reproductive: Fresh Expressions produce additional Fresh Expressions. They remind us that church is, God intentionally, reproductive. Organic reproduction rather than arithmetic thinking is used to describe church growth and vitality. Language of 'natural,' 'healthy' church prevails. Fresh Expressions are young, and it is usually the young who have babies, they reproduce while fertile rather than barren.

9. Engaging with culture: Fresh Expression of church is significant in relation to the constantly changing cultural context. It enables new and different people to become Christian disciples. (Atkins).

Fresh expressions of church include non-verbal and verbal expressions of faith.

For discussion: How do you respond to the story in Matthew 9:36-37.

LECTURE 4: METHODISM–A MODEL OF FRESH EXPRESSIONS OF CHURCH

Who is a Methodist? A Methodist belongs to that company of believers who were and are being added to the Jesus' disciple-band, through the original labours of two brothers, John and Charles Wesley. With the help of many others, both in their own and succeeding generations, who (re)-discovered the evangelical secret that being a Christian is a matter of putting your faith in Jesus Christ as Saviour and Lord by entering into a close and ever more intimate friendship with him.

'EVERY OLD WAY OF BEING CHURCH WAS ONCE NEW.' (Cottrell and Sledge).

'The Spirit is seeking to make the church into the vibrant vehicle of God's tomorrow, not the museum piece of yesterday.' (Stuckey)

EVERY NEW WAY OF BEING CHURCH MUST BECOME OLD

And in turn will give birth to what will follow as the Church responds faithfully to the commission of Christ to proclaim the faith afresh. Every church planted at some point owed its existence to the dedicated ministry of a particular group of believers at a particular time who were seeking to respond to the needs and challenges of their day by establishing some new expressions of Christian life.

The Revd John Wesley (1703-1791) was a clergyman of the Church of England. After a period of service in Savannah, Georgia, he returned to England, where his heart-warming experience took place, in Aldersgate Street, London, on 24th May 1738.

Wesley *'sought no less than the recovery of the truth, life and power of earliest Christianity and the expansion of that kind of Christianity.'* Following the experience in which he received an assurance of his own salvation, John Wesley felt called by God to an itinerant preaching ministry. With the support and help of other like-minded clergy and lay people, he preached in churches, in homes and in the open air (courtesy of Whitefield), offering to his hearers the same salvation and assurance that he had experienced himself. Those who responded to his preaching he organised into religious societies, divided into classes, each with its own leader (Methodist Catechism).

METHODISM'S MANIFESTO.

Eighteen days after Wesley's 'heart' had been strangely warmed,' his preaching at the ancient church of the Blessed Virgin Mary on Oxford's High Street blew the first trumpet-call of the Evangelical Revival.' The trumpet call was: *'For by grace are ye saved through faith; and that not of yourselves; it is the gift of God.' (Eph.2:8).* That was the text on which Methodism was launched. Fresh Expression of Methodism is to make the trumpet call come alive again. **Fresh expression of salvation:** Salvation is the primary need of humanity all the way through history. Every chapter of history tells the story of man's attempt to save himself, his burnt offerings, his ceremonial ablutions, his self-inflicted ordeals, his penances, his disciplines, but none of them avails. Wesley's spiritual background and obedience as a minister of religion was insufficient until his heart-warming experience. The truth dawned. All that had to be done had already been done by Christ, given in grace. In 1745, John Wesley wrote about the nature of fresh expression of salvation:

'By salvation I mean, not barely (according to the vulgar notion) deliverance from hell, or going to heaven, but a present deliverance from sin, a restoration of the soul to its primitive health, its original purity; a recovery of the divine nature; the renewal of our souls after the image of God in righteousness and true holiness, in justice, mercy and truth. This implies all holy and heavenly tempers, and by consequence all holiness of conversation.'

Fresh expression of salvation: Is about restoration of the soul, and recovery of the divine nature. Fresh expression of Wesleyan pattern of evangelism will have no difficulty with salvation theology derived from John Wesley as the basis of our evangelistic activity. This expression is about 'born again' Christianity.

Fresh expression of God's grace: It is easy to illustrate grace as the unmerited favour and love of God. Fresh Expression of the meaning of Grace is an offer of pardon and power, the power of the risen Christ.

Fresh expression of faith: This is the lifting up of an expectant arm to receive the enabling power. An understanding of Peter's fresh expression of God's grace accepted by faith can bring healing to the lame beggar. (Acts 3:1-16).

Methodism was born of God in the warmed heart of its founder. It grew with his growth. All its developments have their correspondence in his experience. Membership is based on personal conversion, the ordinances are ordered for the nourishing of the soul, and all things are made to serve as means in bringing men to the knowledge of the truth.

Wesley preached Christ as he had realized Him in his own soul. The Methodist peculiarities of fellowship, testimony, and progression, were all first exemplified in the religious life of the first Methodist. What John Wesley preached, Charles Wesley sang. The Methodist Hymn-Book is the manual of Methodist theology and the expression of Methodist experience. The hymns everywhere strike the note of universality*(EMHB. 323)*:

'Come, sinners, to the gospel feast, Let every soul be Jesu's guest;
Ye need not one be left behind, For God hath bidden all mankind.' .

LECTURE 5: SEARCH FOR FRESH EXPRESSIONS OF METHODISM IN NIGERIA

1. Open-air worship in Nigeria.
2. Corporate episcopacy.
3. National Congress of Evangelising Methodists (NACEM).
4. Cecil Williamson Outreach from America.
5. Methodist Evangelical Movement (MEM)–Dept. of Evangelism.
6. Fellowship of Methodist Professionals.
7. Methodist Campus Fellowship (MCF).
8. Methodist Praying Partners, Coming Alive and Wesley School of Prayer and Discipleship (WESPLE).
9. Vision Africa.
10. 2006 New Constitution on Methodist repositioning.

HOW FRESH EXPRESSIONS FIT INTO METHODIST CHURCH NIGERIA REPOSITIONING.

Fresh expression of Methodism is the coming alive of its original missional ethos, evangelism and disciple making. The Revival in general and Methodism in particular were the response to a situation where the conventional parish system and parish ministrations had failed to satisfy. Nigerian Methodism is the pioneer of the international church in Nigeria, and pioneer of fresh expressions of open-air worship at Badagry under Agia tree on September 24, 1842. This event marked the Fresh Expression of Christianity and open air crusading in Nigeria. Therefore, one of the needs of Nigeria as a nation is the *raison d'etre* of Methodist Church Nigeria (MCN).

Methodist repositioning has a particular marked significance in the Fresh Expressions of church. The practical challenges of Fresh Expressions of Methodist repositioning are legion, but a genuine vision and mission of the church can give indispensable resources for seeing the church in its fullness and flexibility. The 2006 Methodist Constitution suggests that churches, dioceses, and headquarters need to look closely at their priorities and ask realistic question about best use of resources because the vision and mission of the church need fresh expression. Methodist repositioning according to the church's vision and mission is marked by four characteristics:

- **Spiritually vibrant church.**
- **Consistently win more soul for Christ.**
- **Develop spiritually fulfilled members.**
- **Remain very active in serving humanity.**

Repositioning in verb form is missional, and it goes beyond the vision to be one of the largest and spiritually vibrant churches in Nigeria. It overflows into discipleship. Church repositioning is about participating in God's mission, by enabling others to become Christ's disciples. Repositioning is a call to develop fresh ways of being church in order to bring Gospel to the whole of our society. Fresh expression of Methodist repositioning needs clarity about vision and values. Methodist repositioning as practised by Fresh Expressions of church points to:

1. **Evangelical tradition**: John Wesley's sermons based on his personal experience and the Methodist Hymn-Book will be the best guide to Methodist evangelical tradition.
2. **Growth in discipleship**: *'Discipleship means adherence to Christ and, because Christ is the object of that adherence, it must take the form of discipleship...Christianity without the living Christ is inevitably Christianity without discipleship, and Christianity without discipleship is always Christianity without Christ'.* D Bonhoeffer.

292

Fresh Expression of Wesleyan evangelism is about initiation into discipleship. People who responded to Wesley or his preachers were instructed to join a class. After three months in a class, where they were taught about justification and the new birth they were in a position to be admitted to membership of the Society.

3. **Church growth**: *'Church growth is kingdom growth by the power of the Holy Spirit, the life of the New Creation.'* (Clowney). Church growth is not to be confused with denominational self-aggrandizement or the preservation of a human institution. Behind growth statistics in general is the need for discernment as to what kind of growth is taking place. In church growth, people come into the church three ways: by biological, transfer, and conversion growth. The church growth movement is intended to assist new conversion growth, the kind of church growth that most nearly parallels true kingdom growth (Matt.28:19). For Dr Donald Anderson McGavran, the patriarch and prophet of the church growth movement, *'the whole gospel for all mankind means little, unless it is preceded by stupendous church planting. There can be little hope of sustained signs of the Kingdom in the world without the influence of a sufficient number of sons and daughters of the kingdom.'*

4. **Church planting**: Discipline of creating new communities of Christian faith as part of the mission of God to express God's kingdom in every geographical and cultural context.

One of the main tasks of Methodist repositioning is to ask how it can serve and be a blessing to its local community. This calls for a fresh expression to Methodist liturgy, and renewal of the sacramental character, so as to remain active in serving humanity, by transforming our immediate environment.

Other reasons for utilising Fresh Expressions of church.
1. The pattern of the week has changed: Many people now work or go to school on Sundays.
2. The way we relate to others has changed: Influence of science and technology, especially in relation to communications.
3. Our culture is changing: Numerous recognizable cultures against the former church centrality.
4. Nigerian population is becoming more religious: Spiritual seekers, looking for meaning and answers to life's big questions.

'Every wineskin is destined to serve for a while and then be discarded for the sake of the wine.' (Mclaren).

FRESH EXPRESSIONS IS ABOUT DEVELOPING NEW WINESKINS.

In origin, Methodism was an attempt to make the Church a mission for creating and sustaining 'Scriptural holiness.' Its doctrinal and liturgical emphases were determined by this aim; and its special institutions were designed to make holiness a reality rather than to set up any doctrinaire system of Church polity. We need the grace to overcome the tensions of changing or maintaining a missionary campaign into hierarchical structure.

Methodist liturgy (wineskin) draws life and relevance from what is distinctive about Methodist (wine). Fresh expression of Methodism is about seeking the divine in the daily. Fresh expressions of church encourage movement of mission, and coming alive to a new and still-to-be-discovered future. Fresh expressions of church liturgy depend on the renewing, vibrant power of the Holy Spirit, and can save church traditions from running the risk of becoming full of unnecessary detail and decoration.

Methodist sacramental tradition has the potential and particular gifts and emphases that can widen and enrich the Fresh Expression of Nigerian Methodist repositioning. The Fresh Expressions of Methodist liturgy draws wisdom from the past and translates these insights into the present and future life of the church, its faith, worship, ministry and spirituality.

All can be saved: An inclusive theology.

Living a holy life: Social holiness.

A covenant with God: Covenant service.

Small group: Christians seeking to take their faith seriously and apply it to their lives.

Assurance of salvation: Blessed assurance (Wesley's conversion).

Grassroots movement: Lay people playing major part in the church.

Born in song: Singing our faith.

Methodists and the Bible: The Methodist founding documents emphasise a call to scriptural holiness.

The connexion: A larger connected community.

Fresh Expressions of church liturgy can translate the church from restrictive liturgically informed building, dressing, order of worship and an extremely gloomy and ugly interior into an authentic faith and future runs through the past. Fresh expressions of church through past roots, connection and authenticity in a changing world will help to maintain continuity with historical Christianity as the church moves forward.

1. Fresh Expressions of church divine services including Sunday worship embrace an incarnational spirituality rather than liturgically restricted and routine agenda of the past roots.

2. Fresh Expressions of church acts of worship following prescribed rules can simplify church life to make more space and release gifts and energy for something new. Fresh expression of church divine services encompasses not only those actions that only a clergyman could carry out. The Levitical priesthood was lineal, whereby the existing priests consecrated their successors according to the primary appointment of God, that certain person is devoted to the divine service. Fresh expression of priesthood of all believers is included in the solemn words of the Great commission in Matthew 28:19.

3. Fresh Expressions of church mid-week services and other activities point towards formation and ordering of the spiritual life of the congregation.

4. **Fresh Expressions of the Christian calendar** unfold the whole mystery of Christ from incarnation and nativity to the ascension, to Pentecost and the expectation of the blessed hope of the coming of the Lord. When the Christian year is turned into a mere repetition of the past, we miss the point.

Fresh Expressions of liturgy is a continual evolution of liturgical vitality rather than repetition of the past Victorian glories. Some buildings can pose severe challenge to repositioning or fresh expression of any kind. A noble edifice designed in 18th century, but with interior layout, with fixed pews on slightly raised platform throughout the nave, can restrict the congregation to a very traditional understanding of the congregation's role in worship. We need a truly 'liturgical informed space' that will help the congregation understand who they are. Sunday and weekday congregations must no longer be an audience scattered the length of the north aisle, peering at a distant altar, but a community conscious of one another and interacting with one another in the offering of the liturgy. Fresh Expressions of church are a fresh vision in a relaxed, unhurried atmosphere, liberated from liturgical routine and architectural configuration of an early Christian basilica. Liturgical roles are formed not only for the purpose of fulfilling liturgical tasks, but with the potential to grow into class meetings/house fellowships, where team members could deepen their faith and fellowship (Richard Giles). Fresh Expressions of church promote an authentic church liturgy and true to the apostolic tradition. Fresh Expressions of Methodist evangelical liturgy has the potential to bring new conceptions of God, new expressions of mission and evangelism, and a new sense of responsibility and a baptism of power by which statements and constitution could be transmuted into life.

LECTURE 7: FRESH EXPRESSIONS OF METHODIST SACRAMENTAL CHARACTER

The Methodist doctrines of conversion, assurance, and full salvation can be traced to marked crises in Wesley's own experience of the saving grace of God. Fresh expression of Methodism in Nigeria can bring the needed revolution in Nigeria, as it quickened the Churches, changed the constitution of England, permeated the life of America, freed the slave and inaugurated the missionary enterprise for world mission. Fresh Expressions of Methodist sacramental character are not just about better communication strategy or more up-to-the-minute activities. Practices such as Baptism and Eucharist are where Scripture truly becomes a contemporary happening, that anchors the people in the 'fleshliness' of the Word who became human (flesh!). Fresh Expressions of the ordinances of God (Means of Grace) including the public worship of God, ministry of the Word, either read or expounded, the Supper of the Lord, private prayer, searching of the Scripture, fasting or abstinence has the potential to 'spread the power of Jesus's name.' Baptism (Rom 6: 4). Lord's Supper (Matt.26:20-29, I Cor. 11:23). Fresh Expressions of the Lord's Supper are not simply a record of the past repeated, but a means through which the past is made present, we are truly there. It is a covenant drink and celebration.

Methodist repositioning supports the development of fresh ways of being church through:
1. The stationing and development of lay and ordained people to begin and sustain Fresh Expressions of church
2. Identification and training of suitably gifted lay and ordained people to begin Fresh Expressions of church.
3. The appropriate development and recognition Fresh Expressions of church within.

Local Churches: Fresh Expressions of local congregations of the Methodist Church, meeting together as one for public worship and organised into classes call for revivalistic theology as the basis of the Church Council's supervision and evangelistic activity. To grow Fresh Expressions of a Local Church consisting of Junior members, Members-on-Trial, and Full Members who are enrolled Members of the Methodist Church, Catechumens, and Adherents is based on sowing the seed of the gospel into the lives of individuals. Methodism began in the context of small groups of Christian seeking to take their faith seriously and apply it to their lives and communities. We need to implement practically the mission-centred values built at the heart of the church's new constitution. The stages of admission and training of children and adults into membership of the church must not terminate after the confirmation ceremony. (See MCN constitution, p129-136).

Circuits: Fresh Expressions of Circuits should go beyond compositions of three local churches under the Pastoral care of one or more Ministers. To follow the tradition of Methodism, the Fresh Expression of a Circuit is meant to promote a grassroots movement, a larger connected community, the Connexion. A Fresh Expression of creating new Circuits will help the whole church to catch and live a fresh vision for mission, and not for position or promotion.

Dioceses: Fresh expressions of the Diocese for pioneering lay and ordained ministries and made available in every Circuit will promote church growth and church planting. (MCN Constitution, pp. 92-94). Fresh expressions of Youth Work (Singles and Married), Sunday Schools, Children services, and counselling services are needed in our changing world.

Archdioceses: Fresh Expressions of the Archdiocese will not only act as the executive arm of the Church Government next to Conference Connexional Council, but also initiate a movement of mission and change across the Conference and churches. Fresh Expressions of the Archdiocese will implement evangelical activities, and not only discipline (disciple) Ministers and Officers, but nurture them according to the Word of God.

The Conference: Fresh Expressions of the Conference will renew the vision and mission of the church by promoting growth, developing national network of Spirit-filled workers for Fresh Expressions of Methodist repositioning. Fresh Expressions of Methodism in Nigeria will not only maintain and interpret the doctrinal standard of the church, but will model an immediate, instantaneous, assured work of

297

grace through faith. Wesley's theology was experimental. His statements were formulated from experience. Fresh Expressions of the Methodist Conference can be formulated from members' personal evangelical experience. Truth vitalized by experience quickens and saves. Wesley preached Christ as he had realized Jesus in his own soul.

LECTURE 8: FRESH EXPRESSIONS OF CHURCH LEADERSHIP

The implication of the Fresh Expressions of church leadership calls for the need to equip people who will demonstrate and announce God's purpose and direction through Jesus Christ. Fresh Expressions of church leadership releases the missional imagination present among a community of God's people (1 Pet 2-4), and this goes beyond institutional roles in the church management and worship. Fresh expressions of church leadership are centred on reconnecting the church to the purpose of God by reproducing a community of authentic disciples. Fresh expressions of church leadership are:

Missional rather than attractional: Matt. 23:8, John 13: 5, Matt. 20:21- Fresh expression of church leadership is missional in nature. A 'sent' leader, going and moving in God's Spirit through His people is sent to bring healing to broken situations. Fresh Expression of missional leadership goes beyond the Christendom-mode church approach which is attractional, expecting people to come to them.

Messianic – Inaugurating God's Kingdom (Mark 10:42-44) – Fresh expression of church leadership takes Jesus as the primary model of mission, and the Gospel as the primary texts. Fresh expression of church leadership with Jesus as the model is the principal model for mission, ministry, and discipleship, and the focal point of an authentic New Testament faith. Leaders are partners with God in the redemption of the world

Apostolic and incarnational: Eph. 4:1-16, Acts 13:46-47 The apostolic nature of the church has to do more with sending, than elite legitimacy. Eph 4:1-16 comprehensively describes the five functions of: Apostle, Prophet, Evangelist, Pastor, and Teacher. Fresh Expressions of apostolic leadership in the church is about the rediscovery of the five functions of ministry and leadership in our churches. Vs.12-16:

Apostolic function: Pioneers new missional works and oversees their development.

Prophetic function: Discerns the spiritual realities in a given situation and communicates them in a timely and appropriate way to further the mission of God's people.

Evangelistic function: Communicates the gospel in such a way that people respond in faith and discipleship.

Pastoral function: Shepherds the people of God by leading, nurturing, protecting, and caring for them.

Teaching function: Communicates the revealed wisdom of God so that the people of God learn how to obey all that Christ has commanded them.

The functions are not mutually exclusive. Fresh Expressions of church leadership are relational, cultivating an environment within which God's people discern God's direction. Fresh Expressions of the pure-lineage understanding of apostolic domination has the potential for the church becoming inherently adaptive and flexible, shaping its forms and activities around mission rather than convention (Mclaren).

Fresh Expressions of church suggest the 'called-to-be-sent' and 'blessed-to-be-blessing' understanding of church leadership. The early Methodist response to pastoral problems was the Connexional system of linked societies run under the superintendency of Wesley with lay help; a kind of halfway house between a Religious Society and a church. The Religious Society was discipled and governed piecemeal in an organization for creating and developing Christian holiness, not to promote any theology of church polity. **Pray for the reawakening of our Connexional system and Religious Societies.**

Fresh expressions of church and the Holy Spirit.
The power that is adequate for fresh expression of church, Christian life and work is the power of the Holy Spirit. Without the presence and power of the Holy Spirit, fresh expressions of church may become human efforts (broken cisterns). Confusion and impotence are

inevitable when the Fresh Expressions of wisdom and resources of the world are substituted for the presence and power of the Spirit of God.

The church may have a Fresh Expression of a theology of Holy Spirit, but with no living consciousness of His experience and power. Theology without Holy Spirit experience can amount to faith without work. It is dead. Fresh Expressions of church need the Pentecost experience. Pentecost repositioned the early preachers. (Acts 2) Pentecost brought light, power, and joy to the Church.

Abiding in God's presence is the key to supernatural Fresh Expression of church, because the Church is the Body of Christ, indwelt and controlled by the Spirit. He directs, energises and controls. The resources of the fresh expressions of church are in 'supply of the Spirit.'

E. M. Bounds reminds us: 'Men are God's method. The Church is looking for better methods; God is looking for better men.'

May God make you and me, Spirit-filled vessels that will spread Fresh Expressions of scriptural holiness in Nigeria and throughout the world which is our parish in Jesus' name!

MODULE 5: HOLINESS, SPIRITUALITIES & MISSION

(Revd Dr Jennifer Smith BA MPhil)

INTRODUCTION AND OVERVIEW (INTERACTIVE PRESENTATION WITH KEY DOCUMENTS HANDOUT FOR STUDENTS)

Outline of Lectures with summarised Student Handouts:
1. Introduction and overview
2. Early Methodism and the ideas of John Wesley
3. Wesley and the 'means of grace': works of piety
4. Wesley and the 'means of grace': works of mercy
5. Revision and Reflection: Holiness, Mission, and Wesley
6. 'Holiness' and the mission of the church today I
7. 'Holiness' and the mission of the church today II
8. Revision and Reflection on local issues

Student Responsibilities:
- notes and attendance at lectures
- participation in discussion
- brief daily journal/notes considering
1. What idea or teaching caught your attention today?
2. Was there anything with which you disagreed?
3. Does it have a challenge for your church here?
4. How might the situation or church in which you serve challenge Wesley's (or other) ideas?
5. Does today bring to mind any story or parable from the life of Jesus or other scriptures that might shed light on our questions?

1 INTRODUCTION AND OVERVIEW

a. Definitions: What is holiness?
Tensions between different definitions:
1. Ethical (doing) vs. numinous (being in God)
2. Personal piety vs. social transformation/revolution

b. Why is holiness connected to mission?

c. Holiness and 'Christian perfection' in Methodist history

d. Problems/critical questions to do with holiness and mission

301

i Dangers of antinomianism or 'I can do what I want'
ii Dangers of individualism–reducing to personal piety
iii Dangers of reducing holiness to purity tests

e. Remedy: Isaiah 58–What kind of fast does the Lord require?
How does Jesus behave in relation to the ordinary life and concerns of people around him?

2. EARLY METHODISM AND THE WORLD OF THE WESLEYS

a. History – life of John Wesley and timeline
b. Progress and method of their ministry–open air preaching and organisation of societies, classes, bands.
c. Central ideas of John Wesley: a good churchman!
i Sources of authority: scripture, tradition, reason, experience
ii 'order of salvation': prevenient, justifying, sanctifying grace
iii Arminianism: 'All must be saved, all can be saved, all can know themselves saved, all can know themselves saved to the uttermost.'
iv 'all holiness is social holiness'

d. Controversies
i Arminianism vs. Calvinism
ii Antinonianism and quietism
iii Separate, or within the Church of England?
e. Strengths and weaknesses/critical questions

3. WESLEY AND THE 'MEANS OF GRACE': WORKS OF PIETY

a. Background and relation of works of piety and mercy
b. Sermon on 'the means of grace'/ordinances
   i Prayer
   ii Searching the scriptures
   iii Holy Communion
c. Fasting
d. Christian community
e. Healthy living – should we treat the markers of holiness as fixed, or do they vary with historical and cultural context? Remember what holiness is, and is not. (Consider with regard to alcohol. fair trade in the UK, the position of women in church, the housing of elders in nursing homes, dancing, Sabbath-keeping, status marks of wealth like fancy cars)

4. WESLEY AND THE 'MEANS OF GRACE': WORKS OF MERCY

a. Sermon on the mount VI: works of mercy, works of piety combined in the growth in grace towards 'perfection':

    i 'Doing good'
    ii Visiting the sick and prisoners
    iii Feeding and clothing people
    iv Education–the Foundry
    v Opposition to slavery
    vi Wesley on the use of money: earning, saving, giving all you can

5. REVISION, DISCUSSION, REFLECTION LECTURE: HOLINESS, MISSION AND WESLEY (NO HANDOUT)

What should ministers be doing, for mission?
What should ministers NOT do?
What would you counsel a minister whose church complained that she spent more time:
on non-church goers than on people in the church?
on social/community projects instead of specifically, church activities?

6. 'HOLINESS' AND THE MISSION OF THE CHURCH TODAY I

a. What should the church do to 'spread scriptural holiness?'
    i How are the 'works of piety'/means of grace involved?
    ii What are the issues in which holiness is concerned?
    iii What methods should the church use?

b. How social, how economic, and how political should the church be, in its mission? Cases to consider:

i. Martin Luther King Jr. and 'creative suffering', non-violent civil action for justice
ii. Bishop Ivan Manuel Abrahams, Methodist Church of South Africa:
Proposes Wesley's 'evangelical economics' as an alternative to economic globalisation
Botho/Ubuntu as African expansions of 'holiness'–a prophet to the West
iii. The church in Zimbabwe, opposition to President Robert Mugabe? (Methodist Recorder)

iv. Local problems, burdens, 'dash/bribe' and police tolls

v. Problems with expanded notions of holiness (social, political, economic)

1. When churches disagree internally

2. Persecution/opposition

Remedy: works of piety: Rom 12:1-2, 1 Cor. 2:16, Phil. 2:5 Remaining in the 'mind of Christ'

c. **Other 'cases to consider' in social and political holiness,** in the UK, US, and Nigeria – your examples?

7. 'HOLINESS' AND THE MISSION OF THE CHURCH TODAY II

a. Within the Abia Diocese: the Leprosy Colony, The Royal Cross Methodist Hospital, Renew, Amaudo Itumbauzo, Project Comfort

b. Ozuzu Oke – wholeness – Rosalind Colwill

i. 'Spirituality and Retreat Centre'

ii Ignatian practices of prayer and inclusion of people with disabilities to 'circumcise the heart' (avoid being what Wesley called an 'almost Christian')

iii Unification of works of piety and works of mercy.

8 REVISION AND APPLICATION TO LOCAL ISSUES (NO HANDOUT)

How are we each 'spreading scriptural holiness' in our own place now?

a. What keeps us from it?

b. What pressures do we face?

c. What temptations?

d. What obstacles?

e. What could help us, as Wesley's 'helpers?'

f. What kind of Bishop helps the spread of holiness?

> *...I believe I shall see the goodness of the Lord in the land of the living. Wait for the Lord; be strong and let your heart take courage; wait for the Lord! Psalm 27.13,14*

1. *Do nothing from selfish ambition or conceit, but in humility regard others as better than yourselves. Let each of you look not to your own interests, but to the interests of others.* **Let the same mind be in you that was in Christ Jesus,** *who, though he was in the form of God, did not regard equality with God as something to be exploited, but emptied himself, taking the form of a slave, being born in human likeness. And being found in human form, he humbled himself and became obedient to the point of death, even death on a cross. Philippians 2:3-8 NRSV*

2. 'hōl'y, adjective and noun. consecrated, sacred; morally and spiritually perfect; belonging to, commissioned by, devoted to, God; of high moral excellence.'[1]

3. 'In ordinary English, the term [holy] has acquired associations of "morality", "sanctity," or "purity," which often seem to bear little relation to the behaviour of fallen human beings. The Hebrew word *kadad* which underlies the New Testament concept of "holiness" has the sense of "being cut off", or "being separated". There are strong overtones of dedication: to be "holy" is to be set apart for and dedicated to the service of God.

A fundamental element, indeed *the* fundamental element of the Old Testament idea of holiness is that of "something or someone whom God has set apart". The New Testament restricts the idea almost entirely to personal holiness. It refers the idea to individuals... People are "holy" in that they are dedicated to God, and distinguished from the world on account of their calling by God. ...The term "holy" is theological, not moral, in its connotations, affirming the calling of the church and its members, and the hope that the church will one day share in the life and glory of God.'[2]

---

1 The Concise Oxford Dictionary. (Oxford: Clarendon Press. 1958).

2 Alistair McGrath, Christian Theology: an Introduction, 3rd ed. (Oxford: Blackwell, 2001), pp. 499, 500.

1.　　　　'The Methodist Church claims and cherishes its place in the Holy Catholic Church which is the Body of Christ. It rejoices in the inheritance of the apostolic faith and loyally accepts the fundamental principles of the historic creeds and of the Protestant Reformation. It ever remembers that in the providence of God Methodism was raised up to **spread scriptural holiness** through the land by the proclamation of the evangelical faith and declares its unfaltering resolve to be true to its divinely appointed mission.'[1]

2.　　　　'...it's like a h'urge, like a something you must do, a habit that you can't break. A good habit, a good habit that you can't break. You got to get involved. ...it like an illness but it a good illness. [laughing] Yeah it's an illness but it's something good. Illness is supposed to be something bad, but it a good illness.'[2]

3.　　　　'At Villa Road Methodist Church, holiness is about giving thanks to God with joy in all circumstances, about providing practical social services in the community, about the discipline of worshipping in Christian community, and about nurturing a relationship with Jesus as co-sufferer that acts as comfort in the most grim situations: loneliness, illness, poverty, and fear of violence.'[3]

4.　　　　*Of holy living, in 'the Character of a Methodist,' (1739) John Wesley wrote*: '[a Methodist] keeps all of God's commandments with all his strength, for his obedience is in proportion to his love, the source from which it flows. Whether he stays indoors or goes outside, whether he lies down, or gets up,...Whether he puts on his apparel, or labour, or eat and drink, or divert himself from too wasting labour, it all tendeth to advance the glory of God, by peace and goodwill among men.'[4]

---

1 Paragraph 4, first in section on 'Doctrine,' 'Methodist Church Nigeria Constitution, 1990', p. 1. Also 'Deed of Union of the Methodist Church of Great Britain' Adopted by uniting conference in 1932. Constitutional Practice and Discipline of the Methodist Church, Volume II, (Peterborough: Methodist Publishing House, 2004), p. 213. Emphasis added.

2 Mrs. E. Dixon, 20 Janaury 2005, taped interview 3:00ff, 5:20ff. Villa Road Methodist Church, Handsworth, Birmingham, UK.

3 Jennifer Smith, 'Mary in the Kitchen, Martha in the Pew: Patterns of holiness in a Methodist Church,' unpublished thesis for the MPhil Theology, Birmingham, 2006, p. 35.

4 John Wesley, (Halcyon Backhouse, ed) A Plain Man's Guide to Holiness, (originally A Plain Account of Christian Perfection) (London: Hodder and Stoughton, 1988), p. 25.

Wesley expected holiness to show the love of God and neighbour by keeping to a mesh of moral behaviours marked by self-control in everyday speech, emotion, work, use of money, and service.

5.   *In contrast, for Rudolf Otto, holiness was '…a thrill of awe or reverence, the sense of dependence, of impotence, or of nothingness, or again the feelings of religious rapture and exaltation.'[1] Holiness thus was not 'perfect goodness,' but 'an element independent of the category of the good:' by Otto's description holiness was without moral or ethical dimension, i.e. it was not about what a person DOES but about a sense of 'the numinous' God, withdrawn from ordinary life.*

For Reflection/Discussion: if a church's mission is to 'spread holiness,' how will what the church does, differ with Wesley's definition, versus Alistair McGrath or Rudolf Otto's?

6.   'Others have articulated holiness in more explicitly political or liberation-minded ways: for them the purpose of holiness is social transformation rather than individual or churched piety. For example: Pedro Casaldáliga and José-Maria Vigil wrote of holiness as both revolutionary and socialist, the **hoped-for 'conversion' not to the churches' Jesus Christ but to the needs and perspectives of the poor.**

Even with an explicit definition of holiness as a revolutionary ethic, they kept the importance of 'everyday faithfulness.' However, for them there is no 'everyday' holiness except if people know it is part of their larger revolutionary identity.'[2]

For reflection/discussion: test the different definitions of holiness (Wesley, Otto, Casaldaliga, etc.) on the following question: 'Is how a woman gets water for her family each day a question in which holiness is concerned? (And in which the church should be concerned, if the church is about spreading holiness?)' Is your church concerned with how people get water?

---

1 Rudolf Otto, The Idea of the Holy (English Translation) (London: Oxford University Press, 1923). p. xi.

2 Pedro Casaldáliga, José-Maria Vigil, Political Holiness: A Spirituality of Liberation, (translated from Spanish by Paul Burns, Francis McDonagh) Theology and Liberation Series, (Maryknoll, NY: Orbis Books, 1994), pp. 55-58.

7.   Holiness and Christian Perfection:

a) 'Whenever I have described the church as being without spot or wrinkle, I have not intended to imply that it was like this already, but that it should prepare itself to be like this, at the time when it too will appear in glory.' (Augustine 354-430 ce) That the church will be ...without spot or wrinkle...will only be true in our eternal home, not on the way there. We would deceive ourselves if we were to say that we have no sin, as 1 John 1.8 reminds us.' (Thomas Aquinas 1225-1274 ce)[1]

b) For John Wesley (as we will see in Lecture 2) holiness was about growth in grace towards the entire sanctification of life – that is, being perfected in Christ. This doctrine of his was and is much misunderstood and has been the source of great conflict: it does not mean that people could escape sin, or that moral rules no longer applied to them – holiness for much of Methodist history has included groups of people striving for this perfection in the way that they lived as individuals, and as a group. Thus different 'holiness movements' have sprung up at different times. Below is a summary of his view of Christian Perfection,

From 'A Plain Account of Christian Perfection, as believed and taught by the Reverend Mr. John Wesley, from the year 1725, to the year 1777,' in *The Works of John Wesley* (1872 ed. by Thomas Jackson), vol. 11, pp. 383-385 (Baker Book House edition, 1996). This was originally from the preface of a collection of hymns published in 1742, when Wesley faced much controversy about the doctrine of perfection.

"**(1.)** Perhaps the general prejudice against Christian perfection may chiefly arise from a misapprehension of the nature of it. We willingly allow, and continually declare, there is no such perfection in this life, as implies either a dispensation from doing good, and attending all the ordinances of God, or a freedom from ignorance, mistake, temptation, and a thousand infirmities necessarily connected with flesh and blood.

"**(2.)** First. We not only allow, but earnestly contend, that there is no perfection in this life, which implies any dispensation from attending all the ordinances of God, or from doing good unto all men while we have time, though 'especially unto the household of faith.' We believe, that not only the babes in Christ, who have newly found redemption in

---

1 quoted in McGrath, Op. Cit., p. 499.

his blood, but those also who are 'grown up into perfect men,' are indispensably obliged, as often as they have opportunity, 'to eat bread and drink wine in remembrance of Him,' and to 'search the Scriptures;' by fasting, as well as temperance, to 'keep their bodies under, and bring them into subjection;' and, above all, to pour out their souls in prayer, both secretly, and in the great congregation.

"**(3.)** We Secondly believe, that there is no such perfection in this life, as implies an entire deliverance, either from ignorance, or mistake, in things not essential to salvation, or from manifold temptations, or from numberless infirmities, wherewith the corruptible body more or less presses down the soul. We cannot find any ground in Scripture to suppose, that any inhabitant of a house of clay is wholly exempt either from bodily infirmities, or from ignorance of many things; or to imagine any is incapable of mistake, or falling into divers temptations.

"**(4.)** But whom then do you mean by 'one that is perfect?' We mean one in whom is 'the mind which was in Christ,' and who so 'walketh as Christ also walked;' a man 'that hath clean hands and a pure heart,' or that is 'cleansed from all filthiness of flesh and spirit;' one in whom is 'no occasion of stumbling,' and who, accordingly, 'does not commit sin.' To declare this a little more particularly: We understand by that scriptural expression, 'a perfect man,' one in whom God hath fulfilled his faithful word, 'From all your filthiness and from all your idols I will cleanse you: I will also save you from all your uncleannesses.' We understand hereby, one whom God lath 'sanctified throughout in body, soul, and spirit;' one who 'walketh in the light as He is in the light, in whom is no darkness at all; the blood of Jesus Christ his Son having cleansed him from all sin.'

"**(5.)** This man can now testify to all mankind, 'I am crucified with Christ: Nevertheless I live; yet not I, but Christ liveth in me.' He is 'holy as God who called' him 'is holy,' both in heart and 'in all manner of conversation.' He 'loveth the Lord his God with all his heart,' and serveth him 'with all his strength.' He 'loveth his neighbour,' every man, 'as himself;' yea, 'as Christ loveth us;' them, in particular, that 'despitefully use him and persecute him, because they know not the Son, neither the Father.' Indeed his soul is all love, filled with 'bowels of mercies, kindness, meekness, gentleness, longsuffering.' And his life agreeth thereto, full of 'the work of faith, the patience of hope, the labour of love.' 'And whatsoever' he 'doeth either in word or deed,' he 'doeth it all in the name,' in the love and power, 'of the Lord Jesus.' In a word, he doeth 'the will of God on earth, as it is done in heaven.'

"(6.) This it is to be a perfect man, to be 'sanctified throughout;' even 'to have a heart so all-flaming with the love of God,' (to use Archbishop Usher's words,) 'as continually to offer up every thought, word, and work, as a spiritual sacrifice, acceptable to God through Christ.' In every thought of our hearts, in every word of our tongues, in every work of our hands, to 'show forth his praise, who hath called us out of darkness into his marvellous light.' O that both we, and all who seek the Lord Jesus in sincerity, may thus 'be made perfect in one!'"

"This is the doctrine which we preached from the beginning, and which we preach at this day. Indeed, by viewing it in every point of light, and comparing it again and again with the word of God on the one hand, and the experience of the children of God on the other, we saw farther into the nature and properties of Christian perfection. But still there is no contrariety at all between our first and our last sentiments. Our first conception of it was, It is to have "the mind which was in Christ," and to "walk as He walked;" to have all the mind that was in Him, and always to walk as he walked: In other words, to be inwardly and outwardly devoted to God; all devoted in heart and life. And we have the same conception of it now, without either addition or diminution."

General Resources/Further Study: For a good basic introduction to John and Charles Wesley's ministry and ideas, (with many original sources and attention to his ideas about growth in grace and holiness) if you have an internet connection look up http://gbgm-umc.org/umw/wesley/sitemap.stm and follow the links.

For reflection/discussion: 'Isaiah 58 has much to teach us about what true holiness is, and what the ministry of the church should be.' Discuss—do you agree? Of what does this passage warn the people? How appropriate is this message for the church where you serve today? **How separate from its surroundings should the church keep itself?** Should a church exclude members if their lives appear to show evidence of particular sin? If so, how is the mission of the church carried with those people whose lives exclude them from it? What happens when there is disagreement as to what is sinful?

(ASSOCIATED HANDOUT FOR STUDENTS)

An Account of the Life of John Wesley: this account is from Fox's Book of Martyrs (expanded) and is a very 'friendly' account of his life… it shows how he was viewed by his supporters at the time of his death in 1791.

For reflection and discussion: At what places in this short biography can you see the prejudice of the author? What might a less friendly biography of John Wesley say differently? Do contemporary Methodists need to agree with everything John Wesley preached?

'**Chapter XX:** John Wesley was born on the seventeenth of June, 1703, in Epworth rectory, England, the fifteenth of nineteen children of Samuel and Susanna Wesley. The father of Wesley [right] was a preacher, and Wesley's mother was a remarkable woman in wisdom and intelligence. She was a woman of deep piety and brought her little ones into close contact with the Bible stories, telling them from the tiles about the nursery fireplace. …

… John Wesley was of but ordinary stature, and yet of noble presence. His features were very handsome even in old age. He had an open brow, an eagle nose, a clear eye, and a fresh complexion. His manners were fine, and in choice company with Christian people he enjoyed relaxation. Persistent, laborious love for men's souls, steadfastness, and tranquillity of spirit were his most prominent traits of character. Even in doctrinal controversies he exhibited the greatest calmness. He was kind and very liberal. His industry has been named already. In the last fifty-two years of his life, it is estimated that he preached more than forty thousand sermons….

Edited by William Byron Forbush. The original version of *The Book of Martyrs* (1563) by John Foxe (1516-1587) was expanded after Foxe's death to include John Wesley and others. http://gbgm-umc.org/umw/wesley/foxwesley.stm A Short History of Methodism by John Wesley [As you read it consider: what has he left out, or glossed over? The full text can be found at:
http://gbgm-umc.org/umw/wesley/shorthistory.stm]

1. It is not easy to reckon up the various accounts which have been given of the people called Methodists; very many of them as far remote from truth as that given by the good gentleman in Ireland: "*Methodists*! Ay, they are the people who place all religion in *wearing long beards.*"

2. Abundance of the mistakes which are current concerning them have undoubtedly sprung from this: Men lump together, under this general name, many who have no manner of connection with each other; and then whatever any of these speaks or does is of course imputed to all.

3. The following short account may prevent persons of a calm and candid disposition from doing this; although men of a warm or prejudiced spirit will do just as they did before. But let it be observed, this is not designed for a defence of the Methodists, (so called,) or any part of them. It is a bare relation of a series of naked facts, which alone may remove abundance of misunderstandings.

4. In November, 1729, four young gentlemen of Oxford, -- Mr. John Wesley, Fellow of Lincoln College; Mr. Charles Wesley, Student of Christ Church; Mr. Morgan, Commoner of Christ Church; and Mr. Kirkham, of Merton College, -- began to spend some evenings in a week together, in reading, chiefly, the Greek Testament. ...

5. The exact regularity of their lives, as well as studies, occasioned a young gentleman of Christ Church to say, "Here is a new set of Methodists sprung up;" alluding to some ancient Physicians who were so called. The name was new and quaint; so it took immediately, and the Methodists were known all over the University.

6. They were all zealous members of the Church of England; not only tenacious of all her doctrines, so far as they knew them, but of all her discipline, to the minutest circumstance....

7. The one charge then advanced against them was, that they were "righteous overmuch;" that they were abundantly too scrupulous, and too strict, carrying things to great extremes: In particular, that they laid too much stress upon the Rubrics and Canons of the Church; that they insisted too much on observing the Statutes of the University; and that they took the Scriptures in too strict and literal a sense; so that if they were right, few indeed would be saved.

8. In October, 1735, Mr. John and Charles Wesley, and Mr. Ingham, left England, with a design to go and preach to the Indians in Georgia: But the rest of the gentlemen continued to meet, till one and another was ordained and left the University. By which means, in about two years' time, scarce any of them were left.

9. In February, 1738, Mr. Whitefield went over to Georgia with a design to assist Mr. John Wesley; but Mr. Wesley just then returned to England. Soon after he had a meeting with Messrs. Ingham, Stonehouse, Hall, Hutchings, Kinchin, and a few other Clergymen, who all appeared to be of one heart, as well as of one judgment, resolved to be Bible-Christians at all events; and, wherever they were, to preach with all their might plain, old, Bible Christianity.

10. They were hitherto perfectly regular in all things, and zealously attached to the Church of England. Meantime, they began to be convinced, that "by grace we are saved through faith;" that justification by faith was the doctrine of the Church, as well as of the Bible. As soon as they believed, they spake; salvation by faith being now their standing topic. Indeed this implied three things: (1.) That men are all, by nature, "dead in sin," and, consequently, "children of wrath." (2.) That they are "justified by faith alone." (3.) That faith produces inward and outward holiness: And these points they insisted on day and night. In a short time they became popular Preachers. The congregations were large wherever they preached. The former name was then revived; and all these gentlemen, with their followers, were entitled Methodists.
11. In March, 1741, Mr. Whitefield, being returned to England, entirely separated from Mr. Wesley and his friends, because he did not hold the decrees. Here was the first breach, which warm men persuaded Mr. Whitefield to make merely for a difference of opinion. Those, indeed, who believed universal redemption had no desire at all to separate; but those who held particular redemption would not hear of any accommodation, being determined to have no fellowship with men that "were in so dangerous errors." So there were now two sorts of Methodists, so called; those for particular, and those for general, redemption.

12. Not many years passed, before William Cudworth and James Relly separated from Mr. Whitefield. These were properly Antinomians; absolute, avowed enemies to the law of God, which they never preached or professed to preach, but termed all legalists who did. With them, "preaching the law" was an abomination. They had "nothing to do" with the law. They would "preach Christ," as they called it, but without one word either of holiness or good works. Yet these were still denominated Methodists, although differing from Mr. Whitefield, both in judgment and practice, abundantly more than Mr. Whitefield did from Mr. Wesley.

13. In the meantime, Mr. Venn and Mr. Romaine began to be spoken of; and not long after Mr. Madan and Mr. Berridge, with a few other Clergymen, who, although they had no Bridge with each other, yet preaching salvation by faith, and endeavoring to live accordingly, to be Bible-Christians, were soon included in the general name of Methodists. And so indeed were all others who preached salvation by faith, and appeared more serious than their neighbors. Some of these were quite regular in their manner of preaching; some were quite irregular; (though not by choice; but necessity was laid upon them; they must preach irregularly, or not at all;) and others were between both, regular in most, though not in all, particulars.

14. In 1762, George Bell, and a few other persons, began to speak great words. In the latter end of the year, they foretold that the world would be at an end on the 28th of February. Mr. Wesley, with whom they were then connected, withstood them both in public and private. This they would not endure; so, in January and February, 1763, they separated from him. Soon after, Mr. Maxfield, one of Mr. Wesley's Preachers, and several of the people, left Mr. Wesley; but still Mr. Maxfield and his adherents go under the general name of Methodists.

15. At present, those who remain with Mr. Wesley are mostly Church-of-England men, though they do not love their opinions. Yea, they love the Antinomians themselves; but it is with a love of compassion only: For they hate their doctrines with a perfect hatred; they abhor them as they do hell-fire; being convinced nothing can so effectually destroy all faith, all holiness, and all good works....

Timeline of Early Methodism–source:
Barrie Tabraham, 'The Making of Methodism' (1995)

1688 Samuel Wesley marries Susanna Annesley

1697 Samuel Wesley becomes Rector of Epworth

1703/7 birth of John Wesley/Charles Wesley

1709 Rectory fire

1720 John begins Christ church, Oxford

1725/6 John ordained Deacon/elected Fellow of Lincoln College

1727-9 John Curate at Wroot, ordained Priest, 1728

1729 Charles founds 'holy club', John returns to Oxford

1734 John declines Epworth 'living'

1735 Samuel Wesley dies, John and Charles leave for Georgia, Charles ordained

1738 John follows Charles home after Grand Jury in Georgia, conversion
       experiences

1739 John preaches in open air at Bristol, first Methodist Society meets at Bristol

1742 Classes begin to be formed–to organise payment for 'New Room' at Bristol

1744 First meeting of Conference

1748 First 'quarterly meeting' (Circuit), Kingswood School re-opened
       (G. Whitefield passed resp)

1749 'Christian Library' begins to be published

1766 First Methodist Society in 'new world'

1783 End of war with the American Colonies and independence recognised
       (15,000 Methodists)

1784 Deed of Declaration (Methodism constitutes Conference as the authority after
Wesley's death, and makes itself a church, vs society)

ordinations for America, Wesley's revision of the Book of Common Prayer

1787 Registration of Methodist preaching houses as 'dissenting' chapels

1788 Death of Charles Wesley

1791 Death of John Wesley: 72,476 members, connexional organisation, itinerant
ministry.

1797 Methodist New Connexion (Alexander Kilham, 10,856 members in 1822,
joined 1907)

1806 Independent Methodists–freedom in members & local churches–still survive

1811 Primitive Methodists (Hugh Bourne, William Clowes–north west)–grew from
'camp meetings' Mow Cop, etc. expelled as threat to social order – freedom in
worship, extempore, lay women and men, like Wesleyan Methodism, mainly artisans
(skilled workers), miners, labourers.

1815 Bible Christians (William O'Bryan–Cornwall) not drawing Methodist
members away, but in a Methodist tradition–female itinerant preachers, 1819,
mission–temperance e.g.

1857 United Methodist Free Churches come together–various splinter groups

1907 New Connexion, Bible Christians, United Methodist Free Church=United
Methodists

1932 United Methodist join Primitive Methodists, Wesleyan Methodists to form
the present Methodist Church in Britain.

In 1784 Wesley said, 'I believe I shall not separate from the Church of England until my soul separates from my body' …In 1766 Wesley had warned his preachers not to absent themselves from Anglican worship more than twice a month, and not to end Methodist services with the Lord's Supper. He also insisted that Methodist services should not be held at the same time as Anglican ones, as can be seen by his Journal entry of 24 October 1787:

Tues. 24.–I met the classes at Deptford, and was vehemently importuned [asked] to order the Sunday service in our room at the same time with that of the church. It is easy to see that this would be a formal separation from the church. We fixed both morning and evening service, all over England, at such hours as not to interfere with the Church; with this very design, that those of the church, if they chose it, might attend both the one and the other. But to fix it at the same hour, is obliging them to separate either from the Church or us; and this I judge not only to be inexpedient, but totally unlawful for me to do.'[1]

Useful Terms:
Antinomian: Literally, 'against the law,' an approach to Christian living which minimizes the place of laws and regulations (e.g. the Ten Commandments) instead stressing the importance of the Holy Spirit's guidance. 'Antinomians' emphasized faith alone over Christian behaviour or works.

Arminian: From Jacob Arminius (1560-1609) who opposed Calvinist teaching concerning predestination, that God elected only some people to be saved. Arminius insisted that all people can be saved, but only by the grace of God. His teaching had a profound effect on the Wesleys.

Justification: the word used by St Paul to express God's forgiveness and 'acquittal' (finding innocent) of sinners. In theology, part of the process of salvation–John Wesley equated the term with 'acceptance' and 'pardon', and used it to describe the change in relationship with God in which God took the first step.

---

1 Barrie Tabraham, The Making of Methodism, (London: Epworth, 1995), p. 48.

Prevenient or Preventing Grace: literally, 'going before.' It is the capacity for responding to the love of God, which Wesley believed God had given to all people. Thus, it might be active before a person came to faith. 'No man sins because he hath not grace,' wrote Wesley, 'but because he does not use the grace which he hath.'

Quietism: a passive kind of spirituality which played down the role of human action. At best a tranquil resting in God, at worst denying the value of social action and even, in the extreme, the importance of corporate worship.

Sanctification: the continuing work of God's grace in the heart of a Christian, following justification. As a process of growth in holiness, it marked a real change in an individual's character and life.

For Reflection/Discussion:

Was Methodism right to break with the Church of England?
Should Methodist Churches abide by their Anglican heritage more? How so?

In the UK, often Methodist churches use over-stretched resources on very small attendance services when other churches (frequently similar in theology) are also meeting. Why?

Does anything similar happen in Nigeria?

Many Methodist Churches (including in Nigeria and the US) have Bishops who exercise personal Episcopal authority.
Should the Methodist Church in the UK adopt Bishops? Why or why not?

Would others be better to abandon personal episcopacy in favour of corporate (shared) episcopacy as in the UK church?

Is the holiness of God contained in church? In Christianity?

For what purpose does the church exist, today?

(ASSOCIATED HANDOUT FOR STUDENTS)

Background:

Wesley said that means of grace are: '..outward signs, words, or actions, ordained of God, and appointed for this end, to be the ordinary channels whereby he might convey to men, preventing, justifying, or sanctifying grace.' (From the sermon on 'the means of grace')

For reflection: Wesley was very keen that these 'means,' though necessary, not be confused with 'ends', that is Christ himself. We should guard against these outward signs becoming idols, in other words. As you read, consider: are there times in your own church experience or your observation of another where these 'means' have become idols?

For John Wesley, the 'means of grace' (or way in which people grew in grace and holiness, towards Christ) were 'works of piety' (spiritual disciplines) and `works of mercy' (doing good to others). BOTH were required for the growth in grace or holiness that he desired:

'**...2.** It is by this very device of Satan, that faith and works have been so often set at variance with each other. And many who had a real zeal for God have, for a time, fallen into the snare on either hand. Some have magnified faith to the utter exclusion of good works, not only from being the cause of our justification, (for we know that man is justified freely by the redemption which is in Jesus,) but from being the necessary fruit of it, yea, from having any place in the religion of Jesus Christ. Others, eager to avoid this dangerous mistake, have run as much too far the contrary way; and either maintained that good works were the cause, at least the previous condition, of justification, -- or spoken of them as if they were all in all, the whole religion of Jesus Christ.

3. In the same manner have the end and the means of religion been set at variance with each other. Some well-meaning men have seemed to place all religion in attending the Prayers of the Church, in receiving the Lord's supper, in hearing sermons, and reading books of piety; neglecting, mean time, the end of all these, the love of God and their neighbour. And this very thing has confirmed others in the neglect, if not contempt, of the ordinances of God,-so wretchedly abused to

318

undermine and overthrow the very end they were designed to establish....'
Upon Our Lord's Sermon on the Mount, 7 By John Wesley
(Text from the 1872 edition - Thomas Jackson, editor)

WESLEY ON WORKS OF PIETY:

'The chief of these means are prayer, whether in secret or with the great congregation; searching the Scriptures; (which implies reading, hearing, and meditating thereon;) and receiving the Lord's Supper, eating bread and drinking wine in remembrance of Him: And these we believe to be ordained of God, as the ordinary channels of conveying his grace to the souls of men.' *(From the sermon on 'the means of grace')*
Elsewhere, he also emphasized the importance of fasting and participating in Christian community.

PRAYER

Christians were to pray constantly, without ceasing (1 Thessalonians 5:17).
'...All that a Christian does, even in eating and sleeping, is prayer, when it is done in simplicity, according to the order of God, without either adding to or diminishing from it by his own choice.

Prayer continues in the desire of the heart, though the understanding be employed on outward things...' From *A Plain Account of Christian Perfection*, as believed and taught by the Reverend Mr. John Wesley, from the year 1725, to the year 1777.

For reflection: How have you experienced prayer in your own life?

What different kinds of prayer do you have access to? (silence, contemplation, extempore, traditional set prayers, service, rosary, imaginative Biblical encounter, accompanied, etc.)

Do you agree with Wesley that it is the most important means of grace, more important than the Bible?

319

John Wesley: How to Read the Scripture

'If you desire to read the scripture in such a manner as may most effectually answer this end, would it not be advisable,

1. To set apart a little time, if you can, every morning and evening for that purpose?

2. At each time if you have leisure, to read a chapter out of the Old, and one out of the New Testament: if you cannot do this, to take a single chapter, or a part of one?

3. To read this with a single eye, to know the whole will of God, and a fixt resolution to do it? In order to know his will, you should,

4. Have a constant eye to the analogy of faith; the connexion and harmony there is between those grand, fundamental doctrines, Original Sin, Justification by Faith, the New Birth, Inward and Outward Holiness.

5. Serious and earnest prayer should be constantly used, before we consult the oracles of God, seeing "scripture can only be understood thro' the same Spirit whereby it was given." Our reading should likewise be closed with prayer, that what we read may be written on our hearts.

6. It might also be of use, if while we read, we were frequently to pause, and examine ourselves by what we read, both with regard to our hearts, and lives. This would furnish us with matter of praise, where we found God had enabled us to conform to his blessed will, and matter of humiliation and prayer, where we were conscious of having fallen short.

And whatever light you then receive, should be used to the uttermost, and that immediately. Let there be no delay. Whatever you resolve, begin to execute the first moment you can. So shall you find this word to be indeed the power of God unto present and eternal salvation.

John Wesley Preface to *Explanatory Notes upon the Old Testament*
EDINBURGH, April 25, 1765.

From 'The Duty of Constant Communion,' By John Wesley (1872 edition)

'The following discourse was written above five-and-fifty years ago, for the use of my pupils at Oxford. I have added very little, but retrenched much; as I then used more words than I do now. But, I thank God, I have not yet seen cause to alter my sentiments in any point which is therein delivered. "Do this in remembrance of me."'
Luke 22:19

It is no wonder that men who have no fear of God should never think of doing this. But it is strange that it should be neglected by any that do fear God, and desire to save their souls; And yet nothing is more common. One reason why many neglect it is, they are so much afraid of "eating and drinking unworthily", that they never think how much greater the danger is when they do not eat or drink it at all. That I may do what I can to bring these well-meaning men to a more just way of thinking, I shall,

I. Show that it is the duty of every Christian to receive the Lord's Supper as often as he can; and,

II. Answer some objections.

I. I am to show that it is the duty of every Christian to receive the Lord's Supper as often as he can.

1. The First reason why it is the duty of every Christian so to do is, because it is a plain command of Christ. That this is his command, appears from the words of the text, "Do this in remembrance of me:" By which, as the Apostles were obliged to bless, break, and give the bread to all that joined with them in holy things; so were all Christians obliged to receive those signs of Christ's body and blood. Here, therefore, the bread and wine are commanded to be received, in remembrance of his death, to the end of the world. Observe, too, that this command was given by our Lord when he was just laying down his life for our sakes. They are, therefore, as it were, his dying words to all his followers.

2. A Second reason why every Christian should do this as often as he can, is, because the benefits of doing it are so great to all that do it in obedience to him; viz., the forgiveness of our past sins and the present strengthening and refreshing of our souls. In this world we are never free from temptations. Whatever way of life we are in, whatever our condition be, whether we are sick or well, in trouble or at ease, the enemies of our souls are watching to lead us into sin. And too often they prevail over us. Now, when we are convinced of having sinned against God, what surer way have we of procuring pardon from him, than the "showing forth the Lord's death;" and beseeching him, for the sake of his Son's sufferings, to blot out all our sins?

3. The grace of God given herein confirms to us the pardon of our sins, by enabling us to leave them. As our bodies are strengthened by bread and wine, so are our souls by these tokens of the body and blood of Christ. This is the food of our souls: This gives strength to perform our duty, and leads us on to perfection. If, therefore, we have any regard for the plain command of Christ, if we desire the pardon of our sins, if we wish for strength to believe, to love and obey God, then we should neglect no opportunity of receiving the Lord's Supper; then we must never turn our backs on the feast which our Lord has prepared for us. We must neglect no occasion which the good providence of God affords us for this purpose. This is the true rule: So often are we to receive as God gives us opportunity. ...

II Answer some objections

...**8.** But suppose this were no mercy to us; (to suppose which is indeed giving God the lie; saying, that is not good for man which he purposely ordered for his good) still I ask, Why do not you obey God's command? He says, "Do this". Why do you not? You answer, "I am unworthy to do it". What! Unworthy to obey God? Unworthy to do what God bids you do? Unworthy to obey God's command? What do you mean by this? That those who are unworthy to obey God ought not to obey him? Who told you so? If he were even "an angel from heaven, let him be accursed." If you think God himself has told you so by St. Paul, let us hear his words. They are these: "He that eateth and drinketh unworthily, eateth and drinketh damnation to himself".

Why, this is quite another thing. Here is not a word said of being unworthy to eat and drink. Indeed he does speak of eating and drinking unworthily; but that is quite a different thing; so he has told us himself. In this very chapter we are told that by eating and drinking unworthily is meant, taking the holy sacrament in such a rude and disorderly way, that one was "hungry and another drunken."'

For Reflection/Discussion:

John Wesley believed that God's grace is conveyed through the Lord's Supper and that it is a major way God nourishes us. Has your experience of Holy Communion been nourishing to your spiritual growth?

Are you aware of Christians or Methodists who do not take communion very often?

If so, why do they not? What do you think of Wesley's argument?
Read the entire sermon athttp://gbgm.umc.org/umhistory/wesley/sermons/101/

[The sermon 'sermon on the mount vii' concerns fasting: see text at http://gbgm.umc.org/umhistory/wesley/sermons/27/, also many works repeat the necessity of community–society, bands-as a means of grace, and work of piety for the Christian.]

LECTURE 4: WESLEY AND THE 'MEANS OF GRACE': WORKS OF MERCY

(ASSOCIATED HANDOUT FOR STUDENTS)

1. From John Wesley, 'Upon our Lord's sermon on the mount VI':

'...And, First, with regard to **works of mercy**. "Take heed," saith he [Jesus],"that ye do not your alms before men, to be seen of them: Otherwise ye have no reward of your Father which is in heaven." "That ye do not your alms:" -- Although this only is named, yet is every work of charity included, every thing which we give, or speak, or do, whereby our neighbour may be profited; whereby another man may receive any advantage, either in his body or soul. The feeding the hungry, the clothing the naked, the entertaining or assisting the stranger, the visiting those that are sick or in prison, the comforting the afflicted, the instructing the ignorant, the reproving the wicked, the exhorting and encouraging the well-doer; and if there be any other work of mercy, it is equally included in this direction.'

For reflection/discussion: Notice the way Wesley interprets scripture: he expands the literal meaning (in this case, Jesus mentioned only alms-giving) to take on more of Jesus' full message as demonstrated all across the Gospels – Wesley looks for the sense of the scripture and then to apply it broadly, vs. a close literal interpretation of any specific verse. Thus, he is not a scriptural literalist –because he fears a close literalism will limit the work of the Holy Spirit. Wesley's scriptural guide here is definitely not to treat each verse as a rule in itself, but to test each in light of the whole Gospel and scriptures. Thus, he sees MORE required in holy living than following rules, certainly any thought to derive from scripture.

2. Upon our Lord's Sermon on the Mount, III by John Wesley (1872 edition)

'...Thus far our Lord has been more directly employed in teaching the religion of the heart. He has shown what Christians are to be. He proceeds to show, what they are to do also; -- how inward holiness is to exert itself in our outward conversation. "Blessed," saith he, "are the peacemakers; for they shall be called the children of God." ...

...in the full extent of the word, a peace-maker is one that, as he hath opportunity, "doth good unto all men;" one that, being filled with the love of God and of all mankind, cannot confine the expressions of it to his own family, or friends, or acquaintance, or party, or to those of his own opinions; -- no, nor those who are partakers of like precious faith; but steps over all these narrow bounds, that he may do good to every man, that he may, some way or other, manifest his love to neighbours and strangers, friends and enemies. He doth good to them all, as he hath opportunity, that is, on every possible occasion; "redeeming the time," in order thereto; "buying up every opportunity, improving every hour, losing no moment wherein he may profit another. He does good, not of one particular kind, but good in general, in every possible way; employing herein all his talents of every kind, all his powers and faculties of body and soul, all his fortune, his interest, his reputation; desiring only, that when his Lord cometh He may say, "Well done, good and faithful servant!" ...He doth good, to the uttermost of his power, even to the bodies of all men. He rejoices to "deal his bread to the hungry," and to "cover the naked with a garment." Is any a stranger? He takes him in, and relieves him according to his necessities. Are any sick or in prison? He visits them, and administers such help as they stand most in need of. And all this he does, not as unto man; but remembering him that hath said, "Inasmuch as ye have done it unto one of the least of these my brethren, ye have done it unto me."

3. The last letter that John Wesley wrote was to William Wilberforce, a man who had been converted under Wesley's ministry and who was a Member of Parliament. The letter concerns his opposition to slavery and encouragement for Wilberforce to take action for change.

Parliament finally outlawed England's participation in the slave trade in 1807.

Balam, February 24, 1791
Dear Sir:

Unless the divine power has raised you us to be as *Athanasius contra mundum,* I see not how you can go through your glorious enterprise in opposing that execrable villainy which is the scandal of religion, of England, and of human nature. Unless God has raised you up for this very thing, you will be worn out by the opposition of men and devils. But if God be fore you, who can be against you? Are all of them together stronger than God? O be not weary of well doing! Go on, in the name of God and in the power of his might, till even American slavery (the vilest that ever saw the sun) shall vanish away before it.

Reading this morning a tract wrote by a poor African, I was particularly struck by that circumstance that a man who has a black skin, being wronged or outraged by a white man, can have no redress; it being a "law" in our colonies that the *oath* of a black against a white goes for nothing. What villainy is this?

That he who has guided you from youth up may continue to strengthen you in this and all things, is the prayer of, dear sir,
Your affectionate servant, John Wesley

4. 'This equally concerns every merchant who is engaged in the slave-trade. It is you that induce the African villain to sell his countrymen; and in order thereto, to steal, rob, murder men, women, and children without number, by enabling the English villain to pay him for so doing, whom you overpay for his execrable labour. It is your money that is the spring of all, that empowers him to go on: So that whatever he or the African does in this matter is all your act and deed. And is your conscience quite reconciled to this? Does it never reproach you at all? Has gold entirely blinded your eyes, and stupified your heart? Can you see, can you feel, no harm therein? Is it doing as you would be done to? Make the case your own. "Master," said a slave at Liverpool to the merchant that owned him, "what, if some of my countrymen were to come here, and take away my mistress, and Master Tommy, and Master Billy, and carry them into our country, and make them slaves, how would you like it?" His answer was worthy of a man: "I will never buy a slave more while I live." O let his resolution be yours! Have no more any part in this detestable business.'

From John Wesley, 'Thoughts upon slavery,' 1774.
http://gbgm-umc.org/umw/wesley/thoughtsuponslavery.stm

For discussion/Reflection: Wesley rejected the argument that being involved with the slave trade was a necessity, given how central it was to the economic system of trade between nations. He took opposition to the trade to be a work of mercy required by love of God. Are there injustices now in society where we are tempted to avoid Christian responsibility and say 'I cannot avoid it, if I want to work in the 'real' world?' E.g. cheap imports to the UK, made by children or workers paid very little.

What about the paying of bribes? Or using special influence with the police or courts, even if we have it?

(What about the argument that we can get nowhere without it?)

A very personal example: I have white skin. In many places (not all) white skin gets privileges for no good reason other than prejudice. This privilege is based in sin, because it cannot exist without the prejudice against darker skin. It directly contravenes scripture and what we know of the work of Jesus Christ. Galatians 3.28, etc. I get advantage from this privilege. What should I do with this privilege? How is the 'work of mercy' expressed where you serve? How is it related to the 'work of piety,' and the whole mission of the church?

LECTURE 5: DISCUSSION: (NO ASSOCIATED HANDOUT FOR STUDENTS)

LECTURE 6/7: HOLINESS AND THE MISSION OF THE CHURCH I & II

(ASSOCIATED HANDOUT FOR STUDENTS)

1. A reminder, from the Constitution of Methodist Church Nigeria and UK Methodism:

'The Methodist Church claims and cherishes its place in the Holy Catholic Church which is the Body of Christ. It rejoices in the inheritance of the apostolic faith and loyally accepts the fundamental principles of the historic creeds and of the Protestant Reformation. It ever remembers that in the providence of God Methodism was raised up to **spread Scriptural Holiness** through the land by the proclamation of the evangelical faith and declares its unfaltering resolve to be true to its divinely appointed mission.'[1]

---

1 Paragraph 4, first in section on 'Doctrine,' Methodist Church Nigeria Constitution 1990, p. 1. Also 'Deed of Union of the Methodist Church.' Adopted by uniting conference in 1932. Constitutional Practice and Discipline of the Methodist Church, Volume II, (Peterborough: Methodist Publishing House, 2004), p. 213. Emphasis added.

[The 1990 Constitution of MCN provides for Conference committees concerned with Christian social responsibility, medical health and welfare services, and agricultural and urban development, also outreach and evangelism.]

1. 'The poor and needy may be the recipients of care through a church-run community project, but they are not the primary object of active mission, because the poor, as Jesus insisted, are the likely trigger for the transforming of those who put themselves in the position of caring... our routine assumption is that those who are chronically poor and dispossessed are in deficit, both spiritually and materially, whilst those who respond to their needs are more materially secure and live confidently within the providential nature of God. ...it may be that the secure are likely to receive most from an encounter with the poor and marginalised.

...Community ministry borrows this insight from Liberation theology, where it is the poor and dispossessed who preach the Gospel, in its fullest sense, to the rich and powerful. It is the poor and dispossessed who are likely to be the first to recognise the radical, 'upside-down' nature of the Kingdom of God, whereas those of us who benefit from the taken for granted 'ways of the world' are likely to have the greatest investment in the status quo.'[1]

For Reflection/Discussion: To what extent should the church be concerned with bodies as well as souls, and their social conditions as the centre of mission?
Should the work of evangelism be separated out, or not?
In 'works of mercy,' it who is evangelising whom?
Should our churches be concerned only with Methodists? Only with Christians?

2.   How social/political/economic should ministers or churches be, in mission?: Case 1

The Revd Dr Martin Luther King Jr was an African American Baptist minister and one leader of the US 'Civil Rights' movement during the 1950s and 1960s. He was assassinated in 1968. Many people criticised him because he was interested in social and legal justice instead of just 'church' issues, and because he participated in 'non-violent resistance' to laws that he considered unjust. He

---

1 Ann Morisy, Beyond the Good Samaritan: Community Ministry and Mission, (London: Continuum, 1997) p. 7,8.

was arrested and thrown in prison many times, as were his followers. Here he writes from prison in Birmingham, Alabama USA after a letter from white liberal ministers who asked why he did not 'wait' and 'turn the other cheek' but made conflict with the legal authorities.
(Full text at http://www.africa.upenn.edu/Articles_Gen/Letter_Birmingham.html)

16 April 1963
My Dear Fellow Clergymen:

While confined here in the Birmingham city jail, I came across your recent statement calling my present activities "unwise and untimely". Seldom do I pause to answer criticism of my work and ideas. If I sought to answer all the criticisms that cross my desk, my secretaries would have little time for anything other than such correspondence in the course of the day, and I would have no time for constructive work. But since I feel that you are men of genuine good will and that your criticisms are sincerely set forth, I want to try to answer your statement in what I hope will be patient and reasonable terms…

…In any nonviolent campaign there are four basic steps: collection of the facts to determine whether injustices exist; negotiation; self purification; and direct action. We have gone through all these steps in Birmingham. …

…We had no alternative except to prepare for direct action, whereby we would present our very bodies as a means of laying our case before the conscience of the local and the national community. Mindful of the difficulties involved, we decided to undertake a process of self purification. We began a series of workshops on nonviolence, and we repeatedly asked ourselves: "Are you able to accept blows without retaliating?" "Are you able to endure the ordeal of jail?"

You may well ask: "Why direct action? Why sit ins, marches and so forth? Isn't negotiation a better path?" You are quite right in calling for negotiation. Indeed, this is the very purpose of direct action. Nonviolent direct action seeks to create such a crisis and foster such a tension that a community which has constantly refused to negotiate is forced to confront the issue. It seeks so to dramatize the issue that it can no longer be ignored. My citing the creation of tension as part of the work of the nonviolent resister may sound rather shocking. But I must confess that I am not afraid of the word "tension." I have earnestly opposed violent tension, but there is a type of constructive, nonviolent tension which is necessary for growth. …

We know through painful experience that freedom is never voluntarily given by the oppressor; it must be demanded by the oppressed. ...We have waited for more than 340 years for our constitutional and God given rights. The nations of Asia and Africa are moving with jet like speed toward gaining political independence, but we still creep at horse and buggy pace toward gaining a cup of coffee at a lunch counter.

....You express a great deal of anxiety over our willingness to break laws. One has not only a legal but a moral responsibility to obey just laws. Conversely, one has a moral responsibility to disobey unjust laws. I would agree with St. Augustine that "an unjust law is no law at all."

...Actually, we who engage in nonviolent direct action are not the creators of tension. We merely bring to the surface the hidden tension that is already alive. We bring it out in the open, where it can be seen and dealt with. Like a boil that can never be cured so long as it is covered up but must be opened with all its ugliness to the natural medicines of air and light, injustice must be exposed, with all the tension its exposure creates, to the light of human conscience and the air of national opinion before it can be cured.

...Was not Jesus an extremist for love: "Love your enemies, bless them that curse you, do good to them that hate you, and pray for them which despitefully use you, and persecute you." Was not Amos an extremist for justice: "Let justice roll down like waters and righteousness like an ever flowing stream." Was not Paul an extremist for the Christian gospel: "I bear in my body the marks of the Lord Jesus." ...

For Discussion/Reflection: Should the church encourage people to draw 'creative tension' to make change in society? Is this Holiness?

3.   Case 2: Bishop Ivan Manuel Abrahams, of the Methodist Church of South Africa: recommending resistance to globalisation:

Bishop Ivan suggests that Wesleyan notions of holiness have much in common with African concepts Ubuntu 'the essence of being human which embraces hospitality, caring about others, willing to go the extra miles for the sake of another,' (Archbishop Desmond Tutu) also shown in the proverb 'all members of the family share the head of a locust.' He urges church action in politics and economics, with holiness/Ubuntu as an antidote to economic policies based in market forces and capitalist process. Text is from keynote address, Oxford Institute of Methodist Theological Studies, August 2007, Oxford, UK.

Wesley's economic ethic was more than an ethic of decision or personal choice. The Wesleyan tradition of practical living, homiletics and theological treatise portrays a model of 'holiness of heart and life' that refuses to separate the realms of life into secular and sacred or into public and private. Peter Storey makes the point that 'John Wesley made the revolutionary discovery that you could not really be a Christian unless you engage with the poor of the earth,' and further defines a Wesleyan Christian as, 'one who has made an international option to stand with the poor and marginalised of society, against the principalities and powers that hold all such in bondage.'[1]

So far, so good–but how do we explain the Methodist leadership of the 60s and 70s–certainly until the late 90s in South Africa and Africa-failing to come to grips with the nexus between faith and politics and faith and economics?

I am not suggesting that we take a reconstructed 18th century theological treatise and develop a 21st century reaction to the global economic malaise. What I am suggesting is that we recognise that the poor are caught in a trap of death and despair orchestrated by people who are supposed to be regulating global economics......in the same way that theology undergirded the slave trade in the 18th and 19th century, so also much of our current theology by omission or commission must plead guilty with the purveyors of global capital.'

'It will be more and more difficult for Christians to live their relationship with God in cosy isolation from questions dealing with rising prices, speculation in real estate, or the recrudescence of tribalism. How are we to give an account of the hope that is in us in a society where children are...abandoned in the streets?'[2]

---

1 Peter Storey in P. Malinga and N. Rishardson (eds), Rediscovering Wesley for Africa, (Pretoria: Methodist Church of Southern Africa, 2005) p. 23.

2 Jean-Marc Ela, (translated from the French by Robert Barr) African Cry, (New York: Orbis, 1980), p. 92.

4.   Case 3: Headline from The Methodist Recorder, Thursday Dec 18, 2008:

'Church in Africa accused of failing Zimbabwe'
...at last week's assembly the church was criticised – along with African politicians – for not doing enough to force President Mugabe from his office and for not providing sufficient humanitarian aid...

5.   Upon our Lord's Sermon on the Mount, III, by John Wesley (1872 edition)

'It remains only to inquire, How are the children of God to behave with regard to persecution? And, First, they ought not knowingly or designedly to bring it upon themselves. ...Yet think not that you can always avoid it.... If ever that idle imagination steals into your heart, put it to flight by that earnest caution, "Remember the word that I said unto you, The servant is not greater than his Lord. If they have persecuted me, they will also persecute you." "Be ye wise as serpents, and harmless as doves." But will this screen you from persecution? Not unless you have more wisdom than your Master, or more innocence than the Lamb of God.

LECTURE 8: REVISION AND REFLECTION ON LOCAL ISSUES (INTERACTIVE)

(NO ASSOCIATED HANDOUT FOR STUDENTS)

MODULE 5a: HOLINESS, WESLEYAN SPIRITUALITY

(Revd Kenneth Todd BA MA BD)

RELEVANCE OF JOHN WESLEY'S TEACHING TO THE 21st CENTURY

(Wesley Historical Society lecture, Sierra Leone delivered at St. John's Maroon Methodist Church, Freetown on 8 May 2003, remembering the tercentenary of the birth of Rev John Wesley 17 June 1703)

Born 300 years ago, John Wesley, though small in stature was much bigger than the eighteenth century. Doubtless, the scientific advances of the twenty first century would have fascinated his fertile, inquiring mind. Having travelled a quarter of a million miles on horseback or carriage, he would have relished the use of modern transport to reach the world for Christ. No doubt, he would have maximised the use of modern mass media, computers and the Internet to offer Christ to all people. This man of diverse and remarkable gifts was primarily an evangelist who regarded the world as his parish, often preaching four or five times daily. Having written or edited 400 books, he was essentially a man of one book, the Bible.

Let me, with the help of some quotes, recall four doctrines emphasised by John Wesley and consider their relevance for today.

1: FIRST, THE POLITICAL KINGDOMS OF TODAY NEED AN OPTION FOR THE POOR.

Wars continue throughout the world today. Let us listen to what John Wesley said on the subject of war, which he regarded as a sign of sinful humanity. He wrote: "But, whatever be the cause, let us calmly and impartially consider the thing itself. Here are 40,000 men gathered together on this plain. What are they going to do? See, there are 30 or 40 thousand more at a little distance. And these are going to shoot them through the head or body, to stab them or split their skulls and send most of their souls into everlasting fire, as fast as they possibly can. Why so? What harm have they done to them? O none at all! They do not so much as know them. But a man, who is King of France, has a quarrel with another man who is King of England. So these Frenchmen are to kill as many of these Englishmen as they can, to prove the King of France is in the right. Now, what an argument is this! What a method of proof! What an amazing way of deciding controversies! What must mankind be, before such a thing as war could ever be known or thought of upon earth? How shocking, how inconceivable a want must there have been of common understanding, as well as common humanity, before any two governors, or any two nations in the universe, could once think of such a method of decision? If then all nations, Pagan, Mahometan and Christian, do, in fact, make this their last resort, what farther proof do we need of the utter degeneracy of all nations from the plainest principles of reason and virtue?"[1]

John Wesley saw that our Lord, as well as scripture in general has an option for the poor. He aimed his strategic attack on the Slave Trade with his pamphlet "Thoughts on Slavery" published in 1774 and his well-known last letter to William Wilberforce encouraging his anti-slavery crusade. Wesley denounced the taking of bribes, which was especially prevalent in elections. He also denounced smuggling and the evasion of customs duties. He founded schools for widows and orphans. He challenged the money-making methods of his contemporaries (Sermon 23) and insists that "whoever he is that, owing no man anything and having food and raiment for himself and his household, together with a sufficiency to carry on his worldly business...seeks still a larger portion on earth, he lives in an open, habitual denial of the Lord that bought him."[2]

Wesley described the early days of Methodism in a letter to Revd. Vincent Perronet and spoke of evangelism, then of the organisation of the converts and then of the relief of want. The reading of William Law's "A serious call to a devout and holy life" had influenced him in every way. Arnold Lunn said: Wesley was so obsessed by the eternal values that he completely lost all sense of class values."[3] He believed that when God is personally known, our outward conduct would be transformed. Thus, when Wesley issued his rules for preachers at Conference 1763, and said "You have nothing to do but to save souls", it was not mere pietism but had the expectation that spiritual renewal would produce practical works. A passion for scriptural holiness would result in concern for the poor. The gospel he experienced and expressed was a great leveller. It encouraged generosity by the believing rich and encourages thrift by the believing poor. He wrote to a preacher in Ireland in 1769 "Be active, be diligent; avoid all laziness,

1 John Wesley The Doctrine of Original Sin 2,10

2 John Wesley Sermons on Several Occasions, Epworth Press 1948 p546

3 A Lunn John Wesley Cassell 1929 p.345

sloth, indolence. Fly from every degree, every appearance of it. Else you will never be more than half a Christian... Be cleanly...use all diligence to be clean... Whatever clothes you wear, let them be whole... Let none ever see a ragged Methodist."[1]

In 1752, the Bishop of Gloucester wrote to his colleague in the Irish See of Cloyne: "Your lordship calls this the freest country in Europe. There is indeed freedom of one kind in it...a most unbounded licentiousness of all sorts...a regard to nothing but diversion and vicious pleasures... Our people are now become what they never were before, cruel. These accursed spirituous liquors which, to the shame of the Government, are so easily to be had, and in such quantities drunk, have changed the very nature of our people."[2]

Wesley was a practical Christian who did not intend to be socially subversive, yet G M Trevelyan was able to comment: "A new chapter in the religious, social and educational history of the working class"[3] began with the work of the Wesleys and Whitefield. Dr Albert Outler in his Library of Protestant Thought refers to John Wesley as evangelist, reformer, practical genius." Social conditions in England were similar to those in France, which sparked off the French Revolution in 1789, and a secular historian felt able to claim that Wesley and the Evangelical revival saved England from a bloody revolution.

All the needs of people were included in the Wesleyan gospel outreach. He ministered to their spiritual needs by proclaiming the gospel. He met their educational needs by setting up schools. He cared for their social needs and set up an orphan house in Newcastle, and a home for widows in Dublin. He established a loan Society through which poor and deserving Methodists might be assisted in times of need. No doubt he remembered that his Father, when rector of Epworth was put into a debtors' prison for a while. He ministered to their physical needs. Wesley had studied medicine during his Oxford career and established a sort of medical dispensary in London, Bristol and Newcastle when there was none and he wrote a pamphlet in 1747 called "Primitive Physick" on the treatment for physical ills. Some of his cures were certainly primitive! This influenced his followers to

1 L Tyerman, The life and times of John Wesley, Vol.3 Hodder 1890 p.44

2 Quoted by David Guy in John Wesley, Contemporary Perspectives Epworth 1988 p.116

3 G M Trevelyan English Social History, Longmans 1946 p.362

minister to all the needs of the whole person and to work for social righteousness. The Methodist Missionary Society has since felt the need to bring hospital care and opportunities for education where ever Methodists have been sent.

Rev Dr Edwin Sangster in his famous 1953 sermon which made the headline of Britain's Daily Express spoke in the scriptural spirit of John Wesley when he outlined ten social benefits which would come about if there was a religious revival in Britain. It would he said: *Pay our debts; Reduce sexual immorality; Disinfect the theatre; Cut the divorce rate; Reduce juvenile crime; Lessen the prison population; Improve the quality and increase the output of work; Restore to the nation a high sense of destiny; Make us invincible in the war of ideas; Give happiness and peace to all the people.* He was saying that a revival of religion leads to a moral reformation and that the church is as important as the police station in the defence of society.

2: SECONDLY, THE WORLD TODAY NEEDS SALVATION.

"Humankind's holiness and happiness in God are the ultimate goal of the work of salvation in the life."[1] Wesley's conversion experience at Aldersgate Street on 24th May 1738 radically reordered his theological outlook because it added the dimension of personal experience of God when he felt his "heart strangely warmed", when he was given the "assurance" of sins forgiven, and when he knew he was "saved from the law of sin and death". After Aldersgate Wesley was less interested in a neat theological system but promoted a working theology which became like a recipe for God's plan of salvation. Scripture was, of course, the final arbiter for all his opinions and such authority was backed up by reason, experience and tradition in what has become known as the Wesleyan quadrilateral. He wrote his notes on the New Testament for those who had "a desire to save their souls".[2] People then and now need to be saved because "all have sinned and fallen short of the glory of God" Romans 3v23. The law of sin and death condemns the sinner to hell. The grace of the gospel opens up the gate of heaven to everyone who believes.

---

1 Quoted by Melvin E Dieter in John Wesley, Contemporary Perspectives Epworth 1988 p.166 referring to Albert Outler's Theology in the Wesleyan Spirit.

2 See James T MacCormack Thoughts from a warmed heart- a commentary on John Wesley's Notes on the New Testament Colourpoint Chapter 13

John Wesley, unlike the Calvinists, believed that God's love was all-embracing and that God's saving grace was available to all. So many human systems and groups are exclusive. Wesley read his bible from the perspective that God loved the whole world and that "whosoever" believed would be saved by the atoning death of Christ for all. This impelled him to preach to all, even to be as vile as to preach in the open air, and inspired his global mission, making him to regard the world as his parish. Lest an undue emphasis on human choice may make salvation from sin seem to be a human achievement, Wesley re-constructed the doctrine of "Prevenient grace" which emphasised that in our depravity before conversion, even the capability of repentance was a grace given by God to the sinner, but importantly to *every* sinner.

Wesley's sermons on "Salvation by faith" and "The marks of the new birth" make it clear that any sinner who believed in Jesus upon hearing the good news of God's forgiving love, could be saved from hell and attain heaven. This would happen instantaneously after the analogy of a foetus being born to new life. Such saving faith is more than mental assent but a complete reliance on the saving work of Christ on the cross. There had always been a stress on the importance of good works if people were to please God, but Wesley did not "put the cart before the horse" and called people first to a living experience God's saving grace in their hearts thereby allowing God's indwelling Spirit to complete his work by making them holy and inspiring their service.

Tens of thousands of people responded to the gospel preaching of Wesley and Whitefield and others and were converted. Fifty years after his first foray into "field preaching" Wesley wrote from Dublin and said: "In a course of years, necessity was laid upon me to preach in the open air." John Nelson heard Wesley's remarkable first sermon at Moorfields: "Oh! That was a blessed morning for my soul! As soon as he got up upon the stand, he stroked back his hair and turned his face towards where I stood, and I thought he fixed his eyes on me. His countenance struck such an awful dread upon me before I heard him speak, that it made my heart beat like the pendulum of a clock, and when he did speak, I thought his whole discourse was aimed at me. When he had done, I said, 'This man can tell the secrets of my heart'."[1] Open air preaching may not be as relevant in some parts of the world as it once was, but the passion for the saving of souls continues to win the lost for Christ. May Methodism today, regain that passion.

3: THIRDLY, CHRISTIANS TODAY NEED THE ASSURANCE OF SINS FORGIVEN.

John Wesley described his Aldersgate Street experience in terms of "an assurance was given me that He had taken away my sins, even mine, and saved me from the law of sin and death".[2] People have argued over whether he was converted at that time or whether it was a gift of assurance of salvation. The truth is that John Wesley was now saved and he knew that he was saved. In his sermon on "The witness of the Spirit" he defines assurance as "an inward impression on the soul, whereby the Spirit of God directly witnesses to my spirit, that I am a child of God; that Jesus Christ hath loved me, and given himself for me; and that all my sins are blotted out, and I, even I, am reconciled to God". Objective tests were set to this subjective feeling and the fruit of the Spirit (Galatians 5:22, 23) would be an indication that such claim of assurance was not mere imagination or presumption.

Despite advances today, people live in an insecure world and are often oppressed by stress, depression and self-doubt. We agree with Charles Wesley when he wrote: "My God I am thine, what a comfort divine, what a blessing to know that my Jesus is mine!" (MHB 406)

The 18th century Evangelical Revival recovered this doctrine and experience for the church. Assurance of heaven is something that Roman Catholics may not have so long as they believe in a period of purgatory after death. Formalist Christians will be denied this personal assurance so long as they rely on the mere, dutiful performance of religious rites. Non-Christian religions do not have an assurance of salvation since they do not know the Christ through whom alone the gift is given. Let Methodists preach and demonstrate again this precious evangelical gift of God, that all may know they are saved.

---

1 Quoted by Donald Soper in John Wesley, Contemporary Perspectives Epworth 1988 p.184

2 The Journal of John Wesley Standard edition, Epworth Press 1938 vol.1 p.476

"Our main doctrines which include all the rest are these: that of repentance, of faith and of holiness. The first to these we account as it were the porch of religion, the next, the door, the third, religion itself."[1] So wrote John Wesley in 1746.

Wesley said that Methodists were raised up "to spread scriptural holiness throughout the land". He used differed terminology to describe this experience including Christian Perfection, Entire Sanctification and Perfect Love. Wesley even used the term "Second Blessing".[2] But later explained that the experience could be one of gradual growth as the perfection of a bud, a leaf and a flower at different stages. Christian Perfection seems to have been an unhelpful term and even Mr Wesley had to begin his famous sermon on Christian Perfection by explaining at length that it did not mean "perfection!" In this sermon, he does indicate that the experience means we "do not continue in sin, are made free from outward sin, are freed from evil thoughts and tempers and are delivered from all other inward sin such as pride, anger and self-will".[3]

By emphasising this doctrine, John Wesley was re-capturing for the born-again Christian a new dynamic. Christianity had become formal and static and dutiful. Wesley pointed out that God has always something more for the believer, especially more of his perfect love: 'that love of God and our neighbour which implies deliverance from all sin' and 'loving God with all our heart, soul, mind and strength' which implies 'no wrong temper' and by which all thoughts, words and actions are governed by pure love."[4] Such holiness is our vision and goal. Today the church needs Christians who demonstrate holiness of heart and life as the unbelieving world says: "I might become a Christian if I could see one!"

---

1 John Wesley The Principles of a Methodist further explained, 1746

2 The Letters of John Wesley Standard Edition Vol.5 p.333

3 John Wesley Fifty three Sermons p. 564-581

4 Quoted by Dr William R Davies in John Wesley, Contemporary Perspectives Epworth 1988 p.180 referring to John Wesley A plain account of Christian Perfection Epworth Press 1952 p 41, 42,52

In conclusion, John Wesley used all means to spread the gospel and so can we. He was ceaseless in his personal proclamation of the good news. He encouraged reading and published a fifty volume Christian Library which he edited himself and expected all Methodist preachers to read. He wrote hundreds of tracts defending the faith and many more letters. We refer to "the four all's" of Methodism as: "all need to be saved; all may be saved; all may know themselves saved; all may be saved to the uttermost". We could add a fifth: "the Priesthood of all believers" for he involved, equipped and supported lay people who shared in the work as local preachers and class leaders. Mr Wesley was concerned about Christian unity and did everything in his power to prevent schism. While in Ireland, he wrote his famous Open Letter to a Roman Catholic with the quote: "If your heart is as my heart, give me your hand"; "if we cannot think alike at least let us love alike". He said that Methodists were "the friends of all and the enemies of none".

The Irish Methodist Rev William Arthur in 1888 put it well:

> *(Methodism) rose to national importance and world-wide influence, not by courting either the noble and learned on the one hand, or the populace on the other; but by bringing to every class alike the message of Christ, the Saviour from sin, the Saviour for all, the Saviour now, the Saviour to the uttermost.*[1]

Like Mr Wesley we in our generation must stress the supreme importance of people being led to a warm, intimate experience of God's saving and reconciling love from which all spiritual growth, all fruits of the spirit, all evangelical zeal, all courage in adversity and all hope in death can spring. Such grace is needed and available in 21st Century and the best of all is "God is with us."

---

1 See Norman W Taggart William Arthur Epworth 1993 p.37

MODULE 6: WORSHIP & PREACHING-TRADITIONAL

(Revd Prof Achim Härtner M.A.)

WORSHIP AND PREACHING[1]

LECTURE 1: THEOLOGY OF WORSHIP AND PREACHING–INTRODUCTION

1. WORSHIP AS THE HEART OF CONGREGATIONAL LIFE:

When it comes to questions about church development there rarely is a more central point of interest than the worship service. The worship services traditionally have been characterised to be the "heart" of a congregation's life. A typical worship service says much about the faith practice and theology that shapes the congregation. Therefore, anyone who leads a congregation needs to have a clear perception what a worship service is and be aware of its importance. In the Book of Discipline of the German Methodist Church §401 it says:

"In the worship service the congregation gathers for hearing the Word, for celebrating the sacraments, for confessing their faith, for thanksgiving and intercession in prayer and song, and for giving their offerings. The worship services and gatherings are public. Race, nationality, religion, worldview and social ranking are no means of hindering participants from taking part in them."

In your churches' tradition, you may have a similar statement, saying essential things about worship. Characteristics of worship services as we have heard are the following:
a) Gathering
b) Word, sacraments, confession, prayer, singing and offerings
c) Public character–everyone is invited by God

Now, let's take a closer look on theological essentials of a worship service.

---

1 The lectures are based on the book: Achim Härtner/Holger Eschmann, Predigen lernen. Ein Lehrbuch für die Praxis, Stuttgart 2001; English translation: Konrad Schäfer, 2003.

We start with two questions:
What is it to its content that makes a worship service to be such?
What gives a gathering of people the quality of a Christian worship service?

There are 4 elements that make a gathering to be a Christian worship service.
1. The encounter with God (prayer, songs, sermon, …)
2. The reading and proclamation of the biblical Word (readings, preaching, drama, sacraments, symbols, ...)
3. The fellowship (Singing, prayer, the Lord's supper, time of fellowship, collection of offerings, ...)
4. The sending forth/benediction (Perspectives for Christian practice in everyday live and in public)

Without aiming at an encounter with God a worship service would be reduced to a mere fellowship meeting without the dimension of "the Holy One". That is why Christians celebrate their worship service in the name of God the Father, the Son and the Holy Spirit. We all know that an encounter with God is something we cannot "make", but it is something that we can expectantly pray and long for according to the biblical promises both of the Old and the New Testament.

Without the proclamation of the biblical gospel as living word for today, our worship services would lack the dimension of comforting and directing our lives. We need a word from "outside" in order to help us in our search for guidance and meaning in life. A Christian congregation cannot relinquish the reading and preaching of the biblical message. As the message relates to our lives, it may be delivered in form of a sermon, a drama play, a new song or a shared experience.

Without undergoing fellowship, a worship service would be experienced to be something like a lifeless casing that leaves the individuals alone. Singing together, playing music, dancing, praying and rejoicing will touch and move the hearts of many people. Celebrating God's grace and seeking love by words and signs, symbols and rituals will deepen the spiritual relationship with one another. The Christian "koinonia" (fellowship) will "earth" the

342

heavenly truth. That people will differ in their expectations and opinions shaping their "life together" (D. Bonhoeffer) we will not want to deny.

And finally: without the element of sending forth, the congregation would stay at place and not move forward. Yet, God's promises and benedictions are given to those on the way, those who don't remain in their safe places but go and share what their hearts and minds have been filled with. Worship service and everyday life belong together as the Apostle Paul said in Rm 12:1
"I appeal to you therefore, brothers and sisters, by the mercies of God, to present your bodies as a living sacrifice, holy and acceptable to God, which is your spiritual worship."

Please remember what we have already said about the public relevance of worship. German Reformer Martin Luther in 1526 said about the worship service to be a "public stimulus towards faith and Christianity".

In the sending forth at the end of a worship service, the congregation will be reminded and empowered to go where God directs the individuals to be and to share their faith both with words and with deeds. The benediction which stands at the end of a worship liturgy reinforces the gatherings' consciousness to be nothing less than a crucial part of the Kingdom of God spreading out in a world of darkness and despair. As we may summarize: a worship service is a gathering where God serves us in order that we may serve one another.

3. ONE ISSUE–VARIOUS FORMS:

The way in which Christians want to express and share their faith varies a great deal if we look through the ages and around the world. By this, we recognise that there is always a cultural aspect involved as we worship.

I have heard people say: "we don't want to do anything else but glorify God." Well so, but it just isn't the case: by all we do, we are who we are and do what we are most convinced of being the right thing to do.

343

Let us listen to what the Apostle Paul said in 2 Cor 4:7-8

We have this treasure in clay jars, so that it may be made clear that this extraordinary power belongs to God and does not come from us. We are afflicted in every way, but not crushed, perplexed, but not driven to despair; persecuted, but not forsaken; struck down, but not destroyed; always carrying in the body the death of Jesus, so that the life of Jesus may also be made visible in our bodies.

The gospel message, is not given to us in heavenly purity, which would mean an unearthly way, but is shared among humans in the ways humans interact with each other according to their culture. That's the reasons why we have four gospels in the New Testament– confessing Jesus Christ to be "the way, the truth and the life" (Jn 14:6), but doing it in the manner the hearers and contemporaries of Matthew, Mark, Luke and John may understand it from their cultural backgrounds.

For me personally, coming to this course in Freetown and teaching together with local colleagues and those coming from the British Isles is conjunct with a vital interest in learning from you as you understand and practice worshipping in your own cultures. Thank you for sharing with me!

As we acknowledge a cultural aspect for all worshipping, we acknowledge a given variety in forms of worship as well. The most important shaping factors therefore may be identified to be:
a)   age group and social status (service for children, youth, elderly, families…)
b)   tradition and piety style (more charismatic, more evangelical, more liturgical, more meditative forms of worship)

How much the various forms of worship may differ; yet the four basic elements will have to be identified in one way or the other during the liturgy of a Christian worship service:

- Encounter with God
- Proclamation of the biblical Word
- Fellowship
- Benediction

It is not always easy to accept spirituality practice and worship styles that are different from ours. But we should learn to do as best as we can in what we are convinced of being the appropriate way of worshipping and at the same time be positive about others doing it differently.

In Philippians 1 we read about Paul being imprisoned and getting word from preachers who preach the gospel differently from the apostle: "What does it matter? Just this, that Christ is proclaimed in every way, whether out of false motives or true; and in that I rejoice." (1:18) The important point for me to make here is that all different worship styles in their essence focus on the same issue: *creating a spiritual realm where people may most possibly encounter God's healing and blessing presence within, in a cultural setting that applies to most of those gathering and those not yet reached with the gospel message.*

4. WORSHIP AND PREACHING: THE CORRELATION OF SERMON AND CHURCH SERVICE.

In protestant tradition and theology, the proclamation and hearing of the biblical Word has been identified and stressed to be the core of Christian worship. As we may put our focus on prayer i.e. adoration to be the most important part of a worship service or the reading and proclamation of scripture, so we may want to boldly bring out the fellowship or emphasise the benediction as being the "real thing"–a worship service will need to find its identity in correlation with the biblical testimonies and the denomination's tradition on the one hand and the congregational situation and the actual specific occasion.

Let me highlight six points concerning the relation between liturgy and preaching in a protestant perspective: [1]

1. Liturgy works hand in hand with the sermon, it participates in preaching the gospel. An inviting liturgy can be compared to a key, opening the congregation's hearts to hear God's word.

2. In liturgy the congregation as whole takes part in the capacity of the gospel's proclamation (2 Cor 5:20). Readings, songs and prayers also

---

1 Cf. G. Kretzschmar/ E. Winkler, "Die Gemeinde", in: Handbuch der Predigt revised by K.-H. Bieritz et al, Berlin 1990, p.187.

are vital part of the proclamation of the gospel – to the congregation as much as it is for the liturgists.

3. Through liturgy, the sermon is placed into a supra-individual framework. A sermon is an individual testimony of faith and hope. Liturgy widens the horizon and relates Christians throughout times and ages, nations and cultures (i.e. Lord's Prayer).

4. Liturgy expresses continuity in the relationship between humans and God. It doesn't have to be quite as situation-oriented as the sermon should be. On the other hand, we need to make sure that liturgy can be understood. It doesn't make sense to celebrate a liturgy in which people will not feel "at home".

5. Liturgy helps to communicate the gospel in a more holistic way. Rituals and symbols can reach different layers of human personality than the spoken word most often can.

6. Liturgy focuses on addressing God in thanksgiving, praise and intercession. By this change of perspective, it complementarily replenishes the sermon which is mainly directed towards the congregation.

5. SUMMARIZING OUTLOOK

In this gathering on the topic of worship and preaching, our student and lecturer body consists of a wide range of various spiritual embossments. I assume we may share common ground in this question as we say: Preaching is part of the church service-an important constituent part, but nonetheless only one part. It is important for me to say therefore we should avoid the common notion of the church service as "the frame of the sermon", because it is theologically incorrect. The church service is not merely frame surrounding the sermon. It is itself precious, full of precious elements and possibilities.

What is important is that the sermon is in tune with the service in which it takes place. A clear thread should be recognisable; i.e. scripture readings, hymns, prayers, etc. should relate to one another and to the sermon. In this context, the time of the service within the church calendar should also be considered. Preparing the worship service is a creative act, like preparing the sermon and therefore takes time. Sloppiness in this area can easily lead to boredom or a feeling of confusion. This will also have an adverse effect on the sermon, for "the liturgy participates in the preaching, as do the room in which the service takes place and the whole atmosphere of the service."[1] The sermon and the worship service complement each other and need each other.

This is evident if we contrast the focus of the liturgy with that of the sermon. While the role of the preachers in the sermon involves acting and giving, the worship service offers them salutary relief, as they can, together with the congregation, depend on familiar and given texts and traditions. The liturgical texts provide a larger context for the sermon and may compensate for any one-sidedness. In turn, the sermon can make general statements in the liturgy come to life in the hearts and minds of the hearers.

The various elements in the worship can play a part in ensuring that the gospel is communicated in the church service in a holistic manner. Rituals, symbols and actions in the service appeal to different layers of the human than the spoken word. Finally, the liturgy involves the participants in the service to a greater degree and in a different way than the sermon does: while the sermon is a speech directed towards the hearers, the hymns and prayers, both of intercession and thanksgiving, are directed towards God.

LECTURE 2: THEOLOGY OF WORSHIP AND PREACHING–WHAT ARE WE DOING AS WE PREACH?

1. AN ENCOURAGEMENT TO PREACH

The purpose of our mutual work in this course is to encourage one another to lead worship and to preach. There are various reasons why this is necessary and important. Anyone who leads worship and who preaches the gospel will be keenly aware of the fact that neither leading people in worship nor preaching is an easy business. From the days of Moses, the prophet Isaiah and John the Baptist, from Martin Luther and John Wesley to the present day, preaching has been experienced not solely as a joyful activity, but also as a difficult one.

---

1 G. Kretzschmar/ E. Winkler, "Die Gemeinde", in: Handbuch der Predigt revised by K.-H. Bieritz et al, Berlin 1990, p.187.

The Protestant theologian Karl Barth (1886-1968) once described the dilemma of Christian witness and preaching in the following words: "As theologians we are supposed to talk about God. We are, however, human beings and, as such, we cannot speak about God. We must know both that we should and that we cannot, and it is precisely this knowledge that will cause us to give the glory to God. This is the difficulty we face; everything else is child's play."[1]

A person who preaches will have to withstand this tension but may, at the same time, go forward in confidence, while asking the question, "How do we get to the point, where preaching becomes a joy and where our sermons radiate the calm assurance of faith?" The motive for encouraging people to preach must be the original motive for preaching *per se*: the voice and testimony of God which are not at our disposal. As preachers, we must therefore first and foremost dedicate ourselves to the study of the scriptures and prayer. We may apply Martin Luther's statement to preaching, "Work on our sermon as if all our praying were of no avail and pray as if all our work were of no avail".[2] The preaching of God's redemptive love for our world is an invitation to believe and embrace the Christian life. It is founded on the covenant promise of God in Jesus Christ, whose word applies also to those who preach today and those who will be preaching tomorrow: "And surely I am with you always, to the very end of the age". (Matt. 28:20b)[3]

The appropriateness of preaching as a form of discourse in our modern day church services and the community has been widely disputed for some time both within the church and outside it. "All over the country, so much is being done to proclaim the Christian faith! But is it not, with very few exceptions, institutionalised irrelevance?"[4] Those who believe that preaching has a future will ask the question, how, in the light of such statements, can preaching once again be understood as an opportunity for Christian discourse and become an effective vehicle for communicating the faith?

---

1 K. Barth, Das Wort Gottes als Aufgabe der Theologie (1922). ... in K.-J. Kuschel (Ed.), Lust an der Erkenntnis: Die Theologie des 20. Jahrhunderts, Munich/Zurich 1986, pp. 93 – 110, citation p. 93.

2 H. Hirschler, Biblisch predigen, 3rd Ed. Hanover 1992, p. 43.

3 Bible quotations are taken from the New International Version ...

4 G. Ebeling, Das Wesen des christlichen Glaubens, Tübingen 1959, p.9 (own translation).

Recently, speaking of my home country the encouragement to preach has increasingly been coming from the congregations: people seek and expect a word that will touch them deep inside. A word that interprets the past addresses the present and promises a future. People are once again calling for propagation of the gospel that is biblically founded and, at the same time, relevant to the lives of the hearers. In an age where the pluralism of opinions makes spiritual orientation increasingly difficult, there is a growing demand for basic biblical information and interpretation and teaching that relate to every-day life. Church attendees today need to know, as much as the unchurched, the reason why they should believe the biblical Word and the preaching of that Word. In our opinion, this reason can only be credibly given if preaching is not presented in isolation, but as part of an ongoing process of communicating the gospel (Ernst Lange) which includes the expression of faith, love and hope of the church as a whole.

2. THEOLOGICAL CLARIFICATION REGARDING PRESENT DAY PREACHING

Before discussing concrete steps to prepare a sermon, we need to ask some fundamental questions: "Why do we preach in the church?", "What are the characteristics of a sermon?", "Can preaching be learnt?" These are all questions to which there are no easy and probably no conclusive answers.

I. THE REASON FOR PREACHING

An Ethiopian proverb says: "The word that helps you cannot come from your own mouth." This proverb expresses a basic human experience: in life, we depend on other people, particularly in a time of crisis, to help us break out of our "revolving around ourselves", and to give us new perspectives and show us new opportunities. No one can, in the long run, live without the care and the encouragement of others.

What this proverb says about human existence in general applies especially to the Christian faith. No one can become or remain a Christian by him/herself. Our faith depends on someone telling us of the good story of God and His people - in other words, on someone preaching. "Faith comes from hearing the message," the Apostle Paul wrote in his letter to the church in Rome (Rom.10:17).

German protestant reformer Martin Luther translated this passage: "Faith comes from preaching." Here the word preaching, of course, is not limited to the classical Sunday morning sermon in a church service; it includes all forms of proclaiming the good news. God uses human speech and hearing to make His voice heard, to stir up faith and build His church. Therefore, preaching is not given to the church to be used as and when the church pleases; rather, the church has been commissioned to preach from the very beginning. That is one side of the coin: God commissions people to propagate the gospel in word and deed.[1]

The other side is that people begin of their own accord to talk about that which has liberated them and affects their innermost being. The bible and church history are full of stories where people could not or would not keep their experience of God's love to themselves, but shared it with others. Moved by God's Spirit, they crossed physical and social boundaries to share something of which their hearts were full. To them, spreading the word of the mercy of God and of His coming to His creation is not a burdensome duty, but a heartfelt desire to which they feel compelled.

It is in this tension between gift and responsibility, enthusiasm and commission that our preaching is situated today. As pastors, lay preachers or readers appointed by our churches in the name of the triune God, we are called and commissioned to preach. This can be quite an arduous and agonising experience if one has spent hours over an empty sheet of paper, trying to prepare a sermon but lacking any convincing ideas. However, we endure this only because we ourselves, long before having been appointed by our respective churches, have been touched by the Word of God and feel compelled to share something of the gift of the love of Jesus Christ with others.

For this reason, preaching is primarily a matter of joy and enthusiasm: "Preaching is enjoyable, it is a *delight*. This is the first thing that needs to be taught in a manual on preaching. Point one of paragraph one states: Teaching to preach is teaching to enjoy; preaching should lead to joy! It is in joy that speaking about God fulfils its purpose."[2]

---

1 For a definition of the term "gospel" cf. chapter 7.

2 R. Bohren, Predigtlehre, 4th Ed., Munich 1980, p.17.

II. THE CHARACTERISTICS OF PREACHING

So what is a sermon then? It is a propagation of the gospel, as we have already pointed out. We must, however, distinguish between this broad meaning of the term, and a more specific type of preaching, namely the sermon in a Christian church service. The primary aim of this book is to provide help for this specific instance of preaching, although much of what will be discussed may also be applied to other forms of preaching the gospel.

1. A DEFINITION

The following classical definition is intended to help initially identify what characterises a Sunday church sermon:
"The sermon is a form of speech which must focus entirely on the present, but in which the Christian faith, the 'old' gospel, must speak, within the horizon of the modern-day consciousness, to both the Christian church and society as a whole."[1] What does that mean?

2. THE SERMON AS A SPEECH

In this definition, it is said that a sermon is a speech, thus emphasising its oral nature. There is a difference between reading bible verses, a theological essay or a book about preaching or being addressed by a preacher in a church service. I am usually much more open when being addressed directly and orally. I cannot close my ears as I can my eyes. On the other hand, however, I cannot read the sentences I have heard over again as I can when reading a book, or look up any words that I may not have understood. Due to the sermon's oral nature, rhetorical issues such as structure and organisation, language and form used, and presentation are important. These issues will be covered later in more depth.

3. THE CONTENT

Something else that is said in the above definition is that the content of the sermon is determined by the gospel of Jesus Christ. This is essentially the criterion that distinguishes a sermon from other speeches. A speech can be structured to perfection and presented in the best possible way; but it can only be called a sermon if it tells the good story of God and man. For this reason the Christian sermon must "remain focused on its subject and [must not] want to compete in

---

1 W. Trillhaas, Einführung in die Predigtlehre, 3rd Ed., Darmstadt 1983, p. IX.

fields that have not been entrusted to it for cultivation. And the hearers must be able to rest assured that they will hear in the sermon that which they are in need of, which they cannot be told elsewhere in this particular form."[1] Now, this qualification is not a restriction, because the terms "Christian faith" and "gospel" as definitions of the sermon content are wide. They provide the basis and the scope for the Christian sermon without specifying the concrete individual topic. There are essentially two ways in which the preacher can arrive at a specific topic: either s/he interprets a given passage of scripture or s/he deals with a fundamental aspect of the Christian faith and relates it to the situation of the hearers. S/he may also start with the situation, the circumstances in which the preachers or hearers find themselves, and relate these to statements of Christian tradition. These two approaches are not mutually exclusive. In a context where biblical texts do not have automatic relevance to the hearers (any more), as in the case of evangelistic events, it may be appropriate to start with their circumstances and move from there to the biblical message. This reduces the danger of preaching above people's heads. On the other hand, there is a strong case - particularly in a church service - to begin a sermon as a rule with a passage of scripture. The diversity of scripture helps to prevent monotony which may result from sermons being based for the most part on a given situation. Moreover, the biblical texts have a dynamic and proper motion that can inspire the preacher and the hearers and generate faith.

4. THE SITUATION OF THE SERMON

The third important characteristic mentioned in our definition is that the sermon must focus on the present and take place within the horizon of the modern-day consciousness, as it has been shaped by the political, social and cultural development. A sermon is more than a preservation and constant reiteration of pre-formulated doctrines of faith and more than mere recitation of scripture. A sermon must translate a message which was given at a different time to a different culture, making it relevant to the here and now. A Christian speech can only be called a sermon if it is directed specifically towards its audience.

---

1 H. M. Müller, Homiletik, Berlin/New York 1995, p.204.

A clear understanding of the addressees and their circumstances may be gained with the help of the theologian Ernst Lange's distinction between the "general homiletic situation" and the specific "local situation" according to talking about the weather. "The 'general homiletic situation' includes the macrocosm of the societal order and public life with its constant rapid changes, political events and ideas and, above all, their effects on the people: hopes, fears, resignation, the feeling of impotence in respect of societal developments. The general homiletic situation comprises all those factors that must be accepted more or less as given at a particular time."[1]

These situations vary a great deal from country to country, from rural to urban settings. The preacher learns about the general homiletic situation first and foremost by living attentively. Other sources may be, if available, the mass media (Newspapers, radio, TV, internet…), studies and surveys regarding social issues, and contemporary art which expresses present-day sentiments. The church calendar (Christmas, Lent, Easter, Pentecost…) should also be considered within the context of the general homiletic situation.

The "local situation", in contrast, comprises "those events, relations, conflicts, sentiments, judgements and the prejudice that the preacher does not learn about from the newspapers, as they are relevant alone to the local community and congregation; these factors can only be determined through the preacher's own investigations or from sharing with members of the congregation and from discussions with other church workers, and can be influenced, resolved and changed through the sermon, because they belong to the immediate area of responsibility of the preacher and the church."[2]

In addition to these two ways of understanding the circumstances of the hearers of the sermon, there is a third way which does not result from direct observation. The preacher must perceive his 'opposite' (and him/herself!) from the perspective of the Christian faith, as a person upon whom God has laid his hand, a person whom He has created and reconciled to himself, with whom he walks and for whom he has a destiny. Without this theological perspective, the hearers of the sermon would not be adequately included.

---

1 E. Lange, Predigen als Beruf, 2nd Ed., Munich 1987, p. 38.

2 Loc. cit., p. 38 f.

Finally, the above definition of a sermon states that the gospel should be proclaimed to society as a whole as well as the Christian church. If the Christian church is the addressee of the sermon the propagation of the gospel is directed not at an individual - as it is in Christian counselling - but at the community of the "seeking and the believers"[1]. Although it has proved useful in practice for the preacher to imagine one or at least only a few potential hearers during preparation so as to ensure that the sermon has a clear focus, it must be remembered that preaching in a church service is directed at the congregation as a whole.

The sermon speaks to people who have been brought into fellowship and equipped with various gifts for the benefit of one another. Within this community, there is a mutual giving and receiving, a sharing of joy and grief of which the preaching is a part.[2] Of course, the spiritual gifting of the church congregation and the fellowship between the congregation and the preacher are very often not immediately noticeable. It is therefore necessary - despite and in the midst of all the shortcomings of the church as we know it here and there - continually to recognise these factors in both senses of the word: to identify them, to appreciate and utilise them. Where this happens, the preacher will find helpful words for the church and, vice versa, s/he will receive the support of the congregation.

The fact that the sermon addresses society as a whole as well as the church means that the preaching may be directed at the outside as well as the inside. This does not only apply to preaching evangelistic events, but also to preaching in a church service. The sermon is concerned not only with internal church affairs; it is public by nature and therefore there is and must be room for public concerns. It occurs within a public context. Preaching is, like all the actions of the Christian church, characterised theologically by the interdependence of

---

1 These two terms convey the Methodist understanding of church. cf. Berufen – Beschenkt – Beauftragt, ed. by the Theologischen Kommission des Europäischen Rates der Evangelisch-methodistischen Kirche (EmK heute 68), Stuttgart/Zurich 1991, p.22.

2 Cf. C. Möller, Seelsorglich predigen, Göttingen 1983, pp. 127-150 and U. Nembach, Predigen heute – ein Handbuch, Stuttgart 1996, pp. 135-210.

gathering and sending.[1] In the sermon, edifying, evangelistic, caring and political impulses are closely intertwined. The public nature of preaching is evident from the root of the verb itself: to preach comes from the Latin verb *praedicare* which means to speak publicly and proclaim.

6. THE PREACHER AS AN INDIVIDUAL

In my opinion, there remains one element of preaching that is not emphasised enough in the definition we have used. If one considers the conditions surrounding a sermon, one must also mention the individual who preaches it. It is only through the person of the preacher that the biblical-Christian content becomes a sermon. An individual who preaches must perform the task of a translator. For this reason, preaching has been compared with translating or interpreting: "The preacher seeks to receive the things that touch and affect the hearer into his/her own person and then to relate his/her text to these things. In other words: the preacher seeks to process in him/herself that which his/her text wants to convey and to present it to the hearers as concerning them, so as to prompt them to a response of their own. What the preacher is doing here can be ... compared to the work of an interpreter. Just as an interpreter mediates between two parties in a conversation, thus enabling them to understand each other, the preacher should facilitate a dialogue between the hearers and the testimony of scripture."[2]

To be able to mediate in this way, the preacher needs to have a good understanding of both the bible and the situation of the hearers. In this process of interpreting, the sermons of theologians will differ from those of lay preachers as their understanding of the biblical message and of the hearers' situation differs. While theologians will rely in their sermons to a large extent on their theological competence, the gifting of lay preachers lies especially in their ability, as "experts of everyday life", to relate their experiences in society in general and in the church.[3]

---

1 The order in which the terms gathering and sending occur here is not to be interpreted in a chronological sense (first the gathering, then the sending) but in a complementary sense (occurring simultaneously, and complementing and sustaining each other).

2 H. M. Müller, Homeletik, loc. cit. p.201.

3 Cf. K. H. Voigt, Die Predigt durch Laien in der Evangelisch-methodistischen Kirche damals und heute (EmK heute 51), Stuttgart 1987, esp. pp.26-34.

Are there any other characteristics that preachers must possess or requirements they must meet in order to fulfil their ministry? What is it that gives them their legitimacy? Different traditions have different answers to this question. From a Protestant perspective, the doctrine of the priesthood of all believers means that the commission to preach the gospel is given to every Christian. However, in order to ensure the soundness of the sermon content and judge the suitability of the individual for public proclamation of the gospel, the Protestant tradition too has developed the office of the appointed preacher. This office is to a certain extent the opposite of the congregation, which does not, however, make a person who occupies it, in any theological or religious sense, more important. The calling of an individual to the office of a preacher, be it in full-time service of the church or as a lay preacher, involves two main dimensions, which are ultimately interrelated.

Firstly, there is the calling by the church. This public calling which normally requires some form of training or academic study involves various recommendation procedures and the public appointment to preach by the respective church organisation. This appointment by the church is based on the New Testament principle that the Christian church calls and commissions an individual to preach. It is ultimately the church that has the competence to judge a person's belief regarding Christian doctrine and attitudes to life.[1]

The second requirement for the preaching ministry is a personal conviction that one has been called to this ministry by God. This conviction provides the motivation and enthusiasm required for the joyous and difficult task of preaching. In contrast to the public appointment, this calling of God has no set form; it may vary considerably, depending on the individual's biography and piousness. It will also always remain an "uncertain conviction", as the Christian's faith is tried.[2]

Both these dimensions of the calling to the preaching ministry are equally important and interrelated. In situations where one may doubt

---

1 Cf. M. Luther, That a Christian Assembly has the Right and Power to Judge all Teaching and to Call, Appoint and Dismiss teachers, Established and Proven by Scripture WA 11, pp. 408-416. Luther bases his treatise mainly on John 10. (English translation from www.covenanter.org/Luther/thatachristianassembly.htm)

2 W. Härle, Dogmatik, Berlin/New York 1995, p.61.

one's own gifting, it is helpful to know that the calling and the commission to preach do not rest solely on oneself as an individual. On the other hand, preaching can degenerate into a tedious duty and routine if one is not continuously driven to share the message by the joy of knowing God's love.

In addition to this basic ecclesiastical and personal calling, one may also expect of the preacher that s/he is as credible a witness of the gospel as possible. What may sound like an unattainable ideal here can be stated more precisely and circumscribed by the terms "effort of the heart and of the conscience": "Effort of the heart means a sincere and persistent endeavour to empathise with the people to whom one speaks. The effort of the conscience means having the honesty never to say more than one would say to oneself."[1]

LECTURE 3: THE SERMON – GOD'S DOMAIN OR HUMAN ARTWORK?

In summary, it can be said that learning to preach involves three main factors. Firstly, there is the biblical Christian tradition, the text or the topic on which the sermon is based and which must be translated into the present. Secondly, in this interpreting process, the hearers and their horizons must be considered in order for the sermon truly to reach and touch the hearts of its audience.

Finally, one must consider the preachers and the way they perceive themselves so they can understand their part in the preaching-interpreting process and learn to carry it out in an adequate fashion. These three factors have been described as the homiletic triangle, because they must be viewed not in isolation but rather as reciprocally affecting one another.

I. THE THREE PLACES OF ORIGIN OF A SERMON

Preaching is a process with various stages, involving both the preacher and the congregation. The preachers and hearers take a journey together with the text or topic. Corresponding to the static illustration of the homiletic triangle, there are three more dynamic factors, the three stages of a journey during which the church sermon develops. These stages, work phases or successive homiletic places may be represented by the words desk, pulpit and pew.

---

1 H. M. Müller, Homiletik, loc. cit. p.198.

1. THE DESK

The first place, the desk, stands first and foremost for the groundwork, meditating and unravelling the biblical passage, reflecting on the hearers and the actual organisation of the sermon. This first preparation phase may, in turn, be divided into three steps.

a) There is first of all the step of perceiving, observing and gathering. This step is about perceiving and registering the situation of the hearers and one's own situation in the light of the biblical text or topic which is to be preached. The perception phase begins with one's personal study of the text (or topic) during which ideas and thoughts are written down without being evaluated. This phase is also of spiritual nature; being in silence before God, reading the scripture passage prayerfully and expectantly listening to what God says in many ways is of great importance. This phase goes along with a study of the text with commentaries and other aids and by reflecting on the hearers whom one expects to be present. All this takes place not only at the desk, but also during conversations with church members, while reading the newspaper or while going for a walk.

b) This step of observing and gathering impressions and information is usually followed by a phase of concentration, comprehension, evaluation and collation of ideas. The perceptions of the text, the topic or the situation from the previous step are related, weighted and interpreted. The sermon content is assigned to more general themes of Christian doctrine (e.g. creation, redemption, the church) and contemplated in a more general sense. The previous effects of the text or topic are considered: What results has the topic produced in the past (in church history) and what preconceptions are my hearers likely to have? During this phase of the preparation stage, one has to ask oneself the question, what do I want to achieve with the sermon? This goal should be formulated as clearly as possible before the sermon is written out, so as to ensure that a clear line of thought is recognisable.

c) The third step of the "desk stage" may be described as the production and formulating phase. In this phase, the sermon is verbalised and given a literary form, in the truest sense of the word, which will appeal to the hearers. During this phase, the focus is on the language of preaching, the images and symbols used and the organisation of the sermon. The preacher should also take time to subject his/her sermon once more to a thorough examination with the help of a checklist. As a result, sentences which are too long and therefore not hearer-friendly may be shortened or any incoherence in the use of images rectified. What may sound like an easy and smooth process in the description of these phases is, in reality, usually connected with severe birth pains.

While preparing the sermon, the preacher may experience phases of frustration where s/he almost gets to the point of despair. Research into creative writing has shown that such preaching crises can hardly be avoided. "Not many good sermons have been produced without persistence and earnest seeking ... Blockages and endurance in overcoming them are the *conditio sine qua non* for finding creative solutions. Frustration is the price that must be paid for an idea."[1] The joy over a successful sermon and the positive reactions of the hearers will always compensate for the frustration experienced during preparation.

2. THE PULPIT

The place or stage of the pulpit represents the presentation of the sermon, its delivery. This homiletic element is often underestimated with the result that the sermon is delivered in a monotonous and unimaginative fashion. However, the somewhat flowery sounding words of the theologian August Tholuck (1799-1877) still apply:

"The sermon must be an act of the preacher in his study room, it must again be an act in the pulpit and, descending from the pulpit, he must experience motherly joy, the joy of a mother who has just given birth to a child under the hand of God. It is only when the sermon has been a twofold act of the preacher that it can also be an act in the hearer."

When preparing to deliver the sermon, the possibility of contact and communication with the hearers play a role, as do issues regarding manner and presentation, facial expression and gestures, if necessary and available the use of technical aids and, as the sermon is delivered

---

1 H. Arens/F. Richardt/J. Schulte, Kreativität und Predigtarbeit, 3rd Ed., Munich 1977, p. 30. Cf. also J. Rothermundt, Der Heilige Geist und die Rhetorik, Gütersloh 1984, esp. pp. 143-149. The Latin expression means: a condition, without which something is not possible.

within the context of a church service, what has been called the "liturgical presence" (Thomas Kabel). By this, we mean a spirit of attentiveness to the Holy Spirit according to the biblical promises, a vital expectancy of the preacher that through our message nothing less may happen as that the eternal God may speak to the hearers as it is his will.

Theologian Karl Barth gave some general advice to his friend and fellow-worker Charlotte von Kirschbaum before one of her first presentations: "Be completely with the subject from which you are proceeding and completely with the hearers, whom you want to reach! Let the speech be born on the way from there to here ... Do not be afraid! Forget yourself and remember that it will surely go well!"[1]

Such a conscious forgetting of oneself dispels any fears and tensions. It conveys the message in a convincing way and makes the hearers feel that they are being taken seriously.

3. THE PEW

The third place where the sermon develops is the church pew. It points to the fact that the hearers too are involved in the preaching process. They are involved in deciding, be it consciously or subconsciously, what is heard and what is missed, what is received and what is rejected of that which is said. They influence the way the sermon is processed from the initial acoustic reception right through to putting into practice what they have heard. It may therefore be said that, in the end, there are as many sermons as there are hearers. This does not mean that what the preacher says and how s/he says it is irrelevant, because the hearers anyhow make of the sermon what they want.

The principle remains: the one who preaches must ensure with all diligence that the biblical text or the topic of the sermon is properly interpreted and presented to the hearers in a way that they can understand it. Conscientious preparation will preclude confusion. Nonetheless, the pew as a place of origin of a sermon shows that preachers must be aware of the fact that their sermons are heard, received and put into practice in different ways. Indeed, they should

---

1 Cited in E Busch, Karl Barths Lebenslauf (biography), 3rd Ed., Munich 1978, p.377.

encourage this creativity on the part of the hearers by offering them links "which enable them to transpose the message to their own respective situations and to transform it according to their own specific needs".[1] Where a preacher prevents the hearers from participating creatively through a banal one-track message or an authoritarian style, s/he may jeopardise any congregational response for which s/he may have hoped.

The working of the Spirit of God has been promised for each of the three places or stages mentioned above. The Spirit gives the preacher ideas while s/he contemplates the words of the bible, the Spirit takes what the preacher says and makes it alive to the hearers, and the Spirit directs the hearers in the process of receiving, transforming and putting into practice the content of the sermon. In this whole process, the Word of God is coming into being. This interrelation in the preaching process of God acting and humans speaking, hearing and doing will be discussed in more detail as follows.

II. THE SERMON WITHIN THE DOMAIN OF GOD'S SPIRIT

When God himself speaks in the sermon to comfort, to exhort to call to repentance and to generate faith the sermon becomes more than just an informing activity. It may be said, theologically, that a sermon creates what it attests. Thus, the speaking process is a process of power: "The word in the holy act is filled with holy power." as theologian Manfred Josuttis said.[2] The statement in the preaching definition given earlier that the sermon is "a form of speech which must focus entirely on the present" should be understood not merely in the temporal sense, but first and foremost in the sense that the Spirit and the Word of God are present during the preaching process. God is the "first hearer" of the sermon.[3] It is God who decides what the preaching is worth and God has the final say after the sermon has finished. Everything depends on the way God's presence is manifested."[4]

---

1 I. Reuter, Predigt Verstehen. Grundlagen einer homeletischen Hermeneutik, Leipzig 2000, p.205.

2 M. Josuttis, Die Einführung in das Leben, Gütersloh 1996, p.104.

3 "That is why it is a daring thing to preach: for when I ascend to the holy place – whether the church be packed or virtually empty, whether I take note of this or not: I have a hearer beside those that I can see, an invisible hearer, God in Heaven, whom I can of course not see, yet he can see me." S. Kierkegaard, Einübung ins Christentum (1850), Gesammelte Werke, (Complete works) Vol 26, p.226.

4 R. Bohren, Predigtlehre, 4th Ed., Munich 1980, p. 454.

For the preachers, there are two sides to this statement. On the one hand, it relieves them when it comes to the difficult task of interpreting, because it is the Holy Spirit rather than the human who has the last say and He determines the worth or worthlessness of human words. This knowledge protects against any feeling of resignation, where I notice that something is not coming across the way I meant it to or that I simply cannot find the words to express what is laid on my heart. On the other hand, tremendous demands are made in this statement: if it is ultimately the manifestation of God's presence that decides everything, how can I as the preacher then vouch for his presence, never mind guarantee it? Given these requirements, is it at all possible to learn to preach? After all, God's presence is not at the disposal of us human beings and we cannot administer his grace.

Yet, in putting homiletics on the teaching schedule for this course, we are convinced that indeed there is something that could be learnt with regard to preaching. However, one must take care to distinguish between that which lies within the sphere of the human and that which would go beyond the limits of human ability and may therefore be left to God. The faith of the hearers (and the preachers!) cannot be generated by the human if it is truly the Christian faith. It is God himself who gives faith to us humans through preaching so that we, in turn, can put our trust in God. This frees the preacher from any unrealistic aspirations to be successful. On the other hand, it does not mean that s/he is relieved from the responsibility to work on the sermon. There are things the preacher can do to ensure that the message preached is factually and doctrinally as accurate as possible and as relevant to the situation as possible, that it does not go above the heads of the hearers, but is delivered in a comprehensible and sensitive manner.

If we understand preaching as God's Word and human words or, more precisely as God's Word in the form of human words, the spiritual dimension gains in importance. Preparing a sermon still means to study diligently a biblical text or conscientiously reflect on a Christian theme in order to obtain a message for the sermon. It still involves the study of psychological and societal factors in order to reach the hearers as directly as possible in the world in which they live. In all this, however, the spiritual foundation of these endeavours must be considered.

Manfred Josuttis reminds us that **"Practical pastoral work necessitates a spiritual basis ... Every religious act requires spiritual preparation."**[1] The power to perform a spiritual task such as preaching can only be obtained on the basis of a spiritual existence.

For this reason, prayer plays a vital role in the preparation of a sermon. Yet here too we must be careful: it is not human ability versus the miraculous. The spirit of God must not be an excuse for laziness. The practical theologian Rudolf Bohren introduced the term "theonomous reciprocity" in this context. This term means that, during the preaching process, the Holy Spirit brings what the human does into his service: "Miracles and technology are ... not opposed to one another; they merely indicate different aspects of the theonomous reciprocity. When the Spirit of God works in us, with us and through us, I speak of a miracle. Where we, however, are put to work by the Spirit of God and, consequently, get down to work ourselves, methods are involved, technology is applied, art is performed and science is employed. In the partnership with the Holy Spirit, methods, art, technology, science are not excluded, even if they enter into the κρισις *(krisis)* of the Spirit."[2]

III. THE LANGUAGE OF PREACHING AND TYPES OF SERMONS

Closely related to the above is the consideration whether there is a particular language of preaching which is particularly suited to the character of God's Word in the form of human words. In this question, the American teacher of homiletics Richard Lischer distinguishes between form and language. According to him, no particular norms have been laid down in respect of the form of sermon, either in the scriptures or in church history. **"The Holy Spirit uses all forms, but is not tied to any."**[3] The good story of God redeeming his world can be propagated by lay people and ordained ministers alike, by women or men, by the educated or by the uneducated, whereby each group has its own particular gifting and emphasis. It can be told in an evangelistic, faith generating way or, to the church, in a comforting or socio-politically challenging way. However, Lischer stresses the fact that there is a language, a speech act, with which preaching is

---

1 M. Josuttis, Die Einführung in das Leben, loc. cit., p.48f.

2 R. Bohren, Predigtlehre, loc. cit., p.77.

3 R. Lischer, "Homiletik in der Wissenschaftskrise der Theologie", in: R. Bohren/K.-P. Jörns (Ed.), Die Predigtanalyse als Weg zur Predigt, pp.33-51, p.39.

inseparably connected, i.e. the promise. For the promise has a personal dimension, it is more than a mere message that can simply be dissociated from the sender and the receiver. It contains the assurance of God's presence. This assurance can be trusted because God's name itself is a promise (I am present! Ex 3:14 according to Martin Buber's translation) and because his promise forms the basis of his dealings with His people of Jews and Christians throughout history. This kind of promise is realistic, because it gives the assurance of the grace of God, while not denying the separation of man from God through sin.

The promise opens up the future without having to flee the present with its fragmentary nature. A sermon, which is based on the speech act of the promise, assures the hearer of the faithfulness of God who is with us. One way this can be done is by addressing the opposite directly. The promise may, however, also be conveyed indirectly, i.e. through stories, parables and pictures, enlightening the hearers and opening up new prospects of hope. Whichever of these forms the preacher decides to use depends largely on the bible passage on which the sermon is based and the situation of the hearers.

The fact that the sermon is not inextricably tied to a particular form has resulted in different kinds or types of sermons developing in the history of preaching. According to the content, form and occasion of the sermon, one can distinguish between teaching sermons, pastoral sermons, evangelistic sermons, prophetic sermons, dialogue sermons, narrative sermons and case sermons. These sermon types are not fixed categories and they commonly occur as hybrid forms. Nonetheless, it makes sense to distinguish them, as they can help us to identify once more the main characteristics of the sermon, which they each represent in their own particular way.

(1) The teaching sermon shows us first and foremost that good rhetoric alone does not make a sermon. There are Christian themes which are fundamental to preaching. Teaching sermons appeal to the minds of the hearers and are characterised by a high density of information. These sermons strengthen the church members in their responsibility giving others reason for their faith/hope. (1 Pet. 3:15)[1]

---

1 Further recommended reading regarding teaching sermons: W. Trillhaas, Evangelische Predigtlehre, 5th Ed., Munich 1964, pp.93-107.

(2) The pastoral sermon is a reminder of the fact that God has promised the preacher that he, the God of all comfort (2 Cor. 1:3f) desires to reveal himself and let the people experience his love. The pastoral sermon is more assuring in character than informative or appellative. It conveys a sense of security and comfort and touches the hearers in their innermost being. That is why a pastoral sermon always speaks "about the decisive theme: about God as Lord and the situations relevant to human existence."[1]

(3) The evangelistic sermon brings to our attention the fact that the aim of all preaching is to generate faith and to challenge the people to respond to the redeeming love of God. This type of sermon takes the reality of unbelief seriously and tries to give direction to the hearers so they can get to the point of committing their lives to following Jesus Christ. An evangelistic sermon must especially be "an elementary discourse on God and His redemption on behalf of man".[2] The preacher will formulate his/her sermon in a very personal way to reach his/her hearers, so that they can respond positively to the message of God's salvation and comprehend it with their whole being.[3]

(4) The prophetic sermon emphasises the fact that preaching must be relevant to the present day and challenge the hearers to action. Societal and political controversies, ethical and social issues are addressed from a Christian perspective. As with the evangelistic sermon, the hearers are called to reconsider, to change and to act. The prophetic sermon therefore contains both confrontational and appellative elements.[4]

(5) The dialogue sermon reminds us that preaching is not one-way communication nor is it a one-man affair, but, following the principle of the priesthood of all believers, a "matter of the church".[5] The term dialogue sermon is not meant here merely to describe the complex type of sermon in which two preachers talk about a text, with or without prior consultation. Rather, it comprises all forms of

---

1 H. van der Geest, Das Wort geschieht, Zurich 1991, p.11. Cf. also C. Möller, Seelsorglich predigen. Die parakletische Dimension von Predigt, Seelsorge und Gemeinde, 2nd Ed., Göttingen 1990.

2 W. Klaiber, Ruf und Antwort. Biblische Grundlagen einer Theologie der Evangelisation, Stuttgart/Neukirchen-Vluyn 1990.

3 Cf. W. Bub, Evangelisationspredigt in der Volkskirche, 2nd Ed., Stuttgart 1993.

4 Cf. R Hoburg, Prophetisch predigen, Deutsches Pfarrerblatt, 96(1996) 464ff.

5 Cf. O. Herlyn, Sache der Gemeinde. Studien zu einer Praktischen Theologie des "Allgemeinen Priestertums", Neukirchen-Vluyn 1997, pp.36-59.

participation of the church in the preaching process, be it through discussions before or after the sermon, through questions during the service or through a preaching team.[1]

(6) The narrative sermon is based on the theological realisation that an abstract way of speaking that contains a large amount of theological terminology alone cannot do justice to the biblical testimony of God. God is "a God on the move, a God who is involved in stories. Talking about this God therefore means making his story heard."[2] The most suited form of language to tell God's story with his people is the narrative. The term narrative, however, does not imply that this type of preaching can be successful without diligence and thorough preparation.[3]

(7) Finally, in the case sermon, particular emphasis is placed on the realisation that all preaching of the gospel must give due consideration to the situation of the hearer. As the name tells us, this type of sermon is determined mainly by the case, i.e. the particular circumstances of the people concerned.

Case sermons for special events in the lives of church members, such as baptisms, marriages or funerals, will contain elements of the pastoral sermon, but may also take into account particular doctrinal contents, which is generally associated with the teaching sermon.[4]

LECTURE 4: PREACHING FOR HEARERS

According to scripture as to our own experience, the sermon should effect something in the hearers, it should become the words of the one "who implanted the ear" (Ps. 94:9). In his paper "Pia desideria" (Godly desires, 1675), Philipp Jakob Spener, a theologian belonging to the German Pietist movement, wrote:

"... the preacher must adapt his preaching to the hearers, as they cannot adapt themselves to him: his focus must always be mainly on the simple, so as to include most and not just a few learned ones."[5]

---

1 Cf. M. Hausstein, Sprachgestalten der Verkündigung in: Handbuch der Predigt, revised by K.-H. Bieritz et al, Berlin 1990, pp.459-495, pp.467-471.

2 A. Grözinger, Erzählen und Handeln, p.11.

3 For preaching as narration cf. R. Bohren, Predigtlehre, loc. cit., pp.170-185.

4 For an understanding of special occasions ????????, cf. E. Winkler, Tore zum Leben. Taufe – Konfirmation – Trauung – Bestattung, Neukirchen-Vluyn 1995.

5 P. J. Spener, Pia Desideria, Ed., by Aland, 1940, p.79.

No matter whether we are preaching to the "simple" or the "learned", one fact always remains: we preach for our hearers! They should be able to receive and process the message of the sermon, and what they have heard should affect their lives. In order to ensure this, preachers need to have a better knowledge of the precepts and rules for "handling" their hearers when preaching.

I. MUTUAL RESPONSIBILITY FOR THE SERMON'S QUALITY

Preachers usually know a lot about their text, but often very little about their hearers. Hearers, on the other hand, are rarely able to say what exactly they "gain" from a sermon. This is what the preacher needs to find out. By talking to the hearers, s/he learns what effect his/her sermon has had. In doing so, s/he may come to realise that the huge effort s/he puts into his/her sermons is not in vain. The preacher can learn something by ascertaining reactions from hearers. S/he can learn how s/he can get his/her message across better.

1. THE SHARED RESPONSIBILITY OF PREACHERS AND HEARERS

If a preacher asks his/her hearers, why they want to hear his/her sermons, how they receive them and process them and what they do with what they have heard s/he will usually get very vague answers. The hearers may, for example, confirm to him/her:
- that they have gained something from the sermon (but what?)
- that they like listening to the preacher (but why?)
- that they feel challenged (but what are the consequences?)

Some hearers who have nothing positive to say prefer to remain silent. Others want to voice their criticism to the preacher ("I didn't agree with what you said in your sermon today ..."), but find it hard to do so immediately after the sermon. The hearer senses that the preacher is very vulnerable. S/he has just had to work hard. S/he has, in both senses of the word, "given" something of him/herself and must first "recover" from this before being able to react objectively to criticism.

What must be considered as well is that if the preacher has not handled his/her hearers as successfully as s/he would have liked s/he will have an uneasy feeling. S/he is preoccupied with the question: How could I have better got the gospel across to my hearers? Like an athlete after a competition, the preacher needs to be given time. Hearers who want to offer constructive criticism sense this. In many churches, there are members of the congregation who are willing to bear the responsibility for the preaching with the preacher. Sometimes it may be the spouse of the preacher, or perhaps a close friend. There may be a group of sermon hearers who get together to discuss the preaching, or maybe there is an actual service preparation group who evaluate the service and correspond with the preacher. At this point, we'd like to give some tips how hearers can help their preacher. John Wesley (1703-1791), father figure of the Methodist movement, is said to have read his (very lengthy!) sermons to his maid before preaching them. Every preacher should really have the possibility of rehearsing a sermon manuscript with someone or having it readin advance. However, it would be even more useful if a group of church workers were already involved in preparing the service and the sermon.[1]

Praying together helps us to remember that, in the church service, it is God who serves us humans and not we who serve God. The group select the topic or text for the sermon together. Preaching series are planned in advance and, when planning the services, elements are included that will appeal to the congregation. The preacher can bring into the planning of the worship service what s/he wants to say in the sermon. His/her partners may correct him/her or suggest changes. In some churches, it has been agreed that the sermon manuscript is always checked by team members previously. The idea behind this is not to shut out the Holy Spirit, but to examine the sermon particularly with regard to hearer-orientation and to improve its quality in general. This approach is especially helpful when the sermon is specifically directed towards the unchurched.[2] Even though this shared sermon preparation requires time and energy, the benefits clearly outweigh the inconveniences: many issues can be resolved beforehand.

As a result, any discussions after the sermon has been preached are more objective. The mutual trust that exists within the group supporting the preacher makes it possible to voice criticism. This kind of help will allow the preacher to improve his/her preaching. The preacher's partners will also benefit: they will become better sermon hearers and will acquire more expertise in helping preachers fulfil their role.

---

1 A whole range of suggestions for planning services jointly can be found in K. Douglass, Gottes Liebe feiern. Aufbruch zum neuen Gottesdienst. Emmelsbüll 1998, esp. p.151ff.

2 It may also be helpful to have an abridged written version of the sermon that the hearers can take home. In addition, hearers could be given the opportunity to express their views in writing by way of a "feedback sheet".

Due to their different perspectives, preachers and hearers will have different questions regarding the composition and evaluation of the sermon.

Hearers want to know for example:

- Why did this sermon affect me? Why could I remember a lot of the sermon and why did it mean something to me?
- Why did the sermon upset me? Why did I get nothing out of it?

Preachers, on the other hand, want to know:

- Why was the congregation touched by my sermon? What is it about my sermon that made many of the hearers go home encouraged?
- Why did I not get any responses this time? Why does my sermon affect so little?

There are a number of answers that may be given to such questions. I would like to reflect on your own personal experience with the help of the following exercise (at some point during this course time or later back at home–if possible together with persons of confidence). Please write down what you think of when reading these questions, taking in two perspectives: the one of a hearer and the one of a preacher:

Perspective 1: QUESTIONS FOR HEARERS
Consider how the preacher whom you hear regularly treats you as hearers:

- The sermon affects me/does not affect me, because...
- I can/cannot follow the sermon, because...
- The preacher addresses his/her hearers directly/is vague. I can tell this, because...
- I would enjoy the sermon more if the preacher...

Perspective 2: QUESTIONS FOR PREACHERS

- What did I do best the last time I preached? What didn't go so well?
- Where did I feel that the hearers were following what I was saying? Where did I lose them?
- I found certain parts difficult when preparing the sermon. How did I manage these parts when delivering the sermon?
- Did I know what I wanted to achieve with the sermon, was I clear about my aim?

These questions may help hearers and preachers to become more aware of their experiences with preaching and with understanding the biblical message together. Preachers and hearers can gain something from this, both for themselves and for their part of the preaching process. If these experiences can be shared within a group consisting of preachers and hearers, then both parties, preachers and hearers, can together become experts in the field of preaching communication. They can both learn something which will enable them to fulfil their shared responsibility for the preaching process more effectively and consequently to discuss any issues as partners. In order for this process to be successful, the expectations of the sermon must be clear.

In our congregations here and there, the cultures and habits may differ a great deal; one thing our churches will have in common. People are gathering in worship services because they want to praise God and listen to the biblical word and message. There is a need, a demand, a need for good sermons, which are biblically sound and relevant to the lives of the hearers. Our hearers "want to get something out of the sermon", to be able to follow it consciously, to receive it and to process it. Due to this, it is necessary for the preacher to speak in a way that will encourage people to listen.

We will now take a closer look at the interest people have in preaching. Why do so many people want to hear a sermon? We may suggest the following reasons:

1. The hearers feel that they have a need.
2. Based on past experience, the hearers expect the sermon to be able to satisfy that need, at least to some extent.

Generally speaking, we may assume that only people who have a specific need and know that they can find what they need in the church service and in the sermon will be prepared to listen. A person who wants to hear will not normally be put off for very long from listening to sermons even if s/he has repeatedly had negative experiences in the past. Many have asserted more than once in their anger that they would never again set foot in a church and yet returned after a while. A hearer will not easily be discouraged from his/her expectation that the sermon will satisfy his/her need; for the yearning and searching for security and orientation in life which many people experience today is directed towards God and He can speak and work in church either through the sermon or through other parts of the service.

4. TYPES OF SPEAKING AND HEARING – INTRODUCTION

A condition of need usually leads to seeking actions. This is a general pattern of human behaviour. A person who is cold wants to warm him/herself. A hungry person wants to eat. In the same way, people who want to hear sermons are in search of something specific. The way this search is conducted may differ from one person to another. Nonetheless, we can identify certain types of searches. These different types can, however, only be described schematically. The same applies to types of discourse that correspond to the various seeking actions of the hearers. The types of hearing and speaking may be described on the basis of the experiences that speakers have had in dealing with their hearers over the years. It must be noted, however, that these types usually occur in crossbreed forms. An individual will embody a measure of each of the three speaking and hearing types. Consequently, every hearer and every preacher will have his/her own profile, his/her own way of listening and speaking.

In the following, three types of speaking and hearing will be described. These three types each appeal to different "reception areas" of the human consciousness and consequently have different effects.

Both hearers and preachers can add to their range. They can learn to hear and speak better. The types of discourse described below were already known in Ancient Greece; the Greek philosopher Aristotle described them in his treatise entitled "Rhetoric". While Plato had previously dismissed the art of speaking as an "art of flattery", Aristotle believed that rhetoric was essential to "good living" in any human society.

Seeking actions of hearers	Reference to time	Relevant types of discourse	Reception areas in hearers
Meaning of life	Present	epideictic	emotions
Orientation	Past	judicial	mind
Decision	Future	deliberative	will

- **Epideictic (or demonstrative)** discourse was used to acknowledge the achievements of a statesman or scientist

371

- **Judicial (or informative)** discourse was used in court in order to help the judge through evidence and argumentation to pass a just sentence

- **Deliberative (or challenging)** discourse was used in political gatherings. The hearers were challenged to choose a political party and to act in accordance with his choice.

These types of discourse are not simply the construct of a philosopher, but an aggregation of experiences which speakers have had in dealing with their hearers in particular situations.

The speaker uses them to achieve a particular effect. In the following, we will show how these classical types of discourse can be applied to preaching, where the conditions are quite different.[1]

LECTURE 5: TYPES OF HEARING AND PREACHING

We have already heard about three types of hearing and speaking.

Seeking actions of hearers	Reference to time	Relevant types of discourse	Reception areas in hearers
Meaning of life	Present	epideictic	emotions
Orientation	Past	judicial	mind
Decision	Future	deliberative	will

Let's now take a closer look at those three types, keeping in mind our own experiences as hearers and preachers of the gospel.

1. THE RECEPTION AREA OF THE EMOTIONS

In our days, a lack of security is probably the most important motive for expecting something from a sermon. In many parts of the world the basic demand for food and housing, medical care and education will be most urgently needed. In one way or the other, the question for a liveable future is a question that moves all humans. The hearer of our sermon wants to know what standards to live by.

---

1 For an overview of the multifarious history of the relationship between rhetorik and homiletics, cf. A. Grözinger, Die Sprache des Menschen, Munich 1991, p.70 ff.

S/he has no confidence in his/her world. S/he questions the world in which s/he lives. A particular incident has caused him/her to feel insecure. Therefore, s/he is looking for firm ground on which to stand. Or the hearer has experienced minor or major disappointments: failure at work, problems with his/her children, fear of things that lie ahead. S/he is no longer sure about the meaning of life. S/he cannot cope alone anymore.

The search for meaning in life People who are in search of meaning in their lives come to church. They are looking for a place where they can find tranquillity and shelter. They want to regain any confidence they may have lost. Does the faith that they have had thus far still work? Occasional doubts and the constant anti-sermon of everyday lives have caused them to question its relevance.

QUESTION FOR HEARERS: You probably remember specific situations in your life where a sermon helped you. Try to describe the need that you experienced at the time and what you remember of the sermon, what type of sermon it was, its content, and the preacher (his/her voice, personal appearance, style of preaching).

QUESTION FOR PREACHERS: Describe how you react when someone comes up to you after the service to express his/her appreciation, saying: "That was a lovely sermon today!" or "The service was so touching today!" What do you think of the feelings expressed by the grateful hearer and your reaction to it?

A person who is searching for meaning in life and has the experience of finding firm ground to stand on and being edified and uplifted will be touched first and foremost in his/her emotions. A very unemotional church service and a teaching sermon on problems that do not affect the hearer directly will not appeal to him/her.

The rational world in which the hearer lives already makes strong demands on his/her mind. In the service, his/her will is not waiting to be set new tasks. A person who has had to work hard all week wants to be able to sit back on a Sunday morning and take in something positive.

DEMONSTRATIVE DISCOURSE

Many hearers can be most easily reached through the reception area of the emotions. They are not so much "mind people" or "will people" but rather "emotions people". They experience the world around them

373

not primarily through the actions of the mind or will, in other words, not in a logical order. Neither are they constantly trying to establish such a logical order. Instead, they experience the world in moments, in pictures, in moods.

They register the things they encounter primarily in the sphere of their emotions: in the form of worry, fear, aggression, sorrow, compassion, dedication, joy. They want to be edified and uplifted so they can see the meaning behind the things that affect their lives, not through their minds but through their hearts. What they are looking for is not instruction or admonition, but "spirituality", a spiritual experience that affects the whole person.

The preacher and the hearer searching for meaning in life can meet and communicate. A preacher who is aware of the hearer situation will immediately come up with a series of bible passages that will comfort, encourage and impart joy. Here are some examples:
"Even though I walk through the valley of the shadow of death, I will fear no evil, for you are with me." (Psalm 23:4)
"Praise the LORD, oh my soul, all my innermost being, praise his holy name." (Psalm 103:1)
"In this world you will have trouble. But take heart! I have overcome the world." (John 16:33)
"Blessed are the poor in spirit, for theirs is the kingdom of heaven." (Matthew 5:3)
"If God is for us, who can be against us?" (Romans 8:31)
"Then I saw a new heaven and a new earth, ..." (Revelation 21:1)

In a bible concordance, we can find under the headings *fear, worry, comfort, help, love, rejoice, praise* an abundance of scriptures that will speak directly to people who are searching for meaning in life and give preachers necessary inspiration for demonstrative discourse. The bible passage and the type of discourse should agree. The preacher must therefore consider not only the expectations of the hearers and their need, but also the form of the text to be able to convey the content in an appropriate manner. If, for example, I were to use Psalm 8 as the basis for discussion of the relationship between theology and science, I would be violating this hymn to creation. The account of creation in Genesis 1 with its didactic form would be more suitable for such a topic. A wife and mother put it like this:

374

I am often overcome by fear. I am threatened on every side. My husband - might he get killed in an accident? My children - what will become of them in this sinister world? My friend - she has cancer and has only a few more months to live. Tomorrow, it might be me. Sometimes I stand in front of the mirror anxiously searching for any wrinkles that might be showing in my face. What will I look like when I am 60 or 70? Bitter, careworn or wise and cheerful? Some day this face will no longer smile or weep, some day it will be rigid, turn into dust. My face is only lent to me, just like my life. A gift that I can either waste or make use of.[1]

The hearer finds it easier to identify with the preacher if, like this woman, s/he speaks openly in the first person *"I"* and in the present tense (*I am often overcome ..., I feel ..., sometimes I stand in front of the mirror ..."*). This brings the preacher and the hearer very close to one another. That moment, both are standing before God. The preacher's words can lead on to a prayer without any difficulty. This is what we read in the psalms. Those who pray and profess the words of the psalm describe their hopeless situation and their deliverance from affliction (e.g. Psalm 22). A person is plucked out of his/her state of being forsaken by God and consequently praises God for answering his/her prayer (vv.20-25).

2. THE RECEPTION AREA OF THE MIND

The search for meaning in life and the corresponding demonstrative discourse is all about people being able to get up on their feet again. The aim must be to edify and lift them, to strengthen them and liberate them from the pressures that weigh them down. This psychological relief and strengthening is an important aspect. However, a person who has been helped out of the pit of spiritual and emotional low also needs to be informed about the reason why God helps him/her in this time of need and where s/he can find firm ground from which s/he can proceed further. A preacher will therefore seek to appeal to the mind as well as the emotions. It is not enough for the people attending the service to be drawn into a festive tranquillity. They should learn to find their way in the world in which they live. The hearers should not merely stand on their feet; they should also look around and then move forward.

---

1 Taken from: Unterwegs: Magazin für Reise und Urlaub, 1974, p.22.

The search for direction

If a person lacks meaning in life, s/he is usually not able to take in any new information. S/he cannot see anything, because s/he is surrounded by darkness. S/he therefore searches for light. If s/he finds this light, s/he often thinks s/he now has everything. S/he feels satisfied that s/he has found what s/he was looking for. This applies to many hearers. It is not easy to lead them on any further. As leading people on from where they are is a central objective of Christian preaching, the preacher must work diligently to ensure that hearers who are governed primarily by their emotions continue their search. They need more than just the strengthening of their faith. They should grow in faith, learn something new, and extend the horizons of their lives.

Beside these "emotions people", there is another kind of hearer, whose main aim is to learn something from the sermon. These are "mind people". They want logical conclusive arguments in favour of the Christian faith. They too need something. They are used to understanding the world through the mind. When it comes to matters of faith, however, this is often not possible for them. That is why they come to hear a sermon, to find answers. An individual may, for example, no longer understand particular issues in his/her life. S/he cannot make sense of them. S/he wants to gain an overview, to be able to see through things, to assess and sort the things that s/he does not understand. Maybe the information s/he has had thus far regarding faith and Christian living has come to naught. What s/he now wants to know is: How can my faith be re-established, how can I grow in faith? The hearer wants information that s/he can comprehend with the mind and that s/he can expound to others clearly through logical reasoning. S/he wants to know how his/her present life relates to the past and to tradition, as it relates to today's thinking and reasoning. For this purpose, s/he needs information, interpretations that can withstand the criticism of reason.

The adolescent daughter has argued against the father or the mother: **"The pastor and his stories of miracles-those are all fairy tales that sensible people can't be expected to believe!"** The parents therefore search for information regarding the meaning of Jesus' miracles today. In this condition of uncertainty, the preacher may help the hearer by telling him/her how s/he understands the accounts of miracles, where they feature in his/her conception of the world. Even if the hearer then comes to the conclusion that s/he cannot see it the way the preacher sees it, because many things remain unclear in his/her mind, s/he will respect the preacher's attempt at resolving the issue. The hearer expects a solution with a personal touch, a confession based on information about faith and life.

Thus, a search for direction cannot be satisfied merely by factual information. Logical statements and clearly defined terms alone will not do. The hearer expects something different from the sermon than s/he would expect from a theological lecture. Many preachers find this difficult. They may present theological information in a theologically sound way; the sermon may turn out "dead right" (R. Bohren).

However, they are keenly aware that very little of it is received. Evidently, the big words of the bible are too heavy for the hearers. They are more like stones than like bread. The preaching of the gospel, in contrast, is like a sumptuous meal for which the hearers gladly accept an invitation. If the guests stay away the hosts, the preachers, often resign. Many ask themselves: is there no hunger among the people for the truth of the gospel? (cf. Amos 8:11)

Informative discourse

The same principle that applies to people who are approachable primarily in reception area of their emotions is also valid for people who comprehend the world through their minds. They need to be spoken to in a way that will convey information regarding the Christian faith from the preacher to the hearer. This is not easy. That is why some hearers who need arguments in favour of the Christian faith will prefer a group discussion. Nonetheless, this can be achieved as well through a sermon.

The following example is an instance of informative discourse. In a sermon on the virgin birth of Jesus Christ, Bishop Hans Lilje illustrates how a difficult dogmatic statement may be conveyed to the reader.[1] At the beginning of his sermon, Bishop Lilje responds to the critical questions of his hearers regarding this "incredible story" and refutes existing misunderstandings, and then goes on to explain why in our confession of the virgin Mary we have the "guarantee of our

---

1 Printed in: H.-R. Müller-Schwefe, Zur Zeit oder Unzeit, Stuttgart 1958, pp. 47-55.

salvation". Bishop Lilje presents his information to the hearers so as to allow them to judge for themselves:

Firstly, our Lord Jesus Christ entered into our earthy world. He was born. He became a man. He did the inconceivable in taking our entire human fate upon himself. As much as they may talk about the incarnation of their gods, none of the world religions has dared to say to us what Christians confess of their Lord: that he became as one of us. This means: We have not been left alone in the turmoil of violence, guilt, fear in life and fear of death. God is there. Jesus has come to us.

Secondly, however, this portion of the gospel testifies to us of something that is equally important: Jesus did not merely become our "mate", but our Saviour. And this was possible, because he was not of our nature or of our world.

Everything depends on this. That is why the preaching of a Christ who is of our nature was such an elementary misunderstanding of the Christian message. It is precisely on this fact that everything, absolutely everything depends: the fact that he is not of our nature - God from God, light from light, as the old Nicene Creed declares.

Many preachers find it difficult to argue in such a dogmatic manner. They believe that the hearers cannot be reached with "eternal truths from above". For this reason, a way of speaking was developed at the preaching seminary Loccum which is meant to encourage the hearers to search. They should be able to follow the thoughts of the preacher, in order to come to a decision like a judge in a court case.

3. THE RECEPTION AREA OF THE WILL

A person who can stand on his/her feet and look around is able to go forward of his/her own accord, to take steps of faith. S/he feels strengthened and informed about the foundations of the Christian faith. S/he may now be able to explain these to others in a logical way. This, however, does not necessarily mean that the hearers and the preacher act in accordance with what they know and live the Christian faith, for example by showing love to others, by caring for them in a practical way. Through the sermon, they themselves have experienced the security of love in their innermost being. However, their will has not yet received the impulse to pass on the love they have received in a specific way to specific individuals, to take up the future that has been promised in order to use it creatively. This can be effected through a challenging way of speaking within the reception area of the will.

The search for a decision

Especially young hearers often become impatient if the preacher spends a lot of time on meditative reflection and information about the faith. But there are also other people who understand the world primarily through their will and want an answer: What does that mean in practice, how can Christian faith be lived? Preachers often fail to give answers to these questions, or if they do, then usually at the end of the sermon in a few general statements. The hearers feel that they are "beating around the bush", which is unsatisfactory to them. "Will people" are therefore disappointed and sometimes prefer to get involved in action groups in order to do project work.

There may be quite a number of people in the congregation who are looking for help with practical decisions regarding their present and future. Preachers will recognise this if they get told once in a while: "I followed your advice and did such and such". The preacher may have made some general remarks and is surprised to find out how his/her words were taken in a very different way than they were meant. In the sermon, the hearer who needed to make a decision received an impetus in a particular direction. Thus, the sermon has released the hearer to act, because s/he has related what was said to his/her situation and developed it further.

Such reactions reveal that something is lacking: Many hearers miss a stimulus for putting their faith into practice. Many know what good could be done, but fail to do it, because they do not have the courage or they are unsure, whether they are able to carry it out. This applies especially to big decisions. Many hearers know: If I want to take the sermon seriously, I will have to change my life completely; but I haven't got the courage to do what others have done.

It is like the two boys who climbed onto a wall and got into danger up there. A man called to them: "Jump into my arms!" The one boy jumped and was caught safely. The man who had called was his father. The power of trust that drew him into the saving arms. The other boy had to be taken down from the wall by firefighters.

Challenging discourse

Sermons often fail to call for a decision, at least the ones preached in regular Sunday services.[1] Time and again, we are told that calling people to the faith is "not in keeping with the times". In Europe, many people are offended more by evangelistic activities with the aim of spreading the gospel than by the *de facto* spread of unbelief within large sections of Western society. If we ask critics of evangelistic outreach and faith generating preaching for alternatives, they do not usually have any to offer. In recent times, there has been a rediscovery of the great commission of the church in the independent Protestant churches.[2] Churches are striving for a new evangelistic consciousness and seeking new ways of reaching those who have become alienated from the Christian faith. Evangelism should no longer be an exception, but the rule in the work of the church.[3] In these evangelistic activities, the focus is (once more) increasingly on the ecumenical dimension.[4]

In the context of preaching, challenging discourse is the most difficult of all. It requires good rhetorical skills and great sensitivity when it comes to appeals in the sermon. Many preachers shy away from challenging discourse, because they do not want to "put pressure" on their hearers. Another reason for the reluctance of preachers to challenge might be the fact that many hearers evade the challenge of faith in Christ.

The help offered by the preacher is rejected. S/he urges them, but they don't want to hear. The individual who is addressed directly does not dare to jump even though s/he is assured through comforting words that s/he will land safely in the father's arms. This is what Jesus experienced with the rich young man whom he invited to follow him (Mark 10:17-27). The man decided against it. Jesus had left the decision up to him. For challenging discourse, this means: the preacher

---

1 Cf. W. Bub, Evangelisationspredigt in der Volkskirche, 2nd Ed., Stuttgart 1993, p.140ff.

2 In his introductory paper at the Synod of the The Lutheran Church in Germany held in Leipzig in 1999, the theologian E Jüngel reminded the delegates: "Outreach and evangelism should really be a matter of course for the Christian church. Really, anywhere that even two or three are gathered in the name of Jesus Christ, these two or three should be fervently and passionately committed to reaching others, so that soon four or five will be gathering in Jesus' name ..." (Source: epd-Dokumentationen 4/99).

3 Cf. W. Klaiber, Ruf und Antwort. Biblische Grundlagen einer Teologie der Evangelisation. Stuttgart/Neukirchen 1990, U. Laepple/H.-H. Pompe, Normalfall Evangelisation, Neukirchen-Vluyn 1997.

4 Cf. H. Vorster (Ed.), Ökumene lohnt sich, Frankfurt 1998; EMW/ACK/missio (Ed.), Aufbruch zu einer missionarischen Ökumene, Hamburg 1999.

must not force the hearer to make a particular decision nor seek to manipulate him/her in any way.

The writer Kurt Marti did not do this in his interpretation of the rich young man. The sermon reaches its climax with the statement by the evangelist Mark: Jesus looked at him and loved him (v.21).

At this point, I could really conclude the sermon with an Amen. Is there anything more and better than Jesus loving a person? That is everything, the last and the greatest thing that can happen to us. If Jesus looks at us today and loves us, then this Sunday is a feast unlike any other; we are "cleaned and shined" right through to our hearts; we can then go happily on our way, nothing can befall us any more, we are saved for all eternity. And I really do believe that there are many present today in which Jesus takes pleasure, because they have not aborted the hunger in their innermost being for the living God. I also believe that there are many who are not here and do not go to church at all, but nonetheless are running around, seeking to satisfy this hunger. They too are loved by Jesus, because of their restlessness. It is for us to tell them.

But I still can't say Amen, because our story goes on, because the love of Jesus also goes further, presses further into our lives. That is why he says to that man whom he loves: "One thing you lack. Go, sell everything you have and give to the poor, and you will have treasure in heaven... Then come, follow me." Jesus' love goes further than we think.

Here, however, it seems to go too far. That is why this story doesn't have a happy ending. That is why it ends on an uncomfortable note. Every one of us responds in the same way: that is going too far for me: "Come, follow me". I could accept that, because nowadays we can imagine following Jesus as a matter of the mind. But "sell everything you have ..." no, that is going too far, that cannot be expected ...[1]

The difficulty of challenging discourse lies in the fact that it is directed towards the future. The hearer is to make a decision for the future. S/he doubts whether this decision is right. Is it worth the cost; is it possible to reach the goal set by the preacher? The preacher, too, is often not sure. S/he is making promises for the future. With

---

1 K. Marti, Das Markus-Evangelium, Basel 1967, pp. 214-218.

informative discourse, it is easier. It talks about the past, about history or previously acquired knowledge. Demonstrative discourse focuses on the present. It seeks closeness with God and the people who are present and to whom the preacher wants to be close.

Experience shows that challenging discourse is received best if it succeeds in finding, together with the hearer, the point from which s/he can dare to jump. If we call people to make a decision, we must also be able to tell them how they should live their lives following Jesus after they have made a decision. Challenging discourse must be specific. For this reason, some evangelistic preachers will lead those who are ready to take the step of faith in a "prayer of salvation" in which they "give their lives to Jesus".[1]

Others call the hearers to "come to the front" so as to make a public confession of their new-found faith. Some evangelists invite those who respond to a personal conversation. The idea is to encourage the hearers to take initial steps of faith in an intimate, secure environment. This can take the form of a confession, a prayer, or a blessing. An approach that has proved increasingly successful in recent years is to invite people to take part in a "foundation course" in the Christian faith, at the end of which they are given an opportunity to commit their lives to God in a relaxed atmosphere.[2]

Any evangelistic endeavours must include specific advice as to what the people who are reached with the gospel and generally willing to (re-) commit their lives to God can do from then on. Depending on the situation, a suitable format will be found: what is important is that it happens at all. If a preacher merely calls for a decision regarding a very important matter without showing ways how precisely this can be done, s/he will leave his/her hearers in a grave state of uncertainty. The appeal gets nowhere and may, in the long term, lead to the hearers becoming "immune" to the claim of gospel.

The same applies to political sermons. They must stimulate the hearers to action that can be realised in practice: collection of signatures, public rallies and symbolic acts. Otherwise, those involved will be discouraged or resort to a dangerous activism. The problems of the political sermon are similar to those of the evangelistic sermon, as they are both instances of challenging discourse. During his

---

1 For examples of this, see W. Bub, Evangelisationspredigt, loc. sit., 145f.

2 Cf. K. Douglass, Glaube hat Gründe, 2nd ed., Stuttgart 1999 and B. Krause, Reise ins Land des Glaubens. Christ werden – Christ leiben, Neukirchen-Vluyn 2000.

professorship of theology in Berlin, Helmut Gollwitzer suggested some concrete activities in his political sermons. The references to the political events of his time are clearly recognisable. Time and again, Gollwitzer addresses the individual hearer. If the individual will change, this can have far-reaching personal and political consequences. The hearer's consciousness is changed.

"Jesus says: Ask yourself, what you really lack, what you desperately need, what you are crying out for, what you painfully miss. You may be a very lonely person, you may long, as for your daily bread, for another person who will take care of you, who will listen to you and understand you. Be to the people around you the person that you need - Jesus says - and you loneliness will come to an end. You may be longing for a different spouse, one who is not so selfish, one who is joyful and caring. Be to your spouse the spouse that you long for - Jesus says - and many things will be different in your marriage. You are living in the treadmill of a job that you hate, that leaves you feeling empty. Look around, see how the others in your office and company feel just like you do, and be a person who brings a fresh atmosphere or even a fresh content to that treadmill that you cannot change! Being to others what you need from the others - that is the message of Jesus that, like a key, opens up the door to the lives of other people. It is strange: By looking at yourself, you see others with their needs, you become aware of them. And then you will see: they are suffering even more from a lack of the things that you lack: you need money, you can't afford the things you need, but around you there are many who have even less. You need freedom, justice, a free democratic state under the rule of law and you are grateful if you can live in such a state. In Persian and Turkish prisons, they are tortured and sentenced to death. You need the freedom to openly express your opinion, your political and religious views. In Czechoslovakia, in Greece they are gagged. You are a South African or a Rhodesian White with a house and a garden; the world is open to you. And beside you are the others, with a different colour, forth class citizens, expelled from their land, they need the same things that you have. "So in everything, do to others what you would have them do to you, for this sums up the Law and the Prophets (Matthew 7:12)."[1]

---

1 H. Gollwitzer, Veränderungen im Diesseits, München 1973, p. 52f.

If we make ourselves aware of the difficulties of the challenging sermon, we can preach it in a responsible way. We need courage or, as the fathers and mothers in the faith say, authority. Because we are gripped by God, we can stand up for him and challenge our hearers to act. We can speak with the authority of the imploring Christ (2 Cor. 5:20).

The preacher needs the presence of the Spirit and presence of mind, and also a great sensitivity to speak the right word at the right time. This word is aimed at that which yet lies ahead: following Jesus, changes in the present world, proceeding into an unpredictable future under the promise of God.

QUESTION FOR HEARERS: What do you think of the challenging sermon? Do you desire this type of sermon? Have you had negative experiences with such sermons? If so, what were they? What form would a challenging sermon have to take in order to convince you?

QUESTION FOR PREACHERS: When did you last preach a challenging sermon (evangelistic or political)? Are you reluctant to preach in a challenging manner? If so, what are the reasons for your reluctance? How might they be overcome?

LECTURE 6: STRUCTURES OF SERMONS – INVITATIONS TO LISTEN

If a sermon is to do justice to the hearers, it must have an appropriate structure. This time and in the next session, we will therefore talk about guidelines for structuring sermons. Sermon should be inviting, well planned and well structured. A preacher who carefully plans and structures his/her sermons is like an architect and building contractor who builds a large house and, in doing so, thinks with affectionate of the future residents. They will then enjoy living in the house and do not need to complain about any faults. If we apply this to preaching we can say: Most hearers of sermons would rather follow a diligently prepared sermon than a poorly structured one, and they will be more likely to receive messages and challenges if these are presented in a well-structured manner.

However, if we want to understand the effect of a sermon in its entirety we cannot attribute it solely to the preacher's ability. The hearers sense that something takes place in well prepared speaking and attentive listening, (i.e. responsible involvement in the success of the sermon) that touches them in their innermost being and moves and changes them. On the other, it may happen that a well-prepared and well-delivered sermon does not produce the desired effect. The factors involved in the preaching process are so complex that it is impossible to plan the success of a sermon down to the smallest detail. Yet this will not prevent the preacher from working diligently to ensure that his/her sermons have a good structure. S/he will desire to improve his/her skills in this area, because s/he can assume that it will make his/her sermons more easily understandable.

I. INVITATION TO LISTEN

Sermons should not put the hearers off; instead, they should invite them as to a feast. Jesus often used this picture when speaking of his gospel (e.g. Matt. 22:1-10). He wanted to give his hearers a foretaste of the heavenly kingdom, of the joy of God, which people are to experience here on earth. Many preachers put a lot of effort into grasping the full message of the biblical text and considering the theological problems. Nothing seems to be lacking. Yet that which is said cannot easily be received; there is no invitation to hear. The following extract from a sermon on Phil 4:4 is an example of this:

> *The Lord is near! His nearness already affects the life of the Christian in the here and now, and fills it with joy. Therefore the scripture states: Rejoice in the Lord always. The joy that comes from him is not crushed by the cares and problems of our daily lives; it overcomes them. Our often joyless and depressing existence is neither played down nor idealised; it is genuinely changed, just as Jesus Christ gave new meaning to the lives of the people he met while he was on earth.*

All that this preacher says is correct. However, s/he says far too much in just a few sentences. One dogmatic statement is followed by another. Before the hearers are able to receive and consider what the coming of Christ means for them, they are already expected to rejoice about it, and to leave the things that burden them behind, because their lives now have new meaning. How is anyone supposed to follow? The hearers switch off, their minds begin to wonder. The preacher should not be surprised that the information s/he gives is not received. The gospel that s/he wants to preach is not a gospel, because it cannot be heard.

385

Speeches and texts that are too difficult can be made easier. When it comes to understanding, readers have the key advantage over hearers, that they can read a sentence again. Readers can consult others if they found something difficult to understand and have it explained to them. The hearers of sermons, in contrast, have to understand immediately what they are told. They cannot have it repeated to them.

This is why sermons need to be carefully prepared. In them, the hearers are given known and unknown information. The known information reassures the hearers, the unknown information helps them to understand more and move forward. If the sermon contains a lot of unknown information, the hearers must have sufficient time to process it. They need breaks so that they do not grow weary on the road along which the preacher expects them to travel. The hearers need something that will stimulate them, something that will help them to remain attentive or that will catch their attention. This applies to informed and less informed hearers alike. All hearers benefit when they are presented with known information in a new and more appealing way, and with unknown information in a way that they can comprehend it. That is what the term redundancy means in this context. The Latin root of this word is *redundare*, meaning to flow back, to flow around and to overflow. Here it does not mean that which is superfluous, as in other contexts. We do find this kind of redundancy in sermons as well. It makes them boring. They have nothing to say to the hearers. It is a case of more is not necessarily better.

Usually, however, sermons suffer because the preacher wants to say too much. There is a lack of redundancy, i.e. consolidating repetition. This may be illustrated as follows:

It would be better like this:

Redundancy is as important in a sermon as, for example, in a radio or television news programme. By using background information, stories, interviews and such, news reporters want to arouse his/her addressees' interest in what s/he has to say. There are many ways in which this can be done. Some result from attentively studying the biblical text. Others present themselves as a result of the particular preaching situation.

Various formal and stylistic elements may be employed when interpreting the biblical text in the sermon. Depending on the scripture, these may include:

1. Exact information about a subject matter (Jesus behaved in a completely unexpected way ...)
2. Important background information (The shepherds were on the fringes of society ...)
3. Clear explanation of a term (The kingdom of God is not a political entity, but ...)
4. Brief reference to known facts (Jesus healed the sick ...)
5. Directly addressing a particular issue (Many people have trouble with this saying of Jesus ...)
6. Detailed description of a metaphor (Christ, the light of the world ...)
7. Brief comparison (Christians are supposed to be the salt of the earth ...)
8. Idiomatic expressions and puns (You scratch my back, I scratch yours ...)
9. Narration (from the bible, literature, everyday experience ...)

Of course, there can be too much redundancy. When this is the case, the sermon simply marks time in respect of its content and the hearers get bored. Continual repetition may also be interpreted as an attempt to manipulate, because the hearers are not given room to use their own imagination.

2. NARRATION IN PREACHING

One of the most important tools for structuring a sermon effectively is narration. The preacher unfolds a story to his/her hearers. S/he tells about something that happened to him/her or about a conversation that has been on his/her mind over the last few days. Anyone opening the bible will soon discover that it is first and foremost a storybook. The bible tells stories about life, stories about God and the world. These stories speak of things past and things to come, and in both cases they surprise us, time and again, with things related to our day. The biblical stories tell us of hope and despair, of love and failure, of power and of impotence.

Once a scribe came to Jesus and asked him questions. The people standing around him listen in suspense: What answer will Jesus give him? He tells a story of a man who fell into the hands of robbers somewhere in the hills between Jerusalem and Jericho (Lk. 10:30-35). Jesus uses a common occurrence of that day and makes it into a parable by describing the people who pass by. The account of the "good Samaritan" is one of those biblical stories that become deeply engraved on the mind of anyone who hears them.

Stories can evoke memories and bring long forgotten experiences back to the minds of the hearers and place them in a new light. Stories address deep longings and profound hopes, and raise important questions regarding life. The decisive thing about biblical narratives is that they leave room.

The hearer is not tied down. S/he can decide to what extent s/he wants to take part in the fate of the various characters, with which of them s/he wants to identify. Have I ever "fallen among thieves"? Have I met a "good Samaritan" in my life? Have I ever left anyone "lying by the way side"? ... Sometimes it is the small things, the minor characters, the subplots that touch our hearts and show us new ways how we can act and live our lives.

a) Types of narratives - some rules for storytelling

Before we take a closer look at *everyday narratives* and the *retelling of biblical narratives*, we will begin by introducing some types of narratives and a few basic rules for telling stories.[1] Our aim is, firstly, to give an overview of the kinds of narratives available to the preacher and, secondly, to offer some useful guidelines regarding the structure of narratives as a practical help for telling stories.

Examples of narratives include:

The *retelling narrative* follows the basic direction of the biblical text. It is not necessary to recount all the details of the story, but rather to retain the essential elements: the constellation of characters, the places, the turning-points in the story-line.

---

1 In the following, we will refer to: H.K. Berg, Bibeldialektik, Munich 1993, p. 182ff. and G Adam/R. Lachmann, Metodisches Kompendium für den Religionsunterricht, 1996, pp. 137-162.

The *summary:* The gospels (Mt 15:30; Jn. 7:1) and the Book of Acts (8:1) contain reports in which extended periods or a series of events are summarised. Similarly, the preacher may give a brief overview of the fate of an Old Testament prophet or the Passion of Jesus. Thus, it is possible to show connections between events and put individual biblical statements in context.

The *background narrative*[1] is an attempt to introduce historical background information (e.g. what was the life of a shepherd like in the days of Jesus; why were tax collectors unpopular ...) in the form of a story rather than by way of explanation as in an encyclopaedic article.

The *context narrative*[2] is also concerned with providing the background to biblical events. All the parables of Jesus and most of the prophetic texts of the Old Testament are responses to some specific question or issue. The didactic texts of the New Testament epistles too can be traced back to real situations and questions which motivated the authors to write them. The context narrative serves to illuminate these issues.

In the *perspective narrative* the narrator assumes the role of one particular individual involved in the story and recounts the events strictly from that individual's point of view. As a result, even very familiar stories get a new slant and can touch us in a new way. The story of the "anointing of Jesus by a sinful woman (Lk. 7:35-50), for example, may be told from the point of view of the woman, of Simon the Pharisee, of a guest at the table, or of Jesus himself; in each case, the hearer will get a different perspective of the story.

The *extending narrative*[3] is similar to the retelling narrative, but does not stop there. The hearer is invited to think beyond the biblical text, for example, what may have happened to the "rich young ruler" after the shameful defeat he experience in his conversation with Jesus (Mt 19:22), or what Zacchaeus may have done the week after "salvation had come to his house" (Lk. 19:9).

---

1 G. Theißen gives a good narrative account of the life and ministry of Jesus within the context of his time: Shatten des Galiläers. Historische Jesusforschung in erzählender Form, 13th Ed., Gütersloh 1993.

2 Biblical examples of context narration can be found at the beginning and end of the books of Job and Jonah; in these two books, the "actual" content is sourrounded by a narrative context.

3 Especially W. Neidhard has developed this type of narration in a convincing way. See bibliography.

Important rules for story-telling include:

Choosing the appropriate perspective: Depending on the text and the situation in which the story is told, different persons/perspectives may be chosen. Diverging from usual can increase hearers' attentiveness.

Creating an arch of suspense: Every narrative must have an introduction and a conclusion. In between these two sections, we find the main section, just like in a school essay. In a story (like in a novel or a film), the hearer is kept in suspense if important information is withheld for a while and motives are not immediately revealed, and there is an unexpected twist at the end.

Using appropriate language: The language of narration is characterised by short sentences (as one would speak not as one would write), suitable tenses are the present and the simple past (*then he went*, not *after he had gone*). The use of direct speech (Jesus said: *"Your sins are forgiven"* rather than *They heard Jesus say that her sins were forgiven*) and the active voice make it easier to follow the story. Embellishing adjectives (huge, beautiful) should be used sparingly and evaluations (good, evil) avoided where possible. A good story must leave room for the hearers' own interpretations.

Paraphrase difficult terms: It helps the hearers if the storyteller defines difficult concepts (kingdom of God, judgement, sin, eternity) by means of the action before introducing the term.

Bringing out feelings and motives: Narration speaks to the whole person. Especially the realm of the emotions is affected. A good story does not merely present facts, but it enables the hearers to learn something about the feelings and motives (questions, worries, fears) of the persons involved.

Arousing curiosity and raising questions: God stories are always notable and memorable. They hold our attention and raise questions: What if? How might it continue? What could that mean?

Not solving unsolvable issues and mysteries: Many biblical stories are "always-stories", because they address basic human questions (the meaning of life, the origin of suffering in the world), basic conflicts (good vs. evil; prevailing vs. being defeated) or "matters of life" (growing old, saying farewell). A good narrative tries to let the deeper layers of human existence show through the surface of the action. Mysteries, for example in the account of a miracle, should therefore not be explained, but left as they are. The story focuses more on the effects of the mysterious events on the people concerned.

b) Retelling of a biblical narrative

It is surprising to see how many preachers fail to make use of the forms that the biblical texts offer them. After the initial scripture reading, say a parable of Jesus or a story of a prophet, they do not return to the story. During the sermon, the text appears merely in a fragmented form as extracts: "in verse 17 it says ..." Thus, the context of the biblical story is lost to a large degree. The vivid material of many biblical texts provides enough stimuli to translate the theological contents into the present situation of the hearer. Experiences with church services for all age groups (often referred to as family services) show that adults too appreciate when they are told biblical stories in a graphic way. Even among adults, many biblical stories are hardly known or completely unknown! Every retelling of a biblical account should basically invite the hearers to pick up the "original" in order to find out for themselves "how the story really went".

When preachers retell biblical stories, they do more than just create redundancy. The fact that hearers find it easier to follow a well-told story is merely a side effect. The biblical story is about the message itself, not merely about giving an illustration of an abstract truth! It is to retain this message that the preacher retells the story. The more the need to retell the story can be made plausible to the hearers, the better. The hearer should feel at home in the world of the biblical narrative, to share the feelings of the persons involved, and to identify with what the story claims. In the narrative, an encounter takes place between the hearer and the content of the story. If the hearers allow themselves to be taken by the story it becomes clear, so to speak from the inside, to what extent the message of the narrative concerns them.

Many sermons are perceived by the hearers as too heavy, because they skip the first phase of the invitation to hear and go straight to the reflection and interpretation phase. The sermon then sounds something like this: "What is said about Jesus here means three things to us today: 1.... 2.... 3...." In such sermons, the preacher wants to "teach" the hearers from the very first moment, instead of giving them time to open up. A person who gets involved in a story will quickly be led to the point that the preacher wants to bring across. That is why Jesus told parables. His intention was to confront his hearers with the truth of his person and his message. The truth comes to light. It breaks through; it shines through, as Jesus tells a story.

This is clearly evident in the parable of the labourers in the vineyard (Mt 20:1-15). It would be wrong to impose a particular pattern of thought on this parable, for example the concept of our works versus God's mercy. In this story, we are drawn into a concrete scenario. The story ends with a strange question (v.15). The owner of the vineyard asks his grumbling workers whether they are so angry, because he is so generous. This question decides everything. The aim of the parable is not proclaim the love of God that is above all and available to all; we know that already from the very beginning. It is at this question that I must decide whether I want to entrust myself to the goodness of God that gives what belongs to God even to the poorest and the last, or whether I choose to stand aloof and grumble. The truth of this story cannot be discovered by reflecting on the universal nature of God's mercy, but by trusting this Jesus - preacher and hearers alike - who vouches for the truth of the story with his own life.

By telling us stories from our world, Jesus tells us his own story. By involving us in stories, he involves us in the story of his own life and death. Telling parables is his great art. All of a sudden, the pictures that he paints before the eyes of his hearers become transparent and the truth of his person and his story comes to light. The same way that Jesus uses pictures, comparisons, symbols and gestures in his propagation of the gospel, we can. We will look at this in more detail in chapter 8 of the book.

c) Everyday-life stories

In his parables, Jesus speaks about his world, everyday life and the circumstances of the people. These things are suited for parables of the kingdom of God. The lilies in the field are not merely flowers by the wayside that no one notices; they tell of the robes of King Solomon and preach about God's wonderful provision for me. The tiny mustard seed is as the kingdom of God: at first, it is small, in the end, as a plant, it is big (Mk 4:30-32).

Like Jesus, preachers can make discoveries in everyday life that are suited for parables concerning the truth of the gospel. Finding suitable stories is not always easy. It is best, of course, if the preacher can use his/her own discoveries and experiences. These are close to the preacher's heart and s/he can therefore convey them to the hearers in a convincing manner.

Suspense is not the decisive factor. It will only capture the hearers' attention for a little while. If stories are merely a peg on which nothing hangs, they will distract the hearers from the actual message. If stories do not touch people in the very depth of their existence, they are better omitted altogether.

When we suggest that stories constitute an important element in preaching, we are raising a fundamental question: How will the hearer feature in the propagation of the gospel? How can s/he be involved in the action so that it becomes easier for him/her to comprehend the truth? On the other hand, is s/he still left with enough room to consider what the story means to him/her, despite being so closely involved?

What a good story or account is capable of achieving can be shown by way of the following simple example taken from the diary of the Swiss writer Max Frisch:[1]

> *Today, Ursel, our six-year-old daughter, asked me, in the middle of playing with her toys, whether I liked to die. ' Everyone has to die,' I replied from behind my newspaper, 'but nobody likes to die.' She ponders. 'I like to die!' 'Now?'; I asked: 'Really?' - 'Not now, no, not now!' - I lower the newspaper a little so I can see her. She sits at the table, mixing watercolours. 'But later' she says and draws in silent enjoyment, 'later I will like to die.'*

In this account, experiences that everyone can have, fears and desires that everyone knows, are condensed into one scene. The hearer is left to think about these things. At first, s/he may reject this issue, but somehow the question of dying will not go away: Do I like to die? Why do I not want to think about my own death? What could help me when it's my time to die? Or the hearer may want to know how s/he

---

1 M. Frisch, Tagebuch 1946-1949, Frankfurt/Main (1950) 1977, p. 349. (OFFICIAL TRANSLATION AVAILABLE???)

can help a dying relative. Or perhaps s/he is surprised that a child would ask about death, and wonders what might have triggered the little girl's question.

The preacher's story may sometimes be better than that which s/he has to say about it later in the sermon, and better than his/her responses to any questions that the hearers might ask afterwards. The seemingly innocent scene continues to affect the hearers. This is due to the fact that a well-told story is able to relate to real life and, in doing so, it declares the truth of the gospel. A sermon draws its life from being rooted in the depth of real experience. For this reason, preachers need to learn how to choose and tell suitable stories, whether they be taken from the preacher's own experience or from literature. It is far better to choose something from a collection of stories for one's sermons than to do without any narration at all, because of a lack of ideas.

Any preacher who begins to tell stories in his/her preaching will come to realise how few stories s/he knows that are really suited for a sermon. However, once s/he has begun to discover this valuable resource for structuring sermons, s/he will become increasingly sensitive in this regard. The preacher will experience his/her world through different eyes; s/he will listen and read more attentively. S/he will encounter deep layers of our existence that will unveil to him/her the mystery of the truth of the gospel in our world. This will be felt in his/her sermons.

Exercise:
We will conclude this session suggesting another exercise to find out hearers' reactions to the issue of comprehensibility and redundancy. A difficult passage of a sermon is read to a group made up of hearers and preachers. The hearers are then requested to answer the following questions:
- What have I remembered?
- What did I not understand?
- Where did I switch off and think about something different?

On the basis of the hearers' reactions, the preachers may now work at giving redundancy to the passage and adding to its linguistic form (narrative, example) in order to facilitate comprehension. A second trial will reveal whether this was successful, and how it was achieved?

Usually hearers will reward these efforts by judging the revised passage as being better than the first. In a similar exercise, a group of people analyse a sermon in its written form, specifically in respect of its comprehensibility and discuss where narrative elements might be added to make it clearer and more vivid.

LECTURE 7: THE PREACHER AS ARCHITECT- BUILDING PLANS FOR SERMONS

As we have seen last time, narration is an important element of sermon structure; it is, so to speak, the crystallisation core. Other creative elements for structuring sermons must be added. These include: factual information, background knowledge, and explanation of terminology. Also, references to commonly known facts, a description of a picture, brief comparisons, idiomatic expressions and puns belong to the list creative elements, which can be used at various points in the sermon. The following sermon building plans are meant to correspond to the different types of hearing described earlier in this course: *the search for meaning in life, for direction, and for help with decisions.* Another structural plan is taken from the psychology of learning. This plan takes up elements from the other three models and brings them together into one model.

1. WHAT A STRUCTURAL PLAN CAN AND WHAT IT CAN'T DO

Structural plans help the hearer to understand the sermon in a deeper way, to take in what has been said, to consider it further, and to change existing attitudes and behaviour. However, well-structured sermons do have certain disadvantages as well. A structure may put a natural train of thought in a straightjacket or not be appropriate for the given biblical text. Or it may be that the structure is not suitable for the hearers; they may not feel comfortable in a "house" with such a ground plan and would prefer to move out rather sooner than later.

If the preacher works together with one or several hearers when preparing the sermon, they can select ground plans together that are suitable for the thoughts presented by the preacher and consider their advantages and disadvantages. The preacher can check his/her sermon with hearers, even after preaching it. A comparison with the selected structure will reveal any shortcomings. Moreover, the question can be raised once more, whether a different building plan might have been more appropriate for the given text and that particular congregation.

Not every preacher will immediately feel comfortable working with models. Some opportunities and limitations have already been pointed out. The following three points should be considered in practice:

(1) It is rarely possible to develop a precise building plan from the very beginning of the sermon preparation and then to adhere to it.

(2) A model is, first and foremost, a framework for checking an already completed sermon plan. After having produced an initial version, the preacher considers, on the basis of the structural models known to him/her, how s/he has planned the sermon. Thus, s/he checks his/her draft to see where something is missing and what has to be developed further.

(3) The preacher can use the model as a basis to improve his/her sermon. It can help him/her:

a) to formulate and develop the topic more precisely.

b) to mark the transitions from one section to another more clearly.

c) to summarise the message of the sermon in a conclusion and lead the hearers once more along the route that s/he has taken with them.

(4) Checking the sermon draft against a structural model will show the preacher whether s/he may have burdened the hearers with too much information. This is likely to be the case if the sermon is developed around more than three focal points.

In general, we can say: The building plan must agree with the aims of the sermon. If the preacher is not sure about the aim, the hearers will find it difficult to follow. S/he should consider, for example, how long it will take to acquaint the hearers with the biblical text. Models 1-3 are particularly suited for expounding and interpreting a text step by step. Now let us look at the models one by one:

3. MODELS FOR STRUCTURING SERMONS

Model 1: Expanding circles

At the centre, there is a picture: the tower of Babel, the good shepherd, and the lilies of the field. With its symbolism, the picture appeals to the depth of our emotions. It is suited for silent reflection; we can take it in, meditate on it. The sermon circles around the picture and does very little interpreting. It encourages the hearers to think about the picture for themselves.

The sermon evokes associations rather than following a logical train of thought. The various parts of the sermon are not equally long and equally weighted. They are not closed; the transition from one part to the next is gradual, and the hearers are given room to develop their own thoughts. The preacher keeps leading the hearers back to the picture so they can consider it again and discover something new in it.

Model 2: Perspective structure

Like model 1, this model belongs to the demonstrative and elevating type of discourse. Model 2 draws a clearer line between the various trains of thought. With one picture as the focal point, the sermon reflects in different directions. The various rays may differ in length and lead back to the picture. Before moving on to the perspective development, the preacher may retell the biblical account.

Model 3: Unfolding structure

This model is the most well known and most commonly used form of structural plan. It is suited for the informative type of discourse, which appeals mainly to the mind with the intent of giving direction to the hearers regarding particular problems. It has to do with teaching. The layout (plan) facilitates logical progression. A thematic principle (Example: "Accept one another, then, just as Christ accepted you, in order to bring praise to God". Rom. 15:7) is unfolded in two or three different directions. All the parts are at the same level. They should be equally long as far as possible. At the end of the sermon, the preacher draws a conclusion from the various parts, which s/he then summarises in a few memorable points. These points may be further reinforced visually by means of an overhead projector or a flip chart. This kind of visual plan helps the hearer to know which point in the sermon the preacher has reached. If the hearers can assume that the various parts have approximately the same length (and the last one does not turn out to be the longest, because it was not as concisely formulated as the others) then the attentive hearers' patience will not be worn out.

The unfolding model does have its disadvantages. It tempts many preachers to a deductive approach, whereby they make claims without giving reasons ("That's the way it is, believe it!"). The preacher already has his/her topic, instead of developing it in a dialogue with the hearers. The hearers are not given sufficient time to follow critically what is being said. Besides, frequent use of the unfolding model can lead to the hearers getting accustomed to it and bored, especially if they already know that the quality of parts 2 and 3 will not match that of part 1.

Proposed structural plan for a sermon on Mt 15:21-28 (Jesus' discussion with a Canaanite woman):

Topic: The threefold daring of faith

    I. Faith as an encounter with the person of Jesus
    II. Faith as an encounter with the freedom of God
    III: Faith as an encounter with the future of the world

Model 4: The dialectic structure

I. THESIS II. ANTITHESIS III. SYNTHESIS

First, a thesis is presented and expounded (Example: "Christians are not better, but they are better off!") Then, an antithesis is proposed against this thesis (Are Christians really better off?). Finally, the preacher tries to make a synthesis by combining the thesis and the antithesis in a forward directed manner. This model is especially suited if the preacher wants to call into question a particular thesis or an aspect of the biblical text, for example in the form of an "anti-sermon". This can be done, for example, by referring to individuals (or groups of people) who make such statements ("The other day, my colleague came out with it again: God doesn't exist; he is silent."). This is not about creating the concept of "the enemy". Quite often, the antithesis is present in the hearers or even the preacher him/herself as a trial of their faith!

In the synthesis, the preacher then tries to give answers to the antithesis from the gospel. Thus, s/he equips the hearers with good arguments to counter the antithesis in everyday life or in specific trials. In many cases, however, s/he will not be able to do much more than encourage the hearers to "believe against the facts". The faith of the hearers is strengthened; with the help of the *dialectic structure* model, the preacher can provide them with arguments to defend themselves against trials and animosity for the sake of their faith.

Proposed structural plan for Matthew 15:21-28:

Topic: The silence of God and the promise of Christ

Thesis: Our attitude towards God: the security of "cheap grace" (D. Bonhoeffer)
Antithesis: The silence of God: his resistance against our security
Synthesis: The power of pleading: Jesus will not leave anyone who cries out for help.

Model 5: Progressive-deepening structure

This building plan is suited for both the informative and the challenging type of discourse. The sermon, which again appeals first and foremost to the mind, has a broad and open beginning. Many hearers feel invited. The topic is meant to be interesting; the hearers are invited to think about it. In the two subsequent parts, the sermon goes deeper into the topic. The second part supports the first by giving background information. In the third and final part, the sermon moves on to the core statement. The broad subject is gradually narrowed down until a final judgement is reached. The hearer is supposed to agree with this judgement: "That's really the way it is."

Proposed structural plan for Matthew 15:21-28:

Topic: The test of faith
I. The physical need of the woman and Jesus' harsh rejection
II. Her experience of the limit and the impossibility of help
III. God is overcome and praise from the depth of human existence

The progressive-deepening model is often used in sermons that call for a decision. The hearers may be shown in the first part, for instance, that certain approaches to life (Rom. 2:1ff) will lead them in the wrong direction (legalism). In the second part, the hearers are then shown that salvation is only found in Christ (the gospel; Acts 4:12). Finally, in the third part, they are directly confronted with this message (2 Cor. 5:20). They are challenged to make a decision for Christ, for life, not death. But what does that actually mean? Many preachers who use the progressive-deepening model find this hard to explain. A simple "Jesus is the answer!" will not do. The preacher must be able to show the hearers how the journey will continue after they have made a decision for a life with Christ. Having been lead to the narrow gate, they must now be able to see the open plain, for the call of commitment to Christ opens up the "glorious freedom of the children of God" (Rom. 8:21). The progressive-deepening model makes it possible for the preacher to "get to the heart" of the issue, to present very different alternatives and, finally, to lead the hearers to the point of decision. However, the preacher should be careful not to adopt a "minus-plus theology" that will hardly appeal to a critical hearer.

Model 6: The learning psychology structure

This structural plan, which is currently receiving a lot of attention in the context of the rediscovery of "the sermon as a learning process"[1], will be described in greater detail. This structure takes up elements of models 1-5 and develops them further. Model 6 is the result of research into the psychology of learning.[2] It is intended to help the hearers to enjoy listening to the sermon, to follow it critically, and to stay with it to the end by providing them, every now and then, with opportunities to "take a rest". Listening should not be tedious, it must be made easy.

The learning psychology structure comprises 5 phases:

(1) Motivation. In the first phase, the hearer is "picked up" and invited to listen. S/he should be motivated to listen to the whole sermon right to the end and to open up to the solutions offered at the end. Narratives, dialogues, meditations on pictures, references to current affairs can all serve as tools for motivation. The preacher does not begin by presenting a problem. S/he does not immediately want to teach the hearers something. Instead, s/he leads them to the message one step at a time. S/he wants to get to the place in the lives of the hearers where the problem lies. S/he does this very gently and carefully. S/he approaches them in a personal way, so as to establish a basis of trust. His/her message will be received more readily if s/he manages to build a good relationship with the hearers. This is an important function of the motivation phase.

(2) Presenting the problem. Phase 1 leads to the problem/key question that the preacher wants to address. If the motivation phase

---

1 Cf. H. Arens, Predigt als Lernprozeß, Munich 1972; P. Bulkowski, Predigt wahrnehmen, Neukirchen-Vluyn 1991, p.

31ff; F.T. Brinkmann, Praktische Homiletik, Stuttgart/Berlin?Cologne 2000, 144ff.

2 For up-to-date research results, see: Norbert M. Seel, Psychologie des Lernens, Munich/Basle 2000.

was successful, the preacher should not normally have any difficulty introducing the problem. S/he has already prepared the hearers for it. S/he is now able to unveil an issue that concerns the hearers, or confront them with a current problem. S/he needs to be as precise as possible. The issue must be clearly circumscribed. Any overlap with other problem areas at this point can create disruptive factors that will remain throughout the sermon. The hearers must feel that the preacher him/herself is concerned with the problem as well. S/he does not feel superior to his/her hearers and searches for solutions together with them. Thus, the relationship between the preacher and the hearers is strengthened. The hearers will now find it easier to occupy themselves with the issue at stake and think about it for themselves.

A useful method for this phase is to consider the experiences, events and stories that served as motivating factors with regard to their subject content and/or the scope of the problem they raised. The problem, which was presented indirectly during the motivation phase, is now named and defined. At this point, the biblical text may come into play. It is introduced or, if was read before the sermon, taken up once more. The preacher shows how the text relates to the sermon.

(3) Trial and error. After having introduced the problem, many preachers immediately offer a solution. As a result, the hearers are often not able to keep up. They are still occupied with the issue that the preacher has just addressed and need more time to think about it. Besides, there are very few problems which have only one possible solution. Some hearers want to be involved in the search for a solution. The preacher can help them by suggesting various possible solutions and going through each of them. If the preacher is convinced that a proposed solution will lead to a dead end, s/he conveys this to the hearers. S/he exposes the error. Or s/he may leave it to the hearers to decide for themselves whether the various attempts to find a solution lead anywhere or not.

The aim of the "trial and error" phase is to enable the hearers to enter into a debate with their own convictions and those of others. The more serious the hearers are about their convictions, the easier they will find this process. The hearers need arguments which they can also use in discussions with their friends, relatives, neighbours, and work colleagues. It helps if the preacher illustrates the arguments by means of examples and stories. This will make it easier for the hearers to listen after the sometimes rather abstract introduction of the problem.

It is important in this context that the "trials" introduced in the sermon are taken seriously as trials and are not mere ciphers. An important characteristic of a fair, objective debate is that it treats the very positions that it has to criticise (on the basis of the gospel) with due respect.

(4) Offering a solution. If the preacher has convinced the hearers in the trial and error phase of the seriousness of the issue and of various trials to find an answer, then the hearer will accept or receive the solution proposed by the preacher more readily. It is here that the biblical text, above all, should be allowed to provide an answer. The perspective of faith is made plausible. The fact that this does not lead to easy remedies, but often to more questions and problems, does not need to be explicitly stated in every sermon; it should, however, be remembered. Answers of faith often raise more issues than they can solve. Although this fact cannot be disregarded, the solution phase seeks to strengthen people in their faith, so that it can give them direction and encourage them to change their behaviour. That leads us to the final phase of this sermon structure: the consolidation of the solution.

(5) Consolidating the solution. When the preacher offers a solution to the problem addressed in the sermon, s/he should not do this in the form of a general statements ("Anyone who does not ... cannot expect to ...) or appeals to "everyone" ("Everyone should ..."). Instead, s/he must make specific suggestions that can help the hearers to find solutions to similar problems. It is essential that the preacher applies his/her solution to the everyday world of the hearers and presents them with specific, practical steps that they can take. The preacher illustrates by way of examples how s/he or others might apply the solution in their own lives. S/he points to experiences that people have had in this regard. Or s/he may refer back to the example used in the motivation phase. Thus, the question posed at the beginning is answered. New information at this point would interfere with the progression of thought. The purpose of the consolidation phase is to relate the matter at stake to the everyday lives of the hearers. If this is successful, the sermon will continue to affect the lives of the hearers and urge them to put it into practice.

Generally speaking, anyone who works with models such as the ones discussed above will have to consider what overall direction s/he wants the sermon to take. What is the aim, and how will the hearers be motivated in the direction of that aim?

A preacher who is guided primarily by the deficits of the hearers ("I tell you, what you still lack!") must be aware that, for many hearers, s/he is leading in the direction of a faith that is ultimately motivated by fear. In contrast, a sermon that is guided by the promise of God, by the new life given to us through God's grace and redemption will lead towards a faith that is motivated by fulfilment.[1]

4. LEARNING IN FAITH AND CHANGING ONE'S LIFE

The purpose of preaching God's word is not merely to entertain, inform, or instruct. Although Christian preaching does have the potential to solve human problems ("After all, God's saving presence is for "real life"!), this is not its only purpose. The aim of the sermon as God's Word in the form of human words is to produce faith (Rom. 10:17) and change in the life of both the individual and the community (Phil. 2:12f).

If a sermon has an impact, then that is a gift of God and cannot be credited to psychological or didactic factors. The differences in our understanding, our personal background and our individual aptitude are too great when it comes to dealing with God's word, whether we are preachers or hearers. Preaching can therefore not rely on predictable learning content, learning steps, and learning success.

It is nonetheless legitimate and advisable, in the preaching of the gospel, to keep the obstacles to understanding to a minimum. This entails ensuring relevance to real life and the questions and issues related to it, and an awareness of lifelong learning (sanctification), that must become evident in practical living.

---

1 Cf. B. Grom, Religionspädagogische Psychologie, 5th Ed., Düsseldorf 2000

(1) Motivation	To arouse interest To establish a relationship between the preacher and the hearers To lead the hearers towards the topic (text)	Current examples and experiences Provocative statements Directing thought from the general to the specific and vice versa
(2) Presentation of problem	To establish a relationship between the hearers and the topic (text) The ideal case would be: P=H: Preacher and hearers agree P=T: Preacher and topic (text) agree H=T: Hearers and topic (text) agree	Introducing the hearers to the topic or the biblical text Defining the issue and unfolding the topic (generalising)
(3) Trial and error	To show the complexity of the issue To reflect on the biblical text To get to know various possible solutions To encourage the hearers to a critical debate with the (topic) text	Argumentation Illustrations Texts Pictures Symbols
(4) Offer of solution	To formulate ideas (abstracting) To offer a solution To win the hearers' acceptance of/agreement with the proposed solution	Bringing the biblical message to the point (avoid easy remedies) Formulating key statements or memorable assertion
(5) Consolidation of solution	To apply the proposed solution to everyday life (relevance) To consolidate what has been said at the experiential level	Accounts of experiences Examples of application

The structural plan models described above are not a guarantee for "success" when it comes to the hearers learning and growing in faith and changing their lives; they can, however, facilitate it. Especially the last model introduced is very convincing.

The five steps of the learning psychology model are found already in a similar form in the rhetoric of ancient Greece.[1] They are employed in advertising, in literature, and in filmmaking and television[2]. They

---

1 Cf. A. Grözinger, Die Sprache des Menschen, Munich 1991, p.81ff.; P. Bukowski, Predigt wahrnehmen, 3rd Ed., Neukirchen-Vluyn 1995, p. 30ff.

2 F.T. Brinkmann, Praktische Homiletik, loc. sit., p. 147f., draws a comparison with the structural pattern of many modern-day stories, which is as follows: 1. The hero and his task/ 2. The adversary/ 3. The clash and the victory/ 4.

provide the basis for many sermons without, we may assume, the preacher consciously orientating him/herself referring to the structure!

One more thing must be remembered for preaching practice: the preacher will rarely achieve his/her "learning aim" through one single sermon. This usually happens in a long process in the course of which several sermons take on a special meaning for the hearer. A text or a topic does not have to be covered conclusively in a single sermon. It may be divided up into several sermons, each with a different thematic focus. This used to be practised a lot in the church, for example, in the catechetical sermons. These were a series of sermons, each of which covered one of the main sections of the catechism (the Ten Commandments; the Creed; the Lord's Prayer; baptism; Holy Communion; confession).

A similar approach is advisable when dealing with a series of connected biblical texts. If the hearers are invited to a topical series and the preacher is able to convey to them that they will gain something by continually attending, they will probably follow such a limited series with interest. The preacher should endorse this by announcing the topics beforehand. If this is possible, s/he may take up the topics or texts once more in a mid-week church activity (bible study, youth group, etc.) in order to reinforce them. A spiritual learning process, like any process, requires time. Only repetition can lead to depth and change. It is therefore a good idea to unfold a given topic from different angles.

LECTURE 8: TEN STEPS FROM THE BIBLICAL TEXT TO THE SERMON

INTRODUCTION

Preparing a sermon is, to a certain extent, also a craft involving practical skills. Certain things must be learnt. In this lecture, we will discuss how a sermon can be assembled according to a set plan. We will take the route from text to sermon; a similar way could be sketched out for a second route from topic to sermon. We will concentrate on route one. The sermon preparation process described here does not only take place in the study room where the preacher opens up his/her bible, reads the passage of scripture, meditates on the

---

The return of the hero/ 5. The end. This pattern is clearly very similar to that of the classical drama as well as that of the learning psychology model.

words of the bible in prayer, gathers thoughts for the sermon, develops and consolidates these thoughts and contemplates, what s/he wants to communicate to his/her hearers. Any person who preaches regularly will constantly be working on a sermon, be it consciously or subconsciously. The preacher finds and collates material when visiting members, during random conversations, while reading the newspaper. S/he searches-again consciously or subconsciously-for solutions to problems which seem insurmountable.

Many preachers will wake up at night after receiving an enlightening thought that can serve as the basis of a sermon. Thus, the preacher finds him/herself in a similar situation as an artist, needing creative inspiration. The preacher is dependent on the creative Spirit and must therefore constantly remain open to him. What is important is that the preacher takes time for his/her sermon and does not try to finish it in one go. It is advisable to spread the different steps of sermon preparation over several days of the week or, if there is sufficient time, even several weeks.[1] In most cases, sermon preparation begins with the selection and study of a biblical text. This is followed by further steps that I must take in order to arrive at a sermon that will speak to the hearers. I will not always do all that is suggested below. I will often skip one or more stages and sometimes I will spend more time at a particular point, because I encounter more problems than in the following description. It is like in many board games: sometimes the figure will advance swiftly and reach the finishing mark quickly. At other times, however, the player has to go back some spaces and struggles to get home.

TEN STEPS ON THE WAY TO A SERMON

In the following, I will suggest steps that may be taken when proceeding from the biblical text to the sermon. In doing so, I will include, from the very beginning, the consideration given to the situation of the hearers. I do this in order to show more clearly the strangeness of biblical texts and their reception or rejection in a given hearer situation. I embark on the journey from the text to the sermon with the knowledge I have in respect of my hearers. Thus, my preparation focuses on both the bible and the hearers.

1Cf. K. Adloff, Die Predigtwoche. Ein homiletische Exerzitium, Göttingen, 1988.

1. CHOOSING A BIBLICAL TEXT

There are two basic ways in which a biblical text may be selected. I can either follow the so-called pericope list (i.e. list of assigned readings) which some churches issue and by which they expect their preachers to abide. These orders stipulate a particular bible passage for each Sunday and holiday of the church calendar year on which the preacher must base his/her sermon.

The advantage of such orders is that I do not have to spend time searching for a passage of scripture myself, that the scriptures are selected to suit the time of year, and that relevant up-to-date literature for sermon preparation is available, often including suggestions regarding the liturgical part of the service which are appropriate for the given biblical text or topic.

Another advantage of using a pericope list is that I do not select only my own favourite scriptures, but instead am force to contemplate thoughts other than my own. An argument against these lists, on the other hand, is that they constitute a set pattern according to which the biblical passages are continually repeated at particular intervals. The proposed readings therefore do not always reflect the current issues within the church and society as a whole.

There is a danger that something of the prophetic dimension of preaching may be lost if the biblical word or topic is not selected by the preacher in view of the particular situation.

2. MY FIRST DIALOGUE WITH THE TEXT

This section of the road to the sermon may be subdivided into several individual steps:
(1) When I have found a bible passage: on which to base my sermon I consider the following points during my initial contemplation:

Is the text close to me or far from me? Is it easy or difficult to understand?
Do I feel comfortable with it or is it strange to me? How does it affect me?
After having written down my initial feelings about the text, I proceed along the following stages:

a) I try to rephrase the text in my own words.

b) In the case of narratives, parables and descriptions of situations, I try to put myself in the position of the persons involved and re-enact the passage (maybe even with others).

c) I contemplate the key words of the text or important words that particularly fascinated or annoyed me. I try to grasp the meaning of these words with the help of various dictionaries. I pay attention to the pictures and symbols that occur in the text.

d) I consult various translations of the passage and try to determine how the translators understood particular words and interpreted pictures.

(2) I describe the text with regard to its:

- structure,
- climaxes,
- unclear sections,
- ambiguities.

(3) I try to recall other texts: biblical and non-biblical poems, prayers and stories that I believe have something to do with my bible passage.

(4) I consider the time of my sermon: on this passage in respect of the church calendar and remind myself of the theme, hymns and psalms traditionally assigned to that Sunday.

(5) I note down any questions/issues: that I intend to explore further during my detailed study and exegesis (interpretation of a biblical text according to theological criteria and methods) of the text.

3. MY FIRST DIALOGUE WITH THE HEARERS

When I begin talking to the hearers in my mind, I try to take into account both levels, the specific situation and the "general homiletic weather situation". The following questions may help me during this step:

(1) I imagine how my thoughts for my sermon might affect the hearers. For this purpose, I visualise, as far as possible, one or more specific individuals and also the situation of my church as a whole (make-up and religiousness of the congregation, situation of the church in the community).

(2) I try to determine whether the ideas that I have had based on the bible passage fit the situation in which I am to preach.

(3) I establish which of the issues addressed by the text I would like to talk to my hearers about.

(4) I reflect on conversations or bits of conversations and experiences which I have recently had with the hearers, for example during pastoral visits, or with friends' acquaintances and neighbours.

(5) I try to find out what societal events/global developments are currently of concern to hearers.

(6) I ask myself what I am really hoping to achieve in my hearers when I convey the message of the biblical text: What is my intention as a preacher of the gospel?

All these questions help me with my initial assessment of the homiletic situation, i.e. contemplate what I assume to be the situation of my hearers, the areas affecting their lives and any questions they may have. This subject was discussed in more detail in Chapter 3.

4. EXEGETICAL AND THEOLOGICAL VERIFICATION OF MY IDEAS REGARDING THE TEXT

During this step, I must treat the biblical text as my interlocutor. This means that I talk to my text rather than twist and shape it until it suits me. Consequently, the exegetical and theological verification of my ideas must result in corrections. I am aware that many of you will not largely have theological literature at hand. I encourage you to see, which of the following questions may be helpful:

(1) What was the larger context of the passage at the time and from the perspective of the author?

(2) What goal(s) did the author have in mind and what means (language, style, argumentation, etc.) did he employ to achieve that goal (these goals) in his situation?

(3) What do theological commentaries say about the message and the main statements of the text? Are there significant variations or even irreconcilable differences in the interpretations of the text given by the commentaries?

(4) How does the text fit into the overall testimony of the bible? Does it take up ideas that are frequent throughout the Old and New Testament or does it stand more or less in isolation? What would be missing if this text were not included in the canon of scripture?

(5) To which main areas of Christian doctrine (e.g. creation, justification, discipleship, and church) does the text belong? What can I find out in this regard from encyclopaedias/other theological literature?

(6) Are there significant differences or similarities between the situations and worldviews of then and now?

The results of this third step are summed up in a few core statements. I then know in what way I must represent the text to the hearers.

5. A LOOK AT PREACHING LITERATURE

If I have sermons or meditations in my own library or I am able to obtain good preaching materials elsewhere, I should look at them. With the help of such materials, I can find out how others have interpreted the text before me. I will always benefit particularly from the sermons of preachers whom I have learnt to appreciate, from whose sermons I have received something myself.

The following steps may be helpful:

(1) I establish what the central idea is by which others have linked the bible passage with their own statements.

(2) I decide which of these ideas appeal to me and which of them I find particularly successful.

(3) I write down which stories, images, examples and illustrations I find convincing.

(4) I consider the effects my text has had in the past (Who has used this text throughout church history and for what purpose?) so I can determine whether I can build on a past message or whether I need to refute it.

While plagiarising is forbidden in an academic context, the following rule applies when gleaning from the sermons of others: plagiarism is the mother of all homiletic inspiration or: in this context, theft is permitted. This means that the preacher does not need to state in the sermon from which sources s/he has obtained his/her ideas. The hearers are not usually interested.[1]

---

1 Cf. R. Bohren, Predigtlehre, 4th Ed., Munich 1980, pp. 198-203.

6. PAUSE FOR INSPIRATION

When I have finished gathering material and checking my ideas, it is best not to begin writing out my sermon, but rather take a break and wait for inspiration. The sermon should be allowed to "grow in the womb" until the inspiring thought is birthed.

Going through this inspiration phase may be arduous, because I am not yet clear about exactly how and what I will be preaching. I don't know whether I will come up with something appropriate. I may experience this phase, also referred to as the frustration phase, as distressing. I have to deal with problems concerning my text and my hearers. How can I build a bridge between the text and the situation to ensure that I am not talking above the heads of the hearers?

The arduousness of this phase is usually offset by the joy over the inspiring thought. Once I have checked whether my idea for the sermon will work, I can deal with the material I have gathered in a purposeful way. I am motivated to preach and therefore able to motivate others to listen. I can name the problem and therefore circumscribe it. I have travelled many difficult roads through trials and errors. Now I am able to offer a solution and put on paper my central thoughts for the sermon.[1]

7. ASSIGNING THE BUILDING BLOCKS

I now assign the insights and impulses gathered in steps 2 to 5 to the central idea for the sermon and the main thoughts that I have developed. In doing so, I need to have a dual perspective:

(1) Selection: In studying the available material, I must ask myself what is useful in relation to my main thoughts for the sermon and what needs to be omitted. The same applies to any pictures and examples. If something is rejected as unsuitable for this sermon, it does not mean that it cannot be used for other sermons based on the same passage of scripture. It is therefore a good idea to compile a card index or database for sermons where such findings can be sorted and stored according to the relevant texts or topics.

---

1 Regarding creativity in sermon preparation, cf. J. Rothermundt, Der Heilige Geist und die Rhetorik, Gütersloh 1984, esp. pp.143-149.

(2) Expansion: During this process, which goes in the exact opposite direction to the point described above, the preacher determines which sections of the sermon need to be expanded and what additional illustrations, symbols or texts may be required. At this point, it may be helpful to take another closer look at the preaching literature.

8. ORGANISATION AND WORDING OF THE SERMON

This step is about drawing up various plans to help me develop my sermon. Next, I venture a first draft of my sermon. The following steps may be helpful:

(1) Based on one or possibly several of the sermon models a plan is drawn up for the organisation of the sermon.

(2) The material from the previous steps is fitted into this plan.

(3) A first provisional wording of the sermon is either written down or spoken unrehearsed on tape. In doing so, I must consider what kind of language is appropriate bearing in mind the three factors of the homiletic triangle. In other words, I contemplate whether the language I am using does justice to the biblical text and the sermon content, the hearers, and me as the preacher with my strengths and weaknesses.

(4) I present this first draft to one individual, say a friend or relative, or a small group of hearers. I invite these people to comment on the sermon and make suggestions.

9. COMPLETING THE SERMON AND PLANNING THE SERVICE

The feedback and insights from the conversations regarding the first draft wording of the sermon are recorded and incorporated into the sermon manuscript. Following this, I scrutinise the sermon once more myself with the help of the leading questions so far. Sufficient time and diligence should also be given to planning the liturgical part of the service to ensure that the congregation experience the service as an integrated whole rather than a mixture of incoherent elements. In this context, compare the discussion of the relationship between the sermon and the liturgy that we had during our first session.

10. THE DELIVERY OF THE SERMON

The final step is to deliver the sermon that I have prepared. In most of the literature on homiletics, the delivery of the sermon is given little attention. But in reality, it is very important: the result of our work hopefully is a grasping speech, not a dead pile of paper. We therefore will have a detailed session on the deliverance topic, too.

A brief Outlook: topical sermons

When preaching on a biblical text, much emphasis is placed on diligently interpreting the text. In the case of topical preaching, however, the analysis of the situation and of the audience and also a general theological reflection on the topic are of vital importance. I usually prepare a topical sermon whenever I have an idea that I consider to be so important that I want to produce a sermon on it. I extend this idea into a theme which I then seek to substantiate from a biblical-theological perspective. The steps to be taken in preparation are similar to those above, being aware of a wider context of today's questions and challenges.

LECTURE 9: DELIVERING A SERMON

When asked what they imagine a well-delivered sermon to be like hearers will usually say something like this:
• The preacher should speak as freely as possible and should make "contact" with the hearers.
• The preacher should speak slowly, audibly, and in an understandable way.
• There should be a healthy mixture of lively presentation and calmness.

The answers to this question will, however, differ significantly: according to their age, background and individual conceptions, the hearers will have quite different expectations of the preacher. The success of a speech act depends on various factors. These include:

• thorough preparation of the message content
• an expectant attitude towards that which must be done
• an air of "tense concentration" -in the positive sense, to ensure that the sermon holds the attention of the hearers and is not boring
• an appealing, communicative style that stimulates the hearers to think for themselves, that opens up new horizons and invites the hearers to respond
• clear pronunciation, and appropriate body language and facial expression in the given situation.

Many of these factors can and must be learnt if preaching is to remain enjoyable. Others are giftings that one will have to a greater or lesser degree. They must be discovered, developed and shaped or, in some cases, kept in check. In the following, we will discuss some of the factors mentioned that are relevant to successful sermon delivery.

I. THE MANUSCRIPT

Preaching a sermon without a manuscript is a good thing, provided it is successful, because the preacher can focus more on the hearers than if s/he constantly has to refer to his/her manuscript or even keep his/her eyes glued to it. However, when a sermon is delivered without any notes, there is always a great danger that the preacher will soon get onto his/her favourite hobbyhorse. S/he may also digress, repeat him/herself or get carried away in details, with the result that the hearers will lose the thread. In any case, it would be wrong to assume that preaching without notes is a sign of greater faith or trust in God: "A preacher must always know what s/he is saying, regardless of whether s/he prepares "in passing" or thoroughly, with a clear purpose in mind. The manuscript is then solely a question of the preacher's memory rather than spiritual authority."[1]

There are three main arguments for using a written manuscript:

(1) Producing a sermon manuscript forces the preacher to structure the message clearly and think it through. Thus, unnecessary repetition and "chatting" from the pulpit can be avoided. Moreover, it will be easier to check and evaluate the results of the preaching process.

(2) Having the sermon in a written form gives the preacher sense of security. Even if s/he is very nervous or has a blackout in the pulpit and does not know how to continue, s/he can still finish the sermon by referring to the manuscript.

(3) Finally, a manuscript makes it easier to preach a sermon again. Especially, if the sermon was written on a computer it can always be updated and adapted to the new situation. Thus, a sermon content that was prepared with great diligence can be used with a good conscience on several occasions.

---

1 W. Klippert, Vom Text zur Predigt. Grundlagen und Praxis biblischer Verkündigung, Wuppertal/Zurich 1995, p. 136. While many of the commonly known homiletics manuals provide little information regarding these very practical issues, Klippers book gives a lot of attention to the delivery of the sermon (pp. 136-163). Many important thoughts in this section on sermon manuscripts are taken from this book.

The danger of writing out sermons lies especially in the temptation to read and remain glued to the manuscript. It is also important to be aware of the tendency to use complex "written language" that is likely to overtax the hearers. Adhering to a manuscript can seriously the hinder the spontaneity of the sermon. Wolfgang Klippert states in this context: "The manuscript is a servant, not a master. It must not rob its master of the freedom to incorporate current events and new ideas ... A preacher who makes him/herself the slave of his/her manuscript will miss the *kairos*, God's perfect timing, in key situations. You should basically follow your manuscript and not try to work in every thought that crosses your mind or even interpret it as the "leading of the spirit". You should, however, gladly abandon your manuscript whenever the situation demands it."[1]

In his preaching manual, Horst Hirschler, too, argues in favour of writing out the sermon, but suggests that key words and phrases should then be underlined and highlighted in different colours. The preacher should familiarise him/herself with the prepared manuscript and later, in the pulpit, rephrase every sentence. Hirschler calls this "speaking freely over the manuscript".[2] We neither consider it necessary nor helpful to memorise the sermon, for a memorised delivery is not a genuine communicative act, but the "reading of an inner manuscript" (Friso Melzer).

Besides, there should always be room for discoveries and ideas of the moment, for improvisation and consideration for the hearers. However, in order to use effectively your free leg, you must stand on firm ground with your pivot leg. It is therefore helpful to familiarise oneself with the sermon's structure and the main train of thought.[3]

In his booklet "Frei predigen" (preaching freely)[4], the French priest Albert Damblon gives plenty of advice on how to get away from depending on manuscripts and become a free - not freely drifting! - preacher. However, he argues against producing a fully formulated manuscript and suggests, instead, the use of notes containing key words and memory aids.

---

1 W. Klippert, Vom Text zur Predigt, loc. sit. , p. 138.

2 H. Hirschler, Biblisch predigen, 3rd Ed., Hanover 1992, p. 577.

3 Cf. A. Pohl, Anleitung zum Predigen, 3rd Ed., Wuppertal/Kassel 1976, p. 76.

4 A. Damblon, Frei Predigen. Ein Lehr- und Arbeitsbuch, Düsseldorf 1991.

Damblon lists the following arguments in favour of a free sermon delivery:[1]

(1) The free sermon is a public testimony of the message of Christ. The competence to preach includes the ability to "answer to everyone who asks you to give the reason for the hope that you have" (1 Pet. 3:15) freely and convincingly.

(2) Free speech emphasises in a special way the nature of preaching as a testimony of Christ. Someone speaks freely about the things that "really concern us" (Paul Tillich). In biblical terms: "Out of the overflow of the heart the mouth speaks (Mt. 12:34)."

(3) Free preaching is "speaking while thinking". This shows: the preacher thinks about what s/he says not only while preparing the sermon, but also while delivering it. Thus, there is closer correspondence between the speaking process of the preacher and the thinking process of the hearers. Pauses in speaking are pauses in hearing.

(4) The communicative situation of the sermon requires an appropriate form of language, which is not the written word, but the spoken. The latter is more situational, simpler in style, unique, dynamic, provisional; written language, in contrast, tends to be more static and repeatable.

(5) Free speech establishes contact. Even though the sermon is by definition a monologue, it should be a dialogue in character. The preacher has an inner dialogue with his/her opposite. S/he therefore needs the freedom of speaking, so that the hearer can find the freedom to hear. There are many arguments in favour of free preaching. This, however, requires a considerable presence of mind (as well as the presence of the Spirit!). Like every art, free preaching is both a matter of talent and of diligent practice. Nonetheless, it must be said that free preaching is neither the measure of all things nor everyone's thing.

There are good preachers who are experienced in their use of manuscripts and communicate successfully, because they consciously seek contact with the hearers. Under no circumstances should a lack of preparation be the reason for doing without a manuscript. Werner Jetter comments in this context: **"the Holy Spirit will not make up the overtime that the preacher tried to get out of doing".**[2]

---

1 Cf. loc. sit. p. 25-46.

2 W. Jetter, Homiletische Akupunktur. Teilnahmsvolle Notizen – die Predigt betreffend, Göttingen 1976, p. 106.

So what should a manuscript look like? The best format is A5. While the preacher may find that A4 sheets too large for some pulpits, formats smaller than A5 will require him/her to turn the pages too frequently. If there is nowhere to put a manuscript and the preacher can cope with only a few notes, s/he can always resort to A6 index cards. In any case, the sheets should be numbered with writing only on one side, so that the relevant passages can be easily found.

To ensure that no lines are skipped or repeated, the writing should not be justified. It is also important to use a large font (or large handwriting), especially in dim light or if the pulpit is quite low. Section headings help the preacher to know where s/he has reached in the sermon. The main scripture should, if possible, be read from the bible, not from the manuscript. Thus, it is clear to everyone that the holy scriptures are being cited, and everyone will be able to read the same text again at home in the bible.

(**Editor's Note:** Sheets of notes inserted in plastic display files provide flexibility, easy reading and access for most situations.)

II. CONTACT WITH THE CONGREGATION

We have already touched on this in the previous section: the preacher should be aware of his/her congregation. S/he will notice many things if s/he watches the hearers. S/he will sense and see whether they are following the sermon or whether they are elsewhere with their thoughts. The latter, of course, need not always be negative. When hearers allow their minds to wander, this may actually have been triggered by an interesting statement or picture, and sometimes even be desired by the preacher.

Horst Hirschler suggests that, while delivering the sermon, the preacher should "choose three to five fixed points within the congregation and allow his/her eyes to move calmly from one point to the next."[1] It might be better to speak of faces at which the preacher can look, rather than points. It is always encouraging to see a hearer respond with a friendly smile. Moreover, looking at the hearers gives them the feeling that you are talking to them and not over their heads. The worst thing a preacher can do is focus on a fixed point in the

---

1 H. Hirschler, Biblisch predigen, loc. sit., p. 579.

church building somewhere above or below the hearers' faces. Thus, the preacher reveals that s/he is insecure and creates an atmosphere of anonymity. In contrast, eye contact "creates an atmosphere of openness and personal closeness" and "conveys an impression of honesty and self-confidence".[1]

Indications that the hearers have been lost include checking the time or flicking through the songbook or the bible, rustling sweet wrappers, complete absent-mindedness and, in extreme cases, falling asleep in the pew. All these things can be very off-putting for the preacher. Crying children, too, can distract both the preacher and the hearers, regardless of the fact that parents should feel welcome to bring children and their presence in the service is important. In such situations, the preacher may simply repeat a sentence or passage of the sermon without much ado. The same applies, when someone leaves the room during the sermon. Very rarely, should this be taken personally and understood as a reaction to the sermon. Usually, there are quite natural reasons...

Laughing is good for you – and for the sermon.

A final point in this session is about humour: Christianity, particularly Protestantism, is not exactly known for its humour. Friedrich Nietzsche expressed the criticism that can hardly be dismissed: **"Better songs would they have to sing, for me to believe in their Saviour: more! Like saved ones would his disciples have to appear unto me!"**[2]

Here, we would simply suggest that there are several reasons why it may be helpful if the preacher succeeds in getting the congregation to smile or laugh. It helps the hearers to relax and take a fresh breath, and wakes them up. Any humorous remarks must, of course, suit the situation and the text.

As a rule, one could say it is not a bad idea if the congregation are given at least one occasion to laugh during a church service. You want an example?

---

1 W. Klippert, Vom Text zur Predigt, loc. sit., p. 160.

2 F. Nietzsche, "The Priests" in F. Nietzsche Thus spake Zarathustra II (1883), Translation by Thomas Common (www) OMIT THIS PART IN THE ENGLISH? (Critical Study Edition), revised edition, Munich 1999, p. 118.

A vicar tells his colleague, "I've got a problem with bats in my church. I've tried everything, but I just can't get rid of them. Have you got any suggestions what I could do?" The colleague replies, "Oh yes, I have. I had the same problem. I simply christened and confirmed them, and I haven't seen them since."

III. THE EFFECT OF THE VOICE

"You should accept your voice! ... The mere fact that you accept yourself, including your voice, has such a positive effect on your charisma that you can make good many points in a just a few minutes."[1] Singers know that a good tone can only be achieved if the person singing is at peace with him/herself, if there is an inner balance. Insecurity and fear are obstacles to a good tone of voice and consequently also convincing speech. Now, it is admittedly not easy to accept oneself, nor one's voice, if one is not fond of it. Appeals to accept oneself do not help much in this case. Of more help is the assurance that the ones propagating the good news of the love of God are included in this love. Like everyone else, they are the objects of God's mercy, and therefore they may show mercy to themselves and their voices.

What is important is that the preachers' language sounds as natural and authentic as possible. Put-on emotion and a stilted tone of voice are unconvincing and, after a while, become embarrassing. However, preachers are not usually aware that they do this. It helps to have people in the congregation who give regular feedback regarding this issue (in a loving way!), for it would be wrong, on the other hand, to pay constant attention to one's own voice while preaching. This can lead to excessive self-observation, which will only increase the preacher's insecurity. If the preacher has speech problems that interfere with his /her preaching, s/he can achieve considerable improvement by receiving directed speech training and by working with tape and video recordings of his/her own sermons.

An adequate volume, clear pronunciation and a consistent pace are, so to speak, the golden rules of neighbourly love, particularly when it comes to people with hearing difficulties. However, this rule of adequate volume does not mean that all modulation and lowering of

---

1 E. Wagner, Rhetorik in der Christlichen Gemeinde, Stuttgart 1992, p. 314.

voice should be banned from the pulpit. Some sections must be said quietly or even in a secretive tone to suit the sermon content. Moreover, audibility has to do not only with volume, but also with the precision of speech, i.e. clear articulation. A preacher who doesn't open his/her mouth properly, who mumbles or slurs word endings will not be easily understood even if s/he speaks in a loud voice. If the voice is too low or the speech unclear the hearers suffer, as they have to strain in order to understand what is being said. Consequently, they will grow tired more quickly and "switch off".

The right pace is also very important in preaching. The rule of thumb is that it is always better to speak slowly than fast. The hearers need time to understand and process what they have heard. For this reason, pausing at the appropriate points is important and helps to underline what has been said. On the other hand, overly long pauses and speaking too slowly can also tire the hearers.

Finally, we need to point out that the hearers too have a responsibility in this area. They can make their contribution to hearing and understanding the sermon, by finding a seat where they can hear well and, if necessary, using a hearing aid or a loop system, and by coming to the service with an expectant attitude.

We do not usually give much thought to the way we breathe. Breathing occurs naturally and subconsciously. However, if we are tense or nervous when preaching we often become "short-winded and breath against the natural rhythm." [1] Breathing too quickly can lead to disorder of the carbon-dioxide and CA^{++} concentration the in the blood which adversely affects our circulation and causes us to become dizzy and black out. This can be avoided by making a conscious effort to breathe slowly in a way that involves not only the chest, but also the belly (so-called diaphragmatic breathing).[2]

The author F. Melzer, who studied language and speech over several decades, states that the oxygen volume can be almost doubled through correct breathing. Thus, the preacher will not "run out of breath" while preaching.[3] In any case, the breathing determines the

---

1 W. Klippert, Vom Text zur Predigt, loc. sit. , p. 141.

2 Cf. the practical exercises in: H. Lodes, Atme richtig!, Munich 2000.

3 F. Melzer, Evangelische Verkündigung und deutsche Sprache, Tübingen 1970, p. 6.

syntax. Even if the preacher does not notice when his/her breathing is inconsistent with the syntax, the hearers surely will.

In churches, microphones or sound systems often do not produce a satisfactory result. If this is the case, one should stress the need to invest in new equipment. It is annoying and disruptive when hearers have problems understanding, due to poor sound quality, or when a cold, technical reproduction of the preacher's voice lessens the pastoral effect of his/her words. Just as the acoustics of rooms vary, the effect of microphones and sound systems can vary considerably from one place to another. When being invited to another church as a visiting speaker, it is therefore advisable to check with someone who is familiar with the building how close one should be to the microphone and how loud one should speak, in order to achieve the best possible effect. If possible, the microphone stand or holder should be positioned correctly before the church service. One might also consider whether a microphone is really needed at all. Some speakers limit their elocutionary skills by trusting more in technical aids than in their own vocal ability and charisma. Less technology often means better quality.

IV. GESTURES AND FACIAL EXPRESSION

The sermon does not only begin when the preacher is in the pulpit and it does not end when s/he says Amen. Our entire behaviour before, during, and after the service is part of the preaching process. When opening the service, during the scripture readings and prayers, and during the delivery of the sermon, the preacher's manner, like his/her voice, should be as natural as possible. The preacher should walk to the pulpit upright and at a normal walking pace. Any hectic movements should be avoided. Speaking involves the entire body.

Gestures and facial expressions reiterate the message and lend credibility to that which is said. It is, however, advisable to use gestures sparingly when preaching. You cannot watch a "wriggly" preacher for very long. They make you nervous. Especially movements of the legs and the whole body should be calm. When making gestures, the preacher should look at the congregation. Making gestures to reinforce what you are saying while having your eyes glued to the manuscript usually looks silly. Special attention should be given to the hands. If you don't know what to do with them, you can simply rest them on the pulpit. This appears more natural than grasping the edge of the pulpit as if one were trying to find a hold. A person who feels free and steadfast will be able to use gestures in a natural and consistent way. However, the opposite is true as well: moderate movements can have a liberating effect and reduce nervousness.

By facial expression, we do not mean pulling faces, but looking (in both senses of the word) according to the factual and emotional content. A person who looks bored or distant when delivering the sermon will find it hard to arouse the interest of the hearers. Someone who constantly winks or chews his/her lips, on the other hand, will pass his/her nervousness on to the congregation. Again, we are not usually aware of our quirks. There are preachers whose congregations count the times that they clear their throats, take off their spectacles and put them back on again, take a sip of water, or use a particular filler-word during the sermon. In order to ensure that one uses one's voice, facial expression, and gestures effectively, it is helpful to think of a person one knows in the church building, to turn to that person inwardly and to speak to him/her. This helps to make the preachers' manner more natural and personal.

V. DEALING WITH PREACHING PHOBIA

There is hardly a homiletics manual that addresses the preaching phobia. Rudolf Bohren writes about the preacher's fear of God: "The preacher who fears God does not need to fear man."[1] Although this is true, it is probably not all that can be said on this subject. The most comprehensive discussion on the fear of the preacher is found, again, in Damblon's booklet. He dedicates an entire chapter to this topic. Important findings of his include:

(1) Preaching phobia is normal.

Elocution research found that only 8.8% of those tested were not afraid of speaking publicly. The elocutionists Waltraud and Dieter Allhoff state: "Nearly everyone has experienced public speaking phobia: be it in a speech to a large crowd, or an oral exam, or an unpleasant talk with a line manager. Some "have butterflies in their stomach" or "go weak at the knees", others "have a lump in the throat", yet others get sweaty hands, their heart beats faster, or they find it hard to breathe. All these symptoms are not exactly beneficial for speaking."[2]

---

1 R. Bohren, Predigtlehre, 4th Ed., Munich 1980, p. 262.

2 W. and D. Allhoff, Rhetorik und Kommunikation, 6th Ed., Regensburg 1989, p. 60.

(2) Preaching phobia must be called by name and acknowledged.

On the staircase leading to one pulpit, it says: "Qui ascendit cum timore, is descendit cum honore" - the one who ascends with fear will descend with honour. Thus, preaching phobia is a healthy precondition for preaching, which - provided it does not constantly lead to maladjustments like the psychosomatic reactions described above - contains energy, capable of spurring the preacher to "flight or fight" (i.e. an instinctive maximum performance). The elocutionist Udo Nix states in this regard: "Stage fright is transformed, as spiritual energy, into enthusiasm for the partner and the cause".[1]

(3) The sermon begins with a deep exhalation.

Speaking is tonal exhalation. Preachers must therefore control their breathing; stress can easily lead to extreme upper-chest breathing, and ultimately loss of breath. The church father Augustine is quoted as saying: "Breathe in me, O Holy Spirit, that my thoughts may all be holy" - this could also give modern preachers an inner peace that helps to calm their breathing and preaching and allows that which the sermon ultimately wants to achieve to permeate: i.e. to lead the hearers to the Holy.

(4) The congregation is not the way you think.

What preachers think about their congregation affects the way they preach. Do they perceive the hearers as hungry wolves who are only waiting to tear them to pieces? Or perhaps as innocent lambs expecting tender loving care from their shepherd? We must remember the grace of God which the congregation has already received long before the preacher ascends to the pulpit. If the preacher sees the congregation as a community of people who have experienced God's grace and, with that in mind, involves him/herself in the communication of the liberating and encouraging message of the gospel, s/he will want to give to them that for which they so deeply long: namely, a word from God for the here and now, brought to them by a person who hears it for him/herself and endeavours to live his/her own life accordingly. Bishop Walter Klaiber once asked a pastor who was constantly complaining to him about his congregation: "Do you love your congregation?" A preacher's answer to this question will affect his/her preaching and the way s/he deals with preaching phobia.

---

1 U.H. Nix, Überzeugend und lebendig reden, Landsberg a. L. 1985, cited in Damblon, loc. sit., p. 53.

(5) Thorough preparation.

A preacher who is well prepared can depend on his/her own work. In contrast, a person who lives from hand to mouth will be more likely to fall victim to the stress factor of fear. The rhetorician Maximilian Weller writes in this regard: "First on our list of remedies for inhibitions to speak should be the definite and essential requirement: As a young speaker who is still plagued by public speaking phobia and stage fright, prepare for your topic as diligently as possible, compiling a list of key words, so that you feel you know the topic inside out, that you can produce it "just like that", and you will be free from insecurity, at least in respect of the subject content."[1]

VI. DEALING WITH MISHAPS

Many a preacher will have dreamt in the night before the sermon that s/he goes to the pulpit and finds that the sermon manuscript has disappeared. Others will have experienced that the sound system failed just as they were about to begin the sermon. Whether the preacher has put on two different coloured socks, the flowers are missing, or unintentional situation comedy (a preacher once announced that he would read a few "verses" from a newspaper article) - such mishaps make a perfect event more human. This applies to church services as well.

Thus, mishaps can actually the enhance effect of an event and should therefore not be regarded as something negative. It depends, of course, on the nature and the frequency of the problem. Occasional, minor and therefore non-offensive mishaps rouse a feeling of compassion and empathy in the hearers. Everyone will be relieved and happy when things do finally work out. What is important is that we do not make a drama out of it. Then the mishap is usually quickly forgotten. A little joke relating to the incident may create closeness with the hearers and defuse the situation.

LECTURE 10: THE USE OF SYMBOLS IN WORSHIP AND PREACHING

We have started our series of sessions looking at the whole of a worship service and we will close the same way. After all that we have shared about preaching it should have become clear that we have to consider not only the sermon, but also the "environment", the treasure

---

1 M. Weller, Das Buch der Redekunst, Munich 1989, p. 67.

of shared liturgy and silence. Besides that, there will always be factors that are beyond the preachers influence, such as the church building, the room, and the make-up of the congregation. From this perspective, the propagation of the gospel is most likely to be successful where there is maximum agreement between inner and outer factors, and verbal and non-verbal factors. Using symbols has become to be widely considered in modern theories of worship and preaching.

1. THE LANGUAGE OF IMAGES AS THE MOTHER TONGUE OF FAITH

The girl stood on the shore   And heaved a heavy sigh.
It made her kinda sore   To watch the sunset die.
Hey baby don't you frown,   It happens all the time:
The sun goes down in front   Then pops up from behind.
(Translated by Doug Robinson)

This poem by the German writer Heinrich Heine (1797-1856) illustrates the difference between a purely practical and a symbolic perspective of the same thing.[1] Which perspective is right? Probably both, each in its own way. Nowadays, every child knows that the earth rotates and that sunsets are the result of this rotation. Yet no one ever says: "Look at how beautifully the earth is rotating!", but rather, "What a beautiful sunset!" Beside the mere explanation of facts, we have a deeper symbolic perspective. Depending on the situation and the person concerned, either one will dominate over the other when truth is expressed.

The Old Testament is full of true-to-life metaphoric language.

Thus, for example, the Hebrew word for soul (nefesh) is based on the root word for "throat", the essential place for food intake and inhalation. In important passages, we also find a close connection between speech and symbolic action, especially in the prophetic writings of the Hebrew bible. In the book of Isaiah, for instance, the people of Israel are referred to by means of the speaking image of "God's vineyard" (Is. 5:1ff). At Yahweh's command, Jeremiah (Jer. 27:2) puts a wooden yoke on his shoulders to reinforce his prophecy concerning the yoke of Nebuchadnezzar. Ezekiel runs through the city with his belongings packed for exile in order to underline his message

---

1 H. Heine, Sämtliche Werke (Complete Works), ed. by E. Elster, Vol.1, Leipzig/Vienna 1889, p. 229. OMIT IN ENGLISH?

(English translation: home.olemiss.edu/~djr/pages/translator/german/heine.html)

(Ez. 12:1ff). In the case of Hosea, the prophet's wife (wives) and children are involved in the prophetic assignment - in a way that is hardly conceivable to us today (Hos. 1:2ff).

In the New Testament, it is not much different.

Jesus constantly used comparisons and metaphors, puns and symbols in his preaching. He used everyday things as a starting point for telling his hearers about God within the context of their world (with their reality and their logic). It is only in this light that we can really understand, for example, the parables of the sower (Mk 4:1-20a), the mustard seed (Mk 4:30-34a), the lost sheep, the lost coin, or the two sons who were both lost, each in his own way (Lk. 15). In the same way, the metaphorical "I am's" of John's gospel appeal to the understanding and the reality of the people of the biblical era. All these examples show: "Jesus introduced gestures, symbols, illustrations of the new life and established new meanings ... He not only created friendship but also new expressions of this friendship, making them an example for us: bread and wine, oil and water, blessings and embraces, feet washing and writing in the sand, fasting and drinking all became new gestures of life."[1]

These symbols of life, as we find them in the bible, have been interpreted and employed in a variety of ways throughout church history. For centuries, post-Reformation homiletics with its emphasis on the word was largely "homiletics without symbols" (Horst Albrecht). In contrast, the Roman Catholic tradition had already for some time been more open to the use of symbols in preaching and homiletics. Over the past three decades, Protestants too have begun to pay more attention to the use of symbols in both biblical teaching and preaching from the pulpit.[2] Besides the educational reasons resulting from societal changes[3], this new openness to the use of symbols is mainly due to a theological realisation.

---

1 F. Steffensky, Feier des Lebens, Spiritualität im Alltag, Stuutgart 1984, p. 78.

2 This was prompted largely by the Symboldidactic (The use of symbols in teaching) of the 1980s, in particular the works on religious education by Hubertus Halbfas and Peter Biehl, the former representing the Roman Catholic side and the latter the Lutheran side. Cf. also the standard work by W. Jetter, Symbol und Ritual, Göttingen 1978.

3 The following three examples attest to this: our increasingly multifarious society makes it more difficult to interpret the correlations of life. The number of people who have any biblical knowledge, which could serve as a basis for Christian preaching and teaching, is steadily decreasing. Educational processes are never completed and must not be limited to imparting intellectual knowledge.

The purpose of the communication of the gospel in all its various manifestations is to speak of God, to express that which cannot be said, to depict that which cannot be depicted. This is can only be achieved through metaphoric and symbolic language. When speaking of the absolute and the ultimate, the holy and the eternal, we cannot do without symbols. The language of symbols may be regarded as the "mother tongue of faith".[1] Speaking of the "purpose and the right of religious symbols", the German/American theologian Paul Tillich wrote:[2]

> *"Religious symbols need no justification if their purpose is clear. Their purpose is that they are the language of the religions, the only language by which religion can be directly expressed. We can make statements about religion using philosophical and theological terms, or we can try to grasp the religious through art. Yet, the religious itself can only find expression in symbols or in complexes of symbols which - when combined into a unit - we refer to as myths."*

The use of symbols in this context is not merely about giving illustrations in the sense of superficially increasing the hearers' attentiveness. This will become clear as we consider some of the characteristics of religious symbols, – as the time of the rainy season suggests: exemplified by the symbol of water.[3]

2. FIVE CHARACTERISTICS OF RELIGIOUS SYMBOLS

a) Symbols are part of the finite reality and point beyond it

Symbols are words, pictures, objects, and actions with more than one meaning. They are, so to speak, translucent for a reality that lies behind everyday reality. The visible becomes transparent so the invisible can be seen. Symbols are part of the finite reality and, at the same time, point beyond it. Conversely, we can say: while they have a figurative meaning, it must always be possible to understand them literally as well.[4] Besides the obvious aspect that can be described with the means of the exact sciences, there is an additional symbolic aspect.

---

1 L. Burgdörfer, "Symbolisierend predigen, Studienbrief P1" in Brennpunkt Gemeinde 47. Issue 4/1994, p.2.

2 Taken from: "P. Tillich, Sinn und Recht religiöser Symbole" (German 1961) in P. Tillich, Symbol und Wirklichkeit, 3rd Ed., Göttingen 1986, p. 3 (cf also pp. 3-12).

3 Cf. P. Tillich, loc.sit., p.4ff, P. Biehl, Synbole geben zu lernen, Vol.II, Neukirchen-Vluyn 1993, pp. 116-171.

4 This distiguishes them from metaphors, which are to be understood always in the figurative sense.

This additional aspect is, so to speak, consolidated in the symbol. That explains the meaning of the word: the Greek *symballein* may be translated as "to throw together", or "to unite".

Example: Water. In an encyclopaedia, we would find the following factual information under the entry "water": "tasteless, odourless liquid, colourless in shallow amounts, the oxide of hydrogen, melting point 0°, boiling point 100° ..."[1] which describe water from a scientific point of view as an essential element of life. A look at the semantic field of the word "water" will reveal the abundance of meanings associated with this symbol: water-power, water pollution, holy water, water shortage, water fall, flood water, troubled water, waterway, to water, etc.

b) Symbols are part of the infinite reality to which they point

Symbols often express things that are beyond words, things that can only be sensed or imagined. Symbols stand for realities that are greater than we are. They bring us into contact with realities that we do not fully know, that will always remain unfathomable, no matter how much we try. Symbols unveil mysteries to us; yet these mysteries remain mysteries even after they have become "known". This applies especially to matters of faith.

Let us look again at the example of water. The sentence "Without water there can be no life!" is true in a variety of ways: first in the literal sense and then in the figurative sense. The symbol of a spring reminds us that, even in times of drought, there is hope for life. The symbol of a river points to the fact that nothing is stagnant: "everything flows!"-even our lives flow in a continuous cycle of being born, growing, and passing away. The big wide ocean reminds us of the things that may lie hidden below the surface of our lives: the treasures that must be raised and the burdens that must be buried forever in the deep. As an essential resource of life, water also reminds us of mankind's responsibility to preserve the basis of life, and of the blessing of God on which all life on earth depends every day anew. Thus, Go is referred to in the Old Testament as the "fountain of life" (Ps 36:9). For Christians, water is also a reminder of baptism in the name of the triune God who, being the creator, the sustainer and perfecter of the cosmos, manifests his grace to the individual in the person of Jesus Christ.

---

1 Das neue Fischer Lexikon in Farbe, Vol. 10, Munich 1981, p. 6387.

c) Symbols have a "life": they are born and they die

Mere signs, such as road signs or characters of the alphabet, can be invented, introduced and abolished. They do not necessarily have to have anything to do with the content for which they stand. Symbols, in contrast, are tied to their content. As substitutes, they have a kind of life story; "they are born and they die" (Paul Tillich). A Symbol may sink into oblivion or once again emerge to become topical; its meaning is not fixed forever.

The example of water: throughout the ages and in all human cultures, water has always been a symbol for religious statements and rituals of faith. Thus, water may be regarded as a symbol with a high constancy. As a result of the recent destruction of our environment, the meaning of water as a symbol of life is becoming increasingly prominent again. The more people are conscious in their everyday lives of their complete dependency on water, the stronger the symbolic charge of the word will be reflected in the area of their faith. The bible contains a near endless number of references to water with a wide range of meanings. In the first account of the Creation, the Spirit of God is described as "hovering over the waters" of the chaos (Gen. 1:2f). In God's new world, all who are thirsty may take the free gift of "the water of life" (Rev. 22:17). For the witnesses of the bible, the connection of water with judgement and grace would have been very plausible, as it reflected their everyday experience. This explains the frequent use of the symbol, particularly in fundamental theological concepts.

d) Symbols convey the meaning of reality, particularly where this is not possible through other means.

Our everyday world is determined to a large extent by ideas and behavioural patterns which are based on economic interests and the natural sciences. Logical thinking in the sense of cause and effect takes pre-eminence over everything else. Due to their variety of meanings, symbols are capable of drawing our attention to deeper realities that otherwise lie buried under the surface of mere factual contexts. They are effective where the intellect reaches its limits. They appeal to the whole person, they "give us something to think about" (Paul Ricoeur), but also something to feel and to understand more deeply. This applies especially to religious symbols. Thus, holy writings and pictures, or an encounter in a holy place allow us to partake of the holy itself, yet

429

without it being at our disposal. However, even if we venture a symbolic interpretation of everyday events, we will - often unexpectedly - discover amazing clues regarding the mystery of our world and the meaning of life. This may apply to the individual, a particular community of people, or the world as a whole.

The example of water:

We drink water; we use it to prepare food, to clean our bodies, to wash our clothes. We use water in our daily routine, time and again without giving it much thought. It often takes a disruption of the usual (natural or environmental disaster, a burst pipe) to make us realise how precious every single drop of clean water really is.

On the one hand, the symbol of water reminds us of our dependency as individual human beings, on the other hand, it helps us to recognise larger contexts in the following areas:

- the *social* ("Bread and water") - a symbol for punishment for committing a crime)
- the economic ("share" or "allocation of water"? - this addresses the issue of justice)
- the political (as the most important natural resource of the 21st century, water may be the cause of conflicts and armed hostilities)
- and the religious (constant dependency of all life on factors that are beyond human control).

e) The effects of symbols are not uniform (ambivalent)

According to Tillich, symbols have "power to edify, to order, to subvert, and to destroy".[1] This is true of individuals and the community alike. As varied as the symbols are, they can affect us in very different ways. The function of a symbol is determined largely be its acceptance and use within a given community. In the early days of Christendom, for example, the symbol of the fish[2] quickly became the sign by which Christians would recognise each other. This symbol could only spread throughout Christianity, because people experienced spiritual fellowship and social care in the name of Christ in the churches and supported one another in times of need.

---

1 P. Tillich, loc. sit., p. 5.

2The Greek word for fish (ichthus) was used as an abbreviation for Jesus Christ God's Son and Saviour.

At this point, we have to warn of a danger in the use of symbols: in the first half of the 20th century, the abuse of symbols brought terror and death. Individuals, images, and objects can be built up into idols and used as a means for inhumane propaganda and destruction.

The example of water: as we encounter it in various forms (as a gas, a liquid, and a solid), water is also a symbol of the amorphous, and of adaptation and transformation. In the form of a glassy lake, water can radiate calm and peace; in the form of the "raging sea", it can represent the coldness of the power of death. The symbol of fresh spring water can release. The sunset over the sea can keep the yearning for life and freedom alive in us. In the same way, the symbols of a "burning river" or a "dried-up well" can destroy all hope of life and a future. We also find the multifarious effects of the symbol of water in the bible. Rain is the symbol of bestowed blessings (Ps 65:11). However, in the account of the flood, it is also a symbol of the judgement of God (Gen 7:1ff), which - as expressed in the sign of the rainbow - should not be repeated again (Gen. 8, 22). By turning water into wine, Jesus reveals himself as the friend of life (Jn. 2:1-11). He uses water to wash his disciples' feet (Jn. 13:5f); in baptism, people are united with him in his death and resurrection (Rom. 6).

This variety of effects found in the biblical accounts makes it impossible to interpret the symbol of water in one particular way. The meaning of the symbol, like the substance itself, remains fluid.

In summary: Symbols are meaning-carrying objects which are at home in our finite reality, but point beyond it.

Religious symbols function as bridges between our everyday reality and the reality of God. Due to their surplus and elasticity of meaning, biblical symbols and symbols taken from the world around us are appropriate means to express the religious, without which an experience of faith can neither be grasped nor conveyed. Symbols appeal not only to the mind, but also to the emotions; they are aimed at the whole person. As symbols are situationally determined and ambiguous, it is necessary to have some guidelines for interpretation or a hermeneutic key[1] in order to ensure successful communication. Especially preachers from the Lutheran tradition may find Martin Luther's key for understanding symbols entitled "Was Christum treibet ..." a helpful guide for using symbols in a responsible way.

---

1 The Greek word hermeneuein means to understand.

First, we can differentiate four categories of symbols that occur both in the bible and in our present-day world: language, pictures, objects, and actions.[1] All four categories may be used in preaching:

- *Texts:* Biblical narratives and accounts, prayers (psalms), prophetic texts, doctrinal statements and creeds.[2] Liturgical texts and hymns. Poems, narratives from world literature and songs. Religious writings from various traditions. Current articles from daily papers and periodicals.
- *Pictures:* Religious and secular paintings, graphic arts, prints and art postcards. Photographs, slides, OHP acetates. Films and videos. Computer animations and presentations with the aid of a video beamer.
- *Objects:* Sacred objects and objets d'art found within the church (Cross/crucifix, bible, candles, baptismal font). Any objects brought along by the preacher, such as a clay pitcher, an old wagon wheel, a floppy disk, a tulip bulb.
- *Actions:* Sacred acts in baptism and Holy Communion. Symbolic gestures, such as laying-on of hands for blessing, anointing with oil, crossing, often in connection with special events (e.g. baptism/christening, confirmation/consecration, marriage, funeral). Performing elements in the propagation of the gospel, such as drama, pantomime, dance, symbolic actions, processions, silent marches.

As the above examples show, not every option is suitable for every preaching situation and every preacher. In all cases, the preacher must ensure coherence with the sermon, because not everything is sanctified by its association. The following rules have proved helpful when using symbols and objects in preaching:

a) Focusing on a symbol, on a world of symbols

If we assume that symbols touch people in their innermost being, we should ensure that we do not create a muddle of many different symbols, but rather concentrate on one symbol and its symbolic world. A deeper understanding of the symbol can only be achieved if distracting and disrupting factors are eliminated as far as possible. Now, a surfeit of symbols may actually cause the hearers to become distracted instead of helping them to concentrate on the essential.

---

1 Cf. A. Lorenzer, Das Konzil der Buchhalter – Von der Zerstörung der Sinnlichkeit, 2nd Ed., Frankfurt/Main 1992.

2 In the early days of the formation of Christain doctrines the Creeds were referred to as symbols.

Nowadays in the European countries, we encounter a situation which is aggravated by the fact that we have to cope with an inflation of symbols, for it is not only in church that symbols are used. The advertising industry and the electronic media have also discovered the power of the symbolic. Especially religious symbols are being used (the cross, modified bible quotations, persons dressed in church garments). Trend researcher Matthias Horx states: "The more society turns away from church, the more common religious symbols become in popular culture".[1]

If we want to regain lost Christian symbols for our church activities, we must first and foremost apply the rule: less is more! It is only then that the precious can be recognised as being precious. This of course requires confidence on the preacher's part that the symbol will convey its message.

In his standard work on the use of symbols in teaching published in 1982, the Roman Catholic religious educationalist Hubertus Halbfas voiced sharp criticism of the "thematic problem-orientated religious education" that was prevalent at the time. His admonition regarding the appropriate use of symbols in preaching and teaching still applies:

"What we have been left with is unrefined. All kinds of media are used to the point of overkill. They are no longer carefully explored step by step in respect of their own message; instead a set of predetermined thematic questions is answered. That way, texts, pictures, films, and audiotapes are abused as mere 'pegs', 'visual aids', 'materials for discussion', 'examples for application', while often being deprived of the dignity of having their own meanings. The most shameful example of this is the way in which biblical texts are used as an alibi for discussing a particular issue. As a result, these 'media' are employed thematic functional manner: general perspectives, vague clichés, and sweeping statements prevail. The diligent search for deeper meanings and nuances, for gentle whispers and the unutterable has become the exception."[2]

---

1 Matthias Horx, Trendbuch II, 2nd Ed., Düsseldorf 1996, p. 123.

2 H. Halbfas, Das dritte Auge, Düsseldorf 1982.

433

b) Introducing the symbol

In our fast and ever-changing world, we need to reduce the stimuli to our senses if we want to deal with symbols in a deeper way. We will not be touch in our innermost being in passing and especially not on command. Preachers should therefore not simply thrust a symbol upon the hearers, but gradually introduce them to it. This can be done already when welcoming the congregation to the service, by saying (a few!) linking words in between the scripture readings, but especially in the sermon itself. The preacher then takes his/her hearers step by step along the journey of the sermon and stop for a rest at suitable vantage points.

In the context of using symbols, it has proved useful to prepare the environment accordingly. Such preparation may include appropriate room decorations, purposeful seating arrangements, suitable music, etc. The purpose is to get the attention of the hearers and help them to focus. Experience shows that this can best be attained in an atmosphere of silent reflection.

> *For a sermon on the marriage at Cana (Jn. 2:1-11) in which I discussed the topic "change is possible", I had some clay pitchers put in various places around the church. Beside the pulpit stood a thin pedestal. At the beginning of the sermon, I placed a large clay pitcher on this pedestal and, in a meditative manner, drew some connections between the symbol of the clay pitcher and human life. I then invited the hearers to connect inwardly with the symbol, by asking themselves questions like: What does the pitcher of my life look like? What is inside? By what might the pitcher of my life be threatened (hammer)? Has water ever been turned into wine in my life through God's working? Where is change required, and what can I do myself to change? In the course of the sermon, I brought out the promise of the biblical story: in God's presence change is possible.*

c) Confidence in the symbol

Dealing with the symbol in a deeper way requires time. If the preacher progresses too quickly with the sermon, the hearers may cease to think about the meaning of the symbol. It is also important for the preacher to trust that the symbol will speak for itself, or that it is taken into service by the Spirit of God. Rash, definitive explanations restrain the hearers in their thoughts and emotions. In contrast, careful, expectant moderation encourages them to assimilate actively the content of the symbol.

The use of symbols in preaching appeals, especially to the hearers' imagination. Any minor divergence from the anticipated (e.g. applying the symbol within an unusual context) will normally recapture the hearers' attention. Stark contrasts (introducing a counter-symbol; destroying the symbol) provoke and open up new horizons of understanding to those who receive them. However, if we take this too far we must expect opposition on the part of the hearers.

d) Un-introducing the symbol

If we preach about the wedding at Cana, we must not leave the hearers behind in Galilee. Preaching means making the journey from the here and now to the text, and back! Consequently, a responsible use of symbols entails accompanying the hearers back from their encounter with the symbol to everyday reality.

If we fail to do this, we run the risk that, in the end, everything will remain as it was. Then the Sunday morning church service would be of no significance for everyday Christian service. (Rom. 12:1)

One purpose of accompanying the hearers on their journey back to everyday life is to make them aware of the limitations of their encounter with the symbol.[1]

On the one hand, it is clear that no text, picture, or symbol is capable of saying everything, nor does it have to say everything. On the other hand, some symbols can trigger quite different or even contrary trains of thought. If such ambiguous symbols are used in preaching without any qualifications, they can cause the interpretation of the sermon content to become arbitrary.

This may occur, for example, in the case of a stone, which may be both a positive symbol for steadfastness and perpetuity and a negative symbol for coldness and violence.

---

1 Religious educational theory has adopted the term Symbolkritik (symbol criticism)

We must therefore ask ourselves how this symbol must be interpreted within the framework of the gospel, or more precisely: how it relates to the pivotal symbol of Christianity, the cross. Furthermore, the preacher must consider what prospects may result from the encounter with the symbol for both the individual and the community as a whole.

There are several ways in which a symbol that has been introduced can be un-introduced again. This can be achieved in the sermon itself: In the case of the above example, by saying farewell to Cana. The hearers may be asked to write what they gained from the service on a piece of paper and thus take it home with them in black and white. Or the preacher suggests how that which was said and experienced in the service might affect his/her own life or the lives of the hearers over the coming days and weeks.

Another way of un-introducing symbols is by inviting personal contributions from individual hearers in which they relate personal faith experiences relating to the symbol. Experiences with the symbol may also be brought before God in the intercessory prayers.

e) Securing the harvest

The propagation of the gospel occurs under the promise of God. We may therefore expect God to give his people a deep, life changing understanding when they reflect on the biblical word and the symbols related to it. The fact that this understanding will also prove its power in everyday life is also a spiritual process. We are by no means disputing this, when we draw attention to the psychological realisation that symbols (especially objects) serve to reiterate what is said and help the hearers to remember it.

Psychological research has proved that the average person will retain less than 20% of what s/he has merely heard. If the hearing is accompanied by seeing, this figure increases to more than 50%. 70% of what a person says will normally remain in his/her memory. If seeing and speaking are accompanied by doing, the figure rises above 90%.[1] Thus, it would make sense when using the learning psychology model to add a consolidation phase after the solution phase.

---

1 Cf. K. Witzenbacher, Praxis der Unterrichtsvorbereitung, Munich 1994.

An example of this might be to give each member of the congregation a copy of the symbol used in the sermon (e.g. miniature clay pitcher: "Change is possible-Jn. 2:1-11)" at the end of the service to take home as a reminder. If the hearer then keeps looking at the little clay pitcher, for example on his/her desk, it will serve to reiterate the sermon content.

One could even go further by suggesting concrete action in the sermon to be realised in the form of a project. Examples of this might be:

• carrying out a neighbourhood project or a children's program together with other Christians in the area.

• forming a partnership with a small rural church.

Conclusion:

In the above, we discussed the possibilities of using symbols in preaching. In doing so, we showed the limitations of this endeavour. Symbols should by no means be looked upon as a cure-all for the believers' speechlessness, which is often lamented.

Nonetheless, the language of symbols, the mother tongue of faith, is indispensable for communicating of the gospel with the purpose of attesting God's presence in the world in a relevant and comprehensible way.

We have now discussed some of the most important issues of worship and preaching. Thank you for your patience and attentiveness, your questions and remarks from which I have gained impulses and encouragement to take home to my church and work at Reutlingen.

May the God of love and peace guide you and us all as we become effective tools in God's hand for a ministry sharing God's grace and seeking love at the place where God wants us to serve.

Peace be with you all!

MODULE 6a: WORSHIP & PREACHING-PRACTICAL

(Mr Peter Worrell LP)

LECTURE 1: WHAT IS WORSHIP?

'Christian worship is the most momentous, the most urgent, the most glorious action that can take place in human life.' (Karl Barth)
'The calling of the Methodist Church is to respond to the gospel of God's love in Christ and to live out its discipleship in worship and mission.'
Hebrews 11: 6 reminds us, for worship to be possible *"... anyone who comes to God must believe that he exists and that he rewards those who search for him."* (NEB)

WORSHIP IS:

From the Anglo-Saxon *weorthscipe:* worthship-worship–to attribute worth to something; homage or grateful submission.
sheret/douleia/abodah/lautreia: service as given by a slave or hired servants. Implies total surrender c.f. Luke 17:7-10, an act of allegiance or belonging.
Shachah: a Hebrew word meaning bowing down before God in deep humility and respect Psalm 95:6
Proskuneō: to go forward, to kiss, to act with reverence (John 4:23)
reverence and awe (*phobos*), often used by pagans in relation to their gods as fear and trembling. In OT more drawing back in admiring respect though dread, shaking, trembling, terror may also be appropriate responses.
'When Christians imply that reverence is essentially a matter of one's demeanor in church services, they show little understanding of the Bible's teaching on this subject' *(Peterson D, Engaging with God p17)*

SOME QUOTATIONS:

- the reason for our existence and destiny-*M.Pilavachi*
- an inbuilt condition of our humanity-*LaMar Boschman*
- subversive and counter cultural-*Marva J. Dawn*
- the response of the creature to the Eternal-*E.Underhill*
- to take off the masks and be genuine with God-*M. Witt*
- a gift between lovers-*C. Welton Gaddy*
-

A priesthood orientated theology of worship, based on the liturgy of the Temple in Jerusalem and heavily dependent on the role of the Levitical priesthood. The Holy One is encountered in the temple at Jerusalem. The glory of the Lord resided in the Temple's sanctuary rather than in the people and there is a sharp distinction between the sacred and profane. A few significant differences in Ezekiel (44) (based on Solomon's Temple) emphasise the separation and safeguard from defilement both the holiness of God and the holiness of his dwelling place. Only Levitical priests, only the sons of Zadok are allowed. The king may come as far as the gateway and the people must remain outside. Holiness is not to be touched by un-authorized hands.

A people orientated theology of worship, mainly based on the wider platform of everyday life and more people orientated. Not withdrawal but the faithful discharge of one's duties to one's fellows - obedience to the voice of the Lord; faithfulness to his covenant; caring for the hungry, the thirsty, the widow, the orphan, the stranger, the destitute and the oppressed for the sake of the Lord. The arena as wide as life itself – not a cult of an unapproachable God, but a celebration of Immanuel 'God who is with us'.

c.f. Ex 19:5-6; Deut. 10:12-22; Ps 50:7-23; 51:17-19; Amos 2:6-8; 5:12-15,21-25; Hos 6:4-10; 8:11-14; Is 1L10-17;; 56:6-8; 60,61; Mic 6:6-8; Jer 7:1-12, 22-23; Zech 8:14-23; 1 Sam 15:22-23.The song Moses-Exodus 15:1-18 *(see Encounter with God-Forrester, McDonald, Tellini T&T Clark International)*

The songs of Moses and Miriam-Ex 15:1-18; Ex 15:21
The great song book of the psalms
There is recorded worship for special occasions when ark brought back to Jerusalem by David. 1 Chron. 15:25 when the ark is brought into Solomon's temple 2 Chron 5:7
The songs from the early chapters of St. Luke's gospel
a) of Zech 1:67-79 b) of Mary 1:46-55 c) of Simeon 2:29-32
Acts 2:42; 1 Corinthians 12-14; (more in worship patterns)
In Romans 12, Paul: offer your bodies as a spiritual sacrifice.
In Philippians we worship in spirit and glory in Christ 3:33
The great hymn in Revelation 5.11

"Worship is not to seek spiritual gratification as an end although in worship we are spiritually nourished."

Peterson D-Engaging with God (p17) 'something is seriously wrong when people equate spiritual gratification with worship'

Kendrick G-Condemns this attitude: 'as if the highest achievement of our whole pilgrimage on earth was to enter some kind of praise-induced ecstasy'.

In groups let us look at:

1. **Psalm 95** What does the Psalm tells us about Jewish worship? What does the worship mean? What are the feelings? What actions are going on? Worship in spirit and in truth?

2. **John 4:4-26** Worship in spirit and in truth?

    'Authentic worship still inspires the prophetic vision and attracts people to follow Christ, because it opens new windows onto God's glory and goodness, and provides a holistic context in which the whole of the human personality can begin to respond to everything that God is'. (John Drane, Evangelism for a New Age)

BIBLE WORSHIP HAS BEEN SUMMARISED AS:

God centred; Often noisy in spite of Elijah on Mt Sinai; **Often led**; **A whole body activity**-David danced, the musicians played and sang, the elders fell down; **A celebration**–of what God has done, and who God is. In the NT of who Jesus is. **Being in the presence of God.**

The Bible raises issues between true and false worship c.f. Amos 5:21, 23, 24   What are our idols? Where do we put our trust?

Different aspects of Christian worship[1]

1. Worship as a service to God Many Christian communities have understood public worship as a service to God, a duty which God's human children perform in grateful obedience to the One who is the source of their life and their salvation.

2. Worship as the mirror of heaven For many Christians, worship that takes place in church is an attempt to duplicate, to recapitulate, the worship of God that takes place eternally in heaven. A different dimension of time and space.

3. Worship as affirmation Many Christians are convinced that the primary purpose of Christian worship is to affirm, inspire and support believers in the Christian vocation.

---

1 Susan White, Groundwork of Christian Worship, Epworth:1977

4. Worship as communion Many other Christians believe that in their common worship they are making their relationship with God and with the Christian community a visible, audible and tangible reality.

5. Worship as proclamation Those who think of worship primarily as proclamation wish to highlight the idea that worship is the principal place where Christians gather to make their public affirmation and witness; to declare the mighty acts of God in the power of Christ, crucified and risen.

6. Worship as an arena of transcendence To enter the presence of the living God in worship ... is a highly dangerous enterprise, in which the awesome holiness, majesty and power of God may at any time break into our experience and transform us. A little nervous–well catch your breath! Exodus 3:5 Moses–take off your shoes.
Rudolph Otto and the 'Idea of the Holy'.

To summarise:

The church is called to offer worship to the glory and praise of God

A 'holy priesthood offering spiritual sacrifices acceptable to God through Jesus Christ':'to proclaim the mighty acts' of God. 1 Pe 2:5,9

All true worship is God centred. As we approach the eternal God, Father, Son and Holy Spirit, we are moved to offer our praise and to confess our sins, confident of God's mercy and forgiveness. God's acts of grace and love in creation and salvation are recounted and celebrated, and we respond with thanksgiving, intercession and the offering of our lives.

Worship is a gracious encounter between God and the Church. God speaks to us, especially through scripture read and proclaimed through hymns and prayers and acts of dedication. Worship is the work of the whole people of God. Those who lead worship are called to encourage and, with the help of the Holy Spirit, to enable the whole Body of Christ to participate fully. *(Methodist Sources)*

What is my worship? Psalm 24 Everything in it (v1-2); Clean hands and pure heart (v3-6); Who is he? (v7-10)

While in the heavenly work we join, Thy glory be our whole design,
Thy glory, not our own: Still let us keep our end in view,
And still the pleasing task pursue, To please our God alone   *C Wesley*

(Source Acknowledgements with thanks: Local Preachers' Manual Ian White; Susan White (not-related!)

1. SOME WORSHIP PATTERNS IN THE OLD TESTAMENT

a. The sacrificial system in Leviticus
i) Whole-burnt offerings: (Lev 1:3-9) Used on various occasions, including the twice daily sacrifice offered for all the people in the time of Jesus. Usually a sheep or goat or bull-a male without defect. All of it was to be prepared and burnt-as an aroma pleasing to God. Genesis 22 tells how Abraham felt called to offer his son - a story that not only explores the meaning of faith but expresses the cost of sacrifice and Israelite rejection of human sacrifice.)

ii) Communion sacrifice: (Lev 3:1-5) Where all present share in the flesh of the sacrificial victim, a time of fellowship. In 1 Samuel 9:11-14, Samuel presides over such a sacrifice for the whole city. There was the idea of maintaining right relations with God and they included offerings made in thanksgiving, in fulfilment of a vow or a freewill offering.

iii) Sin/Guilt Offerings: (Lev 4-5) The actual link between sacrifice and forgiveness is not too strong. For example there are examples of people being forgiven without sacrifice. However, with sacrifices for such things as cleansing after childbirth and cleansing after a skin disease, it is likely that the link was one of purification- the animal was consumed / burnt up as a picture of uncleanliness being removed. Note also the provision for unintentional wrongdoing. (Lev 4.22, 27; Lev 5.15, 17) and the person must still make restitution.

A debate about the true meaning of sacrifice.
Proverbs 21:27 speaks of the sacrifice of the wicked as an abomination. Look at 1 Samuel 15:17-23; Hosea 6:6; Amos 5:21-24; Micah 6:6-8; Psalm50:1-23 Do these passages reject sacrifice outright? Do they offer a test for worship? How do we apply this to Christian worship?

b. Festivals
i) The Feast of the Passover Deut 16:1-8 Not an agricultural festival but recalled the deliverance from Egypt. It did not only look back to Ex 12.1-13.16, but by time of Jesus looks forward to future deliverance. Lamb is sacrificed for God's redemption of His people.

ii) The Feast of unleavened bread-Ex 23:15; Deut 16:16 Probably marked the end of the barley harvest but had links with the Passover.

iii) The Feast of Weeks-Ex 34:33 Lev 23:15-16 Deut. 16:10, 16 Seven weeks after Passover/Unleavened Bread (Pentecost). Never gained the same importance as Tabernacles but some groups associated it with Sinai and the giving of the law.

IV) The Feast of Tabernacles (Festival of Booths; Tents). Lev 23:39 This celebrated the gathering of the grape harvest (Ex. 23:16) and was a time of rejoicing (Deut. 16:13-15). Worshippers built booths and slept outside for seven days–Linked to open-air life of the wilderness.

v) Passover was a home celebration, but the three pilgrimage festivals would have involved going to a shrine. Later Solomon's Temple became the only place where sacrifice could be made and Jerusalem would have been crowded (Mk 11:11; 14:14) After the destruction of the temple and the end of sacrifice Passover continued and continues today-celebrated in the home as a celebration of the deliverance of God's people from oppression.

vi) Yom Kippur (Day of Atonement)-in the autumn-see Lev 16-but there are not very many references to it. Note: It is still the most holy day in the Jewish calendar-the day when prayers are offered for the forgiveness of the Jewish nation.

c. The Synagogue and Home

Synagogue worship included

i) The Shema (=hear) (c.f. Deut 6:4-9; Deut 11:13-21; Num 15:37-41)
ii) The Amidah (standing alone prayer–it combines praise and supplication (Also called Tefillah or Eighteen Benedictions
iii) The reading of the Law. From the New Testament we see that there might also be a reading from the prophets or an exposition.
iv) Blessings and perhaps the singing of psalms.

Worship at Home

Jewish people realise the importance of family devotion; celebrate festivals at home; and know the importance of roles for the children and rituals (Mezuzah) The religion changed from *Haggadah* to *Halakah*-from ritual to lifestyle.

Early Christians continued to worship in the temple, many observed the Jewish festivals and as distinctive Christian worship developed it was deeply influenced by Jewish forms and language. Also Christians gathered in their homes and this continued throughout the New Testament period. In the first two centuries there were no church buildings–in Jerusalem, a large house belonging to Mary (Acts 12:12) (upper room in Acts 1:13?). But if Acts 2:41, 4:4 is correct then there must have been numerous groups meeting together. There were house churches in Corinth–Romans 16:23, Ephesus-1 Cor 16:9; Troas-Acts 20:8, Rome–Romans 16:5; Laodicea–Colossians 4:15; Colossae-Philemon v2. There was informality and intimacy-Rom16:23 describes Gaius as host to the whole church at Corinth. Acts 2:42-those who were baptized devoted themselves to the apostles' teaching and fellowship, to the breaking of bread and prayers. It is generally assumed that those who participate in worship are baptized though recognised that sometimes outsiders may be present. (1 Cor 14:24)

a) Jesus and the Temple Luke–Temple as 'my Father's house' (1 2:49) Matt., Mark and Luke all portray Jesus as going to the temple. He is never said to have prayed there or offered sacrifice. (Matt 21:14-23; Mark 12:35; Luke 19:47; 21:37; Christ as High Priest-Hebrews Christ is the key-foundation stone of the new temple not made by hands and composed of living beings.

In Acts 5:6, Stephen fiercely criticizes Temple worship quoting Ex 32:4-6; Amos 5:25-27; Is 6:1 and ends by referring to the Temple as an idolatrous artefact, upon which he was immediately put to death.

i)   **History of Baptism?**
ii) **Prayer and praise were an essential part of synagogue and Christian worship** Acts 22:42-47; 1 Cor 11:4, 5; 1 Tim 2:1, 2, 8
iii) **Ministry of the word** 1Tim 4:13-public reading of scripture, preaching, teaching. Reading and exposition of OT passages.
iv) **The Lord's Supper** 1 Cor 11:23-26; Matt 26:26-30; Mk 14:22-26; Luke 22:14-20
     Meals to remember – when Jesus was alive
     Meals to remember – after the resurrection
v) Liturgical aspect
Echoes of Christian hymns Rev. 15:3-4; 19:1-2; 2 Tim 2:11-13; Eph 5:14; 1 Tim 3:16; Phil 2:6-11 (perhaps inspired writing by Paul)
Brief creeds–Romans 10:9; c.f. Romans 1:3f; 1 Cor 15:3ff

Benedictions 1 Cor. 16:23 2 Cor. 13:14; Gal. 6:18; Phil. 4:23; 1 Thess. 5:28; 2 Thess 3:18; Philemon v.25

vi) Importance of

The Lord's Prayer At the heart of Christian prayer is the Aramaic word Abba-an intimate family term c.f. Mk 14:36; Jesus taught his disciples–my Father Lk 11:2 c.f. Rom 8:15; Gal 4:6

The first day of the week Acts 20:7; The Lord's Day (Rev 1:10)

In the letters we can hear the church at worship Eph 1:3-10; Gal 1:3-5; Rom 16:27; 1 Pe 1:3; 5:11,14. *'much of the New Testament is filled with the fervour of worship'* Moule

vii) Charismatic worship e.g. Church at Corinth. Contribute-a piece of teaching, another a hymn, a creative expression of praise.. Someone would speak in tongues; another would interpret. Another would prophesy. A marvelous sense of freedom but this was abused.

So Paul argues, if something is inspired by the Holy Spirit

Does it proclaim the Lordship of Christ? (1 Cor 12:3)

Does it build up the church? (1 Cor 14:3, 4, 5, 6, 12, 17, 19, 26)

Give scope to the spirit's work (1Cor 14:26-33, 39) but test what is of the spirit (1 Cor 14:29)

Paul also encouraged churches at Thessalonica and Rome to use spiritual gifts (1 Thess. 5:19; Rom 12:8)

John urged readers to test prophetic utterances (1 John 4:1-6)

Luke refers to prophets in Antioch, Caesarea and Judea (Acts 11:28; 13:1; 21:9f)

Even though 1 Timothy is more structured, men are encouraged to contribute (1 Tim 2:8-12, c.f. 4.14)

The New Testament saw no tension between the use of liturgy and the free expression free of spiritual gifts. Freedom testifies to God's grace; liturgy recalls us to the fundamental truths of God's saving actions. **Apart from in the Lord's Prayer,** there is no reference to the confession of sin.

viii) Pattern of Christian worship

A community celebration	-A response to God's saving acts
The Abba relationship	-The presence of Christ, the risen Lord
In the field of the Holy Spirit	-Should be decent and orderly
Intelligible	-Reflect the truth as revealed in Jesus.
Build up the community	-Transcend time

No divide between worship and life.

3. LIFESTYLE AS A PATTERN OF WORSHIP

Continuous Praise; Speech; Actions; Obedience; Presence; Our worship leading should be marked by our leading people to where we are used to being.

4. LECTIONARY

It is important in the worship life of the Church to maintain a feeling about the Christian Year. Lectionaries allow for worship to cover the major themes of our faith as well as to make sure we are celebrating Jesus' birth and not his death at Christmas time. Also makes sure we don't miss out difficult subjects!

What advantages and disadvantages of using the lectionary?

> *'In early worship, an overriding importance was given to praise, proclamation, prayer and communion. Without these elements some would argue it is not historical worship. Some would want to say that as Church History has followed this pattern for centuries we should maintain this pattern today as well.'*

'How shall I thank thee for the grace On me and all mankind bestowed?
O that my every breath were praise!   O that my heart were filled with God!
My heart would then with love o'erflow, And all my life thy glory show.' (CW)

LECTURE 3: THE CONTENT OF WORSHIP

"Worship is running in the spirit up the aisle and being caught up in the arms of God"
"Worship paints the portrait of God" (John Taylor)
"What makes a service an act of worship, is actually not the ingredients but rather a variety of movements, moods or themes in worship, which express different aspects of our relationship with God." (Ian White)

Elements of Worship

Traditionally a service of worship seeks to follow a threefold pattern:
1. Approach to God 1. The preparation   1. Adoration
2. The Word of God 2. The ministry of the Word 2. Celebration
3. Response to God 3. The response   3. Transformation

Recognize the presence of God.   Adore, worship – **God is great**
Recognize ourselves and each other.   Confess, **God Hears**
Be assured of forgiveness.   **God is merciful and loving**

THE WORD OF GOD

The Scriptures – OT/Gospel and Epistle   **God speaks**
Extra canonical reading/ Poem/ music for reflection
Sermon – exposition   **Telling the Old, Old Story**

THE RESPONSE

Thanksgiving
Prayer for others and ourselves
Dedication
Dismissal/Blessing

PRAYERS

"Many people define the church at worship as 'the church at prayer'.
Some go back to the beginning; others are being said for the first time.
A wide variety of sources and many layers of Christian history"

A CALL TO WORSHIP IS A CALL TO CELEBRATION OF:

a) The Old Testament festivals
b) Heaven (celebrations in Revn) & human celebrations in the
   parables
c) Creation, of life, of power, of unity
d) Other people's gifts and abilities, of prophecy
e) God's presence
f) What is at the heart of the way of Christ?

Jesus entered the world on a high note of jubilation: 'I bring you good news of great joy'. Celebration brings joy into our lives, and joy makes us strong. But listen to Richard Foster in Celebration of Discipline:

> *"Joy is not found in singing a particular kind of music, or getting*
> *with the right kind of group, or even exercising the charismatic gifts*
> *of the Spirit, good as all those may be. Joy is found in obedience."*
> *(R Foster, Celebration of Discipline London: Hodder & Stoughton,*
> *1980 p 163)*

447

a) The French word "adorer" means 'to love'. This is the mood of adoration. It is saying, "I love you, God" and spending time enjoying that love. In any relationship, time must be given to enjoying the presence of the other person. It is important to spend time in God's love, not asking, not demanding, but just being

b) Adoration involves all our feeling and emotion, which is why the language of adoration is in poetry, music, art, imagination.

c) Adoration is when we are overcome by the majesty of God, the mystery of God and the undeserved love of God.

Activity: Write a prayer of Adoration

Then question: Does it centre on God—on his glory, greatness and love? Would it help worshippers be lifted into God?

PRAISE

a) Is a celebration of God and perhaps the most spontaneous form of prayer? Rev 19:6; Ps 150

b) A doxology—from the Greek word *doxologia* meaning words of praise.

'Praise God from whom all blessings flow, Praise him all creatures here below.
Praise him above all heavenly hosts. Praise Father, Son, and Holy Ghost.'

c) Another form of doxology often used at the end of psalms

'Glory to the Father and to the Son and to the Holy Spirit ...

d) Promptings to Praise—God's creation; acts; love; mercy; compassion
e) Greater doxology-'Glory to God' at beginning of the Lord's Supper.

PENITENCE WHICH INCORPORATES CONFESSION AND FORGIVENESS

c.f. Is 6:5, Neh 9, Job 42, Ps 51, Lk 3:3, Rev 2:4 But we are all human so can we expect anything else-so not a list of excuses!

Balance of coming to God through Jesus to confess and to receive an **assurance of forgiveness, of restoration and of wholeness.**

Confession can come—At the beginning, as a consequence of adoration, to 'clear the decks' or after the sermon as a response.

2. THANKSGIVING

a) A response to recognising God's active love–the basis for action. c.f. Eph 1.3-14; Revn 5.

b) Focuses on what God does, has done and is doing for the community of faith.

c) Roots in the Jewish past. Jesus was a worshipping Jew; he went to the synagogue on the Sabbath (Luke 4:16-30), prayed at the Temple on holy days (Matt. 21:23-27), celebrated festival meals at home. (Lk 22:7-23)

d) Thanksgiving–God had always been known through concrete acts in the life and history of the community of faith.

e) The Song of Moses (Ex.15:1-18) is an extended prayer of thanksgiving.

f) The primary event for which Christians give thanks is the life death and resurrection of Jesus Christ.

g) Perhaps the best place for thanksgiving is in the response. When God's mighty and saving acts have been proclaimed in the Ministry of the Word then it is natural to say "Thanks".

h) It can come after both adoration and confession.

Activity: **Compose a prayer of thanksgiving.** Examine thanksgiving prayers in the Methodist Service Book; See also MHB 10, 406, 524

3. INTERCESSION

Remembering always that Christ prays for us, part of our response is to pray for others. c.f. Rom 8.33, 1 Tim 2:1, rooted in the confidence that God's ultimate will is that all will be healed, redeemed, freed. Liturgical intercessions are also called the prayers of the people.

Areas

a) the church universal

b) for peace and justice

c) for our own country and community

d) for everyone in need, for specific people and situations

e) prayers of intercession often end by remembering that we are one church, on earth and in heaven

Activity: Make a prayer of intercession now. What specific needs would you include?

a)   Think about what you are asking God to do
b)   Imagine prayer not as an automatic machine, but an exploration into the mystery of God's activity and will
c)   While we assume God's will in general terms, (justice, peace, healing) we do not tell God specifically what should be done.
d)   At the heart of prayer is 'not my will, but yours' **Consider:**
•   A response between each section?
•   A musical response e.g. Taizé or local

4. PETITION

Prayers for ourselves-at the heart of Christian petition is the overwhelming sense of the trustworthiness of God. (Matt. 6:11, 7:9-11) Careful what we ask for–no prayer can be selfish. Thanksgiving to petition–'Give to me Lord a thankful heart' C. Micklem

5. DEDICATION

Every act of worship should open into new commitment, deeper faith and a stronger commitment to serve. Take my life … (MHB 400) How would you develop this into a prayer of dedication?

ADDITIONAL NOTES ON PRAYERS–PUBLIC AND PRIVATE

Private devotion–speaking to God, telling God intimately what we feel, and think and have done. Perhaps saying a 'daily office'. In public, we are seeking to enable everyone to share and own the prayers.
a) Prayers easy to follow, poetic with images people can grasp
b) It is good to give opportunities for response
c) Times of silence for reflection are good
d) Contributions from members of the congregation?
e) Avoid the 'I' word

ANTI-STRUCTURAL PRAYER

Tongues/glossolalia

a) Can be speaking in the air (1 Cor. 13:9b)
b) For building up the church (1 Cor. 14:12)
c) Need for interpretation (1 Cor. 14:15-16)

But note the place given by Paul to this and other 'worship gifts' in the context of 1 Cor. 12-14

Silence
Provision of space within which the spirit of God may move; Waiting for God to speak; Contemplation on the word of God

Written or Extempore Prayers? Discuss the advantages and disadvantages of extempore prayer.

Further Thoughts
- **Worship emerges from life**–people bring their everyday experience into worship.
- **We worship in community**-to encourage, inspire and build each other up.
- **Worship means being honest with God**–sharing our problems, our questions, our doubts.
- **Openness to God's Presence–not 'God in the wings'** It is important _**not**_ to assume that we can come into God's presence, deafen him with our requests and get out before he manages to get a word in edgeways.
- **Time for ministry–worship changes us.**
- **Preparing ourselves to lead. Keep our:**
  Heart right before God:
  Minds free from distractions before leading worship**:**
  Motives and ego in God's hands.
  Actions as those who are sharing in worship
  Leader **Together** with the congregation.

'Those who lead worship are called to encourage and, in the power of Spirit, to enable the whole Body of Christ to participate fully'

LECTURE 4: OPEN TO THE WORD

'The Bible speaks of itself in many different ways–as speech, life, lamp, hammer, food, seed, sword, fire, cleansing water, mirror–and we find many ways of communicating truth, from the visual representation of the Temple imagery, through enacted stories and liturgical drama, to communal reading before worshipping communities and in family settings (Deut 5:1-3, Ex 13:3-8, Josh 24, 2 Kings 22-23, 2 Chron 3-5, Neh 8:1-8, Col 4:16, 1 Thess 5:27, Rev 22:18)' (Sampson p.24)

What does the Bible mean to me?

We read and study the Bible to:
Become familiar with the teachings
Know the saving power of Jesus
Become effective ministers of the Word
See God's truth for the present age
Act on God's truth–for justice, positive change in society, the environment, and serving–Mt 25:31-46
Become like Jesus

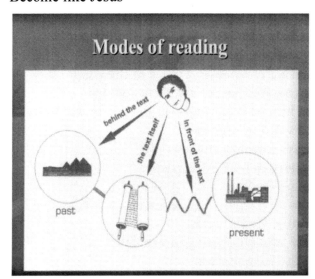

"Of all the possibilities of transformation that one may experience, the most fulfilling is to be transformed into the likeness of Christ as we gaze on him in growing intimacy through prayer, the word and obedience. We have no higher calling than to become like Christ."

(Rt Rev Emmanuel Egbunu, Bishop of Lokoja)

What is our attitude to the Bible in worship? (from Gerald West)
Not a dead letter but a life-giving, transforming force
To be shared creatively, powerfully and liberally!
Think of the response of Israel to God; individuals to Christ, our congregations, you and me

Bible Readings
Words of Introduction can help
Members of the congregation–perhaps dramatized
Congregational Psalm
Music for reflection

NB Page numbers in this lecture refer to book on preaching given to students: *('Learning to Preach Today' Hartner/Eschmann Cliff College Publishing)* **Editor's note: See also Module 6 on Preaching.**

✓ A tradition going back through the centuries.
✓ Old Testament–How beautiful upon the mountains are the feet of him who brings good tidings (Isaiah 52:7)
✓ New Testament–John the Baptist Mk 1:4 John, baptising in the desert-preaching a baptism for the forgiveness of sins.
✓ Jesus in Luke 4:21, reading from Isaiah 61. "The spirit of the Lord is upon me, because he has anointed me to preach good news to the poor
✓ The apostles-"And every day in the Temple and at home they did not cease teaching and preaching Jesus as the Christ" (Acts 5:42)
✓ Paul–'For Christ did not send me to baptize but to preach the gospel' 1 Cor. 1:17
✓ Sermons in Acts-Acts 2, 7, 10:1-11:18, 13:13-41, 17:16-34, 20:17-38, 26
✓ The tradition continues in the early church–Origen earned title of 'Father of the Christian Sermon'

Importance of:
kerygma-message of freedom and reconciliation through Christ.
didache-teaching, implications of the truths declared in the kerygma. 'If religion is grace, ethics is gratitude'. Redemption implies a new way of living.
katachesis-precise teaching about belief and action. Catechism.
paraklesis or exhortation (c.f. 1 Cor 14:3)-particularly the role of the prophet to build up the congregation's faith.

Debate in recent years about the value of preaching, but positive view
• Faith comes from hearing the message (Rom 10:17)
• Faith comes from preaching – Martin Luther

"Our faith depends on someone telling us the good news of God and his people."
"Preaching is a matter of joy, of passion and of enthusiasm."

N.B. WESLEY QUADRILATERAL: 1 BIBLE 2 TRADITION 3 EXPERIENCE 4 REASON

1. Preaching is proclaiming the Bible's witness to the work of God in Christ
2. Preaching reinterprets for today the tradition of the church about its faith
3. Preaching conveys truth through the experience of the preacher and evokes faith within the experience of the congregation
4. By reason, preaching seeks to discover the relevance of the faith to daily life

Preachers are
1. **Heralds**-announcing what God has done, is doing and waiting to do
2. **Witnesses**-telling the truth out of our own experience of god
3. **Messengers**-bringing living words from a living God
4. **Interpreters**-seeking to translate the insights contained in the Bible in words and stories which are relevant to life today
5. **Evangelists**-seeking a verdict on behalf of God who has called us
6. **Prophets**-seeing society and the world as God sees it

Exercise My current definition of preaching is …?Preachers are?

Many different kinds of sermon

Proclamation: not basically an intellectual argument–telling the story
Exhortation: challenge, 'get up off your bottom' type of sermon. Pricks conscience, exposes prejudice, sets a vision of God's kingdom.
Encourage: importance of encouragement and affirmation, often at the feeling level. Affirm the faith a congregation already has.
Teaching: explain some point of faith which helps a congregation; strengthens church members and enables them to give reason for their faith & hope (1Pe 3:15) Appeals to mind, contains much information.
Rebuke: perhaps occasionally necessary but beware, God acts by grace, not by nagging.
Pastoral: (2 Cor. 1:3f) more assuring than informative or appellative. Conveys a sense of security and speaks to the heart.
Comfort: consolation; many need encouragement; people bereaved. Colin Morris– *'to comfort the afflicted and afflict the comfortable'*
Evangelistic: a means of bringing people to a personal faith in Jesus Christ and to respond to the redeeming love of God. A highly personal approach to bring a positive response.

Prophetic: Emphasises that the sermon must be relevant to the present day and challenge the hearers to action. Societal and political controversies, ethical and social issues addressed from a Christian perspective. Sometimes confrontational and appellative elements.

Dialogue: bringing the church into the preaching process through discussions before or after the sermon, questions, a preaching team.

Narrative: The most suitable way to tell God's story with his people is in narrative–this type of sermon requires much thorough preparation.

????Pitfalls for the Preacher to avoid?

THE SERMON

"A sermon is a bridge between the Biblical world and today's world; a two way direction, testing today's experience with the Bible and the Bible with today's experience." (Rev. Dr R. Jones)

PREACHING IS IN GOD'S SPIRIT. (See pp 41-95)

✓ The spirit is with us in the study-can be tedious and hard work
✓ The spirit is with us in the pulpit
✓ The spirit is in the ears of the listener. A passage from scripture-chosen or lectionary

PREACHER

✓ What does the text say to me?
✓ Is it difficult or easy to understand?
✓ Do I feel comfortable with it?
✓ Does it challenge, confront or confirm?
✓ What are the key words and ideas?

PEOPLE

✓ Think of the hearers; what is this particular congregation's experience?
✓ What will be helpful?
✓ Recent personal contacts
✓ What will I hope to achieve in the hearers

WORSHIP

✓ How has the passage been traditionally understood?
✓ Echoes for the liturgical year?
✓ Suitable hymns, creeds, prayers.

EXEGESIS

✓ Look at commentaries and more than one translation
✓ What is the cultural background?
✓ What is the type of literature?

✓   What are the themes and theological ideas?
✓   What do I have that might help–articles, books, sermons etc.
✓   Related texts - Biblical/non Biblical
✓   Questions to explore

Pause for prayer and inspiration-after gathering, pause for hatching.

Sermon structure-three possible structures (Others:see pp 95-125)

a) Introduction - 3 or more points – Conclusion

b) Problem and solution or perhaps 'Thesis/Antithesis/Synthesis' (154)

c) A theme looked at from different aspects or a 'Progressive deepening structure, (154)

d) A topical sermon–especially when there is a lack of Biblical knowledge. Might be an idea, a need, a concern–an event such as a natural disaster. Back up with a biblical text and see how it lies with the faith and theology. A need for knowledge on the topic–abortion, environmental issues. A need to be informed–be sure to research thoroughly!

Useful?

•   Determine the object of the sermon–be sure of your aim
•   Have good examples and illustrations
•   Have interesting material and offer something fresh
•   What is my own story–share and help hearers to identify with.
•   Look at the stories of others–articles, newspapers, sermons

As a preacher

•   Be yourself -many different styles–body language
•   Make contact with the congregation–eye contact is helpful
•   Speak audibly
•   A mixture of lively presentation and calmness
•   A time for laughter if this is for you
•   Accept your own voice–important that the preacher's language sounds natural
•   Audibility has not only to do with volume but with precision of speech, so articulation is as important as volume.
•   Preach with love and regard the congregation as responsible equals (especially the children)
•   Using a microphone is an art!
•   Preaching means a life of study (F. Craddock)

"I have heard hundreds of sermons and remember few but I know that I have been fed"   *"I thank God that I have heard his voice through them and met the living Word, Jesus Christ" (Revd Dr J. Taylor)*

'Don't be drunk with wine, because that will ruin your life. Instead, be filled with the Holy Spirit, singing psalms and hymns and spiritual songs among yourselves, and making music to the Lord in your hearts.' (Eph 5:18,19 NLT)

WHAT DOES IT MEAN TO BE FILLED WITH THE SPIRIT?

OPEN TO THE SPIRIT IN THE OLD TESTAMENT

The Hebrew word=ruach
Wind–Ex 10:13, 19 which blew the locusts; Ex 14:21 which drives back the sea.
Breath– the breath of life Genesis 6:17; human spirit Psalm 31:5
Divine breath-often on individuals and early charismatic leaders.
See Ez 37:7-10 for these three concepts. Old Testament understanding is bound up with an awareness of the spiritual where divine and human make contact; is an encounter with God and is the breath of life.

The Spirit of Yahweh
1. Creating spirit
Hovering, speaking at creation Gen 1:2
Sustaining, renewing Ps 104:29 When you hide your face, they are dismayed; when you take away their breath, they die and return to their dust. 104:30 When you send forth your spirit, they are created; and you renew the face of the ground.
In humans Gen 2:7 as the breath of life
2. Empowering spirit
God himself at work–gives ability but can be abused
Bezaliel–spirit of craftsmanship, skill, ability, knowledge Ex 35.30f
Leaders–Moses, Joshua, Gideon, Jephthah, Samson (can run wild)
Saul –the spirit was withdrawn, replaced with a spirit that troubles him
Need to test the spirit
Marks of spirit shown with Moses–power without pride, power without personal jealousy, power without personal ambition.
The suffering servant Isaiah 42:1
3. Prophetic spirit
David: 'The spirit of the Lord spoke by me, and his word was on my tongue'
The prophets: Compulsion to speak the truth-Balaam in Num 22
Stand for justice- Micah 6:8

457

4. Anointing spirit

Kings were anointed

Saul-but folly and disobedience led to rejection

David–a man after my own heart–mind, will, intention; obedience; doing God's will

Cyrus-a Persian **non believer** was anointed to do God' will

The Servant King-Is 42:1-9; 11:1-9 justice with gentleness, compassion, enlightenment–those in darkness, liberation–the captive

Is 61:1-3 quoted by Jesus in Lk 4:18, 19 "Today this prophecy is fulfilled". The spirit comes on the church-the spirit of Jesus, the spirit of God.

5. The coming spirit and a new era.

Isaiah 32:15-20–recreation and righteousness

Ezekiel 36:26-new heart and new spirit; regeneration

Ezekiel 37:1-14-Can these bones live?

Joel 2:12-17-Genuine repentance; 18-27 forgiveness; 28-32 universal blessing

OPEN TO THE SPIRIT IN THE NEW TESTAMENT

The Spirit comes to fullness with Jesus-to guide us into truth; to convict us of sin; to teach us all things and remind us of the things that Jesus said and did; to empower us – John 14:26, 16:7-16

The Gifts of the Spirit-Ro 12:6-8; 1 Cor 12:8-10; 1 Cor 12:28-30; I Cor 14:1-25; Eph 4:11, 12

All gifts are important (1 Corinthians 12:14-27) though perhaps the prophetic gift is singled out as special (1 Corinthians 14:1).

What gifts do we have personally????????

The Fruit of the Spirit (Gal 5:22) 'A growth in grace through a deepening relationship with God' **Love**, joy, peace, patience, kindness, goodness, faithfulness, gentleness, self-control

"**Gifts** are spontaneous and immediate, but **Fruit** takes time to grow to maturity." RJ

Some symbols of the Spirit

Fire - Matthew 3:11	Dove – Luke 3:22	Wind – Acts 2:2
Water – John 7:38-39	Oil – Luke 4:18	Salt – Mark 4:49-50

Activity in Groups
What symbol do you find most helpful?   Why?
What does it reveal about the Holy Spirit?
When have you seen this symbol most powerfully used in worship?

The Holy Spirit and Worship c.f. 1 Cor 12-14; Eph 4:18 Revitalised hearts–**our own experience. Always based on Jesus**–crucified and risen. **Rebirth of worship**–bringing freedom-Charismatic Movement.

New Songs c.f. Eph 5:18-20; Rev 5: 8-9, 14:2-3; Openness to the new: Emphasis on praise; Deepening experience; Opening out of truth; Dedication; Obedience; Relationships; A calling into action.

"At that time Jesus was filled with joy by the Holy Spirit" (Lk 10:21)
A time to reflect: What is the Holy Spirit saying to me now? Let us treasure what the Spirit has said and act

A time for quiet:

Spirit of the Living God, fall afresh on me,
Spirit of the Living God, fall afresh on me,
Break me, melt me, mould me, fill me,
Spirit of the Living God, fall afresh on me.

LECTURE 6: MUSIC AND WORSHIP

MUSIC

To make music, to listen, to dance;
To join together as community;
To sing our songs and tell our story …

What does music mean to you?

> *'We are almost a nation of dancers, musicians and poets. Thus every great event, such as a triumphant return from battle, or other cause of public rejoicing is celebrated in public dances, which are accompanied with songs and music suited to the occasion.'*
> *Olaudah Equiano 1789*

459

1. Unites us as God's people

The Psalms-By the waters of Babylon (Ps 137) 'How could we sing the Lord's song in a foreign land?' In the Spiritual–they did sing the Lord's song. Nobody knows the trouble I see=importance of lament. All the powers of music bring the music of the heart. (Charles Wesley)

2. Prophetic voice–prophet as poet

Martin Luther King–I have a dream–a music of words 'We shall overcome' from the United States in the 60's. We're marching in the light of God' Nelson Mandela: the voices of little people

3. Inspires faith or is a statement of faith

I gotta home in that rock don't you see

Deepens biblical texts–oratorios, hymns, songs

Christian creeds should be sung; hymns are a natural vehicle for praise

Hymns–we sing **together** (no ipods!)

In hymns, we can discover God, we can learn about God, we can be called to proclaim and witness to his love, and we can learn how to lead Christian lives.

John Wesley: "Sing All"; (Psalms and Hymns for the use of all Christians-1737-encouraging Christians to sing from the depth and breadth of Christian hymnology)

"Learn these tunes before you learn any others; afterwards learn as many as you please.

Sing them exactly as they are printed here, without altering or mending them at all; and if you have learned to sing them otherwise, unlearn it as soon as you can.

Sing all. See that you join with the congregation as frequently as you can. Let not a slight degree of weakness or weariness hinder you. If it is a cross to you, take it up, and you will find it a blessing.

Sing lustily and with a good courage. Beware of singing as if you were half dead, or half asleep; but lift up your voice with strength. Be no more afraid of your voice now, nor more ashamed of its being heard, than when you sung the songs of Satan.

Sing modestly. Do not bawl, so as to be heard above or distinct from the rest of the congregation, that you may not destroy the harmony; but strive to unite your voices together, so as to make one clear melodious sound.

Sing in time. Whatever time is sung be sure to keep with it. Do not run before nor stay behind it; but attend close to the leading voices, and move therewith as exactly as you can; and take care not to sing too slow. This drawling way naturally steals on all who are lazy; and it is high time to drive it out from us, and sing all our tunes just as quick as we did at first.

Above all sing spiritually. Have an eye to God in every word you sing. Aim at pleasing him more than yourself, or any other creature. In order to do this attend strictly to the sense of what you sing, and see that your heart is not carried away with the sound, but offered to God continually; so shall your singing be such as the Lord will approve here, and reward you when he cometh in the clouds of heaven."

John Wimber: *"Historically every move of God has produced new music. Sometimes the music actually precipitated revival, sometimes it occurred during revival, but it was always present in the aftermath".*

SOME EARLY HISTORY

For music–Ju 5.3; Neh *12:27* There are many examples in the Ps 87:7, 92:1, 98.4-5, 108:1, 144:9, 47:7, 149:3, 150 - Let everything that has breath praise the Lord!
Use of Instruments Gen 4:21, Ex 19:13-19, 20:18, Lev 25:9, Num 10:1-10, Jos 6:1-21, Ju 3:27, 7:1-25, 1 Sam 13:3, 2 Sam 6:12-15, 15:10, 18:16, 20: 1,22
Worship leaders-1 Chron 6:31-33 *"These are the men whom David put in charge of the service of song in the house of the LORD, after the ark rested there".*

In life–a natural expression of personal and corporate emotion.
Joy and thanksgiving: Hannah (1 Samuel 2), Mary (Luke 1:46-55)
Grief: David's lament for Jonathon (2 Sam 1)
Sacred and secular festivals: (Is 5:12)
Work songs as people harvested the crops: (Is 16:10)
Expression of love: Song of Songs

NEW TESTAMENT

In Luke, songs surround the birth of Jesus–the heavenly host (2:13, 14); Zechariah (1:67-79); Mary (1:46-55); Simeon (2:29-32).
Entry into Jerusalem (Matt 21:9; Lk 19:38) accompanied by Hosannas
Just one instance-Jesus before Gethsemane *"And when they had sung a hymn, they went out to the Mount of Olives"* Mt 26:30; Mk 14:26

In the book of Revelation–5:9-14, 15:2-4
Music in worship 1 Cor 14:26; Col 3:16; Acts 16:25; Eph 5:19
There are texts which have been identified as hymns for use in worship-Eph 5:14; 1 Tim 3:16; Phil 2:6-11 (often thought of as a hymn, but perhaps inspired writing by Paul?)
Although hymn singing was part of early Christian worship, there was a general prohibition in singing in parts.
Koinonia (fellowship) was expressed by singing in union/unison as with one voice, an offering to God, the source of all unity.
Social events–the return of the prodigal (Luke 15:25)

PRESENT DAY

What is 'Christian worship music'? What style of music is used in your church?

Some comments:

Importance of Hymns–Often express great theological truths *about* God, truths we need to learn; Spiritual songs are songs inspired today by the Holy Spirit-often addressed *to* God. (I love you)
Try to have a breadth of styles in your worship - hymns, modern worship songs, free improvising, different hymn accompaniments, Taizé songs
Not all traditional hymns are good; **not** all modern songs are good
A mixture of old and new, familiar and unfamiliar If a traditional service–make sure the hymns continue the flow of worship Hymns of praise; hymn to follow the lessons; to follow the sermon; prayers of intercession; dedication; pilgrimage; the final hymn. If free, make sure there is direction.
Consider music for reflection–after a reading; after the sermon
Use local music and custom-a rich tradition! **How?**
Music and dance-**how to develop even more in your situation**?
Take advantage of all the musical talent available–don't leave it all to the keyboard/organist/pianist. Different instruments for different styles Be prepared!

"Sing praise in your spirit, sing praise with your soul, that is: give glory to God in both your soul and your body". (Hesychius)

> *'For the word of God is living and active, sharper than any two-edged sword, piercing until it divides soul from spirit, joints from marrow; it is able to judge the thoughts and intentions of the heart.'*
> Heb 4:12
> *(Jesus) opened their minds to understand the scriptures .....*
> Lk 24:45
> *All scripture is inspired by God and is useful for teaching, for reproof, for correction, and for training in righteousness, so that everyone who belongs to God may be proficient, equipped for every good work.*
> 2 Tim 3:16, 17

HOW DOES THE BIBLE TEACH?

It's a great deal richer than a 'handbook' or a 'manual' in its approach

There are complex issues involved in translation

It is intended to be heard and read in community, not read alone

Everyone hears the text through their own experiences and situation

The gifts of interpreting are scattered through the whole people of God

The text is always questioning and challenging us

Interpretation involves us all and our experiences interacting with the diversity of the text. *(M Killingray–Encouraging Bible Literacy)*

BIBLES

Hebrew Bible: Jewish order

Torah (law or teaching) or Pentateuch-considered the most important
Genesis, Exodus, Leviticus, Numbers, Deuteronomy

The prophets follow:
Former prophets-Joshua, Judges, Samuel, Kings–a prophetic interpretation of Israel's history. Prophecy and history go hand in hand.
Latter prophets-Isaiah, Jeremiah, Ezekiel+the Twelve–Hosea to Malachi.)
All the other books were the writings-Psalms, Proverbs, Job, Song of songs, Ruth, Lamentations, Ecclesiastes, Esther, Daniel, Ezra, Nehemiah, Chronicles.

463

There are the same books as our Bible but in a different order and perhaps only one book each for Samuel, Kings and Chronicles. Judaism existed without written scripture for much of its life–it was an oral tradition. It was about the 10th century BC that material began to be set down. By the time of Jesus, the canon was pretty much closed. With many foreign influences at work and Israel suffering from a long period of domination and conquest, preservation of faith became paramount.

Some bibles include the Apocrypha (a title which means 'hidden')
Some writings were hidden because they were not considered good enough; they were questionable or possibly contrary to authorised teaching.
Others were considered so important that only an inner circle should study them
Others were known only in Greek and not in Hebrew
The catholic scholar Jerome included all the books both Greek and Hebrew and the Roman Catholic tradition has recognised them; Protestant tradition has recognised only the books written in Hebrew.
Apocryphal books–Tobit, Judith, Esther (Greek), The Wisdom of Solomon, Ecclesiasticus, Baruch, Additions to Daniel, 1 and 2 Maccabees, 1 Esdras, Prayer Manasseh, Psalm 151, 3 Maccabees, 2 Esdras, 4 Maccabees, Psalm 151

THE CHRISTIAN BIBLE: THE OLD TESTAMENT

Kept the Pentateuch or Law first but saw Joshua, Judges, Samuel and Kings as historical books and classified them with Chronicles, Ezra, Nehemiah, Ruth and Esther.
The poetic books–Psalms, Proverbs, Job plus Ecclesiastes and the Song of Songs.
Lamentations was included because of similarities with Jeremiah
Daniel was included in the prophets. (In the Jewish Bible, Daniel is in the writings.)

THE CHRISTIAN BIBLE: THE NEW TESTAMENT

- 4 gospels
- Acts of the Apostles
- A collection of thirteen letters traditionally ascribed to Paul; nine are to churches, four to individuals. Sometimes Timothy (2 letters) and Titus are called the Pastoral letters.

- Hebrews
- Catholic letters – not addressed to a specific church (James, 1 & 2 Peter, 1,2 & 3 John, Jude
- Revelation

The earliest witness to Jesus is not in the gospels but in Paul's letters. An example is the account of the Last Supper in 1 Cor 15:23-26. Mark is generally thought to be the first gospel to be written. By the time of Origen (185-254 CE), the gospels were thought to represent the crown of scripture and this is why the gospel is traditionally read last.

Note-Paul's Bible was more like the Jewish Bible than the present because it did not include the New Testament which as yet had not been written. Paul and the other New Testament writers also recognised a number of different books not normally included in Protestant Bibles. Originally, each book was written on a scroll and the scrolls would be kept together, so that different churches might have different selections. Note: The invention of the book or codex happened around the 2nd century CE Decisions then had to be made on what was in and what was out and the question of order arose.

INTERPRETATION

Some approaches have emphasized the **divine inspiration** of scripture over the human character of its writing.
Some have been concerned with **human and historical matters**.
Some have stressed questions of **how we hear God speaking to us through the text now.**
The Bible is a multichannel communication. (Derek Tidball)
God speaks through:
History, poetry, philosophy, argument and vision. **Above all the story of Jesus (the living word)** and the early Christians. **It is a living text.** Four gospels for four different communities. What is special for Matthew, Mark, Luke and John?

Jesus fulfils scripture but he also transforms it (Matthew 5:17, 18)

Do not think that I have come to abolish the law or the prophets; I have come not to abolish but to fulfil. For truly I tell you, until heaven and earth pass away, not one letter, not one stroke of a letter, will pass from the law until all is accomplished.

465

But His new interpretation means that Jesus:
Heals on the Sabbath-Mk 3:2
Cuts across family obligations clearly set out in the law-Lk 9:59
Widens the concept of family-Mk 3:31
Supports his disciples gathering grain on the Sabbath-Matt12:1
Mixes among, eats with, and takes it upon himself to clearly forgive identifiable sinners-Lk 7:36
Undercuts whole Jewish categorization of clean/unclean so deeply rooted in the Torah-Lk 11:37-41
Asks provocative questions and gives challenging responses Mk 3:4, Mk 2:27, Matt 9:13, Matt 23:26
Often quotes scripture but is radical, driving straight to the heart of the matter, so that it becomes reforming and life giving.

JESUS IS THE ULTIMATE WORD: Key to understanding the Bible is a relationship with him e.g.
All-embracing Bible: Peter and Cornelius: Acts 10-God-no favourites
It was used in the debate about slavery Equiano–argued against those saying that Bible supported slavery
Every translation into another language brings new insights; every culture its own traditions. For too long the Bible has been western dominated in scholarship and teaching and now is the time for an emergence of new ways and new thinking worldwide. *'To let peoples be religiously informed and religiously themselves.' Lamin Sanneh*
Dalit theology from India–the untouchables: A fundamental passage is Is 53–the concept of a servant God, a God who suffers with and for the people, so that a 'no people' such as the Dalits become God's very own people. c.f. a people on the margins of society are, for God, a chosen people. 1 Pe 2:9
South America: Jorge Pixley writing about victims of violence in El Salvador again relates to Isaiah 53-the servant who suffered and was led to his death for our transgression. In times of social change there are martyrs to violence and oppression but the servant shows how this is life affirming as they play their part toward a better society
Asia: Moonjang Lee who was originally from Korea writes,
We need to articulate the authority of the Bible in Asia in Asian languages in light of Asian religious and cultural experience.' Also, *'As Christianity expands into the global South; our understanding of the Bible will be enriched, for there are teachings of the Bible yet to be discovered.*

Africa: Bishop Egbunu quotes the following passage, *'Most Africans, when they had access to the Bible, were not interested in criticisms of its accuracy. They were fascinated to find how similar the biblical world was to their own, with purifying sacrifices, instructive dreams, important ancestors, the family with a large and extended membership, many wives for patriarchs and kings, disasters through curses, healing through spiritual power, dancing in joyful worship (did not David 'dance before the Lord?') and many miracles after prayer.* You will find excellent expressions of this interpretation in the donated **Africa Bible Commentary.** Also links with a holistic approach to life rather than division between sacred and secular.

THE BIBLE

Bishop Georges Titre: Jesus' prayer for his disciples was, 'Sanctify them in the truth; your word is truth' John 17:17. This means that Christians must be saturated in the word if they are to live holy lives.
John Wesley: 'My ground is the Bible-I follow it in all things, both great and small.'
Itumeling Mosala: 'I decided that I would stop reading books and just read the Bible'
Desmond Tutu: 'They brought us the Bible, and do you know we believed it!'
When we read the Bible. Let us:
Enter into the story, the characters, the situation; we meet all the components of life
Read often for the news of Jesus and His gospel is the most exciting story in the world.
Read imaginatively
Ask questions and share with others
Know the text so that it lives within us (more than rote learning)
Reflect and ponder
Begin, continue and end in prayer
Hear God speak and act–Prof Andrew Walls says theology in all creative times is about doing things.
Serving and transforming society

'LORD THY WORD ABIDETH, AND MY FOOTSTEPS GUIDETH'

'The reality of God that is proclaimed in worship is to be announced for the entire world.' (Darrell Guder)
"Far from being a retreat from the world, worship enables Christians to see what the real world is and enables them to live in it"

Worship and Mission
It is not inside and outside–where we go out into the world-traditional
It is not outside and inside–where we bring the world in-contemporary
It is inside←→out: a unity

A missionary God invites our worship as mission
Mission here means sharing in the life of God, sharing the life of Jesus; proclaiming, sharing, serving - kerygma, koinonia, diakon

'By definition the ekklesia or church is a public assembly, and its worship is its first form of mission'

Meditation-Isaiah 6: 1-8 Listen to the words. Think about our own worship life. What do we offer to God, and what more would we like to offer in our worship? How is the worship connected to mission?

THE UNITY OF WORSHIP AND MISSION (c.f. WORSHIP AND MISSION BY J.G.DAVIES)

IN JESUS

In Jn 12:49, the life and work of Christ are spoken of in terms of mission–"for I have not spoken on my own, but the Father who sent me has himself given me a commandment about what to say and what to speak.
In Jn 6.51, there is the language of worship-"I am the living bread that came down from heaven. ... and the bread that I will give for the life of the world is my flesh."
In Jn 6:57, there is mission and worship-"Just as the living Father sent me, and I live because of the Father, so whoever eats me will live because of me."
Hebrews 3.1 speaks of Christ as both apostle and high priest.- "Therefore, holy brethren, who share in a heavenly call, consider Jesus, the apostle and high priest of our confession."

Ephesians 5:2, "And walk in love, as Christ loved us and gave himself up for us, a fragrant offering and sacrifice to God".

Romans 15:16, "to be a minister of Christ Jesus to the Gentiles in the priestly service of the gospel of God, so that the offering of the Gentiles may be acceptable, sanctified by the Holy Spirit.

2 Tim 4:5, "As for you, always be sober, endure suffering, do the work of an evangelist, carry out your ministry fully. As for me, I am already being poured out as a libation, and the time of my departure has come.

2 Cor 2:15, "for we are the aroma of Christ to God among those who are being saved and among those who are perishing"; Here aroma reflects a Levitical term for the character of a sacrifice which is acceptable to God. (c.f. Lev 1:9,13,17; 2:2,9,12.)

> *'St. Paul does not think of missionary work as an activity completely distinct from worship; rather does he think of his evangelistic labours as an aspect of both the Church's worship and the Church's priesthood ... His very missionary work is itself sacrificial worship in action.' (D. Webster)*

The language of worship is used for daily life and ethical conduct.

> Paul in Romans 12:1 - *"I appeal to you therefore, brothers and sisters, by the mercies of God, to present your bodies as a living sacrifice, holy and acceptable to God, which is your spiritual worship."*
>
> James 1:27 *"Religion that is pure and undefiled before God, the Father, is this: to care for orphans and widows in their distress, and to keep oneself unstained by the world."*
>
> Matthew 5:23 *"So when you are offering your gift at the altar, if you remember that your brother or sister has something against you, leave your gift there before the altar and go; first be reconciled to your brother or sister, and then come and offer your gift."*

Bad behaviour is false worship or idolatry

> Colossians 3:5 *"Put to death, therefore, whatever in you is earthly: fornication, impurity, passion, evil desire, and greed (which is idolatry).*and Ephesians 5:5 *"Be sure of this, that no fornicator or impure person, or one who is greedy (that is, an idolater), has any inheritance in the kingdom of Christ and of God."*

The early Christians

Early Christians did not have sacred buildings such as the Jewish Temple. Their worship was a joyful response to God's actions in Jesus –the divine presence is no longer confined to a building but embodied in a living community.

> 1 Peter 2:4 *"Come to him, a living stone, though rejected by mortals yet chosen and precious in God's sight, **and like living stones**, let yourselves be built into a **spiritual house**, to be a holy priesthood, to offer spiritual sacrifices acceptable to God through Jesus Christ".*

> *'True worship is synonymous with life, because the true God is the creator of the universe, the ruler of all men and nations, the Lord of all life. As such he cannot be fenced in or confined to "the sacred" or "the religious" or excluded from any sphere of life.*
> *(S. Winward)*

Under the Lordship of Christ, there is unity between worship, mission, and daily life.

> *"He seeks Christ without the world, or he seeks the world without Christ. In either case he is deceiving himself" (Bonhoeffer)*

Dangers when worship is separated from mission A church can:

Put its own survival before its mission.

Become preoccupied with internal structures and concerns.

Concentrate on ritual rather than ministry.

Find the worship loses its joy and it can become a religious exercise.

Dangers when mission is separated from worship

> *'a church can forget that it is the servant of Christ and not his proprietor' (R. Orchard)*

The call to mission

Israel was called to be a holy people, to attract people to the worship and service of God (Is. 60.1-4).

Early days saw Jesus sending out the disciples two by two–to the lost sheep of the house of Israel (Lk 13.28 is wider *"And they shall come from east and west, and from north and south, and shall sit down in the kingdom of God).*

It is with the early church that mission opens out. There are several 'Commissions':

1. A royal commission in Matthew 28:18 - And Jesus came and said to them, *"All authority in heaven and on earth has been given to me. Go therefore and make disciples of all nations, baptizing them in the name of the Father and of the Son and of the Holy Spirit."*

2. A liberating commission in post-Mark 16:15-And he said to them, *"Go into all the world and proclaim the good news to the whole creation".*

3. A forgiving commission in Luke 24.46- *'and he said to them, "Thus it is written, that the Messiah is to suffer and to rise from the dead on the third day, and that repentance and forgiveness of sins is to be proclaimed in his name to all nations, beginning from Jerusalem.'* 24:48 *'You are witnesses of these things'.*

4. A continuity of commission between the sending of Jesus by the Father and the sending of the disciples by Jesus in John 20:21-*"As the Father has sent me, so I send you."*

5. The Holy Spirit Commission impels followers of Jesus Christ to mission. As Christians, the Spirit is in our hearts. Gal 4:4 *"But when the fullness of time had come, God sent his Son ... and because you are children, God has sent the Spirit of his Son into our hearts, crying, "Abba! Father!"*

In John 20.22, after the commission, we read, *"When he had said this, he breathed on them and said to them, "Receive the Holy Spirit".* Luke 24:49 ends with a promise, *"And see, I am sending upon you what my Father promised; so stay here in the city until you have been clothed with power from on high."*

From the very first chapter of Acts, the promise for the power of the spirit is closely related to mission. "You will receive power ... and you will be my witnesses". The spirit at Pentecost was the spirit of mission In the house of Cornelius in Acts 10, it was a spirit of mission, breaking barriers. Acts sparkles with the power of the spirit unleashed into mission-the Acts of the Holy Spirit in which the disciples are called to participate.

In Luke's eyes it is, *"a Spirit which impelled to missionary work, in fact a missionary spirit".(Roland Allen)*

"The work of mission is not something alongside the church but its very reason for being." (Myklebust)

(Mission campaigns, church growth, and individual salvation–these have their very important place BUT...)

471

Liturgy in terms of mission

The baptism of Jesus: Anointed for His role; Identifies with people; Baptism points to the cross so mission is inseparable from suffering; Receives the Holy Spirit.

The Lord's Supper: Renews Baptism, acceptance of the covenant, we proclaim the acts of God, we remember what Jesus has done, we anticipate the heavenly banquet. Called into whole mission of Christ.

Prayer: When the church prays, as when Christ prayed, it is engaged in mission. The Lord's Prayer, Praise, Thanksgiving, Intercession, Petition and Re-dedication.

Preaching and teaching For education and to renew dedication to God's mission.

Collection Linked with our fellowship with others and offering of all out 'gifts' in God' service.

The dismissal Always a blessing but can include a commission into God's world.

Ite missa est–Go, it is sent. Go in peace to love and serve the Lord.

"The roots of evangelism in our time lie in new understandings of worship" White J.F.

LECTURE 9: WORDS AND BEYOND WORDS

"Such love renews us: we become new men, heirs of the New Testament, singers of a new song." *St Augustine on St John's gospel*

SCRIPTURE

Scripture permeates worship–both Old and New Testaments include examples of communities at worship. Old Testament prayers were taken over and 'Christianised'. e.g. the first two chapters of Luke. Pliny speaks of Christians 'singing hymns to Christ as to a god.' The language needed was readily available through the scriptures and worship of Israel and Judaism. On the one hand, worship must not become so formalised as to be thoughtless and automatic–there must be a contemporary aspect. On the other, the scriptures have enriched Christian worship through the ages and united us in language and symbolism with the faithful of all ages. Scripture is a major element in worship: Justin–*'on the day called Sunday there is a meeting in one place of those who live in cities or the country, and the memoirs of the apostles or the writings of the prophets are read* **as long as time permits***'.*

Scripture was a major element–gradually the reading of the Word was preceded by praise and prayer but the focus remained. Hearing the Word, responding to the Word, exposition of the Word, response to the exposition.

Synagogue	1 Cor 11/14	Acts 2:42-3:1	Rev 4-5	Pliny to Trajan (112A.D.)	Justin (150 A.D.)	Hippolytus (210 A.D.)
Decalogue	Shared Meal	Apostles' teaching	Hymn	Daybreak service	Reading OT/Gospel	Prayers
Shema	Hymn	Fellowship	Sermon	Praise	Sermon	Readings
Blessings	Word of instruction	Breaking Bread	Prayer	Decalogue	Prayers (standing)	Hymns
Lesson	Revelation	Prayer	Hymn	Meal	Kiss of peace	Sermon
Psalm	Tongue	Wonders			Offering of bread and wine	Blessing
						Intercession
Sermon	Interpretation	Praise			Consecration prayer	Peace
						Thanksgiving
					Sharing of bread and wine	Breaking of bread
Prayers	Prophecy					Communion

Beyond the Word is the encounter with God ....in searching, in prayer, in listening, in doing.

AS A STORY TOLD

Recounting a journey, a meeting, something exciting.

James Dunn–'*many experiences we do not have the language to describe*' Therefore we tell stories. There is action, humour, gesture–unlike a piece of paper that never smiles. The Old Testament is the story of a faith journey for the people called Israel, a story of God's creation. In the New Testament, it is the story of Jesus. After the letters, the gospel writers used narrative and told a story.

The story of Jonah

The power and glory of ancient Assyria, whose capital was Nineveh: wars of imperial conquest including the subjugation of Northern Israel (Jonah's country). Result was the destruction of the country, the ruin of a culture and imposition of foreign ways. Jonah as prophet of the Lord is told to go and preach God's message to this very country–to the people of Nineveh, the Assyrians whom he hated. Jonah does not

473

want his bitter enemies to be saved–he prays for their destruction. The harder Jonah tries to escape God, the more God pursues him and returns him to his task

Jonah returns to his mission with a heavy heart, hoping that he will die before he sees the salvation of his enemies. Even that hope is shattered. Bitterness, hatred, resentment result from suffering. In spite of this, God tells Jonah that his very enemies will receive salvation. The hardness, however natural of Jonah's heart was moved by the voice which said 'Love your enemies and pray for your persecutors; only so can you be children of our heavenly father, who causes the sun to rise on the good and bad alike, and sends rain on the innocent and wicked.' (Mt 5:44-45) c.f. Lk 11:32=the sign of Jonah–but one greater is here.

BEYOND THE WORDS IS THE CHALLENGE FOR THE PRESENT–PREACHING THE GOSPEL IN SITUATIONS OF BITTERNESS AND SUFFERING

Luke as the gospel of stories
Jesus at the home of Simon the Pharisee 7:36-51
The Good Samaritan 10:25-37
'Come, sinners, to the gospel feast' 14:7-24
Lost and found 15:1-32
A situation is recounted and Jesus tells a parable

Beyond the words
Imagining the scene – a visual impact
Being each character in the story–seen from different points of view
Not dumbing down the surprise
Finding a contemporary situation and a contemporary parable

Mark as story
'The narrator speaks from outside the story world. The narrator guides the reader by asides.'
Thereby pronouncing all foods clean
Desolating horror–'let the public reader understand'
Defiled hands are unwashed hands
Sadducees do not believe in the resurrection
The little girl was able to walk–for she was twelve years old
It was not the time for figs
Details such as foreign words and customs

The narrator gives the readers privileged knowledge and establishes a close relationship by letting them know immediately who Jesus is.– 'The beginning of the gospel of Jesus Christ' 1:1 Readers are not bystanders–from the beginning they know that Jesus is the anointed, the appointed one of God

The narrator creates suspense
How will the authorities respond?
Will the disciples ever figure it out?
What will happen when they do?
In the first half, the readers watch the disciples struggle–then after Caesarea Philippi readers learn with the disciples.

STYLE AND TEMPO

Simple and direct using ordinary language to tell an amazing story
Wearing camel's hair; like a dove, among wild animals
Episodes are brief, scenes change often
Euthus-immediately–almost breathless
Little extended teaching–parables from the boat; Mount of Olives

TWO STEPS (REPEATING)–SUGGEST THAT IT WAS MEANT TO BE READ ALOUD

When it was evening - after the sun was set
A Greek-a Syrophoenician by birth
A widow who gave everything she had-her whole living

SANDWICH EPISODES

Jairus/woman with a flow of blood 5:22-5:43
Peter in the courtyard/ the trial of Jesus

THERE ARE MANY QUESTIONS THAT ARE UNANSWERED

Why are you such cowards?
Don't you have faith yet?
How long am I to be with you?
How long am I to put up with you?
Simon are you sleeping?
Weren't you strong enough to watch a single hour?
These questions are unanswered!

Can the attendants of the bridegroom fast while the bridegroom is with them–As long as they have the bridegroom, they cannot fast 2:19

Why does this generation ask for a sign? Surely a sign will not be given 8:12; aren't you greatly misled over this?–You don't know either the writings or the power of God. 12:24

IRONY

Soldiers mock, hailing Jesus as king of the Jews. How ridiculous they thought, but that was who he was!
Others taunt, come down because they thought he couldn't. That he didn't come down shows who He was.
(See 'Mark as story' Rhoads, Dewey, Michie, Fortress Press)
Beyond the words is a vivid and striking encounter

HYMNS: THE OLD TESTAMENT HYMN BOOK OF THE PSALMS

➤ **Thanksgiving by an Individual** 30; 32; 34; 66; 116; **Hymns** 29; 33; 100; 103; 104; 117; 145–50;

➤ **Songs of Zion** where the main theme is YHWH's deliverance and protection of Jerusalem 46; 48; 76; 84; 87; 122;

➤ **Enthronement Psalms** which are characterized by a phrase which has been variously translated as 'The Lord is king', 'The Lord reigns', 'The Lord reigns (now)', and 'The Lord has become king' 47; 93; 96–9.

➤ **Laments of the Community** When famine or defeat in war threatened the nation, a fast would be called and the people would express their grief and call upon YHWH for help (cf. 1 Kings 8:33–40). 44; 74; 79; 80 are examples of the prayers that would be offered;

➤ **Personal laments** 6, 22, 38 88;

➤ **Royal Psalms** These are psalms of various forms which have the king as the central figure, either as the one for whom the prayer is offered or the one who makes the prayer. There is intense debate about the number of such psalms. The absolute minimum number is Gunkel's list of 2; 18; 20; 21; 45; 72; 101; 110; 132; 144:1–11;

➤ **Wisdom psalms** 1, 37, 49;

➤ **Torah Psalms** 119,

➤ **Entrance Liturgies** The question and answer in 15; 24:3–6 suggests that these two psalms may have been the catechism of pilgrims as they approach the temple, whether on an ordinary occasion or, perhaps more probably, for one of the great annual festivals;

➤ **Pilgrimage Psalms** It is commonly accepted that the title 'Song of Ascents' in 120–34 indicates psalms which pilgrims sang as they made their way to Jerusalem;

➤ **History Psalms** Accounts of events in Israel's history play such a large part in 78; 105; 106 that they are often described as history psalms.

➤ **Acrostics** Eight psalms are acrostics, each line or verse beginning with the letters of the Hebrew alphabet in correct sequence 9–10; 25; 34; 37; 111; 112; 119; 145

Plan of Methodist Hymn Book
Beyond the words, hymns are

Devotional–inner growth	to help us discover God
Pedagogical–catechesis	to help us learn about God
Evangelical–mission of Church	to proclaim and witness to his love
Practical–ethical	to discern how to lead Christian lives

Look at the following hymns in terms of the themes outlined above.
MHB 38, 77, 323, 406
To what extent do they inspire, educate and transform us?

If you want life, give your life; if you want prayer, give your prayer; if you want worship; give your worship. (David Watson)

AN AFRICAN READING OF THE BIBLE

Old Testament

Hagar from Egypt	Genesis 16:1
The Cushite wife of Moses	Numbers 12:1
Ebedmelech the Ethiopian	Jeremiah 38:7, 39:16
Tirhakah king of Ethiopia	Isaiah 37:9
Zephaniah, son of Cushi Perhaps	Zephaniah 1:1, 2:12, 3:10
Queen of Sheba	1 Kings 10:1-10
"Out of 'Africa' I have called my son"	Hosea 11:1

Gerald West suggests that the Israelites liberated in the Exodus may have been a racially mixed group of Africans and Asians.

New Testament

The flight into Egypt	Matt. 2:13-22
"The Queen of the South"–	
Another title for Queen of Sheba	Matt 12:42, Lk 11:31
Candace, Queen of Ethiopia	Acts 8:27
The Ethiopian finance minister	Acts 8:27-39

AFRICAN LINKS

The importance of genealogies and ancestors–see Old Testament lists, Matthew 1 and Luke 3:23-38

Gerald West writes,

African traditions and cultures also offer resources for literary and narrative readings of the Bible. The performance of the traditional storyteller and praise poet offer enormous potential for recovering African tools and concepts with which to read the text. The western preoccupation with historical and scientific truth as the only valid forms of truth often leads to a misunderstanding and mis-interpretation of much of the Bible. African familiarity with other forms of truth found in their oral and written literature, which is similar to biblical literature, can complement the predominant Western views and enrich our readings of the Bible. The techniques and strategies of African storytellers and praise poets can also provide us with new critical categories for reading the texts of the Bible.

Itumaleng Mosala reminds us, that ordinary Africans, particularly in the independent churches have **a great oral knowledge of the Bible**. There are stories to be shared together that seize and free the imagination and bring insights which greatly extend and enrich a western dominated academic text reading. (Dialogue between academic approaches and the so called 'ordinary' reader)

Because much of the Bible presents the perspectives of the poor and oppressed, those who experience poverty, oppression, and community solidarity in our context are able to read the Bible from this experience and so uncover themes and symbols of liberation, justice, ancestors, and land in the Bible that have been forgotten or neglected by many western readers.

SOME IDEAS

• **Looking anew with Gerald West and some hard pressed communities in Kwa Zulu Natal, South Africa the widow and her mite-Attempt a Bible study on Mark 12:41-44**

Question 1: Read Mark 12:41 44. What is this text about?

Question 2: Now read Mark 12:38 40, the text that immediately precedes Mark 12:41 44. Are there connections between 12:41 44 and 12:38 40? If so, what are they?

Question 3: Now read Mark 13:1 2, the text that immediately follows Mark 12:41 44. Are there connections between 13:1 2 and 12:38 44? If so, what are they?

Question 4: Jesus comes into the temple at 11:27 and leaves the temple at 13:2. In this literary unit who are the main characters or groups of characters, what do we know about them, and what are the relationships between them? Draw a picture of the relationships between the characters in the temple. What does your picture say about the literary unit as a whole?

Question 5: The temple ordered: Each person's **status** in the social order.

Time through its annual cycle of festivals, including, for example, the Day of Atonement, the Feast of Booths, Passover, Pentecost, and many more.

The **political life** of Israel.
The **economic life** of Israel

1.   How does this text speak to our respective contexts?

2.   What actions will you take in response to this Bible study? (from Gerald West)

SERMONS FOR A VISUAL CULTURE

From static points to imaginative moves

In films, formerly one stationary camera with moving figures; now multi camera with tight editing, rapid cuts and movement of camera angles.

In preaching, a single fixed viewpoint may seem slow to an audience more used to rapid shifts in viewing angles.

In the parables give opportunities for preachers to invite listeners to join in making imaginative leaps-e.g. Luke 10:29-37–stand by the listening lawyer, walk with the religious professionals, and lie in the ditch with the mugged traveller, or 'A view from the inn!'

From monologue to dialogue

Often preaching is simply making deposits of information in the listeners.
Television thrives on disagreement/discussion; producers are expected to represent opposing views and so create dialogue and debate.

The sermon can become a conversation between the congregation and the biblical text Lk 18:9-14–Invite listeners to reflect on the characters. How do they act; what do they say? How relevant today?
Consider inductive-from particular to general rather than deductive–from general to particular. (*Based on thoughts from Fred Craddock*)

Visual imagery

Stories built around pictures are another modern aspect–e.g. television advertising but they need to be carefully edited.

The parables are rich in visual imagery–a sower who spreads his seed Lk 8:5-8; a man who builds his house on a rock Lk 6:48-49, a father who runs, embraces and kisses his profligate son Lk 15:20. Active images can be woven together to create unforgettable stories but there must be order and a logical structure.

'words which you can see, smell, touch, hear and feel' (E.Markquart) Verbal imagery works on many different levels through different parts of the listener's imagination.

The homiletical plot (E. Lowry) – the sermon as a narrative art form

a)   upset the equilibrium Lk 10:30
b)   analyse the discrepancy Lk 10:31,32
c)   disclose a clue Lk 10:33
d)   experience the gospel Lk 10:34,35)
e)   anticipate the consequences Lk 10:36
(Perhaps a scene for each stage)

Lk references from Good Samaritan but translate to the present day.

SYMBOLS

A symbol

Points beyond itself with more than one meaning
Works at non-verbal levels and may appeal to different senses
Has different layers of meaning saying different things to different people or different things to the same person at different stages
Is often used repetitively over a period of time and gathers associations with other occasions
Can be unifying, bringing people together through its common use or in a common expression of faith. (Caution - explanations can lead to divisions!)
(See also 'Learning to preach today' (Hartner/Eschmann) pp 203-216)

A PERSONAL APPROACH

It starts with me c.f. Philip (Acts 8), Paul, John & Charles Wesley.

1. Time and prayer
2. Learning and commitment
3. 'To love as God loves us'
4. 'To serve as Jesus serves us '

A CULTURAL APPROACH

'In both the Old and New Testaments, worship was the one point at which the culture of the day was most strikingly affirmed, and challenged.'

1. Worship that embraces the everyday concerns of worshippers
2. Worship that uses the vision of the creative and visual arts
3. Worship that is not bonded in religiosity, but is culturally accessible to those outside
4. Worship that recognises other people's starting points.
   (Evangelism for a New Age: Faith for the Future John Drane)

A VISIONARY APPROACH

1. The Power of vision: Imagination (entertaining a different reality)
2. The Pain of vision: Grief (lamenting for the present)
3. The Process of vision: Anticipation (seeing 'in part')
4. The Price of vision: Misunderstanding (the cost of subversion)
5. The Product of vision: Hope (the future is 'open')
   (Mike Riddell, Threshold of the future)

THINKING 'OUTSIDE THE BOX.'

New ideas, unusual ideas, unconventional ideas In the UK–Café church, Bread baking;

Fresh expressions of Church not always on a Sunday; but what possibilities are there here?-in your situation?

1. Be bold, not hesitant: Consult, but be ready to step out in faith and confidence when necessary.

2. Explain: Tell people what you are doing, and why. Do it positively-don't say that it is because they are wrong and you are going to put them right!

3. Persist: Resistance to change can lessen after a time, but a single dose of anything is more likely to immunise

4. Be willing to fail: Worship is failing for millions already (UK). At least you will have tried and know what doesn't work.

5. Be understanding: Respect good traditions and what people genuinely like. Be sensitive to how they feel.

6. Avoid false dichotomies: Modern worship songs can be played on an organ and hymns on a guitar. Why is it usually the other way around (at least in the UK)? Make change progressive if possible.

7. Blend the familiar with the new. Avoid a 'slot' mentality. Integrate old hymns with new songs, traditional ways with modern ways, and wider ways with local.

A PERSONAL CHECK LIST

Where have we come from and what do I value? *(Past experience and tradition)* Where are we now? *(Present reality)* What have we lost on the way that needs to be re-discovered? What is missing that needs to be filled? *(e.g. in UK- Songs of Lament, worship for those on the edges of society)* What is my dream? What am I going to do?

Reflection from Dr Daniel T Niles (Sri Lankan theologian)
   'The gospel is like a seed and you have to sow it. When you sow the seed of Christianity in Palestine, a plant called Palestinian Christianity grows. When you sow it in Rome, a plant called Roman Christianity grows. You sow the gospel in Great Britain and you get British Christianity. Now when the missionaries came to our lands they brought not only the seed of the gospel, but also their own plant of Christianity, flowerpot included! So what we have to do is to break the flowerpot, take out the seed of the gospel, sow it in our own cultural soil, and let our version of Christianity grow.'

"Africa is the cradle of humanity"–Archbishop Desmond Tutu

MODULE 7: ENCOUNTERING OTHER RELIGIONS[1]

(Revd Dr Stephen Skuce BD MEd M Phil: Director CCITC)

LECTURE 1: WHAT IS THE JEWISH FAITH?

The Foundation

Around 2,000 years ago, a non-Jew told Hillel, a famous Jewish teacher, that he would convert to Judaism if Hillel could teach him the whole of the Torah in the time he could balance on one leg. Hillel replied, 'What is hateful to yourself, do not do to your neighbour. That is the whole Torah; the rest is just commentary.'

The Founder

It is harder to point to a founder of Judaism compared to other religions such as Buddhism or Islam. Judaism draws its roots in God's creative purpose and his election of a covenant people rather than a charismatic founder or Saviour. Through a series of patriarchs, prophets, kings and judges Judaism has been maintained and renewed as a living faith for a particular ethnic community.

Development

The ancient history of the Jewish community is recorded in what Christians call the Old Testament. It is a story of a community struggling to maintain independence from a variety of relatively local and then international powers, finally disappearing as a sovereign people during the Roman era. More recently, much of the community strength was found in Eastern Europe, partly due to opposition and persecution in many western European states.

A series of pogroms culminated in the Nazi attempt to destroy the community in the 1930s and 1940s resulting in approximately six million deaths in the Holocaust or Shoah. Israel was established in 1948 as a Jewish homeland and, despite political opposition from the displaced Palestinian community and neighbouring Arab states, Israel exists as a visible representation of the Jewish people and faith.

---

1 Much of this material was published originally in Skuce, SF The Faiths of Ireland (Dublin: Columba Press, 2006) and is republished with permission.

Beliefs

Jews combine two different sounding ideas of God in their beliefs: that God is an all-powerful being who is quite beyond human ability to understand or imagine and that God is here with us, caring about each individual as a parent cares for his/her child. A great deal of Jewish study deals with the creative power of two apparently incompatible ideas of God.

Worship

The Jewish Sabbath begins at sunset on Friday and lasts until sunset on Saturday. For observant Jews to ensure that the Sabbath is different, all work in preparation for the Sabbath must be finished before sunset on Friday. People generally dress smartly for Sabbath and go to considerable trouble to ensure that everything is in place to obey the commandment to make the Sabbath a delight. Sabbath candles are lit and there are special Sabbath blessings, prayers, songs and readings. It is traditional for the whole family to attend worship on Saturday although a growing secularism is an issue.

The synagogue or *shul* is a place of study and community centre as well as the main Jewish place of worship. In Orthodox synagogues, men and women sit separately whereas in Progressive synagogues men and women generally sit together. Synagogue services can be led by a rabbi, a cantor or a member of the congregation. Traditional Jewish worship requires a *minyan* or quorum of ten adult males to take place. The synagogue in Cork is only open on High Holy days because of a lack of ten males. For these occasions, Jewish males come from Dublin or England to enable the services to be held. In an Orthodox synagogue the service will be conducted by men in ancient Hebrew with congregational and/or choir singing. The alternative is in a Progressive synagogue where the service will be at least partly in English, often there is a choir and instruments and men and women can sit together. Women can participate as fully as men and women Rabbis are permitted.

In Orthodox synagogues the *Bimah* or raised place, is always in the middle of the hall whereas in a progressive synagogue it is often directly in front of the Ark. In front of the *Bimah* is a lectern where the Torah is placed for readings.

Jewish men always wear hats when they are saying prayers which mention God's name with observant Jewish men wearing some sort of hat almost all the time, normally a small round cap called a *yarmulke* (Yiddish) or a *kippah* (Hebrew). Men over the age of thirteen often wear a *Tallit* or prayer shawl for Morning Prayer, the fringes (called *tzitzit*) on the edges reminding the wearer to observe God's commandments as instructed in the *Shemah*, one of the most sacred prayers.

Each synagogue contains an Ark or cupboard where the Torah scrolls containing the text of the Hebrew Bible are kept. The Ark is named after the wooden chest that held the stone tablets of the Covenant that God gave to Moses on Mount Sinai and the Hebrew words of the Ten Commandments are usually written somewhere above the ark. At the proper moment in the service, the Ark is ceremonially opened and the Torah scroll is carried in procession to the reading desk, unrolled to the reading chosen for the day and laid on the reading desk. Normally the congregation stands whenever the doors of the ark are open. An Eternal Light (*Ner Tamid*) hangs above the Ark. This light is kept burning as a symbol of God's presence and to represent the pillar of fire that guided the Jewish people on their journey through the wilderness.

Jews are supposed to pray three times a day; morning, afternoon, and evening. Much Jewish prayer consists in reciting the written services aloud in synagogue. Observant Jews will say a blessing over everything they eat or drink, and in the face of many natural events to acknowledge that God is involved in all parts of life.

Living the faith

Jews believe that God choose them in order to set an example of holiness and ethical behaviour to the world. Jewish life is very much the life of a community and there are many activities that Jews must do as a community. Judaism is a faith of action and Jews believe people should be judged by the way they live their faith rather than by the intellectual content of their beliefs. **Orthodox Jews** believe that a Jew is someone who is the child of a Jewish mother, and who has not adopted another faith. **Progressive Jews** are prepared to accept as Jewish someone who has a Jewish father or mother.

Holy days

The Jewish calendar is a combined moon and sun calendar, unlike the conventional Western (or Gregorian) calendar, consequently Jewish festivals move about the Western calendar from year to year. The High Holy Days come in autumn, at the start of the month of Tishri. This is the most spiritual period of the year for Jews, a time for looking back on the year just passed, and for taking action to get right with God and with other people. It runs from Rosh Hashanah for ten days until Yom Kippur. These High Holy festivals include:

1. Rosh Hashanah: the New Year festival and commemorates the creation of the world.

2. Days of Awe or Repentance: the ten days between Rosh Hashanah and Yom Kippur during which everyone gets a chance to repent.

3. Yom Kippur: the most sacred and solemn day of the Jewish year which brings the Days of Repentance to a close with a twenty-five hour fast.

The Pilgrimage Festivals commemorate the journey of the Jewish People from Egypt to the Holy Land and mark the dates in Temple times when Jews made pilgrimage to the Temple in Jerusalem for sacrifice. They are:

1. Passover or Pesach: a spring festival marking the escape from captivity in Egypt.

2. Shavuot: marks the time when the Jews received God's laws at Mount Sinai.

3. Sukkot: or The Feast of Tabernacles: commemorates the years that the Jews spent in the desert on their way to the Promised Land and how God provided for them.

Other Festivals include:

1. Purim: marking the defeat of an attempt to wipe out the Jews by Haman during the reign of Xerxes.

2. Hanukkah: or the Festival of Lights: marking the restoration of the temple by the Maccabees in 164 BCE. Hanukkah is celebrated at roughly the same time as Christmas.

3. Tish B'av: is the ninth day of the Jewish month of Av that usually falls in July or August. It is a solemn occasion because it commemorates a series of tragedies that have befallen the Jewish people over the years, many of which have coincidentally happened on this day, most especially two successive destructions of the Temple.

The Foundation

Like many faiths, Islam does not see national or regional differences. Islam is Islam wherever it is. Islam does not want an adjective to modify the faith.

Muhammad was born in Mecca sometime after his father's death in AD 570. Following the normal custom he was sent from his mother for the first few years of life, growing up in the desert with a Bedouin foster- mother, only being returned to his natural mother aged five. A short while later his mother died and Muhammad was raised by a grandfather and then by his uncle and 'guide' Abu Talib. The Quraysh family into which Muhammad was born was the custodian of the existing shrine at Mecca. It was a family of influence in the community although Muhammad had few personal advantages. Upon adulthood he worked on the caravan train of a wealthy widow called Khadijah and aged twenty-five he married Khadijah, becoming a wealthy businessman in his own right. For the next fifteen years, Muhammad traded successfully becoming a respected businessman but also spent time reflecting on the nature of Arab society and the unsatisfactory nature of the polytheistic worship of the people.

From around the age of thirty-five Muhammad began a practice of annual spiritual retreats and five years later, in 610, he had an experience while meditating (or possibly while asleep) alone on a mountain which shaped the rest of his life and that of world history. An angel came to him and said, 'Read'. Muhammad replied with the reasonable comment that he was unable to read but the angel commanded him to read anyway. The words that came to Muhammad in a spiritual state are recorded in the Qu'ran and are held sacred by Muslims and are not to be confused with words he spoke in a normal way which are recorded in the Sunnah of the Prophet.

For the next three years Muhammad preached to his family, friends and the inhabitants of Mecca, with the latter considering him a little mad. The first convert was his wife Khadijah, followed by his cousin Ali, then his servant Zayd. Another early convert was Abu Bakr. After three years, the prophet was guided to go to Mount Safa and warn the tribe of the danger of rejecting the message of monotheism, worship of the one true God, but again Muhammad was rejected. When

Muhammad started to challenge polygamy and idolatry, active persecution began with Yasir and his wife Sumayyah being counted among the first Islamic martyrs. Despite this opposition, there were a few converts to this new understanding of faith with prominent tribesman such as Hamzah and Umar ibn Al-Khattab strengthening Muhammad's position. As the Muslim community grew, other inhabitants of Mecca tried to isolate them through economic boycott and ghettoised them into a small area of the city. The death of his wife and then his protector Abu Talib brought Muhammad to a very low point and a visit to the town of At-Taif brought only more rejection.

In 620, in the tenth year of his ministry, Muhammad was visited by Jibreel who led him on the back of a horse-like animal to Jerusalem. There he prayed for the souls of all who he considered to have been true prophets. He was taken into heaven where he met some of the significant prophets and was brought into the presence of Allah. It was after this experience that the five times a day regular prayer, still followed today by devout Muslims, was introduced. These experiences (*Al Mihraj*) renewed Muhammad's faith, strengthening him in the face of renewed persecution.

Also in 620, Muhammad met six traders from Medina who expressed great interest in his message and the following year they returned with a number of their tribespeople resulting in the establishment of a small nucleus of believers in Medina. Muhammad already knew Medina as he had visited the city as a child, had a number of relatives there and it was the place of his father's death. After a vision, Muhammad instructed his followers in Mecca to leave for Medina and a gradual migration began of the approximately one hundred and forty strong Mecca Muslim community. The Meccans became concerned that Muhammad might establish himself in Medina with the intention of launching an attack on Mecca. An assassination attempt was made on Muhammad, but he escaped with Abu Bakr and reached Medina. Later the Muslims would date the Islamic calendar from this point (622 the Hijrah). It marked a change for the Muslim community from being a small, despised minority led by a religious teacher, into a powerful city-state led by an inspirational political, military and religious figure. In many ways, it is the most significant date in Islamic history.

In Medina, the prophet laid the foundations of the Islamic State. A mosque (the Masjid an-Nabawi) was built and public prayer and preaching was instituted. Prayer had been offered previously facing Jerusalem but after sixteen months in Medina, the prophet received a revelation instructing him to change direction to Mecca, a move strongly criticised by the Jewish portion of Medina. Shortly afterwards the fasting month of Ramadan was established. The Meccan immigrants mixed with the Medina believers and the economic and military might of Islam began to develop.

There followed a period of hostility between Mecca and Medina with the advantage changing several times. During a period of relative peace, Muhammad attempted a pilgrimage to Mecca but was refused entry and had his messenger Uthman murdered. Despite opportunities for revenge, Muhammad held back and the truce of Al-Hudaybiyah was signed allowing no hostilities for ten years; this showed a great contrast to his earlier treatment of the Jewish tribes in Medina. The Jewish tribes of northern Arabia were subdued in this period and an unsuccessful battle fought against the Persians. Muhammad had hoped the Jewish and Christian populations would accept his message but when their rejection became very plain his initial warmth to the 'People of the Book' changed to a condemnation of those who had rejected their own inheritance (Surah 9:30).

In 630, the Meccans broke the truce by attacking another Arab tribe that had a treaty with Muhammad. Leading an attack on Mecca, Muhammad found it relatively lightly defended and the city was captured. He entered the Kabbah shrine, cleared it of idols and established Muslim worship there. With secure control of southwest Arabia, Muhammad's influence began to spread. Tribes came to offer tribute to avoid hostilities and through a combination of threat and attack, the Muslim political and economic influence spread throughout Arabia.

After a final pilgrimage to Mecca Muhammad preached to a vast crowd at Mt Arafat, calling on them to continue the spread of Islam. A brief illness followed during which Muhammad gave instructions that he was not to be worshipped or venerated, and then the prophet died in 632 in Medina, in the company of his favourite wife A'isha.

By the time of Muhammad's death, Islam had political and religious control of most of Arabia, and the next couple of generations saw rapid progress through military conquest, treaties and religious conversion.

Development of Faith

The Prophet was followed by his close friend Abu Bakr (632-34) who consolidated the inherited position and waged war on Syria and Mesopotamia. Umar (634-44) oversaw the capture of Damascus (635) and Egypt (642) and by the time of his murder, the Arabs were a united empire. Uthman oversaw a period of continued political expansion, Cyprus being captured in 649 and Armenia in 652. In 653, the text of the Qu'ran was established but Uthman's corruption and the constant problem of succession led to his murder and a period of civil war between Mu'awaiya and Ali, Muhammad's cousin and son-in-law, married to his only surviving daughter Fatima. During this period, an Arab navy developed and Mu'awaiya's successor Yazid defeated Ali's son, Hussein in a massacre on 10 October 680. This largely resulted in the followers of Ali and Fatima forming the Shi'ite schism in Islam.

The Umayyad Dynasty, based in Damascus, ruled from 661-750 and saw the expansion of Islam both east to Afghanistan, India and central Asia and west to Sicily (667), southern Spain (711) and Toulouse (721). This European expansion was temporarily halted by the Battle of Tours in 732.

The Abbasids (749-847) made Baghdad their capital and completed Arab unity, Arabic became the language of empire and orthodox doctrine was codified. This was a golden period with Caliphs such as Harun al Rashid of Arabian Nights fame. Heading east brought contact with China in 800; moving west resulted in the capture of Palermo in 831. During the next two centuries Yemen, Corsica, Oman and the Punjab were added to the empire, in 970 the great university of Al-Azhar was established in Cairo and a naval victory won over Pisa and Genoa in 1016. But as the centre of influence shifted to Turkey the leadership became remote from the people, Arab territories such as Spain, Morocco, Algeria and Egypt began to act more as independent states and corruption set in once more.

The Seljuq dynasty (1055-1258) did not have as complete overall control as previous families and suffered constant attacks from successive Crusader armies beginning in 1096. The Mongol period from 1256-1517 saw the eastern part of the empire controlled by Mongol rulers who converted to Islam and ruled as far west as the Balkans. In the 13th and 14th centuries large parts of northern India came under Moslem control but in 1492 the last Moslem enclave in Spain, at Granada, was defeated. By this time Java, Sumatra and Sri Lanka all had considerable Moslem influence through Arab traders. In the western part of the empire, the Berber tribes had great influence from the 10th to 16th centuries.

The Ottoman Empire gradually developed from a small Turkish state, via the Balkans and Asia Minor to one of the greatest Islamic empires. Constantinople was captured in 1453 and Syria and Egypt in 1516-17. Then followed Rhodes (1522), Hungary (1526), and in 1529 Vienna narrowly avoided being captured. By 1605, all of northern and central India was under Muslim control with Crete taken in 1669.

The watershed event came in 1798-1801 with the Napoleonic invasion of Egypt. For the first time Islam was faced with a more powerful and militarily sophisticated Europe. The Ottoman Empire retreated and most of the Islamic states were colonised with the exceptions of Iran and Afghanistan. In World War I, Turkey sided with Germany and Austria leading to ultimate defeat and the ending of the Caliphate in post war secular Turkey. The 1917 declaration of a homeland for Jews in Palestine and the subsequent establishment of Israel in 1948 continues to affect world history.

In this brief overview of Islamic history, it is worth noting that Islam spread by the sword no more or less than Christianity. In many areas, people chose to convert to Islam for religious reasons, as well as for factors related to political and economic expediency. Christian history contains similar accounts and similar excesses. Christendom is a description rarely used today as it carries connotations of violence, abuse, enslavement and coercion – none notable Christian virtues. World history tends to show that wherever a religion is dominant, that religion tends to use most available methods to maintain that position and stifle religious opposition. The recent history of Islamic Afghanistan, and contemporary Hindu India and Buddhist Burma and

Sri Lanka tend to enforce this view. Catholic Ireland and Protestant Ulster, in various moments of history, have not been noted for their liberalism or pluralism. Islamic history is no better, but also no worse than this. History does not show a united Islamic world positioned against the Christian west. There has rarely, if ever, been anything close to a united Islamic world nor does the title of Christian west bear much meaningful scrutiny. World War I saw a Christian–Islamic coalition comprising Germany, Austria and Turkey while western European countries, notwithstanding a variety of motives, have militarily intervened to defend Islamic populations in the Balkans and Kuwait in the 1990s. The proposal to admit Turkey to the European Union is a further denial of a pan-Islamic assault on the west, as is the history of conflict between Muslim majority states such as Iran–Iraq and civil wars in what was East and West Pakistan and within post-Sadam Iraq.

Beliefs

'There is no God but God and Muhammad is his prophet.' This simple phrase is all that a new convert need declare to be accepted as a follower of Islam. It is a declaration of strict monotheism and an understanding of faith as delivered through Muhammad. Muhammad considered he was reintroducing monotheism (tawhid) to the world. In the passage of time since its establishment, the shrine at Mecca had become polluted by numerous images to gods while the Christians had developed their trinity, although there is good evidence to consider that Muhammad thought this to be Father, Mary and Jesus. So, Muhammad was calling people back to the monotheism of Abraham. The Christian claim of Jesus as God's son is unacceptable to Muslims as they see it creating a second god and implying that God had a physical sexual relationship.

The Prophet Muhammad is not considered to be a saint, seer, wonderworker or divine incarnation to Muslims; he is not a thoughtful mystic like the Buddha nor a philosopher like Confucius. Rather Muhammad was a simple spokesman for God. His life was normal and contrasts with the virgin birth of Jesus who is viewed as a sort of mystic. The miracle of Muhammad is the Qu'ran. Muhammad is the last prophet and revelation is completed through him (Surah 55:3-4), the life of Muhammad is to be emulated and obedience to the prophet is equivalent with obedience to God (Surah 4:80).

Within Islam, the Qu'ran is considered the speech of God, fully dictated without any human editing. Muhammad could neither read nor write, rather he heard the text of the Qu'ran from Jibreel (known to Christians as Gabriel), supernaturally memorised it and then passed it on to his followers. Hence, Qu'ran means reading or recitation. Inspiration is considered to have been total with the Prophet simply reciting exactly what he was given and having no active input into the words.

Over a period of twenty-three years Muhammad received portions of the Qu'ran from the angel Jibreel, passed them on to his followers who memorised and wrote down the words on palm leaves, leather or shoulder bones - it is to be presumed that a camel's shoulder bone could contain a fair amount of script! Jibreel also indicated where in the expanding corpus of scripture the latest portion should be placed. Tradition has it that every Ramadan Muhammad recited to Jibreel as much of the Qu'ran as he had received to date to check its accurate transmission, and that he recited the entire Qu'ran twice perfectly in his final year.

After Muhammad's death, the task of codifying the Qu'ran fell to Abu Bakr. Zaid Ibn Thabit had been the prophet's scribe and he produced a copy of the Qu'ran, which was checked against other known versions for accuracy, known as the Mus'haf or 'bound leaves'. This task was continued by Umar and then Uthman who passed copies to all the major Islamic cities to establish an authoritative version. All versions that deviated from this script in any way were destroyed and this process was considered completed by 646.

Muslims should only handle the Qu'ran in a state of religious purity and the physical book is treated with great respect, often being wrapped in an expensive cloth and kept in a high place to avoid accidental harm. The exact pronunciation is important and, unlike most Arabic texts, the Qu'ranic script is supplied with the short vowel-sign to ensure the greatest degree of accuracy. Readings are preceded by the phrase 'I take refuge with God from Satan, the accursed one', and followed by 'God Almighty has spoken truly'. It is a spiritual exercise to memorise the entire book, a little shorter than the New Testament.

The Qu'ran is organised into 114 Surahs (literally rows) or chapters, arranged approximately in order of length with the shortest at the end and the longest at the beginning, rather than chronologically or by subject. The main exception to this is the first Surah known as the Fatiha or opening, a seven verse invocation repeated during the five daily prayers. Translations of the Qu'ran into other languages are widespread but do not carry authority; that is restricted to only the Arabic text. The verse structure follows the Arabic breath pauses and does not flow as smoothly in translation.

Of lesser significance but still very important are the Hadiths or the traditions of the Prophet. Tradition as a matter of record is called Hadith; as a matter of obligation and to be acted on it is called Sunna, comprising of all that Muhammad said, did or approved. These are all in harmony with the Qu'ran and rely for verification on the Qu'ran but reinforce and flesh out its teaching. Hadiths are not Scripture, as they did not originate with God but developed as the companions of the prophet taught their successors all that Muhammad had said and done. Authority for this is claimed in Surah 59:7, 'Whatever the Messenger gives you, take it; and whatever he forbids you, leave it.' Sometimes this can be taken to seemingly extreme degrees and so if the Prophet sat to put on trousers and stood while putting on a turban some Muslims will want to emulate this behaviour; the right sandal is put on before the left and so on. To a meticulous degree Muhammad became the norm of true Muslim behaviour and the unconscious source of the manners and total conduct of the community as far as a pattern could be ascertained. The most famous of these books of Hadiths is called 'the Sound Six', the oldest is the Muwatta of Malik and the largest is the Musnad of Ahmad. The authenticity of a Hadith depends on the prominence of who claimed to hear it and the succession it was passed on through. More research is spent on proving the authenticity of this chain than looking critically at the statement itself. A critical tradition, while not absent in Islam, is not as pronounced as in Christianity.

Differences

There are numerous differences within Islam, many of a political nature, but the major difference is that between the Sunni majority and Shi'ite minority. Sunni Islam comprises almost 90% of world Islam, Shi'ite Islam making up most of the rest, being found as the overwhelming majority in Iran, approximately 50% of the Iraqi population and minorities in Bahrain, Afghanistan, Lebanon, Syria and Yemen. Even within Shi'ite belief there are a large number of sub groups ranging from ultra-extreme to that of the Khojas, originally from India, whose members give 10% of their income to the Aga Khan and make pilgrimage to him. What follows is a combination of Shi'ite beliefs rather than those of a particular school.

Shi'ite Muslims believe that after Muhammad there was to be a succession of Imams who were to be considered as divinely appointed and authoritative teachers of Islam. Muhammad's successor was his cousin and son in law, Ali who waged a civil war with Mo'awiya. There had been three successors to Muhammad before Ali but Shi'a considers Ali to have been the second 'Rightly Guided Imam'. He was murdered during Ramadan by a poisoned sword. The third was Ali's son, Hussein. The next in line had been Hussein's older brother Hassan but he, perhaps seeing how history was unfolding, entered into a pact with Mo'awiya and declined his position. The succession of Rightly Guided Imam's continued through descendants of Ali and Muhammad's daughter Fatima down to the twelfth born in 869. Most of the previous eleven met unpleasant ends but the twelfth is considered to be still living but invisible, known as the 'Imam for all times', and one day will return to bring justice to the world. He is said to have disappeared as a four year old boy in a cave in Baghdad in 873. This succession is an approximation with different Shi'ite schools understanding the lineage in slightly differing ways.

Among Shi'ites devotion is given to Hussein. He led his followers into battle when hopelessly outnumbered at Kerbela on the Euphrates, near Baghdad, Iraq in 680. All were massacred. Kerbela is now considered the centre of the Shi'a community while the shrine of Hussein at Mashhad is a popular destination for pilgrimage, rivalling the *Hajj*.

The Festival of Muharran is possibly the best-known feature of Shi'ite Islam. For the first ten days of the Islamic New Year, men refrain from washing or shaving and very passionate and colourful sermons are preached, reminding followers of the suffering of Hussein and his followers. On the tenth day there is a pageant re-enacting the Battle of Kerbela and part of the devotion for some is to cut themselves. In many ways within Shi'a Islam, the figure of Hussein is seen as a type of suffering Christ.

Shi'a law is alive and changing, evolving through the chain of Imams who develop and interpret the Qur'an for today. There is generally a more authoritarian understanding than within Sunni Islam with the interpretation controlled by Ayatollahs, papal like figures with authority and a measure of infallibility.

An approximation to a trinity can be found within Shi'a faith where Muhammad is seen as bringing the revelation of Allah, Ali the interpretation and Hussein the redemption as he is considered to have sacrificed himself to reconcile Allah to humanity. Hussein, Ali and only then Muhammad is the scale of importance, the Hajj is not so significant.

Shi'a doctrine is orthodox in almost all areas with the exception of the perspective on the Imams. Hadiths based on Muhammad are relegated in favour of collections based on the lives and words of Ali, Hussein and their succession. The Qu'ran is interpreted in a very allegorical way that can seem at times to be very tenuously connected with the text. Some sections of Shi'ism are more intolerant than Sunni Islam, an example being that, based on Surah 9:28, a Shi'a Muslim may not wish to be in the company of non-Muslims.

The twelfth Imam disappeared without children, the succession ended but Shi'ites swear allegiance to this unknown or hidden Imam. Just who this Imam was is a source of debate within Shi'ism. The current Imam, as his visible representative, becomes an infallible interpreter of all things and has the right to decide issues with no real place for community consensus.

A further division within Islam is that of the Sufi. If you ever wondered where the 'Whirling Dervishes' came from, then here is your answer. Sufism is a mystical or spiritual movement within Islam that took its name from the coarse woollen garment worn by ascetics. Their main idea is not just to follow God externally in submission, but to know God intimately and eventually lose themselves in the source of His being. To help them do this Sufis generally tried to live simply, although not in separated communities as Christian monks would have done. Sufism discounts intellect and reason and concentrates on the discovery of faith whereby the meaning of faith and truth is given in experimental immediacy to the seeking soul. For the last 100 years,

Sufism has been in decline but it was primarily in this form that Islam entered India and Indonesia and is still influential in this way in West Africa.

Worship

The call of the muezzin from the minaret is one of the characteristics of a Muslim society and community, although this is more likely to be a tape played on a public address system. The call goes out five times a day for Salat or formal prayer, culminating at Friday noon when up to one fifth of the world's population kneels down and prays towards Mecca. The translation of the call is:

God is most great, God is most great. I bear witness that there is no
God except God: I bear witness that Muhammad is the apostle of God.
Come you to prayer.
Come you to good (falah).
Prayer is better than sleep. (only at dawn prayer)
(Come you to the best action.) - only in Shi'ia
God is most great. God is most great.
There is no god except God.

The stated times for prayer are before sunrise, noon, mid-afternoon, just before sunset and early night and this five times a day is a compromise between the twice mentioned early in the Qu'ran (Surah 20:130, 17:78) and the forty times per day prayer that God required from Muhammad (Surah 11:114). The Mihraj and Hadith established prayer five times daily and the specific times. Mosques publish a daily list of prayer times for the faithful as the seasons change.

Formal prayer is an obligation on every Muslim who is sane, responsible and healthy. Children will often start as young as seven and certainly by ten. During menstruation, childbirth and nursing women do not join in public prayer.

Prayer is not so much communication with God as an act of submission. The Arabic words used are standard and formal, a consequence of which is that many Muslims may have limited understanding of the meaning. That is not as important as it might first appear since prayer is primarily an act of submission undertaken in the awareness that Allah is observing. To miss prayer is a sin that needs to be made up later. Private prayer or Du'a can be offered after the

499

formal prayers are over and while this is considered good, it is an addition rather than the main aspect of the prayer time. The formal congregational prayer is considered of greater merit.

Prayer is preceded by the removal of shoes and ritual purification by water (*wudu*). Hands are washed three times up to the wrist, the mouth is rinsed three times, water is sniffed into the nose and expelled three times, the face is washed three times from forehead to chin and ear to ear, both arms are washed up to the elbows three times, then the neck and finally the feet. If water is not available, sand or even rock is acceptable. A clean surface is necessary and so prayer mats or carpets are used (Surah 5:6). Prayer is offered facing Mecca and is accompanied by various bows and formal movements. While a mosque is the ideal place for prayer, anywhere is acceptable, showing the believer the presence of God in the midst of his or her day. A prayer mat keeps the worshipper ceremonially clean and points to the space between the believer and the world. The prayer room in the mosque will generally be large with a high ceiling, decorated by Arabic calligraphy of Qu'ranic verses but no representations of people or objects. There will often be a rich carpet on the floor. The plain walls are only broken by a small indentation in one wall that points the faithful to Mecca, a symbol of Islamic unity as all Muslims are pointed towards the same destination. There will also be some sort of small platform or pulpit for the Friday sermon. This preached Friday sermon is of great importance, only believers will be present and often commentary on social or political matters is given. Music or dancing will not be part of the worship. The English word 'mosque' is a corruption of the Arabic *masjid* that means 'place of prostration.'

Prayer is led by an Imam who may be specially trained but is not a minister or priest in the Christian sense. In smaller mosques, he will have a secular job and the Imam is not essential for weddings or other rituals. The worshippers stand in rows, close to each other. Touching each other, either foot to foot or shoulder to shoulder, is not a necessary part but does increase a feeling of brotherhood. It is congregational prayer as opposed to individual prayers offered together. On Friday at noon, prayer is preceded by a sermon and this is the Muslim Sabbath, although it is not a day of rest as in other religions (Surah 62:9-10). Business will stop from approximately 12noon–2pm and then resume. Men and women are generally separated in prayer for reasons of purity. If praying together in the same room women will be in lines behind the men. Other prayers are offered on occasions such as birth, death and marriage and these prayers are often formal and ritualised. Snatches of prayer, usually Qur'anic verses, are offered spontaneously on numerous occasions such as when entering or leaving a house and starting or finishing a journey.

There is a partial understanding of the role of intercessors in prayer. Some interpretations of Islam consider that prophets, martyrs, saints and angels all can intercede but that Muhammad is truest intercessor. The belief in other intercessors is more marked in Shi'a Islam. A further tradition has it that on the final day of judgement the line of prophets from Adam to Jesus will all disclaim the privilege of intercession that passes on until it reaches Muhammad who will intercede for all the faithful.

Living the Faith

Zakat is the Muslim obligation to share wealth and is administered as a tax in most Islamic countries (Surah 9:11). Private wealth is partially that of the community and only valid for an individual when the generosity of *zakat* is expressed (Surah 2:43, 83, 110, 117, 277). Practices differ as the Qu'ran is not clear on this issue and tax has always been a contentious area in Muslim states. Pakistan introduced special *zadat* stamps to be purchased from Post Offices and ruled that general taxation could not be treated as *zadat*. Taxation is levied on the whole population, whatever their religious position, whereas *zakat* is only for Muslims. *Zakat* can be given directly to individuals or organisations or through the mosque.

Zakat is usually a 'tax' of 2 ½ % on a person's capital and is given to help the poor, widows, orphans and needy within the Muslim community and to promote missionary work. It is not regarded as a charity but as an act of purification and a way to distribute wealth to the poor (Surah 9:34-35, see also 3:180). Additional alms giving are required such as one day's food for a feast at the end of Ramadan. Further acts of generosity that are voluntary are known as *sadaqat* and can be directed towards needy non-Muslims.

Ramadan is a 28-day month (9th month) where Muslims fast from dawn until dusk. As the Muslim year follows a 355 day lunar calendar, this period gradually moves throughout the seasons (Surah 9:37). It appears to have been an Arab tradition before Islam (Surah 2:183) and today is arguably more popular than daily prayer. It commemorates the

501

time of the revelation of the first of the Qu'ran and also the first military victory at Badr in 624. During this month Muslims will abstain from eating or drinking during the daylight hours, times that are defined when a black thread can be distinguished from a white thread (Surah 2:187). The month is to be spent in prayer, attendance at Mosque and studying the Qu'ran while each evening family and friends join for a meal with traditional dishes. This Ramadan meal can be used as an opportunity to invite non-Muslims and hence be an evangelistic opportunity. Ramadan causes a considerable amount of hardship in hot countries and the business life of Islamic countries is considerably affected, but as in most things Islamic it is a test of your submission to Allah and not to be modified. In some ways, Ramadan can be compared to the Christian period of Lent. Asceticism on its own is considered of no benefit, rather the spiritual dimension is emphasised. The dates and exact times for prayer and daylight are published by the mosques with regional differences due to slightly differing sunrise and sunset times. The fast ends with the celebration of 'id al-fitr when visits and gifts are exchanged and special alms given in a spirit of thanksgiving. This has some similarities to the Christian festival of Christmas.

The high point of a Muslim's life is to go on *Hajj* or pilgrimage. At least once, in a believer's life he or she is called to make the *Hajj* unless finance or illness prevents (Surah 3:97). Those that succeed are honoured in the Muslim community and carry the title of Al Haj with their name. The pilgrimage is made during Dhu'lhijah (the last month) but can be taken at other times (Surah 2:196, 3:97). No 'observers' are allowed and non-Muslims are forbidden to enter Mecca. Mecca is the destination for a variety of reasons. It is where creation is considered to have begun, Abraham called by God to journey to Mecca, when Ismail was thirsty his heel struck the ground and a spring of water came out at Mecca and Abraham restored the shrine at Mecca built by Adam around the Kaaba stone. It is believed that Gabriel brought this stone from heaven and the offer of Ishmail in sacrifice was at Mecca - the Dome of Rock Mosque in Jerusalem also commemorates this.

Until the discovery of oil in the 1930s, much of Arabia's income came from *Hajj* pilgrims. At Mecca, they find a circular Mosque with no direction they must face. Instead of pointing towards Mecca, they have arrived at the place one fifth of the world looks towards. Inside the mosque is the Kaaba stone contained in a small building. The room is believed to be a replica of heaven and here believers consider themselves to be closer to heaven than at any other point on earth. Planes are forbidden to fly over Mecca and tradition has it that birds do not fly directly over the stone.

Pilgrims approaching the city stop ritually cleanse themselves and change into plain white garments to show equality. Women are to be unveiled but often choose to wear a veil that does not touch the skin. Upon entering the Kaaba they kiss or touch the building then circle seven times barefoot, before running between two small hills (Safa and Marwa - four hundred and fifty yards apart) seven times to remember Hagar running about looking for water. The pilgrims then go to the tented city at Mina where all stay, a further mark of equality. They travel to Mt Aarafat and stand there from noon to dusk symbolising the last judgement and recalling Muhammad's last sermon. Arafat is also the place where Adam and Eve were separated after the fall and then reunited. The pilgrims return to Mina where they throw stones at three jars representing the three times Satan tempted Abraham over the offered sacrifice of Ishmail. On the final day of the month a goat is sacrificed and the meat given to the poor at the 'Feast of Sacrifice'. This part is celebrated by Muslims worldwide and not just those on the *Hajj*. Upon return to Mecca pilgrims cut their hair, circle the Kaaba once more and the *Hajj* is completed.

Some choose to travel on to Medina and visit Muhammad's mosque and tomb but that is not a necessary part of the *Hajj*.

Islam has no secular/sacred divide and so for Muslims law needs to be Islamic law. For a Muslim to live under Shari'a Law is an attempt to live out your faith and show complete submission to God in all things. In some ways, it mirrors the approach under the English Commonwealth of Oliver Cromwell or John Calvin's Geneva. This approach causes problems when a Muslim majority introduce Shari'a law in a state that has a significant non-Muslim population. Contemporary examples include Sudan and Nigeria. Yet part of the Muslim response is that Shari'a is God's way and while it is obligatory for Muslims, it is also the best way for all to live because it is God's way.

This law, rather than theology, has the prior emphasis in Islam. Broadly, it is obedience to the will of God rather than fellowship in the awareness of God's love. It is considered that it is possible for an individual to follow this law and so show true submission. The true form of the family, state and economy are discovered in the divine will expressed in the Shari'a. No other appeals to human rights or women's rights are of equal relevance because God has revealed the blueprint and the Muslim has to submit and follow.

Shari'a Law is the Qur'an expanded by recognised jurists, the muftis/mullahs who depend on hadiths. It is not codified or uniform in the sense of western law but has been developed and elaborated over the centuries. Arguably, it has never been properly tried; it would seem that it could only work properly in a fully Islamic faith society. This law is applied to cases through the use of *qiyas*, scholarly interpretation often by analogy/precedent or *ijma*, community consensus. Muhammad said, 'My people will never be unanimous in error.'

Ijma can lead to development and change in Shari'a although is generally only used when other roots are not clear. It is tempered by restricting community consensus to a few wise men rather than the full community. At an extreme, this means that Islam is what Muslims define it to be. *Ijtihad* is the process whereby *ijma* is achieved.

Qualified mujtahids or scholars discuss and arrive at conclusions for the people. This deals with the law and not dogma but allows Islamic countries to change laws by a parliamentary type system and claim it as Islamic as it is an expression of the popular will or *ijma*. The Sunna (the way) or legal code binding all Muslims is the result.

Following this law demands complete submission and the law is as concerned with enforcing what is thought as good as it is in stopping what is considered evil (Surah 3:104, 110). Based on the Qur'an and the Hadiths, the words and example of Muhammad are very significant. Even Muhammad's silence on a subject is considered significant implying he did not oppose an act or custom practised by early Muslims. Law can be considered in five categories:

1   what God has commanded
2   what God has recommended but not made compulsory
3   what God has left neutral

4   what God does not encourage but has not prohibited
5   what God has clearly forbidden

In Muslim countries during the latter part of the 19th century and the early years of the 20th century existing versions of Shari'a Law were weakened and secular laws were introduced based on western law codes. However, the rise of a more Islamist approach coupled with the emerging economic strength of Muslim countries has led a number of Muslim nations to reintroduce Shari'a either in part or whole. This is part of a debate within Islam as Shar'ia challenges practices that are common in many conservative Muslim countries, such as hereditary government and the payment of interest.

WHAT IS ISLAMIC FUNDAMENTALISM?

The term 'fundamentalist' was first used in a religious context in the early years of the twentieth century to identify Christians who believed and actively defended a conservative and literalist Protestant Christian belief. A series of booklets called 'The Fundamentals' were published between 1910-15 that opposed those who were accepting the fruits of liberal scholarship and scientific interpretations such as Darwinism. These conservative Protestants used proactive approaches such as publishing articles and organising rallies to raise public awareness of what was happening.

Their beliefs were largely that:

1   They have the true understanding of the faith.
2   Scripture was to be interpreted literally.
3   History was a battle between God and Satan, and they were
        now fighting for God.
4   Traditions were to be upheld, not changed.
5   Political action was part of the faith
6   Their view of morality was to be enforced on all (society
        viewed as in moral decay).
7   Their understanding of faith should be the only view taught.
8   Those that differed were at best deluded and at worst on the
        side of Satan

An important aspect of fundamentalism is the stress on the prominence of religious values and beliefs in social and political contexts and so the religious leader can also become the political leader, or at least the main influence on the politician. Given this particular Christian usage, it is not appropriate to apply the term to Islam. It is more accurate to use Islamist rather than fundamentalist. Many Muslims rightly feel that Islam is being caricatured and that a small extreme minority is being considered as representative of all that is Islam.

Islam believes that faith cannot be forced (Surah 2:256) and that respect must be given in particular to Christian and Jews as 'People of the Book' who worship the same God (Surah 29:46). Tolerance among nations was key (Surah 49:13) and so Medieval Spain under Muslim rule was a refuge for religious dissidents. In Moghul or Muslim ruled India the experience of the majority Hindu population was generally, although not always, one of religious tolerance and pluralism in society. What is sometimes inaccurately described today as Islamic fundamentalism is not the heart of Islam but a distortion of the faith.

Modern Islamism grew in the aftermath of the 1967 war when the Arab nations were defeated by Israel. Before that, some Arab countries had tried to escape western dominance by imitating western institutions. However, 1967 resulted in an alternative approach prevailing, to return to Islamic cultural values and institutions and to reject western influence.

Among the countries changed dramatically were Iran where the pro-western government was overthrown in 1979, and Afghanistan where the Russian dominated government was defeated in a conflict crossing the 1980s and 1990s. As recent history shows, not all these changes are permanent.

Islam has been caricatured as a warlike religion. The reality is that pre-Islamic Arabia was caught up in a vicious cycle of warfare in which tribes fought each other in vendettas. After having to fight for the survival of the early Muslim community, Muhammad brought peace through alliances to Arabia. Many passages of the Qu'ran deal with warfare and can be quoted selectively by those advocating violence, an approach not unknown in Christianity. Thus Surah 4:89 says that Muslims are ordered to 'slay (enemies) wherever you find them.' But a continuation into Surah 4:90 declares 'Thus, if they let you be, and do not make war on you, and offer you peace, God does not allow you to harm them.'

Jihad is not one of the five pillars or essentials of Islam. It means struggle and the greater jihad is the inward struggle to overcome sin and submit to God. The lesser jihad is the physical battle to impose God's rule on society. In the Qu'ran, the only permissible war is one of self-defence. Muslims may not begin hostilities (Surah2:190), warfare is always evil but sometimes you have to fight to avoid the kind of persecution that Mecca inflicted on the early Muslim community (Surah 2:191, 2:217) or to preserve decent values (Surah 4:75, 22:40). It is considered good to forgo revenge in a spirit of charity (Surah 5:45) and hostilities must be as short as possible and stop as soon as the enemy wants peace (Surah 2:192-3).

Almost every religion has aspects of violence in its foundation and early history; some contain aspects of terrorism and genocide or its modern term of ethnic cleansing. The Judeo/Christian history has more than its fair share of such history as does Islam, but it is important to note that Islam is not unique in a connection to violence. The early history of the Islamic community is of a small powerless people being persecuted in Mecca and eventually moving to Medina for survival. Due to spiritual growth and political alliances the community became stronger and eventually military campaigns and what we might today call terrorism were enacted. The subsequent history is one of conquest and defeat, much as any empire and it cannot be argued that Islam is unique in having a partially violent beginning. Where it may differ from Christianity is in a development from an Old Testament to a New Testament understanding. To some extent Islam remains rooted in its 6th century origins and a generally literalist understanding of Scripture does not encourage much development.

When compared to Jesus, Muhammad is a much more worldly, politically and militarily involved character. Christianity does have its own recent history of the apartheid regime in South Africa receiving, for a time, theological justification from section of the Dutch Reformed Church and Irish history shows aspects of legitimation claimed by terrorists of different Christian backgrounds. However, with all the above qualifications, there remains a justification for violence under certain specific conditions within Islam that gives a theological underpinning to extremists that Christian background terrorists cannot have.

Foundation

In the 18th century, the British coined the word 'Hinduism' to describe the religious life of the people of India. Arguably, Hinduism is an artificial construct that seeks to join together various related but independent religious traditions. It is helpful to think of Hinduism as a network of related religions rather than one monolithic faith.

The History of Hinduism

From the Veda scriptures and principally from the Rig-Veda, which was composed by the priests who were responsible for the fire sacrifices, we gain most of our knowledge of these people, from an Aryan race of European origin, that spread as far west as Ireland and as far east as Iran and India, entering India around 1700BC. The gods worshipped were mostly male and often concerned with natural phenomena such as storms and rain.

Links, although far from conclusive, can be drawn between some basic Hindu concepts and aspects of Celtic religion.

These Aryans brought an embryonic caste system, of either two or three tiers. They believed is a cosmic principal, *Rta,* that was precarious and had to be sustained by sacrifice as well as the proper performance of *dharma*. In this early society priests rose to prominence, guided by the *shastras* or manuals concerning the conduct of rituals and the ordering of society. The transmigration or reincarnation of souls was not prominent in Vedic teaching.

When the Aryans arrived in what is now the Indian subcontinent they found dark skinned inhabitants whom they conquered and then intermarried with. The primal religion of this Dravidian community seems to have concentrated on fertility cults with images of the mother goddess and the phallus. Archaeological finds suggest a system of temple worship with ritual washing or purification. It is now common to suggest that these two forms of religion blended and produced early Hinduism that emerged around 200BC, however in a country as vast as India few simple explanations work. What is clear is that beliefs such as rebirth, *samsara* and *karma* are very rarely found in the Vedas yet became prominent in Hinduism.

A major figure in the development of Hinduism was Sankara (788-820AD). He produced commentaries on the Upanishads, founded four still existing monasteries and debated with Buddhists and Jains, winning back to Hinduism many who had been attracted to these other faiths. Hinduism had a series of reformers in the tenth to the fifteenth centuries including Ramanuja, Vallabha and Caitanya. To differing degrees, they promoted devotion within Hinduism, encouraged a form of monotheism and attempted to mitigate the excesses of caste by their own examples.

Islam first encountered Hinduism through Arab traders but it was not until 1001 that Islam made a major impact through the raids of Mahmud of Ghazni who occupied the Punjab. A succession of invasions meant that by 1526 northern India was under Muslim Mughal rule. This rule was generally tolerant, rulers intermarried with Hindu princesses and Hindu practices were allowed at court. While taxes were imposed on non-Muslim subjects, often Brahmins were excluded and temples received government grants. Yet there were exceptions such as Aurangzeb (1658-1701) who demolished temples, built mosques on their sites and closed Hindu schools. This policy eventually led to the decline of Mughal rule as these intolerant practices prompted localised rebellions.

On 20 May 1498, Vasco de Gama sailed into Calcutta and opened up India to western influence. In 1757, the British defeated the French, and so replaced the Mughal Empire as rulers of India until 1947. The British colonialists initially opposed the introduction of missionaries to avoid alienating the Hindu population. Later generations, inspired by the ideals of the Clapham Sect and other leading English evangelicals, opposed various aspects of Hinduism such as *caste*, child brides and the treatment of widows that appeared primitive to a liberal, enlightened European mind. Those same generations were usually not so horrified at British excesses in India. As a living faith, Hinduism has continued to develop and prominent individuals or movements within Hinduism of recent times include:

Ram Mohan Roy (1772-1833) who opposed the practice of *sati* (the burning of widows) and child marriages. He was influenced by Sufism and considered some aspects of Hinduism to be idol worship. Whether Christianity influenced Roy is questionable but his 'reformation' of Hinduism made the faith more attractive to the growing numbers of educated Indians who were being attracted to Christianity. He travelled widely in Britain and Europe. The Brahma Samaj was founded by Roy in 1830 and met on Sunday evenings to worship in a monotheistic way. Its membership was usually high caste and intellectual. After Roy's death Muslim and Christian elements were incorporated into the movement but the rising tide of nationalism in the twentieth century led to the movement becoming marginalised.

The Arya Samaj of Dayananda Saraswati was dedicated to the restoration of pure Vedic religion. Saraswati was born in Gujarat in 1824 and turned against the worship of idols. He attempted to live the life of a *sadhu* or wandering religious ascetic and to reform Hinduism of image worship, *caste* and extreme aspects of village faith. He considered the Vedas to be the oldest and purest scriptures of humanity teaching one complete, eternal, and holy and just God, consequently dealings between people should be based on love and justice. The movement was strongly nationalistic and suspicious of western influence.

Sri Ramakrishna (1834-1886) believed God could be found in all religions and preached a traditional Hindu tolerance. He was prepared to adapt to the dress, food and prayer patterns of whatever group he was with, had a great influence among the westernised educated Indians and led to a return to Hinduism for many who had become attracted to Christianity. He developed a series of Ashrams or open retreat houses. His main disciple was Vivekananda who attended the World's Parliament of Religions in Chicago in 1893 and revealed the riches of Hinduism to a western audience. A fiery speaker, Ramakrishna motivated Indians to have a greater concern for the needy in their own society. Both accepted caste as part of the natural order.

Bhimrao Ranji Ambedkar (1891-1956) was from the untouchable caste. Educated abroad with an American doctorate, upon returning to India in 1917 he discovered his education counted for nothing when compared to his low *caste*. Ambedkar became champion of untouchable rights and opposition to caste, was Law minister in post-independence India and eventually converted to Buddhism with 600,000 followers over the issue of *caste*.

Gandhi (1869-1948) had been influenced by Vivekananda and saw truth as God and non-violence as the path to meeting God. His liberal understanding of Hinduism encompassed all that was good from other religions. *Caste* was rejected and a particular concern expressed for the untouchable groups, wanting them seen as *Harijan* or 'Children of God'. In his ashrams, Gandhi demanded the pursuit of truth, non-violence, abstinence from sexual activity and poverty. He was a devotee of Rama.

Satya Sai Baba (1926-present) has declared himself the incarnation of Sai Baba of Shirdi and teaches that God is beyond form and that appearance is illusion. Love and God are one and so worship consists of devotional songs, many miracles are claimed and values of truth, tolerance and non-violence respected.

There are conservative versions of Hinduism, notably embodied in the Bharatiya Janata Party of India that couples nationalism with a questioning of the traditionally tolerant pluralist nature of Hinduism.

Beliefs

Scripture does not play a central role in Hinduism in the way that it does in Islam, Sikhism or Christianity. Even within a temple copies of texts might be hard to find, more likely words of Scripture will have been memorised by the priest and worshippers and used from memory in acts of devotion. The earliest Hindu Scriptures are believed to have been composed between 1200BC and 1000BC by the Aryan invaders who settled in north-west India around 1500BC. A prolific creation of Scripture occurred between 1200BC and 200BC, known as the Vedic Age. These *Vedas* are believed to have been received as revelation from God and passed on by word of mouth, known as *Shruti* or hearing as they were heard by scholars and are considered as eternal. Today scholars will still often prefer to recite a text from memory rather than use a printed copy. The main exception to this will be when thanksgiving *pura* is performed and, while mantras are recited from memory, the priest will read the story of the origin of the ritual. Two further exceptions are Krishna's birthday and during the Ganesha festival when listening to Scripture being read is considered an act of devotion.

There are four Vedas each composed of four separate parts:

1. *Rig-Veda Samhita* is the oldest and is divided into ten books or *mandalas* and includes 1028 hymns of praise to ancient gods. Various aspects of deity are described and the ultimate answer to life is that Brahman is the one who encompasses all.

2. *Yajur–Veda Samhita* was used as a handbook for priests performing Vedic sacrifices.

3. *Sama-Veda Samhita* consists of chants, melodies and tunes to be sung at special sacrifices.

4. *Atharva-Veda Samhita* preserves many pre-Aryan traditions concerning spells, charms and magic formulae.

Many mantras from these texts are used in modern Hindu worship such as the Gayatri verse from the Rig-Veda, often used in daily worship.

Hindu Scripture is not limited to these four texts. The *Brahmanas* (800-500BC) are prose manuals of ritual and prayer for the guidance of priests. The *Aranyakas* (400-200BC) resulted from discussions in the forests about worship, meditation and ritual. The *Upanishads* (400-200BC) contain mystical concepts of Hindu philosophy, the word meaning 'near sitting' implying that they were delivered as a discourse from a guru to a pupil. In the development of scripture, the physical sacrifices of the Vedas are replaced by internal attitudes. Among the important doctrinal ideas to come from these texts are:

1   The individual soul (*atman*) and the universal soul (*Brahman*) are identical

2   *Brahman* is without form and eternal

3   The visible world is an illusion (*maya*)

4   The soul passes through a cycle of successive lives (*samsara*) and its next existence is determined by the consequences of its actions (*karma*) in the previous existence.

5   The soul is capable of achieving liberation (*moksha*)

6   There is a unity of all things in the created universe

The popular Hindu epics, the *Mahabharata* and the *Ramayana*, are classed as *smriti* texts and include religious, moral and educational writings based on remembered tradition. Composed from 500BC onwards most Hindus accept the teachings of these in as much as they do not contradict the *shruti* texts that are considered to be more directly God's word.

The Ramayana or 'Adventure of Rama' is the story of a Prince from north India who left royal life to meditate with his wife, Sita, in the forest. She was kidnapped by the demon Ravan and brought to Ceylon. Rama, his brother and the monkey god Hanuman followed and after many adventures, the couple were reunited and ruled their kingdom in peace. Possibly based on some historical foundations, Rama became an *avatar* of Vishnu who destroys sin and brings deliverance from trouble while Sita is an example of purity.

The Bhagavad-Gita or 'Song of Krishna' is very popular and accepted as god's word because Krishna is an important incarnation of Vishnu. It can be translated as 'The Song of the Adorable One' and is the sixth book of the *Mahabharata*, the world's longest poem, although some scholars consider it of later construction dating from 200BC – 200AD. *The Bhagavad-Gita* takes the form of a dialogue between prince Arjuna and his charioteer Krishna, an incarnation of the supreme god Vishnu. The setting is the Battle of Kurukshetra where Arjuna wants to back down as he is aware the planned battle will involve killing many of his relatives. Krishna explains that it is Arjuna's *dharma* to fight, *dharma* being the custom or religious duty that cannot be avoided. Following *dharma* is one of the poem's main themes. Other themes include *bhakti* or loving devotion to God and God's love, *samkhya* (theory) providing the analysis of reality and yoga (practice) showing the means of attainment. *Karma* or actions that need to be performed are mentioned as a duty. The focus of the poem is Krishna and devotion to him, which involves the observance of *dharma*. The polytheism of the *Vedas* was replaced by the pantheism of the *Upanishads* and developed into the possible monotheism of the *Mahabharata*.

Three ways of salvation are revealed:
1   The way of knowledge of the *Vedas* (mainly for Brahmins).
2   The way of *karma* or works.
3   The way of *bhakti* or personal devotion which is open to all, irrespective of caste or sex, and which is viewed as the best way.

The *Laws of Manu* (200BC) spell out a system to order every detail of daily life and was *dharma* codified while *Sutras* are short pieces originating from influential gurus and dealing with specific topics.

Hindu sacred literature has no end and is being continually updated. Many Hindus consider Gandhi's commentary on the *Bhagavad-Gita* to be inspiring while the nineteenth century words of Sri Ramakrishna are treasured. Even the words of Prabhupada, the founder of ISKCON, are popular beyond the specific followers of that movement. Some will want to study to understand, others will feel the spoken words have a power as in a mantra.

Hindu Divinity

The search for *Brahman*, Eternal Being or Reality is the pre-occupation of the Hindu mind and to achieve this goal they are willing to renounce the world, family and comfort and go on arduous pilgrimages. Some Hindu schools believe in a personal god, others in an abstract Reality or energy with the physical world viewed as illusion. Most Hindus accept the notion of an all-pervading God and while personal devotion will be offered to a particular deity, that deity may be understood as a representative of a particular characteristic or aspect of the one God. They might refer to God as Bhagwan. This perspective considers Hinduism monotheistic and should be viewed as argument rather than accepted fact. In this opinion, the supreme spirit or Brahman is the ultimate source and the one supreme reality is impersonal energy, possibly more related to monism than monotheism. Consequently, the various gods are explained as representations of the characteristics of *Brahman*. An alternative view sees millions of competing or complimentary gods in a totally polytheistic environment and individuals simply choose their preference – the ultimate consumer society. A more accurate description may be that Hinduism is transtheistic or beyond god.

God always creates out of something or out of himself, never from nothing. Even in the later *Upanishads* and the *Bhagavad-Gita*, where the idea of a personal god is developed, god always tends to be identified with the sum total of creation. The world has neither beginning nor end but is part of an evolutionary cyclical process. These periods are known as 'the days and nights of *Brahman*'. Each day and night last 1000 years and each god year equals 12,000 human years. Each year of the gods is divided into four periods of varying length and we are currently living in the fourth or Kali age. This is the worst age, started in 3102 BC and will last for 432,000 years. A juggling of modern physics can produce some interesting comparisons with dates. Creation is a transit from chaos to order that may or may not involve a Creator God. It can be viewed as the union of primeval male and female, or the birth of the golden seed. The question as to why there is a constant process of recreation is answered as the sport of God.

Broadly speaking, Hindus may be classified into three groups with reference to devotion to god:

1   Those who worship Vishnu and Lakshmi, or Vishnu's important incarnations such as Rama, Krishna and Narasimha.
2   Those who worship Shiva in the form of lingnam or Nataraja (cosmic dancer).
3   Those who worship Shakti the Mother Goddess, variously termed Parvati, Mahalakshmi, Ambaji, Durga or Kali.

There is also a trinity of sorts with Brahma (creation), Vishnu (sustaining) and Shiva (destruction) although the specific worship of Brahma has almost disappeared.

Vishnu was a minor deity of light in the *Vedas* but in modern Hinduism he has come to represent the Preserver aspect of *Brahman*. Often depicted resting on a lotus or under the coils of the serpent Shesha he is usually represented as having a dark bluish complexion, four hands and riding an eagle. Vishnu preserves or protects the universe and is considered to have appeared on earth in the form of twenty-two avatars or incarnations to save humanity in times of crisis. These avatars include Varaha the boar who destroyed the demon Hiranyaksha, Vamana the dwarf who tricked the demon king Bali, Rama whose deeds of valour against Ravana, king of Lanka are described in the *Ramayana*, Krishna who destroyed the wicked, protected the righteous and established a new world order (*dharma*), Buddha the founder of Buddhism and the last avatar Kalki who is still to come as a rider on a white horse at the end of the present 'Age of Darkness'.

Lakshmi appears in her avatars as the partner to the Vishnu avatars. Consequently, she is Padma to Vamana, Sita to Rama and Rukmini to Krishna. Shown as a beautiful woman with four arms rising from a lotus, two hands hold lotus flowers, one hand gives wealth in gold coins and one hand blesses devotees. As goddess of wealth and good fortune, she is offered special worship on the Lakshmi-puja day during the Diwali festival.

The pre-Aryan people of the Indus valley worshipped a male god who is pictured crossed legged surrounded by animals. **Shiva** appears to have grown out of this concept and contains many seeming contradictions. He lives in Mt Kailasa in the Himalayas, has 1008 names and his consort is Parvati and other representations of Shakti (mother goddess). As Nataraja (Lord of the Dance), he is the god of movement in the universe and destruction, yet he is also the god of regeneration and sexuality and usually depicted with one foot on the demon of ignorance and the other foot raised. As Mahayogi, he is the god of asceticism and pictured naked with matted hair and ash; associated with evil he is believed to have a third eye with which he destroyed the god of love.

Shakti is worshipped under many names, stressing her various attributes such as mother goddess and loving wife in Parvati, and terror and bloodshed in Kali or Durga. These goddesses are worshipped in their own right and not just as the consort of male gods. The term Shakti can refer to the female goddess in principal, to any goddess or specifically to the wives of Shiva and is linked to yoga.

The numerous other gods include **Ganesha**, the son of Shiva and **Parvati**, who had his head cut off in a misunderstanding by Shiva and was given an elephant head. He is the leader of the *ganas* or semi-divine attendants and worshipped as a god of good luck, wisdom and one who overcomes difficulties. Prayers are offered to Ganesha at the beginning of a *puja*, at life cycle rituals dealing with marriage, entering and leaving homes and when faced with problems. Ganesha is depicted with a pink body and elephant's head with one tusk, riding on or attended by a rat.

Hanuman the monkey chief, is the son of **Vayu** (wind god) and **Anjana** (semi divine). Renowned for his heroic feats as a helper of Rama, he possesses great strength and agility and the ability to change his shape.

While there are main or prominent gods who can be viewed, to some extent as national or international gods, in villages it is often a very localised deity that will be worshipped. Most of these are female and considered the guardians of the village. The functions of these deities are to give children, food, and overcome sickness and difficulties. There may be other shrines in villages to demons and offerings will be made at these to appease and ward off bad luck. Hindus may have devotion to a minor god from their family or village background, even if several generations ago, and to one or more of the more prominent deities.

Hindu Doctrine

Karma is action or doing and is a moral interpretation of the natural law of cause and effect, extended to the realm of the spirit and to life past, present and future. It applies to good and bad actions; bad actions lead to suffering, good actions lead to freedom from suffering.

Reproductive *karma* is the force of the actions we do which have the power to determine rebirth. Supportive *karma* is the actions that support the reproductive karma and can make life pleasant. Counteractive *karma* obstructs reproductive *karma* resulting in suffering. Destructive *karma* stops the flow of the other forces and so a past action may result in an early death even though there was much other good *karma*.

Much of the teaching concerning *dharma* is found in the *Laws of Manu*, dating from around the time of Christ. It is concerned with the general *dharma* or duty placed on all and the specific duty to those from certain *castes* or arising from relationships. Each has to perform the tasks assigned to them; what is right and wrong is discerned from scripture, other inspired writings, good conduct and conscience. The four separate orders of student, householder, hermit and ascetic are considered and each has certain duties. Each must carry out their own *dharma* and not seek that of another.

Samsara is rebirth or transmigration of the soul. In some ways, the soul is identical with *Brahman*, but migrates from body to body, carrying its load of *karma*. This is a natural principle of the universe amongst all people and animals. Due to a person's actions, they may be reborn as a god, in a different human caste or as an animal. An individual gets exactly what he or she deserves.

Moksha is the goal for a Hindu; finding release from the endless cycle of rebirth and attachment to the material world and attaining peace. There are two traditional theories to explain how this 'grace' operates:

1   Kitten–as a mother cat carries the passive kitten so all is done by god with nothing by the individual.
2   Monkey–this baby clings on to its mother and so there must be a human part in salvation.

This liberation is often seen as merging into *Brahman* rather than reaching a 'Heaven' like state. It comes by knowledge, devotion and action and can be experienced in this life or at death.

One of the strongest distinguishing characteristics of traditional Hinduism has been strict adherence to *caste*, a closed and rigid social group based on heredity. *Caste* origins are uncertain, with a pre-Aryan source possible, but it appears to have grown in significance with the multi-racial and multi-cultural nature of India. In marriage, eating and finding employment, *caste* is a major determining feature. A creation myth describes the origin of *caste* as resulting from the division of the original man. His mouth was the *brahmins*, arms were the *kshatryas* and warriors, thighs the *vaisyas* and the feet were the *sudras*.

Hence the four main caste divisions:

Brahmins= priests and religious teachers   (5% of Hindu population)
Kshatryas=kings and warriors   (6%)
Vaisyas=   traders   (6%)
Sudras=   farmers and servants   (40%)

Within these groups there are about three thousand *jati* or sub groups based on profession and occupation. Beyond the four castes, exist the untouchables or **Dalits**. Several Hindu reform movements have attempted without success to eliminate this distinction. Within India, this community is given extra educational and other opportunities by the government, but still suffers very significant disadvantages.

In former generations, there were mass movements to Christianity, in more recent years movements have been towards Buddhism, such as through Ambekdar. In 2001, there was another significant mass movement of many thousands of *dalits* into Buddhism.

There could be a new caste emerging at present. Some Indian cities, such as Bangalore, have very large Information Technology industries and a well-paid, highly educated middle class of many millions has been developing. In some ways this 'caste' is open to anyone who works in modern industry and falls into a roughly 'middle class' typology. It is too early to consider this the beginning of the end for *caste*, but it is an interesting development.

Worship

The Hindu concept of worship is as varied as the differing expressions of Hinduism. No one word encompasses worship, but the closest may be *puja* that includes ritual worship but is also offered to parents and teachers. In this context *puja* can be interpreted as either worship or offering respect. Most Hindu rituals take place in the home and are generally carried out by women. These include life-cycle rituals and regional festivals celebrating specific deities and those of national appeal such as *Divali* or *Holi*.

Devotion offered to an image is not considered as idolatry as the image is not the deity but rather a symbol and so devotees are praying to or worshipping the deity personified by the image. A simple stone can be as effective as an elaborately carved statue. When a statue is being carved the final moment, when the pupils are added, is known as the opening of the eyes. Some consider this is when some aspect of the divinity enters the statue and part of the power of the divinity is taken on.

Prayer usually consists of the repetition of a mantra a specific number of times, sometimes helped by prayer beads. Usually prayers are for one's own state as to pray for others may be to attempt to interfere with their *karma*. In a home, the household shrine will usually be an alcove in a wall or a cupboard which will contain images of particular gods to which offerings and prayers may be offered daily. It may contain a small lamp and/or joss stick, gains of rice, flowers and powders such as turmeric. Similar shrines will also be common in Hindu run shops, offices and even vehicles.

A more elaborate ceremony may take place in the home during an annual festival. That ceremony may involve an invocation where rice grains sprinkled on a statue (*murti*), grains may be spread in a copper dish below the statue and the *murti's* feet touched by a wet flower to wash them. In a symbol of reverence water and mixture of milk, ghee, honey and sugar may be placed at the *murti's* mouth, fresh water offered and the *murti* symbolically bathed with a flower dipped in water and honey. A red robe draped around the shoulders, a sacred thread wrapped around and sandalwood paste applied to its forehead may honour the statue. Flowers and leaves may then be arranged at the statue's feet, a joss stick and a ghee lamp lit and waved in front. Food, perhaps of copra and raw sugar, may be offered, with fruit and coins placed before the *murti*. Ideally, devotees will circumambulate but if not possible, the devotee will turn around a number of times. Finally, sweet foods may be offered to the *murti* and then shared among devotees, prayers are offered, songs sung and individuals prostrate themselves before the image.

There are sixteen rites of passage although only some Brahmin males will experience all sixteen. Many males will experience about ten, women usually six and almost all Hindus at least three. Regional variations are important but the generally accepted list includes rites for conception, for a son, naming a child, first outing, first solid food, boy's first haircut, piercing upper part of right ear, sacred thread ceremony, starting to learn the scriptures, end of Vedic education, marriage ceremony, householder stage, retirement ritual on 60th birthday and finally cremation.

Annual festivals vary according to regional variations but include the harvest festival of *Navanna*, the spring festival of *Holi* dedicated to Krishna and New Year or *Divali* when Lakshmi, the goddess of good fortune, visits every house lit by a lamp. Often fireworks to celebrate the victory of good over evil will accompany this.

Pilgrimages, often condemned by 19th century Hindu reformers, are still popular today, especially among rural Hindus in India. Some are small scale and involve a journey on foot of perhaps a couple of hours to a town or city temple. The exertion of the journey enhances the spirituality of the occasion. A whole village traditionally was involved and offerings of flowers, coconut and cash will be brought. The sacred rivers of the Ganges and Godavari, and the sacred cities of Banares, Puri and Hardwar attract huge numbers, sometimes numbering millions for specific festivals. *Caste* is temporarily suspended during a pilgrimage and all will bathe together in a sacred river. These are the largest gatherings of people for a single purpose on earth. Many Hindus will return to India to participate in these festivals.

Hindus have been defined as those who accepted the authority of the Brahmin priests and the *Vedas*. The vast majority of priests come from the Brahmin *caste*, although the majority of this *caste* does not enter the priesthood. There is no centralised organisation, rather many priests are attached to a particular temple or, more likely, work only part time as priests.

Sadhus are holy men and women who have taken vows to withdraw from the world. Many live in ashrams were they meditate and follow a very ascetic lifestyle surviving on the gifts of others. *Caste* plays no part in this.

Gurus are spiritual guides who may attract followers with their teaching. They can make Hinduism easier to understand and more personal, they will act as advisers to their followers and may claim miracles.

LECTURE 4 WHAT IS THE BUDDHIST FAITH?

It is useful to note that the word 'Buddhism' can be considered as a western invention, eastern adherents are more likely to talk of *Dharma*. Buddhism can also be read as, to some extent, as a 'protestant' reaction against the practice of Hinduism two and a half thousand years ago, problems that included the expense of sacrifices for participants and the caste system.

Foundation

The founder of Buddhism was not a god, prophet or messiah but rather a normal human being who, by his own efforts, became completely awake, both to his own potential and to the nature of the world around him. **The Buddha was born as Siddhartha Gautama** in the Terai lowlands near the foothills of the Himalayas just inside the borders of modern day Nepal, about 230 miles north of Benares. He traditionally lived from 566-486 BC; as such, he was a contemporary of Pythagarus and Nehemiah although some research would like to place Gautama about 70 years earlier. Discovering 'the historical Buddha' is a difficult task but the following is an approximation of the Buddha's final life.

Siddhartha Gautama was born into a wealthy and noble Hindu Shakya family, probably from the second or warrior *caste*. Married at sixteen, Gautama left home at twenty-nine, became enlightened at thirty-five and spent the next forty-five years as a wandering teacher. More correctly, we should talk of births as the Buddha had many existences going back millions of years and enjoying lives as men, animals and gods. The *Jataka* contains five hundred and fifty birth stories and details of these previous lives. Texts describe how the Buddha was conceived when his mother Maya dreamed that a white baby elephant entered her side, a dream that was interpreted to mean she would bear a son who would be either a great emperor or else a great religious teacher. His mother travelled to her hometown for the birth and she went into labour and gave birth standing up holding on to the trunk of a Sal tree. The gods came to view and the ground shook when the child was laid on the ground. The baby was bathed in a miraculous shower of water, stood up and took seven steps and declared that this would be his last birth. Seven days later the Buddha's mother died and he was raised by his mother's sister, Mahapatjapati. His mother's death is explained that once she had given birth to the Buddha her life was fulfilled.

The Buddha's father wished to protect him from any of life's realities that might cause Gautama to consider the place of religion so that his son would remain in the palace and become King. On rare journeys outside of the palace, the king arranged for only healthy, happy people to be seen. However, despite the luxury and comfort, the Buddha found his life unfulfilling.

On either one trip or four successive journeys outside of the palace, he saw an old man, a sick man, a corpse about to be buried and finally a religious ascetic. These experiences caused him to reflect on his life and the meaning of suffering and decay. On the night, he saw the ascetic the Buddha left his sleeping wife and son (Rahula, meaning chain) and never returned to them, although Mara, the Tempter, tried to get him to return.

The Buddha's decision to leave his family and go in search of spiritual truth has a long tradition in north India and the *samana* movement, a counter-culture of homeless religious mendicants, was already well established by this time. So he was one among many following a similar path. Gautama had five companions on his search and had as his first teacher **Alara Kalama** who introduced him to meditation techniques that induced a profound trance. The Buddha mastered this but found it unsatisfying due to its temporary nature.

A second meditation teacher, **Uddaka Ramaputta**, helped the Buddha to enter into a state of 'neither perception nor non-perception'. Again, while this was appreciated, it did not offer the satisfaction that he needed. Gautama's alternative approach was to attempt a vigorously austere lifestyle. First, there was breath control, but this only produced headaches. Next, food consumption was reduced to an absolute minimum but soon the Buddha could barely sit and his hair started to fall out. This convinced him that these extremes were unproductive and helped him later formulate his 'middle way' doctrine, a path of moderation where appetites were neither denied nor excessively indulged. His five friends left him thinking he had gone soft. Returning to food Gautama began to meditate once more and in the course of one full moon night, while seated under a large pippila tree that would become known as the Bodhi tree, by the banks of the River Niranjana he attained enlightenment. First, he was able to look back through his previous lives; next, he was able to see the death and rebirth of all types of beings in the universe according to their good and bad deeds. After this, he attained the knowledge that his spiritual defilements had been eliminated and that he had overcome his desires and lack of knowledge. Thus, he attained *nirvana* and escaped from the process of rebirth, just as he prophesied at his birth. Legend has a cosmic battle raging between various gods and demons attempting to help or hinder Gautama attaining enlightenment. For part of the time, he was protected by a giant snake that coiled around him. Gautama also experienced many temptations to give up this path, but persevered, events commemorated at *Vesak*.

The gods convinced the Buddha to spread his teaching or *dharma* throughout the world. Supernaturally he realised his former teachers had died but that at Benares on the Ganges he would find his five former associates. These five reluctantly welcomed him and in the Royal Deer Park, the Buddha preached his first sermon in which outlined the essential teachings of Buddhism, known as the 'discourse setting in motion the wheel of truth'. One of the audience immediately glimpsed the truth and entered the stream leading to enlightenment;

eventually the other four joined him. They became monks, were ordained and during the second sermon all achieved enlightenment becoming known as *arahats* or those who attain *nirvana*. The term Buddha was reserved for those who discover the way for themselves. Soon there were sixty *arahats* and the Buddha commissioned them to take the message to the world. Five years later an order of nuns was established. Among the converts were his father, former wife, son and his nephew Ananda who became his companion and helper for the next thirty-five years.

Throughout the rest of his life, the Buddha wandered through towns and villages of north-east India. As he engaged in debates and discourses, the number of converts grew. One tradition has it that when a prince sent one thousand troops to welcome the Buddha they were all converted and became monks. A further one thousand were sent with the same result until the prince could not afford to lose any more soldiers and there were ten thousand new monks. Miracles were ascribed to the Buddha due to the supreme psychic powers he developed and eventually residential centres or viharas were established where the monks would spend the rainy season. While there was much acceptance of his message, at least three attempts on his life appear to have been made.

When aged eighty and in failing health the Buddha explained to Ananda that there he was to have successor as he never saw himself as head of an order, rather the *Dharma* should be the guide. The Buddha died at a small town called Kusinara, lying between two Sal trees that miraculously bloomed out of season. He had suffered from food poisoning just before this but seems to have died of natural causes. Before his death, the Buddha had asked his monks if they had any questions and when three times in succession there were none he presumed that the *Dharma* had been fully explained. His last words were, 'Decay is inherent in all component things. Work out your salvation with diligence.' Ananda declared that the Buddha was dead, but was corrected by a monk who declared that, rather than dead, the Buddha had now entered into the state where both sensations and ideas have ceased to be. The Buddha's remains were cremated, tradition has it that much of this ash took the form of diamond, and the remains were enshrined in a bell like structure called a *stupa*, in a similar way to a king. *Stupas* and statutes of the Buddha are ever-present sights in Buddhists countries.

Development

From the outset, Buddhism was a missionary religion and the Buddha showed that in his own life by constantly travelling for the forty-five years after his enlightenment to spread his message. He had a significant impact in northern India during his lifetime in northern India but the major growth occurred through the influence of Ashoka.

Ashoka became king of India around 268BC and through conquest; he extended the Mauryan Empire, making it the largest Indian empire until the British era. After a very vicious campaign in Orissa in eastern India, he became very remorseful about the cost of life and suffering and turned to Buddhism. He ruled according to Buddhist principles, established the faith throughout India and sent ambassador/missionaries to other countries such as Burma and Thailand, Cambodia, Laos and Vietnam to help spread the faith. His brother Mahinda was sent to Ceylon where he founded a monastic settlement at the capital of Anuradhapura in 250BC.

Buddhism in India flourished for the first half of the millennium but by the year 1000AD Buddhism was in decline and at the end of the 10th century Muslim Turks were able to easily attack the unfortified monasteries. In 1192, a Turkish tribe established rule over northern India and soon Buddhism had virtually died out in the region. The five million Buddhists found today in India are more recent *Dalit* converts from Hinduism, largely as a reaction against *caste* restrictions.

In 83BC, the Pali canon of scripture was first written down on palm leaves and Sri Lankan Buddhists consider that they have a special task to preserve and promote Buddhism throughout the world. Buddhism spread to China from India by the first century of the Christian era through evangelist monks who travelled along the silk route. Buddhism was considered by some to carry on from where Confucianism ended, especially concerning death and the afterlife and soon many Chinese held both faiths, one dealing with this world and the other with the next. Buddhism reached a high point under the T'ang dynasty (618-907AD) and remained as an influential portion of the mixture that is Chinese religion. The post-World War II communist takeover and the 1966 Cultural Revolution placed Buddhism under great pressure, although it has survived and remains particularly strong in Taiwan.

Buddhism came to Japan in the 6th century via Korea but drew much of its inspiration from China. In 593, the ruler became a student of Buddhist and Confucian scriptures and traditional Shintoism was fused with Buddhism. In 1868, a revolution rejected Buddhism because of its close association with dictators but since 1875, there has been freedom of religion. Various Japanese approaches to Buddhism have emerged such as Pure Land and Zen. There has been a strong social engagement and monks marry and take a full part in community life. Zen Buddhism stresses meditation in a calm and relaxed rather than philosophical way, giving significance to various art forms. Doctrinal formulations are not particularly important.

Due to the almost inaccessible nature of Tibet, Buddhism only entered in the 8th century and has taken a particular form known as Mantrayana due to the use of magical formulas and chants. Rich symbolism and various unique religious practices augment Mahayana philosophy. Lamas teach devotees hidden meanings to various magic circles, pentagrams, spells and charms. Tantric teachings can be understood on many levels and various schools developed secret practices. Desire is no longer considered a problem but is harnessed for positive means.

The Dalai Lama encompasses both the religious and political worlds and ruled Tibet since 1642 until the current incumbent fled in 1959, nine years after the Chinese invasion. Since the invasion Buddhism has been systematically persecuted by the Chinese as it is seen as representing the cultural and religious heart of Tibet, a process carried out in order to hasten the destruction of Tibet as a country. Most modern maps no longer show Tibet.

Buddhism began to gain a following in western countries in the 19th century, significantly helped by the publication of the epic poem *The Light of Asia* by Sir Edward Arnold chronicling the life of the Buddha. In 1924, Christmas Humphries founded the Buddhist Society in England and two years later the Maha Bodhi Society was founded and a monastery established for Sri Lankan monks. Scholars were attracted to the Theravada form of Buddhism but in more recent years Zen and Tibetan Buddhism have become influential.

Beliefs

The Buddha's teaching was preserved by his disciples and transmitted orally through the next few generations. There were three general councils in the period from 483BC – 225BC when many points of doctrinal dispute were clarified. Finally, in 83BC King Vattagamani Abhaya of Sri Lanka had the Scriptures written down on palm leaves in the Pali language, traditionally in three parts known as the *Tipitaka* or Three Baskets.

The *Vinaya Pitaka* deals mainly with rules and regulations for the monks and nuns. The *Sutta Pitaka* consists of discourses delivered by the Buddha and some of his more distinguished disciples. This includes the *Dharmapada* containing 423 verses of ethical instruction and the *Jataka* containing events in the previous lives of the Buddha. The *Abhidhamma Pitaka* contains the profound philosophy behind the Buddha's teaching. It analyses phenomena, explaining the nature of mind and matter.

The idea and practice of the three Jewels is central to Buddhists, perhaps having the same place as the *Shahada* within Islam. Buddhists affirm that they take refuge in the Buddha, the *Dharma* and the *Sangha*, or community of Buddhism.

The Buddha was able to recall numerous past lives in considerable detail and Buddhism understands an almost endless succession of rebirths known as *samsara* or endless wandering. All living creatures are part of this cyclic process and will continue to be reborn until they obtain *nirvana*. Hindu concepts underpin much of this area of Buddhism. The main difference between the two faiths is that Buddhism does not recognise a soul that moves from one body to another. Rather it is the consequence of a person's *karma* that transmigrates.

Buddhist thought divides the universe into two categories: the physical universe and the beings that inhabit it. The physical universe is formed by the interaction of earth, water, fire, air and space. Their interaction forms world systems (like galaxies) in six directions (north, south, east, and west, up and down). These systems undergo cycles of evolution and decline lasting for billions of years. The quality of lives of the inhabitants partially determines how long the galaxy survives.

527

A creation story in the *Agganna Suta* tells of the inhabitants of a destroyed world system being reborn as translucent creatures in a new evolving system. As the fabric of this world solidifies, these creatures start to eat and consume it and become more physical. In order to regulate this they elect a king and so a new society is begun. This shows the origins of human suffering in desire.

In the Buddhist cosmology, hell is a place of torment and terrible suffering, both hot and cold but is only temporary and when the bad *karma* has been used up then there is release. The animal realm is not much of an improvement due to their poor quality of life. The ghosts have only a shadowy existence around the edges of the human world. They were too attached to the human world by their desires and now still have these same desires but can no longer fulfil them. Titans are demonic warlike creatures at the mercy of violent impulses seeking conquests in which they find no satisfaction. The human world is a desirable place in which to be reborn and offers a middle way between pleasure and suffering; it also offers the possibility of much further advancement. Beyond this, the twenty-one levels of the gods are wonderful, long lasting existences but it is possible to slip back and be reborn at a lower level. The final five levels or Pure Abodes are for the non-returners who cannot return to the human sphere but will soon attain enlightenment.

Karma is what determines the destination of the individual. Basically, good deeds result in upward movement and bad deeds in downward movement. Rather than a system of divine rewards *karma* is a natural law that involves the moral value of an action as much as the action itself. The moral choices we make help to form our character. Not all the consequences of our actions happen in this life, but can be carried forward to the next or subsequent lives. However, *karma* does not mean everything in life is determined; there is still much freedom of choice. Actions motivated by greed, hatred and delusion are bad and actions motivated by non-attachment, benevolence and understanding are good. Good intentions need to be translated into good actions to make progress.

Much effort is spent in acquiring good *karma* or merit, somewhat like spiritual capital that is locked away until it is needed later. An effective way of obtaining merit is to help the priesthood by gifts of food, robes, by listening to sermons and financial donation. However, doing good deeds to obtain merit would be to act from a selfish motive and so would have the opposite karmic effect.

Everything is dependent on something else; nothing can arise on its own accord. For example, a lamp remains burning because of a wick that depends on oxygen and a sufficient temperature, even oxygen is a combination of elements and a wick is composed of different strands of cotton. This explains the cycle of lives and how a person accumulates *karma* and is reborn through the round of existence as depicted in the 'wheel of becoming'–a wheel of twelve spokes denoting the twelve links of the causal process:

DEPENDENT ON:
- ignorance so intentional activities arise
- intentional activities so consciousness arises
- consciousness so mental and physical phenomena arises
- mental and physical phenomena so the six senses arise
- six senses so contact arises
- contact so sensation arises
- sensation so craving arises
- craving so clinging arises
- clinging so the process of becoming arises
- becoming so birth arises
- birth so decay, sorrow, suffering, pain, grief and despair arises

The ultimate goal of Buddhism is to put an end to suffering and rebirth. Someone who achieves this complete state of self-realisation is said to have obtained *nirvana*, both a concept and an experience. It offers a particular vision of human fulfilment and becomes real in the life of the seeker.

Leading a good life and gaining merit is only part of the pathway to *nirvana*. This needs to be supplemented by wisdom that involves a profound philosophical understanding of the human condition. This is a long process of thought and reflection that eventually reaches full maturity in the complete awakening experienced by the Buddha. In his first sermon in the Deer Park, the Buddha laid out the wisdom that was needed to obtain enlightenment in four basic concepts known as the Four Noble Truths.

Buddhists consider suffering to be an intrinsic part of life. There is suffering of many kinds but the deeper problem is the repeated birth, sickness, ageing and death in numerous lifetimes. Apart from physical suffering, the realisation that we cannot get what we want is a further type of mental or existential suffering. The Buddha did not accept the concept of an individual soul (*atman*) or its cosmic counterpart (*Brahman*), rather an individual's personal moral identity continues beyond a specific death. There are five factors of humanity and they all involve suffering; the physical body, sensations and feelings, understanding, character traits and consciousness.

Suffering comes from craving or desire. It is desire for life and the pleasant experiences it can offer that causes rebirth. This desire will show itself in three ways - desire for sensual pleasure such as taste or sight, desire for existence, desire to destroy or to reject what is not wanted.

All desire is not wrong. There is positive desire such as that for *nirvana* and that others should experience happiness. These right desires enhance and liberate, an example might be related to the desire for a cigarette and the desire to give up smoking.

When desire is removed, then *nirvana* is achieved. *Nirvana* takes two forms:

In this life, such as the Buddha experienced under the tree and at death when the final *nirvana* is reached from which a person cannot be reborn. *Nirvana* literally means 'blowing out', such as in a candle, and what is extinguished in *nirvana* are the greed, hatred and delusion that lead to rebirth. This can be understood in life in a very serene person but it is not so clear at death. It is not annihilation and it is not existence, rather it is an enigma that the Buddha taught was not to be understood but rather to be attained.

An individual passes from the endless wandering of *samsara* to *nirvana* by way of the Noble Eightfold Path-**BY RIGHT:**

1. **View**-accepting the Buddha's teachings
2. **Resolve**-serious commitment to developing right attitudes
3. **Speech**-telling the truth and speaking in a sensitive way

4. Action–not acting wrongly or indulging overly in sensual pleasures
5. Livelihood–not working where harm could be caused to others
6. Effort–controlling thoughts and being positive
7. Mindfulness–constant awareness
8. Meditation–developing deep levels of mental calm

This is the Middle Way because it avoids the extremes of indulgence and austerity. The first two involve wisdom, the next three involve morality and the final three involve meditation. All this is a type of self-transformation process that changes a person intellectually, morally and socially. Through the pursuit of knowledge and moral virtue, ignorance and desire are overcome, the cause of the arising of suffering is removed, and *nirvana* is obtained.

Worship

The common image of the Buddha is of him sitting cross-legged in meditation and it was in this way that Gautama obtained *nirvana*, part of a process whereby a person makes himself or herself into what they wish to be. The Buddha was familiar with the teachings of the *Upanishads* and that of Yoga. What he did was to modify existing practices to suit his understanding.

Meditation can be defined as an altered state of consciousness that is induced in a controlled manner. Daydreams are common to all and show the possibilities of entry into meditation. Types of meditation are found in all religions. In order for the mind to be calm, the body must be composed and the lotus position of sitting cross-legged with the back straight, head slightly inclined and hands in lap is considered helpful. Concentration can be achieved by repeating a silent mantra or focusing on an object. Meditation results in heightened powers of concentration, an inner calm and confidence. Buddhist meditation practices take the individual from detachment to rapture, through peace that leads a person beyond pleasure or pain to an eventual state where there is neither perception nor non-perception.

The Buddha did not view meditation as an escape from the world but rather the generation of insight and the focus in order to sharpen the intellectual capabilities.

In addition to meditation, there are types of corporate worship such as listening to sermons and veneration of relics and religious symbols. Incense, flowers and prostration will be offered. Often the monks will chant in Pali or Sanskrit, making it difficult for lay people to participate fully. In a similar way to Hinduism, most Buddhist homes will have a household shrine with prayers and offerings of incense being offered daily. Pilgrimage to places related to the Buddha's life or where relics are held is also popular.

Living the Faith

The Buddha founded the *Sangha* or community soon after his enlightenment, the first five members of the clergy being the five ascetics who were converted after the first sermons in the Deer Park. Admission to the *Sangha* was open to all without any *caste* restrictions and women were as welcome as men. The *Sangha* has two sections, the first for male and female clergy with a second class for laypeople.

The monks generally live in community and often engage in teaching; they take vows of poverty, shave their heads and wear distinctive saffron robes. There is a sliding scale of regulations for the ordained, rising as they progress to a total of 227. In some countries, such as Sri Lanka, the *Sangha* still has significant political influence.

There are five precepts for lay Buddhists: to refrain from harming living beings, from taking what is not given, from sexual misconduct and misuse of the senses, from harmful speech and drink or drugs which cloud the mind. The newly ordained monk promises to follow these and additionally to refrain from eating after midday, from dancing, amusements, singing with instruments, from perfumes and garlands, from sleeping in comfortable beds and from accepting money.

Differences

After the Buddha's death, the lack of a central leader resulted in the growth of various schools of interpretation. The most serious disagreement occurred about one hundred years into the Buddhist era between a group later designated as the 'Elders' (Theravada) and those known as the 'Universal Assembly' (Mahayana). The disagreement probably centred on the Elders wishes to add to the Monastic Rules and was influenced by the question as to whether expanding Buddhism should adapt or not to new beliefs and practices. Further, some emphasised the words of the Buddha so an extent that the spirit of the message could be lost, with a tendency to view the quest for enlightenment as a selfish personal search. Basically, Mahayana is a more liberal, syncretistic understanding that considers the Buddha a saviour whereas Theravada is a more conservative understanding stressing more the teaching rather than the person of the Buddha. Generally, a Buddhist country will be overwhelmingly either Mahayana or Theravada although within each expression local identity plays a very significant role.

Mahayana or the 'great vehicle' understands itself as the universal way to salvation. It developed around the time of Christ and Christianity may well have influenced it. The ideal is a life dedicated in service to others, helping others find enlightenment rather than concentrating on oneself and by showing compassion in practical ways. Rather than just a teacher, the Buddha is viewed as having three bodies: the human body he had on earth, a heavenly body located upstream in a blissful realm and a transcendent body identical with ultimate truth. There is a belief that a Buddha, known as Maitreya, will appear at the end of the present age when there will be a utopian era when many will achieve enlightenment.

The nucleus of the Mahayana understanding was a series of new scriptures that appeared in the early years of the Christian era. While not claimed as coming from the Buddha's hand, these texts, written in Sanskrit, claimed the Buddha as their spiritual author. The *Lotus Sutra* argues that while the Buddha appeared as an ordinary man, in reality he was enlightened from all time and went through a charade to help people. He had not fully revealed all his teaching as it was beyond people at the time but now it could be fully revealed. He was a type of 'Superman' who could perform many miracles and brought salvation both by his teaching and also in his person. There are other canons of Mahayana teaching that complement these Sutras such as the Tibetan Canon that includes *The Tibetan Book of the Dead* and various Chinese writings.

The path to salvation begins with a moment of enlightenment that could be considered like a conversion experience. Then a vow is taken to lead others to *nirvana*, no matter how long this takes. As the Bodhisattva practices six virtues or Perfections, he/she advances through ten stages towards *nirvana*. These virtues, which can be considered as a reformulation of the Noble Eightfold Path, include generosity, morality, patience, courage, meditation and wisdom. Bodhisattvas who had reached the higher stages of their careers were visualised as enormously powerful beings, virtually identical to the Buddha in his heavenly form. The Tibetan Dalai Lamas are said to be incarnations of the celestial Bodhisattva 'Avalokitesvara' or 'the Lord who looks down in compassion'. A rich pantheon of Buddhas and Bodhisattvas come into being, inhabiting a majestic, unseen universe. A family of five Buddhas became popular. Pure Land Buddhism comes from one of these Buddhas called Amida who took a vow that if he obtained enlightenment he would assist any that called on his name in faith to be reborn in the Pure Land.

Mahayana has a doctrine of emptiness whereby objects do not have any substance in themselves beyond what makes them up. Consequently, there is no such thing as a chair; rather there are legs, a back, a seat and so on. This was expanded to consider that all phenomena or people and things are empty of any real being and so was a middle way between existence and non-existence. Therefore, there is no difference in substance between *nirvana* and the cycle of rebirth. Any difference lies in our perception. Consider a man who is frightened by a coil of rope thinking it is a snake. To liberate us in life, correct vision seeing things as they really are is needed. *Nirvana* is here and now if we could but see it.

Mahayana reinterprets rather than rejects the early teaching of the Buddha with **Theravada** claiming to have recovered the true meaning.

Theravada	Mahayana
men/women as individuals	men/women as involved with others
individuals are on their own	men/women are not alone
emancipation by self effort	salvation by grace
key virtue–wisdom	key virtue - compassion
religion–a fulltime job	religion–relevant to life in the world
primarily for monks	for lay and monks
ideal is the arahat	ideal is the Bodhisattva
Buddha is a saint	Buddha is a saviour
few rituals	many rituals
prayer as meditation	petitionary prayer
conservative	liberal

Zen Buddhism is an intuitive, experimental school of Mahayana Buddhism that spread from India to China and then on to Japan where it became prominent. The legendary transmitter of Zen was Bodhidharma, 28th Patriarch of Mahayana Tradition and 1st Zen Patriarch. However, it was Hui-neng in the 6th century AD who gave Zen its distinctive characteristics, since his time Zen has sub divided into a number of schools.

Zen's most influential time was from the 13th to 16th centuries during which it became the religion of the Samurai ruling classes. Its affirmation of the world made it a driving force in education, government, trade and culture. In the 20th century, DT Zuzuki introduced Zen to the west.

The key to Zen thought and experience is enlightenment. Humanity's basic problem is ignorance about the true reality of the world and in our attempt to understand reality intellectually; we miss the direct experience of life. What Zen teaches is a distinctive intuitive insight into reality or the Buddha nature that is identical with our mind so that enlightenment comes by insight into the Buddha nature and our own self. Enlightenment is the acquisition of a new viewpoint that leads to a new way of life.

Any technique that that leads to enlightenment is valid and care is taken not to replace the goal of enlightenment with a technique. The Rinzai School looks to shock the disciple from his/her old way of thinking by use of a sudden shouted answer or even physical hit. Another popular way is by the use of *koans* – a rationally insoluble riddle posed by a master to a pupil such as 'what is the sound of one hand clapping?' There are approximately 1700 *koans* and a pupil may meditate for years on one before a sudden flash of intuition brings enlightenment.

Tibetan Buddhism consists of five main schools with numerous subdivisions, all holding the main mahayana teachings in common with some small variations. What separates Tibetan Buddhism from other forms is tantra, a teaching to help people link to the Buddha and discover harmony. It is necessary to learn this from a spiritual teacher with the oral transmission considered vital.

Foundation

The title of 'Báb' or 'the door' is given to **Mirza Ali Muhammed,** born in Persia in 1819. His role was similar to that of John the Baptist in Christianity—not a saviour but rather the precursor. Aged twenty-five, Mirza announced he had a new revelation from God and this would be more fully delivered by the imminent arrival of a new 'Messenger'. The Báb gathered a significant number of followers, enough to cause persecution of this new faith community in Persia. After a six-year public ministry, the Báb was executed in Tabriz aged thirty.

In 1844, when aged twenty-seven, **Bahá'u'lláh**, the son of a Persian government minister, became a follower of the Báb. Suffering persecution, it was while in prison that Bahá'u'lláh became convinced he was the messenger who had been foretold. On release from prison Bahá'u'lláh was exiled and he spent the last forty years of his life moving around Iraq, Turkey, Egypt and finally Akka in what is now Israel. Bahá'u'lláh spent these years proclaiming his mission and calling all to recognise the unity of humanity and search for world peace.

History

Before his death Bahá'u'lláh appointed his eldest son 'Abdu'l-Bahá as successor and it was he who oversaw significant worldwide expansion, despite periods of imprisonment and exile. Only free to travel in his later years 'Abdu'l-Bahá helped establish the faith in Europe and America. After his death in 1921, the leadership passed to his grandson Shoghi Effendi, then a student at Oxford. Shoghi Effendi was the real organiser of the Bahá'i faith, developing small local communities into connected groups able to establish institutions to carry out Bahá'u'lláh's vision.

During his thirty-six year control, he put in place the mechanism that today provides the administrative control of the faith. This 'Universal House of Justice' is a nine person body elected every five years who are charged with applying the teachings of Bahá'u'lláh to the Bahá'i community and is based in Haifa in Israel. Effendi also translated Bahá'u'lláh's writings in Arabic and Persian into English, helping to make the faith more accessible to a wider constituency.

After his death in 1957, Effendi was buried in London and the Universal House of Justice took over leadership of the Bahá'i community in 1963.

Differences

There are no significant divergences within the world Bahá'i faith, currently found in approximately 235 nations, although in very small numbers in many of these countries.

Beliefs of the Bahá'í faith.

The central idea of the faith is that of unity, and Bahá'is seek to remove barriers of race, gender, and belief. They believe that people should work together for the common benefit of humanity.

All human beings have a soul that lives forever. All human beings are members of a single race, which should soon be united in a single global community. All human beings are different, but equal. There should be no inequality between races or sexes and all religions have the same spiritual foundation, despite their apparent differences.

The Bahá'i religion has a similar understanding to Hinduism in that it accepts other faiths as true and valid. Bahá'is accept the divine nature of the work of Abraham, Moses, Zoroaster, the Buddha, Jesus and the Prophet Muhammad. They believe each one was a further stage in the revelation of God. Other prophets and divine manifestations are also accepted. God is transcendent and cannot be known directly but is revealed through the lives and teachings of his great prophets, the most recent of whom was Bahá'u'lláh.

Bahá'ís see themselves as a people with a mission to bring harmony and unity in the world, and this is reflected in their spiritual practice with the main purpose of life for Bahá'ís being to know and love God. Prayer, fasting and meditation are the main ways of achieving this and for making spiritual progress. Work performed in a spirit of service to humanity is also considered a form of worship.

The Bahá'í faith has no clergy or sacraments, and only a few rituals; obligatory daily prayers, reciting the prayer for the dead at a funeral and the marriage rite. The emphasis on prayer, meditation and social action in Bahá'í thinking means that congregational worship plays a much smaller part in Bahá'í life than it does in other faiths. Bahá'í services are very simple with readings from the scriptures, along with interpretations and prayers. Hymns and poetry are allowed, but not common. One person will recite prayers on behalf of everyone present because prayer is seen essentially as a private duty. The main occasion for group worship is the devotional portion of the nineteen day feast.

Personal prayer is the significant part of Bahá'í spiritual life. Bahá'ís believe that prayer is conversation with God whereas meditation is akin to a conversation with one's inner spirit. Consequently, they believe that it is not the language that is important, but rather the attitude of mind in which prayer is made. Prayer is intended to help Bahá'ís get closer to God, so its aim is change the person who is praying, rather than to change God. The purpose of the obligatory prayers is to cultivate humility and devotion. There are eleven holy days, of which nine are major holy days. Bahá'ís are required to refrain from work on the three special days of Ridvan and all major holy days unless specifically disallowed in their terms of employment. Children are not to attend school if possible. Bahá'ís are encouraged not to celebrate the holy days of other religions among themselves.

The Ridvan Festival marks the declaration in the Garden of Ridvan in 1863. Naw-Rúz or New Year is celebrated on the 21st March, the first day of spring equinox. Every nineteen days, on the evening before the first day of each Bahá'í month, Bahá'ís meet in a home or their local Bahá'í centre for a shared meal.

The Declaration of the Báb is celebrated 22-23 May from two hours after sunset on the 22nd. The Ascension of Bahá'u'lláh is celebrated on the 29th May, commemorated at 3am in the morning. The martyrdom of the Báb is celebrated on the 9th July at noon and his birth on the 20th October.

The birth of Bahá'u'lláh is celebrated on the 12th November. The minor days, when work is not suspended, include the day of the Covenant on the 26th November and the passing of 'Abdu'l-Bahá on the 28th November.

538

Foundation

The Sikh faith began around 1500, when Guru Nanak from the Punjab began teaching a faith that was distinct from Hinduism and Islam. Nanak had received a revelation telling him that 'there is no Muslim, there is no Hindu'. Nine Gurus followed Nanak, developing the Sikh faith and community. Sikhism was well established by the time of Guru Arjan, the fifth Guru who completed the establishment of Amritsar as the capital of the Sikh world, and compiled the first authorised book of Sikh scripture, the *Adi Granth*. However, during Arjan's time, Sikhism was seen as a threat by the Indian state and Guru Arjan was eventually executed for his faith in 1606.

The sixth Guru, Hargobind, fought to preserve the community, then followed a period of relative peace until the time of the Moghal Emperor, Aurangzeb, who used force to make his subjects accept Islam and had the ninth Guru, Tegh Bahadur, executed in 1675. The tenth Guru, Gobind Singh, recreated the Sikhs as a military group of men and women called the *Khalsa* in 1699, with the intention that the Sikhs should be able to defend their faith. Gobind Singh established the Sikh rite of initiation (*khandey di pahul*) and the five 'K's which give Sikhs their unique appearance.

Development

The first military leader of the Sikhs to follow the Gurus was Banda Singh Bahadur who led a successful campaign against the Moghals until he was captured and executed in 1716. In the middle years of the century the Sikhs rose up again, and over the next 50 years took over more and more territory until, in 1799, Ranjit Singh captured Lahore, and in 1801 established the Punjab as an independent state, with himself as Maharaja. He proved a very capable ruler of a state in which Sikhs were still in a minority. After Ranjit Singh's death in 1839, the Sikh state crumbled, damaged by internal leadership battles and they were finally defeated by the British in 1849. For a while, the Sikhs peacefully coexisted with the British, partly because they came to think of themselves as partners of the British rather than as subjects of the Raj.

At Independence in 1947, the Sikhs were too weak to have their own state and suffered greatly from partition and the huge dislocation of people. The Sikh ambition for independence was something that India would not concede as to do so would have allowed communalism (independent religious groupings) an unbreakable foothold in the politics of what was supposed to be a secular state. However, in 1966, after years of Sikh demands, India divided the Punjab into three, recreating Punjab as a state with a Sikh majority. Yet this did not pacify Sikh anger at what they saw as continuing oppression and the unfair way in which they thought India had set the boundaries of the new state.

As Sikh discontent grew, the conflict gradually changed from political into a violent confrontation between Hindus and Sikhs with Jarnail Singh Bhindranwale the leader of a Sikh extremist movement. In 1983, Bhindranwale and his supporters took refuge in the Golden Temple at Amritsar, the most revered place in the Sikh world. In June 1984, Indian troops attacked the Golden Temple, killing many and seriously damaging the complex. This radicalised many formerly moderate Sikhs who viewed the Indian Prime Minister, Indira Gandhi, as a deliberate persccutor of the Sikh community and faith. Four months after the assault on the Golden Temple Indira Gandhi was assassinated by two of her Sikh bodyguards. Today the Punjab is fairly peaceful, although the recent rise of Hindu nationalism, with its claim that Sikhism is nothing more than a Hindu sect, has renewed tension.

Beliefs
Sikhs believe that human beings spend their time in a cycle of birth, life, and rebirth. *Karma* sets the quality of a life according to how well or badly a person lived previously, basically, you reap what you sow. The only way out of this endless cycle is to achieve a total knowledge of and union with God.

Sikh spirituality is centred round this need to understand and experience God eventually becoming one with God. To do this a person must switch the focus of their attention from themselves to God. They get this state of *mukti* (liberation), 'through the grace of God'. God shows people through holy books, and by the examples of saints, the best ways to get close to him. Sikhs believe that God cannot be fully understood by people, but he can be experienced through love, worship, and contemplation, looking for God both inside themselves and in the world around them.

When a Sikh wants to experience God, they look both at the created world and into their own soul. Their aim is to see the divine order that God has given to everything, and through it to understand the nature of God. Most human beings cannot experience the true reality of God because they are blinded by their own self-centred pride (*haumain*) and desire for physical things.

The three duties of a Sikh are to pray, work and give. Prayer (*nam japna*) is basically keeping God in mind at all times. Earning an honest living (*kirt karma*) is important; since God is truth a Sikh seeks to live honestly, not just by avoiding crime but by avoiding gambling, begging, or working in the alcohol or tobacco industries. The rejection of a couple of these pursuits puts Sikhs on a cultural clash with much of contemporary life. Finally, generosity (*vand chhakna*) is sharing one's earnings with others by giving to charity and caring for others. Sikhs serve God by serving other people and through this; they rid themselves of their own ego and pride.

Sikhs try to avoid five vices that make people self-centred, and build barriers against God in their lives. Overcoming these vices is part of the journey to liberation. These vices include lust, greed, attachment to things of this world, anger and pride. For Sikhs there is only one God, who never takes the form of a human being and is neither male nor female. We know God as he reveals himself and meet God through submission, meditation, the visible world, prayer and living a life of service. Sikhs believe that God is inside every person and so everyone is capable of change.

The main scripture of the Sikhs is the *Guru Granth Sahib*. The tenth and last of the human Gurus, Guru Gobind Singh, declared that nobody would become the eleventh Guru and designated the *Adi Granth* or scripture to be his perpetual successor. Ever since, Sikhs have revered copies of the book as if they were a human Guru. They believe that it guides them through life in the same way as a human Guru. The *Guru Granth Sahib* contains 1,430 pages with all copies having identical page layouts and numbering. The text is in several languages (mainly Punjabi), but written in the Gurmakhi alphabet throughout. Almost everything in the book is in poem form and intended to be sung, containing the hymns of several Gurus and passages from Muslim and Hindu sources.

Despite the great reverence shown to the *Guru Granth Sahib* by Sikhs, they do not worship it since only God is worthy of worship. The reverence to the *Guru Granth Sahib* is not to the book itself, but to the spiritual content, or *shabad*, contained within it. The sacred nature of the *Guru Granth Sahib* means that the sort of textual analysis to which the Bible (for example) is subjected is generally considered inappropriate.

Sikhs are expected to have a place in their home where the *Guru Granth Sahib* can be placed and read. Ideally, this should be a separate room, but space limitations often mean that the book sits in a special portion of a room that is only used for 'uplifting' purposes.

Sikhs can pray at any time and any place, although early morning meditation and liturgical payers are close to the norm. Although God is beyond description Sikhs feel able to pray to God as if to a person with whom they have a relationship.

The Gurdwara or 'residence of the Guru' is the temple where Sikhs meet for congregational worship. It is the presence of the *Guru Granth Sahib* that gives the Gurdwara its religious status, so any building containing the book is strictly speaking a Gurdwara. There are no idols, statues, or religious pictures in a Gurdwara, because Sikhs worship only God, and they regard God as having no physical form.

The focus of attention in the main hall of a Gurdwara is the *Guru Granth Sahib*, which is treated with the respect that would be given to a human Guru. The *Guru Granth Sahib* is kept in a room of its own during the night and carried in procession to the main hall of the Gurdwara at the start of the first worship of the day. The book is placed on a raised platform under a canopy and covered with an expensive cloth when not being read. During a service, a person will usually fan the *Guru Granth Sahib*.

Four doors lead into a Gurdwara: the Door of Peace, the Door of Livelihood, the Door of Learning and the Door of Grace. These doors are a symbol that people from all four points of the compass are welcome, and that people of all four castes are equally welcome. Shoes are removed and worshippers touch the ground with their forehead.

Sikhs do not have a general order of service to be used in the Gurdwara, although there are rules for particular ceremonies. The morning service begins with the singing of *Asa Di Var*. Other hymns from the Guru Granth Sahib are then sung, accompanied by instruments. A sermon or talk, usually based on a theme from Sikh history comes next followed by the singing of *Anand Sahib*. The congregation then stands with eyes closed facing the *Guru Granth Sahib* for prayer. During the prayer the word *waheguru* (Punjabi for 'praise to the Guru') is often said, having much the same role as the word 'amen' in Christian services. After the prayer, the service ends by opening the *Guru Granth Sahib* to a random page and reading the hymn found at the top of the left-hand page. Food is then normally offered to the congregation. Every Gurdwara has a *Langar* or kitchen attached to it where simple food is served to anyone without charge. Although Sikhs are not required to be vegetarian, only vegetarian food is served in the gurdwaras.

Sikhs do not have ordained priests, and any Sikh (male or female) can lead the prayers and recite the scriptures to the congregation. Each Gurdwara has a Granthi or custodian who organises the daily services and reads from the Guru Granth Sahib.

Sikh festivals include those that are associated with the lives of the Gurus, celebrated with an *akhand path* or complete reading of Sikh scripture taking 48 hours and finishing on the day of the festival with the Gurdwara specially decorated for the occasion. Other festivals include: the birthdays of Guru Nanak and Guru Gobind Singh, and the martyrdoms of Guru Arjan and Guru Tegh Bahadur. *Vaisakhi* or New Year is celebrated on 13 or 14 April, this also commemorates the founding of the *Khalsa* in 1699. *Divali* is celebrated by both Sikhs and Hindus.

The majority of Sikh customs are associated with the *khalsa*, the body of initiated Sikhs to which most adult Sikhs belong. Sikhs who have been through the *Amrit* ceremony of initiation wear the symbols of the five 'K's and take new names; men take the name Singh meaning lion and women take the name Kaur meaning princess.

The five 'K's date from the creation of the *Khalsa Panth* by Guru Gobind Singh in 1699. He introduced them to identify members of the *Khalsa*, bind the community together and symbolise that the wearer has dedicated himself to a life of devotion and submission to the Guru.

Kesh or uncut hair, including beard, indicates that one is willing to accept God's gift as God intended it and symbolises adoption of a simple life, the denial of pride in one's appearance and a symbol of one's wish to move beyond concerns of the body to attain spiritual maturity. A Sikh should only bow his head to the Guru and not to a hairdresser. It is a highly visible symbol of membership of the group and follows the appearance of Guru Gobind Singh, founder of the *Khalsa*. Sikh women are just as forbidden to cut any body hair.

Kara or steel bracelet is a symbol of restraint and gentility reminding a Sikh that he or she should not do anything of which the Guru would not approve. It is a symbol of God having no beginning or end, of permanent bonding to the community and of being a link in the chain of *Khalsa* Sikhs. The *Kara* is made of steel rather than gold or silver as it is not intended to be an ornament.

Kanga or wooden comb symbolises a clean mind and body and the importance of looking after the body that God has created. This does not conflict with the Sikh's aim to move beyond bodily concerns; since the body is one's vehicle for enlightenment one should care for it appropriately.

Kachha is an undergarment that must not come below the knee. It was a particularly useful garment for Sikh warriors of the 18th and 19th centuries, being very suitable for warfare when riding a horse, although clearly less so today. It is also a symbol of chastity.

Kirpan or ceremonial sword plays an important part in the initiation ceremony into the *Khalsa* when it is used to stir a mixture of sugar and water that the initiate must drink. There is no fixed style of *Kirpan*, and it can be anything from a few inches to a metre long. It is kept in a sheath and can be worn over or under the outside clothing. The Kirpan symbolises spirituality, the defence of good and of the weak, the struggle against injustice and is a metaphor for God.

The *Amrit* ceremony is the initiation rite introduced by Guru Gobind Singh when he founded the *Khalsa* in 1699. A Sikh can go through this initiation as soon as they are old enough to understand the commitment that they are making. The ceremony takes place in a

Gurdwara, before the *Guru Granth Sahib* and in the presence of five initiated Sikhs. During the ceremony, hymns are recited from the Sikh scripture, prayers are said, and the principles of Sikhism are affirmed. The candidates for initiation drink some *amrit* (a mixture of sugar and water that has been stirred with a double-edged sword) from the same bowl, and have it sprinkled on their eyes and hair. Each then recites the *Mool* mantra (the fundamentals of Sikhism).

There are readings from the Guru Granth Sahib and an explanation of rules of Sikhism. The ceremony ends with the eating of the ceremonial *karah parshad*.

Foundation

It could be argued that this section should be dealing with Chinese faiths in the plural, in the same way as Hinduism encompasses a collection of associated religious traditions. Confucianism, Taoism and Buddhism are all part of this Chinese mix. Yet what may be more significance than the distinctive streams of understanding is the Chinese-ness of these expressions. While China has been exposed to Judaism, Islam, Zoroastrianism and a number of varieties of Christianity, these appear to have remained as foreign religions with only Buddhism an exception. In China individuals did not normally associate with an exclusive religious tradition, rather they appropriated religious beliefs to help in different aspects of life. Doctrinal disputes, part of western Christianity, do not exist in traditional Chinese belief as doctrinal orthodoxy has never been a feature. Even Buddhism, with a set of core beliefs, found itself changed by this encounter rather than changing Chinese society. In some ways, Chinese religion is more a cultural expression than a religion in any traditional sense.

The early Chinese world-view was of a natural world following a cyclical pattern, a pattern of growth and decline understanding the reality of opposites. This view of opposites, or bipolarity, is a specific characteristic of Chinese metaphysics expressed through *yin* and *yang*.

Nature existed through the interconnectedness of heat and cold, light and dark, male and female. The *yin* and *yang* are not closed states but rather discernible phases in the constant flow of life.

A belief existed in a Supreme Ruler in Heaven, often written as Heaven, although this concept appears somewhat less than the Judaeo-Christian understanding of God. *Tao* is the way and as such is concerned with ethical and religious truth. It also has a broader understanding of the reality behind or within truth although again is not considered as Deity. Beyond the natural world was an unseen world of spiritual beings; ancestors and those who had been wronged in their earthly life. To protect against the actions of these malevolent beings, a series of charms, firecrackers, mediums, prayers, burning of incense and exorcisms existed to offer protection. All this led to a mysticism based on an understanding of *Tao* rather than on a Divine Being.

Towards an Authentic Wesleyan Inter-Faith Understanding[2]

INTRODUCTION

In Wesley's generation, the British of the "long eighteenth century"[3] were starting to become more aware of non-Christian religions, but the level of accurate knowledge was relatively low.[4] The European interaction with Islam had centred around the crusades, with the final expulsion of Muslims from Spain occurring in 1602.[5] In 1683, only twenty years before Wesley's birth, the Ottoman Turks had laid siege to Vienna. This violent engagement with Muslims continued immediately after Wesley's death through Napoleon's Egyptian campaign from 1798-1801.

The British East India Company controlled much of India for the duration of Wesley's ministry. Knowledge of Hinduism and Buddhism was increasing, but, as with Islam, the interaction occurred in an atmosphere of conflict and perceived Western cultural superiority. Awareness of Chinese and Japanese religion dated back to at least the middle Ages through the journeys of traders and Catholic missionaries but accurate knowledge was scarce, partially due to the distance between Britain and the Far East but also due to Chinese and Japanese policies of isolation.[6] In the North American colonies, very little attention was paid to the religious understanding of the Native Americans. (See McDermott 2000)

---

1 This material was originally published in Skuce, SF 'A Firm and Generous Faith: Towards an Authentic Wesleyan Inter-Faith Understanding' Studies in Interreligious Dialogue, No 19, Vol 1 (2009) and is republished with permission.

2 When reflecting on the life of Gordon Wilson, Irish Methodist peace campaigner and survivor of the Remembrance Day bomb attack in Enniskillen in 1987, the then President of Ireland, Mary Robinson, commented on Wilson's "firm and generous Methodist faith" (Mary Robinson, "Foreword," in: McCreary 1996: xi.

3 An accepted designation among historians to refer to the period between the Glorious Revolution of 1688-89 and the Parliamentary Acts of 1828-9 when Roman Catholics and dissenters received emancipation.

4 People of other religious and ethnic backgrounds were paraded as curiosities for amusement and interest. Oglethorpe, for example, brought a group of Georgian Native Americans to England in 1735 to provide "exotic publicity for the project" (Rack 1992: 112).

5 When the Turkish siege of Malta was lifted in 1565, Anglican prayers celebrat- ing the perceived deliverance referred to "that wicked monster and damned soul Maho- met" (Vitkus 1999: 210).

6 Wesley alludes to Chinese antipathy to foreign influence in Works, Vol. 18, Journal, 2 December 1737.

The first systematic study of other religions published in Britain was Edward Herbert's De Religione Gentilium (1683). His argument was that clergy and priests had distorted all religions, and he wrote to attack the contemporary role of clergy within Christianity.[1] A few years earlier the Puritan Richard Baxter gave a fairly positive assessment of people of other faiths when he wrote, "I find not in myself called or enabled to judge all these people as to their final state, but only to say, that if any of them have a holy heart and life, in the true love of God, they shall be saved."[2]

Joseph Pitts[3] Faithful Account of the Religion and Manners of Mahometans (1704) gave a sympathetic and accurate portrayal of Islam but still argued for the supremacy of Christ. By Wesley's death in 1791 William Robertson was publishing A Historical Disquisition Concerning the Knowledge which the Ancients Had of India, giving a positive image of Hinduism when compared to ancient Greek religion.

The general British inter-faith view in the eighteenth century can be summarised as one of Christian supremacy supported by little accurate knowledge of other faiths.[4] Yet this was starting to change. The upsurge in Protestant missions at the end of the eighteenth and throughout the nineteenth century resulted in numerous publications on the religious beliefs of the peoples being evangelised. Colonial explorers and administrators potentially had a more objective perspective than missionaries; the work of Sir William Jones, who founded the Asiatic Society of Bengal in 1784, and the Asiatick Researches journal in 1788 being outstanding examples of this. Jones' work facilitated Western access to the original sources of Indian religion and culture and so overcame the problem of writers using biased secondary accounts and consequently repeating the errors and distortions of earlier authors. Because many of the early commentators on other religions were Christians seeking to validate

---

1 Alexander Ross' Pansebeia (1653) surveyed world religions but attributed a positive role to clergy.

2 From The Reasons of the Christian Religion (1667) quoted in Pailin 1984: 156.

3 Joseph Pitts (1663-1735) was captured at sea and sold to Muslim traders as a slave; forcibly converted to Islam, before his escape he was one of the first Englishmen to go on Hajj to Mecca.

4 For a more positive view of the Western Christian interaction with other reli- gions see Nederman 2000, Wheatcroft 2003 and Grady 2005.

internal Christian arguments, these commentators often had little first-hand knowledge of other faiths and were content to perpetuate the errors of their predecessors (Blanks 1999: 22). It was only by the end of Wesley's life that this approach was being superseded by a more accurate appraisal.

John Wesley

Objectively defining the inter-faith view of John Wesley is a difficult task since "Wesley's writing is so voluminous in scope that selective quoting could back up almost any argument" (Harris 1997:53). Additionally, in considering Wesley's writing and experience to discern his inter-faith understanding it needs to be borne in mind that he was not a systematic theologian but rather "an experiential Christian thinker interested in the doctrines relating to experience" (Whaling 1995: 18). A further issue is the need to avoid using Wesley as a "guru" by simply quoting him as the definitive voice that concludes any argument. Rather, Wesley should be seen as a "mentor" where his contextual perspective gives underlying principles for contemporary study rather than specific answers (see Maddox 1992). This approach allows the development of Wesley's thought beyond the confines of his limited experience, and allows an authentically Wesleyan perspective to develop rather than creating a fossilised snapshot from history.

Experience had a very significant impact on Wesley's theological reflection and his direct experience of other religions was primarily that of Native Americans in Georgia and Jews, the latter in Britain, Rotterdam and Georgia. That said, he was able to write in his sermon "On Faith" that *"with Heathens, Mahometans and Jews, we have at present nothing to do" (Wesley Works, Vol. 3, Sermon 106 "On Faith").*[1] In his writings, Wesley used language that could not be considered appropriate today, describing heathens as *"inferior to the beasts of the field" (Wesley Works, Vol. 2, Sermon 63 "The General Spread of the Gospel").* While it may be unfair to judge a man of the eighteenth century by the norms of the twenty-first, some of Wesley's statements do little for inter-faith harmony. Wesley never wrote about

---

1 This can be considered to be Wesley's mature reflection, preached on 9 April 1788 when Wesley was aged eighty-four. It was the first time Wesley was recorded as preaching on Hebrews 11:6.

other religions in a systematic or detailed way; rather, as Miles highlights, most of Wesley's comments on other faiths "are rhetorical devices used to persuade his Christian listeners to be better Christians," the general approach in eighteenth-century Britain (Miles 2000: 66).

Despite his early hopes, Wesley had relatively few contacts with Native Americans in Georgia.[1] He initially considered them to be *"as little children, humble, willing to learn and eager to do the will of God; and consequently they shall know of every doctrine I preach whether it be of God". (Wesley Letters, Vol. 1, 10 October 1735 to John Burton)*[2] In July 1736, Wesley was able to question five Chickasaw Indians about their religion and report a factual account to the Georgia trustees (Wesley Works, Vol. 18, Journal, 29 July 1736). His relatively positive assessment of Chickasaw religion was amended after discussions with a Frenchman who had lived for some months among them (Wesley Works, Vol. 18, Journal, 9 July 1737). By late 1737 Wesley considered various Native American religions in a uniformly negative way, considering them little more than a licence for immorality and that *"They show no inclination to learn anything, but least of all Christianity, being as fully opinionated of their own parts and wisdom as either modern Chinese or ancient Roman" (Wesley Works, Vol. 18, Journal, 2 December 1737).*

Eventually, Wesley's opinion of Native Americans was that they,
"torture all their prisoners from morning till night, till at length they roast them to death; and upon the slightest provocation, to come behind and shoot any of their own countrymen". (Wesley Works, Vol. 2, Sermon 38 "A Caution Against Bigotry")[3]

---

1 Wesley met some Native Americans before he left for Georgia. Oglethorpe brought them to England, but "it is not known if they were represented as savages come to repentance or zoological exhibits" (Hattersley 2002: 99).

2 Wesley published an abridgement of the life of his near contemporary but much more successful missionary to Native Americans, David Brainerd, who worked in Pennsylvania from 1743 until his death in 1747. For perspectives on how Native Americans viewed missionaries see Ronda 2000 and Cogley 1999.

3 In Works, Vol. 18, Journal 9 July 1737, Wesley shows his awareness of William Wollaston's The Religion of Nature Truly Delineated (1722) in his comments. Similar treatment, although with no personal knowledge, was given to others such Pacific islanders who were slightly above wolves, Africans who were as sheep and the inhabitants of India who were in a dark and cruel place, in Works, Vol. 2, Sermon 69 "The Imperfection of Human Knowledge."

An important strand in Wesley's theology can be deduced from this change. Wesley was, to a large extent, an experiential theologian and allowed experience to help mould his theology, not vice versa. His experience of lived religion challenged his conceptual knowledge of Native American religion. The mature Wesley may well have written differently about world religions if he had had greater exposure to Islam and Hinduism. The fluidity of Wesley's understanding can be seen in his attitude to Jews. In Savannah he recorded that, *"I began learning Spanish, in order to converse with my Jewish parishioners; some of whom seem nearer the mind of Christ than many of those who call him Lord" (Wesley Works, Vol. 18, Journal 4 April 1737).* By the following year Wesley's opinion of Jews in Rotterdam was radically different: *"Having waited till past four in the afternoon, we stepped into the Jews' Synagogue, which lies near the water-side. I do not wonder that so many Jews (especially those who have any reflection) utterly abjure all religion. My spirit was moved within me at that horrid, senseless pageantry, that mockery of God, which they called public worship. Lord, do not thou yet "cast off thy people!" But in Abraham's "Seed" let them also "be blessed!" (Wesley Works, Vol. 19, Journal, 4 September 1738)*

Open to the influence of experience, Wesley was able to write in a very different vein thirty years later: *"I was desired to hear Mr Leoni sing at the Jewish synagogue. I never before saw a Jewish congregation behave so decently. Indeed the place itself is so solemn, that it might strike an awe upon those who have any thought of God." (Wesley Works, Vol. 22, Journal 23 February 1770)*
In Sermon 113, "The General Spread of the Gospel" Wesley argued that Christianity needed to be reformed and only then:

> *The Mahometans will look upon them with other eyes, and begin to give attention to their words. And as their words will be clothed with divine energy, attended with the demonstration of Spirit and of power, those of them that fear God will soon take knowledge of the Spirit whereby Christians speak .... The poor American savage will no more ask "What are the Christians better than us?" —when they see their steady practice of universal temperance, and of justice, mercy and truth. (Wesley Works, Vol. 2, and Sermon 63 "The General Spread of the Gospel")*

What tempers some of Wesley's strong language towards Islam[1] and other religions is the knowledge that he levelled similar accusations at nominal Christianity. As Cracknell comments, "Despite all the eighteenth century prejudices about the people who were called 'Mahometans,' John Wesley was able to see Islam as a form of true religion" (Cracknell 1998: 77).[2] Various religions were considered as having their own dispensation of grace, of having access to prevenient grace with a series of covenants stretching from Adam through Moses and the Jews to John the Baptist and finally through to Jesus (Wesley Works, Vol. 2, Sermon 63 "The General Spread of the Gospel").

Wesley's understanding of prevenient grace helped him to consider positively that God could be at work outside of and beyond the conscious understanding of an individual. Wesley understood the universal phenomenon of conscience to be a sign of the universality of God's grace meaning, that it is found *not only in all Christians, but in all Mahometans, all pagans, yea the vilest of savages" (Wesley Works, Vol. 4, Sermon 129 "Heavenly Treasure in Earthly Vessels").* A measure of the grace of God was available to other traditions through the media of their own dispensations (Whaling 1995: 23). Taken to an extreme, this view can understand God to be fully at work in other faiths but that was not Wesley's position. Prevenient grace was how the initial awakening occurred in an individual's life. Justification and sanctification describe the divine action and the human response that was necessary to this grace.

---

1 Wesley's knowledge of Islam came from reading rather than personal en- counter; c.f. Works, Vol. 18, Journal, 22 and 24 January 1737 and Works, Vol. 22, Journal, 23 November 1767. Among the works read was Fontenelle's Entretiens sur la Pluralite des Mondes (1686) and Brerewood's Enquiries Touching the Diversity of Languages and Religions through the Chief Parts of the World (1614). It can also be presumed that Wesley was familiar with Isaac Barrow's Sermons (1678) and Richard Baxter's The Reasons of the Christian Religion (1667). Other information came via "travelogues" from sailors, merchants and explorers who were more interested in presenting the exotic nature of others rather than a systematic account of their beliefs and practices. Given his quantity and breadth of reading, it is to be assumed that Wesley was as well informed about other religions as most people in eighteenth-century Britain, even if much of his information was inaccurate.

2 Wesley's positive use of a Muslim example of faith in Sermon 106 "On Faith" supports Cracknell's assertion. However, it should be noted that Wesley wrote at length against Henri de Boulainviller's attempt to present Islam as an alternative to Christianity in Works, Vol. 22, Journal, 23 November 1767.

The God Wesley served was *"not the God of the Christians only, but the God of the Heathens also" (Wesley Works, Vol. 2, Sermon 41 "Wandering Thoughts").* In Dublin, he declared that Methodism was to *"stir up all parties, Christians or Heathens, to worship God in spirit and in truth" (Wesley Works, Vol. 24, Journal, 12 April 1789).* There was hope for all because, *"I do not conceive that any man living has a right to sentence all the heathen and Mahometan world to damnation" (Wesley Works, Vol. 4, Sermon 130 "On Living Without God").*[1] The great Methodist emphasis "for all" included the benefits of Christ's death which:

> *.. not only extended to such as have the distinct knowledge of his death and sufferings, but even unto those who are inevitably excluded from this knowledge. Even they may be partakers of the benefit of his death, though ignorant of the history, if they suffer his grace to take place in their hearts, so as of wicked men to become holy. (Wesley Letters, Vol. 2, 10 February 1748 to T. Whitehead)*

Arguably, Wesley was helped to this opinion by his respect for the early church theologians who made no complete separation between general and specifically Christian revelation, seeing both as based in God's grace. General revelation progressed through stages before finally and essentially culminating in Jesus (Wesley Works, Vol. 3, Sermon 106 "On Faith"). Faith was considered to be in evolution; from the faith of a materialist, to that of a Deist, to a Heathen (which included the Muslims), to a Jew, to that of John the Baptist, to Roman Catholicism and finally to Protestantism (Wesley Works, Vol. 3, Sermon 106 "On Faith").[2] While only living faith in Jesus gave the faith of a child, there was hope for others who had the faith of a servant; a faith the mature Wesley considered he had prior to Aldersgate Street.

With this opinion other religions were not without hope and so he wrote about Acts 17:26 that the hymn of Cleanthes to the Supreme Being is *"one of the purest and finest pieces of natural religion in the whole world of pagan antiquity" (Wesley Notes on the New*

---

1 The question of salvation is a Christian concern that does not easily translate into other religions and in many ways is an unhelpful position in seeking inter-faith understanding (Forward 1995: 48).

2 William Carey used a similar descriptive way of separating religions but, like Wesley, he seemed more interested in the differences between Christians than those between religions; see (Pailin 1984: 46).

Testament). [1] Marcus Aurelius was considered to be acceptable to God (Wesley Works, Vol. 20, Journal, 11 October 1745) and in his sermon "On Faith" Wesley went on to declare:

> *But many of them i.e. the ancient Heathens, especially in the civilised nations, we have great reason to hope, although they lived among Heathens, yet were quite of another spirit; being taught of God, by his inward voice, all the essentials of true religion. Yea, and so was this Mahometan, an Arabian, who, a century or two ago, wrote the life of Hai Ebn Yokan. The story seems to be feigned; but it contains all the principles of pure religion and undefiled. (Wesley Works, Vol. 3, Sermon 106 "On Faith")*

All religion was considered to share a common core:

> *"True religion, in the very essence of it, is nothing short of holy tempers. Consequently, all other religion whatever name it bears, whether Pagan, Mahometan, Jewish or Christian: and whether Popish or Protestant, Lutheran or Reformed; without these is lighter than vanity itself." (Wesley Works, Vol. 3, Sermon 91 "On Charity")*

Yet Wesley could still write of Islam: *"how far and wide this miserable delusion spread over the face of the earth!" (Wesley Works, Vol. 2, Sermon 63 "The General Spread of the Gospel").*

In summary, Wesley's view of other religions was that their followers were in the same place as all others in needing grace and salvation: that all people had an awareness of God leading to an understanding of good and evil; that followers of other religions were in the same state as nominal followers of Christianity and; that the Gospel should be preached to all but only when the time was right. Wesley had, in some senses, an enlightened view for his time, pointing towards the possibility of a more developed opinion. This was reinforced in his charitable work where there was no preference given to those of a particular faith or denomination. As Turner comments, "The impact of the reality of God in other religions ... was just over [John] Wesley's horizon" (Turner 1985: 47). Despite his

---

1 In a similar way Socrates is quoted approvingly (Wesley Works, Vol. 3, Sermon 71, "Of Good Angels."

limited accurate knowledge[1] and historical context, Wesley could see value and faith in other religions, compared them favourably with nominal Christianity and left an adherent's eternal destiny in God's hands.

Finally, there is the question of Wesley's practice as well as his theology. Before his evangelical conversion Wesley was eager to preach to the Native Americans. Subsequent to his evangelical conversion, Wesley did not personally attempt any missions to non-Christians and only reluctantly gave limited support in 1786 to Thomas Coke's Address, a missionary programme that was not implemented during Wesley's lifetime. Part of the answer may involve the pragmatic Wesley consolidating work in Britain and among the Methodist diaspora. Yet there is still the possibility that Wesley, content to leave the fate of non-Christians in God's hands, was not as enthusiastic as others to evangelise such people. Wesley makes no "missionary" comments in his Notes on the New Testament on Matthew 28:19 or Acts 1:8.[2]

Perhaps his parish was really only the nominally Christian world and Methodism was a renewing force within Christianity rather than a mission to the world, even though that view tends to discount the great emphasis in Charles Wesley's hymns that Christ died for all. Would a twenty-first century Wesley have been an evangelist to every country in the Billy Graham mould? Or would Wesley have sought for renewal within British Christian life, supporting others in world mission but not participating himself?

One of the intriguing issues that remains is that the pre-Aldersgate Wesley was a missionary to the world, albeit a failure, whereas the post- Aldersgate Wesley was at best ambivalent towards this task.

---

1 Wesley had an uncle who lived in India while a merchant with the East India (Hattersley, 2002: 24, 45). While Wesley probably had little contact with this relative he could as easily have been a source of inaccurate information as much as accurate.

2 Wesley's comment on Mark 16:15 does include an implied challenge to take the Gospel to all, but it is not with the force expected of one who saw the world as his parish.

There is no definitive Wesleyan inter-faith understanding despite the very significant inter-faith reflection undertaken by international Methodism. British, American and Sri Lankan Methodism have all produced prominent inter-faith theologians, a number of whom radically stress the generosity of the Methodist understanding.

The British list of names includes Geoffrey Parrinder, Kenneth Cracknell, Martin Forward and Elizabeth Harris. Sri Lankans include Wesley Ariarajah, Lynn de Silva and Ajith Fernando, while currently prominent in the USA is Diana Eck. This disproportionate influence in inter-faith thinking and practice can be paralleled to a similar disproportionate leadership in the ecumenical movement.[1] Many Methodist Conferences have produced documents to help their members understand these questions, but most tend to be more pragmatic than theological, seeking to address specific issues rather than primarily reflect theologically.

An embryonic Wesleyan theology of religions exists in the work of Philip Meadows, a task that has still to be developed (see Meadows 2000). Others include Rebecca Miles who analysed the potential impact of John Wesley in twenty-first century inter-faith dialogue (see Miles 2000).

Yet, despite the influential reflection and practice of those and many more named here, there is yet to be a received Wesleyan theology of religions. Therefore, based on the DNA of Wesley's thinking and practice, what might a sketch of an inter-faith theology look like?

TOWARDS AN AUTHENTICALLY WESLEYAN INTER-FAITH UNDERSTANDING

Theology

God can be viewed as being in relationship with many peoples. Wesleyans can understand that there are different degrees of relationship between God and the peoples of the world, with the acknowledgement that God is in relationship with some people beyond Christianity. Without a significant shift from theological orthodoxy, the positive implications of this understanding can be

---

1 Three of the six general secretaries of the WCC have been Methodists.

embraced with a breadth acknowledged whereby there is "a wideness in God's mercy" (see Pinnock 1992).

Wesley's understanding of the work of God beyond Christianity can be developed but more in richness than in an increasing wideness. For example, Celtic Christianity contains an openness to other religious perspectives yet still maintains the centrality of Christ and the offer of a saving relationship (Mackey 1995: 1-21). Marrying the depths of Wesleyan evangelical inter-faith theology to the openness of Celtic theology could develop a rich Wesleyan inter-faith theology.

PNEUMATOLOGY

The Holy Spirit is acknowledged as one who blows where he wills. The Spirit is not captive to any Wesleyan understanding, recognition or desire. The Spirit is at work beyond Christianity which is a part of the Missio Dei. The God of mission has a church of which the Wesleyan family is a fragment.

Wesley's doctrine of prevenient grace enables a positive understanding of God at work beyond Christianity. Prevenient grace acknowledges that before an individual enters into a saving relationship with God through Jesus Christ, God is at work in his or her life, bringing an awareness of his presence. This is the initial stage of a relationship and points to the need for a fuller relationship based on a faithful response. Humanity is unable to enter into such a relationship by individual initiative. God necessarily takes the initiative and is consequently at work in all people. Wesleyans can engage with the peoples of the world with the understanding that God is already at work and in a relationship with all. Yet this is not necessarily a saving relationship. There can be a positive awareness of the work of God beyond Christianity while still understanding the need to offer Christ so that all may have the opportunity to enter into a full and saving relationship with God through Christ.

CHRISTOLOGY

Jesus should be understood as not just owned by Wesleyans and other Protestants. That Jesus is authentically at home in Roman Catholicism was a twentieth-century discovery for many Protestants. In the present century, it is necessary for Wesleyans to recognise that

557

Islam has a clear opinion on Jesus, that aspects of Hinduism can incorporate an understanding of Jesus within its pantheon of deities, and that Judaism has its own perspectives on the teacher from Galilee. The person of Jesus is a fruitful area with which to engage in dialogue. Wesleyans should not seek to dismantle their Christology; indeed, a firmness of faith does not allow this. Yet a generous faith is confident enough to allow this perspective to be challenged by others. As Methodists talk to their neighbours in the dialogue of life, conversation can turn to who Jesus is and his meaning for all. Mission is dialogical and Wesleyan activism can engage in mission through this discussion.

SOTERIOLOGY

The salvation of people who are not Christians is a matter on which contemporary Wesleyans can remain agnostic. Indeed, this is an appropriate Christian perspective that acknowledges that it is for God alone to pronounce on a per- son's spiritual state rather than for individual Christians or churches to pass judgement. Wesley believed an individual could know with certainty their own spiritual state but that there could be an ambiguity as to the spiritual state of others. Not all who claim a saving relationship with God need necessarily be in such a relationship, nor is it for Wesleyans to judge this. The generosity is seen in the ability not to judge negatively the spiritual state of some who do not explicitly claim such a saving relationship. This awareness allows for positive encounters between Wesleyans and others without the need to claim spiritual superiority or be condemnatory. It is for God to judge. Wesleyans can engage confidently with others, pointing all to Jesus, without needing to condemn the faith or practices of non-Christians. Heaven can be conceived of generously, leaving such decisions to God alone.

A Theology of Narrative

Story-telling has a long tradition in Wesleyan culture. The stories of Wesley's life and the heroes of the Wesleyan movement are regularly retold, if not as regularly as in a previous generation. Indeed, Methodism has been quicker to document its history than to write blueprints for its future. Encouraging others to tell their stories and providing a listening ear with a desire to learn is one of the important roles that Wesleyans can play. The evidence of inter-faith history contains much that is positive. This needs to be told in contemporary Britain.

A Theology of Risk

Inter-faith leadership is risk-taking in the sense that not all in the Wesleyan family fully understand the motivation and need for such gestures. There is a danger that some, without fully reflecting, may be antagonised by such initiatives. It is to be expected that some fundamentalist Christians would use such initiatives as an opportunity to criticise others. The resultant level of controversy that inter-faith initiatives might bring could be creatively used by Wesleyans to highlight general inter-faith issues in the awareness of clergy, church members, and even the general public. Such leadership may be provided by those from the Wesleyan family but is not restricted to this community. It is leadership that seeks to lead all into a firm and generous understanding.

A Theology of Hospitality

If Wesleyans are *"the friends of all and the enemies of none"* then a theology of hospitality becomes an imperative rather than just a possibility. Methodists should be generous with their premises. In common with most established Christian denominations, Methodism has a large number of generally well appointed buildings in addition to worship centres. Such premises could be offered to non-Christian faith groups for their community events. It is against British Methodist regulations for church buildings to be used by other faith groups but, given the current range of activities held in Methodist owned buildings, an expansion to include non-Christian faith groups should be possible.

While local congregations, as gathered faith communities, may be wary of this, it may be that there is a particular role here for Methodism's city missions with their broader ministry. They are not public spaces in the sense of a cathedral, but they do occupy an acknowledged place where a wide variety of community and support groups meet. It would be potentially less problematic for property such as this to be offered.

When the author of this article was a mission partner ministering in Maradana Methodist Church in Sri Lanka, a pre-school play group run by the congregation, which already had a large majority of non-Christian community children attending, invited a Muslim to serve on the management committee that formerly had been exclusively Methodist in membership. The Christian content of this group was not compromised, nor were the various evangelistic events associated with this group. Rather, an embrace of hospitality was offered that opened further opportunities for Methodist-Muslim encounter and created a space where clear presentations of the Christian message were welcomed by those outside of the Christian family. It was an outworking of a personal and denominational firm and generous faith. Could such hospitality extend to offering premises to other faith groups to use for their worship? The purpose of the regulation is primarily to safeguard the orthodoxy of Methodist faith by not allowing a form of Christian worship to happen in Methodist premises that departs from the firmness of the Methodist faith. While it is unlikely, but not impossible, that non-Christian worship cause such confusion, the generosity of Methodism does not reach to the encouragement of worship that is not Christian within premises that are devoted to Christian worship. Wesleyans should act with great hospitality, but not to the point where Christian worship could potentially be confused with that of other faiths.

A Theology of Dialogue
The Wesleyan family should be a community that develops small-scale local inter-faith groups. Dialogue, at its best, needs a firm faith commitment by the participants. A weak faith perspective that is quick to deny central tenets of belief rarely makes for a dynamic engagement. Yet, an openness is required to allow for the possibility of being convinced by the other's point of view. Less than this is to have two or more mutually exclusive monologues.

That said, formal dialogue is an important but peripheral activity when compared to the ongoing dialogue of life. Wesleyans enter the breadth of dialogue with the   hope of meeting Christ in unexpected places and the confidence that they can share Christ with all.

A Theology of Engagement

The contemporary world context is witnesses a "clash of civilisations" be- tween differing faith-based perspectives. When considered historically and globally, Christians have generally lived in a context of religious plurality. Those following Wesley can act first and then reflect. Theological justification can be a secondary motivation and not every answer needs to be known. The journey is a necessary part of the reflection and the Wesleyan DNA encourages participation.

There are specific areas of inter-faith engagement that are particularly appropriate for Wesleyans. Methodism has a traditional temperance/total abstinence view on the use of alcohol. While other Christians also share this perspective, for Methodism this has been a traditional denominational perspective. A rediscovery of the importance of this view may lead to areas of fruitful participation with Muslims who share a similar perspective. In local communities when, for example, applications for "twenty-four hour alcohol licences" are debated,

Muslims and Methodists may well share a similar opinion and therefore can act together. Related areas of particular shared concern include issues related to gambling and sexual morality.

The Wesley Historical Society regularly organises pilgrimages to sites of Methodist interest. Pilgrimage is a very significant tradition and religious experience in Islam and Hinduism. It would be a challenge to find a place of joint significance, but there is scope for encounter on the theme of pilgrimage and what the experience means to members of the various faith groups.

A Theology of Evangelism

Wesleyans need to build on their traditional evangelical understanding and see the need to engage evangelistically with members of other faiths. There is a clear Methodist history of

561

evangelism towards other faith communities through the missionary movement. It should hardly need to be added that such evangelism should be carried out with appropriate respect and consideration. To do so is in keeping with the Wesleyan tradition. Wesley firmly believed that all people needed to be saved and it is a matter of putting this into effect given the opportunities in contemporary Britain rather than needing a change in theological perspective.

The Wesleyan "Four All's" allow for optimism in evangelism. Understanding that no one is excluded from the possibility of meeting the grace of God charges Wesleyans with bringing the good news to all. The implication of such optimism is that Wesleyans cannot withdraw from an evangelistic inter-faith engagement and remain true to their traditions and understanding.

There is nothing incompatible with an evangelistic encounter complimenting other inter-faith approaches (Jones 2003: 159-83). The various theological and practical developments detailed here are in the stream of Wesleyan tradition and understanding. Indeed, such an evangelistic understanding is necessary in order to authenticate these other developments. Wesleyans do not engage with people of other faiths solely to create opportunities for appropriate evangelism; their theological understanding is broader than that. But within a positive engagement, opportunities for such authentic sharing faith occur.

An Understanding of Life as a Minority
More than many major Christian movements Wesleyans understand what it means to live as a religious minority. The Roman Catholic Church is in a religiously majority position in much of Europe; the Church of England has a history as an established faith with the Reformed faith sharing a parallel his- tory in Scotland. Each of these three denominations, in different eras and areas, has had very significant political influence to complement their religious ascendancy. Methodism shares none of these histories. Methodism has always been a minority faith and has never sought or had the opportunity to establish its own version of Christendom in Britain.
This understanding of living as a minority religious community allows Wesleyans to empathise with the experience of other faith communities that stand where Methodism has stood throughout its history. A theology of minority status gives the final impetus to

Wesleyans to act in the present to welcome the stranger, accept the outsider, listen to stories of faith and share the story of new life through Jesus Christ.

Conclusion

Wesleyan faith is firm and the evidence cited in this study demonstrates that it is within the evangelical mainstream. In order to be true to its traditions, history and understanding it is necessary for the successors to Wesley to maintain such a firmness of faith. But, as this study has made clear, such faith is also generous. There is a breadth within the Wesleyan movement, both historically and contemporarily, that not all other Christians share. The generosity of this faith can be developed in the future without losing its firmness. It is a creative tension that offers much to Christianity and wider Methodism. This is the heart of Methodism, but it needs to be taken positively. The boundaries of this generosity need to be pushed without sacrificing the firmness of faith that is a hallmark of the MCI.

It remains to be seen if Methodists and the Wesleyan movement have the courage to live out their firm and generous faith in the contemporary inter-faith context.

LITERATURE

Blanks, D.R. (1999). "Western Views of Islam." In: D.R. Blanks and M. Frassetto (eds). Western Views of Islam in Medieval and Early Modern Europe. New York: St Martin's Press.

Cogley, R.W. (1999). "Pagans and Christians on the New England Frontier: A Study of John Eliot's Indian Dialogues (1671)." Mission Studies XVI-I: Pp. 95-110.

Cracknell, K. (1998). Our Doctrines: Methodist Theology as Classical Christianity. Calver: Cliff College.

Forward, M. (1995). "Pure Universal Love Thou Art: God, Christ and the World's Religions." In Macquiban, T. (ed.). Pure Universal Love: Reflections on the Wesleys and Inter-faith Dialogue. Oxford: Applied Theology Press. Pp. 45-60.

Grady, F. (2005). Representing Righteous Heathens in Late Medieval England. Basingstoke: Palgrave, 2005.

Hattersley, R. (2002). A Brand Plucked From the Burning. London: Little Brown.

Harris, E. (1997). "Wesleyan Witness in an Interreligious Context." In P.R. Meadows (ed.). Windows on Wesley: Wesleyan Theology in Today's World Oxford: Applied Theology Press. Pp. 53-85.

Jones, S.J. (2003). The Evangelistic Love of God and Neighbor. Nashville: Abingdon.

Mackey, J. (1995). An Introduction to Celtic Christianity. Edinburgh: T&T Clark.

Maddox, R.L. (1992). "Wesley and the Question of Truth or Salvation Through Other Religions." Wesleyan Theological Journal 27: Pp. 7-29.

McCreary, A. (1996). Gordon Wilson: An Ordinary Hero. London: Marshall Pickering.

McDermott, G.R. (2000). Jonathan Edwards Confronts the Gods. Oxford: OUP.

Meadows, P.R. (2000). "'Candidates for Heaven': Wesleyan Resources for a Theology of Religions." Wesleyan Theological Journal 35: Pp. 41-66.

Miles, R.K. (2000). "John Wesley as Interreligious Resource: Would You Take This Man to an Interfaith Dialogue?" In: M. Forward et al. (eds). A Great Commission: Christian Hope and Religious Diversity. Berne: Lang.

Nederman, C.J. (2000). Worlds of Difference. University Park, PA: Pennsylvania State University Press.

Pailin, D.A. (1984). Attitudes to Other Religions. Manchester: Manchester University Press, 1984.

Pinnock, C. (1992). A Wideness in God's Mercy. Grand Rapids: Zondervan.

Rack, H. (1992). Reasonable Enthusiast: John Wesley and the Rise of Methodism. London: Epworth.

Ronda, J.P. (2000). "'Indians' Views of Christian Missionaries." In P. Allitt (ed.). Major Problems in American Religious History. Boston: Houghton Mifflin.

Turner, J.M. (1985). Conflict and Reconciliation. London: Epworth.

Vitkus, D.J. (1999). "Early Modern Orientalism: Representations of Islam in Sixteenth and Seventeenth-Century Europe." in D.R. Blanks and M. Frassetto (eds). Western Views of Islam in Medieval and Early Modern Europe. New York: St Martin's Press.

Wesley, John (1984 -) The Works of John Wesley Bicentennial Edition. F. Baker (ed.) Nashville, TN: Abingdon

Whaling, F. (1995). "John Wesley's Premonition of Inter-Faith Discourse." In: T. Macquiban (ed.). Pure Universal Love: Reflections on the Wesleys and Inter-faith Dialogue. Oxford: Applied Theology Press.

Wheatcroft, A. (2003). Infidels: The Conflict between Christendom and Islam. London: Viking

MODULE 8: MINISTRY LEADERSHIP-HISTORIC

(Revd Prof David Dunn-Wilson MA M.Phil BD Ph.D FRSA)

LECTURE 1: "THE KEYS OF THE KINGDOM 1"1

CHANGES IN CHRISTIAN LEADERSHIP: "FROM BETHLEHEM TO ROME"

INTRODUCTION: WHY BOTHER?

There is one thing that binds us all together. We do not deserve it; we may not have sought it; we will never be worthy of it or do it as it ought to be done. That bond is the fact that we have all, in various ways, been called to be leaders in Christ's Church and the reason we have gathered is that we want to be the best leaders we can be. We are here to discover, what authentic Christian leadership is and how we can exercise it for the glory of God and the benefit of those whom he has entrusted to our care.

It would seem arrogant for me as an outsider to ask you to consider this were it not for the fact that it appears already to concern you. I came across an unattributed article analysing the challenges facing this great country and was impressed by the fact that it was entitled, *"The Leadership Crisis in Nigeria"* and concluded with these words, "There is a need for a leadership with the courage to face the challenges of allowing the societies of Nigeria to rediscover their values." If that is so, then it is a matter of great concern and another Nigerian writer reminds the Church has a paramount part to play. In his *Task of Christian Leadership,* asserts that "A Christian leadership "style is "Imperative" and that we are right to explore the nature of authentic leadership.

But how are we to tackle such a vast subject? Here again I have found wisdom in Nigerian sources. I have encountered the studies of Professor Adiele Afigbo, the charismatic lecturer in the University of Nigeria who died in 2009, and I was impressed by the way in which he

---

1 For further lectures by Prof David Dunn-Wilson and Revd Richard Jackson on historic mission themes: See 'Then & Now of Church Mission' published by feedaread 2015 isbn 978-1-78510-583-8

warned against seeking 'quick fixes' to Nigeria's challenges. There is a foundational truth in all his writings and it is this: those who seek to meet any challenge must accept what he called 'the primacy of historical understanding'. In other words, researchers must be prepared to go back into history to discover how the present situation has arisen. The late Professor Bruce was right. As leaders of our churches' missiological thinking, we need much more than a superficial knowledge of our task. If we are to serve the present age, we must have explored our common past in order to understand our present and plan for our future.

So I want us to take those two Nigerian insights as our guiding lights. Firstly, to assert that it is important that we discover authentic Christian leadership and secondly, that we avoid 'quick fixes' and take time to search for that authentic leadership in the roots and growth of the Christian Church. There are many ways to approach our subject but I ask you to think of Christian leadership as a cord, woven together over the centuries from several different strands.

1: THE ROMAN LEADERSHIP STRAND

ROMAN POWER-LEADERSHIP:

So let us begin, even before that moment when Jesus of Nazareth, a young, dynamic preacher came out of divinely-devised obscurity to begin his three years of public ministry. Even before he was born, Jesus had experienced an alien form of leadership. He was already caught up in the supreme fact of First Century Jewish existence – they lived in Roman province. His poor pregnant mother had to travel for three days to cover the seventy miles from Nazareth to Bethlehem at the whim of a Roman Emperor. That census was only one terrible symptom of the Roman concept of leadership and we might almost say that Jesus' first cry was a cry of protest!

The Roman authorities were interested in the numbers of people for one purpose only and that was the raising of taxes, the tools of tyranny. Not only was the whole idea of the census an insult to the Jews (remember that it was Satan who tempted David to conduct a census) but taxation paid to a foreign power was a symbol of slavery and it would eventually drive the Jews to revolution under Judas of Galilee.

That census opens the door to the whole imperial system of leadership – virtually the only form of leadership which was known to the world of Jesus. It was basically a pyramid of power with the Emperor at its apex whose supremacy was supported by seventeen glorious titles. He was accorded religious authority with his own religion and temple.

The whole Roman conception of was about power. There were even two words for it –*potentia* (personal power) and *potestas* (political power). - and the power of the Emperor had to be ruthlessly protected. Great and bloody fights were held in the Roman arenas to show the fate of criminals and 'outsiders' (later including Christians) and to be a safety valve so that the people could express their aggression without turning it revolution.

JEWISH POWER-LEADERSHIP:

Now, all this had a profound effect upon the Jews. Their leaders plotted to harness as much of that power as possible for themselves. The squabbles between the Temple-controlling Sadducees and the Pharisees were legendary. A rich Jew could wield power if he became a *publicanus* – by buying the right to become a Chief Tax Collector for the Romans. He farmed out his power to lesser tax-collectors. What kudos it gave them! They could stop any man in the street and tax him for what he was carrying, adding a little extra for their own pocket. Yes, contemporary Judaism also loved power-leadership.

2: THE JESUS LEADERSHIP STRAND

It was against this background that Jesus called a group of red-blooded, macho young men to follow him. Most of them were rebellious Galileans. Several were probably already freedom fighters and all were looking for adventure. Do you think that they responded to Jesus call for sophisticated spiritual reasons? Surely not! It is more likely that they believed that they had been recruited by the long=awaited national deliverer from the yoke of Rome. They were ready for blood and fire like young patriots in any age.

Remember that they had only one model of leadership in their minds. Leadership was about power. They showed their hand when a Samaritan village refused entry to Jesus. "Lord, do you want us to command fire to come down from heaven and consume them, just as Elijah did?" No wonder they argued about who was going to be most powerful when the Kingdom was won! No wonder that that proud mother sidled up to Jesus to 'have a word' on behalf of her boys – James and John! Would Jesus please appoint them as his Prime Minister and Chancellor of the Exchequer when he finally came to power?

Jesus had to teach them a completely different definition of leadership. He sets a child in the midst of them – the word used is diminutive – a very little, insignificant child – to upset their scale of values. And he says, "He that is least among you all (like this little child) will be great". (Lk. 9:47) They were not to seek the best seats at feasts like important Jews did. (Mt.23:11ff.)

They were to reject the modes of leadership that surrounded them. "You know that the rulers of the gentiles lord it over them and those who are great exercise authority over them, it shall not be so among you but whosoever desires to be great among you let him be your servant. And whoever desires to be first among you let him by your slave. Just as the Son of Man did not come to be served but to serve." He drives home this lesson by the foot-washing at the Last Supper but, even then, swords were carried into the Garden of Gethsemane.

One of the most helpful suggestions is that Jesus is resurrecting the old image of the leader as the Shepherd and Servant of others. He describes himself as the Good Shepherd, the one who cares for the sheep. (John 10:4)

After the resurrection, he establishes this as a pattern by commissioning Peter to be a shepherd to his followers. Certainly, the early church retained its vision of Jesus as the Good Shepherd. (Heb. 13:20, I Pet. 2:25, 5:4) and the title *Shepherd* is retained for church leaders (Ephesians 4:11, I Peter 5:1-3. They are urged not to 'lord it over' their flocks. So there was now an alternative strand on offer. How did it fare?

3: THE APOSTOLIC LEADERSHIP STRAND

LEADERSHIP TENSION IN THE EARLY CHURCH:

The Jerusalem Church, founded by the apostles led by Peter, enjoyed halcyon days after Pentecost. They met to worship in the Temple's Solomon's Colonnade and lived a life of communal charity

However, that honeymoon period was not to last and as the great Professor F.F. Bruce showed in his careful study, another leadership style was lurking in the wings to re-assert itself when the apostles' widening mission took them away from Jerusalem into other fields.

The Adventist scholar Robert Johnson identifies what he calls the challenge of 'Familial Leadership'. At some point, the unbelieving brothers of Jesus (Mk.3:31ff.) had become believers and the leadership of the church had been vested in the family-line, the so-called 'Master's People', with James as their head – a pre-eminence which had been confirmed by his being accorded a special visitation by the Risen Christ.

The title 'James the Righteous' indicated his stance with regard to the Christian faith. He saw it primarily as a Jewish Messianic Reform Movement. Many converts came from among conservative Pharisees who were proud to be 'zealots for the Law' and, if Bruce is right, they established a ruling council for the church modelled on the Jewish Sanhedrin. They wanted to preserve the purity of the faith by establishing a strict, authoritarian leadership-style. It was no wonder that the conversion of the gentiles appalled them and that they wanted to impose Jewish rites and customs upon them. The story of church leadership might have been very different had not
James been stoned to death in 62 AD and, faced by persecution, his successor Simon bar Clopas, had not led the survivors of the Jerusalem Church out to Pella and beyond.

DEVELOPMENT OF THE IDEA OF APOSTLESHIP:

Meanwhile the influx of gentiles into the churches helped to establish the idea of Apostolic Leadership. The eleven original apostles were the natural leaders of the churches but the choice of Matthias to fill the vacancy left by Judas the Traitor introduced an important new idea. True, he had accompanied Jesus throughout his ministry, had witnessed his resurrection and had been selected under the guidance of the Holy Spirit but the fact remained that a new principle had been established. The title 'apostle' no longer applied only to the original Twelve called by Jesus. It was possible to create an apostolate by appointing suitable candidates much as, in Judaism at that time, a synagogue could commission 'apostles' to undertake tasks on its behalf.

Paul arrives on the scene humbly claiming to be a graciously 'appointed apostle'. He insists that he has been 'called to be an apostle' (Romans 1:1) by Christ himself and he frequently stresses the fact. Moreover, he told Timothy that he had been 'ordained as an apostle' (I Tim.2:7) In other words, it was possible for the church to nominate and commission candidates for the apostolate. Paul affirms Apollos, Silvanus, Timothy and several others as appointed apostolic leaders.

The next step comes when, in order to free the apostolic preachers for their evangelistic ministry, the church decides to appoint what amounts to a second order of ministry. Stephen and six other men 'of good reputation, full of the Holy Spirit and wisdom' were appointed as 'deacons' – servant-leaders to care for the needy. Notice that it is no casual affair. They are properly ordained by the laying on of hands

4: THE EPISCOPAL LEADERSHIP STRAND

THE EUROPEAN FOCUS:

To understand the full significance of appointed Apostolic leadership, we need to remember the effect of one of their most famous dreams. On his missionary journey through Galatia, Paul comes to Mysia and plans to go East into the Roman province of Asia but he is thwarted and spends the night in Troas. That night he dreams about a man from Macedonia appealing to him to come and preach the Gospel there. DO you see the immense implication of this decision?

Paul had brought the Gospel into western Europe! He was proud of being a Roman citizen and his goal was to plant the Gospel in Rome itself, the centre of the known world. Irenaeus says that the Roman church was founded by Peter and Paul. As we will see, the significance of focussing the Christian Church in Europe and in Rome in particular was to have profound and lasting consequences.

THE GROWTH OF EPISCOPACY:

In view of all that we have said, Paul must have seen his imprisonment in Rome as a sort of victory. He had arrived at his goal and, from his prison cell he could send messages along the 50,000 miles of Roman roads to guide the congregations of the Empire. It is in the opening verse of one of these messages–*The Letter to the*

Philippians–that he drops something of a bombshell. He sends greetings to "all the saints as well as to the bishops and deacons." So uncomfortable is this early reference to a two-tier leadership that many scholars regard it as a later addition. However, this is unnecessary.

I have no intention of becoming embroiled in the argument about bishops and presbyters but it seems to me that, initially at least, *episcopos* (overseer) and *presbyteros* (elder) probably refer to the same office. Suffice it to say that it is clear that churches had begun to appoint and commission their own local leaders.

There was no neat development in episcopacy, for many years different churches developed their own forms of church leadership. However, it seems clear that Ignatius of Antioch (c98-117) tells congregations "Your bishop presides in the place of God" and so should be honoured as safeguards of unity in the churches. At some time during the next half century, it became common for each town or area to have its own bishop supported by a council of presbyters – the so-called *monarchical bishops.*

CONSTANTINE AND THE BISHOPS:

Whatever the process, we know that, when we leap to 312 AD when Constantine became Emperor, he found the Christian Church firmly established. To avoid religious problems in his empire, he established a working relationship with the Christian bishops who represented 10% of the Empire's population. Unlike pagan priests were not appointed by the state or drawn from an obedient elite. Especially, with great tact, he bought the support of its Bishop Militades with generous gifts and the Lateran Palace as his official residence in Rome,
which until he built a new Christian capital at Byzantium in the East, was Constantine's headquarters.

The Emperor's programme brought about a profound change in the nature of the bishops' leadership. He gave them the same privileges that pagan priests enjoyed–exemption from government service, gave them government stipends and freedom from taxes. He made them judges to sort out squabbles in state-recognized church courts and accepted them as a potent force in the political life of the Empire. He also placed them in charge of the Church's growing wealth.

571

It was not surprising that there was an unseemly scramble for the richest dioceses. The church was becoming materialistic and many bishops developed luxurious life-styles. The way they governed the church began to reflect that of Roman officials and they used their power, backed by Roman law, to tyrannize opponents and defend their privileges.

THE SUPREMACY OF ROME:

It is here that we must that we must notice something very important. We saw how Constantine gave special treatment to the bishops of Rome (he dealt with four of them during his reign). Paul's dream of outing Rome at the centre of the Church had come true and now it needed historical and theological undergirding. Church writers pointed out that Christ himself had declared Peter to be 'the rock on which I will build my church' and claimed that Peter had been the founder of the Roman church. He had personally appointed Linus to be his successor, so establishing a succession which had the authority of Peter the apostle. Bishops that followed Linus must also have inherited that apostolic authority.

Over the following years, the primacy of Rome and its bishops became an established belief, supported by Church fathers like Irenaeus, Tertullian and Cyprian. It faced fierce competition from the Eastern Church but eventually, the Emperor Theodosius II declared the Bishop of Rome to be, "rector of the whole church" and, by the fourth century Bishop Damasus (366-384) took the title Pope (previously used in the Eastern Church for quite humble clergy) as the sole right of the Bishop of Rome.

THE CITY OF GOD:

It was then that something unimaginable happened–the great Roman Empire collapsed! Within less than forty years, Alaric and his Visigoths had occupied the city of Rome and it seemed that the end of the world had come. It was in the midst of the chaos that one of the greatest of all Christian books Augustine's *City of God.* Augustine urged Christians not to be afraid – this was all part of God's plan. He had to remove the old sinful City of Man (the Roman Empire) so that he could bring in his reign on earth –The City of God. Now was the time for Christians to act because they were the citizens of the new City of God–the Church. The name for this divinely created political and spiritual state was Christendom–the Kingdom of Christ.

Their task was to bring everybody into the Church, like rescuing people from the sea and bringing them on board the ship of salvation. The City of God had two parts, there was the Spiritual Part which was the Church and there was the Secular part which was the political state. The two must co-operate in God's work. This was an idea of immense importance. Now secular rulers –kings, princes and governors, were commanded to defend the church and ensure its victory. Emperor Theodosius the Great (347-395) sounded a sinister note when he condemned non-Catholic Christians as "demented and insane" who would be "punished in accordance with our displeasure."

Years later (1381) Pope Boniface spelled out what this meant. *Outside the Church there is neither salvation nor remission of sins and in the Church's power there are two swords, namely the spiritual and the earthly. This authority is divine, reaffirmed to Peter's successors. Therefore, whoever resists this power resists the command of God.* The meaning was clear. Those who did not accept the authority of the Church would be ruthlessly dealt with.

5: THE CHRISTENDOM LEADERSHIP STRAND

CRUSADES AND COERCION:

During the ensuing centuries, the power of the Popes to impose Catholic Christianity on everybody grew and, by the eleventh century, matters came to a head. Islam had risen as a counter-force to the church and had to be conquered. In 1096, in Claremont in Southern France, Pope Urban II summoned a great gathering of clergy, political leaders and common people. There he preached a fiery sermon to launch a Crusade to drive Islam from the Christian Holy Places in Palestine. The congregation responded with a road, "God will it!" and the idea of "God's War" was launched.

So the Church's fight for soul was being waged on two fronts–the infidel Moslems in Palestine and heretics in Europe. The Popes left the fighting to the Crusaders but they formed a spiritual army from among the monks and nuns who had embraced a disciplined Christian life. In 1216, Pope Honorius created his Dominican Order of Preacher to fight heresy wherever they found it. This they did both with brilliant argument and also with ruthless cruelty.It was believed that human beings were composed of bodies and souls and that it was the supreme task of the clergy was to save souls by 'educating the body'. If this meant hurting the body, it was a price worth paying even if it killed the person being so 'educated'. So the Church developed organizations like The Spanish Inquisition which used sophisticated torture and death to make its victims accept the Catholic Faith.

EUROPE REIGNS!

But something else was happening. Christendom was being given a geographical identity. Dr Denys Hayes has the interesting suggestion that the idea of Europe as a geographical area originated in a letter from Pope Pius II to Mohamet II his great Moslem rival. In the letter, the Pope threatens to crush Mohamet by "the resources of the Christian people" and then he gives a list of Christian countries, Spain, Britain, France and so on. In other words, Christendom and Europe were identical and, therefore, Europe had a right and a responsibility to convert the rest of the world.

In March 1493, two tiny battered ships–*The Pinta and The Nina*– docked in Barcelona in Portugal with a miraculous cargo of riches from the New World. The priests who had accompanied Christopher Columbus and Martin Pinson, told stories of wild heathens waiting to be converted. It was then that the two great sea-powers, Spain and Portugal persuaded the Pope, as the supreme spiritual and political head of Christendom, to divide the world between them.

So the strands of leadership were firmly woven together to bind the missionary work of the Church. The Pope and the European Church had been divinely entrusted with the task of bringing the whole world to the Catholic faith by every spiritual, economic and military means available. Within the European Church was light: outside it was darkness which must be attacked and dispersed. Priests and soldiers set out to conquer the world together.

6: THE NIGERIAN CONNECTION:

I was interested to discover the work of Ade Ajay and his Ibadan School of historians who devoted so much care and skill to reveal the external forces which have shaped West African history because, a little more than sixty years after the Pope had divided the world, the force of Christendom's leadership style was to make itself here.

This is a story that you will know better than I but we need to hint at because it shows the Nigerian connection to our studies. The Portuguese lost no time in sending explorers to find a sea-route to India and, on their ships, they carried missionary priests. One of the most zealous was a Dominican called Gaspar da Crucis who worked in many parts of the Portuguese Empire but was appointed as Bishop of Sao Tome. In 1555, he sent Augustinian monks to Warri and a Portuguese priest Father Francisco a Mater Dei began to evangelise the Itsekiri. He baptized a young man called Olu and gave him the name Sebastian who allowed his son to go to Portugal to be trained as a priest but he married there and never returned home. All attempts to establish an indigenous Catholic priesthood failed because priests were expected to be unmarried and, therefore, the first Christian mission to Nigeria failed.

Many reasons have been given for this but surely; we need look no further than the fact that the Portuguese missionaries came in the armed ships of the slave-traders. Some actually profited from the terrible traffic in human flesh but even the most enlightened believed that they could never convert Africans until they had been brought out from the so-called Dark Continent into the light of Christendom. For those who remained stubborn, Gaspar set up an active branch of the Portuguese Inquisition on Sao Tome to torture them into faith.

So, you see what has happened. The history we have been studying has become your history too. The Christendom mind-set declared that the European Catholic Church had the right and the responsibility to convert all other races to Christianity (by force, if necessary) and to destroy paganism and heresy wherever it was found. That was what brought the first missionaries to your shores. But the story was far from over...

CHANGES IN CHRISTIAN LEADERSHIP: "FROM CONSTANTINOPLE TO LAGOS"

1: THE NON-CONFORMIST STRAND

THE CHALLENGE TO THE POPE'S LEADERSHIP:

You will remember that in our discovery of the strands that were twined together over the centuries to form the cord of Christian leadership, we had reached the point at which the power of the Popes in Rome was supreme. At least in their own minds, the Popes ruled the world and were given authority to bring everybody into the fold of the Catholic Church, whether they liked it or not. Of course, this brought them into fierce conflict with the Eastern Orthodox Churches – but that is another story which we cannot pursue in our short time together.

At the end of our last lecture, I hinted that, although everything looked smooth on the surface, underneath there were rumbles of another kind of leadership. We need to trace these because, eventually they revolutionised Christian leadership and profoundly changed the spiritual conformation of the Western world. I have labelled this other kind of leadership 'Non-conformist' because it sprang from strong individuals who refused to *conform* to the official dictates of the Catholic Church. We saw how the Christendom style of leadership demanded the total trust and obedience of its people and, therefore, any kind of nonconformist thinking was a dangerous challenge.

CHRISTIAN PROPHETS:

To find the roots of this non-conformity, we need to go back to the earliest days of the Church because there we find those mysterious Christian prophets who were certainly a law unto themselves and very non-conformist. True, some, like Agabus and the daughters of Philip, attached to local congregations but others who drifted from church to church to bring congregations claiming to bring messages straight from the Holy Spirit. St Paul certainly urged the Thessalonian Christians to respect prophets but it is interesting that Jesus himself warns about those who would 'prophesy in his name' (Mt 7:22) The second generation of Christian leaders took up this caution and warned their congregations to be wary of wandering prophets (*Didache c90)* and always to consult their bishops about their reliability(Ignatius).

This non-conformity needed official control and perhaps it was because it lacked official approval that, eventually, it died out in the early church.

MONTANISM:

Nevertheless, prophetism is never so easily extinguished and it burst into flame in a much more potent form around the middle of the Second Century. In Phrygia, a recent convert called Montanus and his helpers Maximila and Prisca claimed a prophetic role, declaring that the Holy Spirit was giving them direct revelations. They lived very strict lives and, at first many bishops supported them so that their influence spread widely – especially in Northern Africa. However, the Church could not bear their non-conformity and drove them out to Pepuzza where their leaders died. Even that was not enough and, centuries later, their shrines were destroyed and their books burned by the Emperor's decree. Once again, the Pope had crushed non-conformism.

CATHARISM:

Just to show how tenacious prophetism is, we move forward to the eleventh century where, in Southern France, a group of nonconformists called Cathars arose. With tones reminiscent of Old Testament prophets, they condemned to Rome and its priests as "the Church of Wolves' they gained many followers to a life of discipline and poverty and when Rome sent its best scholars to root out 'The Great Heresy', the Cathars out-argued and humiliated them.

In 1208, the Pope could no longer tolerate the situation and he ordered a crusade of terror to be waged against the Cathars. When asked how his soldiers were to distinguish between innocent citizens and heretical Cathars, the Pope ruthlessly replied, "Kill them all! God-will know his own!" –and half a million men, women and children were slaughtered. The Dominicans and the inquisition moved in to torture and execute ruthlessly and, by the fourteenth century, another group of nonconformists had been destroyed. Nevertheless, these eruptions of nonconformity show that, from the beginning, there was an alternative, Spirit-led strand of leadership which was in constant conflict with the authoritarian Christendom strand.

THE SACK OF CONSTANTINOPLE:

Hitherto the Church had managed to stifle nonconformist strands of leadership but in Italy there were nonconformist forces at work which would prove irresistible. They were let loose in the strangest of ways. In 1453, the Pope's enthusiasm for crusades back-fired when, instead of being defeated, the Moslem Turks captured Constantinople, the Christian capital, massacred its inhabitants and brought the 1000 year Roman Empire to an end. The Turks closed the great University in Constantinople and its scholars fled aboard on merchant ships.

One the major trade routes led to the Italian city of Florence where the great Medici family welcomed artists and scholars. These scholars brought with them the riches of the ancient world, the writings of Greek and Latin geniuses like Plato and Aristotle of which Western scholars knew little. It began literally a 'new birth' of learning –a 'renaissance- and the Church hated it for one reason in particular.

HUMANISM:

For centuries, the Church had taught people that the only knowledge worth having was knowledge of God and that that was the business of the clergy. However, the great Greek and Latin writers of ancient times saw things differently. They believed that the priority was for human beings to understand themselves and their world, so they were called 'humanists–scholars who studied history, moral, philosophy and rhetoric. They encouraged people to test information and to think for themselves, saying that human beings were the height of God's creation and He had placed their destiny in their own hands. (Pica da Mirandola 1463-1494)

Now we meet a great writer called Petrarch who travelled far and wide collecting ancient documents. What makes him so important is that he began to apply these new ideas to Christian doctrines and soon many Christian scholars were thinking in a 'humanist' way about the faith. When humanist ideas moved northwards in Europe, they became even more concerned with religion and the Catholic Church was terrified.

One development frightened them above all others!

Among the ancient documents that had been discovered were copies of the Bible in Hebrew and Greek and the great Dutch scholar Erasmus used these original texts to correct the Church's official Bible, Jerome's Latin Bible which for a thousand years had been the *Vulgate* which means the commonly used translation'. This had been open only to the clergy who could read Latin; it was not for common people. This was only the beginning. Humanists believed that education was the way to self-discovery and, all over Europe; people were beginning to want books in their own language. Why should the Bible be any different?

In England an Oxford scholar John Wycliffe (c1330-1384) took up the task. Like a good humanist, he believed that every individual was personally responsible to God. How could they know what was right if they could not read the Bible? He said that the Bible exposed the corruption of the Church, the riches of the monks and the falsehoods of the Pope, who immediately condemned him as a heretic. Nevertheless, he won many supporters, even though the Church later burned his body and attempted to blot out his memory. But it was too late!

3: THE PROTESTANT LEADERSHIP STRAND

INDULGENCES:

The spark that eventually caused the explosion was struck in the strangest way. Mad with power and short of money, the Popes claimed that their authority extended beyond this world and that they had power to forgive the sins of the dead. Needing funds to complete his great church in Rome, the Pope sent 'pardoners' far and wide to sell these tickets of pardon which cancelled sins. These were called 'indulgences' and their slickest salesman was John Tetzel who arrived in the town of Wittenberg in Germany with his carefully organized 'road-show'. He assured the local people that they could purchase forgiveness, not only for themselves but for their loved one pining in Purgatory.

Seeing his parishioners deceived and robbed of their money the local priest, Martin Luther, was furious and the spark that blew Europe apart was set when he went to the Church in Wittenberg and nailed to the door thirty-five matters that needed to be debated.

The date is June 15th 1520 and Pope Leo X is furious. His scribes cower as he strides up and down, trying to find the right words. Finally he breaks out, *Exurge Domine, Arise, O Lord and judge your cause...you committed the rule of the Vineyard to Peter and his successors. The wild boar from the forest seeks to destroy it...Rise Peter...give heed to the cause of the Holy Roman Church.* Of course, the wild boar was Martin Luther and no wonder the Pope was furious.

At every point Luther contradicted the Roman church, declaring that it was only man-made and that the True Church was spiritual –that was the True Christendom. He condemned the Pope for boasting that he was the head of the Church and for his condemning all that refused his authority. He declared the principle that everybody was saved by grace through faith and he insisted that truth was to be found only in the Bible. He believed that, guided by the Holy Spirit, every true Christian could read and interpret the Bible. Consequently, in 1522 he published his own version of it in German for his people to read.

So now, it was clear that Europe was divided. There were, in effect, two Churches–the Catholic Church which subjected individual opinion to the authority of the Pope and the Protestant Church (mainly divided between Luther's Lutheran and Calvin's Reformed churches) which stressed the authority of the Bible and the importance of every individual to study it for themselves. There followed years of furious warfare between the two Church as each struggled to extend their influence.

PIETISM:

Sadly, as time went by, the Protestant Church became almost as hard and intolerant as the Catholic Church it had challenged and it was time for a new revival. In France, there lived a boy who had been brought up by a godly grandmother. His name was Philipp Jacob Spener (1636) and he realised how dry Lutheranism had become. He studied theology in Strasburg and began religious meetings in his house for Bible-study and prayer. He wrote a great book calling for the reform of the Lutheran Church and, since it was entitled *Pia Desidiria* his followers became known as 'Pietists'. In spite of great opposition from the traditional Protestant Churches, Spener's work continued and spread under the guidance of another great leader August Herman

Franke who founded an orphanage and a new university at Halle. However, one of Pietism's greatest contributions to our story came through Spener's god-son Count von Zinzendorf.

A hundred years before Luther made his stand, in what is now the Czech Republic, Jan Hus (1269-1415) a brilliant priest-philosopher was so impressed by Wycliffe's non-conformist teachings that he began to preach the same truths. The outraged Catholic authorities lured him to his death, burned him at the stake and drove his followers from the country. Some of them fled to Moravia and became known as The Moravian Brethren. They finally found a home in Germany on the estate of the Pietist Count Nicholas von Zinzendorf where they built their own town at Herrnhut. There, on 13th August 1727, they had a wonderful experience of the Holy Spirit and began to meet in small groups for Bible study and prayer.

The result of this was that they became a fervent missionary church, taking the Gospel to many parts of the earth. In 1727, one of their groups sailed from England to America and, on the ship, they met a young Anglican missionary. Their ship, *The Simmonds,* ran into great storms and everybody was terrified – except for the Moravians who calmly read their Bibles and prayed, so impressing the young priest that, when they reached their destination in America, he continued to study their way of life. That young man was John Wesley, the founder of Methodism and so your history and that of the Moravians began to come together.

When he returned to England, John Wesley felt that compared with the Moravians, he was not a true Christian so he began to seek their guidance. On May 24th 1738, he went to one of their meetings held in Aldersgate in London. He writes,

'I felt my heart was strangely warmed. I felt I did trust in Christ, Christ alone for my salvation and an assurance was given me that he had taken my sins even mine and saved me from the law of sin and death.' About the same time, his brother Charles had a similar experience and the Methodist revival was born.

John Wesley declared, "I look upon the whole world as my parish" and he travelled thousands of miles on horseback in the British Isles, preaching and creating Christian communities very much like those of the Pietists and Moravians. Just before his death, John Wesley ordained Dr Thomas Coke to go to America and he is called 'The Father of Methodist Missions' because he travelled abroad creating Methodist fellowships. In 1813, the Methodists in general caught the enthusiasm for missionary work and in 1818, a committee was formed to organize it.

4: THE SECULAR LEADERSHIP STRAND

Now, we must go back to those Renaissance and humanist scholars that we met because there is another important strand of leadership that needs our attention. You remember how the value of every individual was established by Reformers like Wycliffe, Luther and Calvin who declared the right of individuals to study the Bible for themselves and to discover their own personal relationship to God. But there were others who developed individualism in a radically different way.

THE RISE OF ATHEISM:

On a cold day in 1620, an ex-soldier who dabbled in mathematics and philosophy took refuge from the bitter Swedish winter in a room with a burning hot stove. There, the great philosopher Rene Descartes vowed, "never to accept anything as true which he did not know to be true". He emerged with the conviction that the only thing he could be sure of was that, in order to doubt things, he must exist, so he adopted as his motto. "I think, therefore I am." Now you can see what had happened. The Catholic Church declared that *Doubt* was the supreme sin but Descartes was saying that doubt was the great virtue, that human beings learn by doubting because it makes them search for the truth. Descartes remained a faithful Catholic but the focus had been changed. Now human beings were placed at the centre of the search for truth and the seeds of religious doubt had been sown.

Another philosopher David Hume (1711-1776) took matters further. He created what he called 'the science of Man' and he was convinced that human behaviour was caused by what we want rather than by what we think. He was very sceptical about Christianity and was not sure that human needed God at all.

Other great philosophers like the Frenchman Voltaire (1694-1778) and the German Emanuel Kant (1724-1804) thought that we might need some remote Supreme Being but another French philosopher Denis Diderot (1713-1780) declared his belief that God did not exist. He was joined by a whole group of French atheistic writers but what was worse was the fact that thousands of people in Europe believed the atheists.

When the French people revolted against their rulers, one of the first things that they did was to abolish Christianity. They turned Notre Dame Cathedral into a Temple of Reason and appointed a chorus girl as the Goddess of Reason for the new religion. Within a few years, the German philosopher Nietzsche (1844-1900) was declaring "God is dead!" and Karl Marx (1818-1883) the architect of Communism had begun his movement which eventually plunged half of Europe into deep atheism.

THE RISE OF THE 'NEW INDIVIDUALISM':

Even in non-Communist countries secularism and atheism spread. For many ordinary people caught up in two world wars the idea of a loving God seemed a bad joke. After the Second World War, war-weary people were no longer ready to be pushed around by authorities and the age of new individualism was born

In our own time, this thinking has come to full fruition. We have entered the time of what has come to be known as post-modernism which says that there are no universal truths which everybody has to accept. Everybody makes their own 'Truth'–whatever is true for them at any time. In the same way, since there is no universal Right and Wrong, everybody makes their own morality. Nobody can tell you what is right or wrong for you.

So you can see why the Western Church has had such a difficult time for the last fifty years. It represents everything that the New Individualists hate. It claims an authority figure–God; we respect an organization–the Church. We declare a universal Truth–the Gospel. The Church seems to represent the sort of tyranny to so many people who, if they think of it at all, prefer to create their own religion out of bits and pieces of mysticism, Buddhism, paganism, fairies, angels, prisms and so on.

THE GREAT DISILLUSION:

So far the spotlight of leadership was focussed on Europe (plus increasingly America but that is another story) whose churches saw themselves as being divinely responsible for taking the light of the Gospel to the whole world. Many of the noble army of missionaries gave their lives in order to take the Gospel, education and health to remotest lands. In 1910, a huge gathering of missionary societies met in Edinburgh to organize their work on a global plain. It was a great achievement but it eloquently demonstrated the supremacy, perhaps the unwitting arrogance of the Western churches. Of the 1,335 delegates, less than 20 came from the so-called 'younger churches'. The message was clear: Europeans were the teachers and everybody else were the learners.

However, events were about the change that leadership style. Scarcely had the Edinburgh Conference ended than the 'Christian' European powers were killing each other in the First World War, drawing thousands of men from their colonies into the terrible work. Thousands of these were killed but those who returned home were profoundly changed. Not only had they seen that it was possible to defeat Europeans and learn their warfare skills but their idealist view of the European church had been smashed by seeing Christians saying their prayers and then killing one another. Their disillusionment was completed when they became embroiled in the Second World War.

THE 'REJECTION' OF EUROPE:

The causes of the resulting nationalism are complicated, suffice it to say that, within ten years of the end of the Second World War; nearly thirty countries (including Nigeria) had claimed their independence. Their churches followed suit and, in The All-African Conference of Churches in Nairobi pointed to European missionaries as perpetrating, "a distorted view of the mission of the Church in the world". And the 1973 World Council of Churches meeting in Bangkok accepted a motion to stop European churches sending missionary personnel or funds. It is now widely understood that the hub of Christianity has moved away from the European/North American axis to Africa, Latin America and Asia, which leads us to the question of Nigerian Christian leadership.

I think that we can now see that the history of the Church in the Western world is important for the church in Africa. There is a sense in which our history is your history too. In a previous lecture, we saw how Catholic missionaries came to these shores, binding Europe and Nigeria in a disastrous embrace and making our history your history too. Never again could Africa and Europe ignore each other's existence.

PROTESTANT MISSIONS:

However, it is with the rise of the missionary zeal of the Moravians that this joint-history takes a much healthier turn. Inspired by the Moravians, the Methodists also sought to spread the love of Christ throughout the world. In 1796, Thomas Coke had sent missionaries to Sierra Leone where, after a poor start, by 1804 a small Methodist society was formed in Freetown. Significantly, among the first converts was a young Yoruba called Joseph May, whose son became an eminent educator. In 1838, one of the greatest Methodist missionary pioneers, Thomas Birch Freeman, was sent to the Gold Coast and he lost no time (1824) in forging ahead into Nigeria where he established Methodist societies (1842) at Badagry and Abeokuta. In this, he was helped by William de Craft whom he left in charge of the work.

The rest of the story you know better than I. In 1881, Halligay developed the work among the Yoruba and, ten years later, the Primitive Methodists began their work in the East. The Training Institute was opened at Ibadan in 1905; Ilesha Hospital (supported by The Wesley Guild) in 1912 and so the relationship has continued through to 1962 when the Nigerian Methodist Church became autonomous-and here we are today!

THE ISSUE OF AUTHENTIC CHRISTIAN LEADERSHIP:

But let us turn the spotlight on a particular issue–the search for authentic leadership. The late Professor Adiele Afigbo exposed the influence which the Western churches have had on traditional African leadership patterns. He said that 'Christian missions destabilized communities because wherever missions planted their feet the society split into pro-mission (so-called 'progressive') and anti-mission (so-called 'conservative' elements)"

How true that is, you will know better than I, but it does raise the question, "What is the kind of leadership needed by the contemporary Nigerian churches"–an issue which lands firmly in your lap!

It seems to me that there is both a spiritual and a social challenge here. For instance, spiritually, it must have seemed odd that we spent so much time looking at non-conformist prophets like Agabus and Montanus but nothing could be more relevant to the issue of authentic Nigerian Christian leadership than the question of prophecy. This whole strand of prophetic leadership is very much alive in West Africa. 'Prophet' is a popular title for religious leaders in Nigeria. The Danish scholar Niels Kastfelt describes a 'prophet' as "a charismatic man who better than others perceives the problem of his society and preaches a course of action founded on revelation" (*African Prophetism and Christian Missionaries in North-East Nigeria* Journal of Religion in Africa).

The Yale academic Matthew Kustenbauder notes how often the 'abundant' Christian prophets in Nigeria have an uneasy relationship with mainline churches. Methodist friends in many parts of Africa have told me of their regret that many of their members are deserting them for the 'spirit churches'. Without checks and balances false prophetism thrives but what are the authentic Nigerian elements in Pentecostal prophetism that the mainline churches need to learn?

Here is another challenge, a social one. In an article entitled *Societal Values and the Leadership Crisis in Nigeria* the unacknowledged writer says this, "I am convinced that the kind of leadership that Nigeria needs is one that would have the courage, integrity and ability to address once for all those factors which have allowed corruption and inequality to be institutionalised in the country." If this is true and the Christian Church stands for Truth, honesty and respect for every individual, what kind of leadership is necessary to make our churches champions for these things in society?

You are the leaders who must guide Nigerian Methodism into the future, what do you see as the priorities of leadership which must be grasped?

MODULE 8a: MINISTRY LEADERSHIP-PRACTICAL

(Revd Richard Jackson MA BD International Coordinator CCITC)

LECTURE 1: BIBLICAL LEADERSHIP: OLD TESTAMENT

Four important factors affect our thinking and learning about leadership in the Old Testament.

1.   All leadership and authority is derived from God who created all things.
2.   All leadership styles noted relate to a particular social context.
3.   All leadership in the Old Testament context is in essence Patriarchal.
4.   All leadership has a political and religious dimension.

FRIEND OF GOD: ABRAHAM

(2 Chr. 20:7; Is 41:8; Ja.2:23) Lessons from the life of Abraham:
Gen. 12 Going out in faith and obedience. (c.f. Heb.11:8) Importance of worship. (Gen 12:8)
Gen. 13 Generosity of spirit in relationships with Lot. (c.f. Gen. 14)
Gen. 15-18 God's Covenant with Abraham and its effect on their relationship. (Gen. 18:16-33)
Gen. 21 A promised fulfilled in the birth of Isaac.
Gen. 22 Obedience tested in the challenge to sacrifice Isaac.

LESSONS TO BE LEARNED FROM THE LIVES OF ISAAC, JACOB AND JOSEPH

Gen. 24-50 Polygamy; favouritism; man's choice; God's choice; leaders as learners.

CALLED OF GOD: MOSES

Ex. 1 God's preparation.
Often discerned when looking back from a later point in time.
Ex. 3-4 God's call.
Confirmation of call sometimes worked out in process of responding.
Ex. 5-13 God's confirmation.
Experience of leadership under God's breeds new expectations.
Ex. 14-17:7 Learning to lead.
The highs and the lows of working with people.
Ex. 17:8-19 Learning to lead.
Lessons to be learned when working with people.

Ex. 19-31 Reinforcing the relationship.
Relating to each other and to God.
Ex. 32-33 Dealing with problems.
People problems and those of the leadership team. (Num 11-16)

LESSONS TO BE LEARNED FROM THE LIVES OF JOSHUA, GIDEON AND SAMSON

Jos. 1-24; Ju. 1-21 The calling of God and the equipping of leaders.

A BIBLE STUDY OUTLINE ON THE LEADERSHIP OF NEHEMIAH

The book of Ezra describes the return of some of the Jewish exiles from Babylon and the restoration of life and worship in Jerusalem. This preserved the religious heart of Israel and their social identity as a nation.

Nehemiah is credited with the rebuilding of Jerusalem as the foundation for a renewed city/state. Nehemiah had risen to high rank in Persia as the 'Cup Bearer', to Artaxerxes 1, who lived about 500 years before Jesus Christ.

CHAPTER 1 NEHEMIAH'S CONCERN AND HIS RESPONSE

1:3 Survivors in Jerusalem in great difficulty with no walls to protect them from their enemies. True leaders have a concern for the conditions faced by their own people.
1:4 Weeping, mourning, fasting and praying consecrated sorrows by bringing them to God. 'Commit your way to the Lord; trust in him, and he will act.' Psalm 37.5 Handed over to God with willingness to respond to God's guidance. Nehemiah, the leader, first turns to God.
1:5 Acknowledges greatness of God in prayer. Rehearses faith in power of God before taking action.
1:6-7 Prayer, begins with confession. Personal & corporate as Nehemiah identifies with the people and begins to lay foundation for a right relationship with God and with his people.
1:8-9 Brings to mind God's promises as part of the process of faith building for himself (and others).
1:10-11 'Lord, these are your servants, your own people'. Affirms Covenant relationship and gives Nehemiah the confidence to make a brief, but specific prayer, 'Give success to thy servant today, and grant him mercy in the sight of this man.'
Note: Artaxerxes is only 'this man' in relation to God.

2:1-8 About four months of fasting, praying and no doubt thinking followed before opportunity presented itself before the Emperor, by which time Nehemiah was prepared with his response and able to articulate clearly what God was wanting of him. 'Fools rush in!

2:9-10 Opposition, yes, but stifled by careful preparation. Pray as though everything depends upon God, plan as though everything depends on man. Balance here between agonising & organising.

2:11-16 Nehemiah does his own research into the situation to assess what is required.

2:17-20 Nehemiah, establishes credentials as God's servant, enlists helpers and deals with opposition.

CHAPTER 3 NEHEMIAH ORGANISES THE WORK WITH TEAMS OF PEOPLE

CHAPTER 4 NEHEMIAH ENCOURAGES THE PEOPLE DIFFICULTIES/OPPOSITION ARISE

CHAPTER 5 NEHEMIAH RESPONDS TO THE PRACTICAL CONCERNS OF PEOPLE

CHAPTER 6 NEHEMIAH STAYS FOCUSSED AND IS DEAF TO SOME ADVISORS

CHAPTER 7 NEHEMIAH BUILDS COMMUNITY AS WELL AS COMPLETING CITY WALLS

CHAPTER 8-13 NEHEMIAH ESTABLISHES GOD'S WORD AT HEART OF COMMUNITY

OT history passes through the 'Kings' phase and closes with the 'Servant' image of Isaiah. Both Ezekiel and Jeremiah are concerned about religious and political leadership. Today, they are separated and those in political leadership rarely lead as under 'Divine Authority'. Discuss!

LECTURE 2: BIBLICAL LEADERSHIP: NEW TESTAMENT-GOSPELS/ACTS

SERVANT OF ALL: JESUS (JOHN 13.1-38)

Lessons to be learned from the life and example of Jesus:
Servant ministry and necessary humility demonstrated in John 13
Doulos = servant/slave under orders
Diakonos = servant/friend offering willing service
Lifetime of learning/teaching brings Jesus and his disciples to this moment in time.

TRACE THE LIFE OF JESUS IN THE GOSPELS TO DISCOVER INFLUENCES UPON HIS LIFE AND MINISTRY.

Born to be different: c.f. Birth stories of Matthew & Luke. Visit to Temple Lk. 2:41-51
Baptised and tempted as one of us: Mt. 3:13-17; & Matt & Lk 4
Humanity of Jesus-weariness & human emotions. Jn. 4:6; 11:35
Divinity of Jesus-sinlessness & representative role. Jn. 8:46; Mt 16:13f

Who is the greatest? 'Whoever wants to be first of all must place himself last of all and be the servant of all' **Mk 9:35**

Be like a child! 'The greatest in the Kingdom of heaven is the one who humbles himself and becomes like this child.' **Mt 18:4**

Practice what you preach! 'Whoever makes himself great will be humbled, and whoever humbles himself will be made great.' **Mt 23:12**

Don't ask of others what you are not prepared to do yourself. 'Foxes have holes and birds have their nests, but the Son of Man has nowhere to lie down and rest.' **Mt 8:20**

Work out for yourself (& with others) what the vision of Jesus means for your ministry/situation.

The Kingdom of God: The herald-John the Baptist. The sign of the Kingdom-Jesus

The Ministry of Jesus: **Lk 4:16-27** Jesus links his ministry with the message of Isaiah 61 and goes on to use two illustrations from the Old Testament to spell out the unexpected and radical nature of his ministry

Followers filled with the Spirit: **John 14-16** Jesus lays the foundations for a continuing relationship with his followers through the influence of the Holy Spirit. Dying He lives!

KEY LEADERS OF THE EARLY CHURCH

Leaders in the Acts of the Apostles, the second part of Luke's telling of the Gospel (hi)story are influenced by the life, teaching and example of Jesus.

Peter-Lessons from his life.

Peter is the one who preaches at Pentecost but what is known of him prior to Pentecost?

His Call-**Jn. 1:41; Mk 1:16** From being a fisherman.

His Status-First name mentioned in lists. Part of the inner circle of three. **Mk 5:37; 9:2**

His Faith-Affirmation at Caesarea Phillipi Mk.8.29 Confidence at Supper **Mk 14:29**

His Failures-Caesarea Phillipi-**Mk 8:33** Denial of Jesus **Mk14:66-72**

His Commission-The rock **Mt. 16:18ff**; The follower restored into leadership **Mk.16:7; Jn 21:15-19**

Early Church-Lessons learned.

Acts 1:8 'But when the Holy Spirit comes upon you, you will be filled with power, and you will be witnesses for me in Jerusalem, in all Judaea and Samaria and to the ends of the earth.' Acts 1:11 'Galileans, why are you standing there looking up at the sky?'

Acts 1:21 'So then someone must join us as a witness to the resurrection of the Lord Jesus.'

Acts 2:4 'They were all filled with the Holy Spirit'

Acts 2:44 'All the believers continued together and shared their belongings c.f. **v42-47; 4:32-37**

Acts 6:3 'So then, brothers, choose seven men among you who are known to be full of the Holy Spirit and wisdom, and we will put them in charge of this matter.'

7:54-8 'The witnesses left their cloaks in the care of a young man named Saul. They kept on stoning Stephen as he called out to the Lord, "Lord Jesus, receive my spirit!"'

Paul-Lessons from his life.

Saul the Jew becomes Paul, Apostle to the Gentiles, after the Damascus Road experience.

Phil 3:5 'I was circumcised when I was a week old. I am an Israelite by birth, of the tribe of Benjamin, a pure-blooded Hebrew. As far as keeping the Jewish law was concerned, I was a Pharisee, and I was so zealous that I persecuted the church.'

Acts 21:39 'I am a Jew, born in Tarsus (a Roman citizen-see 16:37) in Cilicia, but brought up here in Jerusalem as a student of Gamaliel.'

Acts 8:3 'But Saul tried to destroy the church; going from house to house, he dragged out the believers, both men and women and threw them into jail.'

Acts 9:3 'As Saul was coming near to the city of Damascus, suddenly a light from the sky flashed around him. He fell to the ground and heard a voice saying to him, "Saul, Saul! Why do you persecute me?'

Acts 9:26 'Saul went to Jerusalem and tried to join the disciples. But they would not believe that he was a disciple and they were all afraid of him. Then Barnabas came to his help...'

Peter and Paul-Discuss their relationship with Jesus and responses to each other as very different leaders of the early church.

(Especially note the role played by Barnabas and others.)

Three sections of the Epistles are turned to when any discussion of the character of those called by the church into leadership takes place. They have been summarised as follows:

1 Timothy 3:1-7
Above reproach
1) Husband of one wife (includes wife of one husband or single people)
2) Temperate
3) Self-controlled
4) Respectable
5) Hospitable
6) Able to teach
7) Not given to much wine
8) Not violent but gentle
9) Not quarrelsome
10)   Not a lover of money
11)   Manages family well (obedient, respectful children)
12)   Not a recent convert
13)   Good reputation with outsiders

Titus 1:5-9 (additional qualities)
1) Children behave as members of a Christian household
2) Not overbearing
3) Not quick-tempered
4) One who loves what is good
5) Upright
6) Holy
7) Disciplined
8) Holds firmly to God's word
9) Encourages others by sound doctrine
10)   Refutes those who oppose it

1 Peter 5:1-4 (adds some further comments the about motivation of those offering)
1) Not because you must, but because you are willing
2) Eager to serve
3) Not lording it over those entrusted to you, but being examples

Any reflection on the principles of Biblical Leadership found in the first three lectures would suggest that as church leaders/ministers/you are:

Committed to God with:
1. An awareness of God at work in your life
2. A mature faith in God as revealed in Jesus Christ and experienced through the Spirit
3. An understanding of God's will and purposes
4. A growing maturity as God's grace nurtures the fruit of the Spirit in your life
5. A personal discipline that is the foundation of discipleship
6. A listening ear that allows you to learn from God and from other people
7. An experience of a relationship with a living God demonstrating the gifts of the Spirit

Committed to the church with:
1. A sense of the call of God upon your life
2. An awareness of God's love for you
3. A willingness to work as a servant of God in the life of the church
4. An integrity that is demonstrated in all your relationships with other people
5. A love for God's people working in and for the church
6. An ability to say 'no' as well as a willingness to say 'yes'
7. A combination of gifts and graces in your living that sets you apart

Committed to the 'Missio Dei' the mission of God for the whole world with:
1. An understanding of what your ministry is meant to be
2. A willingness to fight against temptation in all its (dis)guises
3. A determination to do what God wants you to do outside the church as well as within it
4. An ability to recruit and build up others in a team working for God
5. A heart big enough to cope with hurt/betrayal and offer forgiveness
6. A mind that is alive to every opportunity for reaching out into God's world
7. A strength that perseveres through success and seeming failure because you trust in God

In examining Biblical Principles in this way and combining the attributes required of a Christian leader, we may perpetuate the myth of the super-powered minister. A quiet meditation on the faults and failings of biblical leaders would suggest that all (excepting Jesus) were fallible human beings.

Nehemiah's discipline, 'I reprimanded the men, called down curses upon them, beat them, and pulled out their hair' Neh. 13.25 would not find favour today!
Peter and Paul may be saints of the church, but along with other 'saints' they were not without fault. The Apostle Paul gives ministers/leaders hope by insisting:

'We say this because we have confidence in God through Christ. There is nothing in us that allows us to claim that we are capable of doing this work. The capacity we have comes from God; it is he who has made us capable of serving the new covenant, which consists not of the written law but of the Spirit. The written law brings death, but the Spirit gives life'. ***2 Cor. 2.4-6***

LECTURE 4: CALLED TO BE MINISTERS

A minister in non-technical terms is quite simply: 'A person who is called to exemplify the ministry of Jesus Christ.' This definition makes Jesus our reference point at all times, but it does not answer all the questions for us. Those called to ministry, lay or ordained, like all the people of God are on a spiritual journey. Ordination, as with baptism and full membership/confirmation in the church is a stage on the journey. In the ordination ritual of the Early Church and in the Methodist the Church today there is a point in the ordination service when people shout, 'They are worthy' as they acknowledge that the people concerned are fit to be ordained. That is not a fact but an act of faith on the part of God's people!

Paul Beasley-Murray quotes Evelyn Underhill from an earlier generation saying:

The very first requisite for a minister of religion is that his own inner life should be maintained in a healthy state. The man whose life is coloured by prayer, whose loving communion with God comes first, will always win souls; because he shows them in his own life and person the attractiveness of reality, the demand, the transforming power of the spiritual life ... The most persuasive preacher, the most devoted and untiring social worker, the most up-to-date theologian-unless loving devotion to God exceeds and enfolds these activities-will not win souls.

And James Taylor insisting:

No higher reputation should, or can, he desired by a Christian minister than that possessed by the prophet Elisha in the mind of the Shunamite woman. 'I perceive', she said, 'that this is a holy man of God who is continually passing our way' (2 Kings 4.9). No matter what other gifts a church fellowship may admire in their minister this is, in the final reckoning, what they most desire him to be. All other virtues are virtually irrelevant and most other faults are forgivable if, to them and in their midst, he is a 'man of God'.

Writers on ministry draw attention to several aspects of Jesus' own life and ministry.

Jesus was controlled by a relationship that trusted in God's purposes:

'Do not worry about tomorrow… **Mt 6:24-34**

'Jesus was in the back of the boat sleeping with his head on a pillow' **Mk 5:35-41**

'Let us go off by ourselves to some place where we will be alone and can rest for a while' **Mk 6:30-32**

Also, Jesus worked long hours in fulfilling God's purposes:

Mk. 1:21-39 Highlights a long day of ministry followed by early morning personal prayer.

Mt. 4:1-11 In the temptations and elsewhere we find Jesus tired and hungry. Jn. 4.4-8

Mark's Gospel suggests that Jesus (and his followers) walked long distances whilst engaging in a demanding ministry of preaching, teaching and healing.

Jesus was not driven by his mission, but worked out his ministry in tune with God's will:

Jesus prayed alone and escaped from the crowds when he needed to. **Jn. 6:24**

Jesus' spiritual life based on Judaism, with synagogue and Sabbath, but freed up. **Mk 2:27**

Jesus protected time for training his closest followers: the three Mk. **5:37**; the twelve **Mk 9:30-1**.

Jesus understood what his ministry was about at each stage. **Mk 1:38; Mk 8:31-8; Lk. 9:51.**

Jesus lived out his understanding (Lk. 4:14-27) of his calling to ministry by:

Being what he was meant to be-In a right relationship with God and with people.

Teaching what he was meant to teach-We cannot teach it if we do not know and understand it.

Showing a way of living that contrasted with what could be seen in the lives of some religious and political leaders of the time.

Throughout this Course on Leadership, we will be looking at what good leaders 'do', but as with Jesus, much of what leaders are able to accomplish depends upon what kind of people they are. The humility and compassion of Jesus are foundational to the practice of Christian Leadership. What Jesus as a leader is able to accomplish is a direct consequence of the kind of person he is.

HUMILITY

Phil 2:1-18 esp. v8 'He was humble and walked the path of obedience all the way to death-'

Jesus was secure in his knowledge of himself, who he was and to whom he was obedient.

In inviting the followers of Jesus, 'to be humble towards one another, always considering others better than yourselves.' v4 Paul is encouraging us to have a positive attitude towards others, to value their discipleship and to find ways of supporting and affirming them. Humility uses Jesus as its standard; pride tends to compare others in their weakest areas with us in our strengths. **'The attitude you should have is the one that Christ Jesus had:' v5**

COMPASSION

Mt 9:35-8 esp. v36 'As he saw the crowds, his heart was filled with pity for them, because they were worried and helpless, like sheep without a shepherd.' Cf. **Mt 14:14; 15:32; 20:34**

Compassion breeds in a heart full of God's love and determines the character of your life, your teaching, your preaching, your worship and your leadership.

Probably the best known parables of all, the Good Samaritan and the Prodigal Son find their focus in the one whose 'heart was filled with pity' **Lk 10:33 and Lk 15:20.**

Much of the thinking in the first part of this lecture is based on writings by John Adair who is an Anglican layman and was Britain's first Professor of Leadership Studies.

KNOWLEDGE/EXPERTISE ATTRACTS FOLLOWERS.

Leadership flows towards the person who knows what to do in a given situation. (Situational)

People are willing to follow those who seem to know what they are doing.

Leaders earn respect if not popularity by giving direction, setting an example and sharing hardship.

Leadership includes management, but transcends it by encouraging and inspiring followers.

Leadership skills can be learned.

Leaders recognise three distinct, but overlapping or interacting areas of need.

A good leader works with followers to:

1. Achieve a common task-failure in the task affects the other areas.

2. Maintain the team-breakdown in the team affect the other areas.

3. Meet the needs of individuals-disappointment for the individual affects the other areas.

Action Centred Leadership in the Industrial Society of Great Britain suggests that we can Achieve a Task, Build a Team and Develop Individuals by following their Ten Commandments:

1. Set the task of the team; put it across with enthusiasm and remind people of it often.

2. Make leaders accountable for 4-15 people; practise and instruct them in the three circles.

3. Plan the work, check its progress, design jobs or arrange work to encourage the commitment of individuals and the team.

4. Set individuals targets after consulting; discuss progress with each person regularly but at least once a year.

5. Delegate decisions to individuals. If not consult, those affected before you decide.

6. Communicate importance of everyone's job; explain decisions to help people apply them; brief team together monthly on Progress, Policy, People and Points for action.

7. Train and develop people especially those under 25; gain support for the rules and procedures, set an example and 'have a go' at those who break them.

8. Where unions are recognised, encourage joining, attendance at meetings, standing for office and speaking up for what each person believes is in the interest of the organisation and all who work in it.

9. Serve people in the team and care for their wellbeing; improve working conditions and safety; work alongside people deal with grievances promptly and attend social functions.

10. Monitor action; learn from successes and mistakes; regularly walk round each person's place of work, observe, listen praise.

DISCUSS THE IMPACT OF SUCH SUGGESTIONS ON:
The leadership of a church in Nigeria
The leadership of a village in Nigeria
The leadership of all levels of government in Nigeria.

WHEN WE HAVE SET OUT SOME OF THE:

1. **Task Functions as**-Defining the task; Setting objectives; Making a plan; Allocating work and resources; Controlling quality and tempo of work; Checking performance against the plan; Adjusting the plan.

2. **Team Functions as**-Setting standards; Maintaining discipline; Building team spirit; Encouraging; Motivating; Giving a sense of purpose; Appointing sub-leaders; Ensuring communication within the group; training the group.

3. **Individual Functions as**-Attending to personal problems; Encouraging individuals; Giving status; Recognising and using individual abilities; Training the individual.

We have only begun to itemise what is a dynamic and interactive process between leaders and followers with differing characteristics and personalities.

Writers on leadership produce many different lists of qualities that are required in a good leader, but all writers agree that such lists are given life as the 'word becomes flesh' in the performance of the individuals.

Integrity-honesty/trustworthiness are as important in leaders as they are to personal relationships

Vulnerability-trusting others makes leaders vulnerable, but the invulnerable leader is on her own

Discernment-sensitivity that sees through the public face and hears the underlying murmur

Awareness of the human spirit-people positive relational leadership precedes professional skills

Courage in relationships-compassionate leaders cannot avoid making tough decisions

Sense of humour-ability to laugh at oneself and with other people defrosts serious situations

Intellectual energy and curiosity-learning and discovery keeps us humble in our relationships

Respect for the future, regard for the present, understanding of the past-the life cycle of past present and future keeps us journeying towards news goals.

Predictability-reliability in the leader helps the team with a common ethos pursue goals/vision

Breadth-allows contributions from unlikely (maverick) sources

Comfort with Ambiguity-acceptance rather than agreement allows for some chaos during growth

Presence-being where the people are builds relationship and encourages free flow of information

'Called to be leaders' implies that others are called to be followers. In any church, there are many capable people who quite rightly object to the notion of the 'Omni competent' minister leading and the people of God following. Thinking **'Task, Team and Individual'** should prompt us to see individuals as colleagues, companions, partners, working together as a team. After all it was Jesus who said to the team he had put together, 'My commandment is this; love one another, just as I love you. The greatest love a person can have for his friends is to give his life for them. You are my friends if you do what I command you. **I do not call you servants any longer, because a servant does not know what his master is doing. Instead I call you friends....'** Jn. 15:12-15

Leaders who love their people and are acknowledged as friends will find many who are willing to journey with them on a road that is not always as clear to others as it is to them. Vision-building comes next!

A BIBLICAL UNDERSTANDING OF VISION

(Gen 15:1) 'After this, Abram had a vision and heard the Lord say to him….' It all sounded impossible, but **(Gen 15:6)** 'Abram, put his trust in the Lord, and….'

In the Old Testament, the visions described are given to men, like Abram, Jacob, and the boy Samuel. In the New Testament we can think of Zechariah in the temple, Paul and Ananias, Peter at Joppa and Paul at Troas. The New Testament suggests also that visions can be shared, as with the two women at the tomb (Lk) and the disciples at the Transfiguration (Mt)

Visions in the Bible often lead into conversations where the recipient questions God or an angel about what is being proposed.

Peter Brierley in 'Vision Building' argues that visions are stronger and more focussed than dreams; very often detailed; associated with physical elements like Isaiah's 'burning coal cleansing his lips'; and very clearly the word of the Lord. **Proverbs 29:18 (AV) 'Where there is no vision, the people perish.' (NIV) 'Where there is no revelation, the people cast off restraint.'**

One, particularly helpful, definition of vision which I want us to think about suggests: **'Vision is the self-revelation of God. It is God's activity of revealing his nature and purposes to men and women who are open to hear from him.'**

VISION AND CLIFF COLLEGE

Cliff College in England is the product of a God given vision. Cliff House from 1835 belonged to James Hilton Hulme, a Congregational layman from Manchester. It was destined to fulfil his late-life vision, as his hoped for missionary training college became a reality in 1875, as his friend, Henry Grattan Guinness established a centre for training lay missionaries in practical skills as well as biblical studies. Here the Cliff story and Sierra Leone/Nigeria is linked up through one of the great Methodist preachers of the 19th Century.

Thomas Champness came as a missionary to Freetown in 1857 and later in 1860 to Abeokuta, Nigeria (where his first wife nee Mary Archer died on 23/09/1862)). On his return he was given responsibility for newspaper entitled Joyful News that soon became 'The Joyful

News Training Home and Mission' in Rochdale which later moved to the present Cliff College site. The Guinness and Champness stories coincide in 1903 when Methodism took over and Cliff College was born.

VISION AND SIERRA LEONE

I learned a great deal about vision during my time in Sierra Leone from 1969 to 1979. Senior Medical Staff at the Nixon (Methodist) Memorial Hospital opposed the visionary thinking of Dr Mary Groves who established the Sandaru Clinic in a remote part of SL on the grounds that it could not be serviced from Segbwema. A succession of minister's wives, who were nurses and doctors, kept the clinic going for over thirty years until in 1979 the clinic was left in the safe hands of a well-trained Sierra Leonean nurse.

I was among those who opposed the visionary thinking of a missionary minister with a farming background, Dwin Capstick who neglected the so called 'normal work' of a minister to establish the pioneering Tikonko Agricultural Extension Centre. The work of the Centre continues albeit in a limited way today.

It wasn't missionaries who founded the Methodist Church at Tongofield, but semi-literate Christian visionaries who established a church on the veranda of a house. The church eventually built to accommodate over two hundred people was unacceptable for many years to the main denominations because its three of its four founders were polygamists. If you make a list of church initiatives in villages with schools and clinics and towns with churches and Community Centres, you will find that one person's vision began the project.

I learned an important lesson about God's vision in SL which has been borne out in my experience of ministry since that time. The visionary, (often seen as a maverick), in almost every sphere of work including the church is often opposed.

The scriptures and the history of the church bear witness to the difficulties that many face when they challenge others to believe that God is doing a new thing.

601

My vision in May 2001 on the return journey from Freetown to London prompted me to jot down on a sick bag (which I still have-empty of course!) ideas as to how we might do something different in delivering a refresher re-training course for ministers of all denominations in post-conflict Sierra Leone.

Your attendance on this course, following on from the success of the SL programme has helped to fulfil the vision (almost word for word), which has become the Cliff College International Training Centre. People tell me that the way in which the project has come together and the Courses are being delivered in such a short space of time is nothing short of miraculous. I think to myself, **'Vision is the self-revelation of God. It is God's activity of revealing his nature and purposes to men and women who are open to hear from him.'**

The key that unlocks the door to the vision is being *'Open to hear from him'.* For academic thinking about vision read the books. To experience vision, think big thoughts about God, yourself and your people and take the risks (and sometimes the hurt) associated with being a visionary leader. Without some God-given vision of where you are going, you will become a manager rather than a leader.

LECTURE 7: CALLED TO BE THEOLOGIANS

VISION GIVES US DIRECTION; THEOLOGICAL REFLECTION MAKES SURE THAT WE DO NOT LOSE OUR WAY.

Traditionally theology is defined as teaching about God, summed up by Thomas Aquinas: *'Theology is taught by God, teaches of God, and leads to God.'* Historically, it is qualified by a word such as 'Biblical', 'Evangelical', or 'Liberation' which suggests its orientation. The contemporary way of 'Doing Theology', described as 'Theological Reflection', 'begins with the lived **experience** of those doing the reflection; it correlates this reflection with the sources of the **Christian tradition**; and it draws out **practical implications for Christian living**.' (Kinast)

Each of the terms highlighted requires further discussion of what is understood by their use. Robert Kinast in 'Theological Reflection' argues that there are 'styles' of 'Doing Theology'.

The style a person adopts indicates what that person values and prefers, how the person responds to other people and situations, what that person's feelings and tendencies are and ultimately who the person is. Regarding theology, a confessional or evangelical style proclaims theological truth for others to accept, whereas an apologetic style argues for the cogency of theological beliefs so that others may be convinced. A devotional style accents the affective dimension of theology, whilst a scholastic style emphasis the cognitive. A dogmatic style suggests authoritative definition, whereas a liberal style suggests a toleration of all viewpoints, and an ecumenical style implies openness to diverse opinions with a view towards consensus.

Similarly a theological reflection style is determined by the type of experience practitioners of that style focus on, how they correlate it with the faith tradition and what sort of praxis they envision emerging from their reflection.

In Kinast's book, he looks at five 'styles': Ministerial; Spiritual Wisdom; Feminist; Inculturation; and Practical.

The 'Ministerial Style' is based on the teaching of James & Evelyn Whitehead, who understand theological reflection to be, 'the process of bringing to bear in the practical decisions of ministry the resources of the Christian faith.' They understand the complex nature of human beings and society and look for a method of doing theology that will be **'portable so that Christians can carry it into their daily lives, performable so they can translate their reflections into action and communal so they can face today's challenges together.'**

The Whiteheads' model begins with the **faith tradition**, with scripture central, but embracing the whole Christian tradition as being the ways in which people have experienced God in history. It moves away from individualism/clericalism by emphasising **both personal and communal experience** and pays serious attention to the impact of contemporary culture on religious beliefs. Theological reflectors under the ministerial model are not only ministers, but lay people, willing to take seriously the study of theology leading to confirmation or change in how we practice our faith today. What practical issues might be discussed and acted upon in your church situation?

Read the two International Study Guides by John Parratt, 'A Guide to Doing Theology' and 'A Reader in African Christian Theology'. Study the Notes and Introductions to both books. Here (as earlier) we focus on 'The Theological Method' and note the different 'styles' used.

Canon Harry Sawyerr from Sierra Leone insisted that 'Doing Theology' should begin with an understanding of traditional Christian theology. Connections can then be made between Christianity and traditional African religious thought. Sawyerr is wary of theologies that do not take account of important doctrines like Christology and Atonement. For Sawyerr it is the Christian faith handed down that controls the 'indigenisation' or 'Africanisation' of the church. So he uses a quotation from Tom Beetham to ask,

'Have the roots of the Christian Community gone sufficiently deep in African society, with its traditional belief in the Supreme God and the spirit world, it ritual for purification, and consequent protection of individuals from harm within the family or clan.'

Sawyerr critiques the 'Independent Churches' characterised in Turner's study as 'A Place To Feel At Home' with concerns drawn from Turner's study of the Aladura Church which admits that it is 'devoid of theological or historical understanding'. Sawyerr's 'style' makes him defensive in responding to theologies that begin with Africa but concludes,

'In spite of the difficulties inherent in the term African, there is a strong case for a Theologica Africana which will seek to interpret Christ to the African in such a way that he feels at home in the new faith...To the present writer, the answer lies in the rigorous pursuit of Systematic Theology based on a philosophical appraisal of the thought forms of the African peoples.' p22

Both John Pobee from Ghana looking at the 'Sources of African Theology' and Bishop Tshibangu from Zaire adopt the 'style' of Sawyerr and agree on fundamentals with him.

On the other hand, Bishop Desmond Tutu recognises the distinct contribution that 'Black Theology' makes in the South African situation with its concerns about liberation, reconciliation and true humanity. Tutu acknowledges the dogmatic condemnation of 'Black Theology' by John Mbiti, but Tutu's 'style' allows him to be much more sensitive to the cultural context as challenging traditional Christian theology and he concludes,

> *'I myself believe I am an exponent of Black Theology, coming as I do from South Africa. I also believe I am an exponent of African Theology, coming as I do from Africa. I contend that Black Theology is like the inner and smaller circle in a series of concentric circles.....' p43*

Dr Isabel Apawo Phiri from Malawi has her own ''feminist style' in, 'Doing Theology as African Women' she highlights the problems associated with a Bible 'written by inspired men within a patriarchal culture.' p54; and theological concerns dominated by males, because:

> *'First, there have been more African male than female scholars and theologians. Second, scholars have usually been concerned with issues in which men play a more active part than women.' p45*

> So, *'the sources for many African women theologians are whatever uphold women's and men's humanity in the Bible, in African traditional religion, and in African culture.' p49*

Theology here then, begins with the woman's perspective, is justifiably suspicious of the male influence, and begins to examine (re-examine) the Bible, traditional theology, and traditional culture with its rituals from a female point of view.

LECTURE 8: CALLED TO BE PASTORS

The Apostle Peter (1 Pet.5:1-4) encourages pastors: **'I, who am an elder myself, appeal to the church elders among you...to be shepherds of the flock that God gave you and to take care of it willingly, as God wants you to, and not unwillingly. Do your work not for pay, but from a real desire to serve...And when the Chief Shepherd appears, you will receive the glorious crown which will never lose its brightness.'**
Pastors need to be reminded that, 'The Lord is my shepherd' applies as much to them as to their people.

Paul Beasley-Murray in, 'A Call to Excellence' assesses the missionary Paul's Pastoral Leadership Model which I have reproduced in full with my own highlighting:

*'Pastoral care has many aspects. This comes out very clearly in the way in which Paul approached the pastoral task. Interestingly, in his letters Paul never described himself as a 'pastor' (but see Eph. 4:11; also Acts 20:28). Instead, **he used the imagery of the parent-child relationship.** Tender and loving as a mother (1 Thess. 2:7-8), he was anxious to see his children grow in the faith (Gal. 4:19-20). As a father, Paul believed that both encouragement (1 Thess. 2:11-12) and correction (1 Cor. 4:14-21) were necessary for healthy development within the Christian family. For Paul **discipline was not reserved as a final resort** for gross moral error, but rather was perceived to be an essential part of Christian nurture, by which individuals and churches were built up in the faith (see Col.1:28).*

*Significantly, Paul was concerned **not just for the corporate health of the churches in his care, but also for the well-being of individuals.** People counted for Paul: hence in Romans 16 Paul takes the trouble of greeting over 27 people by name. The personal character of Paul's pastoral work comes to the fore in 1 Thessalonians 2:11 and Colossians 1:28. All this is in line with Luke's account of Paul's speech to the Ephesian elders, which suggests that his normal practice was to combine preaching to the church at large together with the visiting of individual church members (Acts 20:20).*

*Although Paul was clearly a very dominant figure, **he never operated as a solo pastor.** Rather, he constantly surrounded himself with colleagues who could share in the pastoral task. It is reckoned that, if one adds all the names found in Acts and in Paul's letters, then at various times some 100 people were associated with the Apostle. What is more, Paul also **encouraged his converts in general to be involved in pastoral care.** Likening the church to a body, he spoke of the members having 'the same care for one another' (1 Cor. 12:25). Paul urged the Galatians to 'Bear each other's burdens', which in turn involved caring for those straying from the faith, restoring the backsliders (Gal. 6:1-2). Within the context of death and bereavement the Thessalonians were told to, encourage one another and build up each other' (1 Thess 5:11). Indeed, Paul expected the Thessalonians to share in every aspect of pastoral care: 'admonish the idlers, encourage the fainthearted, help the weak' (1 Thess. 5:14). Similarly, the Colossians were to 'teach and admonish one another in all wisdom' (Col. 3:16).*

Pastoral care was not exclusive to a particular cadre in the church: all were involved in the work of ministry' (see Eph. 4:12, 15-16).'

People are God's concern and Pastoral Leaders must care about people.

Bible Study on Abram's role as a Pastoral Leader (Gen 12.1-13.18)

12:1 God calls and appoints leaders who are pastors taking their people with them. The call to both leader and people is to 'go out' and do what God wants of you

12:2 We are called to be obedient and to trust the promise of God for the outcome

12:3 We are given authority to 'bless and curse' (c.f. Jn 20.23) Huge responsibility

12:4-5 Our 'flock' are people that God wants us to lead and care for on God's journey

12:6-7 They are part of a larger flock to be gathered in (c.f. Jn 10.7-18 esp. v16)

12:8-10 We move forward in general direction (vision) without knowing final destination

12:10 Neither the good times or not so good times are entirely the pastor's responsibility

12:11-13 A Pastor will have difficult decisions to make and will not always get it right

12:14-20 Crossing borders risky, but may be the only way to spiritual/numerical growth

13:1-4 We may need to revisit places we have already been to re-establish our bearings

13:5-7 Growth without delegation leads to conflict unless appropriate structures in place

13:8-13 Good humour, flexibility and trust in God resolves problem in Abram's favour

13:14-18 Faithfulness to God's purposes leads to a fruitful outcome

The role of a Pastoral Leader though having similar characteristics is in some ways different from the role of a Pastor.

Though called to be a pastor in relating to people, the leader will be conscious of her responsibility in modelling the pattern of Jesus by training his closest followers in the vision and goals of ministry.

Traditional ways of doing this tend to follow a training pattern:
1. I model – I do it.
2. I mentor – I do it and you watch me.
3. I monitor – You do it and I watch you.
4. I motivate – You do it.
5. We multiply- You do it and train someone else.
   N.B. (Each one teach one in literacy projects!)

Questions have been raised as to whether this 'learned behaviour' is as helpful as it might be when rapid change means that most models of training date so quickly. Perhaps, Interactive teaching/learning based on traditional models will produce 'transformed Christians' finding fresh ways of being the leaders/pastors that God wants us to be.

LECTURE 9: CALLED TO BE (AD)--MINISTRATORS

Who am I/are you? Personal background: Home; School; Work; Theological College; Ministry.

A. PREPARE YOURSELF - TAKE TIME TO MAKE TIME

YOUR WORKSHOP

Office/Study-Discuss! You are the most important 'Thing' in your study. Everything in it should relate to what is most helpful for you to be able to work efficiently. Basic principle-Organise for yourself.-anything that you use regularly, including your Bible, you should be able to reach what is an important tool by stretching out your arm.

YOUR WORKING ENVIRONMENT

Health & Safety at Work!   Seating-comfort and control.
Lighting-natural over left shoulder.   Desk lamp alone-not good!
Heating-performance affected by temperature, draughts and sunlight.
Disturbance-of noise, neighbours, necessary and unnecessary callers.
Keep your feet on the ground with breaks, relaxation to avoid stress.
Working from home-family come first, at least sometimes!

YOUR TOOLS OF THE TRADE

Use them, don't lose them!

BOOKS-Library and reference system-Mark inside and out-
? Sacrilege!! tear pages out for pulpit use, esp. prayers.
PAPER-Handle each piece of paper once. Simplify paperwork. 'If in doubt, throw it out'.
FILES-File things to find them-Procrastination/waste bin best file of all!
LETTERS/TELEPHONE CALLS-Answer question being asked and keep brief as possible. Standing up keeps calls brief and stretches body
COMPUTERS-Use other people as much as possible even if computer literate and maintain personal contact by face-to-face meetings.
IDEAS-Plagiarism on Academic Course not acceptable but can be time-saving common sense in Theology/Ministry. Don't reinvent the wheel!
SERVICES-Hymns/Prayers/Orders linked with Lectionary or themes-Prepare and preserve.
SERMONS-Never, 'all your own work'. Use resources available and keep-ABANDON before perfection is reached

TAKE TIME TO MAKE TIME FOR GOD

Office/study same room, change mode and/or seating position.
Few people at work have our opportunities to switch off and switch on to God!

Discipline, variety and discipline to maintain devotional ministry for self and to others.

B. AP(PRAISE) YOURSELF–(AD)MINISTRATION AS MINISTRY

YOU AND YOUR TIME

Personality traits and training: Early Bird or Night Owl.

Job description: Be specific-own it-have others own it. 50 words!

Mission statement: Shared process-group owned-specific annual targets.

Determine priorities: What will really make a difference. How much evangelism and people training?
How do you spend your time at present?

Make sure you know where your time goes. Don't depend on memory!

Time log for one week to check on your priorities: C:Committees, T:Telephone, P:Pastoral, S:Sermon, W:Worship etc. Does your time allocation reflect your own priorities and/or God's?
Plan your use of time to link with your priorities

Annual Calendar-Preparing first time is the most difficult-drive or be driven-review and amend, but plan for progression.

Quarterly Plan-Look on a big map. Study leave, Retreats, Holidays.

Week Planner-Fixed points-Can others share in this?

Day Planner-Must it be done. By me? Now? How much time do I have? 'Make your day with your diary.' Diary for anniversaries including family/personal time! God's diary for your leadership where you are!

TIME-WASTERS

You: (Look in the mirror!) A-ction I-nformation R-eading S-crap: your need/theirs.
Other people: G-reet R-eceive A-ccompany C-onfer E-mbrace S-ee off
Bad Management: Unclear objectives. If you drawing a circle round your shot you will have hit the target? Target progress you plan to make.
Procrastination is the thief of time. Do it now-especially unpleasant.
Abdication v delegation. Dump what should not be delegated.
Administration v orchestration. Conductor does not make music!
Committees that never commit "More said than done" v intentional and time conscious working parties taking action.
Inability to say no is often linked with desire to be liked.

TIME SAVERS-TEN COMMANDMENTS

1. Daily discipline of time management. Start today not tomorrow!
2. Be clear about what you are trying to achieve. My task is to..
3. Do only what you alone can or should do. Guilt is energy leak!
4. Focus on achievements. "It works for me."
5. Review regularly. Is this/was that the best way? Ignatian Examen!
6. Make progress with one time-saver at a time. Habitual behaviour!
7. Share your priorities to enlist support. You need help of others!
8. Trust others and let them grow. Support them and let them show!
9. Stop and note-task finished. Tick through the item listed.
10. Follow up. Appraisal with approval for self and other people.

BEWARE BURNOUT-TEN CAUSES OF STRESS FOR CHURCH WORKERS.

1. Job never finished.	Abandon it!
2. Not easy to see results except building!	Practical leisure!
3. Work repetitive and cyclical.	Challenge yourself-end goal!
4. High expectations-your own and others.	Let go let God!
5. No escaping your problem people.	Make your own mates!
6. Drain of giving pastoral transfusions.	Protect renewable source!
7. Stop stroking at Your peril.	Have you died to self?
8. The 'Man (woman) in the Mask'.	To your own self be true!
9. Fighting against failure.	God/Elijah after Carmel!
10. Preoccupation with time management.	Who you are/what you do!

Priorities, Planning and Paperwork by Peter Brierley Marc/Monarch isbn 1-85424-119-2

LECTURE 10: CALLED TO BE—WHAT?

ESTABLISHING PRIORITIES FOR YOURSELF AND YOUR MINISTRY

1.Setting priorities means deciding which activities, opportunities, etc. are of primary importance.

2.Ask yourself: What needs to be done first, next, at once, later, by someone else, not at all?

3.Whatever helps us to best to fulfil the vision/reach our goals should be considered a priority.

4.Once a priority has been set, we should try and keep it until priorities are reviewed periodically.

5.We need to learn to say 'no' to what is not in line with the priorities we have decided upon.

6.We ought to invest our time (and that of the church) in proportion to the order of our priorities.

7.Those who lead others must be especially careful in selecting priorities that impact on others.

N.B.   The good is the greatest enemy of the best!

The urgent is the greatest enemy of the important!

Priorities for Christians to:

1. Love God (Mt 22:37-38)
2. Glorify God (Eph 1:12-14, 1 Co 10:31)
3, Seek God's kingdom and His righteousness (Mt 6:33)
4. Feed on God's Word (see Mt 4:4)
5. Pray (1 Ti 2:1, Eph 6:18)
6. Be filled with the Holy Spirit (Eph 5:18)
7. Pursue holiness (Heb 12:14)
8. Grow into Christ-likeness (Ro 8:29)
9. Lead a godly family life (see Eph 5:21-6:4)
10. Share the Gospel with all the world (Mk 13:10,16:15)
11. Make disciples (Mt 28:19)
12. Rest (see Ex 20:8-11, Mk 6:31)

Priorities for Christian Leaders:
Christian leaders should model their own priorities:

Joshua:	relative to serving God	(Jos 24:14-15)
David:	relative to praising God	(2 Sam 23:1-4)
Ezra:	relative to God's Word	(Ez 7:10)
Jesus:	relative to prayer	(Mk 1:35, Lk 5:15-16)
	relative to God's will for His life	(Lk 22:42)
Paul:	relative to his preaching technique	(1 Co 2:1-5)
	relative to his spiritual growth	(Ph 3:7-14)

Whatever priorities we set for ourselves and our ministry the scriptures remind us that even Peter (Acts 10:1-11:18) and Paul (Acts 16:6-10) had to be open to adjust their priorities to God's priorities.

Discuss with your group what our priorities should be in ministry: number what follows in order 1-14.

Use this set of priorities (produced by the Bible Society some years ago) adapted for your own situation and cut up into single cards as an exercise for sharing with leaders who share work with you in the life of the church. It helps leaders when you are clear as to your own priorities and when through this exercise they see what church work is their responsibility if priorities are to become realities in your church.

VISITING Calling on members of the congregation in their homes. Visiting others in village/neighbourhood. Shop, workplace or prison visits.	**COMMUNITY LEADERSHIP** Involvement in secular community organizations and politics so that the church is represented and shows its concern by making a positive contribution.
TEACHING Expounding the Scriptures and relating them to daily living. Ministers are expected to give time to prayer and preparation for Worship, Sunday sermons, developing teaching programmes for groups within the church and speaking at other meetings.	**CONGREGATION LEADERSHIP** Serving as the available leader in the congregation: the person to whom members turn for advice and guidance on all aspects of the life and work of the congregation.
COUNSELLING Counselling individuals on personal and spiritual problems. Couples planning to be married, those who are in hospital. Other people on personal and vocational problems. Bereaved and their families.	**PERSONAL DEVELOPMENT AND IN-SERVICE TRAINING** Developing devotional life, pastoral teaching, and management skills. Reading, studying and keeping up-to-date in biblical, theological and other studies.
ADMINISTRATION Serving as 'managing director' of the congregation, working with planning and finance committees. Ensuring that plans are implemented.	**DENOMINATIONAL, INTER-DENOMINATIONAL OR RELIGIOUS COUNCIL RESPONSIBILITIES** Carrying fair share of denominational responsibilities, participating in inter-denominational groups (CCSL) and other co-operative bodies.
EVANGELISM Calling on the uncommitted people in the community and sharing the Good News. Preaching, leading evangelistic missions to people outside the church.	**LEADING WORSHIP** Planning and conducting public worship, and working with worship leaders, musicians and others who help to lead corporate worship.
TEAM LEADERSHIP Serving with the lay leadership team – each with their own unique gifts and special responsibilities. Learning together about leadership.	**ENABLING** Helping others identify their own special gifts, call to service and ministry, and enabling them to respond to that call.
TRAINING Planning/executing training programmes for leaders who will teach groups, perform pastoral functions, & engage in evangelism. Prepare people for baptism, membership, preaching and evangelism	**DENOMINATIONAL, INTER-DENOMINATIONAL OR RELIGIOUS COUNCIL RESPONSIBILITIES** Carrying fair share of denominational responsibilities, participating in inter-denominational groups (CCSL) and other co-operative bodies.

We beg you, our brothers (and sisters), to pay proper respect to those who work among you, who guide and instruct you in the Christian life. Treat them with the greatest respect and love because of the work they do. Be at peace among yourselves. We urge you our brothers, to warn the idle, encourage the timid, help the weak, be patient with everyone. See that no one pays back wrong for wrong, but at all times make it your aim to do good to one another and all people.

Be joyful always, pray at all times, be thankful in all circumstances. This is what God wants from you in your life in union with Christ Jesus. Do not restrain the Holy Spirit; do not despise inspired messages. Put all things to the test: keep what is good and avoid every kind of evil. May the God who gives us peace make you holy in every way and keep your whole being-spirit, soul and body-free from every fault at the coming of our Lord Jesus Christ. He who calls you will do it because he is faithful.

1 Thess 5.12-2

MODULE 8b: MINISTRY LEADERSHIP-PENTECOSTAL

(Dr Ben Pugh)

WHAT IS DISTINCTIVE ABOUT PENTECOSTAL (CHARISMATIC) LEADERSHIP?

Pentecostals borrow a number of things from traditions that preceded them but what is truly distinctive of them in the area of leadership – and to some extent unique about them – are the following three things:

LECTURE 1: PENTECOSTALS BELIEVE THAT LEADERSHIP IS CHARISMATICALLY ORDAINED

Pentecostals and Charismatics have had a longstanding aversion to formal training, ordination and employment routes into ministry. For newer Charismatic streams, in particular, the very idea of advertising for a leadership position in the Christian press, interviewing a set of candidates whom you have never met before and then appointing one of them to a position of responsibility over your people, is almost blasphemous. It is a process that, to them completely excludes the Spirit who is deemed to be the only one with the right to summon and anoint people, not just to leadership as a vocation, but to any given position of leadership. They also find the idea of putting a near-stranger in charge of a congregation very unnerving. Home grown leadership, even within those older denominations that have a Bible college and a route to ordination, is always the ideal.

Pentecostals see charismatic ordination being played out vividly in the Bible: 1Sam.16:1, 12-13, 1Kings 19:15-16; Jer.1:4-5; Isa.6:8-9; Amos 7:15; Acts 13:2-4. Let us take a closer look at this concept biblically.

The Old Testament: Kings

The Office
The office of king in ancient Israel was marked out by the permanent anointing of the Spirit of God (1Sam.16:13; 2Sam.23:2; Isa.11:2). It is the permanence of the presence of the Spirit that is the distinctive thing being expressed here, as distinct from the Judges on whom the Spirit came for particular feats of strength (Othniel 3:9-10; Gideon 6:34; Jephthah 11:29; Samson 14:6, 19; 15:14). Charismatic

anointing had always been the main qualification for leadership in Israel, rather than political succession and Firth associates the language of the Spirit with new strands of leadership, as opposed to already well institutionalised offices.[1]

David

In particular, the emergence of David is highlighted as a new thing that carried a new kind of anointing, so that 'God was with him.' (1Sam.16:18). It is clear that David was specially chosen by God as a man after God's own heart: 1Sam.13:14. The element of divine calling is crucial.[2] The chronicler seems to edit out the facts surrounding David's humble background while the author of 1Samuel seems to use these facts to underline the divineness of the call and does not shield our eyes from David's moral failings after ascending the throne, presumably with the same aim in view: to draw attention to the sovereign work of God.[3] Not only was David a shepherd boy but, while on the run from Saul, became a brigand, a leader of one of the raiding gangs that were notorious in the area but which were also a valuable source of leadership.[4]

The Old Testament: Prophets.

The prophets could all boast of a direct special calling from God that often found them reluctant (Isa.6, Jer.1, Ezek.2) or in humble circumstances (Amos 7:15): 'They have not simply made a carefully considered career choice.'[5] The last of the judges, Samuel, was distinct in that he had the anointing of a prophet. He alone of all the judges was able to lead Israel to a completely new place and break the cycles of failure and restoration.

---

1 David Firth, 'The Spirit and Leadership: Testimony, empowerment and Purpose', in Presence, Power and Promise: The Role of the Spirit in the Old Testament (Leicester: Apollos, 2011), pp. 260-61

2 D. Block, 'The Burden of Leadership: the Mosaic Paradigm of Kingship (Deut.17:14-20),' p. 277.

3 So Von Rad, Old Testament Theology Vol 1 (New York: Harper & Row, 1962), p. 309.

4 'In troubled times…when civil insecurity was widespread and political configurations were liable to quick and unpredictable changes, these 'leaders of raiding gangs' represented an attractive source of leadership', they were leaders who had 'proven themselves capable of resisting, evading, and otherwise reckoning with more powerful enemies.' P. Kyle McCarier Jr., 'The Historical David', Interpretation 40/2 (1986), pp. 121-2. McCarier sets great store on David's military success based on his personal private army as the main thing that propelled him to success: 'At one time or another he had been an Israelite soldier, a brigand, a Philistine mercenary, and a king – but he had always been a warrior. In an age of conflict that produced many talented war leaders…David was the best.' McCarier, 'The Historical David', p. 129.

5 Bruce C. Birch, 'Reclaiming Prophetic Leadership', Ex Auditu (2006), p. 14. Birch speaks for many in urging a return, in the context of church ministries today, to 'the voicing and hearing of God's call.'

New Testament Leadership

In every case the New Testament writers seem to be at pains to point out that leaders were led supernaturally into their positions;[1] they did not choose them: e.g. Peter: John 21:15-23, Paul: Acts 9:10-19, 27; 11:25-26. Jesus says to the Twelve, probably minus Judas: 'You did not choose me but I chose you.' (John 15:16). 'Peter, Paul, and their contemporaries never run for election to office.'[2] To the contrary, they all seem to have detailed stories to tell of how they were divinely led and commissioned: 'True leaders in Christ will be those who can most convincingly articulate to the larger church the ways in which they themselves have been led by Christ.'[3]

Charisma

The word that Paul tends to use to describe the giftedness to minister to others is charisma,[4] literally a grace or a grace-gift. Kasemann defines this as 'the specific part which the individual has in the lordship and glory of Christ.'[5] This is a radical concept and was, as far as we know, completely without precedent either in Judaism or Greco-Roman religion. Even the word charisma or its plural charismata does not appear at all in Classical Greek and even in Paul's day was only ever used in a non-religious setting to refer to the giving of presents.[6] It is part and parcel of a much greater whole and that was Paul's understanding of grace. Paul understood that all of God's dealings with humankind, including the church, bore the nature of an undeserved and free gift that elicited a well spring of thankfulness from those that were on the receiving end of it.[7]

In view of the biblical evidence, it appears that the Pentecostal emphasis on charismatically ordained leadership is the recovery of a right emphasis. The downside is that Pentecostals emphasise home grown leadership to the point of neglecting the proper training of

---

1 So John Koenig, 'Hierarchy Transfigured: Perspectives on Leadership in the New Testament', Word & World XIII/1 (Winter 1993), p. 28.

2 Koenig, 'Hierarchy Transfigured', p. 28.

3 Koenig, 'Hierarchy Transfigured', p. 29.

4 It was Kasemann that led the way in the recovery of this emphasis on the charismata in Paul: Ernst Kasemann, 'Ministry and Community in the New Testament,' in Tr. W.J. Montague Essays on New Testament Themes (London: SCM, 1964).

5 Kasemann, 'Ministry and Community', p. 65.

6 Banks, Paul's Idea of Community, p. 91.

7 Banks, Paul's Idea of Community, p. 92.

leaders. There is an over-reliance upon a leader's calling and anointing to see him or her through. The challenges that such poorly trained leaders face yields such shocking statistics as those of Assemblies of God: only 10% of leaders are still in full time ministry by the time they reach retirement age.

LECTURE 2: PENTECOSTALS BELIEVE IN PLURALITY IN LEADERSHIP

Restorationist charismatics, in particular, believe in plurality in leadership, believing this to be reflected in the church at Antioch: Acts 13:1.They believe that in a leadership team there would ideally be representatives of all five ministry gifts of Ephesians 4:11, accepting, of course, that some individuals might, for instance, be gifted as both a prophet and a teacher.

Apostles and Prophets

Apostles and Church Planting

Foremost of Christ's gifts to the church was the office of apostleship, often paired with the work of the office of prophet as being the two essentially mobile, foundation-laying, church-planting ministries upon which a sedentary team of elders (which in turn might itself include emerging ministries of a similar kind) would build a local church. Not all Pentecostals have tried to retrieve the office of apostle, though, under the influence of the apostolic networks in the UK, most streams have at least been influenced by this way of thinking. Classical Pentecostals seem more comfortable with the term 'apostolic' than the title 'apostle.'

The retrieval of apostolic ministry has resulted in a revolutionary approach to mission. This is a complete break with church tradition and an attempt at restoring the biblical model. The Apostolic Networks began during the House Church movement of the 1970s. In Britain, the leading network now is Terry Virgo's New Frontiers International. The first important thing to note here is that this is not a missionary organisation but a Church, or rather a collection of churches who exist in a fairly informal relationship to their apostles. The second important thing to note is that it is the apostles themselves who go out into an overseas situation to initiate missionary work. They then call upon their home churches for the necessary support. So the Apostolic model is driven from the top, from its very most senior people, rather from the bottom, and, like Faith Missions, driven from the field rather than from the home base. The third thing to note is that the main task the apostle carries out in the field is the planting of churches. No parachurch organisation ever develops. The one priority overseas is to do exactly the thing the apostle has done so successfully back home: plant and design congregations and set in elders.[1]

Apostleship and Suffering

Paul's apostleship is especially interesting in that the whole concept of being an apostle, in Paul's mind, is linked to suffering. Some have linked this to the way the Corinthian crisis 'struck a blow to his apostolic authority.'[2] It is thought that his 'theology of the cross' in which he identifies himself with the suffering Jesus, dates back to this time. Sumney prefers the view that an awareness of his own weakness and frailty within the role of apostle can be seen in his very earliest epistles.[3] A context for this may be the expectation in Greco-Roman culture that a philosopher would live out his message. For instance, austere Cynics were always much more severe in their rhetoric than mild Cynics and Lucian is scornful of those who merely dress like philosophers but conduct themselves in a way that did not match.[4] This is one aspect of apostleship that Pentecostals and Charismatics have not sought to emulate.

Apostles and Prophets

The word 'apostle', as is well known, is the noun form of a verb that signified sending away or even chasing off.[5] Hence, an envoy or delegate.[6] Outside the New Testament, the term could refer to ambassadors of kings or even traveling philosophers sent by a god.[7]

---

1 William Kay, "Apostolic Networks and Mission," EPTA Vol. 26:2 (2006).

2 Ralph Martin, WBC: 2Corinthians (Waco, TX.: Word, 1986), p. lix. Also D.A. Black, Paul, Apostle of Weakness: Asthenia and its Cognates in the Pauline Literature (New York: Peter Lang, 1984), p. 101.

3 Jerry Sumney, 'Paul's "Weakness": A Integral Part of his Conception of Apostleship', Journal for the Study of the New Testament 52 (1993), p. 71-72.

4 Sumney, 'Paul's "Weakness"' p. 72-73. We can also see points that marry up in the whole matter of means of support for traveling teachers such as himself. Among the traveling philosophers, the options were: charge students, enter a household, beg or work. Paul chose the last and least desirable of these. He supported himself through tent-making. Sumney, 'Paul's "Weakness"' p. 73-74.

5 D. Müller, 'Apostle', in Colin Brown (ed) New International Dictionary of New Testament Theology Rev Ed., Vol.1, (Carlisle: Paternoster, 1986), p. 126.

6 Müller, 'Apostle', p. 127.

7 Müller, 'Apostle', p. 127.

Apostles were those with the power to gather a church. Some scholars say there were two kinds of missionaries in the early church: traveling charismatics and community gatherers. Paul's apostolic circle qualified as community gatherers. Wherever a local church has been initiated, the New Testament understands that the work of an apostle is behind it. The on-going work of an apostle would be the oversight of a number of churches that look to him or her for guidance, whether planted by that apostle or not. The church in Colossae, for example, was not planted by Paul but chose to come under his oversight.

This kind of ministry is echoed today by the ministries of NFI, Pioneer etc. In these settings, there was, in the early days, some debate about whether prophets should have the primacy as those who speak for God and to what extent an apostle should listen to his prophet or prophets. A quasi husband-wife kind of relationship seemed to emerge from the discussions in which the mutuality of apostle and prophet was agreed. It was contended that, without a prophet, an apostle will only create a 'glorified civil service.' It is the prophet that urges a continual return to the model of Jesus Christ and the New Testament. Apostles, it is held, are men with a grand view of the church as an organisation. Prophets bring direction to that organisation.

Apostles and Prophets and Postbiblical Church History
Historically, it appears that the original mobile charismatic ministries gradually evolved into sedentary, monarchical ministries. It is believed that Apostles and Prophets were gradually replaced by Bishops, Presbyters and Deacons. Apostles and prophets were the mobile, church-planting wing of church ministry, who set in 'elders' or 'deacons' as the permanent, sedentary oversight of a local church. Deacons, it is thought, gradually took over from the charismatic office of Teacher. By the early 2nd Century, apostles and prophets were themselves being replaced by stationary, elected, and increasingly powerful, bishops and presbyters.[1]

Pastors, Teachers & Evangelists
The remaining five-fold ministry gifts of Ephesians 4 form part of the treasured Pentecostal and Charismatic concept of 'plurality in leadership,' though, in truth, there is not often any great effort to

---

1 See Didache XV.1-2.

ensure that every gift is represented within a leadership team. There tends to be a preference for prophets.

This plurality can result in any of the three models of church government:

Episcopal: The Tall Pyramid

Episcopal systems would normally claim a long line of succession that goes all the way back to the Twelve, especially to Peter. Pentecostals who use an episcopal system would make no such claim. A Pentecostal bishop is simply a very senior overseer that has trans-local responsibility. This model is only found among black Pentecostal groups.

Presbyterian: The Flat Pyramid

This is government by means of a Presbytery, or body of elders. This is a central body, often representing churches at a national level. Presbyterians are keen to maintain the headship of Christ alone over His Church. This, of course, has strong support from Scripture: John 15:1-8; Eph.1:10, 20-23; 2:20-22; 4:15; 5:30; Col.1:18; 2:19; 3:11.

In the Presbyterian system, the authority that Christ has as Head and King of the invisible and visible Church is invested in the Church as a whole but is expressed by the officers elected by the people to represent them. These local officers, or pastors, then represent their church at the regional or national 'session,' 'synod,' 'presbytery' or 'assembly' (elders seem to have had a similar function at the Council of Jerusalem: Acts 15:2). This system endeavours to honour the autonomy of the local church at the same time as maintaining unity and accountability among the churches.

Elders are supported by deacons. All ministers, however, are seen as being of equal status. The larger Pentecostal churches, such as the Christian Centre, Nottingham, use this model so as to avoid excessive democratic wrangling with the congregation. The leadership team is a team of elders who make democratic decisions on behalf of the congregation. The congregation's role in decision-making is limited.

Congregational: No Pyramid

This is government by the whole local congregation. No governing body has any rights over the local congregation. These congregations, do, in practice, however, consult with and appoint ministers via a

621

wider organisation such as one of the apostolic networks. Leaders are, in theory, on the same level as their congregations, with leadership teams consisting of pastors and deacons. In non-Pentecostal Congregationalist churches, the congregation is consulted about all major decisions and will often be given the opportunity, especially in Baptist churches, to vote. In Charismatic contexts, the result is something more like a theocracy in which the congregation all seek to discern the will of God through exercising the gift of prophecy.

Within this system, Charismatics have a 'restorationist' tendency. There is a desire to restore the primitive church and to move as far away as possible from Episcopal hierarchies and state control. The re-introduction of apostles and prophets into this congregational mix can have the effect of leading us back, full-circle, to the Episcopal model as there is, in practice, no difference between a charismatic view of the role of an apostle and an Anglican or Catholic view of the role of a bishop. There is thus a tendency in restorationist churches towards the Animal Farm predicament: "Everybody's equal, but some are more equal than others."

LECTURE 3: PENTECOSTALISM HAS A STRONG BELIEF IN 'SPIRITUAL AUTHORITY.'

The late '60s saw the rise of the Civil Rights movement and the 1968 riots. The baby boomer generation began questioning everything.[1] In particular, 'question authority' was the key phrase. There was a deep suspicion of the establishment. In the business world, the CEO leadership style was the best way to adapt to this change. The CEO was a vision-caster, inviting his or her organisation to buy into the vision and work towards it. The dominant value was productivity. How to motivate better productivity by spurring on the work force was the main objective.

Within churches, a reaction to 60s anti-authority libertarianism was the 'Shepherding Movement.' The ideas of the Shepherding Movement originated with the Argentine evangelist Juan Carlos Ortiz. Ortiz pioneered 'covering' and 'shepherding' terminology.

---

1 Howe and Strauss provide an illustration of generational differences in this regard: In 1950, 'question nothing' was the approach. By 1970 (the boomers), it was 'question everything.' In 1990 (the Xers), the approach was 'question questions.' They predict that the new generation (Millennials / Gen Y) will say, 'enough questions!' Neil Howe & William Strauss, Millennials Rising: the Next Great Generation (New York: Vintage, 2000), p. 348.

I've heard Christians say very proudly, 'I don't follow any man–I follow Christ.' That sounds pious, but it's really a great mistake. It means the person wants to do his own will; he doesn't even realize what it means to follow Christ.[1]

There is no formation without submission.[2]

He commanded, and they did it. That is how disciples are formed.[3]

This kind of teaching provided an answer for church leaders whose religious authority was diminishing in a libertarian age.[4]

Watchman Nee was also highly influential, and, with the title of one of his books, appears to have coined the term 'spiritual authority':

To reject delegated authority is an affront to God.[5]

Whether the one in authority is right or wrong does not concern us since he has to be responsible directly to God.[6]

Further to this, American charismatic renewal had resulted in the same leakage of renewed Christians from the denominations as had been experienced in Britain and around the world. Charismatic Christians were forming independent prayer groups and churches.

There was concern over the individualism of these Christians. People needed to belong, to be a part of something. There was a widespread cry for personal discipline; people hungered to get their lives together.[7]

---

1 Ortiz, Disciple, 101.

2 Ortiz, Disciple, 111.

3 Ortiz, Disciple, 111.

4 In the UK, the 1960s saw an unprecedented undoing of Christian values in government legislation: the Obscene Publications Act of 1959; the legalisation of Abortion and Homosexuality in 1967; the Theatre Act of 1968. Added to this was the advent of the contraceptive pill in 1965. These factors all contributed to the removal of restraint in society and, because it was happening at such a high level, caused religious leaders to feel powerless.

5 Nee, W., Spiritual Authority,71.

6 Nee, Spiritual Authority, 71.

7 Bob Mumford, Christianity Today (19 March 1990).

The Fort Lauderdale Five

The Fort Lauderdale Five (Ern Baxter, Derek Prince, Charles Simpson, Don Basham, Bob Mumford) began what became known as the 'Shepherding Movement', whose ideas are still widespread today.

They felt the need to ensure that every believer had someone to whom they were accountable, a 'covering'. That person in turn would be answerable to a higher leader who, via a chain of command, would be under the authority of one of the Five.

Restoration

There was a parallel movement going on in the UK in the form of the restorationist House Church movement. Various horror stories began to emerge,[1] especially from Bryn Jones' Covenant Ministries. People were required to submit their holiday plans, romantic intentions, financial plans – everything, to their shepherd. Members of Noel Stanton's Jesus Army were not even free to leave.

During the 1980s, teaching on authority in British Charismatic churches chimed with the tough right-wing Thatcherism of the day and enjoyed a strong following among the middle class businessmen and their families that formed the bulk of most charismatic congregations.

Critique

Among the more thoughtful critiques of the shepherding movement are the following:

One of the most immediate problems is that under close-knit shepherding individuals did not find the opportunity to learn to hear God for themselves or to make their own mistakes.[2]

Personal responsibility to make decisions before God is both a basic freedom and a basic necessity in the churches. To rob man of that in the name of eldership is abuse of office.[3]

---

1 There are some in Scotland, Charismatics, 93-94. See also, Johnson, D & J. Van Vonderen, the Subtle Power of Spiritual Abuse, (Minneapolis, Bethany House, 1991), 17-19, 21-22. Most such stories would probably be found in the popular Christian press, e.g. Christianity Today.

2 Scotland, Charismatics, 101.

3 North, G.W., (known as Wally North, a pioneer of early Restoration) Eldership, (Exeter: Paternoster, 1986), 87.

The New Testament and Worldly Models

Of all the distinctives of Pentecostal and Charismatic approaches to leadership, it is easily this one that is the least biblical. It runs contrary to the New Testament attitude towards leadership, which is one of subverting worldly infatuations with power and privilege. Jesus warns of taking our cue from worldly models of lording it over others, saying, '...not so with you.'[1] One writer goes so far as saying, 'To say that Jesus was lukewarm on the subject of leadership is...something of an understatement.'[2] Former military leader John Adair identifies humility as the thing that marked out the leadership style of Jesus from other leaders of his day.[3] This was against a Greco-Roman cultural setting in which, 'Those of higher status expected deference and obedience; they were in charge and expected no challenge from those below them.'[4]

We can see how the Corinthian church had fallen foul of a worldly approach to leadership, only recognising the impressive and the powerful: 'The Corinthians thought their leaders should demonstrate their endowment of the Spirit with their powerful demeanour and impressive lives.'[5] Paul turns this completely on its head: 1 Cor.3:5-10; 4:1. His language is deliberately drawn from the world of manual labour, the work of the lower classes.[6] In 2 Corinthians, this battle against the wrong model of leadership seems to have intensified with the arrival in Corinth of 'super-apostles' (2 Cor.11:5). Most of that letter is taken up with combating the seductive appeal of their flair and impressive oratory skill. In contrast, Paul compares the true minister to a clay jar–the equivalent to a jam jar or Styrofoam cup (2 Cor.4:7-12).[7]

The New Testament and Servanthood Jesus needed to correct in his own apostles the desire for prominence, honour and position. Each time he warns of his impending death he then also has to contend with speculation about who will be the greatest. It is then that he launches

1 Finney, Understanding Leadership, p. 44; Watson, Fourfold Ministry, p. 14.

2 Watson, Fourfold Ministry, p. 14.

3 Adair, The Leadership of Jesus and its Legacy Today (Canterbury Press, 2001), pp. 17-26.

4 Jerry Sumney, 'New Testament Perspectives on Ministry', Lexington Theological Quarterly, 37/1-2 (Spr-Sum 2002), p. 28. See also: Andrew Clarke, Serve the Community of the Church: Christians as Leaders and Ministers (Grand Rapids, MI.: Eerdmans, 2000).

5 Sumney, 'New Testament Perspectives', p. 29.

6 Sumney, 'New Testament Perspectives', p. 29.

7 Sumney, 'New Testament Perspectives', p. 31.

his devastating critique of the status quo, insisting on an inverted hierarchy within the Kingdom of God: Mark 9:35-37. Those who want to be greatest are to be diakonoi.

> *'Wanting to claim authority over others is diametrically opposed...to the kind of leadership to which Jesus calls men and women.'*[1]

There is some debate in the literature surrounding the Greek word diakonia, from which we get the word 'deacon' and which, in its verbal form, means 'ministry.' Some emphasise that the word typically referred to table service[2], which would tie in with, for example, Paul referring himself by a still more extreme title: doulos, 'slave': Rom.1:1; Gal.1:10; Phil.1:1. Others point out that diakonia often referred to positions of prestige.[3] People were known to sell themselves into slavery in order to enter the service of a very high standing person. Likewise, in many households, servants could reach positions of such authority and honour that they were second in command to the master – still in bondage though. In support of this, it is important to note that the New Testament usually refers to people as servants 'of God' and only rarely servants of people.[4]

SUMMARY

Supernatural, charismatic ordination, plurality of leadership gifts and a strong belief in God-given authority are the emphases that Pentecostals and Charismatics have introduced to the Church.

So widespread has been the influence of these attempted retrievals of New Testament teaching that it seems there is no going back from here. Much as the New Testament principles of anointed, diverse, authoritative leadership have been applied in flawed and faltering ways within the movement, there is widespread recognition of their validity as reflecting biblical insights.

---

1 Sumney, 'New Testament Perspectives', p. 35.

2 Sumney, 'New Testament Perspectives', p. 33.

3 Koenig, 'Hierarchy Transfigured,' p.30. For more on this view see: John Collins, Diakonia: Reinterpreting the Ancient Sources (Oxford: Oxford University Press, 1990).

4 Finney, Understanding Leadership, p. 45. Apparently, it is 18x and 2x respectively.

MODULE 8c: MINISTRY LEADERSHIP-PASTORAL

(Revd Dr Heather Morris MA)

MISSION AND PASTORAL CARE

MODULE AIMS

- To develop students' understanding of the nature of pastoral care
  Biblical basis; Contemporary developments
- To develop students' self-understanding of themselves as pastors
- To develop students theoretical basis/skills in theological reflection
- To develop the students' pastoral skills in specific contexts

LECTURE 1: THE NATURE OF PASTORAL CARE: THE PASTOR AS SHEPHERD

INTRODUCTION:

Beginning with your experience, what forms of pastoral care does the church offer? What does pastoral care look like in your context?

Why do we offer pastoral care?
- Response to human need
- Response to Gods action
- As a missional activity- Christian pastoral care reveals the nature of God in the world
- Obedience

THE PASTOR AS SHEPHERD

Thomas Oden claims that the shepherd is "the pivotal analogy of ministry". The image of shepherd was a natural one for Israel to adopt both as a description of their God and of their own human leaders. They belonged to a pastoral economy and the role of the shepherd was fundamental to their existence. Because the land was so dry, shepherds were always on the move leading their sheep in search of new and fresh pastures. Shepherd is, of course, a description of God. Gen 48:15, 49; 24, Ps 23; 1 and 80:1 are direct references to God as shepherd. Tidball points out that "Behind even the darkest and most bewildering experiences of their (the children of Israel's) history was a God who called, led, pastured, healed and carried His people. This belief served as a foundation for all their praying (Ps 28:9) and their hoping (Is 40:11)" (1997:31).

Behind the idea of God as shepherd is a stress on the leadership, provision and guidance offered by God. (Ps 23:3, 68:7, Jer 50:19). The image comes to the fore when the people of God were on the move, in the wilderness they are told not to be like "sheep without a shepherd (Numbers 27:17). Similarly in declaring the exile over God showed himself to be the one who "tends his flock like a shepherd: He gathers the lambs in his arms and carries them close to his heart; he gently leads those that have young" (Is 40:11) The image of shepherd was broad enough to encompass the blessed and comforting side of their experience (Ps 28:9,85:7, 100:3, 121:4) and also its tough and terrifying aspects (Ps 44:11: 80:1).

ISRAEL'S HUMAN SHEPHERDS

Among the people of the ANE, the title of "shepherd" was commonly used for their kings and rulers. It was viewed as a role which required the exercise of real authority- so Ps 78:70-72 refers to David the king as "the shepherd of his people Israel" An echo of that authority of also seen in Psalm 23 where as well as carrying a staff to comfort the shepherd carries a rod which is a sign of authority and leadership.

The prophets, for example, Jeremiah, Ezekiel and Zechariah, use the image of shepherds negatively to describe the failures of human leadership. Jeremiah says that rather than protecting the flock they destroyed it and scattered the sheep (23: 1-5). Under these foolish shepherds, the sheep became lost, left to roam and wander over the hills without any sense of where their true home is. Ezekiel accuses the shepherds not just of negligence but of deliberately killing the sheep so that they might themselves benefit from the wool and meat "You have not strengthened the weak or healed the sick or bound up the injured. You have not brought back the strays or searched for the lost" (34:4) God's delegation during this period of the work of leading, protecting and guiding Israel ended in momentous failure. Human shepherds had been unable to resist the temptations inherent in their role and had abused both their power and their sheep. We need to learn the lessons of this period. "The abuse of power and privilege, speaking our own words while claiming them to be the word of God, and spiritual indifference which allows the sheep to stray down dangerous paths, remain potent temptations which trap many pastors" (Tidball 1999:137).

Read Ezekiel 34–from the prophet's accusation of bad shepherds and description of God as shepherd what can we learn of what a good shepherd should do and be? *(restoring, teaching, encouraging, listening, healing, counselling, rebuking, strengthening and exhorting)*

JESUS

So when Jesus spoke of himself as a shepherd (Jn 10:11) it is not surprising that he needed to qualify it with the word "good". Shepherds had a dubious reputation by this time. They were thought of as being dishonest, people were forbidden to buy anything from them because it was presumed that anything which they had had been stolen. They were not accepted as witnesses in court. Furthermore, because they were on the move they could not worship regularly at the Temple, so they were considered as unclean. They were listed among those who practiced a despised trade. This makes Jesus' use of the term shepherd surprising. First of all, in using it he is clearly making a messianic claim. He is the true shepherd of Israel and fulfilling the prophecy of Ezekiel and Jeremiah that God would shepherd his people himself. But what does Jesus mean when he describes himself as a good shepherd? **John 10: 1-18**

1. Jesus is good because there is a close relationship between the shepherd and His flock. He knows them by name they follow him because they know his voice (3-4)

2. As the gate of the sheep he is good because he provides security, salvation and pasture (7-10)

3. He lays down his life for his sheep (11, 15, 17-18). This is not the way a hired hand would behave- when a wild animal comes he protects his own life first and runs away, but Jesus sacrifices his life to preserve the life of the sheep

4. The role of the good shepherd is to gather sheep into one flock (16)

SO WHAT THEN, ABOUT THE ROLE OF UNDER-SHEPHERDS?

Jesus commissions Peter to "Take care of my sheep" Jn 21:16. Paul warns the Ephesian elders "Keep watch over yourselves and all the flock of which the Holy Spirit has made you overseers. Be shepherds of the church of God which he bought with his own blood" (Acts 20:28) 1 Peter 5:2 and Ephesians 4:11-12 We are accountable servants who must one day give an account and therefore we are not free to rule the flock as we like. So in the light of this wealth of Biblical material how does the image of shepherd inform our pastoral care?

Close relationship with God and sheep: the character of the shepherd is vital, he leads rather than guides the flock (Hebrews 2:10). The shepherds concern is entirely focussed on those entrusted to his care, even to the point of surrendering His own life-"thus leadership is expressed in great compassion, sensitivity to need and a knowledge of what is life-sustaining and wholesome" Campbell:30

Courage: In his book "Rediscovering Pastoral Care" Alastair Campbell calls us to see courage as an essential characteristic of the shepherd. "Anyone who has entered into the darkness of another's pain, loss or bewilderment and has done so without the defences of a detached professionalism will know the feeling of wanting to escape...caring is costly, unsettling and even distasteful at times" (1986:26) It is a courage which is based on trust in God-listen to young David as he tried to convince Saul that he is capable of fighting Goliath 1 Sam: 17: 34-37. The courage of Jesus has a quality to it that is both strong and gentle; above all, it is a courage for others, not a courage for its own defence or aggrandisement. There is courage in the teaching of Jesus, in the action of Jesus when he touches lepers; there is courage in the suffering of Jesus.
IN WHAT WAYS DOES YOUR MINISTRY CALL FOR COURAGE?

Tough: pastor called to enter the valley of the shadow, staying with people through illness, taking questions. Tender: Isaiah 40:11, Ezekiel 34:16 Care for those in the fold: Acts 20:28, all of them are valuable to God- they belong to God – Ezekiel gave us an insight into the range of care demanded- we picked that up when we looked at the passage–restoring, teaching, encouraging, listening, healing, counselling, rebuking, strengthening and exhorting.

John 10:14 also highlights that **a good shepherd will have a sound knowledge of his sheep**-demands getting to know them and listening to their concerns. Searching for those outside the field: the good shepherd will take the initiative in going out to search for lost sheep. Luke 15:1-7 "Pastors who abdicate their work as evangelists cannot be faithful to their biblical calling"(Tidball 1999:146). Campbell claims that "Jesus uses the shepherd image in his teaching to describe God's strenuous and often surprising concern for those who have gone astray (Matt 18:12-14).

630

Have you experience of times when as you exercised your pastoral role God brought people to faith? What are the dangers in recognising a link between pastoral care and evangelism?

There has been criticism of the image of shepherd. Stephen Pattison (2000:8) writes that "The metaphor of wise shepherds leading or guiding silly sheep has been challenged as dangerously one sided, misleading and unhelpful"

QUESTIONS FOR REFLECTION: DOES 1 PETER 5:2-4 CHARACTERISE YOUR MINISTRY?

LECTURE 2: THE NATURE OF PASTORAL CARE (2)

WHAT IS PASTORAL CARE?

Pattison begins his book with an anecdote about a TV programme which brought to light the fact that patients in a large psychiatric hospital were being abused by some of the nursing staff. As part of the follow up to that programme a radio interviewer asked the hospital chaplain "How do you see your role in the hospital in the light of recent events" The chaplain replied "I do not see my role, I just do it" Pattison goes on to say that that response is totally inadequate. "What is pastoral care?"

What is pastoral care: Ideally think of a time when you experienced pastoral care and then form a definition.

1. PASTORAL CARE AS HELPING ACTS

Clebsch and Jaekle (1967) Pastoral Care in Historical Perspective Harper Torch Books

The ministry of the cure of souls or pastoral care consists of helping acts done by representative Christian persons directed towards the healing, sustaining, guiding, and reconciling of troubled persons whose troubles arise in the context of ultimate meanings and concerns.

As you thought about "What is pastoral care" you may well have come up with a list of activities as your answer: visiting the sick, comforting the bereaved, responding to family crises".

There is a strong tradition underlying that view of pastoral care. The work and writing of Richard Baxter is a good example of it.

Baxter lived from 1615 to 1691. One of his best known works is "The Reformed Pastor". In it, he sets out his understanding of pastoral care. For him pastoral care pastoral care is the responsibility of the ordained minister, who has oversight of the congregation and has three main concerns:

1. That the pastor pays attention to their own relationship with God
2. That conversion is a primary aim of pastoral care; preaching well he believed was not enough- but in relationship with the congregation God could work to bring about spiritual awakening
3. That the pastor takes heed to all of the flock Acts 20;29

In his book "The Reformed Pastor" Baxter lists seven pastoral functions. They are conversion of the unconverted, advice to enquirers; building up of the already converted; oversight of families in the congregation; visiting the sick; reproof of the impenitent; exercise of discipline. If pastoral care focuses on what is done, then change is recognised as being a significant motive. Pattison points out that pastoral care is part of changing the world as well as simply being in it. So he highlights action and change in the definition which he constructs: *"Pastoral care is that activity, undertaken especially by representative Christian persons, directed towards the elimination and relief of sin and sorrow and the presentation of all people perfect in Christ to God."*

If you ask many people "What is pastoral care?" you may well have been given a list of activities as your answer: visiting the sick, comforting the bereaved, responding to family crises". The pastor and pastoral care was generally thought of as the preserve of those in ordained ministry, it was in essence a problem solver.

CHANGE IS UNDOUBTEDLY A VALID AND SIGNIFICANT MOTIVE FOR PASTORAL CARE.

But what are the dangers in seeing change as a motive?

1. There is a danger however in seeing change as the only motive for pastoral care. There may be situations where change does not occur. Why bother visiting a confused elderly person when there is unlikely to be any change evidenced as a result of your time spent with them.

2. Another danger with the identification of pastoral care with helping acts is that pastoral care can become identified with technique, and pastoral care becomes good works performed through ever more sophisticated techniques. This is an ever present danger in pastoral care training. There is always a pressure to let training in pastoral care become simply a series of lecture in "how to" care in different contexts. And while you need to know the how to, you also need to know that pastoral care is more than helping acts.

3. Pastor being only a problem solver

PASTORAL CARE AND RELATIONSHIP

Alastair Campbell's definition of pastoral care is *"pastoral care is embodied care, care incarnate"*. For Campbell the essence of pastoral care is the pastoral relationship. His claim is that that pastoral relationship does not depend primarily on the acquisition of knowledge or the development of skills but on a truly loving and caring attitude to others which comes from our own experience of pain, fear and loss and our release from their grip through the work of God in our lives" He writes "the carer and the cared for are not on two sides of a divide which must be bridged by expertise on the part of the one who cares. Pastoral care is grounded in mutuality; it is possible because we share a common humanity. If I can find some courage, hope and transcendence in the midst of life, then I can help my fellow man to find that same wholeness" In his book, Campbell picks up a number of interesting images and applies them to pastoral care but the one I want us to think about for a moment is that of the wounded healer. **The image of the wounded healer** is central to an understanding of the death of Jesus:

> *"For God was pleased to have all His fullness dwell in Him, and through Him to reconcile to himself all things, whether things on earth or things in heaven, by making peace through His blood shed on the cross" (Col 1: 19 and 20)*

Jesus was a wounded healer and it is Campbell's contention that there may be occasions when God gives us wisdom though our experience of loss or hurt which He may choose to use as we offer pastoral care.

As we seek more deeply for those resources of help and guidance which we have to offer others in pastoral care we find them in a surprising place–in our vulnerability. It is natural for us to suppose that we must help out of our strength...Pastoral care however is not correctly understood if it is viewed within the framework of professionalism...pastoral care is a relationship" (1995:37) Christ, the wounded healer, restores the fractured relationships between God and human beings. "Such wounded love has a healing power because it is enfleshed love, entering into human weakness, feeling our pain standing beside us in our dereliction.

Strengths:
Reaction against skills; Emphasis on Gods strength; Takes account of the reality of pain and grief; pastoral relationship as the medium whereby biblical truth can be communicated

Weaknesses:
Over-empathy

PASTORAL CARE AS PRESENCE

John 1:1-5, 14; Philippians 2:1-11
At the heart of Christian faith is the incarnation. What can we learn from Jesus' incarnation which can help us to understand the nature of pastoral care? Is the church a sign of God's love and commitment to the world?

Athanasius, the great fourth-century theologian, in his beautiful little book *On the Incarnation of the Word,* shows that the entire world benefits from the incarnation of the Word even before being aware of it.

You know how it is when some great king enters a large city and dwells in one of its houses; because of his dwelling in that house the whole city is honoured and enemies and robbers cease to molest it. Even so it is with the "king" of all; he has come into our country and dwelt in one body amidst the many, and in consequence the designs of the enemy against mankind have been foiled, and the corruption of death that formerly held them in its power, has simply ceased to be. For the human race would have perished utterly had not the Lord and Saviour of all, the Son of God, come among us to put an end to death.

The Word was made flesh; incarnation is a crucial picture applying first and foremost to Jesus but not only to Jesus. The eternal Word was and longs to be made flesh. Seen to be part of, relevant to and in the world. The pastoral care we offer is one way in which flesh is put on the gospel.

John Patton (2005:21) puts it like this:

> *Christian faith affirms God's presence with us–God's remembering and hearing us wherever we are. The pastoral carer is a reminder of this affirmation by his remembering and hearing the person cared for...The pastoral carer...is present to the person cared for in a particular kind of relationship–one that "re-presents" the presence of God through relationship to the person cared for. ...Pastoral carers affirm by their action that God continues to hear and remember them"(2005:22)*

The derived understanding that the Christian pastor should seek to be with people. So, for example, I would understand the spirituality of someone like Sheila Cassidy as being very much within this paradigm. She writes:

> *"So the spirituality of those who care for the dying must be the spirituality of the companion, of the friend who walks alongside, helping, sharing and sometimes just sitting, empty handed, when he would rather runaway. It is a spirituality of presence, of being alongside, watchful available; of being there."*

Patton (2005) claims that in this **ministry of presence** that God is "re-presented" most effectively when:
1. The carer is fully present and s/he is aware of themselves and their own feelings
2. The carer is fully aware that s/he represents more than themselves
3. S/He is aware of and able to experience as much as possible of the person to whom care is offered

Mark 14: 32-41 When Jesus was in the Garden of Gethsemane facing the horror of his death he brings the disciples who were closest to him with him and what does he ask of them. He doesn't ask that they would make the situation different, that was not in their power, he asks that they would stay and keep watch. He asks for a ministry of presence. But they can't do it, they fall asleep. A ministry of presence demands commitment to God and the other person. What would a ministry of presence look like in your context?

Despite it being culturally widespread and acceptable in Africa, a ministry of presence is not universally accepted as valid, Wesley Carr claims that the idea is vague and often produces vacuous if well intentioned behaviour. He claims that it is unsatisfactory just to be there as this does not let people a latching on point to his ministry or message, they then find it difficult to know what form of association is expected or appropriate, are you friend, counsellor, priest etc.

PASTORAL CARE AS COMMUNITY ACTION

The individualism which has characterized pastoral care is now developing as the significance of context and community is recognized.

> *The communal contextual paradigm views pastoral care as a ministry of the Christian community that takes place through remembering God's action for us, remembering who we are as God's own people, and hearing and remembering those to whom we minister.* John Patton

Patton's premise is that the concept of community is basic to pastoral care, that God created human beings for relationship and continues in relationship with creation by hearing us, remembering us and meeting us in our relationships with one another. Therefore, as we offer pastoral care we do not simply offer companionship, understanding, whatever our primary paradigm may be, but our pastoral care also signals that they are a significant, valued member of a community. He gives an example of a woman he calls Natalie. She said:

> *I grew up in this church. A lot of these people were here when I lost my father, and they gave me something I didn't even know I needed. I guess you could call it a sense of being part of a group that cared. When I visit people I want to give them that same kind of thing, a feeling that there is something important that they are part of.*

The church, Patton claims may be characterized as a community of action, of relationship and of meaning, *"the church exists to facilitate care of the earth and of the human beings that inhabit it, through offering genuine relationship and enabling persons to discover meaning in life and the world" (1993:25)*

An American Methodist bishop, Will Willimon writes about how he came to faith in Jesus; looking back over his life he recognises the way in which the people of God held on to him and did not give up on him when he rebelled, he writes:

The folks at the church just wouldn't let me go my own way, took time for me, put up with me...Looking back I can't believe that church people believed in God enough to believe in me.

They believed in God enough to believe in him. Do we believe in God enough to regard no-one from a human point of view? Do we believe in God enough to believe that no one and no situation is beyond redemption? Do we believe in God enough to believe that God still loves the Church and that God still loves the world? Pastoral care therefore is an action of the community which may be nurtured and led by the ordained pastor, but which is first a responsibility of the community.

Bonnie Miller-McLemore emphasises the importance of community in pastoral care. She suggests that we are all part of a living human web. The wider community, of which the person is a part will also influence the stories being told, will also influence valid pastoral responses. If, for example, the story of an individual is being influenced by racism, then an individual response which simply focuses on the individual experiencing racism is inadequate a valid and necessary pastoral response becomes community and societal change.

So pastoral care takes account of the community, allows the community to care for its members. It also means that appropriate pastoral care may demand prophecy, speaking out the truth into the wider world, that God loves and cares for those who are on the margins, that God loves people who have HIV/Aids. To do this is to take up the OT prophetic role.

In what ways does the community influence pastoral care?
What needs to be spoken out in your community? Corruption?

"What is required is pastoral care which is lay corporate and adventurous" Lambourne 1971 Lambourne is asserting that pastoral care is not just the task of the ordained minister, or indeed that of the main pastor, but of the whole people of God. Burck (1982) cites Thornton who claims that "the church itself ought to be the shepherd" How would you argue for this emphasis?

BODY MINISTRY AND JOHN WESLEY

Again and again, the writings of John Wesley remind us that God has more invested in our ministry than we do. God makes power available (there must be thousands of spiritual gifts) to each of us that we might minister effectively within our own spheres of influence. Since our spheres are different, our gifts will be different. I do not covet your gift and you do not covet mine; but, together we are the body of Christ. Let God arise! Robert G Tuttle

Would you argue against it? Who offers pastoral care in your community? Should others be encouraged to use their gifts in this way? What would need to happen in order for others to serve in this way?

LECTURE 3: PASTORAL CARE AND EVANGELISM

Introduction: Time for a quick review…. What have you brought with you from yesterday?

PASTORAL CARE AND EVANGELISM

Pastoral care which has a role in proclaiming the truth about God. All understanding of pastoral care takes its starting point from the ministry of God to God's people. In pastoral care, human beings partner with God in God's ministry. Therefore, pastoral care must have mission at its heart because God is a God of Mission. Why is mission essential to the nature of pastoral care? Because mission is essential to the nature of God.' As Revd Dr Martyn Atkins shares:

Whatever God is perceived to be like, the Church, if it is being true and faithful, will embody and emulate. If God is encountered and experienced as the supreme missionary, going before, searching out, inviting and receiving in, abiding with, then those very characteristics will be found in the Church of such a God.

God still loves the world and because of that, because of who God is, the Church is called to be missional, to be outward looking. Stan Hauerwass hits the nail on the head when he claims:

The only way for the world to know that it is being redeemed is for the church to point to the redeemer by being a redeemed people. The only way for the world to know that it is the world, namely fallen, corrupt, broken and greatly loved by God is through the presence in its midst of a saved and being redeemed community, the church. That truth is there at the beginning of first Thessalonians (1:5), writing about how those who are now the church experience salvation the writer says, "you know how we lived among you for your sake". The Church living as a redeemed community in the world, for the world.

If we cease to be missional, we cease to be Christian. When we settle down and become content with who we are; when we grow so comfortable with each other that we cease to be a welcoming community; when all our concerns are inward; when we cease to reach out with Christ; when we stop being curious about the new things that God is doing in the world; when as one writer puts it we are not being hammered by the world for having lunch with people like Zacchaeus; it's not just a pity, we deny an essential aspect of our identity.

There are a range of opinions as to the most effective ways of making the covenant love of God visible. For Eduard Thurneysen the most effective way of doing that is verbal proclamation. He defines pastoral care as:

A specific communication to the individual of the message proclaimed in general in the sermon to the congregation.

He sees pastoral care as proclamation, as part of the gospel proclaiming task of the church. Its function is to bring the individual into direct and explicit contact with the Word of God. Within this view psychological perspectives, while recognised as having their own integrity, were seen as having no contribution to make to a theological understanding. "we shall really understand man" claimed Thurneysen "only when we understand him from the Bible".

Strengths:
1. Discipline and instruction
2. Commitment to truth: Campbell: integrity "being incapable of compromising that which we believe to be true"
3. Leadership from pastor

Weaknesses:
1. Paternalistic and patronizing
2. Ignore valid insights from other disciplines:
3. Foskett and Lyall in Europe pastoral theology and secular therapies developed in isolation from one another

Elaine Graham, would I think agree with Thurneyson that pastoral care speaks truth about God into the world. Her preferred method of that proclamation is different however. She sees God's covenant love being proclaimed through the action of God's people:

Pastoral care may be understood as the expression of fundamental values of the Christian community, and their enactment in human terms is the means by which Christians disclose the purposes and actions of God in human affairs.

This definition highlights the revelatory nature of pastoral care, that as we care through our actions the truth of the kingdom of God is revealed. Working within this model pastoral care is offered simply as a response to God and becomes by necessity an act of witness to Him. Can you think of an example from your own experience of pastoral care which revealed the nature of God?

Thus, Christian pastoral care and evangelism are inextricably linked. But it's a relationship which requires thought.

A RELATIONSHIP OF CONGRUENCE AND CHALLENGE

John Patton (2005:117)

Our care of each other is based in God's care for us. The ministry of pastoral care grows out of the Christian affirmation that God created humankind for relationship with God and with God's other creatures.

Laurie Green entitles the last chapter in "Doing Theology" "Spirituality: the risks of conversion". There he suggests:

A holy spirituality might be understood to mean that state of affairs whereby people become so open to the transforming touch of God in their total experience that other people become hungry for God when in their company. (129)

Thus, it seems clear that as we offer pastoral care and as we "live among people for Christ's sake" that the Holy Spirit may use our lives to draw people into relationship with himself.

1. As Christians, we are honest that our desire for others is that they experience salvation; new life in Christ.
2. We ourselves are invited to such a deep relationship with God that our lives have integrity, dark is acknowledged as is the power of God; lives which in the power of God's Spirit speak of wholeness, steadfastness; and God.

Evangelism is one aim in pastoral care but not the only aim. Needs to be handled sensitively. And this brings us to a crucial question. Look back at the material we have covered so far. What are some of the aims of pastoral care? 1. Proclamation   2. Revelation:

DISCUSSION:

Should evangelism be a primary aim in pastoral care, should it be intentionally evangelistic?

On one side can argue that the only way to wholeness, peace salvation is in a relationship with Jesus therefore pastoral care must have evangelism as a primary aim.

On the other side could argue evangelism is not primarily a human activity, it is God's work. Our part is to live faithfully and trust that God will take our actions and use them to point people to His Son.
You could argue that it is dishonest to offer pastoral care with the aim of evangelism- I will serve you for what I can get out of you.
What are the possible dangers in having evangelism as a primary aim of pastoral care: get fed up and frustrated, they are never going to make a commitment

Gula asserts that: *"A significant moral dimension of the pastoral relationship is the inequality of power" (1996: 66)* Now by a pastoral relationship Gula means one where a minister or representative Christian person is "acting as a representative of the church so that people can draw from his or her special authority to meet a religious need"

Social scientists define power as the capacity to influence others. Power can be positive, a liberating influence that releases the goodness in others and allows it to flourish. The dark side of power is associated with a controlling and dominating style of leadership. Having authority gives us the right to be heard and heeded but is also carries the correlative duty to use power and authority for the good of the community, God's glory and not for personal gain. The power which representative Christian people have is significant. We have a role in defining reality from a theological perspective, of interpreting experience in the light of faith. *"Our way of seeing things is taken as the way the Church sees them, ...or as the way God sees them"* Gula *(1996:68).* Gula gives an example of a young woman who was a victim of her pastor's sexual abuse. When she looked back on how she experienced her pastor's power she said: *"He had a lot of power over me personally too, in terms of naming me. I was still very young, I was trying to figure out who I was. ...at the time whatever he said was gospel"*

This has significant implications for preaching, teaching and pastoral care. James and Evelyn Whitehead suggested that pastoral power comes from 3 sources- institutional, personal and symbolic: in some people's minds ministers can be thought of as speaking for God. That is why many see ministers as worthy of trust without having done anything to show that. When someone comes seeking pastoral care they are recognising their inability to satisfy their needs on their own and they entrust their needs and themselves to the carer. When they do that they give the carer great power over their lives. How that power is exercised becomes a key moral issue in the pastoral relationship, so that for example, we ensure that vulnerability is not exploited and that the needs of the other person are served rather than our own needs.

Spiritual abuse takes place when: *"a leader with spiritual authority uses that authority to coerce, control or exploit a follower thus causing spiritual wounds"* Anderson (1997:191) Rollo May describes 5 kinds of power in human relationships:

Exploitative power	Power over
Manipulative power	Power over
Competitive power	Power against
Nutritive power	Power for
Integrative power	Power with

1. Acknowledge the power
2. "The greater burden of moral responsibility falls on the one with the greater power" Gula (1996:76)
3. Use power to enable others and not to manipulate them

How does the recognition of power in pastoral relationships impact on evangelism and pastoral care? It means that we need to take care, desire is that people come to living faith aware of the dangers of manipulation, that people may make a commitment because they want to please us, and pressure.

SUMMARY

1. Evangelism may be an aim in pastoral care
2. It is not the only aim
3. Evangelistic opportunities must be handled with immense pastoral sensitivity and with a mature awareness of the dynamics of the pastoral relationship.

CONCLUSION

1 Peter 3: 15-16a Lovely balance in these verses. First, note that they contain an expectation that people will ask questions about your faith...why will they ask, because they see in our lives something attractive, something of Jesus. When they ask be ready to give an account, but do it with gentleness and reverence, with respect and graciously. William Willimon notes:

"...simply to care for other people is not our chief pastoral goal. To care in the manner of Christ is pastoral carer's greatest challenge"

Write a definition of pastoral care!
What makes Christian pastoral care Christian? Does your definition reflect that?

INTRODUCTION

Experience can cause us to think about what we believe.

For example, what questions about God are raised when part of the world is devastated by an earthquake and many people die?

......these are theological questions.

What options do we have when experience raises theological questions? Try not to think about it; Mess; Two different sets of beliefs; engage.

A place to begin: All methods of theological reflection refer to and guide the discipline of integrating theology and practice. All carry two important implications.

➤ The first is that theological reflection means that there is no practical situation in the world or the Church that does not need a reflection that is theological.
➤ Secondly, it suggests that there can be no true theology that is abstracted and pursued in isolation from experience and practice.

Theology and practice in a relationship which is complex, and dialogical

In an unpublished paper, James Fowler claims that this is a pattern which we can see in the Bible:

(a) The experience in Corinth was of factions developing within the Church, division and disorderly worship and so Paul writes theology about unity, and order in worship. **1 Corinthians 1**

(b) Knowing that his imprisonment would raise questions for some, why would God let this happen, he writes to Christians in Philippi : **Philippians 1:12**

So Fowler claims that the letters of Paul need to be: *"seen afresh as inventive, inspired, practical theology"*. He goes on to say that we need to see the theologians of the Reformation as practical theologians, trying to re-shape the practices and teachings of the churches in their eras, in the light of new historic circumstances and challenges.

Theology therefore becomes "a vibrant and exciting tool for those who want to connect the traditions of the Christian faith with the issues of daily life" (Green 2009:39) It is a process by which explicit connections are made between belief and practice (Thompson 2008:3) Methods of Theological reflection help us to do that "connecting" in a disciplined way. Viewing theology in this way has great potential- but there are dangers....too subjective, not valuing Bible,.... So how do we do it?

AN INTRODUCTION TO THEOLOGICAL REFLECTION

Numbers of models exist whereby experience and theology are brought into relationship. If you want a good overview Thompson's (2008) book is a good place to begin. We are going to focus on three models for the purpose of this module.

1. THE "DOING THEOLOGY" SPIRAL This approach to theological reflection has its basis in work done in the field of experiential education, including for example, Kolb's learning cycle; a helpful emphasis which it beings from Kolb is the stage of standing outside the situation so that it can be analysed with a measure of detachment. This approach to theological reflection has also been influenced by liberation theology. A number of cycle models exist.

EXPERIENCE

Starting from where we are. Being aware of events and needs which demand a response.

To be useful, as the basis for action, experience needs to be tested, broadened and refined. Anecdotes are not enough!

Similarly, gut reactions and emotions need acknowledging lest they take over our actions consciously or otherwise. So perhaps the first thing we need to do is analyse the experience and our reactions.

By the time (you have) finished this first Experience phase of the work, (you) should...have begun to discern what is involved in the issue...(you) should be able to say how (you) feel about it and how is touches (you), and why it is (you) feel gripped by the subject (Green 2009:49)

You should also acknowledge prejudices hopes and fears, and consider theological and faith commitments with which you come to the theme. You now move to factual analysis.

EXPLORE

This stage demands gathering as much precise information about the issue as possible. Green (2009) suggests the following areas for exploration:

Areas of analysis
Historical
Geographical
Social   community issues or who are the people affected
Economic how money relates to the issue
Cultural
Religious

What other areas might we add?
- psychological
- ?
- ?

Then look for connections, values and causes. Between experience and analysis a "thick description" is developed.

REFLECT

If there is to be a response to experience in terms of Christian action, then that response will need to be informed and shaped by Christian belief. What Scripture says, either in particular principles or in stories similar to our own. What Tradition and other Christians have to say-past and present. We need to consider all of these and we need to remember to listen to voices that differ from our own, not just the views we agree with.

And then we need to weigh up and assess the material. Do some views have more weight than others. How do we decide?

RESPOND

Theological Reflection that doesn't have any effect on us and doesn't result in any change or further action is like the mindless debates of which Paul complains.

AN EXAMPLE: APPLYING THE "DOING THEOLOGY" SPIRAL

You are a minister. A number of people in the town where you are stationed have HIV/Aids. You decide that it would be good to open the church to those who have this illness and offer counselling and support. However, your circuit steward comes to you to say that if you do this you are supporting sexual promiscuity and that if you go ahead he will leave the church.

1. The Experience. Summarise the experience you are reflecting on
What is happening- what are the facts
How do you feel?
Why does the situation bother you?
Clearly identify the issue. What are the facts? How do you feel?
Possible reasons for feelings including personal prejudices

2. EXPLORATION

Developing a 'thick description'
Areas of analysis
Historical
Geographical

Social	community issues or who are the people affected
Economic	how money relates to the issue
Cultural	
Religious	
Others	

Are there different interpretations of the "facts"?

Reasons of which you hadn't thought for the practice being as it is?

3. REFLECTION

What key insights from theology and faith need to be included?

What resources can you draw on to help you answer the questions?

Scripture	*Other Christians Ideas (Past & Present)*

N.B. Once you have drawn up the list-does it include views you don't agree with? Allow these insights to come into dialogue with one another

4. RESPOND

What would you now say, what changes will you now make, what do you now need to do as a result of having theologically reflected on this experience?

2. THE CRITICAL CONVERSATION; PATTISON

When you had coffee with your friends this morning what was going on? Brainstorm a list of several 'happenings' during this time.
? ? ? ? ? ? ? ? ?

(a)   Participation in a conversation implies the legitimacy of all the participants, that "all have something to say" that is relevant and significant. That's why it's important that you think about who comes to the table.

(b)   The participants in a conversation are changed- both by what they learn and by the process of conversing with other participants

(c)   Conversations allow participants to discover things about themselves and each other which they did not know before

(d)   The concept of conversation does not necessarily imply that participants end up agreeing at every point or that the identity of one over-rides the character of the others. PT is not a tidy discipline, we will be addressing difficult questions, we may well be left with loose ends. In that sense it is a very honest discipline that doesn't simplify scripture or experience, instead it seeks to bear witness to the truth and relevance of religious experience in dialogue with the contemporary world. As a result, PT must be prepared to admit and to live with gaps in understanding and experience. Pattison gives the example of suffering: it's one thing to have developed a theology of suffering in the safety of a classroom, it's quite another to live that if your own child is dying of cancer. John Drane, miscarriages

(e)   Conversations don't go on for ever: The longest of conversations will eventually end and you will return to action.

So PT begins in experience and returns to experience. Its goal is not the formulation of abstract understandings or principles, its aim is the modification of practice so that it is more adequate and a more faithful witness to Christ. Thus, PT is transformational: in process and in outcome it aims to make a difference to peoples, understanding and situations in the contemporary world. As he gathers resources together, **Pattison groups the participants of critical conversation into three main groups:**

(1) Your own ideas, beliefs, feelings, perceptions and assumptions
(2) The beliefs, assumptions and perceptions provided by the Christian tradition, including the Bible
(3) The contemporary situation which is being examined

An example: Applying critical conversation

There is a strong practice of witch craft and traditional medicine in your town. You have preached against this for years because it involves ancestor worship. Your own son gets ill and someone comes to tell you that he will not be healed unless you go to the witch doctor because they believe that an evil spirit has caused this.

The beliefs, assumptions and perceptions provided by the Christian community????

The contemporary situation being examined?   ?????

Your own ideas, beliefs, feelings, perceptions and assumptions? ?????

Questions that remain for me?   ?????

3. REFLECTION THROUGH IMAGINATION AND SPIRITUAL WISDOM: KILLEN AND DeBEER (2002)

Killen and deBeer (2002:51)

The discipline of exploring our individual and corporate experience in conversation with the wisdom of religious heritage. The conversation is a genuine dialogue that seeks to hear from our own beliefs, actions and perspectives as well as the tradition. It respects the integrity of both. Theological reflection, therefore, may confirm, challenge, clarify and expand how we understand our own experience and how we understand the religious tradition. The outcome is new truth and wisdom for living.

For Killen and deBeer this conversation is facilitated by identifying the feelings which underlie experience and crystallising them into images that connect with scripture and tradition.

PROCESS

1. Think of experience and enter into it, allowing feelings associated with it to emerge.
2. When those feelings and sensations have come into focus, allow an appropriate image to arise which gives shape and form to them
3. Stay with that image and allow connections with theological themes, insights and narrative to emerge.
4. Identify new ways of thinking and acting based on those insights.

DEFINITIONS OF THEOLOGICAL REFLECTION

The process of bringing to bear in the practical decisions of ministry the resources of the Christian faith. Whitehead and Whitehead 1995:9

A critical conversation which takes place between the Christian tradition, the student's own faith presuppositions and a particular contemporary situation. Pattison 2000:136

The habitual, conscious, methodical and purposeful correlation of some of the insights and resources of the theological tradition with contemporary situations and practice, resulting in a continuous process of critical awareness, transformation and action. Thompson 2008:28

The discipline of exploring our individual and corporate experience in conversation with the wisdom of a religious heritage. The conversation is a genuine dialogue that seeks to hear from our own beliefs, actions and perspectives, as well as from those of the tradition. It respects the integrity of both. Theological reflection, therefore, may confirm, challenge, clarify and expand how we understand our experience and how we understand the religious tradition. The outcome is new truth and meaning for living. Killeen and Beer, 2002:15

To think about....In what ways do these models differ? What similarities are there?

THE DISCIPLINE OF THEOLOGICAL REFLECTION

What are the strengths in seeing theology like this? (Add to lists!)
- Real life
-
-
-

What are the weaknesses?
- Too subjective
- Not valuing scripture
-
-

What questions do you have?

-
-

Exodus 3:7-10: Acts 9: 1-5 God who hears the cries of His people, Jesus who feels it when His people suffer as if it were His own suffering.

Switzer (in Hunter RJ (1990:472) defines grief and loss like this:

> *The complex inter-action of affective, cognitive, physiological and behavioural responses to the loss by any means of a persons, place, thing, activity, status, bodily organ etc., with whom (or which) a person has identified, who (or which) has become a significant part of the persons own self.*

Muller and Thompson 2003 point out that grief has physical, emotional and spiritual implications. Parkes (1996) contends that bereavement results in emotional, cognitive physical and behavioural changes.

These researchers highlight a number of significant points for us:

1. Grief is complex: "affective, cognitive, physiological and behavioural"
2. Grief is a response to loss of any sort: example loosing job, diagnosis of HIV/AIDS...Doehring highlights 6 general areas of loss: material, relational, intrapsychic, functional, role, systemic
3. Grief is "normal" – even for a Christian. It was Ambrose who stated that: *"grief is a natural, acceptable and necessary response to loss"*. Faith does affect the grieving process, that is recognised objectively by all researchers, but that needs to be held alongside fact that grief is necessary. The fact that a Christian grieves does not mean that they do not have hope in God. The Bible makes it clear that God understands and stands with His people when they mourn: Psalm 89, 103, 136.

What losses have you experienced? With those experiences in mind:
1. What was grief like?
2. How did it affect your relationship with God?
3. What helped?
4. What did not help?

Our response to death and dying of others will necessarily be affected by our own views and experience. That may be something that you want to think about and reflect upon. Norman Autton points out that before we can begin to respond adequately to the needs of others who are dying and bereaved we need ourselves to become reconciled to our own deaths. That is not easy-people like Freud would say that it's well-nigh impossible. However, Autton writes:

> *Not until we ourselves have worked out fully the purpose of life and the meaning of its end, can we hope to be of assistance to those who find themselves in "the valley of the shadow". Death can never be a private matter, for each death reminds us of our own.*

A PROCESS MODEL:

Some researchers and practitioners, having worked with grieving people over a long period of time delineated what they called a grieving process, whereby they proposed that there were certain common stages which people worked through following loss. Parkes (1986) puts it like this: "Grief is a process and not a state. Grief is not a set of symptoms which start after a loss and then gradually fade away. It involves a succession of clinical pictures which blend into and replace one another". Elizabeth Kubler-Ross stages were developed though her work with people who were terminally ill. These stages have been found to be broadly relevant to the grieving process as well.

Denial: KR calls her first stage denial. Everyone who gets that diagnosis has to make a painful transition from thinking of themselves as perfectly healthy people to thinking of themselves as people who might die, to seeing themselves are people who are going to die. Thus, almost everyone who faces a threat of terminal illness goes through a stage of shock, it may be for a short time, hours or days- or it may be a phase so long that they never seem to emerge from it completely. "Even though she has died it won't really affect me"

Disbelief: Is the stage when the person cannot incorporate the news into their world view. Almost always, the believing of bad news seems to come and go intermittently, one day the person seems to accept it and the next they are wondering if it was all a bad dream.

Shock: Implies a bigger impact on the person's ability to think and behave, and like disbelief, it waxes and wanes. The most common symptom of shock is an inability to make decisions, also forgetfulness, clinging and a lack of independence. This can be a distressing time for the individual especially if they feel that they are not coping, and feel that they should be able to snap out of this but can't.

If disbelief is the feeling of "I can't take this on board" denial is "I'm not going to take this on board". It can occur even if the person is well informed and can be characterised as a conflict between knowledge and belief: the persons mind may be telling them that this is real, but they just can't believe the facts that the mind is feeding them, and denial results. Denial is a normal coping mechanism, and it usually fades in time allowing the person to accept the bad news without being swamped by it.

There are a number of psychological theories which attempt to explain why grief is so devastating. Some of them are based on attachment theory: they say that as a child develops it has significant attachments most importantly with the mother but with others as well, and that a sense of self, who you are, is developed from the perceived attitudes of significant others to you. So that when significant others die, there is a sense of the loss of aspects of oneself- those reference points are taken away.

Combined with that is the sense that many people go through life with the conscious or unconscious feeling that tragedy will not happen to them so that when it does that defence mechanism is torn aside. One young woman whose father is dying said to me the other night that it's a whole new world that most people are protected from normally- and that while you might think about it is different because you are now going through it.

That stage can include emotional numbness, occasional outbreaks of pain and tears, a lack of awareness of external events and conversations, and difficulty in thinking clearly. Parkes research indicates that the usual period of time for this stage is 5-7 days. Ainsworth-Smith and Speck suggest up to two weeks for a close relationship.

654

Time to talk-watch both collusion and confrontation. Do not leave the person in isolation- signal that there are no taboo areas. At this time of acute grief, the appropriate pastoral response is a ministry of presence. Our willingness as pastors to sit with someone at this stage is important in its own right but also is a sign of the presence of God, is a sign that what they are feeling is acceptable to God- God does not reject us when we grieve, (Psalm 34: 18 "The Lord is near to the broken hearted, and saves the crushed in Spirit") and it is a sign of their inclusion in the faith community.

The book of Lamentations and many of the Psalms are significant here-the OT scholar Kathleen O' Connor writes that "the laments of the Bible are prayers that erupt from wounds, burst out of unbearable pain and bring that pain to language." "Although laments appear disruptive of God's world they are acts of fidelity. In vulnerability and honesty, they cling obstinately to God and demand for God to see, hear and act". John Patton points out that in Lamentations God does not respond to the laments that are expressed "Lamentations...invites the reader into pain, chaos and brutality, both human and divine. It conveys the effect of trauma, loss and grief beyond tears." So at this stage the task of the carer is to be present in the darkest valley. The covenant faithfulness of the pastor who is willing to stay up late and watch and pray is an example and a reminder of Gods own faithfulness.

Bargaining: "Why me?" may then develop into "why now?" So the person has moved to the point of admitting yes this is happening, but there is a "but". Often during this time, the person begins to deal with unfinished business- will, care of the children. In many ways, bargaining can be seen as a battle between hope and despair, so like denial, it is one means by which the mind adjusts to the threat of dying and accepts it in small pieces rather than being over-whelmed by it.

KR experience is that the reactions of dying people at this stage may be revealed to those who represent faith, and particularly clergy more often than to other people as the dying person may see a minister as a confidant who will not laugh at their request and their attempt to gain extra time. The minister may also be seen as someone who may be able to persuade God to agree with the request, "I suppose you couldn't put in a good word upstairs..?"

PASTORAL RESPONSE:
Listen but do not collude with unrealistic hopes. Bargaining takes a lot of energy, person may be glad to give it up

Anger; People who have been bereaved can feel very angry with themselves, with the medical staff, with God, and with the person who has died. Most researchers suggest that the central issue which gives rise to anger is loss of control, specifically the feeling of powerlessness over one's own body.

Anger is often divided into three types:
Anger at the rest of the world-anyone who isn't ill-why me-which is more often a cry of anger than a question.
Anger directed at what he calls "any recognisable form of fate-for people of faith this may take the form of anger against God for letting this happen, or for not intervening to bring physical healing. There may also be a real sense of disappointment with God, an individual who feels that they have lived well, and don't deserve this; or there may be a sense of guilt- that this illness is being inflicted as a punishment for past wrong-doing.
Anger at anyone who is trying to help

PASTORAL RESPONSE: Allow the person to express anger.

Guilt: People can also experience guilt. Sometimes guilt is expressed as "If only" statements... and sometimes folk feel guilty because they feel relieved that the person has died. **Three types of guilt: real, irrational, and existential.** Relationships that have been difficult often leave a legacy of guilt. Guilt may also be a significant feature when AIDs is diagnosed or when the death occurs as a result of HIV/AIDS

PASTORAL RESPONSE: Allow space for person to talk through feelings

Depression: Facing up to the probability of the end of life is a monumental task. Despair, like anger, fear and denial is a very common phase in facing the threat of dying. Despair really means the loss of hope, often despair comes in waves.

KR suggested that people go through a stage of depression. First, she suggests they may go through a stage of reactive depression in which they mourn past losses and then a stage of silent grief or preparatory grief, when they mourn not just past losses but future ones. KR says that at this stage people do not talk as much because it is hard to verbalise anguish. One thing which people may need to know at this stage is that they will not be forgotten-that is not the same as being asked to make promises like not marrying again. But the dying person may need to know that their life made a difference was significant. **At this stage, a pastoral response may be to talk about the person who has died.**

For those who are grieving, depression also a reality-simple tasks may feel like a burden and there may be a sense of futility and isolation. Another sign of despair may be excessive busyness.

Acceptance: KR describes acceptance as a feeling of outer and inner peace, a submission to things that cannot be changed- but a very different thing to resignation. For those who are grieving acceptance is a stage of letting go but not forgetting. As acceptance grows, there may well be a sense of true sadness. At this stage, the person begins to see the possibility of a hopeful future without the physical presence of the deceased. **Parkes study indicated that after 13 months the majority of his subjects had not reached this stage.**

Socially at this stage, the bereaved person begins to resolve a new identity and feel that they can make social contacts and enjoy themselves without feeling disloyal. This stage may also involve the taking on of new roles. It is significant to recognise that this stage is about adjustment to a new reality. Life will never be the same again, to expect that is unrealistic. They now have to build a new life, in which memories of the dead person are a part, but lives which are not defined by the dead person. "forged by that loss but not stunted by it" In Parkes research the majority of people that he talked to were still at this stage a year after the loss.

Other aspects of grieving are:
Pining: whereby the person may feel an intense longing for the deceased, may be preoccupied with them. It is at this stage that people

may feel as if they have seen the person, may dream about them. Crying and feelings of physical emptiness are common, as is anger.

Disorganisation and despair: (Ainsworth Smith and Speck): At this stage while some of the characteristics of the previous stage- like crying- may diminish, other emotional reactions develop. People may feel or appear apathetic and aimless, may find it difficult to see a positive future.

In your pastoral or personal experience, which aspects of grieving have you seen most frequently?

SOME CONDITIONS AND COMMENTS:

1. Understanding grief as a process is a reminder that movement is happening, so behaviours, which may appear strange to us as they appear during the process are usually normal. So for example people may say that they have seen the dead person, even hallucinations if they do not persist, do not seriously interfere with daily activities, and if decisions and behaviour are not being based upon them, are not to be feared.

2. Individual differences.

3. People can move backwards as well as forwards in this process. In fact stages may be skipped.

4. Grieving following a death is influenced by many factors: these include the abruptness of the loss and opportunity for preparation, and the nature of the relationship between the bereaved person and the person who has died.

5. Human beings are capable of experiencing several different emotions at the same time

6. Watts, Nye and Savage point out that there is some question about how universal stages are as different cultures emphasise different parts of the grieving process

What are some of the Biblical resources we bring to understanding grief and loss?

An affirmation of the humanity of Jesus: Bayley "Jesus was misunderstood and rejected by his family (John 7:2-10, rejected and condemned by rulers of the nation (John 11.47-53); ridiculed, stigmatized, tortured and finally executed in public by a shameful, protracted and brutal method reserved for slaves...He was greatly distressed and troubled and longed to escape His fate"

Looking at the crucified Christ, we can see that God is not indifferent to our agonies. Derek Tidball states "God is not indifferent to our suffering but has Himself experienced, in Christ, the depth and anguish of it. Hebrews 2:9 speaks of Christ tasting death in solidarity with all humanity and thereby providing human beings with a way of defeating death. 1 peter 4:1 stresses that Christ actually experienced suffering in his body and the whole of Peter's first letter provides an assurance that God sympathises with us in suffering. "As Christ entered into the darkness of human suffering in His incarnation, we too are often called to share the burden and anguish of another person's suffering. We are often to do so silently (Isaiah 53:7) without rushing to easy explanations or justifications of God.

Resurrection: "We believe that Jesus died and rose again, and that it will be the same for those who have died in Jesus: God will bring them with Him" 1 Thess 4:14. This is one ground for Christian hope, that in the death and Resurrection of Jesus death, which scripture calls the final enemy, is conquered.

"Nothing is needed more in ministry to the dying than the gospel: Christ dies for sinners to take away the curse of death and guilt, to redeem death from its emptiness and terror by offering the faithful eternal life" (Oden) The pastor is called to state the good news as Wesley often said "plain and home" Thus Christians do not despair in the face of death. They trust in God who has made himself known in Christ and throughout history.

CHILDREN AND GRIEVING

Children also grieve and it is important to take their needs into account. Detailed notes in the hand-out.

CHILDREN'S UNDERSTANDING OF DEATH

The following information describes children's understanding of death and behaviours which may be exhibited during infancy, school age and adolescence. The suggestions for 'what you can say/do' may apply across more than one age level. You may want to read through these several times to decide what is most applicable for your child.

Children's understanding of death	Possible related behaviours	What you can say/do
Infancy		
This age has no understanding of death but reacts to: **1.** Fear of separation- is mostly disturbed by loss of physical/ loving presence of parent. **2.** Parents' emotions: infants are very in-tune with parents' anxiety level.	**1.** Crankiness **2.** Crying **3.** Slight skin rash **4.** Clinging	**1.** Talk about your feelings and concerns with available personnel. **2.** Let family and friends help with care and household tasks. **3.** Try to spend some of each day with your child to keep the feeling of security intact. **4.** Provide much loving/ patting/ holding. **5.** Keep baby's routine as consistent as possible.
Preschool Age - 2 ½ - 5 years		
1. Death is NOT seen as permanent, but rather, as reversible and temporary. **2.** Death may be confused with sleeping or being away, with the belief that the person will return. **3.** Death may be seen as punishment for some wrongdoing.	**1.** May show little concern at times. **2.** May go back to: bedwetting thumb-sucking baby talk fear of dark. **3.** May show fear of separation from significant others: - at bedtime -attending preschool.	**1.** Tell them about what they can expect, how things might look and what might happen: - house filled with people - funeral arrangements - traditional routine broken - parents/family grieving **2.** Encourage anyone explaining the death to this child to use the terms 'dead/death'. **3.** Do NOT use these phrases as they give mixed messages: - passed away - sleeping - taken from us - resting

4. Child considers self as centre of universe (egocentric see all as either caused by or related to themselves).
5. Death may be seen as caused by a death wish, or that anger may produce death. These are examples of magical thinking.
6. Child may think he might catch the same thing.
7. Child may think dead people live underground.

4. May need to talk about the death a lot, often at what seems inappropriate times. This repetition helps make it real for a pre-schooler. Child may need to repeat the fact of death. He may say such things as,
"We're all going to the zoo, but not Daddy, he's dead," or,
"Ben doesn't need a plate, he's dead," or,
"Ben can't use his dump truck anymore 'cause he's dead."

e.g., "Ben is sleeping in the arms of God," - the child may have subsequent sleep disturbances and be afraid to go to bed;
"Ben was so good God wanted him to come to live with him," - child might react with bad behaviour to avoid death or develop fear of God;
"Ben is just away",-the next person who goes away may not be trusted to come back.
4. Respond to the child's security needs
-concerns about "Who will take care of me?" - reassure him regarding routine activities, schedules.
5. Keep explanations short, simple and truthful. They may need to be repeated over and over again. "Ben was VERY ill. The doctors and nurses could not make him better, although they tried everything they knew. They are sad, too. But Ben's body could NOT work anymore. His breathing stopped. Being dead doesn't hurt."

5 - 9 years **1.** Death seen as possible, but not for them, only for others. *9 - 11 years* **2.** Death now may include them. **3.** Child may begin to understand irreversibility death. **4.** Death becomes more real, final, universal and inevitable. **5.** Child can differentiate between living and non-living. **6.** Child may show interest in biological aspects of death and details of funeral.	**1.** Crying **2.** Anxiety **3.** Headache **4.** Abdominal pain **5.** Separation anxiety at time of going to camp, away to school **6.** Denial of death **7.** Hostile reactions toward deceased **8.** Guilty - blame someone other than self **9.** Poor grades **10.** Day dreaming **11.** Lack of attention **12.** Loss of manual skills **13.** Withdrawal **14.** Fear of continuing friendship bonds - might lose friends **15.** Try to fix things and find solution to death **16.** May fear will die at same age **17.** Display similar symptoms of deceased person	**1.** The suggestions for the preschool age child may also apply to the school age child. **2.** Explain that everyone has different reactions to death at different times. It, (the reaction), might not hit until the funeral or two weeks later or on Christmas or other special occasion. **3.** Give permission to cry through words and example - or let them know it's okay not to cry if the child doesn't usually react in that way. **4.** Give an honest explanation for the person's death - again avoiding previously outlined statements. **5.** Encourage attendance at funeral as a final ceremony-as a way to say goodbye. Abide by the child's wish and be sure to understand reasons if child chooses not to go. **6.** Be a good listener. **7.** Let them know their feelings are very important.

Adolescents 12 - 18 years		
1. Child begins to think more like adults. **2.** Child is able to think more abstractly; now understands more fully the implications of death. **3.** Child may view suicide as a means of getting back at someone, but also see it as reversible (because some survive it) and re-occurable (because some try it more than once). **4.** Can acknowledge that life is fragile.	**1.** Want to assume more adult role **2.** Anger **3.** Preoccupation with death: - taking on mannerisms of deceased - aggression **4.** Regression: - idealism of deceased **5.** Practice denial of death by risk-taking **6.** May be very critical of parents' handling of financial arrangements, funeral traditions etc.	**1.** Review suggestions for school age children for 'What you can say/do". **2.** Encourage communication first in family, but may also find it beneficial to involve a trusted friend or counsellor. **3.** Important to have physical touch and "I love you" spoken often. **4.** Discuss role changes which may occur in family structure.

Sickness is an issue which runs through the pages of Scripture. In the Old Testament, we have the stories of Naaman, David's new born child and Job, and Kelsey reports that almost one fifth of the gospels are devoted to the subject of healing.

Care for those who were sick was an integral part of Jesus earthly ministry, and Jesus' own ministry set a pattern which those who follow him were encouraged to follow. (Mt 4:23, Mk 6:13, John 4:46). A major biblical instruction for ministry to those who are ill is to be found in James 5:14 "Is any one of you sick? He should call the elders of the church to pray over him and anoint him with oil in the name of the Lord". Oden claims that "visitation of the sick remains a primary task of the representative ministry"

As we seek to offer pastoral care, it is vital for us to think about what we theologically we believe about sickness. Oden (1983:224) states that "the parishioner has a right to expect that the pastor has thought deeply about the coalescence of God's power, love and human suffering". Pattison goes so far as to say "a theology which cannot speak to the issues raised by disease and suffering could well seem a theology not worth having" So what can be affirmed theologically?

1. **Christianity speaks boldly of God's own active participation in our suffering:** This fits well with models of pastoral care which stress the metaphor of journey in pastoral care. As we care, we have the privilege of journeying with the person who is ill, but far more significantly the journey through illness can occur in companionship with God where it can become a means to growth. And of course, the Cross speaks powerfully of the fact that Jesus understands and has himself experienced human suffering.

2. **Sin and sickness:** Job's comforters wanted him to believe that all his problems were the result of his personal sin. Job himself discovered that this was not the case. In Luke 13:3-4 and John 9 Jesus directly contradicts the view that sickness is a direct punishment for individual sins. At times it seems straightforward to see a relationship between sin and sickness, as for example between drinking and liver disease, but it is helpful to bear in mind the Hebraic assumption of the social matrix of sin and sickness.

One person drives carelessly and knocks down a pedestrian who was crossing the road carefully. This is an important area for all who are involved in pastoral care to think through, as from time to time we may encounter people who believe that their illness is a result of some past sin and will make comments like "I don't deserve to get better".

Nor does a careful examination of the Biblical evidence point to a link between sickness and a lack of faith on the part of the person who is ill. Sometimes in the gospels, people did get better because they personally believed that Jesus would heal (woman with the issue of blood). There are other examples of people other than the one who is sick having faith (several examples of parents who told Jesus about their sick children and saw them healed), and then in the Garden of Gethsemane the servants ear was healed even tough no-one had faith except Jesus. The Bible therefore while speaking of the reality of physical healing does not support those who would claim that sick people are always out of God's will or lacking in faith.

I do not believe that Christians are exempt from sickness, or that physical healing is the inviolable right of every Christian. However, some people do and that may well raise pastoral issues which you may be called upon to deal with.

Example: Parents with ill child. Healers insisting, "by His stripes you are healed". Just as Jesus has made salvation a reality on the Cross for those who believe that physical healing is also available for those who believe, but it needs to be claimed. Should they go?

3. **Health and full functioning are God's basic intention for us:** Sickness is a part of life; few people go through life without experiencing some sickness. The Bible recognises that illness can cause psychological as well as physical stress.

Therefore, we can pray in good conscience for healing. Luther also makes the important point that pain should not be regarded as an absolute evil out of which no good could ever come. Therefore, Speck cites the Archbishop of Canterbury's commission who say that "Those who are called to minister to the sick have the duty of setting free all of God's resources for health". Those resources include prayer and Bible reading, the Sacraments and corporate acts of worship.

Pain The profound and disturbing effects of pain must be understood. Some researchers claim that purposeful pain is more endurable than pain for which one sees no purpose. Thus, the pain following an operation and leading to healing is different in quality to the pain experienced as a result of secondary cancer growths.

Pain can affect mood, blur thought, vision and understanding, can cause deep depression and can have a disturbing effect on a person's walk with God, producing prayerlessness, robbing them of joy and the ability to read the Bible, and it can make the sufferer irritable and cause them to withdraw from fellowship.

Speck writes of one young woman who had been hospitalised several times and who said that the greatest cause of emotional distress was that when she really wanted to or needed to pray she was too tired or in pain, "It's as if the resource that you take for granted is whipped away just when you need it most." It might be helpful in sits like that to lead the person in simple acts of meditation focussing on the psalms for example, or to give them prayer cards with clearly printed scripture texts which can be read even when you are lying down. It may also be helpful for you to be prepared with bible readings which apply to particular sits but beware what those readings are saying or may be taken to be implying about the persons illness. Psalm 34 good.

Sense of low self-esteem one of the effects of illness and of hospitalisation in particular is loss of control. The person who is ill loses control of the time table of the day, and indeed loses control of their own bodies. This may be experienced as profoundly frustrating or can give rise to a sense of hopelessness. Feeling alone in their fears and suffering can cause people to withdraw, become uncommunicative and abandon self-worth. Low self-esteem can also be fostered by the effect of the illness or the treatment. People may have their appearance altered by chemotherapy, and feel that no-one could love them like this. People may lose control of their bodily functions and feel that they have lost all dignity; it can be profoundly upsetting for someone to suffer from diarrhoea. In the face of these understandable feelings, we can bring a ministry of loving acceptance that counteracts any belief that God and others could not love them.

Surgery can also represent a major disruption of people's body image, and some people describe the experience as being mutilated or invaded. People may have all sorts of fears surrounding surgery; beware of your own assumptions. Listen to the person for what surgery means to them, not what it would mean to you if you were in their situation.

Anger with God and those who represent Him

If the sick person feels let down by God because they have become ill they may feel or express anger towards Him. Alternatively Christians may adopt a stoical approach which they do not really feel-" 1 will show people how believers cope with illness".

Others may find it very difficult to deal with the faith questions that illness raises for them: Why me? Why not others? Why does God choose not to intervene? This may lead them to feel, and perhaps to express that God is remote or irrelevant.

Effects on the family

The family of someone who is ill will need pastoral support. What sorts of feelings might they need to express? There will be changes in family routines, changes in roles within the family, which can create fatigue, irritability and worry. Sometimes in an effort to protect one another, the family refuse to discuss their real feelings and fears with one another, pretending instead that all is well.

Your own experience of illness

Pattison claims that the vast majority of contemporary Christians respond to illness and healing in ways which are in-distinguishable from their non-Christian neighbours. Is that your experience? If anything distinctive was offered, what was it?

Historical Responses:

Kelsey states that the institutional church withdrew its interest from the area of the physical healing of the body after the first few centuries of its existence. After this time, the church concentrated on the life of the spirit and preparing people for the world to come.

There were a number of different factors involved in this withdrawal:

1. Most Christians since the Middle Ages have accepted that medical means would be the primary way of bringing about healing. Therefore, the priority for the church was to ensure that those means were available and the church became a provider of hospitals.
2. There is the OT idea that God sends sickness and uses it for His purposes, example-Book of Common Prayer 1662 "Wherefore, whatsoever your sickness is, know certainly that it is God's visitation"
3. Dispensationalism; God performed miracles through the early church to establish it and he then withdrew his power

A PASTORAL RESPONSE

Look back at the material in the first 3 lectures. What models of pastoral care help you as you think care for those who are physically ill?

What therefore do you think will be important elements of a pastoral response?

1. Listen: to the person's story, for their priorities, are there unfinished tasks which need to be completed, relationships to be restored; listen to the persons fears about death and dying; is there fear of judgement- for ex in the case of someone dying with HIV or Aids- confess, be anointed; listen to the family, remember that we are all part of community (Miller-McLemore)

Remember that even when close to death it is best to assume that the person can hear.

2. Patton (2005;74) "What is essential for pastoral care in situations of illness is the carer's knowledge, presence and guidance...she needs to find the best ways to be present in spite of the separation from community that illness creates"
3. Be alert to the questions about God which illness may raise- am I being punished? Does the fact that I have HIV/Aids mean that I am rejected by God? Bayley points out that these questions and the fears which underlie them may well be exacerbated by the rejection which many people with HIV and Aids actually experience from family and friends
4. Remember the grieving process. People when given their diagnosis may experience aspects of grieving

What practical steps have proven useful, in your own experience, when helping men and women to cope with fears of witchcraft?

What traditions exist in your own community for care of people who are about to die? In what ways have churches altered and adapted tradition?

LECTURE 8: CHARACTER AND LISTENING

EXERCISE

Think for a moment someone who helped you though a difficult time in the past. What was it about those people that made them most helpful?

Divide into twos

Ask each couple to make a list of the qualities that make a good carer

- To listen
- To accept
- To be available
- To be patient
- To keep confidences
- To be honest
- To learn from one's experience
- To be sensitive
- To offer hope and encouragement

QUALIFICATIONS FOR CHRISTIAN SOUL CARE

Benner David G (1998) "Care of Souls" Paternoster

Those who care for souls should possess a deep and genuine love for people:

Oden "Neither analytical skill nor theoretical knowledge can have positive effect if there is no genuine and compassionate care for others"

(a)   For ordinary people: not just the ones who challenge us

(b)   As they are

1. Those who care for souls should be people who are trustworthy and who are capable of trusting others:
(a)   Trust in God, because all growth and healing comes from Him
(b)   Trust in the person, as being genuine in their seeking
(c)   Trustworthy: confidences

2. Those who care for souls should be spiritually and psychologically mature.
(a)   possessing a well-developed capacity for empathy that never confuses the experience of the other with that of the self
(b)   having a reasonable base of self-confidence
(c)   being relatively free of a need for the love of those they seek to help
(d)   being able to learn from their own experience as well as the experience of others
(e)   having a deep and ever deepening relationship with God; soul guides can only lead others to places they themselves regularly inhabit

3. Those who care for souls should be characterised by genuineness.
In "Rediscovering Pastoral Care" Alastair Campbell writes about pastoral care as integrity. He suggests that when someone seeks help from another person they will look for someone who has integrity because these are difficult issues to be faced and we need a genuine trustworthy companion "All genuine care for those assailed by doubt and guilt proceeds from this integrity and without it no ecclesiastical role or counselling technique will be of help to others". (1995:12)

So we must ask therefore, what are the characteristics of this integrity? Honesty and steadfastness: *"to possess integrity is to be incapable of compromising that which we believe to be true...(it) is to have a kind of inner strength which prevents us from bending to the influence of what is thought expedient, or calculated to win praise"* (1995:13)

4. Those who care for souls should have a deep experiential knowledge of God's grace. Otherwise, we work out of a mind-set that emphasises self-justification and works righteousness –

"Church, why would I ever go there? I was already feeling terrible about myself. They'd just make me feel worse"

670

Those who seek to follow this God by caring for his children must acquire His heart and offer his care through his Spirit.

5. Those who care for souls should be characterised by deep faith that light will eventually overcome darkness.
Not talking about a starry eyed optimism here. Faith that God will see others through their dark nights. This faith that light will ultimately overcome darkness gives the soul guide the ability to enter the pain, distress or anxieties of others without the need to fox things, content to be on the journey, perseverance: journey with children

6. Those who care for souls should be characterised by wisdom and humility.
Wise and humble! Prepared to offer advice but, *"sparingly, chiefly on invitation and with full respect for the conscience and self-directive resources of the other person"* Tolerant of silence

What other characteristics would you want to add to this list?

Who can do all this, Oden: *"It is only in the companionship of grace, drawing on resources beyond one's own, that wisdom is found for the task"*

LISTENING:

Introduction:

Beginning with experience: think of a time when you needed to talk about something really important and you weren't listened to.

How did it make you feel when person didn't listen?

Listening as a theological activity.

John 4: what effect does it have on the woman as Jesus listens to her? Can you think of other Biblical examples where God listens?

God who listens: we belong to a God who listens: 2 Kings 20: 4-5 "And before Isaiah had gone out of the middle court, the word of the Lord came to him "Turn back and say to Hezekiah...I have heard your prayer, I have seen your tears, behold I will heal you" Exodus 3

Why does listening matter?

What theological messages does listening send?

1. Acceptance
2. Worth
3. Listening is a missional activity

Bonhoeffer "Life Together"

Being a good listener demands sincere interest in others; patience, reliance on the Holy Spirit: Frank Lake cites Taylor Caldwell who wrote that: *"man's real need, his most terrible need, is for someone to listen to him, not as a 'patient' but as a human soul"*.

"He who answers before listening- that is his shame and folly" Proverbs 18:13

Do be prepared to work hard at listening (not the same as normal conversation):

1. Do beware of hearing only what you want or expect to hear, and don't make assumptions about what people are going to say (or feeling..home from hospital).

2. Do listen to how things are said, but don't spend your time mentally criticising).

3. Do ask for clarification if you haven't understood.

4. Don't think about your next contribution while another person is talking.

5. Don't interrupt, and don't finish other people's sentences for them. You could be wrong.

Listening is a basic but demanding skill. Jacobs puts it slightly differently when he says that listening stresses the "calm acceptance" of the other

Guideline 1. Listen with undivided attention, without interrupting

Purpose of active listening is to see into another person's world and help them to explore it; in order to do that we need to pay attention to and try to understand the thoughts and feelings of the other.

The aim of this is simply to practice listening, without any need to respond.
Divide into pairs. A and B
The person listening is not allowed to say anything to the speaker must not comment or ask questions.
A speaks for 5 minutes about last week- time to go into detail but no pressure to speak of anything you don't want to divulge
Time 5 minutes and then B speaks

Feedback:
What did it feel like to speak without interruption?
Which role was easier for you?

Guideline 2: Remember what has been said, including the details

Exercise: Hearing and remembering

Feedback for 3 minutes

Feedback:
How accurate was each person's memory?
Was anything omitted which felt important to the speaker?
Was there any reason why some aspects of what was said were easier to remember than others?

It is often the little things, the tiny phrases and subtle emphases which enable the listener to hear more than the obvious- ex substitution of 'but' for 'and' can make a big difference.

"I went to that lecture and I enjoyed it" is fairly innocuous- to say "I went to that lecture but I enjoyed it" is a different thing entirely.

Barriers to listening

It is easy to admit that listening is important, there are however barriers to listening. In normal conversation what are some of the things that can impair our ability to listen?

External factors

Internal factors

When listening to what the other person is saying, we may be thinking about what we are going to say next, wanting to get in with our own story, we may be distracted and thinking about something else, wanting to get away. Something the person says may trigger off our own memories, or they may say something which irritates us.

Prejudice
Jumping to conclusions
Worrying about how to respond
Not remembering

Guideline 3: Listen to the "bass line"- what is not openly said, but possibly is being felt.

Michael Jacobs describes this as "listening for the bass-line". …This then is the third level at which I am going to invite you to listen.

An interesting piece of music will have a strong melody, and when we listen the first time that may well be what we hear. But listen repeatedly and you begin to notice other features, the bass line perhaps. When a person speaks, especially when they speak about emotional matters there will be a main melody, but also a bass line.

It is often when there is a conflict between the main emotion and bass line emotions that people will seek a listening ear. It is important for the listener to be able to listen at different levels so that less acceptable, less easily expressed emotions can be brought into the open, as well as the obvious feelings.

Exercise: Listening for the bass-line

The task for the listener here is again to say nothing, except to give a few minimal prompts until the speaker has finished their story.

Speaker: How they feel about being here today

What are the feelings which you find it most difficult to hear or deal with when listening?

Empathy: not sympathy

Imagining how we would feel in a specific situation is not empathy in itself. But it is a first step. Empathy begins when we leave behind what we might think and move into what the speaker might be thinking and feeling.

Empathy is not the same as sympathy- you may or may not be sympathetic to the situation being described.

Thus empathy begins with listening to yourself- what would I feel? it moves on to finding out more information, and then enables the question to be silently asked- what is this other person feeling in this situation?

Finishing the module

As we finish this module on mission and pastoral care, think of three things which you have learnt which you want to carry with you.
1.
2.
3.

GUIDELINES FOR LISTENING AND RESPONDING *From Michael Jacobs (2000) "Swift to Hear" SPCK*

GUIDELINES FOR LISTENING

1. Listen with undivided attention, without interrupting.
2. Remember what has been said, including the details.
3. Listen to the "bass line"- what is not openly said, but possibly is being felt.
4. Watch for body language, non-verbal clues that help you to understand feelings.
5. Listen to yourself, how you might feel in a described situation, as a way of further understanding- this is a first step towards empathy.
6. Try to tolerate pauses and silences that are a little longer than is usual in conversations.
7. Create a comfortable and relaxed setting so that you can give attention to each other

GUIDELINES FOR RESPONDING

1. Use words carefully; be as accurate as possible in describing feelings and ideas that you perceive.

2. Use your empathetic understanding, again making this accurate.

3. Keep questions to a minimum unless:
You need precise information, in which case ask precise questions.
You want to open up an area, in which case ask open-ended questions.

4. Use minimal prompts "Mm", "yes" or repeat last few words.

5. Paraphrase or reflect accurately as:
    *   A way of prompting.
    *   An indication that you have been listening.
    *   A way of checking that you have heard accurately.

6. Avoid making judgements or loaded remarks.

7. Avoid changing the subject or interrupting unnecessarily.

MODULE 9: SOCIAL RESPONSIBILITY & MISSION

(Revd Albert Beah MA)

LECTURE 1: CONCEPT OF MISSION FOR COMMUNITY DEVELOPMENT

Definition:

Participants discuss their concept of mission generally (both theological and sociological perspectives) and from a pastoral perspective specifically.

A WORKING DEFINITION OF MISSION:

i) How we define *mission* determines what we do and how we do it. For example, some mainline churches state their *mission* as *To make Disciples of Jesus Christ* thereby referring concerns about hunger, social justice, and healing to other stakeholders in the business of promoting the attainment of more dignified human conditions for all men. This perspective suggests that some Christians put more premiums on *making Disciples* than on establishing *shalom*–peace and justice –for all in the world.

ii) Mission is sharing the new life in Christ. When we are baptized with Christ, we are incorporated into his death for the sins of the world. (Latourette, 1937; c.f. 2 Cor.5:17; Rom.6:8).

iii) The Messianic proclamation of the Good News with the invitation to discipleship, and insistence on the freedom people should have to respond to it (Ariarajah, 2001; *cf.* Mtt.28:19; Mk16:15)

iv) Mission is the consequence of, and a witness to, the sending of the Son by the Father, in the power of the Holy Spirit. It is a graceful response to Christ and a confession of faith. It is the response to a mandate to being called by God (Lamara, 1969).

A THEOLOGICAL PERSPECTIVE OF MISSION:

Participants discuss the story of the original sin of Adam and Eve in the Garden of Eden-the initial disobedience that caused the temporal separation of man from his creator God (Gen.3:1ff).

677

In the Old Testament period, when Yahweh (God) was the ruler, the children of Israel came to Samuel and said, "We want a king so that we can be like other nations around us." (Dt. 17:14-16, 1 Sam.8:5ff). Samuel does not hesitate to tell them what will happen when they are under the kingship of someone other than Yahweh, to point out the kinds of demands that the king would make upon them.

But the Lord said, if they want a king, give them a king. And sure enough, the rest of the prophetic witnesses – up to the time of Jesus, to the time of the early church and even today – are the record of God's struggling with his people who have asked to be put under the reign of Caesar rather than the reign of Yahweh. Today, direct parallels can be drawn from the kinds of things that Samuel warns against to the kinds of kingship that people in many parts of the world are experiencing under the rule of something, or somebody, other than God himself (c.f. 1 Sam. 8:11-18).

MISSIO DEI

The following questions come to mind:

What really does God intend for the world to which He has revealed himself in Jesus?

What is the ultimate goal of the mission Dei?

Both the Old Testament and the New Testament God, by both His Words and Deeds, claim that God's intention is to *bring the kingdom of God to expression* and *restoring His liberating domain* of authority in His kingdom on earth. The kingdom of God is the goal of the *Missio Dei.*

What is the kingdom of God?

OLD TESTAMENT PERSPECTIVE SPIRITUALIZES THE KINGDOM OF GOD.

Includes only the inner life of the individual

Includes the satisfaction of man's spiritual needs

Involves the forgiveness of sins

In my estimation, this was mission that was focused on liberating the soul of men without much attention being paid to liberating that body that houses the soul.

In the New Testament, the model of *mission* changes with the advent of Jesus. Jesus marked a significant change in the concept of *mission* as was understood in the Old Testament.

678

Jesus' ministry was characterized by *inclusiveness* and *breaking down barriers between people* (Bosch, 1996). His goal was directed toward all Israel rather than only the remnant of the faithful.

This is why one of the well-known missionary texts, the Great Commission (Mt. 28:19-20; Mk.16:15-16), cannot be divorced from the rest of the gospels.
E.g. **Matthew** envisions a mission to both Jews and Gentiles characterized by discipleship and a call to challenge *social justice.*
Luke understanding of mission highlights repentance and forgiveness as well as economic justice and peace-making;
Paul's understanding of *mission* focuses on the church as an eschatological community which works for the improvement of society while awaiting the ultimate renewal of all things with the *parousia.*

THE NEW TESTAMENT PERSPECTIVE DOES NOT LIMIT THE KINGDOM OF GOD TO THE SPIRITUAL ASPECT OF MAN.

Involves a *proclamation* and a *realization* of a **total salvation**, one which covers the whole range of human needs and destroys every pocket of evil and grief affecting mankind. It embraces heaven as well as earth, world history as well as the whole universe.

The kingdom of God is that *new order* of affairs begun in Christ which, when finally completed by him, will *involve a proper restoration not only of man's relationship to God but also of those between sexes, generations, races, and even between man and nature.* This is the message of the prophets, and this is what John saw in his visions recorded in the book of Revelation. This too is the testimony of the Apostles who join Peter, *We await a new heaven and a new earth in which righteousness dwells* (2 Peter 3:13).

Bosch emphasized that *mission* is ultimately multidimensional as a result of six *Salvific events* that are recorded in the New Testament (Bosch, 1996).
1. Christ's *incarnation*-by which he fully experienced the challenges and struggles of being human;
2. Christ's *crucifixion*-which signifies the completeness of His service and self-sacrifice;

3. Christ's *resurrection*–which conveys a message of victory and hope for humanity;

4. Christ's *Ascension*–which calls Christians to work for a new order here on the earth which issues from above;

5. The *Pentecost*-which inaugurated the era of the church as a distinct community where social renewal is made manifest;

6. The *Parousia,*-which sets the sights of the church on the imminent and full realization of God's reign.

THE LATIN CONCEPT OF MISSION.

The Latin concept of *mission* is related to what we now understand as *Missionary Work* has its origin in the *Jesuit 'Missiones'* now referred to as Latin-America. They implied from their observation of the *practice of* mission that missions go from the Christian West to the non-Christian world, to the Gentiles, the Barbarians, who were to be reached by propagating the Christian Gospel from *'the haves'* to *'the have-nots.'* (Lamara, 1969). It was, as if to say, *we have been blessed so let us share the blessing* (cf. Lk. 22: 32).In their concept, mission through the centuries were Western realities and were all the time loaded with Western connotations. To them Westernized Christianity came as a religion of the Western powers, and when Christianity appeared, the Western colonizers and their clerical counterparts themselves experienced the faiths and cults of the subjugated people as their religion. They suggest that because of the western connotation to mission, the existence of African culture was not acknowledged, hence at baptism, African names were not accepted and had to be replaced with more *Christian names.*

They contend that the whole idea of religion is Western and was superimposed upon the rest of the world. Hence, they understand *mission* as the expeditions from the *western corpus christianum* into a world that was regarded as *void* – a world full of heathenism and was be replaced by Christianity. This conception of *mission* lasted up to the 19th century when the terms *Home Mission* and *Foreign Mission* and *World Mission* emerged. Whatever, connotation is given to *mission;* it meant that *mission* was a specific arrangement designed by Christians to expand the influence of Christianity in the non-Christian world. The main ideology behind this *mission was* that the Christian world from which these *missions* were sent out was aimed at *proclaiming* the Goods News to *other* nations and to include them under the *Lordship* of Christ. This concept of mission suggests that *mission* and *missions* have been and are part and parcel of the Western expansion and dominance which had its *Spiritual counterpart* in *the expansion of Christianity* in most cases through the work of *Missionary Societies.*

For them, *mission* is understood as that work which is done by missionary organizations and their personnel. Anything they do is *mission,* either *home-mission* or *Foreign Mission* or *World Mission.* The principal aim was to strengthen the general situation of Christianity at home and abroad and so missionaries went over-the-seas to proclaim the gospel of Christ. The missionary had power at his disposal, the power of knowledge, power of possessions and perhaps also the power of the institution in his missionary work. Therefore the churches that grew out of this system have developed the idea that *mission* can only be accomplished with the acquisitions of these powers of knowledge, possessions, and the institutions.

Given the fact that there are worldwide economic structures that create the poverty of these countries, the result is that the churches in these countries will always remain poor and condemned to being dependent on the rich countries that helped to bring them into being. However, evidence gathered from the experience of African churches – churches that have sprung up without the help or the instrumentality of foreign m*issionary* churches, have given the proof that it is possible to build on a different structure.

These churches are showing more rapid growth indicators than those of our churches which have been created by foreign missionaries. The fact that the *missionary activity* is believed to have emerged as part of the mercantile (connected with trade and commercial affairs) world: the fact that the *mission* themselves are structured from the very beginning as corporations; that the model (a simple description of a system used for explaining how something works) for modern *missionary* movement is the corporate (recognized by law as a single unit) model; and therefore that they are the companions from the very start of the whole capitalist (a person who owns or controls a lot of wealth and uses it to produce more wealth) expansion; helps us to better understand the new form that the *missionary* work has taken.

Just as we have the internalization of capital, so today, we have the internalization of *mission*, with a type of structure which is a counterpart to the multinational company. The phenomenon of *third world mission* is a worldwide phenomenon. Mission coming from Asia, from Africa, from Latin America is the new trend in *mission* today. The missionary expressions coming from third world missions are the fruits, as it were, of the poor churches. The missionaries from these countries have gone out in very heroic manner with very limited resources to win souls for the Lord.

ATTEMPTS TO REFORM THE LATIN CONCEPT OF MISSION.

In recent times, energetic attempts have been made to reform and renew the Latin concept of *mission* by unloading it of its *imperialist, colonialist Western connotations.* One of the several attempts has been to integrate *mission* and *Church* and understand *mission history* as the *mission of the Church.* However, this orientation is yet to diminish greatly the Western nature of *mission.* The question still remains as to whether the commission to *mission* is accepted as the responsibility of the Whole Church or are Christians viewing it as the responsibility of some members of the church only? Or is it just a matter of words? Have our churches actually become instruments for the *mission of God?* The factual situation is that the *mission-oriented* church has not changed much. It is believed to have retained the same principles and practices that brought it into being – caring for its own members – in most cases the respectable members, not the lost sheep, the social outcastes, the victims of wars and natural disasters and social injustice. Instead, we still have the same old parishes, same church structures, same liturgies and dress codes that do not quite reflect the cultural codes and belief systems of host communities and the current dynamics of the world it is meant to service. Consequently, the church is believed to be reproducing not by virtue of *evangelization* or *mission work* but by virtue of *nature* and *biology, just as ancient Israel did.*

WHY MISSION?

The dynamic (characterized by constant change) of the church's mission comes from a *deep awareness of the suffering of a human race* steeped in *ignorance of God,* torn apart by *hatred and conflict of every sort,* alienated by material and spiritual poverty *in all its forms.*

Together with the whole of creation, man experiences a profound *nostalgia* (longing for things of the past) for a *paradise lost,* in which *justice, well-being* and *peace* would prevail. The church's responsibility is to bring to this tormented and enslaved world the vigorous response of God to its questionings and rebellions. This response is the living Truth of Christ which reaches down into the very depths of man's being and liberates him. It is also the gift of the infinite love and compassion of God who ignores no human suffering and distress, and towards whom the blood and tears of the oppressed arise in mute appeal.

WHOSE MISSION?

The mission is God's mission revealed to us in God, the son, Jesus Christ; and in the church, the Body of Christ; and is powered by God, the Holy Spirit. The *mission is God's,* he could have done it without our involvement but he has allowed us to participate in the kingdom building process because we are co-heirs and co-possessors with Jesus of His Kingdom.

Mission to whom?
✓   Initially meant to restore the broken relationship of Israel (the lost sheep of the house of Israel) with God (Matthew 15:24).
✓   After His resurrection, Jesus sent his disciples beyond the frontiers of Israel (Mt. 28:19)
✓   To bear witness to the ends of the earth (Acts 1:8)

WHAT POWERS MISSION?

God, the Holy Spirit–But he commands them to wait in Jerusalem until he sends upon them the *Father's promised gift* and they are *armed with the power from above.* (Luke 24:49).
Rejoicing therefore, in the communion of the Holy Spirit and marvelling at the resurrection, the church proclaims to the world the reign of *Jesus Christ crucified (1 Cor. 2 :2), the reign of* him who is and who was and who is to come (Rev.1:4; 1:8; 4:8)

MISSION FOR HOW LONG?

Until the reign of God has come (through the incarnation of Jesus Christ) and is coming (through the second coming of Jesus Christ) to the world by the community of repentant and pardoned sinners, the Church. However, since the church is given the presence of the Holy

Spirit as guarantee, the kingdom is in our midst, the END–is already accessible to the world. The kingdom is already at work in the world, what a joyful hope.

HOW SHOULD CHRISTIANS PARTICIPATE IN MISSION?

The calling to *mission* should remind us that God is not the answer, but the source of the call, the call to be, to follow the way of Christ and through Christ, to be sent to the very ends of the earth, to proclaim God's reign, to forgive and to heal. It is *mission* out of concern for others especially those who are weakest.

Those who are called to participate in the *mission* of God are to speak personally to Christians (for Christians too need renewal) and non-Christians alike, inviting all to *bet* their lives on Jesus Christ. The invitation of the king is *to follow him, to suffer with him, to hope with him*. Indeed the struggle of the kingdom is too serious to be left to *nominal Christians*. For this, we need individual commitment.

The battle of Jesus Christ is to deliver humankind from the power of darkness and commit our lives to the communication of the good news of this liberating king to our neighbours. Our personal commitment to Jesus should include *legislative lobbying; dispute counselling; labour; education; visitations (home meetings, hospitals , hospices, prisons, ghettos, universities, colleges and schools, etc.) network formations; public advocacy, etc.*

Conclusion:

The desire of God for *mission* is that:

the God of love, not ourselves is the acting subject of *mission*

The crucified and risen Jesus, not ourselves, is the entire content of mission.

For God was in Christ reconciling the world to himself (2 Cor 5:19) Therefore, to be in Christ our saviour is to be connected to all. That is to Jesus, the crucified and raised son of God to whom belongs *all authority* in heaven (Mtt.28:18). All power belongs to him by right of his obedience to God, serving others even to death on the cross. This is our witness. The future belongs in no human hands. It is in the hands of the one who declared, *I am with you all the days*. That promise is our assurance as we obediently go, singing Alleluia and seeking everyone to participate in the kingdom building work of God.

(Participants discuss their concept of ministry.)

The Christian ministry refers to the religious services of individuals or congregations of redeemed and repentant people of God, the Church.

In the *Old Testament, the word ministry* was used to highlight the exclusive privilege of a priestly caste that ministered to the spiritual needs of the people of Israel. (Numbers 3: 10ff; 3: 5ff – they carried the Ark and the tabernacle of the Lord). They entered the Holy of Holies in the temple to offer sacrifices on behalf of their communities and themselves for the remission of their sins.

In the *New Testament, however, ministry* describes the *more excellent* ministry of Christ (Heb. 8: 6 - 13). Today, the meaning of *ministry* can be applied to the spiritual service rendered by prophets, teachers and preachers (Acts 13:2; Rom. 15: 16) or the body of believers as a whole (1 Peter 2 : 9).

In essence, ministry is a generic term that refers to all forms of *spiritual service* within the church.

Originally, the term *ministry* was understood to refer to the *mission* of Apostles and Evangelists whose *principal responsibility* was the proclamation to the God News to all nations, baptizing and teaching those who believed them and accepted the free invitation they pronounced for the believers to inherit the Kingdom of God together with Jesus Christ (*cf.* Mark16:15; Mtt.28:19).

This position, however, took the form of a more permanent local ministry of *Pastors, teachers, administrators and helpers* who appear to have been appointed by the apostles (Acts 6). However, Rom.12 and 1Cor.12 imply that the church as a spirit filled community produces its own organ of ministration. Ephesians 4:11 also suggest that the ministry is given to the church by Christ. Therefore, while Christ is the *source* of all *authority* (Mt. 28: 18) and the *pattern* of *all service*, the church as a whole is only a recipient of His divine communion. We need to note here that God does not need us to fulfil his purpose on earth but that He has given us an opportunity to participate in the kingdom building process with Jesus, our co-heir and co-possessor of the kingdom of God. The choice is ours to either grab or let-go this divine opportunity to serve God.

CHARACTERISTICS OF THE MORE EXCELLENT MINISTRY OF CHRIST:

The pattern of the Christian ministry is provided by the life of Christ who came not to receive service but to give it by laying his life as a ransom for many (Mt.20:28; Mk. 10:45; Jn. 13:4ff). The ministry of Christ, following the example of his Father, renders a humble but *loving service* to the needs of humanity at large in the same spirit as that in which angels (Mt. 4:11; Mk. 1:13) and women (Mt.27:55) ministered to the Lord.

Such services included –
a. Service to Jesus on earth – such service is rendered to the persons of the needy (Mtt.25:44). E.g. The *poor; sick; insane; beggars; touts; victims of wars, rape, natural disasters; prisoners of conscience, political discrimination; injustices of society, etc.*
b. Service to the saints (Rom 15:25; 1 Cor 16:15; 2 Cor. 8:4;, 9:1; Heb. 6:10)
c. A mutual service within the fellowship of Christ's body (1 Pe 4:10)
d. A proclamation of the gospel (1 Peter 1:12)
e. Service of reconciliation (2 Cor.5:18)

WHO POWERS THOSE WHO ARE CALLED TO THE MINISTRY OF GOD?

Ministry is a gift of God (Acts 20:24; Col. 4:17; 1Tim. 1:12; 1 Pet. 4:11; Rom. 12:7; I Tim. 3:8; 2 Tim.4:5**). This work of service has as its great object, the edification of the body of Christ (Eph 4:12) and it is God Himself who calls men to His exciting service that empowers them through the work of the Holy Spirit. The God who calls men to service equips and sustains them through His grace in the service.

Types of Ministry
In its earliest form, the Christian ministry is *charismatic* (A spiritual gift or supernatural endowment whose exercise witnesses to the presence of the Holy Spirit. Some missiologists consider it as a repeat of the Pentecostal experience -Acts 2). This is why when Paul laid his hands on some ordinary believers after baptism, they were able to prophesy (Acts19:6).

Paul gives us three lists of spiritual ministry in his epistles to the churches in Rome; Corinth; and Ephesus as following:

Romans 12:6-8	*1Cor.12:28*	*Ephesians 4:11*
Prophecy	Apostles	Evangelists
Service	Prophets	Apostles
Teaching	Teachers	Prophets
Exhorters	Miracle workers	Pastors
Contributing to almsgiving	Healing	Teachers
Aiding-doing acts of mercy	Helpers	Visitation of sick/poor
Administrators	Speaking in tongues	

The various gifts listed in these passages should be considered as functions or ways of *serving* rather than regular or stereotyped offices. One may act in several capacities but his/her capacity to fulfil any depends on the prompting of the Holy Spirit. All Christians are in effect called to minister in their various capacities (Rom.15:27; Phil.2:17; Phm13:1; 1 Peter2:16) and it is for this reason that God equips people with special talents (Eph 4:11ff). Accordingly, there are Christians who minister to congregations; others are in the caring ministry, e.g., development, relief work, while some others still are in specialized ministries. Methodists believe in the *Priesthood of all believers.* Today we talk about:

A. *APOSTOLIC MINISTRY:*

Include the *ministry of the 12 Apostles;* Paul; James (the Lord's brother who also saw the risen Lord – Gal 1:9); Barnabas – Paul's fellow evangelist (Acts14:14; 1Cor.9:5ff); Andronicus and Junias (Rom.16:7).

Primary qualification of an Apostle included:
✓   must have been an eye witness of Christ's earthly ministry especially of the resurrection (Acts1:21-22);
✓   must have been in some way commissioned by Christ *either* in the days of his flesh (Mtt.10:5; 28:19) *or* after He was risen from the dead *(Acts 1:24; 19:5);*

The work of an Apostle included:
1. Apostles and elders met in council to decide a common policy for the church (Acts15:6ff)

2. Apostles are sent out as delegates from the original congregation to superintend some new development in another locality (Acts8:14ff);
3. The main work of an apostles was to act as a missionary for the propagation of the gospel in which capacity their labours should be confirmed by signs of divine approval (2 Cor.12:12)

B. EVANGELISTIC MINISTRY

The work of an evangelist is similar to that of apostles as they exercise unrestricted mission except in so far as it lacks the special qualifications for the higher function of apostles (e.g., **Philip**, Acts12:8; **Timothy**, 2 Tim 4:5).

C. PROPHETIC MINISTRY

A gift of intermittent occurrence even though some individual were so regularly endowed with it that they formed a special class of prophets such as were found in Jerusalem (Acts15:320; Antioch (Atcs13:1); Corinth (1 Cor14:29). Other prophets named included Judas and Silas (Acts 15:32); Agabus (Acts12:10); Anna (Luke 2:36); and the pretended prophetess Jczebel (Rev.2:20). Their work in essence was to provide *edification, exhortation* and *comfort* to their communities. As such a prophet's message must agree with the fundamental teaching of the gospel as contained in 1 Cor 12:1-13; 1 Thess 5:20; 1 John 4:1-3.
Work of a Prophet included:

o   Could issue specific direction (Acts13:1-2)
o   Could foretell the future (Acts 11:28)
o   His messages were more profitable than *glossolalia*

The work of prophets was extremely controlled by those possessing it, otherwise prophets could be dismissed as one of the false prophets/pretenders whose coming had been foreseen by Christ (Matt.7:15). Other ministries include:
Healing; Teaching; Administrators; Helpers; Deacons/Deaconesses, etc.

D. PASTORAL MINISTRY:

Is connected with the *care of the flock* as an outstanding part of ministerial duty (Jn 21:15-17; Acts 20:28; 1 Pe 5:2); with the preaching of the word (1 Cor.3:1-2) as the bread of life (Jn 6:38); with pure nourishing milk (1 Pe 2:2). Christ the good shepherd (Jn10:11), the great Bishop of man's soul (1 Pe 2:25) is the pattern of the ministry. The parable in Luke 12:41-48 implies that this ministry is to continue in the church until Christ's return.

Pastoral ministry should therefore be conceived as a lifelong activity that requires the Christian minister to live as a parable (a short story that teaches a moral or spiritual lesson, especially one of those told by Jesus as recorded in the Bible) or as an open book read and interpreted by everyone for guidance and inheritance of the kingdom of God. Therefore, the pastoral ministry must mirror the critical issues in the life and ministry of Christ from the desert experience to the entry into Jerusalem, in terms of his incarnation, temptation, crucifixion, resurrection, ascension, and the parousia. This is the central principle in pastoral ministry, and the one that integrates every pastoral duty.

Clergy Ethics:
The underlying questions: 'Who ought clergy to be' and 'what clergy ought to do' should be discussed by the class to share their experiences in the pastoral ministry.
The term clergy: refers to all ministers, ordained or licensed, who have standing in the Christian Church (Disciples of Christ) and who minister within their communities for Christ.

We note, however, that different religions and denominations have different standards for the behaviour of their clergy. For example, a Catholic priest can drink alcohol, but not get married, while many mainline churches hold precisely opposite requirements–expecting their ministers to *drink for their stomach's sake* and can *get married.* Most frown on sex outside of marriage. These behaviours and several others must be handled carefully by church management in order not to give the wrong impressions to outsiders.

The whole church receives the call of God to embody and carry forth Christ's ministry in the world. For the sake of the mission of the Jesus Christ and the most effective witness of the Gospel, and in consideration of their influence as representatives of Christ, ministers should be willing to dedicate themselves completely to the highest ideals of Christian life and standards. Furthermore, we must note that

689

the church workers are called to exercise responsible self-control in personal habits, and to be persons in whom the community can place trust and confidence. Violation of the ministerial relationship by unethical behaviour is a sin against God and an offense to the Church (*Ref.* Constitutions of the various churches).

Clergy ethics is understood to be imposed upon clergy by their vocation (calling), of which ordination is an outward sign of professional status. For Amitai, ordination is a promise of God's character-forming work in the life of the vocational minister (Amitai, 1993). A lot of emphasis is put on the *cruciality of character* for faithful Christian ministry not because clergy are fated to be some upper crust of morally exemplary Christians, but because their vocation, as leaders of a countercultural community, demands certain morally strenuous attributes.

The whole of Paul's letters in Romans, Corinthians, Ephesians, and Philippians are full of examples of moral teachings that Jesus demands from His followers. I have singled out the following to help our reflection on this crucial and sensitive topic in the life of the clergy.

As (God) who called you is holy, be holy yourselves in all your conduct ... tend the flock of God that is in your charge ... Not under compulsion but willingly ... Not for sordid gain but eagerly ... Do not lord it over those in your charge, but be examples to the flock. You know that we who teach shall be judged with greater strictness. (1Peter 1:15; 5:2-3; James 3:1b, NRSV).

Be perfect, therefore, as your heavenly Father is perfect (Matt5:48); and Be merciful just as your Father is merciful (Luke 6:36, NIV).

These verses demand that all Christians must display their heavenly Father's mercy and even his moral perfection.

He reflects the glory of God and bears the very stamp of his nature, upholding the universe by his word of power (Heb.1:3; cf. 1Cor.11:1); Therefore, be imitators of God, as beloved children. And walk in love, as Christ loved us and gave himself up for us, a fragrant offering and a sacrifice to God. (Eph.5:1ff). This verse confirms that Jesus bears the *stamp* of the Father; the call to imitate him comes with equal force to all Christians.

So whether you eat or drink or whatever you do, do it all for the glory
of God. Do not cause anyone to stumble, whether Jews, Greeks or the
church of God–even as I try to please everybody in every way. For I
am not seeking my own good but the good of many, so that they may
be saved. Follow my example, as I follow the example of Christ
(1Cor.10:13-11:1).

But just as you excel in everything–in faith, in speech, in knowledge, in complete earnestness and in your love for us, see also that you also excel in this grace of giving (2Cor.8:7).

Do nothing out of selfish ambition or vain conceit, but in humility consider others better than yourself (Phil.2:1-11).
Flee from sexual immorality. All other sins a man commits are outside his body, but he who sins sexually sins against his own body (1Cor.6:18).

Jesus said, Feed my lambs, Take care of my sheep ... Feed my sheep... (Jn21:15–19).

Sadly, today both clergy and lay are sometimes feeding on God's children instead of feeding them the word of God through:

Flagrant, repeated, or serious violations of ministerial codes,
Violation of confidentiality,
Failure to be truthful in sharing information provided to church authorities, congregations, our employers in the secular jobs;
Unauthorized use of church/employer funds, for personal purposes,
Substance abuse,
Professional misconduct of a sexual nature, which may occur both within and outside the marriage relationship.

TODAY, WE HEAR ABOUT:

Clergy dating those directly served by their ministry-Sexual contact and/or sexual harassment between a minister and a congregant, client, employee of the congregation, student, intern, Child or anyone whom

691

the minister has a professional or pastoral relationship is sinful, unethical, and unprofessional. Various sources on the subject of clergy sexual abuse estimate that 15-20% of clergy have sexually abused someone but that sadly, many of such cases are unreported ignored, allowed to continue, or hidden by church leadership. As a matter of fact, it has been observed that many churches do not even have established policies for handling sexual abuse allegations.

Whether the victim is a child, teen or adult, the harm caused by sexual abuse in the ministerial relationship can last a lifetime. In recent years, the problem of sexual abuse by clergy and other religious leaders has surfaced in the media and the courts. Unfortunately, our religious institutions, whether due to ignorance, denial or deception, have not always responded to support victims and hold perpetrators accountable.

The result is that trust is betrayed, boundaries are violated; body and soul are broken and victims of abuse often feel abandoned by God. Some have even taken their own lives out of frustration and shame.

CHALLENGES FOR MINISTRY IN OUR WORLD:

The world is experiencing a population explosion. Recent population statistics has put the population of the world to a little over 6.5 billion people. This rate in the population boom of the world has so far exceeded human imagination and population scientists are trying to discover new ways of controlling the world's population so that our world does not spin out of its orbit. Similarly, the world is believed to be experiencing an Evangelism explosion giving rise to the emergence of many charismatic churches, majority of them are Pentecostals.

Unfortunately, the spiritual activities of some of these new churches are such that they are, in my estimation, only fishing in the ponds of mainly mainline churches. Consequently, only very few members of their congregations are new converts. Nevertheless, research has shown that the rate at which the population explosion is increasing far outweighs the evangelism explosion and this has resulted in a huge gulf between the reached and the unreached for *mission* and *ministry* of the Church. The mission of the church is to cater for the spiritual and material needs of those that are yet to be reached through the *ministry* of the church.

The fast growth of Christianity in Africa is reported to be second only to China which has a population of 1.3 billion people among whom are 202 million children (BBC News, Science in Action programme, May 2006). Statistics have shown that in some African countries up to 90% of their population is claiming to be Christians (Amitai, 2004). Development research results have indicated that Africa is a continent that is blessed with vast deposits of natural and human resources for her empowerment. But just as its natural resources are exploited by more development nations so also experience has shown that Africa is being drained of her enlightened human resources (her productive population) for want of better conditions of service. While this estimate is true, Africa ironically is heavily besieged by *social, economic and ecological problems* some of which are beyond description of any type. I reckon that, Africa has carved out for herself a unique socio-economic position on the world's economic scale.

TODAY IN AFRICA

If Africa is not last from the top, then Africa is first from the bottom *of every measurable index of economic development in the world.* As one travels across Africa, one can easily see evidence of poverty in: the destruction of lives and properties as a result of avoidable wars; extreme hunger and famine; diseases of various descriptions and dimension; malnutrition; high mortality and low life expectancy rates; low human development indexes; poor infrastructural development; poor shelter; poor health facilities and unhealthy sanitary conditions. And the list goes on and on, and on…..

In effect, Africa has been described in some circles as a continent of deprived people (deprived of their culture and wealth) who are emotionally, psychologically, and spiritually fragile and dangerously vulnerable to the challenges of the dynamics of this world.

SOME OF THE QUESTIONS PEOPLE, INCLUDING CHRISTIANS ARE ASKING TODAY INCLUDE:

What has caused these unbearable conditions in a continent that is experiencing exponential Christian growth?

Why is it that the church's values we continue to present to the world are not having maximum positive impact on the attitude of people and therefore not affecting Africa?

Is the Gospel good news for Africa?

Where is the abundant life that Jesus promised His followers in Africa?

Are Africans to expect abundant life only in heaven?

Why have the teachings of Christian values not helped to wipe out corruption, injustices, exploitation of employees by employers through bad labour policies in our societies today?

Why are national elections not conducted freely and fairly in most parts of the continent?

Why have new waves of constitutional reviews and the concept of third *termism* emerged in our political agenda?

Do Christians not care if Africa perishes?

Is it because Christians are too preoccupied with leading their congregations along the paths of righteousness for his name's sake (*cf.*Ps23:3) without caring much about providing the necessary conditions of life that would empower the body which carries the souls of the less privileged members of our societies so that they too would feel that they belong to the human race and could share not only in its woes and sorrows but also in its joys and peace?

HOW CAN THE CHURCH MINISTER IN SUCH A SITUATION?

It is my considered view that the responsibility of the church to ensure that her ministers are **healthy *psychologically, emotionally, and spiritually,*** so that they are less likely to be at risk of unethical conduct or professional misconduct of any nature, should be taken more seriously by the management of our churches. For example, they should make sure that:

Ministers, have adequate preparation and education for helping those under their care. We should be reminded of the common joke that the *Pew* is becoming much stronger than the *pulpit.* Whatever the interpretation of this statement is, it should be given the attention it deserves if ministers are to be given the due recognition and respect they deserve from their congregants.

Ministers, are encouraged to participate, at least every three years, in refresher training programmes organized by the church, with the hope of establishing and maintaining appropriate boundaries in ethical training and guidelines.

The church ensures that ministers understand that it is their professional responsibility to set appropriate boundaries and preserve the sacred trust of their office, and that confidentiality is strictly maintained.

Discipline is maintained within the constitutional provisions of the church without fear or favour.

LECTURE 3: CONCEPT OF COMMUNITY

(Participants discuss their concept of a community and list some examples of communities in their environment.)

WHEN THE TERM COMMUNITY IS USED, THE FIRST NOTION THAT TYPICALLY COMES TO MIND IS A PLACE IN WHICH PEOPLE KNOW AND CARE FOR ONE ANOTHER.

Some definitions:

a)   A group of people living in a particular local area having ethnic or cultural or religious characteristics in common–e.g. The Christian Community of the apostolic age–they share ownership of property/possessions and interest.

b)   A set of people with some shared elements – in a particular group who live in the same area. The substance of shared element varies widely, from a situation to interest, to lives, to values. The term is generally used to evoke a sense of collectivism.

c)   The aggregation of populations of different species within a specified location in space and time. A society of people having common rights and privileges, or common interests, civil, political, etc. or living under the same laws and reputation.

d)   The aggregation of persons with common characteristics such as geographic, professional cultural, religious, or of socio-economic similarities.

e)   A group of people who reside in a specific location, share governments and often have a common cultural and historical heritage.

f)   A collection of individuals who are bound together by natural will and a set of shared ideas and ideals. (Virtual library-virtual communities)

Manifestations of a community:
- Location (area)
- shared interests, challenges, common bonds
- generational considerations e.g. race, ethnicity, age, family
- collectivism / aggregation

CHRISTIAN PERSPECTIVE OF COMMUNITY

In order that God's will may be done on earth as it is in Heaven (Mt.6:9ff) the joys of the kingdom of God must be experienced by all who come to know Him as their saviour and Lord. In order that men and women may come to the knowledge of God, there must *first of all be a community*. It is in a community setting that a person meets his/her God mainly through the sharing of experience with one another. (Acts 1:1-11 – a family meeting of Jesus and Disciples; Acts2:42-47 – fellowship of believers; Acts4:32-5:11 – sharing of possession; Acts6:1-7 – the appointment of seven deacons)

Christians are a chosen race, a royal people, a people appointed by God, a holy nation, a people belonging to God and must be seen as a community that is set aside for the purposes of God (Jn15:16,19; 1 Peter 2:9; Ps33:12; 2 Th.2:13). Christian mission should therefore take the form of a community, an environment:

- in which God's rule is recognized,
- where the values of;
- justice
- peace and   } operate
- love

In this way, the mission of the church then becomes one of invitation into the community, and within the community, to sharing, solidarity. The Christian mission becomes one of creating that environment in which God's rule is – recognized; to which people are welcome; and in which, if they so desire, can belong to it.

When Jesus formed the twelve disciples into a community, He taught them to pray saying "Our Father" (Mtt.6:9ff); He sent them out two by two (Mk6:7). He spoke of his intention to build a church (Matt.16:18). Several of His teachings in the synoptic gospel (e.g., Mt.18:15ff and Mt. 10:41-45) assume that the disciplines will have a community existence. I am of the opinion that the aim here was to constitute a community worthy of the name of the people of God, which would become a force in history for the achievement of God's purposes.

One of the most obvious facts is that individuals must be seen in the context of a community. Even though men and women are called to be individual Christians they are, as a matter of fact, called into the body of Christ, the people of God. So in relating to the world, the basic Christian identity is community. This means that the basic theological concern has to do with the Christian Community in the structure of society. In this way, pastoral nurture and political involvement, personal devotion and public witness, evangelism and social action, are brought together.

I believe that for Christian mission to be very effective, it must be done through a team approach. The congregation that does not have roots in the world cannot be a community in which man meets his God, for the simple reason that man lives in this world and cannot meet Him elsewhere. Hence, for mission to be effective, it must deal with people in the context of their life situations.

COMMUNITY SOLIDARITY AROUND CHRIST

Conversion means turning to Christ and identifying with him; it also means community solidarity around Christ. In other words conversion to Christ means that a new convert *takes his/her place with other members of the community around Christ Jesus*. As a matter of fact, the *most authentic way for anyone* to express identity with Christ is to *share Christian solidarity with those around Christ*. The solidarity of Christians around Christ is meaningful only if the centrality of Christ amidst his community is a realized fact. It should be a community in which Christ is recognized for his divinely wise counselling and Christian instruction to the non-Christian. A community in which Christ becomes the centre of all that goes on there, in other words, a Christian community is one in which everything revolves around Christ.

In the Christian community, Christ becomes the wise and counselling leader around whom life and all activities of the community find meaning, and where all are equal in the sight of God.

The solidarity of Christian was characteristic of the primitive church in Jerusalem, Antioch (Acts11:26) and other early churches. Luke gives us an idea of what happened to those who were added to the primitive church each day in Jerusalem. "They devoted themselves to the apostles teaching and fellowship, breaking of bread and prayers … And the Lord added to their number daily those who were being saved." (Acts2:42). Indeed a characteristic of conversion is a willingness of the converts to be involved in the Christian communities where they find themselves. Today, Christians participate in sharing their experiences in small groups such as Class meetings, Local preachers, Bible study groups, Prayer groups etc.

In the New Testament, proclaiming the messianic message is always accompanied by gathering, preserving and adding to the people of God (c.f. Lk 9:17). When Jesus invites us to become his disciple, he calls us to join a community and become members of the people of God, and not to stand isolated alone. Jesus calls *Zacchaeus a son of Abraham (Lk19:9)* and the woman he healed in the synagogue, *Abraham's daughter (Lk13:16)*. His interest was not merely in converting individuals but in forming a new people. Having seen that the synagogue *establishment* rejected him, he immediately began to form a new community and called the Apostles out from the ranks of his disciples to become the founders of this new fellowship (Lk6:13).
The apostles carried on the work begun by Jesus. They established new communities of faith among the various people they met. It was a community which bore the stamp of God's own possession. The factors which united them were not the economic or political or cultural ties which usually bind human communities together; instead, they emerged from the ranks of Israel and Gentiles by the words, deed, and spirit of the Messiah and existed only in complete dependence on him, its shepherd and King.

Jesus calls it, cares for it, and frees it through the forgiveness of sins and the renewal which proceeds from him. It is these people that he desires to employ as means of realizing his world embracing plans. Peter reminds us '… but you are a chosen race, a royal priesthood, a holy nation, God's people that you may declare the wonderful deeds of him who called you people; once you had not received mercy but now you have received mercy" (1 Pe 2:9-10).

Our responsibility to new converts:

Christian converts need to feel welcomed as they take their place in a community gathered around Christ and are empowered to share their solidarity with stronger members of the family. They need to feel that there are those who are prepared to share their personal burden with in confidence and receive their attention and can respond in such a way that others are led to experience a life changing condition in Him. New converts should be given the opportunity to perceive the reality of Christ in their own lives as they participate in the solidarity of the community gathered around Christ.

LECTURE 4: CONCEPT OF DEVELOPMENT

WHAT IS DEVELOPMENT?

(Participants discuss the meaning of development.)

Development is an overused term and its meaning vary from one community to another and among individuals including development practitioners. For some people, development means increase in national wealth, for some others it represents improving the wellbeing of the majority of the population, for some others still, it means increasing the economic security of people.

Whatever definition one adopts, development is a process that should lead to a positive changes in the socio-economic and environmental conditions of people in their communities. Such developments can be temporal or permanent (sustainable – it goes on for a long period of time).

A brief historical Perspective of Development.

In the 1940s and 1950s, development concept was associated with purely economic processes that increased the production or consumption level of a nation or region. In fact, the term consistently used was economic development, leaving aside any discussion of social, personal and other aspects especially when most writings on the subject came from applied economics whose main concerns were for the rebuilding of the production systems in the countries that were devastated by the 2nd World War, and thereafter, in the world's poorest countries, now generally referred to a developing countries.

However, this understanding of development was limited in that:
Indicators of wealth which reflect the quantity of resources available to a society, provide no information about the allocation of these resources. For example, there is usually limited information on:
Ratio of distribution of income among social groups; about shares of resources used to provide free health and educational services; about the effects of production and consumption on people's environment,

This implies that even tough countries can have similar average incomes they can differ substantially when it comes to determining the quality of life of their peoples in terms of: Access to education, health care, employment opportunities, availability of clean air and safe drinking water, the threat of crimes, and so on, as different countries have different priorities in their development polices.

The aim of development:
The aim of development is to raise the income level or welfare needs of beneficiaries and development aid should help to reduce inequalities that are created as a result of bad governance or geographic conditions.

Sustainable Development:
Sustainable development is a term widely used today even though the notion is still rather new and lacks a uniform interpretation. Important as it is, the concept of sustainable development is still been developed and the definition of the term being revised, extended, and refined. Main components of sustainable development include:

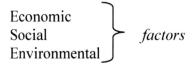

Economic
Social   } *factors*
Environmental

I perceive sustainable development as initiatives that are ongoing; or can continue along the same line for long period even when external interests are minimized or stopped. The commonly accepted classical definition among development specialists is that development is sustainable if it

"meets the needs of the present generation without compromising the ability of future generations to meet their own needs" (UNWCED, 1987).

This definition implies that current development initiatives must be planned in such a way that the values enjoyed by present generation in both built up or natural environments are not prejudices or sacrificed for short term goals so that future generations too would benefit from it. Development initiatives should ensure that the sum total of decisions taken today do not substantially deny future generations the best of today's environment.

Sustainable development demands that both project proponents and potential donors and the public, including project beneficiaries are fully aware of and gainfully participate in the administration/decisions of the development process. Where this is not the case, it can be hard to conceive that such development could be sustainable as people would fail to claim ownership of the development process and therefore willingly participate in its sustenance.

SOME SPATIAL THEORIES OF DEVELOPMENT.

The drive for improvements in human conditions, personal and social wellbeing of individuals and communities have always being the concern of researchers, governments, governmental functionaries, civil society movements and other social groups. It has also been the concern of development theorists who seek to understand the combination of variables involved in development practices with a view to controlling them to enhance sustainability of community programmes. Accordingly, some theories have been advanced to explain why some nations development faster than others and how development impulses move across international, national, regional and district boundaries to improve the socio-economic conditions of people living in distant communities.

Two spatial version of development models have been extensively used to explain how development, starting in one place moves out to other places using capital, land and labour, as the basic factors of development.

The **Right wing (RW)** and **Left wing (LW) Models of regional development** use capital and labour, the two mobile factors of development to explain the main causes of regional imbalances in the distribution of the economic wealth of the world.

A: RIGHT WING MODEL: (2 SPATIAL VERSIONS–GROWTH POLES AND CENTER-PERIPHERY VERSIONS):

(Neoclassical; Liberal View, Orthodox view–Proposed by Williamson 1965; François Perroux 1966; Priedmann 1966): These development scholars proposed that regional inequalities arise through the working of normal forces in the course of capitalist development, and disappear also through the working out of the same economic forces.

They described how countries change over time in their degree of income variations between centres and indicated that interregional difference are thought to be small at the early stages of development. They proposed that as some development impulse is felt at one point, perhaps a port city or the main industrial centre, differences grew between the regions, as the other regions, perhaps rural regions, maintained the practice of subsistent agriculture.

They reasoned that as the development process reaches a high point in presumably the central region (due to say technological advances); the development impulse begins to diffuse to the other regions which had remained at the level of subsistence. In this context, the development impulse moves across regions.

As a consequence, the centre may set up the first manufacturing industry and accumulate wealth which affects the build-up of services and administration in the centre city and over time, the centre attracts the productive population and raw materials from the rural areas. The reason is that it is the centre that has the technology to process raw materials and employ more labour to increase production – a process referred as centripetal movement of resources from the centre to the peripheral areas.

When growth poles begin to experience high build ups they begin to send back their products to where the process began and when the excesses explodes, the development process is reversed to the areas outside the core – a process referred to as centrifugal movement of resources due to the very forces that attracted them to the care areas.

This idea can be diagrammatically presented as follows:

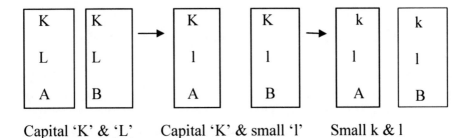

Capital 'K' & 'L'   Capital 'K' & small 'l'   Small k & l

A – REPRESENTS THE GROWTH POLE/CENTRE;

B – THE PERIPHERY AREAS;

K – CAPITAL;

L - LABOUR.

For the diffusion of development, the agents of development are centres, most typically large cities and from them development impulses spread out to periphery areas. In these cities or centres is accumulated wealth, market structures, advance technical know – how and information system, entrepreneurship, management skills, Etc.
They become responsible for the innovation of technology and for their diffusion outwards in a process of modernizations. The industries of these centres offer the high wages that attract migrant labour and take the productive human resources of the country from the rural areas centre.

In the long run, however, labour and skills acquire higher value in the periphery and are attracted away from the centre to the regions.
Capital too, which was accumulated at the centre in various ways in the initial stages of development moves out to other regions because of the higher returns there:

Friedman (1966) postulates that the:

Outward movement of CAPITAL in the form of factories which are too confined in the centre and see CHEAPER labour and LAND in the periphery in the outer response and inward movement of labour as migration from rural areas.

It is these movements that tend to reduce the inequalities of income between regions. Industries move to areas with slight populations but massive natural resources.

B. The Left Wing model – (A dependency model or Radical view).

Based on the conception that as one region continues to develop, it creates dependency tendencies so that other regions become permanently depended on it. The proponents accepted the explanation given by the RW model for the unequal distribution of the world's wealth among different regions of the world but that for it to be complete, it must take on board the crucial element of *power play* of individuals and organizations that are involved in controlling the course of development.

They argued that development especially in the third world does not depend too much on the matter of abstract capital and labour and land, but that it depends crucially on the controlling forces at play. They identified for example, the *landowners; Administrators of colonial land; Colonizing forces of the metropolitan county (Internal colonialists)* as the main forces that determine which areas develop faster than others.

They argued that if power is equally possessed between states, there would be equal development and that the wealthier nations use *power* to create a dependency syndrome forcing poorer nations to remain poor and become dependent on them. They argued that the power structures of the less developed world are oriented in such a way that internal colonialists promote the interests and policies of the more developed nations on whom they depend for their survival. In their view, missionary work was part and parcel of the mercantile world which began with the *explorers, then came missionaries, then the traders, and finally the colonial administrators.*

BIBLICAL PERSPECTIVE

The story of the missionary journeys recorded in the Acts of the Apostles–the seed for this journey was sown in Jerusalem and was extended to other parts of the world.

(Participants discuss their concept of Community Development.)

All communities have numerous distinct groupings of people. Through these groups, people act to achieve various interests and goals. Finding common needs and connecting these individual groups is central to community development. Meeting these general needs contributes to the greater well-being of the entire locality, while significantly enhancing local structures and/or institutions as well as the environment for small business, entrepreneurial efforts, and other locally based economic development initiatives. Each of these groups presents an enormous range of skills, experiences, and methods of addressing local needs and problems. Bringing together these local assets allows for the maximization of local resources and development programmes.

The need for development initiatives to be done at community level is a widely recognized concept even though there is inconsistency in the definition, usage and general understanding of what community development actually represents. Without a clear and consistent definition of community development, one can hardly meaningfully undertake community initiatives that would maximally contribute to the overall improvement and well-being of communities.

For some development specialists, community development '*represents* **economic development** and is characterized by efforts to establish industries and render services: In this context, it is perceived as a dynamic process involving diverse social groups' (Wilkinson, 1991; Luloff and Swanson, 1995; Luloff and Bridger, 2003). For others, Community development is seen as 'action that is purposively directed towards altering local conditions in a positive way' (Wilkinson1991; Luloff and Bridger, 2003).

The aim of community Development:
The principal aim of community development is to ensure that a usable level of skills, personal and professional relationships, and resource mobilization skills among community members becomes effective. Therefore, every development effort must aim at maximizing the diverse skills, knowledge, experiences and resources that exist within targeted communities.

The development of community:

Community is important in that it contributes to individual and social well-being by:

- *establishing and maintaining* channels of communication
- *organizing resources* to meet local needs
- *providing* a framework where the collective view is more than the sum of its parts (Williamson, 1991)

ASSUMPTIONS FOR COMMUNITY DEVELOPMENT

It is assumed that when the diverse skills, knowledge, experiences and resources that exist in a given location are combined together, they would maximize the social wellbeing and self-actualization of the community members. This implies that a community is enhanced when residents work together to address common issues. However, for development to be most effective and to maximize its impact, within the locality, it must incorporate both social and economic needs:

IN UNDERSTANDING A COMMUNITY DEVELOPMENT CONCEPT, A DISTINCTION MUST BE MADE BETWEEN *DEVELOPMENT OF* AND *DEVELOPMENT IN* COMMUNITY.

DEVELOPMENT IN COMMUNITIES:

This concept is associated with the establishment of industry and other economic structures within a community. It is often characterized by attempts to enhance specific social components and structures. In this context, community is seen as a given entity while development is said to enhance this existing entity. (Wilkinson, 19991; Summer, 1998; Bridger and Luloff, 2003) An example would include the establishment of a community bank by a local community government.

In this context, a process exists in which plans are made to assess both local conditions and the potentially positive impact that a banking facility would have locally. If it is determined that the facility is desirable, appropriate steps would then be taken to encourage the location of the facility within the community. In this exercise, development plans focuses on the successful establishment of this facility. The corporate decision to locate the facility or not, signals the success of failure of local development efforts.

However, it must be noted that the development of specific community areas and systems, while contributing to the enhancement of the local community, is not sufficient enough to lead to the sustenance of community as it does not increase the social and cultural connections between residents or to communicate needs and opportunities throughout the locality.

DEVELOPMENT OF COMMUNITIES:

The development of a community concept seeks to enhance the social interests and relationships between people (Summers, 1986).

It is the process of *interaction, communication, and collective mobilization of resources that signal the development of a community.* Central to the *development of* perspective is the establishment of relationships and networks among diverse community members (Wilkinson, 1991; Luloff and Bridger, 2003).

An example is the establishment of a local Inter-religious Christian Council. Such an effort would begin by bringing together diverse and representative groups of the local population in a routine and focused setting. This process allows channels of communication to be established that cut across class and other dividing lines. Through the purposive assessment of *skills, needs, and opportunities for action, locally based plans for community and economic development that reflects the community, can be prepared.* The success of individual plans in this setting is irrelevant. Through this development *of* community, a framework is presented that allows future efforts to be attempted. This model allows for long term community based collective action to take place.

Such efforts are purposive and serve as the basis for interaction that benefits the overall.

'It must be emphasized that it is only through community actions and the purposive interactions of community members that the development of a community takes place.' (Luloff and Bridger, 2003). This process provides a basis for social and economic development which benefits the entire community by representing all segments of the locale. By building and maintaining channels of communication and interaction, the development of community takes place. Wilkinson observed that 'without a local basis for economic structural change, wide ranging and beneficial efforts cannot be expected' (Wilkinson, 1991; Luloff and Swanson, 1995).

The development *of* community and *in* community can, and should, take place together. One does not preclude the other. It is only by developing strong, local social bonds can more effective, focused, and reliable economic development plans be established. Accordingly, Communities must communicate with one another to share best practices, educate themselves about different programmes, and band together to advocate for their communities. This ensures that community development practices do not occur in isolation, but touch the entire community and go even further to benefit communities everywhere.

Strategies for Community Development:
Five critical elements:

1. Vision and Community Ownership:
Community members must fully understand and have a clear *vision* of their development drives, and this can only be achieved if the members are familiar with and are dedicated to achieving community needs through a clear definition of the *vision* for community initiatives, the required level of involvement of community members and by paying constant attention to changes that are taking place in their community. Lack of mutual understanding among community leaders and their people would lead to disastrous consequences that would destroy the total fabric of the development initiative. Hence, community members should be given enough time or training and education to be able to address adequately the needs of their community. Active community participation and involvement of all members of a community is important to assuring *individuals to feel a sense of ownership.* A Strong vision and a sense of ownership of development initiatives by beneficiaries will enhance effective community development.

2. Comprehensive Programming leads to community competence:
This is the process of empowering communities to be able to independently identify their challenges; analyse them, find solutions with minimal input from outside; develop programmes/strategies to alleviate them; develop capital to monitor and evaluate their interactions; and put new strategies/interventions in place to address gaps identified from the evaluation of their performances.

Must have the following features:

Must take into consideration the diverse strengths and needs of a community; remove barriers to development; increase development opportunities; recruit a wide variety of community members and participants to enhance quality of human networks within the organization; must have a clear understanding of the needs of their communities. When an organization's activities are predicted on a true understanding of the community, a wholistic experience will increase participants' economic, social, physical well-being.

3. Learning Opportunities:

A community that provides a variety of learning opportunities for its members is most effective at undertaking community development programmes. **Nevertheless, planners must always note that** community members have diverse needs and interests that stem from their diverse individual differences, hence learning opportunities should be so designed that they reflect the total learning needs of the majority of the members so that they could more positively and proactively influence development initiatives within their communities. Where feasible, the establishment of different learning opportunities that provide a variety of learning experiences that cater for the improvement of the diverse talents and skills of most of the members of the community are the best ways of meeting the needs of all participants and the community as a whole.

4. Self-Reliance

A community that has diversified funding, ownership of capital, and efficient use of resources is said to be *self-reliant*. Such communities can sustain their programmes over time and in a particular location thereby creating lasting relationships within the community. In this context, *efficiency* means more resources to deliver programmes while *Self-Reliance* enables the community structures to develop the capacity of their members, staff, and the community.

5. Social Capital

Social capital describes the power generated from creating the combined efforts/energies/capabilities of individuals/groups available in a community. Communities that build social capital are more effective at developing community competence. The disruptive effects of poverty and crime manifested in substandard physical resources, rob communities of their interpersonal and inter-organizational networks that sustain community members. By bringing together people with similar needs and diverse assets, communities could create interactions and relationships that form the bedrock of successful community growth and development. Every effort should therefore be made to encourage cross community relationships with other members within their areas for bridging neighbourhood to one another.

It is also advisable that communities create alliances with other communities with similar needs in order to contribute to disadvantaged community's collective empowerment. This enhances an effective way of helping the larger community to teach the values of interconnectedness. Through such alliances, communities would generate *bonding capital for her* members and would also create a *bridging neighbourhood* to one another. However, community members should be cautious in engaging in collaborative work with other communities as it may pose the following challenges:

Misappropriation of resources by partners; lack of transparency and accountability in the use of funds; lack of professional capacity to assess the needs of their communities and gainfully plan for them.

SUMMARY

a) *Vision and Ownership:*
Have volunteers and staff who are personally invested in the community.
Proactively incorporate community input.
See itself as an integrated part of the community.
Foster a sense of ownership in participants and other community members.
Give community members the power to make decisions.

b) *Comprehensive Programming*
Offer diversified programme that meet participants needs and reduce barriers to learning,
Have resources available to include participants, staff, and volunteers with special needs.
Do testing and re-testing of the organization's assumptions about the members served and what their needs are.

c) *Learning opportunities*

Provide engaging and relevant content, encouraging members to use the opportunities available to them for benefits that make sense to them. Have an open atmosphere, in which learners and tutors form supportive relationships to enhance learning. Provide a variety of programmes at a variety of times.

d) *Self-Reliance*

*H*ave permanence and control of location

Maintain a diverse mix of funding sources by avoiding dependence on any single source.

Attract and retain qualified workers by providing opportunities for professional development and continuing challenges that make the work interesting.

Encourage and develop volunteers as a resource for all areas of operation.

Have expertise available within the community for troubleshooting, repairing, and upgrading the different functionaries of the organization.

e) *Social Capital*

*B*e familiar with the other service delivery institutions in your area and be able to refer members in need of different services to them

Form multiple partnerships with other communities.

Create bonding between members by encouraging them to work collaboratively.

Encourage participants to be aware of the world outside their communities and solve problems using available outside their normal sphere of activity.

Encourage participants to form strong ties to their community.

BIBLICAL PERSPECTIVE

THE STORY OF NEHEMIAH: Read again and learn the lessons!

BRIEF HISTORY OF STRATEGIC PLANNING:

The history of strategic planning began in the military. It was "the science of planning and directing large-scale military operations, of manoeuvring forces into the most advantageous position prior to actual engagement with the enemy" (Coombs, 1980). The key aim of strategic planning here was *to achieve competitive advantage*. Since it had its root in military settings, strategic planning reflected *"the hierarchical values and linear systems of traditional organizations and mainly used the top-bottom approach to planning. Once this was done, the actual work of implementation – which was considered a separate, discrete process, began." (Freire, 1972).* According to Freire, strategic planning in organizations started in the 1950s and soon became very popular and widespread in the 1960. In recent years, subsequent newer versions of strategic planning have evolved that are mainly focused on adaptability, flexibility, and importance of strategic thinking and organizational learning.

What is planning?

A formalized procedure that is intended to produce a clearly defined result from a combination of interdependent decision making procedures is referred to as planning.

Woelk observed that thinking about and attempting to control the future are important components of planning (Woelk, 1992).

Why Plan?

Planning is required when the future state we desire involves a set of interdependent decisions–i.e. a system of decisions–(Tumwine, 1989)

What is a strategy?

A strategy determines and reveals the organizational purpose in terms of long-term objectives, action plans, and resource allocation priorities.

What is strategic Planning?

Strategic planning is a complex and continuous process of organizational change. It involves planning where one wants to be. It can be defined as an organized way of doing things based on an analysis of the competitive advantage each alternative has over others in addressing the issues of concern to the individual or to a group of persons or institutions. Strategic planning is the process of developing *strategies* to achieve defined *objectives.*

It involves projecting current activities and programmes of an institution/organization into a revised view of its externalities, thereby describing results that will most likely occur. Strategic planning creates more desirable future results, by either *influencing the external conditions* or by *adapting current programmes* and *actions* to have outcomes that are more favourable. Strategic planning can occur in a wide variety of activities including military, business, government, election campaigns, athletic competitions, games, etc.

An effective strategy will:
Have the capability to obtain the desired objectives
Fit well both with the external environment and the organization's resources and core competencies, it should appear feasible and appropriate.
Have the capacity of providing an organization with a sustainable competitive advantage – ideally through uniqueness and sustainability.
Provide dynamic, flexible, and able to adapt to changing situations.
Suffice on its own–specifically providing value or favourable outcome without the need for cross-subsidization.

Methodologies:
Most strategic planning methodologies depend on a 3-step process **(STP):**
1. Situation: evaluate the current situation and how it came about
2. Target: define goals / or objectives (end-state)
3. Path: map a possible route to achieving the set goals/objectives

Alternative strategic planning Methodologies (Draw-see-think-plan methodology-DSTP):
1. Draw: what is the ideal image or *the desired end-state?*
2. See: what is today's situation? *What is the gap from the ideal and why?*
3. Think: what specific actions must be taken to close the gap between today's situation and the ideal state?
4. Plan: what resources are required to execute the activities?

Steps in strategic Planning:

This process must begin with the identification of the vision and mission statement of the organization as every strategic planning process is uniquely designed to fit the specific needs of a particular organization. When these are clearly identified, the following steps may be adopted:

1. Clearly state objectives (end-state) to be pursued. Note that objectives must be SMART (**S**pecific; **M**easurable; **A**chievable; **R**ealistic; **T**ime-bound),

2. Gathering and analysing available of information using perhaps SWOT analysis,

3. Evaluation of the feasibility of the objectives in the light of the SWOT analysis;

4. Strategic Development–must attempt to answer the following questions:

a. How can the weaknesses be minimized using the strengths identified?

b. How can the opportunities identified be used to achieve the defined objectives taking into consideration the threats highlighted,

5. Development of an action plan that takes into consideration advantages of the strategy, significance of the strategy to the institution and other stakeholders, actions to be taken, by whom, when and for how long, location, implementing strategies, resources available in terms of – human, money, information, etc.; performance-related-pay, contingency plans for other programmes that may emerge from the implementation of the initial programme.

6. Implementation, monitoring, adjustments and control measures.

Why Strategic Plans fail?

The major causes for the failure of strategic plans can be grouped under two main headings:

Inappropriate Strategy: *These may arise due to the following causes:*
Failure to define objectives clearly.
Incomplete SWOT analysis with respect to the desired end goals.
Lack of creativity in identifying possible strategies.
Strategies poorly designed and are incapable of obtaining the defined objectives.
Poor fit between the external environment and organizational resources infeasibility.

Poor Implementation: *These may arise due to the following causes:*
Over estimation of resources and abilities,
Poor coordination of activities of various stakeholders,
Ineffective attempts to gain the support of others or resistance,
Underestimation of time, personnel, or financial requirements;
Failure to follow the plan

SOME MANAGEMENT TOOLS:

Organizations sometimes summarize goals and objectives into *a mission statement* (**purpose,** reason for being) and/or a *vision statement* (An **image** of the future they seek to create): **The three basic tools organizations use to define themselves are statements describing:**

a) Core values; b) Vision; and c) Mission.

Together, these three statements comprise the foundation upon which organizational strategy is built. These are three interrelated components of defining and describing an organization's essence as they convey *who* and *what* the organization is and they tell a story about the organization. Mission/vision statements: There are many definitions for both mission and vision statements. Hence, there are many definitions as there are varying conceptions of the use to which the meaning of these terms are applied. There is no one accepted definition for either of them. They are simply management tools if used appropriately, have the potential to help improve the probability of the success of the organization.

a) Core Values:

They describe the ***principles*** **the organization** *turns to* when making its most critical decisions. They describe ***simply*** and ***concisely*** how ***individuals are expected to approach*** any situation. Core values must be stable, not shifting as conditions change. It describes the principles upon which the organization acts.

b) Vision statement: (talks about what the organization would like to be).

A *vision statement* should describe in graphic terms *where* the goal-setters want to see themselves in the future. It may describe how they see events unfolding over a specific period should everything be done as exactly as hoped. It is specific in terms of objectives and time frame. It describes the future state of the organization in *vivid, compelling* terms that inspire all involved in it to achieve it. It is a snapshot of the future. It allows leaders to communicate persuasively where the organization desires to go, and motivates everyone to work towards the same end. It can be described as a picture of the future. It communicates where the organization wants to be-its **destination**.

c) Mission Statement: (talks about purpose/direction of an organization).

A *mission statement* defines the *purpose* or *broader goal for being in existence or in business.* It serves as a guide in times of uncertainty, vagueness. It has no time frame. It is a simple, short statement that clearly communicates the purpose of the organization to its stakeholders. It can be described as the **journey.** It clarifies the organization's purpose. The mission statement declares why the organization exists and, therefore, what it strives to do in every transaction and decision it makes. The mission should be understood by everyone in the organization and used practically daily to:
Communicate the direction of the organization. Help make day-to-day operation decisions. Keep organization focused. Motivate employees.

COMMUNITY PARTICIPATION

Community Participation: (The involvement of people in decisions about development)

Definition 1: Community participation is the process by which individuals and families assume responsibility for their own welfare and those of the community, and develop capacity to contribute to their and community's development. They come to know their own situation better and are motivated to solve their common problems.

This enables them to become agents of their own development instead of passive beneficiaries of development aid. This implies that community people would become involved in both delivery of and decisions about development interventions in their location in order to provide the type of care most appropriate to their own needs and circumstances (Rifkin, 1986)

In this context, the term *Community* is used to refer to people grouped together on the basis of geography, common interest, identity, or interaction or exposed to a particular risk. Similarly, the term:

Participation is used to mean:
Collaboration – e.g. contribute land or labour, or other resources, hence some form of stakeholder) *or*
Target Beneficiary – just receiving programme benefits, *or*
Involvement – political process of gaining information, understanding, skills and power necessary to articulate their concerns, ensure that action is taken to address them and, more broadly, gain control over their lives.

Definition 2: Community participation in development is ,essentially a process whereby people, both individually and in groups, exercise their right to play an active and direct role in the development of appropriate development services, in ensuring that the conditions for sustained better services, and in supporting the empowerment of communities for service development' (WHO,1991). It has become an umbrella term for people-centred approach to development.

Tenets of genuine community participation:
Active and genuine involvement by community people in defining problems/issues/challenges of concern to them; deciding priorities for action; formulating policies to address then; designing plans; implementing; managing; monitoring solutions; and evaluating outcomes–all of these must be done in an empowerment frame.

Two approaches to community Participation:

Note: Top/up-bottom/down; and Bottom/down-top/up Approaches.

Top-Bottom Approach:
The professionals have the predominance in decision-making process. They decide on what is good for the poor, plan interventions for them, implement, monitor and evaluate themselves using their own standards and measuring tools, they report on their behalf, most times without sharing any information with such beneficiaries. In this context, the beneficiaries become recipients and not participants in their development.

Bottom/Top Approach:
Emphasis is put on the importance of community people learning to decide what is best for them and participating in the processes of how to achieve the change they desire for themselves.

So is community participation an abused concept?

A). YES

1. When it is used as a cosmetic label, to make what is proposed or what is done appear good. In such cases, imitators of programmes require participatory approaches and consultants, planners, and managers say that they will be used, or they have been used, while the reality has been top-bottom in the traditional style.

2. When used as a co-opting practice, to mobilize local labour or materials and reduce costs–meaning 'they' (the local people) participate in 'our' project.

B). NO

1. When used as an empowering process which enables community people to do their own analysis, to take command in terms of design, planning and action, to gain confidence and self-esteem, and make their own decisions; albeit with the experts acting as facilitators of learning than teachers.

Who should be involved? All stakeholders including:

Governmental Organizations; NGOs; CBOs; Civil Society;

Specialized institutions; The Church; Donors;

Beneficiaries; Community Leaders; Programme staff.

BIBLICAL PERSPECTIVE
The triumphal entry into Jerusalem (Mt. 21:1-11); the healing of the paralyzed man (Mk. 2:1ff); Peter and Cornelius (Acts 10:48); Philip and Ethiopian Eunuch (Acts 8:26-40).

SOME TECHNIQUES FOR MEANINGFUL PARTICIPATORY PLANNING

SWOT analysis

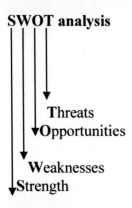

Threats
Opportunities

Weaknesses
Strength

PLEST Analysis

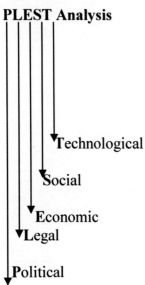

Technological

Social

Economic
Legal

Political

Situational Analysis:
This involves an analysis of an organization and its operational environment *as at the moment* and *how it will be* in the future – a process referred to as the analysis phase of the strategic planning process.

Gap Analysis:
Process of estimating the difference between the current position and desired future of an organization is referred to as *Gap Analysis.* It

evaluates the difference between the organization's current position, and its desired future. Gap analysis results in development of specific strategies and allocation of resources to close the gap (CSUN strategic planning leadership retreat, April 1997).

Benchmarking:

Measuring and comparing the organization's operations, practices, and performance against others is useful for identifying *best practices.* Through an ongoing systematic process of measuring and comparing an organization's operations, practices, and performance against the other organizations: It is used within the strategic planning process to guide the management of organization's human, social, and technical resources (Lerner, Rolfes, Saad, & Soderlund, 1998).

Strategic issues:

Are the fundamental issues that the organization has to address to achieve its mission and move towards its desired future.

LECTURES 8 & 9: PROGRAMMING FOR SUSTAINABLE DEVELOPMENT

PART (A) SUGGESTED FORMAT OF A PROJECT PROPOSAL

1.   Project Basic Information
- Project title;
- Name of organization/content
- Mailing address and street address
- Telephone and fax numbers, as well as e-mail address

2.   Introduction/Background
- Context, rationale and background of the project

3. Description of the Project
- Objectives and the nature of the project;
- Types of participants/beneficiaries and the reason for their participation
- Dates and venues (location of the projects);
- Management approach/implementing strategy/capacity of the implementing agency;

4. Expected Results.

Short Term Results–for example, organize and hold a conference; summarize and analyze the comments made. At the conference, prepare any next steps that may be required, forward results to local government and sponsoring authorities

Medium Term Results–for example, local government and sponsoring authorities are better aware of the recommendations of the conference participants and civil society organizations are recognized as effective participants in the development process

Long Term Results–for example, the sponsors programmes reflect the recommendations of the project/conference and civil society organizations are more involved in the implementation of sustainable programmes

5.   Detailed Budget:

Outline expenses required for the project. For example rental of venue, travel and accommodation, fees for resource persons, administrative costs. **Note:** that some sponsoring agencies do not pay equipment or other revolving costs and in most cases, the budget should be presented in internationally recognized currencies, e.g. British Pounds sterling or US Dollars.

6. Description of organization submitting the project.

- Objectives ;
- Legal status; management structure ;
- Funding sources;
- Number of employees;
- Summary of organization's activities
- If the organization is new, please provide two references
- and the resumes of Board Members and/or key personnel

7. Annexes

- Proposed programme;
- Proposed list Participants/beneficiaries;
- Other relevant documents.

....

....

1. Basic Project Information
Title of Project;
Name of organization
Overall Project Budget
Duration of project

2. Description of the Project
Objectives;
Nature of Project
Types of participants and reasons (s) for their participation;
Topics covered;
Dates/venues; Management approach (incl. who managed the project).

3. Summary of Results:
Discuss expected results and actual results;
Analysis of any gaps between expected and actual results;
Analysis of the gender equality measures and their contribution to the project
Sustainability of results achieved.

4. Detailed Budget:
Lessons related to achievement of results
Lessons related to implementation to the project

5. Financial Report and Reconciliation:
Detailed expenses;
Report on unused funds. Any unused portion of the funds and/or related interest not used for the purpose of the project must be returned to the sponsors.
Funding sources;
Number of employees;
Summary of organization's activities
If the organization is new, please provide two references and the resumes of Board Members and/or key personnel

6. Annexes
Actual programme
Actual list of participants/beneficiaries;
Other relevant documents.

BIBLICAL PERSPECTIVES

1. The story of Joseph in the household of Pharaoh. (Gen.41:39-57)
2. Feeding of the five thousand. (Jn 6:1-15)

THE STORY OF Joseph provides a graphic account of Pharaoh's dream of the seven cows and the seven lean cows; seven healthy ears of corn and seven withered ears of corn. After Joseph had interpreted the dream for him, a process of participatory and strategic management began to unfold. Pharaoh appointed Joseph to the second highest position in the empire – ruler over all the land of Egypt. Joseph accepted the awesome responsibility delegated to him by Pharaoh and used the authority entrusted to him to organize the citizens of Egypt in storing adequate goods during the seven years of plenty for the seven years of famine. Participatory leadership and strategic planning averted famine in Egypt and other countries. Joseph utilized his innate leadership qualities in articulating the vision, embodying the values, defining the national culture, creating the appropriate environment and empowering others for participatory leadership.

The Feeding of the five thousand demonstrates some sound management practices and principles.

1. Jesus took the loaves of bread and the fishes and blessed them. He acknowledged and thanked God for his gracious providence.
2. He instructed the people to sit down in rows of fifty. He divided the crowd into small management units. This ensured order and discipline, coordination and monitoring.
3. He distributed the available resources to the disciples and the disciples distributed them to the people. He involved the disciples in a process of participatory leadership by delegating responsibility and authority to them.
4. He advised that the leftovers should be collected. A process of recycling and prudent stewardship was initiated. Surplus food should not be wasted while others are hungry. Thus appropriate management practices were utilized to avert what might have been a chaotic situation.

The mission of the church was demonstrated in concrete terms and by prudent management of its resources.

GOD INTENDS THAT THE GOSPEL BELONGS TO ALL NATIONS ESPECIALLY THE MASSES OF POOR PEOPLE TO WHOM IT HAS BEEN ANNOUNCED.

Jesus replied, "Go back and report to John what you hear and see. The blind receive sight, the lame walk, those who have leprosy are cured, the deaf hear, the dead are raised, and the good news is preached to the poor." (Matt. 11: 4 – 6; cf. Isaiah 35:4-7; NIV.).

The ministry of John Wesley, the founding father of Methodism, was later summarised as the *Four All's of Methodism in* this way:

All need to be saved
All can be saved
All can know that they are saved
All may be saved completely

The fact that so many poor people in the world do not have any access to the true knowledge of God's grace manifested in Jesus Christ should be a challenge to our Christian conscience today. The gospel to the poor is a dynamic call, a call to the kingdom, to discipleship, to enlistment in the struggles of the kingdom in history.

1. How can we together actualize the intentions of God for this troubled world? How can we engage the clergy and Lay Faithful to rise up to their responsibilities by becoming more aggressive and obedient to the great commission of Jesus in our world today?

2. How can we build upon the demonstrated excitement of African Christians to participate more meaningfully in the kingdom building process of God through the evangelism explosion that we now experience in the continent of Africa?

3. How can Christians enable people to claim the promises of God for the whole community by linking their personal and communal stories to the stories of Jesus?

4. How can Christians live today in a pluralistic situation, side by side with people belonging to different religious persuasions or ideologies

without losing our identity as a people called by God for service to humanity? How do we proclaim God's kingdom in relation to the hopes of people of other faiths?

5. In our living together, working together, sharing together, how can we build upon our strengths and weakness to overcome the many threats to our mission and gainfully use the God-given opportunities open to us in Christ to increase the possibilities for shaping a better tomorrow?

6. How can the Lordship of Christ, the reality of the kingdom be confessed among our neighbours of other faith and ideologies?

7. How can we stimulate Christians to experiment with new ways to witness from within their cultures to the glory of God?

8. How can we appropriate the unsearchable riches of Christ (Eph.3:8) to the realities of life in human communities and society at large?

9. How can we be both Salt and Light in the troubled world?

10. How can the Christian mission become one of creating an environment in which God's rule is recognized, to which people are welcome and in which if they so desire, they can belong?

11. What is the attitude of the churches today to the mission of new religious movements? Is it one of collaboration, accommodation, antagonism, or hate?

In my estimation, these questions cannot be ignored or avoided
Whatever answers we give to such crucial questions will border around *Responsibility*. It will have to deal with specific actions or non-actions on the part of individuals or members of the Christian family. **I am proposing the following points for our consideration:**

A We need church management systems that have the capacity to identify, develop and utilize the total resources of their churches in efficient, effective, transparent ways using easily accountable principles, practices and strategies that would build the confidence of their members to trust them bountifully.

B.   Christians should be able to develop strategies that would make enable them to resist peacefully the manipulations of Christianity by some governments in other to achieve their politico-socioeconomic ideologies which seek to maintain discriminatory tendencies in governing their people.

C.   If being a Christian should mean anything to those concerned the promotion of the work of the church, then sacrificial identity with Christ is an absolute necessity.

D.   The church needs to develop a *New Theology* and *praxis* which accommodates other new religious movements in the kingdom building process.

E.   For mission to be more effective, the Christian messages must be expressed in *national and cultural* patterns with our liturgy, church music, dance, drama, and even the building structures accentuating national features.

F.   Those church/theological institutions maintain church management as a separate course of study in their curriculum as it would help to introduce church workers to the scientific approach in identifying, developing and utilizing the total resources of the church in more efficient and effective ways.

G.   If the church is to make the transition from a maintenance church to a dynamic community, then it should assess and re-evaluate its current management systems and practices and other applications to structures that produce and perpetuate poverty, cooperate greed, injustice, conflicts, deteriorating social services and escalating crime and violence.

H.   Because of the central importance of leadership to the integrity of mission, leaders of the church should develop and utilize appropriate behaviours. The challenge facing the church today requires leadership that is sensitive, flexible, motivational and exemplary. Hence, under the guidance of the Holy Spirit, the church must discover new ways of participating more meaningfully in the struggle for justice, peace, freedom and sustained development of our communities.

CONCLUSION:

The whole argument about contextualizing Christianity is about whether in the process the *biblical and historical* doctrines of Christianity can be preserved without compromise.

Personally, I have no doubt that Christians would endeavour to *listen, evaluate, and be open-minded* to different theological views in contextualizing mission without compromise.

To be able to do this, I believe that:

We must be faithful to the gospel.
We must proclaim the gospel in love as the apostle Paul exhorts saying:

"Be on the alert, stand firm in the faith, act like men, be strong. Let whatever you do be done in love" (1 Cor.16:13-14);

"... for our God is not a God of disorder" (1 Cor.14:35).

We must recognize and appreciate the fact that the mission is God's and His grace will always sustain us in His exciting ministry.

MODULE 9a: COMMUNITY MINISTRY & MISSION

(Revd Cameron Kirkwood MA CNAA)

LECTURE 1: A COMMUNITY CHURCH IS INCARNATIONAL

Every Church context is unique and no two Churches are exactly the same. Each one has a story to tell about how it came into being, the successes and failures. It is important that we understand something of that story and attempt to apply the gifts and insights into that experience, rather than to "import" them for somewhere else and expect it to work. What works in one place, may not work somewhere else. Think of situations you have been in previously and how your ministry developed there in particular ways, but this has not been repeated where you are now.

Exercise and Reflection: Think of a Church you know well. Why was it established where it is? What do you know about its history? Is the community in which it is set different or the same as in previous years? Is the change that has taken place within the local community reflected in its life and mission?

WHAT DO WE MEAN BY INCARNATIONAL? *IT IS NOT THE CHURCH OF GOD THAT HAS A MISSION IN THE WORLD, BUT THE GOD OF MISSION WHO HAS A CHURCH IN THE WORLD.*

As Christians, we believe that God entered our world in Jesus. God took human form for our salvation. Jesus was born into and exercised his ministry in a specific cultural identity. God revealed himself for all cultures, by entering into one specific culture. The story of the early Church is that it did not remain culturally static. The Gospel was translated out of the original language and culture of Jesus as the Church begun to plant itself and welcome into its life non-Jewish languages and cultures.

Churches need to take seriously the context in which it is located just as Jesus took seriously the social and cultural circumstances of the men and women among whom he lived. A Church needs to shape its life in relation to the culture in which it is located and to which it is called.

Reflection: What will that mean for how leadership is exercised? How might styles of worship, ways of working, community outreach be affected? Will different situations require different leadership models and skills or do you think that there is one model of leadership which should be applied in all situations?

Critical Engagement:
The story of salvation is one of faithfulness and obedience leading to death. Jesus demonstrates the importance of belonging to as well as challenging the culture of which he was a part. To what extent do you feel yourself to be part of the local culture where you are ministering? Should ministers be seen to be alongside people and therefore "one of us", or should our calling and role require us to be different in some way? Think of ways in which you think we should be seen to be different.

Reflection: How do we get alongside people but also challenge those things about their life that seem to deny the Gospel? Jesus calls us to discipleship which includes self-denial.

Important points to remember:
1. It is important to identify with the local context and culture
2. To express within the life of the Church God's loving concern for each individual
3. To bring the demands of the Gospel to bear on that culture and context in a critical way.

Learning from St Paul: The Christian life, as argued in St Paul's writings, is to imitate Christ. St Paul saw his own life of discipleship as a way of demonstrating to others the person and nature of Christ. For St Paul, this was a crucial way to share the Gospel with others.

Action:
Study 1 Corinthians 9 v 19-22. What might these verses mean for you in your Church situation?

Reflection: The Church is most true to itself when it gives itself up and to be reformed among those who do not know God's son. In each new situation, the Church must give up its life (to die) in order to live.

The aim of this lecture is to show that a key foundation block for mission is when a Church has a clear sense of what is important within its life and how those values underpin its relationship with the wider community.

Reflection: Does the Church to which you belong have a clear sense of what it wants to share with your neighbours? Is there are shared sense of why it is there and what its priorities are?

Defining what those priorities are: It is important that congregations spend time thinking about what is important at this point in our life together. What are the issues and needs of the community around; what are the skills and gifts we have and how can all our work and effort be focussed on towards that aim. One simple way is by encouraging a congregation to match resources with people.

We divided into groups and played a simple game. The game was about matching situations and people's needs against what we either do, or could offer to our community." (Dudley Wood Church) From this exercise, the congregation looked at: **Isn't it a shame that…., Isn't it good that…. and Wouldn't it be good if….**
A local church with mission centred values at its heart will ask these kinds of questions of itself. If the questions emerge from values and from a vision of God, then the local church will be prepared to put its own shape in the melting pot to develop an answer to them.

Reflection: If you were asked to help a congregation to think about what its values are and how those values might help the congregation to engage in mission, what would be some of the questions you would want to ask the congregation to try and answer?

A Strategy with a human face
There doesn't have to be anything mechanistic about this process. But the word 'strategy' is a good one. This helps to focus on those things you feel are important for your life together in a particular place. Values enable the church to express the heart of God, whilst at the same time ensuring that the focus of church life is geared towards ensuring that it leads to action rather than just conversation. "Walking the walk as well as talking the talk".

Reflection: Ideas, lead to prayer, which leads to a deeper understanding of God. From this values are discerned, structures are put in place, plans emerge. What has been your experience of carrying out such an exercise? How easy or difficult was it to come to agreement? If things went wrong, why did that happen?

BRIXTON CIRCUIT LONDON MISSION STATEMENT

We came to four important values that we felt expressed our life together and why it was important to be where we were doing what we did.
1. Sharing the Good News
2. Expressing Christ's Love
3. Growing as Christians
4. Working with others

What came out of the exercise was the realisation that we cannot do everything and it is necessary to say no to some things we felt were important. It was also necessary to recognise that we had to return to these four values to keep asking ourselves whether they needed to be revised in the light of our experience of implementing them.

The place of values as an antidote to panic or arm-chair discussion

In the western world, Christians live in a society where getting on and getting things done is highly prized. This has impacted on the church where getting on with God's work and doing it as quickly as possible, grabbing the latest ideas from somewhere else and trying to put them into practice without thinking for too long about whether they are appropriate for this context, is a common problem. Mission and evangelism are then seen as practical active things for Christians to do, if you like that sort of thing. Mission can so easily become a fringe activity, even an optional extra based on new ideas, frantic activity, very little ownership or continuity.

Many churches set up evangelism or mission groups and never do anything but talk with little or no action. Churches that take seriously the discerning of their values know that such an exercise requires them to stop and look around, at their context and their potential. A church that prays through its mission values, teaches them, makes them its own and is willing to place them at the centre of all that it does, may just begin to be seen by the wider community as an authentic community of God's people.

Exercise: If someone in your community asked you what the values of your church were, what answer you would give and how would you be able to demonstrate them?

Introduction

Our day-to-day lives are lived out somewhere. We live in a particular community; we might also work in that same community or perhaps somewhere quite different. Where we live now maybe where we have always lived or perhaps our roots and family are somewhere different. The Church where we minister is also part of a local community where stories, history, changes and experiences have helped shape it over the years. This Bible Study is a way of helping you to look at your community and through the sharing of stories, memories and experiences help you to understand how you can engage in mission. This exercise can be done either over four sessions or by spending part of a day together. Someone in the group should have the responsibility of writing down the main points of the discussion and any decisions reached.

STUDY ONE: HOME AND JOURNEYS

Ask each person to bring with them to discuss an object of their choice which describes for them something about the local community. Be willing to talk about why this object represents for you something of the local community. Share together your various examples.

Spell out the name of the place where you live. Example: UMUAHIA/SAGAMU and for each letter think up all aspects of the place that you particularly value. This can be anything from a part of the natural world to a tradition or something that might seem quite trivial.

Questions to discuss after reading Luke 15 v 11-32:

1. What immediately jumps off the page as you listened to this story?
2. How do home and journeying feature in this story? Do any connections occur to you with life where you live?
3. What parts do property and wealth are represented in this story? Do they find any resonance where you live?

STUDY TWO: BEING OUT OF PLACE

On a piece of paper, draw a rough map of your local community, the main roads and buildings. This does not need to be elaborate, but it should include as many of the main buildings or places where people meet that you can think of. If there is a map of your area, so much the better.

On the map, each person in turn should mark the places they go to on a day-to-day or very regular basis. Using different colours each person should mark on the map those places they think of being sacred, those places they see as of contest, conflict or dispute. Share together what you have all put on the map.

Questions to discuss after reading Luke 2 v 41-52:

1. What immediately jumps out of the story for you?
2. The story represents the family going to Jerusalem. What rituals/celebrations/activities are celebrated where you live? Have these changed over the years? If so, why?

STUDY THREE: RIPPLES UNDER THE SURFACE

On a piece of paper, list what you consider to be the strengths, weaknesses, opportunities and threats for your Church and the local community in your area.

Questions to discuss after reading Luke 8 v 22-39:

1. In the story various elements are stirred up, the sea and various people. How do people in your community react to being stirred up? Do things/people get healed or do things/people get driven out?
2. Legion is often said to represent land occupied by an outside power. What threatens your place?
3. What action can you take to liberate your place from the treats you have identified?

STUDY FOUR: THE CALL TO MOVE ON

As a group think about the key people within your community. Who are they? How have they gained that position? In what ways do they contribute to the positive well-being of the community? Are they people you admire?

Questions to discuss after reading Luke 9 v 46-52:

1. What do you make of the saying "Foxes have holes....."? Is it good or bad to have a strong sense of home or place?
2. The idea of following is a key theme in the context of this story. Who or what is followed in your context?
3. What is the urgent concern for the future of your place? What demands from you "hands to the plough"?

Conclusion

As a final short exercise bring together your responses to the four sessions and discuss together:

1. What have we learned about our place that we were not aware of before?
2. What are the main issues that we have to face?
3. How might we as the people of God respond to those challenges?

Bibliography

Lawrence, L. J. (2008). Contextual Bible Studies Resources on Place. Expository Times, Volume 120 Number 3, pp 131 -132.

LECTURE 4: A COMMUNITY CHURCH IS INVITATIONAL

The aim of this lecture is to recognise that people will sometimes come to the Church, or seek support from the Church for a variety of reasons. From the perspective of mission, the issue of importance is how we respond. We shall look at three ways in which people come to the Church for support and explore how we engage with people at such times. What might be good practice in such situations?

Baptism

A frequent request made to the Church is for infant baptism. Such requests often come from people who have little or no on-going relationship with a Church. Why do people not come back afterwards is an important mission question. This is an issue many congregations discuss and come to few conclusions. One way is to look at the liturgy being used on such occasions, which might use language which those unfamiliar with religious language might be able to relate to. But what might be the dangers with this approach? What do we understand baptism, particularly infant baptism to mean?

Reflection: How is pastoral care offered to families who request baptism before, during and afterward the event? How difficult is it in your current appointment to ensure that there is an on-going relationship with families? God's mission in Jesus was to shape himself around the humanity he was entering. God came in Jesus, because God sought to live among and save humanity. Read Philippians 2 v 7.

Baptisms are a sacrament of relationship, between God and the child, the child and the Church and God and the parents. Do you agree that in our practice of baptism we are provided with the opportunity to demonstrate the generosity of God's grace?

Weddings Again, the reasons for asking for a Church wedding vary. It is important that the Church seeks to respond in a gracious and loving way. Some of those ways might be:
Use liturgy in creative ways, making it personal to particular couple.
Invite guests to renew promises to each other as well as the couple.
Recognise the leaving of one family relationship and the creating of a new family.
Speak openly and honestly about the nature of God's love.
Recognise complexity and difficulties of married life and faithfulness.
Be honest about how the church has experience of brokenness within its own life and how the glory of God can bring healing.

Reflection: How can we help people to celebrate and share their feelings for one another? How can we make the occasion special for them as individuals and their families? How can links with the couple and their families be maintained after the ceremony?

Funerals In the UK, it has been suggested that more people enter a Church for a funeral than any other single reason. How then can funerals become part of a Church's mission strategy? By being honest about the person who has died, their failings and mistakes as well as their strengths and achievements.

By providing an opportunity for sadness and grief to be expressed as well as thankfulness for the gift of life. What is God's word through this service to the family and wider community?

Reflection: Funerals are primarily a pastoral rite. Are funerals an evangelistic opportunity or a pastoral response to a specific need? In some situations, valuable partnerships can be developed which enable the church to engage pastorally with families who have lost contact with the church.

The Importance of Follow-up

Contact with family members before, during and after funerals is important for a mission-focused Church. Being there for the family, when everyone else has gone! Many in pastoral ministry say that the Church's most important role comes after the funeral has taken place.

Reflections and Important Questions

Think of a Baptism, Wedding for Funeral you attended recently. What contributed to it being a good experience, how might the experience have been improved? What cultural rites are you expected/required to offer as part of the pastoral ministry of the church. What issues do these sometimes raise for you?

Conclusion

We need to see requests for baptism, weddings and funerals not as something more that has to be done but as an important invitation into the lives of individuals, families and sometimes communities. Such requests are a gift to a mission-focused Church. Through them, we can go a long way to open people to the grace of God.

LECTURE 5: A COMMUNITY CHURCH IS RELATIONAL

The aim of this lecture is to show that a key foundation block for mission is when Church members are willing to work on friendship with one another. Read John 15 v 15. This verse points us to a particular understanding of relationship which lies at the heart of our life together.

Reflection: "The creation of living, breathing, loving communities of faith at the local church level is the foundation of all our answers. Proclamation of the gospel, charismatic gifts, social action and prophetic witness alone do not finally offer any real threat to the world as it is. The church must be called... to rebuild the kind of community that gives substance to the claims of faith." (Sojourners Magazine Volume 9 September 2002)

What do we mean by Relational?

How well do members of congregations know each other? In some cases, people have attended the same church for many years but know one another very little. Yet friendship flows from the heart of the Good News of the Gospel. Jesus sets out in his teaching what life shared together with others means. It is Relational. We are called together and a commitment to deepening friendship should be a priority.

In the Gospels, we see how Jesus brought together at the start of his ministry a group who would be required to learn from each other (Mark 1 v 13-20). They also learned the need to reject self-importance (James and John seeking places of honour).

Open Friendship

Read Luke 7 v 34. In this verse, we see how the willingness of Jesus to extend friendship to all, even those considered to be beyond God's care and concern brought criticism and complaint.
"What would it be like if congregations were no longer to regard themselves as the communion of saints or as a congregation of the faithful, but as a community of friends?" (Jürgen Moltmann).

Reflection: Friendship is more than a warm welcome. It is a willingness to get to know someone at a deep level. How good are our churches at taking friendship beyond just a warm welcome? Where are the signs within the life of churches you know where this commitment to one another is being demonstrated?

Prophetic Friendship

When friendship is offered within the life of a congregation this is a challenge to the increasingly private and individualistic lives people are living. It is counter-cultural. It challenges how people normally do things. Some writers on Church life suggest that much of the opposition and discontent about various forms of change arise out of an unwillingness to engage with a Church agenda that seeks to bring people close to one another in friendship.

Reflection: How is friendship demonstrated in the life of your Church? Think of examples. If a visitor came into a congregation, how would they know that it was a community of friends? What would be some of the signs they might look for?

Organising for friendship

This is about recognising the need to arrange groups and opportunities for people to meet together. Friendship does not just happen it has to be worked at. Consider Jesus and the disciples and our own personal experience. Those Churches where such meetings do not take place are impoverished. They lack something fundamental to their life in what it means to be the Church.

There needs to be recognition that such organising is not easy. Today it seems that both short-term and flexibility are the key.

The experience of friendship is an essential contribution to the mission of the Church in a particular place.

Reflection and action Think of the friends you have. What do you value most about that friendship and why are friendships so important to us? Jesus gathered friends around him from the very beginning of his ministry. They learned from each other, argued with each other, betrayed and forgave each other. They also learned that there is no greater gift than to lay down one's life for a friend. In the New Testament, we see a strong emphasis on a community life based on love, of the need to lead an authentic life and that the friendship found within the life of a church community would inspire Christians to a life of service.

What is your experience of Church as a:

Worship centre? That is a place to which Christians come for worship and possibly some fellowship, but there is little real sense of belonging and of people being committed to one another.

Community of friends? That is a group of people who spend time getting to know each other and working on their relationship as the people of God in a particular place.

LECTURE 6: A COMMUNITY CHURCH IS A MINISTERING COMMUNITY

The aim of this lecture is to see that ministry belongs to the whole people of God. A shift needs to take place from communities focused around a minister to the creation of ministering communities. This is not an easy transition to take place since many people, both those ordained and those not, have very clear ideas about who a minister is, what they should be doing and where authority lies.

Lessons from the New Testament

When we look at the New Testament, we find that a wide variety of people were exercising ministry. Look at the following passages: Matt 20 v 26b - 28, 1 Pe 4 v 10, Eph 4 v 11 - 12, and Rom 12 v 4 - 8. What picture of ministry emerges? How is ministry understood? What we learn from the New Testament is a realisation that no one person can do ministry for everybody.

Each individual is given gifts which are offered as ministry to the whole group. Words used to describe forms of service include deacon, shepherd, apostle and minister. All these terms have a servant dimension to them. To exercise ministry is to be someone who is serving God's people to enable them to carry out God's will.

The Need for Order In the letters of St Paul we find him writing to different communities to deal with issues that arose within the life of these new Churches. They were very often circular letters and so would be passed on from one community to another. These writings, alongside those of James and Peter, had different emphasis which over a period of time led to different shades of theological thought, e.g. the first Council of Church Leaders in Jerusalem was set up to discuss and resolve some of these differences.

Read Acts 15. Eventually a threefold order of ministry emerged. Deacon, who was seen as a messenger/spokesperson; priest (presbyter), who was responsible for the ordering of the life of the Christian community and bishop, whose main task was maintaining the integrity of the Christian community and keeping the faith. A further responsibility of the bishop seems to have been that of evangelism. Over a period of time, a clear distinction between those ordained and those not ordained emerged.

Reflection: Pope Gregory 16th (1831-46) "No one can deny that the church is an unequal society in which God destined some to be governors and others to be servants. The latter are the laity and the former the clergy". To what extent do you think this clear distinction between ordained and non-ordained has been a help or a hindrance to the mission of the church?

Our shared Calling to Ministry

We are all called to exercise ministry. It is important to return to the ministry of Jesus as the model for our own lives. God calls the Church to ensure that the ministry of Jesus is available in a recognisable way in each local community, with each member offering the gifts that God has given to them.

Reflection: Many Christians see ministry as something done to and for them rather than something done by them. How can you encourage members within your congregation to see themselves as having a ministry to offer?

We are called to be a sign of God's Kingdom, to model and to respond in life-giving ways to what God is doing in his world. This means that all of us have a task, gift and responsibility to live a life of service. God calls the Church to ensure that this ministry of Jesus Christ is available in a concrete and recognisable form in each local community. The effectiveness of that ministry depends upon every member of the Church offering the gifts that they have received in service for both the life and mission of the Church.

Reflect on Ephesians 4 where the gifts of the Church are listed and each member of the church is given grace as part of the huge generosity of God. The task of those with gifts is to equip the saints to do the work of ministry, to build up the body of Christ.

Important Questions

Who exercises ministry in your Church setting?

Does your Church have a vision for its ministry?

How is that vision practised?

How different might each Church look if it saw itself as having 50 ministers instead of 1 minister and 49 members?

What would you see as being the disadvantages and difficulties of such a model adopted in your situation?

Such an understanding of the church as a ministering community demands a huge change in our thinking, in the practice we undertake and in the responsibility that we accept. No longer should members of our churches think of themselves as passive consumers of religious experience, but rather as those whom God has stirred to share his love and care in a sensitive way.

Our day-to-day lives are lived out somewhere. We live in a particular community; we might also work in that same community or perhaps somewhere quite different. Where we live now maybe where we have always lived or perhaps our roots and family are somewhere different. The Church where we minister is also part of a local community where stories, history, changes and experiences have helped shape it over the years. The Bible Studies shared earlier are one way of helping you to look at your community and through the sharing of stories, memories and experiences will help you to understand how you can engage in mission. These exercises can be done either over four sessions or by spending part of a day together. Someone in the group should have the responsibility of writing down the main points of the discussion and any decisions reached so that they can be followed up with your church and community.

Questions:

1. In the area where you live, what form of Church might realistically be developed that could relate to people who are not currently in contact with Church?

2. Do we need more and different Churches, or simply better existing Churches, or both? (See 1 Corinthians 3, v 10-16)

3. With what we have learned, how can we help integrate the church(es) for which we are responsible with the communities in which we are called to minister and mission.

MODULE 10: APPLIED EVANGELISM PROJECT

(Supervision by MCN Lecturers & Diocesan Staff)

Requires students to reflect upon and write up a programme related to mission/evangelism which they have initiated as a consequence of undertaking this course. The projects written up so far have included church planting; social & community development initiatives; evangelistic events; as well as a variety of teaching/training programmes relating to different aspects of the church's Ministry and Mission.

ONE FINAL WORD!

Preachers are noted (notorious!) for saying 'and finally' more than once! I make no apology here for repeating as an appeal the conclusion to the earlier Preface.

As indicated earlier the International Coordinator or Director of CCITC will happily respond by email to anyone seeking further information. Cliff College will be pleased to receive any donations that will help to promote and extend this programme. With untapped short-term training resources and funding provided through bi-lateral relationships as well as nationally through the World Church Relations Office and the CCITC, 'The world is my parish' might again become our Methodist watchword in the UK. Supportive friends/sponsors continue to help us respond to the training needs of our partner churches in the 21st Century. There is no copyright on the concept of 'Doing Training There, Together with Them'. Our hope is that our pioneering work will help the church(es) multiply, partnership in training initiatives because:
'MINISTRY & MISSION MATTERS'.

Richard Jackson (Revd)
International Coordinator,
Cliff College International Training Centre (CCITC)

APPENDIX 1: CORE TEAM-INVITED TRAINERS

(2002-14)

CORE TEAM (ORGANISING, LEADING TEAMS & LECTURING ON A VARIETY OF SUBJECTS AT DIFFERENT TIMES IN SEVERAL COUNTRIES)

Atkins Revd Dr Martyn BA *(Former)* Cliff College Course Director
Principal Mission/Evangelism-Then and now
Blake Revd Dr Chris MA BSc Principal of Cliff College;
Pastoral & New Testament
**Dunn-Wilson Revd Prof David Dunn-Wilson MA M.Phil. BD Ph.D
FRSA** Methodist Mission Partner & College Lecturer: Church History
Hall Mrs Sylvia Methodist LP Formerly Nigeria & MCSL,
Teacher & Network Leadership, Lay Trainer
Hall Revd Gilbert Methodist Minister, Formerly Nigeria & MCSL,
Chair of District (retired), Lay trainer
Jackson Revd Richard MA BD International Coordinator of CCITC
(Ret'd) Methodist Minister & PG Tutor
Kirkwood Revd Cameron MA (CNAA) Methodist Supt Minister,
Brixton, London Community & Mission
McCall Revd Dr Malcolm BA MA Methodist Minister
(Ret'd) Shetlands, missionary teacher & Naval Chaplain
McCall Mrs Janet BA (Hons) Methodist LP, Teacher in Africa;
French & English as second language skills
Mellor Revd Dr Howard Former Principal of Cliff College
Mission Lectures & graduations
Phillips Mr Keith CQSW Anglican, VSO in Sierra Leone
Social Worker in Child Care field: Logistics/administration
Skuce Revd Dr Stephen MPhil BD Irish Methodist Minister
Cliff College Dean of Studies & CCITC Director
Smith Revd Dr Jennifer BA MPhil Methodist Minister
Lecturer Wesleyan Holiness & Mission, Politics and Religion
Thompson Revd Dr Michael MA BD Methodist Minister
Former Missionary Ghana, Religion & Mission Theology – OT
Todd Revd Kenneth BA, BD, MA Irish Methodist Minister,
Past President of Conference & Mission Partner SL
Walls Prof Andrew Methodist Missionary Statesman
Church History and Mission in Africa
Worrell Mr Peter Methodist LP Ret'd violinist with Halle Orchestra;
Lecturer on Worship & Adult Learning

Atkins Mr James BA (Hons) TV Production
Experience of filming: Sierra Leone, Sri Lanka & Nigeria
Baxter Mrs Margaret BA (Hons) PGCE Anglican Trainer
Author-Adult Learning
Beah Revd Albert MA BA Secretary of Conference to the MCSL
Particular expertise in Community Development
Bolas Revd Pamela BA (Hons) Methodist Chaplain, Leicester
Involved in HIV/Aids awareness and Counselling
Burns Major Alan MA Salvation Army Officer
Particular responsibility for evangelism in Norwich area
Clark Revd Peter MA PGCE Methodist Minister
Former Mission Partner overseas, Dev & Social Work
Clarke Revd Phil MA BA Methodist Superintendent Minster
Former Director of Evangelism, Cliff College & Methodism
Claye Mr Michael Communication
Camera & DVD production assistant
*{Cooke Revd Dr Dennis (late) BA BD MTh Methodist
College Principal, Belfast; Reconciliation following Conflict}*
Cree Revd Dr John Anglican Rector Chorley
Being the Church in the World: Contextualisation
Emery-Wright Revd Dr MDiv BA Methodist Minister,
Lecturer in Missions, Cliff College, Youth Work Research
Ensor Revd Dr Peter MA Methodist Minister
CC Director of UG Studies: Lecturer in New Testament
Eze Very Revd John MA Nigerian Methodist Minister,
Cliff College Graduate, Mission & Evangelism
Garnett Mrs Susanne MA, MEd Anglican
Cliff College Lecturer-Spirituality in Ministry
*{Garnham Capt. Nicola (late) MA BSc Salvation Army Officer
Lecturer at William Booth College in London}*
Gibson Dr Jenny Hospital Doctor
Long term missionary in Africa-Responding to HIV/Aids
Habib Revd Dr Usman MA Postgraduate Research Student; Nigerian
Lecturer on New Generation Churches
Härtner Revd Prof Achim MA United Methodist
Prof of Evangelism at Reutlingen Seminary, Worship & Preaching
Härtner Mr Lukas United Methodist from Germany; Youth &
Logistics

Hensman Mrs Audrey MA Methodist Local Preacher
Former Social Worker-NT Evangelism
Jackson Dr Carole Methodist Conf. Medical Committee;
Psychiatrist-special interest in adult learning disabilities
Jackson Chris MEng (Hons) ACGI AMIMechE
Camera/Video Producer with team in Nigeria
Kirk Mrs Janet MA (CQSW) Methodist Local Preacher; Social
Worker with training experience
Klaiber Revd Dr Walter Presiding Bishop UMC Germany;
Church & Mission Theology - NT
Morris Revd Dr Heather Irish Methodist Director of Ministry,
Edgehill Theological College, Belfast (Born in Nigeria)
Okegbile Revd Dr Deji MA MCN Presbyter; PhD Research Student
Lecturer on Fresh Expressions of Church
Olabimtan Revd Dr Kehinde BTh MTh Baptist Minister-Lagos:
Lecturer in West African Church History
Parker Miss Amy BA (Hons) Student Liaison,
Evaluation and Promotion, Marketing Expertise
Parker Mr Douglas IT Lecturer;
Cameraman on training visit to Cuba
Richardson Revd Dr Neil MA BA MLitt Former College Principal
& President of UK Methodist Conference-NT Lectures & graduations
Stapleford Mr Mike IT Assembly & Computer Training
Community Development projects
Yambasu Revd Dr Sahr Sierra Leonean Methodist serving in Ireland
West African Church History

*NB Whilst our thanks are being expressed to the people listed above we want
to pay tribute to the leaders of the churches, coordinators, resource persons-
lay and ordained, lecturers/Principals in Sierra Leone, Cuba and Nigeria for
their hospitality and encouragement.*

*With unfailing good humour, they have supported the ITC programme as
an add-on to their ongoing responsibilities and helped us, as visiting
lecturers, in countless different ways. As visitors, we are welcomed during
our brief visits, but it is the day to day work of student supervision
undertaken so graciously by our partners in this enterprise that has produced
such successful outcome(s).*

*Those listed above want to say, thank you to our friends for their
partnership in this programme which has enhanced our ministry as well as
theirs!*

APPENDIX 2: ASSOCIATED BOOKS

ALREADY PUBLISHED
BY THE SAME AUTHOR

"GOING AND GROWING"
(ISBN 978-1-78510-355-1)

A companion volume to this new collection of lectures included in 'Ministry & Mission Matters' shares the inspiring story of the growth of the Cliff College International Training Centre (CCITC) from 2001-14.

From its pioneering programme undertaken in post-conflict Sierra Leone in 2002, the CCITC has developed 'partnership in training' programmes together with churches in Sierra Leone, Cuba, Nigeria and Uganda.

"THEN & NOW OF CHURCH MISSION"
(ISBN 978-1-78510-583-8)

These lectures by Professor David Dunn-Wilson and Revd Richard Jackson are focused on the, 'Then & Now', because we believe that understanding the ministry and mission of the church in the past leads into more effective ways of practising it in the present.

Lightning Source UK Ltd.
Milton Keynes UK
UKOW02f1936180515

251791UK00001B/45/P